The MacLeods of Prince Edward Island

The MacLeods of Prince Edward Island

Harold S. MacLeod

SELKIRK

STORIES

Library and Archives Canada Cataloguing in Publication

MacLeod, Harold S., 1927-, author

The MacLeods of Prince Edward Island / Harold S. MacLeod. -- Revised edition.

ISBN 978-1-926494-10-4 (softcover)

1. McLeod family.   2. Scottish Canadians--Prince Edward Island—Genealogy.
3. Prince Edward Island—Genealogy.   I. Title.

CS90.Mc73 2017   929.20971   C2017-902553-8

TABLE OF CONTENTS

Harold S. MacLeod—x
From the Publisher—xi
Introduction—xii
Immigrant Ships—xiv
John MacLeod of Park Corner—16
Kenneth MacLeod of New London and Tignish—23
Hugh MacLeod of Spring Valley—29
John MacLeod of Long River—30
Roderick MacLeod of Darlington—33
Donald MacLeod of Tyne Valley—35
Alexander MacLeod of Hartsville—42
James Townsend MacLeod of Bay View—45
Donald MacLeod of Stanhope—48
John MacLeod of Darlington and Hartsville—49
Angus MacLeod of Glen Martin—50
Allan MacLeod of Hartsville—53
Norman MacLeod of Hartsville—55
Neil MacLeod of Cape Traverse—57
Roderick MacLeod of Ebenezer—58
John Scott MacLeod of Dunstaffnage—62
Alexander "Tailleur" MacLeod of Kinross—65
Murdoch "Tailor" MacLeod of Orwell Crossroads—79
Archibald MacLeod of Kinross—85
Angus MacLeod of Kinross—88
Donald MacLeod of Kinross—92
Donald MacLeod of Montague—93
John MacLeod of Pisquid and Dromore—95
John MacLeod of Glenwilliam—97
Neil MacLeod of Orwell Head, Grand River, and Cumberland Hill—98
Angus MacLeod of Bellevue—102
Murdoch MacLeod of Dundas—103
Murdoch MacLeod of Mermaid and Murray River—105
George MacLeod of Beach Point—118
Donald Mor MacLeod of Point Prim—121
Letter from John MacEachern to Michael MacLeod—126
Roderick MacLeod of Grandview—127
Norman MacLeod of Valleyfield—133
Angus MacLeod of Belfast—135
Archie MacLeod of Whim Road—139
Angus MacLeod of Valleyfield—142
Samuel MacLeod of Murray River—152
Malcolm MacLeod of Pinette (Glashvin)—156
John Torquil MacLeod of Little Sands—159
Articles by Father Bennet MacLeod—161
A Rona (Skye) Family in Canada—161
Article by Catherine McLellan—168
John MacLeod of East Line Road—170

Autobiography and Journal of Rev. Donald MacLeod—177
Donald MacLeod of Lorne Valley—184
James MacLeod of Uigg—192
Archibald MacLeod of Bellevue—193
Letter from John MacLeod of Cardross to Donald MacLeod—194
Letter from Malcolm MacLeod, Isle of Raasay, Scotland—196
John MacLeod of Melville, Montague and Cardross—197
Donald MacKay of New London Area—204
Donald McLeod of Hopedale—205
Donald MacLeod of Iris and Hopefield—206
Donald Ban Oig MacLeod of Murray Harbour Road—210
John MacLeod of Caledonia and Iris—213
Allan MacLeod of Melville—216
Malcolm MacLeod of Valleyfield—218
George MacLeod of Long Creek—222
Murdoch MacLeod of Strathalbyn—224
Murdoch MacLeod of Glasgow Road—226
Neil Hugh MacLeod of Glen Martin and Valleyfield—227
Donald MacLeod of Clyde and Springton—228
The Pioneers of South Granville—229
Roderick MacLeod of South Granville—231
Donald MacLeod of Meadowbank—238
John MacLeod of Lyndale—240
Gordon MacLeod of Long River and Brae—241
Hugh MacLeod of Scotland and Prince Edward Island—243
Donald MacLeod of Orwell Cove and Earnscliffe—244
Malcolm MacLeod of Earnscliffe—245
Murdoch MacLeod of Orwell Cove—265
Roderick MacLeod—289
List of Master Mariners—307
Alexander MacLeod—308
Letter from Ewen MacLeod to his Mother—314
John MacLeod of Glen William—315
Norman MacLeod of Uigg—317
The Uigg School—335
Murdoch MacLeod of Uigg—336
James MacLeod of Uigg—340
Donald MacLeod of Surrey—341
John MacLeod of Colville Station and Charlottetown Royalty—343
Angus MacLeod of Malpeque—344
Letter from Donald MacLeod to Mrs. D. MacLeod—345
John MacLeod of Head of Montague—346
Allan MacLeod of Darlington—347
John MacLeod of Heatherdale—350
Murdoch MacLeod of Raasay, Scotland—356
Alexander S. MacLeod of California and Hawaii—358
Norman MacLeod of Culloden—359
In Memoriam: Doctor Donald MacLeod—360
William MacLeod of Valleyfield—362
John MacLeod of Isle of Lewis and Canada—364
Peter MacLeod of Albion Cross—366

John or Norman MacLeod of Darlington and Alliston—368
William and Ronald MacLeod of Point Prim—374
Angus MacLeod of Lorne Valley—376
Norman MacLeod of High Bank—378
William MacLeod of Wigmore Road—384
John MacLeod of Bonshaw—388
Murdoch MacLeod of Hartsville and Primrose—389
John MacLeod of the Isle of Skye—391
Obituary of William McLeod—400
John MacLeod of Dundas—401
Hector MacLeod of Charlottetown—406
Short Genealogies of MacLeod Families—408
Donald MacLeod of Darlington—409
Donald MacLeod of Victoria Cross—413
John MacLeod of Hartsville—415
John MacLeod of Hartsville—417
John C. MacLeod of Hopedale—419
Donald MacLeod of Springton—422
Heads of Families, Belfast Church, 1811—424
Excerpt from *Skye Pioneers and the Island*—425
Remarks by the Hon. A. B. MacKenzie in July, 1895—426
The MacCrimmon Pipers by Madeline MacCrimmon—431
Extract from *The Canadian Men and Women of the Times*—434
Letters from Descendants of Robert MacLeod and John MacKay Macleod—435
MacLeod Families of Rona and Nearby Districts—437
Red John MacLeod—439
Cemetery Transcriptions—441
 Alberton, Hillcrest United Presbyterian—441
 Alberton, Old Dock Cemetery—441
 Alberton, St. Peter's Anglican Cemetery—441
 Alexandra Baptist—441
 Appin Road Cemetery—441
 Annandale (Presbyterian) United Church—441
 Argyle Shore Cemetery—441
 Bangor, Free Church of Scotland—442
 Beach Point—442
 Belfast, St. John's Presbyterian—442
 Belle River—448
 Belle River Pioneer Cemetery—448
 Bideford United—448
 Birch Hill, Free Church of Scotland—449
 Brae, Immaculate Conception Catholic Cemetery—449
 Brae United Presbyterian—449
 Breadalbane, St. Elizabeth's Anglican—449
 Brookfield Presbyterian—449
 Brooklyn Church of Scotland (Anglican)—450
 Brudenell Baptist Cemetery—451
 Caledonia Presbyterian—451
 Canoe Cove Presbyterian—452
 Cape Traverse Free Church of Scotland—452
 Cardigan All Saints Roman Catholic Cemetery—452

Cardigan, St. Andrew's Presbyterian—452
Cavendish United—453
Central Lot 16, United Church—453
Charlottetown, Elm Avenue, St. Paul's Anglican—453
Charlottetown People's Cemetery—453
Charlottetown Roman Catholic—456
Cherry Valley, Christ Church (Anglican)—456
Cherry Valley United (Methodist)—456
Clyde River Presbyterian—457
Clyde River Restored Pioneer Cemetery—457
Cornwall United (Methodist)—457
Crapaud, People's Cemetery—457
Crapaud, St. John's Anglican—457
Cumberland, St. Martin's Roman Catholic—457
Dundas Community Cemetery, Protestant—457
Dundas United Church (Presbyterian)—458
Dunstaffnage Central United—460
Flat River Presbyterian—460
Fort Augustus, St. Patrick's Roman Catholic—460
Foxley River Anglican—460
Fredericton Community—460
Freeland Presbyterian—461
French River, Yankee Hill Cemetery—461
Georgetown United—461
Hampshire United Cemetery—461
Hartsville Cemetery—461
Hunter River Presbyterian Cemetery—465
Kensington People's Cemetery—465
Kelly's Cross, St. Joseph's Roman Catholic—465
Kingsboro United Baptist—465
Little Sands—465
Long Creek, United Baptist—467
Lorne Valley—467
Lower Montague, United (Methodist)—468
Margate United—468
Marie Community—468
Marshfield, St. Columba Presbyterian—468
Meadowbank, Hyde and Crosby Pioneer Cemetery—469
Mermaid, Calvin Presbyterian—469
Midgell Cemetery—470
Milton Anglican—470
Montague Community Cemetery—470
Mt. Buchanan, Polly Cemetery—471
Mt. Herbert United—471
Mt. Pleasant Cemetery, Church of The Nazarene—471
Mt. Stewart People's Cemetery—472
Mt. Stewart, St. Andrew's Roman Catholic—472
Murray Harbour English Church Cemetery—472
Murray Harbour North Presbyterian—472
Murray Harbour South—472
Murray River, Gladstone—473

Murray River (Wilmot)—474
New Dominion, Presbyterian—475
New Glasgow Cemetery—475
New London, Geddie Memorial—475
New London Protestant—478
New London, St. Thomas Anglican—479
North Bedeque, United Presbyterian—480
O'Leary, St. Luke's Anglican Cemetery—480
Orwell Corner, United Presbyterian—480
Orwell Head, Church of Scotland—482
Peters Road Presbyterian—484
Portage (Brackley Area) Pioneer—484
Port Hill, St. James Anglican—485
Pownal—485
Princetown United (Presbyterian)—485
Rustico Road, Fairview Baptist—485
St. Catherine's, Shaw Cemetery—485
St. George's Roman Catholic Cemetery—485
Seven Mile Bay, St. Peter's Roman Catholic—486
Sherwood—486
Souris West Cemetery United—486
South Granville Presbyterian—486
Springfield, Summerfield United—487
Springfield West United Baptist—487
Springton—488
Springvale, Princetown Road United—488
Sturgeon United (Methodist)—488
Summerside, People's Protestant Cemetery—489
Tignish, United Church Cemetery—489
Tryon People's—489
Tyne Valley Presbyterian—489
Uigg Baptist Church Cemetery—489
Uigg, Church of Scotland—491
Valleyfield United (Presbyterian)—492
Vernon, St. Andrew's United—495
Vernon River Memorial Cemetery, United Methodist/B. Christian—495
Victoria West United Church, People's Cemetery—496
Westmoreland Baptist—496
Wheatley River, United Church—496
Winsloe, Highfield Presbyterian, Lower Malpeque Road—496
Wood Islands Presbyterian—496

In Memoriam
Harold S. MacLeod

The measure of a man is not where he stands in moments of comfort and convenience, but where he stands at times of challenge and controversy.

Martin Luther King Jr.

Farmer, soldier, railway stoker, carpenter, bricklayer, sawyer, teacher, maintenance supervisor, administrator, Mayor, presentor, singer, traveller, genealogist, writer, etc. Before you think "Jack of all trades," be assured that he was master of all those vocations, and excelled in each and every one of them.

Harold Sinclair MacLeod was born February 23, 1927, in Lyndale, PEI. The youngest child of Roderick and Margaret [MacNeill] MacLeod, he was predeceased by his parents and siblings, Ellen Taylor, Reginald, Wendell, Hector, Marion Leafe, and Ewen.

March 29, 1952, was the beginning of a joyous and love filled life as he married Tilly Compton. Their children, Stephen and Janis were beloved additions to this union. Sadly, Stephen succumbed to cancer in June 2007. Tilly was laid to rest in Orwell Head Cemetery in June 2009. Janis and her husband, Marty Samms, are long distance truck drivers based out of Alberta.

Music, family research, and an abiding faith in their Lord were the mainstays of their lives together. They left a legacy in the recordings of songs they loved and sang for churches, concerts, funerals, and many other occasions. Genealogy researchers have been blessed by the books they compiled on the MacLeods, Lamonts, MacNeills, Curries, Comptons, and other family histories. But it was in their faith and knowledge of the presence of a Higher Power that sustained them throughout their lives. Faithful members and participants in the life and work of the Free Church of Scotland, Montague. they also attended services in churches across North America, Great Britain. and in Israel. On one of their journeys to Florida, they noticed cars gathering for Sunday service at a church in South Carolina, so they pulled in off the highway to worship there. At the conclusion of the service, a lady seated in front of them stood up and said, "I don't know who these people are, but I want everyone here to hear their beautiful voices." So they sang several pieces before the congregation would let them carry on with their journey.

Harold had a fantastic memory for names and the families with whom they were connected. He could also recall many anecdotes of people and funny things that had happened to them. He loved visiting and having visitors drop in at any time. He was faithful in keeping daily journals of events in his life going back to 1980. He embraced computer technology and revelled in researching as well as entering family data on the latest gadgets as soon as they became available on the market. He mastered the keyboards and rapidly became a two fingered typist in no time.

A brilliant mind and voice has been stilled, and we will miss him greatly, especially when we think, "Oh, I must ask Harold about that."

Written by his niece; Margaret [Taylor] Campion

Preface
From the Publisher

This edition of *The MacLeods of Prince Edward Island* by Harold S. MacLeod is based on computer files (titled "MacLeods 97") typed by Tilly MacLeod and left behind after Harold MacLeod's death in 2014. According to the metadata included with the files (its "properties"), this is the 176th revision of a document created in 1993 and last edited in 2005. A comparison of this edition with the last printed edition of the book shows that considerable additions have been made to certain family trees. However, with a few exceptions, Harold MacLeod made little effort to update what he had done, so most of the genealogies are out of date, and do not include the many births and deaths that have occurred since the book was last printed. In addition, the photographs and whimsical drawings included in previous editions of this book are absent from this book.

The transcriptions of cemetery markers made by Tilly MacLeod and included in previous editions of this book were not part of the digital files left by Harold MacLeod at his death. The publisher scanned the corresponding pages of the 1996 edition and used optical recognition software to turn the scanned pages into editable documents. For easier reference, the publisher has also arranged the cemeteries in alphabetical order.

Since previous editions of *The MacLeods of Prince Edward Island* were printed and bound locally, on Prince Edward Island, there were limited press runs. Used copies are hard to find and command high prices. This edition, because it is being published in a print-on-demand format, will be easily available to anyone, anywhere in the world, who wishes to purchase it through an online retailer. It will remain in print perpetually, or at least until it is replaced by an updated edition.

However, some changes have been made. The way that Harold and Tilly MacLeod set up their book for printing made it difficult to incorporate revisions into family trees. They were sometimes added as addenda later in the book, such as a note about the family of Catherine MacLeod, found on page 391 of the 1996 printing of the book. This note more properly belongs with the genealogy of John MacLeod of Hartsville, page 343 of the 1996 printing. It has now been moved to its proper place. Spelling of place names has been standardized, and abbreviations (such as C.B. for Cape Breton) have been spelled out for the benefit of readers unfamiliar with Atlantic Canada. In addition, any obvious oversights of spelling or punctuation, such as are inevitable in any printed book, have been corrected. Any errors that remain are the responsibility of the publisher, not the author.

We hope that by producing this book we are able to render a service to the many descendants of the MacLeods of Prince Edward Island throughout North America and the world, and to all those interested in genealogy and family history.

THE MACLEODS OF PRINCE EDWARD ISLAND
INTRODUCTION

There were three MacLeod families on Prince Edward Island in 1798 according to the census of that year.

Murdoch McCloud was living on Lot 48. His family consisted of five males and one female under sixteen years of age, and one male and one female between sixteen and sixty, for a total of eight.

Ser. McCloud was living in Royalty, Charlottetown with three males and two females under sixteen years, and a male and a female between sixteen and sixty, for a total of seven.

Alex McCloud resided in Lot 37 with one female under sixteen and a male and a female between sixteen and sixty.

The total population of P.E.I. that year was forty-five hundred people. The next fifty years, however, were to witness a flood of immigrants from the Highlands of Scotland. The first wave came in 1803 with the arrival of three ships: the *Polly*, the **D***ykes*, and the *Oughton* from the Hebrides, bringing some eight hundred people, under the sponsorship of "the great colonizer," the Earl of Selkirk, and landing at Belfast, P.E.I. There were a number of families with the name MacLeod in this group. In the year 1811, some of the heads of families of the Belfast Parish, presented Dr. Angus MacAuley with a letter of thanks for his services to the parish. The list of names included eleven MacLeods, among others. This flow of immigration from Scotland to Prince Edward Island, however, had slowed to a trickle by 1850.

The early settlers were a healthy and prolific group. Families of sixteen children were not uncommon, so that the land available after that date was, for the most part, taken by the descendants of the earlier settlers.

An example is Bangor and other sections in that area which was settled at a later date by the Grants of Brooklyn, the Comptons of Belle River and the MacDougalls of Nine Mile Creek, among others. In Prince County, Milo, Hebron, Brae and the surrounding districts received an influx of families from the DeSable area—MacNevins, MacQuarries, MacDonalds and others.

The mid-eighteen hundreds also witness the beginning of the migration of native-born sons and daughters to all parts of the U.S.A., but chiefly to Massachusetts. This migration continued for about eighty years until the great depression of the 1930s when the United States closed the "line" because of widespread unemployment among their own people.

About 1852 a large tract of land, known locally as the "Queen's Bush," in the Huron and Bruce counties of Ontario, was surveyed and made available for settlement. A number of families, including MacLeods, holdings and moved to that region. The 1861 census for Turnberry Township, Huron Co., Ontario, lists:

MacLeod, John, farmer, born Scotland, ch. Scotland, 33 years, M.
>Christian, born P.E.I., ch. Scot., 28 years, F.
>Angus, born P.E.I., ch. Scotland, 8 years, M.
>Duncan, born Ontario, ch. Scot., 6 years, M.
>John, born Ontario, ch. Scot., 4 years, M.
>Donald, born Ontario, ch. Scot., 2 years, M.

Living in a one story log house.

MacLeod, John, school teacher, born Nova Scotia, ch. Scot., 21 yrs, living on the farm of Andrew Mitchell.

MacLeod, John, farmer, born Scotland, ch. Scot., 63 yrs.
>Ann, born Scotland, ch. Scot., 60 yrs.
>Donald, born P.E.I., ch. Scot., 19 yrs.

Living in a one story log house and they had 3 cows and 6 sheep, livestock valued at $70.00.

Among those taking up land in Turnberry Twp., was John Lamont, brother of Ewen of Lyndale. He married as his second wife, Sarah Lamont, Grandview, daughter of John and Euphemia (MacLeod) Lamont. John and Sarah's son Malcolm is the author of *Bush Days* in Ontario in which he gives a vivid account of the day to day activities and the difficulties of carving a home and farm out of the virgin forest.

Patricia Lamont Schwenke, professor and Chair, Dept. of Education, Carroll College, Wakesha, Wisconsin, U.S.A., is also a descendant of this John and Sarah Lamont.

Another wave of emigrants left P.E.I. circa 1874 for the Great American Plains when the U.S. Government offered land for settlement in Nebraska. There were MacLeod families in the group as well. The Donald Bhan Oig MacLeod family of Lyndale was among them and the son Donald Bhan MacLeod afterwards studied for the ministry and carved out a distinguished career, holding pastorates in Orwell Head, Charlottetown and other places. Another son returned to P.E.I. and farmed in Uigg. Two of his grandchildren are in Uigg, Malcolm MacLeod living on his grandfather's farm, and Louise, R.N., married to Arnold MacLeod, living on a neighbouring farm.

When the Canadian Pacific Railway was completed in 1885, this opened up the Prairies for settlement and many of the young men took advantage of the "Harvest Excursions" to make a few dollars gathering the harvest in Western Canada. A number of them homesteaded, and their descendants can be found in many parts of the Canadian and American west.

The sea also called them. The shipbuilding industry, which was a profitable venture on P.E.I. for many years, gave many a young man an opportunity to become a member of a ship's crew, and travel to all parts of the world. Of the family of Donald "Horo" MacLeod, Orwell Cove, there were five brothers who were Master Mariners.

Some of those who went to sea eventually settled in foreign countries and their descendants can be found there to this day. Others spent many years before the mast and later settled on farms on P.E.I., eventually to marry and raise a family.

After World War Two, work was available in Ontario and Western Canada, consequently there was a steady flow of young people in that direction. Perhaps one of the disadvantages of being a small island is that some have to move where there are more opportunities.

Someone has said that the most valuable export of P.E.I. is young people. Certainly, over the years, a great number have left the place of their birth to make their homes in other parts of the world. It is my hope that this book will be of some assistance to their descendants and others in compiling a history of their families.

We have checked and re-checked in an effort to eliminate errors. Alexander MacLean Sinclair, the noted Gaelic scholar and historian once concluded an article of research by stating: "In what I have written there may be errors, but a few errors. They may, indeed, be useful in setting men and women of knowledge to think, to talk about things old and collect facts."

It is my wish too, that this may be just a beginning. Much more information can be gathered to add to what is between these covers and perhaps others will carry on to provide us with a more complete record of the various MacLeod families of Prince Edward Island.

Harold S. MacLeod

IMMIGRANT SHIPS

The earliest vessel leaving the West Highlands with immigrants for the lower provinces seems to have been the *Annabella*, which landed a party of seventy families of Kintyre settlers at Malpeque, P.E.I., in the year 1770. In the summer of the same year, two agents, Montgomery and Stewart, brought one hundred and twenty families to Cove Head and Three Rivers, and in 1771, a still further settlement from Argyllshire took place on the west side of Richmond Bay, P.E.I. In the following year the *Alexander* sailed from Loch Boisdale, Uist, with two hundred and ten immigrants and dropped anchor in Charlottetown Harbour in the latter part of June, 1772. These settled for the most part in the districts around Panmure Island and Cardigan, where their descendants still live. Some thirty years later, in 1803, came the Selkirk Settlers to the Belfast district, on the *Polly*, the *Dykes*, and the *Oughton*.

It was not until 1840 that the Valleyfield district was opened up for settlement. In that year immigrant ships sailed from island of Skye bound for Prince Edward Island. One was a full-rigged ship, the other was a brig. Both vessels left Loch Snizort of Uig Bay about the last week in July. The ship took on board four hundred passengers, and the brig, two hundred and twenty five. Although they left the shores of Skye within a short time of one another, the brig arrived in Charlottetown Harbour almost a month ahead of her larger companion. It would appear that the captain of the ship was not a good mariner as he went far off his course to the north. Fortunately, however, there was on board among the passengers, an experienced deep-sea captain who remonstrated with the captain of the ship that if he did not change his course he would fetch about the south end of Greenland. The passengers could not understand such cold weather in mid-summer.

Soon, however, they noticed a change as the ship steered southward and the setting sun began to go down on the other bow. Both vessels called at Sydney, C.B., and discharged some of their passengers and then sailed for Charlottetown where the remaining passengers were safely landed. The brig crossed the Atlantic in thirty-one days while her companion was eight long weeks on her zig-zag course. Of the four hundred passengers on the ship, nine of them died during the voyage and were buried at sea. Four or five babies were born on board. A number of the passengers travelled east from Charlottetown and took up land in Green Marsh, Grand River, Cardigan and High Bank. Others settled west of Charlottetown. Many of those, though they took up land, did not build houses during the first winter, but stopped with kind friends who had come to this country a few years previous.

In the following summer another ship sailed from the Island of Skye, having on board some eight hundred and fifty passengers. She was called the *Washington*, and hailed from Liverpool, England. She was 1660 tons burden and one of the largest, if not, indeed, the very largest sailing vessel ever to enter the harbour. The *Washington* made a very quick passage. She left Uig Bay on the 6th day of July and dropped anchor in the three tides of Charlottetown on the 28th day of the same month being twenty-two days out. Her passengers were from Snizort, Kilmuir, and the east side of Skye. Two passengers died on the way out. One, an old woman, was buried at sea. The other, a Mr. MacKay, died off the coast of Newfoundland. Seeing the sailors pulling hard in setting up a large topsail, being used to that kind of work, he ran to lend a hand, but immediately after letting go of the halyards he took a heavy hemorrhage and, in a very short time, died. His body was placed in a coffin and taken to Charlottetown where he was buried.

It was always customary on board emigrant ships to hold worship morning and evening on the Sabbath day on the deck of the vessel. Most of the families also kept family worship regularly each day.

On arriving in Charlottetown the passengers left in groups for different parts of the Island. Many went to the Scotch settlement as it was then called, and quite a number settled in Brown's Creek and Douse's Road.

In that same year, 1841, and on the 26th of June, the barque, *Ocean*, also hailing from Liverpool, England, left the town of Portree, Skye, with four hundred and fifty passengers, the majority of whom came from the Island of Raasay. They were thirty-six days on the way and came direct from Portree to Charlottetown. There were no deaths among her passengers. Two children were born on the voyage. The usual fare charged each adult passenger was three pounds sterling. For children under the age of twelve the fare was one half. A number of passengers of the *Ocean* settled in Brown's Creek.

From the "History of Valleyfield," by Rev. D. M. Sinclair.

JOHN MACLEOD
JOHN MACLEOD AND MARY MACPHERSON OF PARK CORNER

A   John MacLeod, of Durness, Sutherlandshire, near Assynt, Scotland, m. Mary MacPherson. She was the daughter of Hugh MacPherson of Sargoe. They were married on Dec. 8, 1789. He was described as "little farmer and fisher" in the Scottish census. It is likely that he had been dispossessed of his land in 1797 or 1798. In the baptismal records of 1798 and 1804, the family address is Caennibin. They emigrated with their children to P.E.I in 1805 on the ship *Polly*.They first settled in St. Peters and moved to Park Corner (New London area) in 1809. Their farm became known as the "Cove Farm" and descendants known as the "Cove MacLeods" in that area. John was born 1761–died 1836. Their children were:

B1   Christian MacLeod, born Dec. 30, 1790. She probably died in infancy as another daughter was given the name in 1798.

B2   Isabel MacLeod, born June 12, 1793, m. George MacKenzie, died in Wisconsin, with issue:
     C1   George MacKenzie.

B3   Hugh MacLeod (Col.), born Aug 12, 1795, died about 1865. Buried at Yankee Hill, New London. He m. Nancy Burke. With issue:
     C1   John MacLeod, m. Margaret Stewart.
     C2   Isobel MacLeod, m. Capt. James Lamont, with issue:
         D1 Hugh John Lamont, m. Eliza Duggan, with issue:
             E1   Donald Lamont.
             E2   Jean Lamont.
             E3   Ema Lamont.
             E4   Minnie Lamont.
             E5   Maisie Lamont.
     C3   Margaret MacLeod, m. Cpt. Joseph Palmer.

B4   Christian MacLeod, born Oct. 17, 1798, m. George MacKay, with issue:
     C1   George MacKay.

B5   Donald MacLeod, born July 27, 1801. Died at French River about 1860, m. Amelia MacKay. They settled on a 150 acre farm in what is now Springbrook. Their family was:
     C1   Barbara MacLeod, 1837–1919.
     C2   Mary MacLeod, 1840–1905.
     C3   William Hugh MacLeod, 1826–1898.
     C4   John Donald MacLeod, known as J.D., 1832–1913.
     C5   Andrew MacLeod, died in Minneapolis. He was born Feb. 8, 1831.
     C6   Hugh MacLeod, 1846–1882.
     C7   Benjamin MacLeod, 1848–1925, m. 1) Emily Sims.
         D1   Amelia Harriet MacLeod (Hattie), taught school for over 65 years. Never married.
         D2   Daniel Fenwick MacLeod, died at age 24.
         D3   John Daniel MacLeod, died at age 19.
         D4   Heath Fulton MacLeod, m. Kate Bernard in 1906. She died in 1909. Afterwards Heath lived with his sister Harriet. In 1926 they returned to their father's farm until it was sold. They then bought the late Capt. Alfred MacLeod's home.

Benjamin m. 2) Catherine <u>Fraser</u>, with issue:

D5 Hector John MacLeod, received his Ph.D.from Harvard University in 1921 and in 1943 was awarded the O.B.E. (The King's Birthday Honours, 1943) for valuable public service in connection with scientific research.

D6 Horace MacLeod, became a successful rancher.

D7 Ernest MacLeod, drowned in 1915.

About 1895, the family moved to Kensington, then to Alberta in 1900.

C8 Ann MacLeod, born 1828, died in infancy.

C9 Penelope MacLeod, born in 1843, died in infancy.

B6 Andrew MacLeod, 1804–1839, m. Catherine <u>MacIntyre</u>, with issue:

C1 Catherine MacLeod, died at an early age.

C2 Lemuel MacLeod, went to U.S.A.

C3 Kenneth MacLeod, went to U.S.A.

C4 Bruce MacLeod, went to U.S.A.

C5 John MacLeod, Capt., known as "Johnny Garland," 1831–1873, m. Sophia <u>Sims</u>, 1834–1916. He perished in the wreck of the schooner *Carrie P. Rich*, of which he was Commander. It foundered during the "Great August Gale" of 1873. It was estimated that forty P.E.I. vessels and countless lives were lost in that storm. Their family was:

D1 Herbert MacLeod, went to U.S. where he and his brother were raised by an uncle.

D2 Margaret MacLeod, m. Alvin <u>Glover</u>, with issue:

　　E1 Horace Glover, m. Ruth <u>Davidson</u>, with issue:

　　　　F1 Elaine Glover.

　　E2 Cecilia Glover, m. Harris <u>Blackeney</u>, with issue:

　　　　F1 Kenneth Blakeney.

D3 Elizabeth MacLeod, "Janie," 1861–1933, m. William Andrew <u>Pidgeon</u>, 1849–1936, with issue:

　　E1 John Pidgeon, 1882–1963.

　　E2 James Pidgeon, 1884–1907.

　　E3 Pearl Pidgeon, 1886–1963.

　　E4 Lillian Pidgeon, 1888–1978.

　　E5 Carmen Pidgeon, 1890–1919.

　　E6 Ernest Pidgeon, 1894–1962.

　　E7 Franklin Pidgeon,1896–1973, m. J. Vern <u>Leslie</u>, 1900, with issue:

　　　　F1 Thelma Pidgeon, m. Lowell <u>Clark</u>, with issue:

　　　　　　G1 Barry Clark, m. Heather <u>Herl</u>, with issue:

　　　　　　　　H1 Andrea Clark.

　　　　　　　　H2 Adam Clark.

　　　　　　　　H3 Daniel Clark.

　　　　　　G2 Brian Clark, m. Anne <u>House</u>.

　　　　F2 William Pidgeon, m. Gerry <u>Flowers</u>, with issue:

　　　　　　G1 Cathi Pidgeon.

　　　　　　G2 Vicki Pidgeon.

　　　　　　William m. 2) Marilyn <u>MacMullen</u>, with issue:

　　　　　　G3 Debra Pidgeon.

　　　　　　G4 Darlene Pidgeon.

　　　　　　G5 William Pidgeon.

　　　　F3 Robert Pidgeon.

D4   John Andrew MacLeod, 1868–1946, m. Cecilia <u>Caldwell</u>. According to his obituary which appeared in the "Canadian Banker," was born at Park Corner, P.E.I., and entered the bank at Summerside in 1887, becoming Manager at Harbour Grace, Newfoundland, in 1895. In 1897 he was made Assistant Manager at Chicago and subsequently Manager at St. John's, Newfoundland, Boston, Havana, and Chicago. He was appointed Chief Superintendent of Branches at Toronto in 1913, Assistant General Manager in 1917, General Manager 1923, Vice-President 1927, President 1934, Chairman of the Board 1945. He served as President of the Canadian Bankers Association in 1932–33, and during his term ably represented the banks before the MacMillan Commission on banking and currency. In recognition of these services he was elected Honourary President of the Association in 1934.

C6 Andrew MacLeod, m. Elizabeth <u>Paynter</u>, with issue:

D1   Chelmsford, "Chem," MacLeod, 1878–1944, m. Amelia <u>Profitt</u>, with issue:

E1   Marion MacLeod, m. 1) Hollis <u>Warren</u>, with issue:

F1   Marlene Warren, m. Robert <u>Wilcox</u>, with issue:

G1   Julia Wilcox.

G2   Lisa Wilcox.

Marion m. 2) Everett <u>Webster</u>.

E2   Vera MacLeod, m. Scott <u>Sinclair</u>, with issue:

F1   Bruce Sinclair.

E3   Bruce MacLeod, m. Georgie <u>Campbell</u>, with issue:

F1   Carl MacLeod, RCMP Officer in Toronto.

F2   Beverly MacLeod.

D2   Mary Ann MacLeod, m. Garnet <u>Profitt</u> (brother of Amelia), with issue:

E1   Lottie Profitt, m. Fulton <u>Pierce</u>, with issue:

F1   John Pierce.

E2   Hazel Profitt, m. George <u>McCubrey</u>, no children.

E3   Jane Profitt, m. William <u>Gendron</u>, with issue:

F1   Robert Gendron.

F2   Catherine Gendron.

E4   Fred Profitt, m. Ferne <u>Hutchinson</u>, with issue:

F1   Sylvia Profitt.

F2   Gail Profitt.

F3   Jackie Profitt.

F4   Uta Profitt.

F5   Maxine Profitt.

D3   Myra MacLeod, m. Dan <u>Wedlock</u>, with issue:

E1   Roy Wedlock.

E2   Keith Wedlock.

E3   Wanda Wedlock.

E4   Muriel Wedlock.

D4   Ella MacLeod, died at age 18, never married.

D5   Hannah MacLeod, m. ___ <u>Taylor</u>, no children.

D6   Bruce MacLeod, m.___, no children, lived in Saskatchewan.

D7   Lemuel MacLeod, m.___, no children, lived in Saskatchewan.

C7   George MacLeod, Capt., 1843–1905, m. Alice Cornish. He was in command of the ice-breaker *Stanley*. They raised his brother John's two sons, Herbert and John Andrew, in addition to their own children:

D1   Eveline MacLeod.

D2   Beatrice MacLeod.

D3   A girl, m. William Profitt.

D4   Everett MacLeod, m. Johanne Stewart, with issue:

    E1   Harold MacLeod, 1919–1972, m. Isobel Hulme, with issue:

        F1   Ronald MacLeod.

        F2   Gerald MacLeod.

    E2   Fred MacLeod, lives in Summerside, m. Frances Green, issue:

        F1   Adele MacLeod.

        F2   Marion MacLeod.

    E3   Florence MacLeod, m. Arthur Johnston.

    E4   Ethel MacLeod.

D5   Duncan MacLeod.

B7   Jennie MacLeod, apparently born on the *Polly* in 1805.

B8   John MacLeod, born at Greenwich Farm, St. Peters in 1809. He died at the Cove in 1895. Married to Isabella McKie, born 1815. They inherited the family farm. Their children were:

C1   Jane Louise MacLeod.

C2   Henrietta Marie MacLeod, died 1912, aged 70 years.

C3   Lucille Matilda MacLeod, born c. 1849.

C4   Lucy MacLeod, born c. 1859, never m., bed-ridden with arthritis.

C5   Artemus MacLeod, 1847–1889. The eldest son m. Lucy Sims, with issue:

D1   Wallace Merrill MacLeod, 1879–1958, Capt. known as "Med," m. Amelia A. Stewart, 1879–1940, with issue:

    E1   Ralph Stewart MacLeod, 1910–1947, m. Mary Ellen Found, 1910–1994. He drowned in 1947, issue:

        F1   Barbara Christine MacLeod, m. Gordon Sutherland, died in 1973, son of Robert and Cassie (MacLeod) Sutherland, Seaview. Their children were:

            G1   Lynn Sutherland, m. Joe Bulger.

            G2   Kenneth Sutherland, m. Wilma Bell, with issue:

                H1   Brandon Sutherland.

                H2   Colton Sutherland.

            G3   Cindy Sutherland, m. Douglas Costain, with issue:

                H1   Mellissa Costain.

                H2   Ryan Costain.

                H3   Stephanie Costain.

            G4   Elizabeth Sutherland.

            G5   Marla Sutherland.

            G6   Corey Sutherland.

        F2   Clayton MacLeod, m. Annie Grace Campbell, daughter of Arthur K. and Gladys Campbell, Seaview. They live on the Wigmore Road. Their children:

            G1   Arthur Ralph MacLeod, m. Cathy Mitchell, daughter of Lawrence and Irene Mitchell from

Manitoba. Ralph and Cathy live in Calgary and have two daughters:

    H1   Irene Grace MacLeod.

    H2 Melissa Dawn MacLeod.

    H3 Clayton Lawrence Ralph MacLeod.

    H4 Mitchell Gordon MacLeod, 1993.

G2 Gordon Leigh MacLeod, m. Pamela Doris Brander, daughter of George and Dot Brander, with issue:

    H1 Barbara Gail (Waldner) MacLeod, m. Kirk Hill, with issue:

        I1   Tristin David Hill.

        I2   Shawn Michael Hill.

    H2 Jay Gordon (Brander) MacLeod, adopted by Gordon.

    H3 Chad Arthur MacLeod.

    H4 Lucas Allan MacLeod.

G3 John David MacLeod, m. 1) Olive Stewart, with issue:

    H1 John Douglas MacLeod, m. Shauna Witmack (or Witmark), with issue:

        I1   John Dyman Preston MacLeod.

John David m. 2) Heather Porter.

G4 Ronald Earl MacLeod, m. Nancy Cole, daughter of Charles and Jessie Cole, Spring Valley, with issue:

    H1 Ronald Charles Clayton MacLeod.

    H2 Tammy Nancy MacLeod.

    H3 Andy Earl MacLeod.

G5 Garth Ian MacLeod, m. Lesley Jane Thompson, daughter of Carl and Norma Thompson, Margate, with issue:

    H1 Courtney Wendy (Gill) MacLeod.

    H2 Hillary Barbara Olivia MacLeod.

    H3 Kaeleigh Ellen Jane MacLeod.

G6 Barbara Ann MacLeod, m. John Lynn Dickieson, issue:

    H1 Jaclyn Anne Dickieson

F3 Annie Beryl MacLeod, m. Donald C. MacLeod, Granville, son of Jack and Lillian MacLeod, they had four children:

    G1 Heather MacLeod, m. Charles Lymus.

    G2 Elaine MacLeod, m. Gerald Arsenault, with issue:

        H1 Kristie Arsenault.

    G3 Mark MacLeod.

    G4 Dwight MacLeod.

E2 Lucy Jane MacLeod, m. Henry Bishop, who was owner of Bishop Transport, Summerside, with three children:

    F1 Sylvia Bishop, m. John Sutherland, with issue:

        G1 Steven Sutherland, m. Jayne Williams, with issue:

            H1 Sarah Sutherland.

                H2 Mellissa Sutherland.

       F2 Merrill Bishop, m. Lillian <u>Hansen</u>, with issue:
            G1 Karen Bishop, m. Woodrow <u>Hynes</u>, with issue:
                H1 Bryan Hynes.
            G2 Anthony Bishop.
       F3 Helen Bishop, m. Charles <u>Myers</u>, with issue:
            G1 Shawn Myers, m. Sherry <u>Olsen</u>, with issue:
                H1 Scott Myers.
                H2 Brett Myers.
   E3 Helen MacLeod, m. Albert <u>Walker</u>, they live near Toronto, Ontario. Their children are:
       F1 Patricia Walker, m. Evan <u>Franklin</u>, with issue:
            G1 Andrew Franklin.
            G2 Sarah Franklin.
       F2 Alan Walker, m. Elaine <u>Stewart</u>, with issue:
            G1 Emily Walker.
            G2 Nicholas Walker.

C6 Wallace MacLeod, m. Mary <u>Bearisto</u>. He was superintendant of the postal service in Western Canada for many years.

C7 Henry Collingwood MacLeod, 1851–1926. General Manager of the Bank of Nova Scotia beginning 1897. He m. 1) Sarah <u>Davison</u> from Charlottetown. After her death in 1881, he m. a daughter of Hon. Daniel Gordon of Georgetown, a former Premier of P.E.I. Hector MacLeod, in "Family Records," states that Henry Collingwood MacLeod, was also the author of a number of works on banking, including "Bank Inspections," "The Necessity of External Examinations," "The Best System of Banking," "The Economic System of Great Britain" and others. He retired from the Bank of Nova Scotia in 1910, and was summoned from Europe by the Borden Government to assist the Banking and Commerce Committee of the House of Commons in the formation of the Bank Act of 1913. He was also an enthusiastic yachtsman and amateur designer. He designed the *Minota* for the Canadian Cup Race in 1889 and commanded and navigated the *Amorita* in the New York–Bermuda ocean race in 1909, establishing a new record for the course. He died in 1926 at his winter home in Camden, South Carolina.

   D1 Vernon MacLeod, took over the Cove Farm after his father's death in 1926. The farm was later sold to Garnet Campbell.

C8 Newton MacLeod, 1848-1937, m. Elizabeth <u>Blackeney</u>, with issue:
   D1 Elmer MacLeod.

C9 A. Cuthbert MacLeod, 1852-1931, m. Agnes <u>Ross</u>, with issue:
   D1 Fred MacLeod, died in WWI.
   D2 Harold MacLeod, died in WWI.

C10 Captain Alfred MacLeod, 1860-1944, m. twice, no family.

C11 Leslie MacLeod, 1862-1899. Single, died in New York, described as a talented writer.

C12 There is also evidence of a twelfth child. Louise MacLeod, in her memoirs, states that John had twelve children.

Information supplied by Thelma Clark, including obituary of John Andrew MacLeod, Clayton MacLeod and Grace MacLeod, Kensington. Also from Marion

Webster, Community History of French River and Park Corner, census and cemetery transcripts.

The following is an extract of a letter from John D. Robinson, Belgrade Lakes, Me., U.S.A. (August 20, 1986)

My Great Grandmother, Jennie MacLeod, m. Thomas Robertson, son of Henry Robertson and Mary Boyd Robertson of Cavendish. According to the Marriage Book, 1832-1840, page 69, the marriage took place 18th July 1833 and was performed by Wm. Cundall, J.P. Witnesses were John MacLeod, Sen., Hugh MacLeod, Jr., Henry Squarebridge, and others. Prior to the marriage, a bond was signed by John MacLeod and Thomas Robertson for the sum of 100 pounds sterling, on July 13, 1833. A card exists in the Master Name File, indicating that they were m. at St. Paul's Anglican Church in Charlottetown by Rev. Walpole. No such record exists at the church and Rev. Walpole not a Rector of that Church. (Rev. Walpole did, however, for a short time perform marriages in the New London area at the time.) It is my opinion that the evidence is rather convincing that this Jennie MacLeod was a daughter of John MacLeod and Mary MacPherson, born at sea on the way over on the brig *Polly*, and a sister to Isabel, Hugh, Christie, Donald and John. This family lived on the Cove Farm, Park Corner, New London. A report of the "Family Records" by Hector J. MacLeod does not mention Jennie as far as her husband and children are concerned, and an article written in 1933 by Malcolm MacQueen, indicates that Jennie died in Iowa. This latter article, also states that John MacLeod was "highly intelligent ... well educated." He certainly appears to have been "highly intelligent," but his will (allowed 14 July 1836) was signed with an X. That is to say that this article may also have been incorrect as it indicates that Jennie died in Iowa. The Jennie that m. Thomas Robertson of Cavendish on July 18, 1833, is buried in the United Methodist Cemetery in North Granville as Jenetta, beloved wife of Thomas Robertson, died May 16, 1844, aet. 73. It is my opinion that the presence of Hugh and John MacLeod, Sr., at her wedding, the signature of John MacLeod on the marriage bond, are more convincing than the slight age discrepancy which appears to exist, especially during a time when ages were frequently distorted for whatever the reason.

KENNETH MACLEOD
KENNETH MACLEOD AND NANCY MORRISON OF NEW LONDON AND TIGNISH

A   Kenneth MacLeod, 1759-1841, age 82, m. Nancy Ann <u>Morrison</u>, 1780-1841, Kenneth was born in Sutherlandshire, Scotland, and married Nancy in Scotland. They left with their children from Thurso, North Britain, on the ship *Elizabeth and Ann* of Newcastle, bound for P.E.I. They arrived on P.E.I. on Nov. 8, 1806, and settled in New London in 1808 and had a farm of 58 acres. Kenneth and Nancy are buried in the Pioneer Yankee Hill Cemetery, New London. Their gravestone inscription reads "Emigrated from Parish Durness, Sutherlandshire, Scotland." Their children's names and ages from the passenger list are as follows:

B1   John MacLeod, age 12, born in Scotland in 1794. He emigrated with his parents. He was a farmer in New London and owned about 100 acres of land. He married Catherine <u>MacKay</u>, who was born in Scotland about 1800. They are buried in New London. John and Catherine had eight children:

C1   Duncan MacLeod, 1818-1887, m. Dollina <u>MacKay</u>, 1823-1912, settled at Graham's Road, with issue:

D1   James MacLeod,1852-1937, m. Georgina <u>Fife</u>, 1872-1951, of Stanley Bridge. They carried on the farm at Graham's Road and had one son:

E1   George Preston MacLeod, m. Margaret Frances <u>Munn</u>, of Marshfield They have one daughter:

F1   Anne MacLeod, m. John <u>Coles</u>, Milton, P.E.I.

D2   George MacLeod, was a twin to Mary.

D3   Mary MacLeod, born 1857, neither twin married.

C2   John MacLeod, 1819-1897, m. Johanna <u>MacKay</u>, with issue:

D1   Christy MacLeod, m. William <u>Campbell</u>.

D2   James MacLeod, m. Grace <u>MacKay</u>.

C3   Kenneth MacLeod, 1824-1897, m. Sarah <u>Whitehead</u> and lived on the home farm at South West River. They had at least five children.

C4   Anne MacLeod (Kenneth's twin), born Oct. 31, 1824, died 1892. She was first m. to John <u>Nisbet</u> from New Glasgow, P.E.I., son of George Nisbet and Martha (Hart) Nisbet from Scotland. They were married in 1848 and lived in the Tignish area where they had two girls: Catherine Nisbet, 1849, and Martha Hart Nisbet, 1850. John died in 1851 and was buried in Cavendish Cemetery. Ann remarried to Capt. John <u>Ireland</u> in 1856, they lived in Tignish. They had a family of five: Edward James, John, William, Andrew, Agnes St. Clair, and George Drillis. Agnes married the Hon. J. <u>Agnew</u>. George Drillis was a Minister.

C5   Elizabeth MacLeod, 1826-1917, m. David <u>Cole</u>, New London, and had at least five children.

C6   Barbara MacLeod,1833-1917, m. Robert <u>McKay</u>, Clifton, four daughters.

C7   George MacLeod, birth and death dates unknown. He was a sea captain and moved to Buffalo, U.S.A. He married in the States, with two children.

C8   Margaret MacLeod, 1838-1912, m. George <u>McLeod</u> in the U.S.A. and lived in Buffalo. He was drowned off Gloucester, Massachusetts, in approximately 1883. Margaret was buried in New London.

D1   Wesley McLeod, died at the age of eighteen of T.B.

D2   William Duncan McLeod, 1871-1954. He was twelve years old when his father was drowned. He and his brother Wesley, with their mother, moved to Alberta after their father's death. William was born in French River, m. Annie <u>Dawson</u> on Dec. 19, 1917. Annie was born Aug. 14, 1894. She was from Christopher Cross. Issue:

E1   Lloyd MacLeod, born 1919, m. Stella _____.

E2   Roy MacLeod, m. Margaret (Peggy) <u>Lambert</u>. They had three children.

E3   Margaret MacLeod, m. William <u>Strawbridge</u>.

E4   Edith MacLeod, m. Reg. <u>Eldershaw</u>.

E5   Chester MacLeod, m. Danielle _____.

B2   Marion McLeod, born c. 1796, m. Andrew <u>MacPherson</u> of Irishtown.

B3   Angus McLeod, born c. 1800, did not marry.

B4   George McLeod, m. Sophia <u>MacKay</u>, 1794-1890, with issue:

C1   Catherine MacLeod, m. James <u>Sheen</u>. They moved to the MacLeod home where James was a farmer and shoemaker. George had willed the farm to James and at his death to his grandson George. His joiner's tools were to be divided between his sons Kenneth and John. After James' death in 1901, his wife and family moved to Boston, Massachusetts. Their family were:

D1   George Sheen, was a violinist.

D2   Annie Sheen.

D3   Augusta Sheen.

D4   Ila Sheen.

C2   Kenneth MacLeod, died July 8, 1893, aged 66, m. Margaret <u>MacPherson</u> who died Oct. 28, 1900, at age 66. They were married Jan. 15, 1853, at St. Eleanor's Church. They lived with her parents, Mr. and Mrs. Andrew MacPherson. Kenneth left this house to his son George, who lived there all his life. George left it to his son James. When James left in 1955 he sold the farm to his brother Kenneth, who later sold it to Freeman Simmons.

D1   William H. MacLeod (adopted), d. May 30, 1893 aged 11.

D2   Annie MacLeod, 1853-1943, m. Albert <u>Stewart</u> and moved to Park Corner.

D3   Eliza MacLeod, 1861-1944, m. William <u>Champion</u>, a widower from Spring Valley, with issue:

E1   Kenneth Champion.

E2   Elwin Champion.

E3   Margaret Champion.

E4   Lena Champion.

E5   Edgar Champion.

D4   Alma MacLeod, 1866-1951, m. William <u>Sheen</u>, with issue:

E1   Lila Sheen, m. Will <u>McNevin</u>.

E2   Roland Sheen.

E3   Elga Sheen.

E4   Nelson Sheen.

D5 Andrew MacLeod, 1856-1951, married Joanna <u>Profitt</u> of Eel Creek. In 1893 he bought a farm to the south of the Irishtown Road from John Burke. He lived there until his death at the age of 95. His children were:

E1 Emeline MacLeod, 1885-1964. Never married.

E2 William MacLeod, 1887-1983, spent part of younger life in Western Canada. He m. Margaret <u>Brown</u>, who was a teacher in the Irishtown School. He farmed in Norboro and then moved to Mt. Herbert where he managed the P.E.I. Orphanage Farm. Later he operated Checkers Court Fur Farm in Central Royalty. He then was a Fruit and Vegetable Inspector of P.E.I. After retirement he lived in Parkdale, his children were:

    F1 Marion MacLeod, m. Eric <u>Coffin</u> of Montague, issue:

        G1 Roger Coffin, m. Janice <u>George</u>, with issue:

            H1 Jennifer Coffin.

            H2 Eric Coffin.

        G2 Malcolm William Gary Coffin, m. Sandra <u>Mac-Donald</u>, with issue:

            H1 Victoria Coffin.

    F2 Irene MacLeod, m. George <u>Rogers</u> of Charlottetown, issue:

        G1 George Jennings Rogers m. Teresa <u>MacKrow</u>.

        G2 Alan Trenaman Rogers, m. Brenda <u>Stewart</u>.

        G3 Margaret Jo-Anne Rogers, m. Kevin <u>Whitrow</u>.

            H1 Anna June Whitrow.

E3 Heath MacLeod, m. Elizabeth <u>Cousins</u>, Park Corner. They lived on the family farm, with issue:

    F1 Mildred MacLeod, m. William <u>Heaney</u>, of Clinton, with issue:

        G1 Harold Heaney.

        G2 Jean Heaney.

        G3 Kenneth Heaney.

    F2 Margaret MacLeod, m. Milner <u>Hill</u>, Fredericton, issue:

        G1 James Hill.

        G2 Harold Hill.

        G3 Ronnie Hill.

        G4 Barbara Hill.

        G5 Mary Elizabeth Hill.

        G6 Phillip Hill.

        G7 Kent Hill.

    F3 Harold MacLeod, m. Olive <u>Buchanan</u>, of Albany, issue:

        G1 Beryle MacLeod, m. Carlyle <u>MacEachern</u>, Freetown, with issue:

            H1 Carey MacEachern.

            H2 Brett MacEachern.

        G2 Linda MacLeod, m. George <u>Boyle</u>, of Hunter River, with issue:

            H1 Geoffrey Boyle.

            H2 Robert Boyle.

         G3   William MacLeod, m. Wendy Jacklyn, of Shilo, Manitoba, with issue:
             H1   Krista MacLeod.
             H2   Cara MacLeod.
         G4   Alan MacLeod, m. Shirley Bryenton, Malpeque.
             H1   Wade MacLeod.
             H2   Corey MacLeod.

D6   George MacLeod, 1858-1952, m. Hannah Bernard, with issue:
    E1   Leta MacLeod, died in 1907 at age 16.
    E2   Kenneth MacLeod, 1895-1962, m. Hattie Tuplin, 1895-1962. They bought the Don Bernard farm and also the farm of William H. Campbell, their children were:
         F1   John MacLeod, m. Ruby Cole. They lived on the family farm. Their children were:
             G1   Clifford MacLeod, m. Carol Anderson. They live in Edmonton, with issue:
                 H1   Kenneth MacLeod.
                 H2   Glen MacLeod.
             G2   Thelma MacLeod, m. Clayton Leary, Carleton.
                 H1   Karen Leary.
                 H2   Wade Leary.
                 H3   Jason Leary.
             G3   Lois MacLeod, m. Elwin Sharpe, of St. Eleanors.
                 H1   Todd Sharpe.
             G4   Leta MacLeod, R.N., m. Erwin MacEwen, RCMP.
                 H1   Aaron MacEwen.
             G5   Donald MacLeod, m. Mary Thomas, with issue:
                 H1   Shelley MacLeod.
                 H2   Fern MacLeod.
                 H3   Heather MacLeod.
             G6   Myra MacLeod, m. Roger Clark, Kensington.
                 H1   Curtis Clark.
    E3   James MacLeod, m. Lina Tuplin. They inherited the family farm. Issue:
         F1   George MacLeod, m. Marguerite Paynter. Moved to Langley, British Columbia, with issue:
             G1   Wendell MacLeod, m. Linda Osborne. They live in British Columbia.
                 H1   Karen MacLeod.
                 H2   Jamie MacLeod.
             G2   Donna MacLeod, m. Gerald Bernard, live in Alberta.
                 H1   Gerry Bernard.
                 H2   Kirk Bernard.
                 Donna m. 2) Orest Makowsky in Saskatchewan.
                 H3   Jenny Makowsky.
D7   Edgar MacLeod, 1863-1946. Never married.
D8   Barbara MacLeod, 1868-1963, m. John MacGougan, with issue:
    E1   Lillian MacGougan, died aged 5.
D9   Amelia (Minnie) MacLeod, twin to Barbara, 1868-1955, m. Hugh Campbell, with issue:
    E1   John Eddie Campbell.

C3 Barbara MacLeod, m. George Bishop.

C4 John MacLeod, moved to Summerside. He was a shoemaker.

C5 Margaret MacLeod, m. John Gregg.

B5 Donald MacLeod, born 1802.

B6 Kenneth MacLeod, [died?] 1883. He m. Catherine MacIntyre, with issue:

C1 Lemuel MacLeod, moved to California.

C2 Andrew MacLeod, m. Elizabeth Paynter Cousins.

C3 Kenneth MacLeod, lived in Brockton, Massachusetts.

C4 George MacLeod, was a captain. He m. Alice Cornish of Park Corner.

C5 Ann Marie MacLeod, m. John Franklin MacNeil of Cavendish, P.E.I.

C6 Catherine MacLeod, never married.

C7 Duncan MacLeod, m. Miss Jones, and lived in Spokane, Washington.

B7 James MacLeod, born 1805.

B8 Nancy (Ann) MacLeod,1805-1888, m. James Pidgeon, died Dec. 18, 1886.

B9 William MacLeod.

B10 Murdock MacLeod, 1808-1885. He m. Ann Hardy, she died in 1898, aged 84. Murdock and Ann lived in the Belmont area, but moved to Park Corner some time prior to 1860. They leased the land from a Mr. Holland of Charlottetown. The deed showed the property was bought in 1860. Their children were:

C1 Andrew MacLeod, farmer at Park Corner. He died in 1905 at the age of 46 of a heart attack. He m. Priscilla B. Bell, she died Feb. 4, 1948, aged 80 years. Their children were:

D1 Ada Blanch MacLeod, died June 25, 1900, aged 17. She died of T.B.

D2 Glenwood MacLeod, died Dec. 8, 1900, of spinal meningitis.

D3 William Preston MacLeod, 1887-1953, died of Parkinson's disease. He m. Belle Fife, 1885-1980, with issue:

E1 Glenwood MacLeod, 1916-1982. He was killed in a farming accident. He was m. to Anna M. Warren, born Sept. 29, 1919. They were m. on Oct. 13, 1937, issue:

F1 Wallace MacLeod, m. Lois G. Stavert, with issue:

G1 Katherine MacLeod, m. David Brown, issue:

H1 Philip Brown.

H2 Katerina Brown.

G2 Cheryl MacLeod, m. Delmar Noonan, living in Searletown.

G3 Glennamae MacLeod.

G4 Stavert MacLeod.

F2 Myrna MacLeod, m. Jim MacKay, with issue:

G1 Shawn Patrick MacKay.

G2 Kelly Coleen MacKay.

F3 Alberta MacLeod, m. Ronald Somers, with issue:

G1 David Somers.

G2 Jeffrey Somers.

G3 Murray Somers.

E2 Annie MacLeod, m. Lloyd Carr. They live in Miscouche.

F1 Ronald Carr.

F2 Maybelle Carr.

E3 Nina MacLeod, m. Robert Taylor, they live in Clearwater, British Columbia, with issue:

F1   Shirley Taylor, m. Robert <u>Haywood</u>. They live in Vancouver, they have one son and two daughters.

F2   Sandra Taylor, m. Robert <u>Rayner</u>. She works in a bank in Clearwater, British Columbia. Issue: one son and one daughter.

F3   Janice Taylor, m. Adrion <u>Damini</u>. Living in Kamloops, British Columbia, with issue:

    G1   Aaron Wade Damini.

    G2   Daryl Wayne Damini.

C2   John MacLeod, a bachelor in Park Corner, died March 5, 1911, aged 55.

C3   Martha MacLeod, m. _____ <u>Mofatt</u>, they lived in Boston.

C4   James MacLeod.

C5   William MacLeod and his brother James (C4) were in partnership with a cousin by the name of MacLeod, and their company went bankrupt. They later left this country and it is believed that one went to the Klondike, and the other one to Southern U.S.A.

C6   George MacLeod, buried in Plaster Rock, New Brunswick, m. Elizabeth <u>Graham</u>, died Nov. 9, 1913. The family disapproved of the wedding and the family disowned him, which was not uncommon in those days, issue:

    D1   John A. MacLeod, 1880–1966, is buried in Geddie Memorial Cemetery.

Information from Edith Douglas, Little Sands; Edith Eldershaw, Kensington; George P. MacLeod, New London; Elda Sharpe, and Blanche Heaney on behalf of James MacLeod, Kensington; and Anna MacLeod, Kensington.

HUGH MACLEOD
HUGH MACLEOD AND MARION WALL OF SPRING VALLEY

A   Hugh MacLeod, 1829-1917, born in French River, m. Marion Wall, 1843-1881, daughter of James and Susanne (Adams) of Sea View. In 1874 Hugh and Marion moved to Spring Valley, where he was a fisherman and farmer. They are buried in New London Geddie Memorial Cemetery. They had five children:

B1   Hugh James MacLeod, 1865-1935, m. Jane Champion, she was born in 1877 to George and Elizabeth (Day) Champion of Baltic. They lived in Spring Valley where Hugh James was a farmer and a fisherman. They had seven children:

C1   George MacLeod, 1896-1969, m. Annie Woodside, daughter of Bennie Woodside, Malpeque. George was a fisherman. They had no family.

C2   Ertel MacLeod, 1898-1969. He was a fisherman and lived with his uncle George in Darnley, never married, buried in Princetown United Cemetery.

C3   Lila MacLeod, 1889-1985. She was an R.N. and received her training in Summerside. She moved to U.S.A. In 1957 retired and moved back to P.E.I. with her brother Neil.

C4   Russell MacLeod, born 1901. He m. Jessie Black in U.S.A. and owned and operated a poultry farm. They had two sons:

D1   Russell MacLeod.

D2   Kenneth MacLeod.

C5   Edward MacLeod, 1903-1979. He was a fisherman, farmer and labourer. He never married.

C6   Lucy MacLeod, born in 1905 and died the same year.

C7   Neil MacLeod, born in 1908. Moved to U.S.A. and in 1957 retired and came to live in Traveller's Rest. Later he built a home for him and his sister Lila in Baltic.

B2   Elizabeth MacLeod, born 1873, m. Johez Tuplin son of John and Margaret (Marks) Tuplin, Margate. They had three children:

C1   Claude Tuplin, 1891-1927. He never married and lived in British Columbia.

C2   Ethel Tuplin, m. Howard Daws in U.S.A. They had no children.

C3   Edith Tuplin, m. Nelson Zachews and later m. Richard Adams, and lived in U.S.A. They had no children.

B3   George MacLeod, 1876-1955, m. Mary (Polly) MacKay, 1864-1919, daughter of Alex MacKay and Ellen (Pickering) MacKay. They farmed the MacKay farm and they had no children, but George's nephew Ertel lived with them. They are buried in Princetown United Church Cemetery.

B4   Eliza MacLeod, 1869-1954. She was a bookkeeper in U.S.A. and never married.

B5   Jessie MacLeod, 1874-1926, m. George Ganong, and lived in U.S.A., with one son.

C1   Keir Bradford Ganong.

Information received from Emily Douglas, Kensington, through Jim MacLeod, Idaho, and cemetery transcriptions.

JOHN MACLEOD
JOHN MACLEOD AND MARGARET MACLEOD OF LONG RIVER

A1   John MacLeod, born 1770, Isle of Skye, m. in 1794 to Margaret <u>MacLeod</u>. Margaret was the daughter of Hugh MacLeod. Their children were:

    B1   Allan MacLeod, m. [?].

        C1   Malcolm MacLeod, Graham's Road, near Kensington, P.E.I.

    B2   Mary MacLeod, apparently blind, lived with nephew Malcolm. During the voyage there was an outbreak of smallpox. Marion recovered but remained blind. Murdock was alive when the ship landed but succumbed to the disease later. When the ship arrived with smallpox aboard, the authorities refused to let them land, which was understandable. They set up a tent camp for them on the shore where they were forced to remain until the disease subsided.

    B3   Roderick MacLeod, 1810-1889, m. Jan. 29, 1836, to Catherine <u>McInnis</u>, 1815-1907. She was the daughter of Lauchlin and Catherine McInnis of Skye. Scottish Census 1861 lists Roderick in Portree, Skye, as a farmer. Roderick and Catherine emigrated to P.E.I. in 1871, apparently with all the children except Mary and Neil. Roderick farmed at Long River and was buried at New London, their children were:

        C1   John MacLeod, died in infancy by falling into the fireplace.

        C2   John MacLeod, 1838-1928, m. Priscilla <u>Marks</u>, 1842-1928. Scottish Census of 1861 lists him as a tailor.

        C3   Lachlan MacLeod, 1834-1889. Also listed as a tailor, m. Mary <u>MacLean</u> on Dec. 24, 1862, in Scotland. She was born in 1841 and died 1938, which was 49 years after her husband's death. Her death wish was that her husband be exhumed and she buried beneath him. Her son Murdock reluctantly complied with the request and told his cousin that the corpse was reduced to piles of dust. (Nothing was said of the bones.) Their children were:

            D1   Rachel MacLeod, 1880-1935, m. Charles <u>MacKay</u>. With issue:

                E1   Chester MacKay, born 1911, m. Ruth <u>Campbell</u>.

                E2   Mary Irene MacKay, 1915-1936.

            D2   Margaret MacLeod, 1881-1906.

            D3   Murdock MacLeod, 1884-1976, m. Bessie <u>Johnstone</u>, with issue:

                E1   Jean MacLeod, m. R. <u>Jones</u>.

                E2   Margaret MacLeod, died in infancy.

            D4   Christina MacLeod, m. A. <u>Sterling</u>, with issue:

                E1   Violet Sterling.

                E2   Ralph Sterling.

                E3   Neil Sterling.

                E4   Marjorie Sterling.

                E5   Mary Sterling.

                E6   Jean Sterling.

                E7   Ruth Sterling.

        C4   Mary MacLeod, 1841–1872, m. John <u>Shearer</u>, they stayed in Scotland. They had issue:

            D1   Elizabeth Shearer, single, lived with a brother in Edinburgh.

            D2   Rod Shearer, single.

C5 Rachel MacLeod, 1843-1937, m. John <u>Forbes</u>.
C6 Murdock, 1844-1872. Died of smallpox.
C7 Neil MacLeod, 1853-1934, m. Dec. 27, 1886, to Ada <u>Ramsay</u>, daughter of William B. Ramsay of Summerside. She died March 2, 1932, at age 64. Neil MacLeod came to P.E.I. in 1873, two years after the rest of his family. He had been employed in the post office in Glasgow, Scotland, and after his arrival on P.E.I. he attended the Fanning Grammar School at Malpeque, where he obtained a scholarship which entitled him to two years at Prince of Wales College. He began teaching in Malpeque in 1877 and then was Principal of the Eastern District School in Summerside. He became Superintendent of Schools in 1879 and retained that position until 1893 when at the age of forty he began to study law in the office of J.H. Bell. In 1899 he became an attorney and was admitted to the bar the following year. He was appointed King's Counsel in 1917.
  D1 Norman MacLeod, 1887-1958, m. Sarah Hannah <u>Ching</u>, 1895-1941, with issue:
    E1 Norman Erskine MacLeod, m. Nettie Kathleen <u>Chase</u>, issue:
      F1 Norma Irene MacLeod, m. Thomas <u>Lipsock</u>.
      F2 Joyce Ellen MacLeod, m. Clarence <u>Ferrish</u>.
      F3 Catherine Ann MacLeod, m. Lawrence <u>Johansen</u>.
      F4 Susan Flora MacLeod, m. Robert <u>Groalchman</u>.
    E2 Ada Verna MacLeod, m. Eville <u>Gorham</u>, with issue:
      F1 Ann Kerstin Gorham, m. Todd <u>Bartholomary</u>.
      F2 Sarah Vivian Gorham.
      F3 Jocelyn Shirley Gorham.
      F4 James Neil Gorham.
    E3 William Stephen MacLeod.
    E4 Neil Roderick MacLeod, m. Janet <u>McPhee</u>. No family.
  D2 Donald L. MacLeod, 1889-1934. He died from a fall from a horse at Thorold, Ontario. He m. Marion <u>MacLean</u>, with issue:
    E1 John M. MacLeod.
    E2 Donald D. MacLeod.
  D3 William F. MacLeod, 1891-1980, m. Alice <u>Martin</u>, with issue:
    E1 Allan MacLeod, m. Jeanne Marie <u>Smith</u>, with issue:
      F1 Keith MacLeod.
      F2 Barbara MacLeod.
      F3 Lynne MacLeod.
    E2 Frank S. MacLeod, m. Beryl <u>Griffin</u>, with issue:
      F1 Ian MacLeod, m. Doris Lei <u>Jones</u>.
      F2 Brenda MacLeod (adopted), m. Eric <u>Anderson.</u>
  D4 Reginald MacLeod, 1894-1965.
  D5 John Malcolm MacLeod, 1896-1916. He was in the McGill University Contingent of the Princess Pat's Canadian Light Infantry. He died at Sanctuary Wood, Ypres, Belgium, on June 2, 1916.
  D6 Allan R. MacLeod, 1896-1917. He was a gunner with the 747 C.G.A. B.E.F. and died of pneumonia while in Halifax in 1917.
  D7 Neil MacLeod, 1900-1935, died in a car accident. He was a doctor and pathologist at the University of Pennsylvania and was not married.
  D8 Kenneth MacLeod, born 1905, m. Ella <u>Juergenmeyer</u>, with issue:

E1   Donald MacLeod, m. 1) Lynda <u>Forbers</u>.
   F1   Christopher MacLeod.
   Donald m. 2) Marilyn <u>Houseman</u>.
E2   Lorraine MacLeod, m. Joseph <u>Snearson</u>, with issue:
   F1   Mark Snearson.
   F2   Glen Snearson.
C7   Marion MacLeod, 1853-1933. She was blinded by smallpox.
C8   Catherine MacLeod, 1857-1937, m. Spurgeon <u>Burns</u> of Chicago.

Information provided by Frank S. MacLeod.

Roderick MacLeod
Roderick MacLeod and Catherine MacLean of Darlington

A   Roderick MacLeod, 1817-1861. Roderick was from Raasay, m. Catherine MacLean, also from Raasay. She died Dec.16, 1890, age 71. They lived in Darlington and are buried in Hartsville, P.E.I. They had issue:

B1   Norman MacLeod, 1840-1924, m. Margaret Drummond, 1848-1908. They are buried in Springvale Cemetery. Their children were:

     C1   Alex MacLeod, went to Bangor, Maine.

     C2   John MacLeod, went to Maine.

     C3   Margaret MacLeod, lived in U.S.A.

     C4   Walter MacLeod, 1882-1970, m. Bertha Sentner, 1885-1960. They lived in Brookfield, and had the following children:

         D1   Margaret MacLeod, m. 1) Robert MacKinnon, with issue:

            E1   Harvey MacKinnon.

            E2   Joyce MacKinnon.

            E3   Gloria MacKinnon, m. R. Piggot.

            E4   Blair MacKinnon.

         Margaret m. 2) Max Benson, no children.

         D2   Gordon MacLeod, m. 1) Edna Holms, no children.

         Gordon m. 2) Helen Robertson, with issue:

            E1   Ruth MacLeod, m. Lawson Thompson.

     C5   Sadie MacLeod, 1884-1922.

     C6   Angus Leslie MacLeod, 1886-1892.

B2   John R. MacLeod, 1843-1929. He did not marry and is buried in Hartsville.

B3   Donald MacLeod, 1845-1914, m. Margaret Morrison, they are buried in Brookfield. Their family was:

     C1   Rod MacLeod, in British Columbia.

     C2   John (Jack) MacLeod.

     C3   William (Will) MacLeod.

     C4   Effie Ann MacLeod, buried in Brookfield, m. Louis MacPherson, they lived in Darlington, and had issue:

         D1   Donald MacPherson, m. Mamie Nicholson, with issue:

            E1   Donald Weir MacPherson.

               F1   Heather MacPherson.

               F2   Laurie MacPherson.

         D2   Wendell MacPherson, m. Dot Mar, with issue:

            E1   David MacPherson.

            E2   Beverley MacPherson.

            E3   Barry MacPherson.

         D3   Lloyd MacPherson, m. Jean MacPherson, with issue:

            E1   Garry MacPherson.

            E2   Blane MacPherson.

B4   Ann MacLeod, 1847-1914, m. Daniel MacDonald, 1847-1914, they had no family and are buried in Hartsville.

B5   Isabella MacLeod, 1852-1935, m. William MacLeod, they are buried in Royal Oak Cemetery, Vancouver, British Columbia. They lived in Hartsville until 1910, then moved to Vancouver. (See Cornwall, the family of Malcolm and Mary).

B6   Angus R. MacLeod, 1854-1935, never married and is buried in Hartsville.
B7   Effie MacLeod, 1858-1923, m. Donald MacLeod. They are buried in Harts-
      ville. With issue:
      C1   John A. MacLeod, 1884-1925, m. Flora MacKinnon, with issue:
            D1   Edith MacLeod, unmarried.
            D2   Sterling MacLeod, m. Winnifred Haslam, no children.
            D3   Finley MacLeod, m. Connie Holroyd, with issue:
                  E1   Keith MacLeod.
                  E2   David MacLeod.
                  E3   Donna Gwen MacLeod.
                  E4   John MacLeod.
            D4   Helen MacLeod, m. W. Roberts, with issue:
                  E1   Gail Roberts.
                  E2   Donald Roberts.
                  E3   Elizabeth Roberts.
                  E4   Doreen Roberts.
            D5   Jean MacLeod, 1919-1919.
            D6   Keith MacLeod, died 1923.
      C2   Catherine MacLeod, m. Amos Rodd. They are buried in Milton, issue:
            D1   Gordon Rodd, m. Anna _____, with issue:
                  E1   Dianah C. Rodd.
                  E2   R. James Rodd.
            D2   Anna Rodd, m. Lorne Thompson, with issue:
                  E1   Nancy Thompson.
                  E2   Bob Thompson.

Information provided by Elizabeth and Ronald MacLeod of Darlington, P.E.I.

DONALD MACLEOD
DONALD MACLEOD AND JESSIE NICHOLSON OF TYNE VALLEY

A1 Donald MacLeod, born 1808, Isle of Skye, died 1884 in Victoria West, m. Jessie Nicholson, 1814-1900 also from Skye, with issue:

B1 Bella MacLeod, 1845-1929, m. Henry Mooney.

B2 Mary MacLeod (big), died 1921, aged 72, m. Samuel Dyment. She is buried in Victoria West. They had an adopted son:

    C1 James Dyment.

B3 James MacLeod, 1853-1925, m. Harriet Elizabeth Campbell MacDougall, 1869-1924. She was descended from the Harriet Campbell, who was descended from the noble House of Argyle. (See *Skye Pioneers*, page 42.) They are both buried in the Victoria West cemetery, issue:

    C1 Donald MacLeod, 1889-1974, m. Lilla Belle Ramsay, 1896-1940, from Northam, they lived in Wellington Center, with issue:

        D1 Donald MacLeod, m. Verda Allen, they lived in Ottawa, issue:

            E1 Allen MacLeod, married in Ottawa, with five children.

        D2 Myrtle MacLeod, m. Lloyd Deavy, Ottawa, with issue:

            E1 Donna Deavy, m. Douglas Sprecht, two children.

            E2 Cheryl Deavy, m. Garry Harris, Ottawa, two children.

            E3 Mira Deavy, m. David Clark, one child.

            E4 Lynn Deavy, m. Paul Sharpe, two children.

            E5 Ronald Deavy.

        D3 James Clarence MacLeod, married a girl in Ottawa, three children.

    C2 Annie MacLeod, 1890-1989, never married.

    C3 Alexander MacLeod, 1893-1977, m. Lulu Ramsay, 1902-1952, sister of Belle (above). They lived in Victoria West and had issue:

        D1 Priscilla MacLeod, m. John W. Myers, Carleton.

        D2 Freda Maude MacLeod, m. Horace Jewell, from Bedeque. They lived in London, Ontario, with issue:

            E1 Elizabeth Jewell.

            E2 Helen Jewell, m. Ivan Cablek, London, Ont., issue:

                F1 Joshua Cablek.

                F2 Jesse Cablek.

        D3 Annie Blanche MacLeod, m. Ivan Craig, Bedeque, they lived in Victoria, with issue:

            E1 Leigh Craig, m. Joyce MacKay, with issue:

                F1 Darren Craig, m. Tracy Richard.

                F2 Trevor Craig.

            E2 Sandra Ann Craig, m. Bruce MacFarlane, Fernwood, issue:

                F1 Kimberley MacFarlane, m. Steven Townsend.

                F2 Krista MacFarlane, m. Jay____.

                F3 Arron MacFarlane.

            E3 Eileen Craig, m. James Bagnall, they live in Montague, where he is a member of the Provincial Legislature, issue:

                F1 Douglas Bagnall, m. Glenda McCabe.

                F2 Craig Bagnall, m. Nancy Penny.

                F3 Tara Bagnall.

    F4 Tanya Bagnall.

   E4 Evelyn Craig, m. Reigh <u>MacEachern</u>, Appin Road, issue:

    F1 Stacy MacEachern, m. Paul <u>Ferguson</u>.

    F2 Stephen MacEachern, m. Jennifer <u>MacFarlane</u>.

    F3 Andrew MacEachern.

    F4 Lindsey MacEachern.

   E5 Brenda Blanche Craig, 1952-1975, never married.

   E6 William Craig, m. Elizabeth _____, living in St. John, New Brunswick.

   F1 Falen Craig.

   E7 Robert Craig, m. Susan <u>MacFayden</u>, living in Victoria West.

    F1 Bobby Craig.

    F2 Jason Craig.

    F3 Matthew Craig.

   E8 Susan Elizabeth Craig, m. Derek <u>Richard</u>, Appin Road.

    F1 Craig Richard.

    F2 Logan Richard.

  D4 Muriel Catherine MacLeod, m. Eric <u>Pearson</u>, Victoria, British Columbia.

   E1 Victoria Anna Pearson, m. David <u>Coates</u>, from British Columbia.

   E2 Ruth Novella Pearson, m. Mark <u>McLaughlin</u>, with two children.

   E3 Barbara Ethel Pearson, m. Philip <u>Masini</u>, with issue:

    F1 Peter Masini.

    F2 Brian Masini.

   E4 Nancy Lou Christine Pearson, never married.

  D5 Ramsay MacLeod, m. Verna <u>Ellands</u>, living in Victoria West.

   E1 Linda MacLeod, m. Fred <u>Pike</u>, St. John, New Brunswick, issue:

    F1 Fred Pike, Jr.

    F2 Heather Pike.

   E2 James MacLeod, m. Cindy <u>MacPhee</u>, living in Summerside.

    F1 Katie MacLeod.

   E3 David MacLeod, m. Paula <u>Gillis</u>. He was killed in a car accident in 1977, leaving a five week old son:

    F1 Colin MacLeod.

   E4 Brian Ramsay MacLeod, m. Carole <u>Roy</u>, in Ottawa.

   E5 Douglas MacLeod, m. Janet <u>Matthews</u>, they live in Victoria West, with three children.

   E6 Catherine MacLeod, m. 1) Lyndon <u>Noye</u>, with issue:

    F1 Lindsay Noye.

    F2 Ryan Noye.

    F3 Amanda Noye.

    Catherine m. 2) Scott <u>Cooling</u>, living in Enmore.

   E7 Melissa Dawn MacLeod, living in Charlottetown.

  D6 Helen MacLeod, m. Gordon <u>Murray</u>, Harmony, with issue:

   E1 Alex Gordon Murray, m. Frances <u>Smith</u>, with issue:

    F1 Graham Murray.

    F2 Amanda Murray.

   E2 Raymond Murray.

E3 Sheila Diane Murray, m. John <u>Manderson</u>, Lot 16, with issue:
    F1   Jackson Manderson.
    F2   Sarah Manderson.
    F3   Nancy Manderson.
E4 Laurie Murray, m. William <u>Dawson</u>. They live in Scarborough, Ontario, with issue:
    F1   Megan Dawson.
E5 Alan Murray, m. Myrna _____, with issue:
    F1   Shara Lee Murray.
    F2   Bryson Murray.
E6 Priscilla Anne Murray, m. Kevin <u>MacMillan</u>, West Cape, issue:
    F1   Jennifer MacMillan.
    F2   Jessica MacMillan.
    F3   Lou MacMillan.
E7 John Murray, not married.

D7 Leaman Alexander MacLeod, m. Jennie <u>MacWilliams</u>, they live in Victoria West, with issue:
E1 Myles MacLeod, died when a few months old.
E2 Arthur MacLeod, m. Gail <u>Arsenault</u>, with issue:
    F1   Ryan MacLeod.
    F2   Jeremy MacLeod.
E3 Rose MacLeod, living in Summerside.
E4 Lulu Blanche MacLeod, m. Gordon <u>Whitlock</u>, they live in Summerside, with issue:
    F1   Corolyn Whitlock.
    F2   Paul Whitlock.
E5 Jarvis MacLeod, Victoria West.
E6 Barry Ross MacLeod, Summerside.
E7 Marlene MacLeod.
    F1   Spenser MacLeod.
E8 Vivian MacLeod, m. Charles <u>Herrel</u>, Summerside.
    F1   Ashley Herrel.
    F2   Jason Herrel.
E9 Kelly Jean MacLeod, m. Michael _____. They live in Summerside, with issue:
    F1   Chelsey ____.
    F2   Luke _____.
Leaman and Jennie also had twin girls who died at birth.

C4 John MacLeod, son of James MacLeod, was in the 1st World War. He was a prisoner of war in Germany where he met a German girl called Anna _____, whom he eventually married. After the war they moved to San Francisco, they had no family.

C5 Roderick MacLeod, m. Clara <u>Phillips</u>, she had been married to Dan MacLeod, from Mt. Pleasant and they had two children named Charles MacLeod and Jennie MacLeod. Roderick and Clara's children were:
D1 Carmen MacLeod, m. Frank <u>MacKinnon</u>, from Springhill, with issue:
E1 Carol Anne MacKinnon, m. Sam <u>Evans</u>, Charlottetown.

F1   Alexandria Evans.
F2   Vida Evans.
E2   Earlene MacKinnon, m. Robert <u>Gray</u>, Stratford. They are both teachers, with issue:
F1   Matthew Gray.
F2   Tristan Gray.
E3   Donald MacKinnon, m Noelle <u>Laing</u>. He is a banker. They live in Halifax.
F1   Sarah MacKinnon.
F2   Emily MacKinnon.
E4   David MacKinnon, m. Wendy _____, lives in British Columbia.
E5   Douglas MacKinnon, lives in Borden, P.E.I.
E6   Gladys Elizabeth MacKinnon, m. Alvin <u>Price</u>.
F1   Kate Price.
F2   Donald Price.
E7   Richard MacKinnon, m. Marie <u>May</u>, in the U.S.A.
F1   Elana MacKinnon.
D2   Corinne MacLeod, m. Earl <u>MacLaurin</u>, Enmore, with issue:
E1   Dawn Marie MacLaurin, died at 3 months of age.
E2   Clara Anne MacLaurin, living in Toronto, Ontario.
E3   Devern Roderick MacLaurin, m. Ann Marie <u>Gallant</u>.
F1   Amanda MacLaurin.
F2   Nathan Roderick MacLaurin.
E4   Charles Robert MacLaurin, m. 1) Debbie <u>Murray</u>.
F1   Michelle MacLaurin.
Charles Robert m. 2) Dorothy <u>Adams</u>.
E5   Warner Earl MacLaurin, m. Darlene <u>Murray</u>.
F1   Robert MacLaurin.
E6   Russell Geoffrey MacLaurin, m. Heather <u>Bernard</u>.
F1   Peter MacLaurin.
F2   Todd MacLaurin.
E7   Earla Maxine MacLaurin, m. Dale <u>Davignon</u>.
F1   Marc Lucien Earl Davignon.
F2   Annette Dominique Desiree Davignon.
D3   Earl MacLeod, m. Lois <u>Kirkpatrick</u>, living in Don Mills, with issue:
E1   Kent Douglas MacLeod.
D4   Roderick MacLeod, 1937-1995, m. Joanne Elaine <u>Gleason</u>, in Moncton, New Brunswick.
E1   Roderick MacLeod III, living in Florida.
E2   Scott MacLeod, m. Debbra Ann <u>McCluskey</u>, they are living in St. John, New Brunswick, with issue:
F1   Hillari Lauren Quinn MacLeod.
F2   Ethan Jak Prescott.
D5   Harriet MacLeod, m. David <u>Gilpatrick</u>, living in the U.S.A., with issue:
E1   Dawn MacLeod, m. Larry _____.
E2   Elizabeth MacLeod.
C6   Archibald MacLeod, 1897-1939, lived in the U.S., buried in Victoria West.

C7   Douglas MacLeod, 1901-1946, lived in the U.S., buried in Victoria West.
C8   Jessie MacLeod, m. John Heskett, Brownville, Maine, with issue:
     D1   Robert Heskett, a Baptist minister, married in Maine.
     D2   Pauline Heskett, m. Andrew Michaud, Maine.
     D3   Shirley Heskett, married in Maine.
     D4   Mary Heskett, m. John Thomas, in Maine.
     D5   Gerald Heskett, married in Maine.
     D6   Geraldine Heskett, a twin of Gerald, is married in the U.S.A.
C9   Mary Belle MacLeod, lived in the U.S., never married.
C10 Carmen MacLeod, lived in Lowell, Massachusetts, never married.
C11 Stirling MacLeod, lived in the U.S., m. 1) ____ Cotton, from Springhill, their children were:
     D1   Joan MacLeod, m. Richard Henshaw, Danvers, Massachusetts.
     D2   Barbara MacLeod, married in the U.S.
     D3   A girl.
     Stirling m. 2) Priscilla _____, with issue:
     D4   Reginald MacLeod, accidentally killed when a child.
     D5   A son.
C12 Everett MacLeod, m. 1) Dorothy _____, with issue:
     D1   A son.
     Everett m. 2) _____, no family.
B4   Roderick MacLeod, born 1853, m. Mary Ann Gillis, with issue:
     C1   Murdock MacLeod, 1871-1953, m. Mary J. Curry. They lived in Springhill, with issue:
          D1   Lorne MacLeod, never married.
          D2   Oliver MacLeod, m. Irene Enman, they lived in Macadam, New Brunswick.
          D3   Gladys MacLeod, never married.
          D4   Aletha MacLeod, m. Ralph Campbell.
          D5   Glenda MacLeod, m. _____ Pridham.
     C2   John MacLeod, died in 1896 of tuberculosis.
     C3   Jessie MacLeod, 1876-1904, also died of tuberculosis.
     C4   Dan MacLeod, m. Margaret Belle Smith, they lived in Victoria West, issue:
          D1   Margaret MacLeod, died young.
          D2   Wesley MacLeod, m. Arthinese (Artie) _____.
          D3   Lila MacLeod, m. Bruce Coulson.
     C5   Christy Ann MacLeod, 1881-1965, m. Alfred Long Frost, 1883-1966, they lived in Enmore, and had issue:
          D1   Marjorie Frost, 1905-1998, m. 1) A. Lawrence Stetson. They lived in the U.S.A., with issue:
               E1   Lloyd Stetson, m. Zilla, with issue:
                    F1   John Stetson.
                    F2   Carol Stetson.
               Marjorie m. 2) Les Noye.
               E2   Ruth Noye, m. Lucien Eliot, with issue:
                    F1   Elizabeth (Beth) Eliot.
                    F2   Victoria Eliot.
                    F3   Katherine (Katie) Eliot.
          D2   Jessie Frost, 1906-1997, m. Francis J. Olsen, U.S.A., with issue:

E1   Christine Olsen, m. Robert <u>Meeken</u>, with issue:
    F1   Deborah Meeken, m. Robert <u>Wright</u>.
    F2   Donald Meeken.
    F3   David Meeken.
E2   Ken Olsen, m. Joan _____, with issue:
    F1   Susan Olsen.
    F2   Lynn Olsen.
    F3   Mark Olsen.
E3   Gary Olsen, m. Diane, with issue:
    F1   Inge Olsen.
    F2   Ethan Olsen.
D3   Charles Frost, 1908-1986, m. May <u>Enman</u>, with issue:
    E1   Charlene Frost, m. Ellsworth <u>Campbell</u>, Summerside, with issue:
        F1   Charles (Chuck) Campbell.
        F2   Deborah Campbell, m. Doug <u>MacAusland</u>.
        F3   Nancy Campbell, m. John _____.
        F4   Marilyn Campbell.
        F5   Karen Campbell, m. _____ <u>Johnston</u>.
        F6   Leila Campbell, m. _____ <u>MacDonald</u>.
    E2   Betty Frost, m. Blair <u>Strongman</u>, Summerside, with issue:
        F1   Doug Strongman, m. Joyce ____.
        F2   Bobby Strongman, m. Cheryl ____.
        F3   Barry Strongman, m. Barb <u>Haslem</u>.
        F4   Darren Strongman.
    E3   Ethel Frost, m. Russel <u>Ellis</u>, Summerside, with issue:
        F1   Brian Ellis, m. Cathy <u>Newson</u>.
        F2   Ricky Ellis, m. Diane <u>Newson</u>.
        F3   David Ellis, m. Georgia <u>Burleigh</u>.
        F4   Stephen Ellis, m. Kelly <u>Poirier</u>.
    E4   Alfred Frost, m. 1) Marilyn _____, with issue:
        F1   Elizabeth Frost.
        Alfred m. 2) Pauline <u>Maynard</u>, with issue:
        F2   Geoffrey Frost.
        F3   Paul Frost.
    E5   Robert Frost, m. Evelyn <u>Yeo</u>, Enmore, with issue:
        F1   Angela Frost, m. Terry <u>Carragher</u>.
        F2   Michael Frost, m. Cheryl <u>Lynch</u>.
        F3   Susan Frost, m. Gary <u>Arsenault</u>.
        F4   Christopher Frost.
    E6   Sidney Frost, m. Linda <u>Colwell</u>, Norboro, with issue:
        F1   Andrew Frost.
        F2   Cory Frost.
        F3   Robert Frost.
    E7   Anna Jean Frost, m. James <u>Dyment</u>, Northam, with issue:
        F1   Todd Dyment, m. Denise _____.
        F2   Mark Dyment.
        F3   Melanie Dyment.
        F4   Heather Lynn Dyment.
    E8   Doris Frost, m. Dan <u>MacLean</u>, Northam, with issue:
        F1   Malcolm MacLean.

        F2   Amanda MacLean.

        F3   William MacLean.

    E9   Heather Frost, m. 1) Barry Webster, with issue:

        F1   Greg Webster.

        F2   Jamie Webster.

        Heather m. 2) George Mitchell.

D4   Eva Frost, m. Dale Simonds, U.S.A., with issue:

    E1   Linda Simonds, m. Bruce Webb, with issue:

        F1   Matthew Webb.

        F2   Samuel Webb.

    E2   Sara Frost Simonds, m. Jim Bourque, with issue:

        F1   David Bourque.

        F2   Ross Bourque.

        F3   Diana Bourque.

D5   Anna Frost, 1912-1996, m. Tom Walsh, U.S.A.

D5   Lloyd Frost, m. 1) Jean Martin.

    E1   Margaret Frost, m. Barrie Phillips, Arlington, with issue:

        F1   Christie Laura Phillips, m. Jeff McNally.

        F2   James Alfred Phillips.

    E2   Martin Frost, m. Jo-Ann Brown, with issue:

        F1   Catherine Jean Frost.

        F2   Eric Christian Frost.

    E3   Frances Frost, lives in O'Leary.

    E4   Patricia Frost, m. Wendell Gillis, Ellerslie, with issue:

        F1   Timothy Lloyd Gillis.

        F2   Ethan Wendell Gillis.

    E5   Jessie Frost, m. William Wicks, Charlottetown, with issue:

        F1   Amy Marguerite Frost-Wicks.

        F2

    Lloyd m. 2) Doris Forbes, Summerside.

C6   Malcolm MacLeod, 1886-1960, m. Mary MacKenzie, with issue:

   D1   Flora Belle MacLeod, died at 24 years.

   D2   John Alec MacLeod, m. 1) Vivian _____ m. 2) Mariah_____.

   D3   Annabelle MacLeod, m. Frank Brown.

Source of information: Carman MacLeod, Richmond; Jessie Frost Wicks, Charlottetown; Priscilla Myers, Charlottetown; and Eileen Bagnall, Montague.

ALEXANDER MACLEOD
ALEXANDER MACLEOD AND FLORA MACKENZIE OF HARTSVILLE

A   Alexander MacLeod, born in 1816 in Raasay, Scotland, died 1905 in Hartsville. Emigrated to Hartsville area in late 1830s. He m. Flora MacKenzie, born 1816 in Wallace, Nova Scotia, she died 1885, age 66, in Hartsville. Both are buried in Hartsville. Their children were:

B1   Roderick MacLeod, born Dec. 31, 1858, in Hartsville, m. Catherine MacSwain of Pleasant Valley, on Nov. 23, 1889. She was born March 3, 1868, and died June 7, 1949. She is buried in Pleasant Valley. Roderick died Sept. 13, 1933, and is buried in Hartsville. Their children were:
    C1   Donald MacLeod, killed in action in WWI.
    C2   Flora MacLeod, m. William Horne, they lived in Marble Head, Massachusetts. They had no children.
    C3   Murdock MacLeod, m. Mary MacDonald, of Montague. Murdock farmed the original homestead in Hartsville. Their children were:
        D1   Catherine MacLeod, lived in Hartsville, never married.
        D2   Florence MacLeod, R.N. in Massachusetts. Never married.
        D3   Donald MacLeod, lived with sister Catherine.
        D4   Margaret MacLeod, m. Edward Gilsky, they live in New Jersey.
        D5   Joan MacLeod, m. Frank Levy. They live in Mahone Bay, Nova Scotia.
    C4   John MacLeod, m. Bessie Barrett, they lived in Hunter River and had no children.
    C5   Archibald MacLeod, m. Jean Taylor. They lived in Edmonton, with issue:
        D1   Donald MacLeod, lives in Ottawa.
    C6   Isabel MacLeod, m. Russell Seller, of Charlottetown, with issue:
        D1   Frederick Seller.
        D2   David Seller.
    C7   Malcolm "Lloyd" MacLeod, m. Florence Ward, with issue:
        D1   Roderick MacLeod, m. Phyllis Parker, with issue:
            E1   Diane MacLeod, m. James Boswell, with issue:
                F1   Andrew Boswell.
            E2   James R. MacLeod.
            E3   Carolyn MacLeod.
            E4   Andrew MacLeod.
            E5   Anita MacLeod.
        D2   Marilyn MacLeod, m. William Kennedy, with issue:
            E1   Dawna Lee Kennedy.
            E2   Debra Lynn Kennedy.
            E3   Sandra Kennedy.
            E4   Scott Kennedy.
            E5   Blair Kennedy.
B2   Kenneth MacLeod, born 1856, moved to Montana with brothers Daniel and Murdock.
B3   Daniel or Donald MacLeod, born 1861.
B4   Murdock MacLeod.
B5   Jessie MacLeod, m. Lauchlan MacLeod of Hartsville, with issue:

C1   Janie MacLeod, m. ____ MacMillan.
C2   Florrie MacLeod.
C3   Lottie MacLeod.
Lauchlan died at a young age and Jessie moved with her children to Montana where she kept house for her brothers.

B6   Effie MacLeod, m. John MacLeod, teacher known as "John Teacher." John was born in Hartsville and had a brother William MacLeod. They and all their children moved to Massachusetts.
C1   William B. MacLeod, m. Jessie MacLeod, in Quincy, Massachusetts, with issue:
D1   Rita MacLeod, m. George MacDonald. They had three children.
D2   Ruth MacLeod, m. Ed Jenkins, they had six children.
D3   Chester Arthur MacLeod.
D4   Jean MacLeod, m. Ed Gehrke.
D5   Catherine MacLeod, m. Joe Bruton, they had two daughters and one son.
C2   John Alexander MacLeod ("Alex"), m. Mannie Christian. They lived in Lynn, Massachusetts.
C3   Dr. John Malcolm MacLeod, m. Ann Cummings, with issue:
D1   Gordon MacLeod, m. Ann Cochrane, with issue:
E1   Gordon Avery MacLeod.
E2   Douglas Malcolm MacLeod.
E3   William Bruce MacLeod.
E4   James Redyard MacLeod.
D2   John MacLeod, m. Amy Ela, with issue:
E1   John Malcolm MacLeod.
E2   Barbara Ann MacLeod.
E3   Robert MacLeod.
C4   Flora MacLeod, 1874-1960, m. Rev. J.W. MacKenzie, Charlottetown. with issue:
D1   Katherine MacKenzie, born 1905, m. Mr. Justice George Tweedy, with issue:
E1   Gordon Tweedy, m. Carol MacKenzie.
E2   Jean Tweedy, m. Roger Perry, with issue:
F1   Jennifer Perry.
D2   John MacKenzie, born 1908, m. Betty Probert, with issue:
E1   Scott MacKenzie.
E2   Linda MacKenzie.
D3   Jean MacKenzie, born 1910, was a nurse in New York.
D4   Evelyn MacKenzie, born 1912, m. Wilson Becket, with issue:
E1   Heather Becket, m. Gordon MacLean. They had one child.
E2   Joanne Becket.
E3   Wilson Becket.
D5   Anna Gordon MacKenzie, m. Don Rathbone, with issue:
E1   Gordon Rathbone.
E2   Debbie Rathbone.
C5   Mary MacLeod, 1873-1938, m. in 1911 to Angus Martin, Quincy, Massachusetts.
D1   Edna Martin, m. John Beeman.
D2   Florence Martin, m. Bob Sealy.
D3   John Martin, m. Laura _____.

       D4 Ruth Martin, m. Richard <u>Turner</u>, with issue:
           E1 Mary Ann Turner, married in Montague, with issue:
               F1 Jennifer.
           E2 Jane Bruce Turner.
           E3 Richard Turner, Jr.
           E4 Bruce Aerich Turner.
       D5 Howard Martin.
       D6 Marjorie Martin.
   C6 Neil Murdock "Murt" MacLeod, m. Belle <u>MacFee</u> (this is the way this name was spelt), Quincy, Massachusetts, with issue:
       D1 June MacLeod.
       D2 John MacLeod, married.
       D3 Cuyler MacLeod, married.
       D4 Gloria MacLeod, m. ___ <u>Cline</u>, with four children.
   C7 Catherine MacLeod, 1880-1964, m. Rev. Angus B. <u>MacLeod</u>, 1874-1952.
       D1 Bessie Jean MacLeod, 1914-1987, lived in San Diego and retired to Vancouver where she lived with her sister Heather.
       D2 Heather MacLeod, 1918-1990, m. Jack <u>Gillies</u>, 1917-1970. They lived in Vancouver, British Columbia, with issue:
           E1 Bruce Gillies, works for the Dept. of External Affairs.
   C8 Isaac Newton MacLeod, 1882-1950, m. Effie <u>MacKenzie</u>. They lived in Quincy, Massachusetts, with issue:
       D1 Newton MacLeod, m. Peggy _____. They lived in Nashville, Tennessee.
       D2 Eleanor MacLeod, m. Lincoln <u>Foster</u> in 1967, with issue:
           E1 Caroline Anne Foster.
           E2 Paula Jane Foster.
           E3 Debra Drew Foster.
           E4 James Lincoln Foster.
       D3 Malcolm M. MacLeod, m. first wife (name unknown) and had one child possibly named June. His second wife was Shirley <u>Green</u>.
 B7 Mary Ann MacLeod, m. Angus <u>Nicholson</u>, with issue:
   C1 Allan Nicholson.
   C2 John Nicholson.
   C3 Alexander Nicholson.
   C4 Malcolm Nicholson.
   C5 Florence Nicholson.
   C6 Sarah "Sadie" Nicholson, died young.
   C7 Margaret Nicholson.
   C8 Annie Nicholson.
   C9 Murdoch Nicholson, moved to California.
 B8 Catherine MacLeod, m. John <u>MacLean</u>. They had no children. Catherine died in childbirth.

Information from Lloyd MacLeod, Hartsville, Hartsville Church records and cemetery transcripts.

JAMES TOWNSEND MACLEOD
JAMES TOWNSEND MACLEOD AND MARY BELL OF BAY VIEW

A James Townsend MacLeod, died Sept. 30, 1892, age 73. He m. Mary Bell, they lived in Bay View, P.E.I. Their children were:

B1 Cassie MacLeod, 1854-1883, m. James Simpson, with issue:

C1 Blanche Simpson, born Oct. 21, 1878, m. Allan Stewart after Winnie passed away. (See B7 below.)

D1 Allan Stewart, 1907–1971, m. Catherine Cameron, they lived in Owen Sound, Ontario.

D2 Marjorie Stewart, born Aug. 17, 1908, m. Phillip Meek, they live in Peterborough, Ontario.

C2 Mary Belle Simpson (Birdie), 1880-1957, m. Andrew Glen, 1886-1970, issue:

E1 Muriel Glen, m. Alex Henderson, living in Africa, with issue.

E2 Douglas Glen, born Sept. 27, 1910, died Jan. 3, 1938.

E3 Reginald Glen, m. Kathleen Parsons. They are missionaries in Africa.

E4 Marion Enid Glen.

After Cassie's death James m. Mary Wares, they had seven children.

B2 Robert MacLeod, 1856-1909, m. Amelia MacEwen, with issue:

C1 Ira MacLeod, 1883-1967, m. 1) Margaret Bell MacKay, 1883-1921, issue:

D1 Emily MacLeod, born April 21, 1921. She m. Alex Douglas, with issue:

E1 Wendell Douglas.

E2 Janet Douglas, m. Brian Campbell.

E3 Judy Douglas, m. Gregory Sedguick, Sept. 11, 1976.

Ira m. 2) to Laura Morrison Dixon, 1892-1943, 3) to Pearl Underhill MacKenzie. No family from these marriages.

C2 George MacLeod, 1888-1928, m. Clara Stewart, 1889-1926. They went West and then returned to the old home in Spring Brook. George was a sea captain. After his wife died, his mother came to help him with the children. About sixteen months after she came, George was drowned. Their maternal grandmother, Mrs. Annie Stewart in Sea View, took the girls.

D1 Annie MacLeod, m. J. Weeks Murphy, with issue:

E1 Wallace Murphy, m. Lucy Melissa.

E2 Max Murphy, m. Jean Brown.

D2 Cassie MacLeod, m. Robert Sutherland, with issue:

E1 Gordon Sutherland, m. Barbara MacLeod.

E2 John Sutherland, m. Sylvia Bishop.

E3 Claire Sutherland, m. Maureen Gillis.

E4 Lee Sutherland, m. Isabel MacMillan.

E5 Garth Sutherland, m. Debbie _____.

D3 Lillian MacLeod, m. Reginald Hiltz, with issue:

E1 Elizabeth Hiltz, m. Rod Aitken.

C3   Pearl MacLeod, m. John Campbell. They lived most of their life in Hollister, California.

C4   Myrtle MacLeod, m. Dan MacNeill from Village Green, P.E.I. They lived most of their life in Detroit, with issue:

D1   Parker MacNeill, m. Virginia Dorman in California, with issue:
E1   Doreen MacNeill, m. Marven Vaughn.
E2   Carole Ann MacNeill, m. A. Stonewood.

D2   Irma MacNeill, m. Ray Ruhela. They lived in Detroit, with issue:
E1   Joan Ruhela.

D3   Keith MacNeill, m. Betty Henry and they lived in Detroit, with issue:
E1   Sandra MacNeill.
E2   Judy MacNeill.
E3   Dannie MacNeill.
E4   Robert MacNeill.
E5   Barbara MacNeill.
E6   Lori MacNeill.

C5   Ivan MacLeod, m. Etta Middleton from Charlottetown. They lived first in Saskatchewan and in Manitoba in 1939. They lived in Tiner, Saskatchewan, in the dried out 30s. Etta passed away in 1935 and Ivan and the family moved to Swan River, Manitoba. Their family was:

D1   Jean MacLeod, m. George Townsend, Victoria, British Columbia, no family.

D2   Doris MacLeod, m. Albert Klemmer, living in Rosetown, Saskatchewan, issue:
E1   Eloise Klemmer, m. Ken Johnson.
E2   Carol Klemmer, m. Keith Wilkinson.
E3   Frank Klemmer, m. Cheryl _____.
E4   Norman Klemmer.

D3   Myrtle MacLeod, not married, lives in Saskatoon, Saskatchewan.

D4   Robert MacLeod, never married, died in 1973 in Swan River, Manitoba.

D5   Betty MacLeod, m. Charles Williams, living in Victoria, British Columbia, issue:
E1   Gail Williams.
E2   Lesley Williams.
E3   Michelle Williams, is Lesley's twin.

D6   Leah MacLeod, m. Lloyd Hanson, they live in Swan River, with issue:
E1   Valarie Hanson, m. George _____.
E2   Delores Hanson.
E3   Karen Hanson.
E4   Leonel Hanson.

D7   Yvonne MacLeod, m. William Pohl, they live in Bawsman, with issue:
E1   Marlene Pohl.
E2   Donald Pohl.
E3   Robert Pohl.
E4   Sheldon Pohl.

B3   Jessie MacLeod, m. John MacEwen, with issue:

C1 Bertram MacEwen, m. Ada <u>Simpson</u>, and lived on the farm in New London, later moved to Charlottetown, with issue:
    D1 Claude MacEwen, m. Glennie <u>Bernard</u>, they live in New London.
        E1 Elda MacEwen, m. Hillard <u>Thompson</u>.
    D2 Leigh MacEwen, m. Muriel <u>Montgomery</u>, living in New London.
        E1 Ruth MacEwen, m. Robert <u>Brown</u>, with issue.
        E2 Montgomery MacEwen, m. Linda <u>Strong</u>.
    D3 Lorna MacEwen, m. Donald <u>MacEwen</u>, New London, with issue:
        E1 Hodge MacEwen, not married.
        E2 Jessie MacEwen, m. Bud <u>Thompson</u>.
        E3 Dean MacEwen, m. Marilyn <u>Oliver</u>.
        E4 Alan MacEwen, m. Sarah Doven <u>Reeves</u>.
C2 Laura MacEwen, m. James <u>MacAdam</u>, with issue:
    D1 Mary Belle MacAdam, m. 1) Harry <u>Martinson</u>, 2) Murray <u>Yandt</u>.
    D2 Bill, m. Vera _____ .
    D3 Jack, m. Ann _____ .
C3 Ella MacEwen, never married, lived in Saskatchewan, died 1936.
B4 Wallace MacLeod, died July 28, 1897, age 36 years, on a train from British Columbia, near Winnipeg.
B5 Mary MacLeod, died July 31, 1899, age 24 years.
B6 Leopold MacLeod, died Dec. 13, 1865, age 7 or 8 years.
B7 Winnie MacLeod, 1872-1903, m. Allan <u>Stewart</u>, Charlottetown, with issue:
C1 Winnifred Stewart, died Nov. 4, 1903, 8 months old.
B8 Laura MacLeod, m. Sandford <u>Crowe</u>, Vancouver, British Columbia. They had no family.
B9 Ida MacLeod, m. Henry <u>MacMillan</u>. They lived in Stanley Bridge and later moved to Vancouver, with issue:
C1 Jean MacMillan.
C2 Louis MacMillan.
C3 William MacMillan.
C4 May MacMillan.
C5 Jack MacMillan.
C6 Edgar MacMillan.

Information received from Emily Douglas, Kensington, through Jim MacLeod.

DONALD MACLEOD
DONALD MACLEOD AND FLORA SHAW OF STANHOPE

A   Donald MacLeod, died 1888 in Dakota. He came to the Island and settled in Belfast area, later he moved to Bradalbane and lastly to Stanhope. He m. Flora <u>Shaw</u>, she died in 1874. Flora was the daughter of Marion and Duncan Shaw. The 1871 census shows Donald living in Stanhope with two sons:

B1   Malcolm MacLeod, died May 1932, and is buried in Covehead Cemetery. He was given the deed of the land from his father and brother James. He m. Isabella <u>Lawson</u> (Belle) and had the following family:

C1   James MacLeod, died at four years of age.

C2   A daughter died in infancy.

C3   Harry MacLeod, born June 10, 1910; baptized Jan. 2, 1913. Harry was adopted. He m. Dorothy <u>Humphrey</u>, an English lady, in April 1945. She was a widow with two girls and one boy. Harry and Dorothy had one son:

D1   Gary Leslie MacLeod, born Dec. 8, 1946.

B2   James MacLeod, was a teacher, he and his father moved to Lead City, Dakota. James worked as a foreman in the mines. He was known as a bully and was murdered in his bed by a fellow worker with a shovel. He died in 1908 and is buried in Lead City, Dakota.

Information provided by Shirley Lawson, Stanhope, P.E.I.

John MacLeod
John MacLeod of Darlington and Hartsville

A   John MacLeod, m., wife's name unknown, with issue:
B1   John B. MacLeod.
B2   Allan MacLeod, m., wife's name unknown, with issue:
    C1   Alexander MacLeod, m., wife's name unknown, with issue:
        D1   Allan MacLeod.
        D2   Murdock MacLeod.
        D3   Bruce MacLeod.
        D4   Earl MacLeod.
        D5   Dan MacLeod.
        D6   May MacLeod, m. _____ Campbell.
        D7   Everett MacLeod.
        D8   Elmer MacLeod.
        D9   Julia MacLeod, m. _____ Waddell.
        D10 Borden MacLeod.
        D11 Lillian MacLeod, m. _____ Galbraith.
        D12 Vernon MacLeod.
        D13 Kathryn MacLeod, m. _____ Farquharson.
    C2   John MacLeod.
    C3   Mary MacLeod, m. _____ Matheson.
    C4   Jessie or Jeanette MacLeod, m. Angus Campbell.
    C5   Annabella "Belle" MacLeod, m. Malcolm Cummings.
    C6   Kathryn MacLeod, m. George Morrison.
    C7   Euphemia "Effie" MacLeod, m. _____ Johnson.
    C8   Mary Ann "Annie" MacLeod, m. John Nicholson.
    C9   Dan or Donald MacLeod, died 1896.

Information provided by Kathryn Farquharson, Charlottetown.

ANGUS MACLEOD
ANGUS MACLEOD AND MARY MACKAY OF GLEN MARTIN

A   Angus MacLeod, 1830-1915, and his wife Mary <u>MacKay</u> emigrated from Sealt, Isle of Skye, sailing from Portree on the barque *James Gibb* in 1858. Angus had a sister Catherine, m. John <u>Martin</u> who also came to P.E.I. at that time, both families settling in Glen Martin. Angus was born in Breakra [?], Stensholl, Isle of Skye. Mary was born in Balmaqueen, Trottenish, Isle of Skye. Their children were:

B1   Lauchlin James MacLeod, m. Catherine Euphemia <u>MacLeod</u>, daughter of Roderick MacLeod and Isobel Nicholson of the Isle of Raasay and Hopedale, P.E.I., with issue:

    C1   Donald MacLeod, born 1894, married in the U.S.A. with a family.

    C2   Mary Isobel MacLeod, born 1901, m. _____ <u>MacDonald</u>, and had a family in U.S.A.

    C3   George McLeod, born 1903, lived in Massachusetts.

    C4   Florence MacLeod, born 1904, m. _____ <u>Schmitz</u>, U.S.A.

    C5   Jessie MacLeod, 1906-1925, buried in Walleston, Massachusetts.

B2   Hugh MacLeod was 5 months of age when he left Skye with his parents.

B3   Catherine MacLeod, 1860-1933, m. Donald <u>MacDonald</u>, Glen Martin, they have descendants on P.E.I.

B4   Peter McLeod, 1870-1915, never married, buried in Valleyfield.

B5   Angus Adwood McLeod, 1877-1956, was a miner in the Yukon and died in Vancouver.

B6   John Alexander McLeod, 1861-1929, died in Providence, Rhode Island, m. Sarah <u>MacLeod</u>, 1861-1949, of Culloden, P.E.I. They emigrated to Providence in 1897 and are buried in the North Burial Ground, Providence. Their children were:

    C1   Marina McLeod, 1894-1982, born in Caledonia, P.E.I., m. Wallace Smith <u>MacKeil</u>, 1892-1945, from British Columbia. They lived in North Kingstown, Rhode Island, and are buried in the Quidnessett Memorial Cemetery, in North Kingstown. Marina, along with her brothers Norman and Edwin, founded the McLeod Optical Company, Inc., a highly successful company with its head office in Warwick, Rhode Island.

    C2   Norman Angus MacLeod, 1900-1982, m. Bertha M. <u>Nelson</u>, 1901-1965. He served with the 26th division in France during WWI. They are buried in Quidnesset Memorial Cemetery, Rhode Island. Their children were:

        D1   Norman A. MacLeod, m. Norma A. <u>Slocum</u>, they live in Warwick, Rhode Island. Their children are:

           E1   John A. MacLeod, m. Kathy <u>Kubert</u>, with issue:

              F1   Henry A. MacLeod.

              F2   Abbey M. MacLeod.

           E2   Joyce MacLeod.

           E3   Susan M. MacLeod, m. James <u>Nagle</u>, with issue:

              F1   Sarah M. Nagle.

              F2   Katherine M. Nagle.

E4   Laurie A. MacLeod, m. Paul <u>Pirozzi</u>, with issue:
       F1   Emily L. Pirozzi.
       F2   Samuel M. Pirozzi.
E5   Sandra M. MacLeod, m. Dean <u>Famiano</u>, with issue:
       F1   Bryce M. Famiano.
       F2   Ethan M. Famiano.

D2   Karol B. MacLeod, 1936-1936.

D3   Wallace N. MacLeod, m. Linda R. <u>Tedrow</u>, they live in North Kingstown, Rhode Island, with three children:
    E1   Scott W. MacLeod, m. Erin <u>McGee</u>, they live in North Kingstown, with issue:
       F1   Scott W. MacLeod, Jr.
       F2   Patrick G. MacLeod.
       F3   Ian W. MacLeod.
    E2   Roderick N. MacLeod, m. Michel <u>Henly</u>, they live in North Kingstown, Rhode Island, with issue:
       F1   Tiffany MacLeod.
       F2   Gabrielle MacLeod.
       F3   Emily MacLeod.
    E3   Heather L. MacLeod, m. Allan <u>Fiddes</u> from Aberdeen, Scotland. They live in Norfolk, Massachusetts, with a daughter:
       F1   Cameron R. Fiddes.

C3 Edwin A. A. McLeod, 1898-1961, m. Gladys <u>Lane</u>, 1897-1961, they are buried in North Kingstown, Rhode Island, their children are:

D1   Edwin A. McLeod, m. Shirley <u>Rachko</u>, living in Warwick, with issue:
    E1   Janet McLeod, m. Kenneth <u>Rosenfield</u>, they live in Massachusetts, with a son and two daughters:
       F1   Cory Rosenfield.
       F2   Hannah Rosenfield.
       F3   Emma Rosenfield.
    E2   Douglas E. McLeod, m. Barbara <u>Sprott</u>, living in Warwick, with issue:
       F1   Alexander McLeod.
       F2   Andrew McLeod.
    E3   Donald J. McLeod, m. Donna <u>Poole</u>, they live in Augusta, Maine, with issue:
       F1   Stephen McLeod.
       F2   Ryan McLeod.
    E4   Robert S. McLeod, m. Jennifer <u>Armstrong</u>, living in Westerly, Rhode Island, with issue:
       F1   Alyssa McLeod.
       F2   Brianna McLeod, twin to Alyssa.

D2   Jane F. McLeod, m. Autino <u>Maraia</u>, living in North Carolina, with three children:
    E1   Susan Maraia, m. Phillip <u>LeFave</u>.
    E2   Mark Maraia, m. Robin <u>Curtis</u>, with issue:
       F1   Jennifer Maraia.
    E3   Lynda Maraia.

D3   Marie McLeod, m. Donald <u>Arsenault</u>, he died in 1971, she lives in North Carolina. Their children are:

      E1   Donna Arsenault, m. Keith <u>Darling</u>, living in Idaho, with issue

             F1   Kieta Darling.

             F2   Kelsie Darling.

      E2   Toni Arsenault, m. Clyde <u>Campbell</u>, with issue:

             F1   Jesse Campbell.

             F2   Jacquline Campbell.

      E3   Lori Arsenault, m. Robert <u>Wade</u>, with issue:

             F1   Alexandra Wade.

             F2   Kelly Wade.

      E4   Denise Arsenault, m. Paul <u>Boushell</u>, with issue:

             F1   Molly Boushell.

C4   Austin L. H. McLeod, 1904-1950, m. Virginia <u>Kelly</u>, he was a veteran of WWII, having served in New Guinea in the South Pacific, and is buried in the North Burial Ground, Providence, Rhode Island. Austin and Virginia had a daughter:

      D1   Joyce McLeod, 1929-1998, m. William <u>Searby</u>, they lived in California, and had a son:

            E1   William Searby, Jr.

C5   Florence McLeod, 1902-1993, m. Graham J. <u>Smith</u>, 1896-1975, they lived in Norwich, Connecticut, but are buried in Quidnesset Memorial Cemetery, North Kingstown, Rhode Island. Their children were:

      D1   Richard Smith, 1930-1972, m. Randi <u>Nilsen</u>, they lived in New York City, and had one daughter:

            E1   Karen Smith, m. Richard <u>Pavone</u>, they live in Denver, Colorado, with two children:

                 F1   Andrew Pavone.

                 F2   Blaire Pavone.

      D2   Graham J. Smith, Jr., m. Roberta <u>Charlton</u>, they live in Scotch Plains, New Jersey, and have a daughter:

            E1   Ellen Smith, m. Donald <u>LaFronz</u>.

C6   Marion MacLeod, died as an infant.

B7   Mary Ann MacLeod, died in 1930 in Massachusetts, m. Donald G. <u>MacPhee</u>, who died in 1929. They had a family all of whom are in the U.S.A.

Source of information: Elva Whiteway, Murray River; Catherine Gallinger, Walnut Creek, California; Wallace N. MacLeod, North Kingstown, Rhode Island; and Norman A. MacLeod, Warwick, Rhode Island.

ALLAN MACLEOD
ALLAN MACLEOD AND MARGARET MCINNIS OF HARTSVILLE

A Allan MacLeod, died Feb. 22, 1871. His stone was erected by his son Duncan. Allan and his wife Margaret McInnis came from Raasay, Scotland, to Charlottetown in 1840. From there they went to the Skye Settlement on the Dock Road. The three oldest children were born in Raasay, the dates of births and death are not known.

B1 Alexander MacLeod, born 1835, died at age 22. Buried in Hartsville Cemetery.

B2 Ann MacLeod, born 1837, died at age 22. Buried in the Hartsville Cemetery.

B3 Roderick MacLeod, born 1839, died during the period 1861-1865. He and a neighbour Robert MacKinnon joined the 12th Marine Regiment during the American Civil War. He died while a member of the Union Army and is buried in the army cemetery in New Orleans.

B4 Duncan MacLeod, 1841-1922, m. Jessie MacLean of Belle River on Aug. 8, 1881. He was born in Springton schoolhouse while the family was on its way to Skye Settlement (now Hartsville). They lived in Hartsville and are buried in Hartsville Cemetery, with issue:

   C1 Allan MacLeod, 1881-1965, m. Florence MacLeod of Darlington, 1887–1945. She was the daughter of Duncan and Mary (MacSwain) MacLeod of Darlington, she had a brother Malcolm, sisters Mrs. Catherine Johnston and Mrs. Margaret Sutherland of Wollaston, Massachusetts. Allan and Florence had issue:
      D1 Margaret MacLeod, m. Arthur Burgess.
      D2 John MacLeod, unmarried.
      D3 Alexander MacLeod, m. Grace _____. Died Nov. 14, 1979. Buried in United Cemetery, Plumbsweep, New Brunswick.
      D4 Ira MacLeod, unmarried.
      D5 Douglas MacLeod, married.
      D6 Oliver MacLeod, married.
      D7 Mary MacLeod, m. Ronald Howard.
      D8 Stanley MacLeod.

   C2 John Angus MacLeod, 1883-1967, m. Florence Ferguson of Cape Breton. They lived in Halifax, Nova Scotia. (Both Allan and John served in the army in WWI. Allan became Lieut. Colonel.) Their children were:
      D1 Gordon MacLeod, married.
      D2 Douglas MacLeod, killed in WWII.
      D3 Frank MacLeod, married.
      D4 Jean MacLeod, m. Richard Smythe.

   C3 Roderick Alex MacLeod, 1885-1976, m. Ester Martin, of Bridgeport, Illinois. They were missionaries in Batang, Tibet, also in White Swan Indian Mission near Yakima, Washington. Served as pastor in Haddam, Connecticut. Lived in Geneva, New York. Their children were:
      D1 Flora MacLeod, m. John Natti.
      D2 Duncan MacLeod, married.

        D3   Shelton MacLeod, m. ___, died June 1979, buried in Kettering, Ohio.

    C4 Katherine A. MacLeod, 1886-1972, m. Wallace F. <u>MacLeod</u> of Dundas. They lived in Boston and Melrose, Massachusetts, with issue:

        D1   Sarah MacLeod, unmarried.

        D2 Duncan Wesley MacLeod, unmarried.

    C5 Margaret MacLeod, 1888-1906. Buried in the Hartsville Cemetery.

    C6 Belle MacLeod, 1890-1967, m. James <u>Locke</u> of Nova Scotia on June 5, 1918. They lived in Sommerville, Massachusetts and Florida. Buried in Peabody Lawn Cemetery. They had no family.

    C7 Anne MacLeod, born Jan. 23, 1893, m. William J. <u>Bailey</u>. They lived in Brighton and Dorchester, Massachusetts, and in Cincinnati, Ohio, with issue:

        D1   Margaret Bailey, m. Gilbert <u>Ross</u>.

        D2 Robert Bailey, m. _____.

  B5 Sarah MacLeod, 1843-1935, m. John <u>Corbett</u>, Granville. Buried in South Granville along with her husband and family, issue:

    C1 Hector Corbett, born Jan. 20, 1882, died 1957. Single.

    C2 Margaret Corbett, 1884-1938, m. Joseph <u>Thompson</u> from the U.S.A. Their daughter Sarah lived with grandparents.

        D1   Sarah Thompson, m. Percy <u>Lowe</u> of Nova Scotia and lives in Dover, issue:

            E1   Margaret Lowe.

            E2   Edward Lowe.

            E3   Robert Lowe.

            E4   Thomas Lowe.

            E5   Donald Lowe.

Information provided by Mary Dugas, Little Sands, and Sarah MacLeod, Kennebunk, Maine.

NORMAN MACLEOD
NORMAN MACLEOD AND MARY MACKAY OF HARTSVILLE

A   Norman MacLeod, born 1844 in Hartsville, died of pneumonia in 1888. Most of his family history is unknown to the descendants since his children were young at his time of death. It is thought that Norman's father came to P.E.I. from Scotland. Norman m. Mary MacKay of Hartsville, 1839-1925, with issue:

B1   Neil Dan MacLeod, born in Hopedale in 1883, died 1972, m. Eliza Almanda Ross of Hunter River, with issue:

    C1   Mary Florence MacLeod, m. David Stewart Sherren, with issue. (She is buried in Crapaud.)

        D1   David Sherren, died young, m. Bonnie ____, from New Brunswick.

            E1   David Sherren.

            E2   Mary Ann Sherren.

            E3   Michelle Sherren.

    C2   Alma MacLeod, m. Vernon Ford, with issue:

        D1   Verna Lee Ford, m. Alan Dalziel.

        D2   Guy Ford.

        D3   Ada Ford, m. Ronnie Peterson.

        D4   Glen Ford.

    C3   Norma MacLeod, m. Duncan MacIntosh, with issue:

        D1   Allister MacIntosh, m. Jean Boyce, with issue:

            E1   Scott MacIntosh.

            E2   Lisa MacIntosh.

            E3   Amanda MacIntosh.

    C4   Greta MacLeod, m. Ralph MacPhee, with issue:

        D1   Donnie MacPhee.

        D2   Jean MacPhee.

    C5   Allison MacLeod, m. Ella Crossman, no family.

    C6   Orville MacLeod, m. Catherine Burgess, with issue:

        D1   Charles MacLeod, m. Linda Barlow.

        D2   Harold MacLeod, m. Karen Gallant, with issue:

            E1   Jamie MacLeod.

            E2   Steven MacLeod.

        D3   Kenneth MacLeod.

    C7   Betty MacLeod, m. Gordon Dingwell, with issue:

        D1   Ross Dingwell, m. Mary Ann ____.

    C8   Harold MacLeod, twin of Betty, died at birth.

    C9   Ruby MacLeod, m. 1) Bernie MacDonald, with issue:

        D1   Deborah MacDonald.

        D2   Danny MacDonald.

        Ruby m. 2) Cecil Stewart.

B2   Alex MacLeod, born 1872, never married, buried in Manor, Saskatchewan.

B3   Roderick MacLeod, born 1874, m. Gertie Kirk, buried in Brewer, Maine, issue:

    C1   Mary MacLeod.

    C2   Evelyn MacLeod.

B4   John "Jack" MacLeod, born 1879, war vet, m. Ida <u>Younger</u>, with issue:
  C1   Girl, died young.
  C2   Norman John MacLeod, building contractor in Charlottetown.
B5   Norman MacLeod, m. Helen Nelson <u>MacKay</u>, died in Imperoyal, Nova Scotia, issue:
  C1   Lawrence MacLeod.
  C2   Mae MacLeod.
  C3   A boy.
B6   Kate MacLeod, born 1876, m. Alex <u>MacLennan</u>. No children.

Information provided by Neil Dan MacLeod and 1881 census.

NEIL MACLEOD
NEIL MACLEOD AND JANET CAMPBELL OF CAPE TRAVERSE

A Neil MacLeod came from Miramichi after the fire of 1825. He m. Janet <u>Campbell</u> in Jan.1840. She was from Cape Traverse. Their children were:

B1 Margaret MacLeod, born 1841, m. Thomas <u>Bishop,</u> Wellington, P.E.I. They are buried in the Church of Scotland Cemetery, Cape Traverse. Thomas was a ship's carpenter and came to Cape Traverse from Murray Harbour to work in the shipyards owned by McLeods. They moved to St. Eleanors and then to Wellington, where Thomas is listed as a farmer in the 1881 census. They had issue:

C1 John Bell Bishop, born March 6, 1866.

C2 James Bishop, 1868-1952, m. Mary <u>MacLure</u>, with issue:

  D1 A. Helen Bishop, born 1897, m. Mr. <u>Wright</u>, with issue:

    E1 Mary Wright, m. Mr. <u>Bradshaw</u>.

C3 Daniel Bishop.

C4 Thomas Bishop.

C5 Mary Bishop, m. Fred <u>MacLure</u>.

C6 Robert Bishop.

C7 Harry Bishop.

C8 Sadie Bishop, m. James <u>Chappell</u>, Sherbrooke.

B2 Mary MacLeod, m. John <u>Andrews</u>, of St. Eleanors. She died of T.B.

B3 Donald MacLeod, was in the State of Oregon in 1908, married with two sons.

B4 Lauchie MacLeod.

Source of information: Mrs. Mary Bradshaw, Summerside, P.E.I., Beaconsfield files, Charlottetown.

RODERICK MACLEOD
RODERICK MACLEOD AND MARGARET MACINNIS OF EBENEZER

A   Roderick MacLeod, 1813-1902, m. Margaret MacInnis, 1823-1899. In 1880 Roderick MacLeod owned 50 acres of land on the Glasgow Road in Ebenezer, P.E.I. This land was handed down from generation to generation and is presently owned by his great-grandson J. Daniel MacLeod. Roderick and Margaret's children were:

B1   Murdock MacLeod, went to U.S.A.

B2   James MacLeod, went away, couldn't write and never came home.

B3   Charles MacLeod, also went away and never returned.

B4   John MacLeod, 1853-1900. He never married and stayed at home on the farm. In 1900 on his way home from a neighbour's, his team of horses ran away. He was thrown out on the frozen ground and was killed.

B5   Angus MacLeod, 1861-1934, m. Christine Ann Campbell, 1867-1956. They lived on the Glasgow Road. Later moved to Charlottetown and bought a store on the corner of Queen and Bayfield Streets, they lived over this store for many years until his death. Their children were:

C1   Alexander MacLeod, born Aug. 1887, m. "Bert" Doyle of Charlottetown. They farmed in Ebenezer for a few years but exchanged roles with brother Archie in 1916—Archie moved from, and they moved to, Charlottetown. They had issue:

D1   Aggie MacLeod.

D2   Edith MacLeod.

D3   James MacLeod.

D4   Stan MacLeod.

D5   William Alfred "Jiggs" MacLeod.

D6   Emily MacLeod.

C2   J. Archibald MacLeod, 1890-1950, m. Sarah Isabell Coles, born in 1894. With issue:

D1   Margaret Matilda MacLeod, born in 1914, m. Raymond A. Andrews, with issue:

E1   Frederick A. Andrews, m. Daphne Shaw, with issue:

F1   Sherri Andrews, m. John David MacLean, with issue:

G1   Jason MacLean.

G2   Jeffrey MacLean.

G3   Juston MacLean.

F2   Allan Andrews.

F3   Daniel Andrews.

D2   John Daniel MacLeod, born in 1916, m. Inez Stevenson, with issue:

E1   Margaret MacLeod, m. Kenneth Jones, with issue:

F1   Kent Jones, m. Lynn Roblee, with issue:

G1   Carla Jones.

G2   Kirk Jones.

G3   Kris Jones.

E2   Jean MacLeod, m. Louis Ranahan, with issue:

F1   Pamela Ranahan.

F2   Patricia Ranahan.

E3 Donald John MacLeod, m. Helen <u>MacNeill</u>, with issue:
    F1 Scott MacLeod.
    F2 Dwayne MacLeod.
    F3 Helena MacLeod.
E4 Lloyd MacLeod, m. Marilyn <u>Currie</u>, with issue:
    F1 Marsha MacLeod.
    F2 Angela MacLeod.
    F3 Tyler MacLeod.

D3 Frederick Angus MacLeod, 1917-1966, m. Helen Elizabeth (Betty) <u>Holman</u>, with issue:
  E1 Barry Wayne MacLeod, 1947-1975.
  E2 Lynn MacLeod, m. Leonard <u>MacNeill</u>, with issue:
    F1 Angela MacNeill.
    F2 Jeffrey MacNeill.
    F3 Sara MacNeill.
  E3 Roderick (Roddy) MacLeod.

D4 James Emerson MacLeod, m. Joyce Alma <u>Auld</u>, with issue:
  E1 Gail Joyce MacLeod, m. Millar A. <u>MacQuarrie</u>, with issue:
    F1 Wendell MacQuarrie.
    F2 Dwayne MacQuarrie.
    F3 Morgan MacQuarrie.
  E2 Shirley June MacLeod, m. Phillip <u>Weatherbie</u>, with issue:
    F1 Tammy Weatherbie.
    F2 Penny Weatherbie.
  E3 Gary Emerson MacLeod, m. Diane <u>Ling</u>, with issue.

D5 Allison Archibald MacLeod, m. Annette <u>Stewart</u>, with issue:
  E1 Eric MacLeod, m. Lois <u>Hansen</u>, with issue:
    F1 Jeffrey MacLeod.
    F2 Laurie MacLeod.
  E2 Judy MacLeod, m. Roland <u>Vessey</u>, with issue:
    F1 Julie Vessey.
    F2 Stephen Vessey.
    F3 Pamela Vessey.
  E3 Robert MacLeod, m. Ellen <u>Golling</u>, with issue:
    F1 Terra MacLeod.
    F2 Jerrod MacLeod.
    F3 Shailee MacLeod.
  E4 Frank MacLeod, m. Debbie <u>Dereau</u>, with issue:
    F1 Ryan MacLeod.
  E5 Aubrey MacLeod, m. Darla <u>Simpson</u>, with issue:
    F1 Dewer MacLeod.
    F2 Barrett MacLeod.
  E6 Randy MacLeod.
  E7 Kevin MacLeod, m. Wanda <u>Madore</u>, with issue:
    F1 Blair MacLeod.

D6 Leitha Jean MacLeod, m. 1) Robert <u>MacKenzie</u>, with issue:
  E1 Ella MacKenzie, m. Jack <u>Pound</u>.
    F1 Jill Pound.
    F2 Mark Pound.
  E2 Carol MacKenzie, m. Eugene <u>Wynn</u>, with issue:
    F1 Stephen Wynn.

F2   Susan Wynn.
F3   Peter Wynn.
Leitha m. 2) David <u>Moreside</u>. Two stepchildren were:
E3   Beverly Moreside.
E4   Michael Moreside.
D7   Charles Claude MacLeod, m. Roma <u>Dickieson</u>, with issue:
E1   Paul MacLeod.
E2   Debbie Ann MacLeod, m. Melvin <u>Ling</u>, with issue:
F1   Matthew Ling.
F2   Craig Ling.
E3   Charles MacLeod, m. Barbara <u>Mason</u>, with issue:
F1   Devon C. MacLeod.
E4   Sandra MacLeod, m. David <u>Hiscock</u>, with issue:
F1   Holly Hiscock.
F2   Emily Hiscock.
E5   Adam MacLeod.
D8   Isabelle Ann MacLeod, m. Arthur <u>Campbell</u>, with issue:
E1   Carol Ann Campbell, m. Jim <u>Eager</u>, with issue:
F1   Troy Eager.
F2   Jeff Eager.
F3   Chris Eager.
F4   Stephen Eager.
F5   Jennifer Eager.
E2   David Campbell, m. Patsy <u>McKenna</u>, with issue:
F1   Tommy Campbell.
F2   Jackie Campbell.
F3   Mikael Campbell.
F4   Patrick Campbell.
D9   Louella Susanna MacLeod, m. Edward <u>Kuntz</u>, with issue:
E1   John Kuntz.
E2   Pamela Kuntz.
E3   Allan Kuntz.
D10 Carl Arthur MacLeod, m. 1) Pat <u>Oakes</u>, with issue:
E1   Penny MacLeod.
E2   Michael MacLeod.
E3   Mark MacLeod.
Carl later m. 2) Opal _____.
C3   Roderick MacLeod, was an electrician and worked in Massachusetts and Minnesota. He m. Agnes <u>MacInnis</u> from the Murray River area, she died in 1934 and he returned to Charlottetown with his son:
D1   John Bruce MacLeod, m. Margaret <u>Budge</u>, of Glace Bay, Nova Scotia, they live in Kingston, Ontario, with issue:
E1   Trulie Ann MacLeod, m. Stephen <u>Hunter</u>, with issue:
F1   Cameron Gordon MacLeod Hunter.
F2   Anna Jane Hunter.
E2   Cathy Margaret MacLeod, m. Brian <u>Beavis</u>, with issue:
F1   Matthew MacLeod Beavis.
F2   Katherine Sarah Beavis.
E3   Laurie Hope MacLeod, m. James <u>Smith</u>.
C4   Margaret MacLeod, died at almost a year old
C5   Leitha MacLeod, born July 1900.

C6 Margaret MacLeod, died young (named after the other baby who died).

C7 Ena MacLeod, born 1908.

B6 Catherine MacLeod, born 1846, died Jan. 25, 1934, age 88 years.

Information provided by a family member and John Bruce MacLeod, Kingston, Ontario.

JOHN SCOTT MACLEOD
JOHN SCOTT MACLEOD AND 1) MARY MACDONALD AND 2) MARY JANE STEWART OF DUNSTAFFNAGE

A   John Scott MacLeod was born in 1814 in the Isle of Skye. He came to P.E.I. with his widowed mother around 1820. They bought a small farm on the Suffolk Road and later obtained a grant of land in Dunstaffnage. John Scott was a wealthy man. He bought farms or paid for education for the members of his family. The daughters and sons were given $1,000.00 cash each. The first pipe organ brought here by Miller Bros. was bought by him for his daughter Mary Jane, who was organist in the church at Dunstaffnage. He m. 1) Mary MacDonald who was born in 1813 and died in 1869 in Marshfield. They married in approximately 1835. Their children were:

B1   Henry Morpeth MacLeod,1837-1899, m. Sarah Anne Stewart, 1836-1910. She was the daughter of John Stewart (of the Five Mile House Stewarts) and Flora Cameron. Their children were:
　　 C1   Mary Agnes MacLeod, born 1865, died Jan. 17, 1891.
　　 C2   Flora Cameron MacLeod, born 1867.
　　 C3   Herbert Stewart MacLeod, born 1868, died Sept. 10, 1892.
　　 C4   Bruce Morpeth MacLeod, born 1870.
　　 C5   Sarah Malinda MacLeod, born 1873.
　　 C6   Henry Stainforth MacLeod, born 1875.
　　 C7   William Wallace MacLeod, Nov. 4, 1877 - Nov. 28, 1878.
　　 C8   Alberta Bessie MacLeod, born Dec. 18, 1878.
B2   John MacLeod, born 1840, died April 24, 1877, m. Lizzie MacDonald.
B3   Hector MacLeod, dates of birth and death unknown, m. Matilda Stewart.
B4   George MacLeod, dates of birth and death unknown, m. Sophia Godfrey, issue:
　　 C1   Emily MacLeod.
　　 C2   Girl, m. Dr. Bovyer.
B5   James MacLeod, m. Anna Allen.
B6   Hannah Spencer MacLeod, 1852-1917, m. Peter McNair Robertson, on Dec. 27, 1876. He was born 1851 and died 1931, with issue:
　　 C1   Alexander Preston Robertson, born Oct. 22, 1877.
　　 C2   John Ernest Robertson, born Jan. 20, 1880.
　　 C3   Norman MacLeod Robertson, 1881-1903.
B7   Alexander MacLeod, 1853-1921, m. Katherine R. Rodd, 1868-1965, issue:
　　 C1   Henry Allison MacLeod, born 1901. Never married.
　　 C2   Helen M. MacLeod, 1905-1947, m. Fenton Court.
　　 C3   John Eric MacLeod, 1908-1961.
　　 C4   Margaret Ethel MacLeod, born 1912.
B8   William MacLeod, m. Mary Verity of Boston, with issue:
　　 C1   Elsie MacLeod.
　　 C2   A girl.
　　 C3   William MacLeod, Jr., M.D.
B9   Katherine MacLeod, never married.
B10 Robert C. MacLeod, born May 1851, m. Madge (Margaret) MacRae, of Kingston, Ontario. Robert was a prominent businessman and politician, representing 5th district in P.E.I. Legislature. Their family were:

C1 A. Gwendolyn MacLeod, 1896-1899, buried in Dunstaffnage.
C2 Lionel Stanley MacLeod, born 1894, moved to U.S.A. around 1913 with brother Henry, after attending Prince of Wales College.
C3 Marion MacLeod, born March 4, 1889, m. Fred Jenkins in Calgary. They lived in Edmonton, with issue:
    D1 Margaret Ruth Jenkins, m. John DePeyre, no family.
    D2 Helen Louise MacIntyre Jenkins, m. Louis Neely, and lived in Kirkland Lake, Ontario. They had three children.
    D3 Robert Frederick Jenkins, m. ____, and lives in Edmonton.
C4 Henry Morton MacLeod (also used name Frederick Henry), 1894-1942, buried in National Cemetery in Minneapolis, m. Emma Caroline Olson, with issue:
    D1 Beverly Margaret MacLeod (school secretary), m. Robert Allyn Peterson. They had seven children and lived in Minneapolis.
C5 Marjorie Gordon MacLeod, born 1896, m. Rudolph Davis Niven. They live in Calgary, with issue:
    D1 Murray Frederick Niven, m. ____, with four children.
    D2 Roberta Francis Niven, m. Bert Hutchison, and have two children.
B11 Matilda MacLeod, m. James Wyatt, March 28, 1878, with issue:
    C1 James Bismark Wyatt, 1880-1880.
    C2 Esther Elizabeth Wyatt, born 1881.
    C3 Mary Elsie Wyatt, 1883-1977, m. Herbert C. Nelson.
    C4 Ambrose W. Wyatt, born 1885.
    C5 Matilda Catherine Wyatt, born 1890.

John Scott m. 2) Mary Jane Stewart, born 1832, died June 10, 1905, in Marshfield. (Her name is not on the stone.) Her parents were Alexander Stewart and Annie Robertson Sinclair.

B12 Mary Jane MacLeod, 1873-1897, m. Hector Darrach, buried in Marshfield.
    C1 Scott Darrach, 1897-1981, at Braintree, Massachuetts, m. Rhoda Ward, issue:
        D1 Howard Scott Darrach.
        D2 Orlin Darrach, m. Marjorie Pearson on Sept. 5, 1953.
        D3 Ian Darrach, born June 28, 1936.
        D4 Lucian Darrach, adopted her sister's son.
B13 Annie Robertson Sinclair MacLeod, 1877-1971, m. on March 18, 1903, to Walter Charles Munn, 1877-1964. His parents were Donald Munn and Mary Jane Smith and grandfather was Neil Munn (born 1798, Scotland, died 1889, Mermaid), with issue:
    C1 Vernon Stewart Munn, 1905-1971, m. Margaret Myrtle Stewart, 1899-1982. With issue:
        D1 Marjorie Eleanor Munn, m. George Crosby, with issue:
            E1 Douglas Stewart Crosby, m. Lynn Elizabeth Levy in 1975.
            E2 Eleanor Shirley Lynn Crosby, m. Fred Smith in 1972.
            E3 Brian George Crosby, m. Janeth Drake in 1973.
            E4 Ian Scott Crosby, 1959-1976.
            E5 Marsha Elaine Crosby, m. Charles Robert Bryenton in 1984.
            E6 David Lawson Crosby.
        D2 Annie Phyllis Munn, m. Arthur E. Brown, in 1960. No children.
        D3 Velma Shirley Munn, m. Ernest Wood in 1959, with issue:
            E1 Patricia Lynn Wood.

E2   Ronald Cecil Wood.
E3   Roger Ernest Wood.
C2 Jean Munn, born 1907, m. Morley F. Smith, born 1902, with issue:
D1   Elda Ida Smith, m. in 1946 to John George Jay, 1922-1976, with issue:
E1   John Jay, Jr., m. Helen Carroll.
E2   Judith Jay, m. in 1977 to Scott Henderson.
E3   Donna Jean Jay, m. in 1979 to Robert Kyte.
D2   Stanley Smith, m. Edith DeRoche, living in Boston, with issue:
E1   Brian Morley Smith, M. Linda MacKin.
E2   Coleen Ann Smith, m. Wesley "Wes" Orcutt.
E3   Lynn Marie Smith, m. Steven MacDonald.
E4   Blair Stanley Smith.
E5   Pamela Jean Smith, m. Raymond Adelsberg.
E6   Laura Lee Smith.
C3 Hildred Ethel Munn, m. Clarence Walker on March 23, 1932, with issue:
D1   James Walker, m. Joan Lewis in 1955, with issue:
E1   Bruce Walker.
E2   Kent Walker, m. in 1983 to Tanya Denise Waddell.
E3   Robbie Walker.
E4   Lindsay Walker.
C4 Elinor Munn, m. Russell D. Matheson on June 18, 1937, with issue:
D1   Deanna Elaine Matheson, m. Donald Victor Campbell, with issue:
E1   Brian William Campbell.
E2   Brian Andrew Campbell.
E3   Carolyn Ruth Campbell.
D2   Linda Carol Matheson, m. James Gavin Harding, 1944-1976, issue:
E1   Daniel Gordon Harding.
E2   David James Harding.
E3   Margaret Elinor Linda Harding.
D3   Marlene Gail Matheson, m. Francis William J. Bolger in 1974.
E1   Michael Francis Bolger.
E2   Krista Lynn Bolger.

Information provided by Linda Carol Harding and Beverly Margaret Peterson.

TAILLEUR MACLEOD
ALEXANDER "TAILLEUR" MACLEOD AND 1) _____ MACLEOD AND 2) MARY MACLEOD
OF KINROSS

A   Alexander "Tailleur" MacLeod emigrated from Raasay in 1821 to P.E.I. While
     he lived in Raasay for two years he was a brewer and a tailor. He m. twice, both
     women believed to be MacLeods from Skye. He was believed to have been
     born in Glenmore, Skye. His children were all grown when they emigrated to
     P.E.I. He purchased 500 acres of land on the Kinross Road. His children from
     his first marriage were as follows:
B1   Murdock MacLeod, m. Miss Martin of Orwell Cove, P.E.I., with issue:
     C1   Donald "Stonehouse" MacLeod, 1825-1905, married in 1853 to Jessie
          MacDonald. She died on March 6, 1855, age 33 years. This informa-
          tion was taken from the stone from the Uigg Church of Scotland
          Cemetery. The year must be 1865 because the births of the children
          are after 1855. Their family were:
          D1   Malcolm MacLeod, m. Margaret MacLeod, born Sept 27, 1854,
               issue:
               E1   John MacLeod, died in U.S.A. serving in WWI.
               E2   Milton MacLeod, was killed in New Brunswick woods.
               E3   Elija MacLeod, m. Miss Hickey, P.E.I. They lived in Mas-
                    sachusetts and had two children.
               E4   Jessie MacLeod, m. Mr. Dawes of Massachusetts. With
                    three or four children.
               E5   Wallace MacLeod.
          D2   Donald "D. D." MacLeod, 1856-1939, m. Catherine Penelope
               Enman, Grandview, 1859-1940, with issue:
               E1   Herman MacLeod, born Jan. 26, 1880, m. Nellie Clow, issue:
                    F1   Helen MacLeod, m. Edward Godfrey, Ontario.
                    F2   Alice MacLeod, m. Charles Jones.
                    F3   Penelope MacLeod, m. Michael Dickinson, two boys.
               E2   Jessie Catherine "Daisy" MacLeod, born Oct. 2, 1881,
                    unmarried.
               E3   Artemas MacLeod, died Aug. 20, 1884, at two months old.
               E4   Ernest MacLeod, 1885-1958, m. Christine MacLeod, born
                    1906. They were married on Sept. 12, 1928, with issue:
                    F1   Donald Beverly MacLeod, died in New York.
                    F2   John Clifford MacLeod, m. Shirley West MacDonald.
                         G1   Donald Clifford MacLeod, m. Carla Dykerman,
                              living in Orwell Cove, with issue:
                              H1   Orin Donald MacLeod.
                         G2   David Ernest MacLeod, born in North Bay,
                              Ontario, m. Anne Nelson, Dartmouth, living in
                              Lower Newtown, P.E.I.
                    F3   Mildred Penelope MacLeod, m. Charles Compton,
                         Charlottetown, with issue:
                         G1   Jo-Anne Compton.
                         G2   Beverly Compton.
                         G3   Jayne Compton.

G4   Kathleen Compton.
G5   Janet Compton.
E5   Susan Elizabeth MacLeod, 1887-1975, never married. The name recorded on the baptismal record is Susanna.
E6   Maude MacLeod, born Dec. 1888, unmarried.
E7   Amos MacLeod, lived on the Gillis farm in Orwell Cove, never married.
E8   Penelope "Pansy" MacLeod, born Apr. 6, 1894.
E9   Fanny MacLeod, born 1896.
E10 Bertha Blanche MacLeod, born Jan. 10, 189[?].
E11 Donald Stanwood MacLeod, 1902-1971, m. Mildred Petrie, they had no family.
D3   Murdock MacLeod, 1863-1890.
D4   Christy MacLeod, 1861-1902.
D5   Mary Ann MacLeod, born March 15, 1858.
D6   Jessie MacLeod, born Dec. 19, 1864, m. _____ MacLean. They had ten children, two of whom were Isobel and Maude.
D7   John MacLeod, 1859-1899, m. Catherine MacPherson, she died in 1932. They were married in April 1889, with issue:
E1   Jessie MacLeod, born March 1890, m. Murdock MacPherson, Dundee, with issue:
F1   Bertha MacPherson, m. Harold Wood, Vernon River and Charlottetown, no family.
F2   Edna Mae MacPherson, m. James Halliday, Eldon, issue:
G1   David Halliday.
E2   John D. MacLeod, m. Catherine Bruce, with issue:
F1   Munro MacLeod, m. Irene MacLeod from the family of Murdock "Tailors."
F2   Louise MacLeod, a noted author in Ontario, m. Ralph Reynolds, with issue:
G1   Rennie Reynolds.
G2   Carol Reynolds.
G3   Garry Reynolds.
G4   Jackeline Reynolds.
F3   Ruth MacLeod, m. Mac Carver, Vernon River and Ontario.
E3   Samuel A. MacLeod, m. Mae MacPherson, he was a merchant and postmaster at Kinross, their children are:
F1   Stanwood MacLeod, m. Merlene McNeill. They live in Kinross, with two boys:
G1   Brian Alexander MacLeod, m. Helen MacLean, Kinross, with issue:
H1   Jacquline Stacy MacLeod.
H2   Christy Michelle MacLeod.
G2   David Allan MacLeod, m. Judy Warren. They live in Charlottetown, with issue:
H1   Jennifer MacLeod.
F2   Edward MacLeod, m. Cecilia Currie, Vernon River, issue:
G1   Karen MacLeod, m. Don Chandler, with issue:

> > H1   Lisa Chandler.
> > H2   Gillian Chandler.
> > H3   Tim Chandler.
> G2   Dianne MacLeod, m. Neil Anderson, with issue:
> > H1   Derek Anderson.
F3   Weston MacLeod, m. Agnes MacLean, with issue:
> G1   Cheryl MacLeod, m. Dave French, with issue:
> > H1   Mark French.
> > H2   Tammy French.
> > H3   Lorra French.
> G2   Roberta MacLeod, m. 1) Sandy Briant, with issue:
> > H1   MacLean Briant.
> > H2   Heather Rose Briant.
> > Roberta m. 2) Rob Bignall.
> G3   Cathy MacLeod, m. John Payne, with issue:
> > H1   Jeffrey Payne.
> G4   Heather MacLeod, m. Mark Govain, with issue:
> > H1   Scott Govain.
> > H2   Eric Govain.
> G5   Pauline MacLeod.
> G6   Joan MacLeod.
> G7   Dianna MacLeod.
E4   Etta MacLeod, m. Stanley Lee, with issue:
F1   Stanley Lee, Jr.
E5   Ruth MacLeod, never married, a nurse in the U.S.A.

Donald "Stonehouse" m. 2) Mary Ann Slate, daughter of a British officer from Newfoundland. He operated a telegraph office in White Sands, with issue:

D8   Samuel Alexander MacLeod, 1866-1948, m. 1) Frances Perkins, 1868-1897. They are buried in the People's Cemetery in Charlottetown. Their children were:
E1   Frances MacLeod, died May 11, 1956, m. Hal Bourke, issue:
> F1   Frances Isobel (Billy) Bourke, born 1926, m. 1) Ron Smith, in 1948, with issue:
> > G1   Glenn Edward Smith m. Sharon Rose McAulay of Charlottetown, with issue:
> > > H1   Kellie Smith.
> > > H2   Craig Smith.
> > G2   Barbara Lynn Smith, m. James Malcolm Phillips.
> > > H1   Robert Malcolm Phillips.
> > Frances m. 2) Robert MacLeod, with issue:
> > G3   George Douglas Henry MacLeod.
E2   Wilfred MacLeod, 1897-1986, m. Florence McKendrick, 1899-1983. They lived in Charlottetown and are buried in Clyde River.
> F2   Phyllis MacLeod, m. William Bently, with issue:
> > G1   Wilfred Charles Bentley, Kingston, Ontario.
> > G2   Susan Louise Bentley, Kingston, Ontario.
> > G3   James William Bentley, lives in Kingston, Ontario.
> F1   Donald MacLeod, m. Shirley McCoy, with two children:

> > > G1 Mary Margaret MacLeod.
> > > G2 Allan Andrew Lewis MacLeod.
> > F3 Allan MacLeod, m. Charlotte Jane MacEachern, from Appin Road, they live in Charlottetown, with issue:
> > > G1 Nancy Lynne MacLeod.
> > > G2 Timothy MacEachern MacLeod.
> > Wilfred and Florence had two infant sons who died at birth in 1920 and 1921. They are both buried in Clyde River Cemetery.
>
> > Samuel Alexander m. 2) Elizabeth Wyatt, she died Jan. 10, 1944, and is buried in People's Cemetery, Charlottetown.
> D9 Charles MacLeod, born April 19, 1869, lived in California.
> D10 Allan MacLeod, killed by a ram in childhood.
> D11 Fanny MacLeod, m. _____ Allen of Vancouver. Died Dec. 1936.
> D12 Wallace MacLeod, born Jan. 6, 1876.
> D13 James MacLeod, born June 7, 1879, died of asthma in childhood.
> D14 Bertha MacLeod m. 1)Arthur Wentworth, with issue:
> > E1 Arthur Wentworth.
> > Bertha m. 2) Charles Rankin.
C2 Malcolm MacLeod, died in Western Canada.
C3 Mary MacLeod, m. Peter Finlay MacDonald. They had five children.
B2 Alexander "Og" MacLeod, born 1789, in Raasay, Scotland. Died Aug 17, 1867, and is buried in the Church of Scotland Cemetery, Kinross. He married Isabella Gillis, she died Feb. 28, 1868, age 64, and is also buried in the Kirk Cemetery, Kinross.
> C1 Murdock MacLeod, m. _____ Dewar, of Brudenell. They lived in Somerville, Massachusetts, and had issue:
> > D1 Mary Jane MacLeod.
> > D2 Elizabeth MacLeod.
> > Two sons.
> C2 Ronald MacLeod, m. 1) Euphemia Gillis, Lyndale, with issue:
> > D1 Eva Ellen or Evangeline MacLeod, nurse, unmarried.
> > D2 Ronald MacLeod, m. Emily Wheeler, with issue:
> > > E1 Ronald MacLeod, m. Emily Hitchcock, Boston.
> > > E2 Harry MacLeod, m. Ruth MacMillan, New Brunswick, with two children.
> > > E3 Virginia MacLeod, m. Clayton Sawyer, Boston.
> > > E4 Eva MacLeod, m. _____ Gerann or William Swann of Pittsburg.
> C3 Donald MacLeod, born Nov. 28, 1827, m. Emily_____, Colorado Springs, no family.
> C4 William MacLeod, married in Texas.
> C5 Alexander J. MacLeod, born March 9, 1832, m. Margaret MacLeod of Belle River, P.E.I. Alexander was a tailor. They had no family.
> C6 Mary MacLeod, m. John Archibald MacLeod, known as "John Archie." He was an 1829 settler with Uigg emigrants, on Murray Harbour Road. With issue:
> > D1 Isabella MacLeod, m. Richard Ward, born Feb. 4, 1866, issue:
> > > E1 Savina Mary (Mae) Ward.
> > D2 Alexander J. MacLeod, 1862-1920, m. Christy MacDonald, Bellevue, with issue:

E1 John Cameron MacLeod, 1899-1918, killed in WWI.
E2 Alexander Cameron MacLeod, born July 1900.
E3 Alexander Leavitt MacLeod, 1901-1953, m. Evelyn Cahill.
    They lived in Quincy, Massachusetts, with issue:
    F1 Alice MacLeod, m. Putman Borden, with issue:
        G1 Allison Borden.
        G2 Kenneth Borden.
        G3 Holly Borden.
        G4 Neil Borden.
    F2 Kathleen MacLeod, m. Paul Lunetta, with issue:
        G1 Lynn Marie Lunetta.
        G2 Paul Lunetta.
        G3 Mark Lunetta.
        G4 David Lunetta.
        G5 Michael Lunetta.
    F3 Joan Marie MacLeod, m. Joseph Cicco, Connecticut,
        with issue:
E4 Ewen Stanley MacLeod, 1902-1943. He died in England,
    WWII.
E5 Mary Florence MacLeod, born May 19, 1903, m. Wilfred
    Furness, Vernon, P.E.I. He died 1973. Their children were:
    F1 Russell Furness, m. Dorothy Isobel MacLeod, daugh-
        ter of Angus (Sandy John), Kinross, with issue:
        G1 Donald Furness, m. Jean Wilson, with issue:
            H1 Cathy Furness.
            H2 Jason Furness.
            H3 Lauren Furness.
        G2 David Furness, m. Ann Marie Villa, with issue:
            H1 Lea David Furness.
        G3 Sheila Furness, m. Robin Barker.
    F2 Lloyd Furness, m. Kay MacNeill (MacDougall), with
        issue:
        G1 Ralph Furness.
        G2 John Furness.
        G3 Gordon Furness.
    F3 Marion Furness, m. William Platts, with issue:
        G1 Susan Platts.
        G2 David Platts.
        G3 Douglas Platts.
E6 Angus Russell MacLeod, m. Marion MacLaren, with issue:
    F1 Carol Jean MacLeod.
    F2 Joyce MacLeod.
    F3 Marion MacLeod, m. James Early, with issue:
        G1 Matthew Early.
        G2 Russell Early.
        G3 Brooke Early.
E7 Christine MacLeod, m. Ernest MacLeod. Ernest is the son
    of D. D. MacLeod and Catherine P. Enman. They had issue:
    F1 Donald Beverly MacLeod, died in New York.
    F2 Clifford MacLeod, m. Shirley West MacDonald, with
        two boys.

F3   Mildred MacLeod, m. Charles Compton, they have five children.

E8   Kathleen Isobel MacLeod, born Dec. 16, 1908. She was a nurse in Montreal.

E9   Alexander Edison MacLeod, m. Ann MacLean, Head of Montague.
        F1   Judy MacLeod.

D3   Donald (Dan) MacLeod, m. Emma Nelson, with issue:
    E1   Lillian MacLeod, living in old home, Riverside, California.
    E2   Verna MacLeod, m. Arnold Shutter, no family.
    E3   Mildred MacLeod, m. William Weiner, with issue:
        F1   William Weiner, Jr.
    E4   Alice MacLeod, m. Clyde Rex.

D4   Archibald MacLeod, born Nov. 1, 1860, m. 1) Ann Robbins, no family, m. 2) Mary Belle Pringle, with issue:
    E1   Mary Belle MacLeod, m. _____ Cundy, with issue:
        F1   Carol Frances Cundy.

D5   Laughlin MacLeod, born May 24, 1864, m. May _____, with issue:
    E1   Lillian MacLeod, unmarried.
    E2   Annie MacLeod, unmarried.

D6   Sarah Ann MacLeod, 1856-1867. She is buried in Kinross Cemetery ("Old Kirk"), single.

D7   Catherine MacLeod, 1868-1905, m. James Nicholson. No family.

D8   Christine MacLeod, m. Angus MacLeod, 1873-1963, with issue:
    E1   Ward MacLeod, deceased.
    E2   Margaret MacLeod, m. Carl Holmgrain.

D9   Margaret Euphemia MacLeod, m. Frank J. Leavitt, 1875-1930. They had no family.

D10   Angus John MacLeod, m. May Manril, born March 28, 1878, issue:
    E1   Helen MacLeod, m. Francis St. John, Florida.
    E2   Christine MacLeod, m. John Keith, Florida.

C7   John "Sandy" MacLeod, died Nov. 21, 1901, age 77, m. Mary MacLeod, she died March 1, 1923, age 84. Mary was the daughter of Donald MacLeod, 1829 pioneer. In the Hutchinson's 1864 Directory, John is listed as a farmer in this area. Their children were:

D1   Catherine MacLeod, m. Sam Campbell, as his first wife, with issue:
    E1   Etta Campbell, m. Alan Stewart from Grandview and British Columbia.
        F1   Hazel Stewart, m. Norman MacLeod, from Glasgow, Scotland. Norman MacLeod was a Metallurgical Engineer and spent some time with the American Army where he designed the "Claymore" land mine, a lethal weapon of war, used extensively in Vietnam. It was named Claymore after the Highlanders' short sword. Apparently it was designed to spray shrapnel in a sweeping circular manner and could be hung in trees as well as concealed in the ground and also could be operated by remote control. They have five children.

F2   Campbell Stewart, m. with a family.
F3   Donald Stewart.
F4   John Stewart.
E2   Mabel Campbell, deceased.
E3   Ada Campbell, m. Bill <u>Benson</u>, Boston, with issue:
F1   Barbara Benson, m. <u>Caldwell</u>, with two children.
E4   John Campbell, m. Edith <u>MacNeill</u>, Little Sands. She is the granddaughter of Ewen Lamont, Lyndale. Their family is:
F1   Samuel Ewen Campbell, m. Norma <u>Trodden</u>, they live in Smith Falls, Ontario, with issue:
    G1   John Campbell.
    G2   Donald Campbell.
    G3   Douglas Campbell.
    G4   Marilyn Campbell.
F2   Donald Roy Campbell, Professor and former Dean of Education at U.P.E.I., m. Maida <u>Harris</u>, R.N., Ontario.
    G1   James Campbell, an engineer in Nova Scotia, m. Virginia <u>Brown</u>, with issue:
        H1   Corey Campbell.
    G2   Ian Campbell, M.D., practising in Montreal.
    G3   Cathy Campbell, m. Michael <u>Ungar</u> of Montreal.
    G4   Heather Campbell, m. Joseph <u>Driscoll</u>, with issue:
        H1   Vanessa Driscoll.
F3   Rebecca Campbell, m. Ron <u>Williams</u>, lived in British Columbia, issue:
    G1   Cathy Williams.
    G2   Elizabeth Williams.
    G3   Winton Williams.
    G4   Andrew Williams.
F4   Clarence Campbell, M.D., m. Dot <u>Bussey</u>, R.N., of Newfoundland. They live in Little Sands, with two children:
    G1   Evelyn Campbell, m. Steven <u>Miller</u>, M.D., they are living in New Glasgow, Nova Scotia, with one child.
    G2   John Campbell.
F5   Sheldon Campbell, living in Charlottetown.
F6   Eva Campbell, m. Marcel <u>Pronovost</u>. He played with the Detroit Red Wings, for a number of years and is in the Hockey Hall of Fame.
E5   Wilfred Campbell, m. Mary <u>MacLean</u> of Caledonia. They lived in California, with issue:
F1   Buddy Campbell.
F2   John Campbell.
F3   Everett Campbell.
F4   Donald Campbell.
F5   Cheryl Campbell.
E6   Eva Campbell, m. Sam <u>Cantelo</u>, U.S.A., with issue:
F1   Joan Cantelo, m. Dwight <u>Kellogg</u>.
    G1   David Kellogg.
    G2   Kim Kellogg.
    G3   Another child.

D2 Daniel or Donald MacLeod, died in 1925 in Calgary. He was m. to Agnes <u>Cowan</u>, Colorado Springs, with issue:

  E1 Donald MacLeod, M.D., m. in Jackson, Wyoming, they had two children.

D3 Angus MacLeod, died in California.

D4 Isabella MacLeod, m. Angus <u>Gillis</u>, Head of Montague, P.E.I. They had at least:

  E1 Lendel Gillis.

  E2 Alex Gillis, Calgary.

  E3 Malcolm Gillis, Detroit.

  E4 Mabel Gillis, R.N., m. Charles <u>Nicholson</u>. He was the son of Donald Charles Nicholson, Orwell Cove. They had a daughter:

    F1 Carol Nicholson.

D5 John MacLeod, married in Colorado Springs and had one daughter.

D6 Malcolm MacLeod, 1879-1921. He was on the old homestead and m. Isobel <u>MacLeod</u>, 1879-1918. She was the daughter of "Sandy" John MacLeod, of Kinross. They are buried in Uigg Church of Scotland, with issue:

  E1 Blair MacLeod, 1907-1929.

  E2 Alexander MacLeod, m. Kay _____ in Calgary. They lived in Victoria, British Columbia. He served as Captain in WWII. They had two daughters. Alexander was raised by uncle Angus Alexander MacLeod and wife Catherine Lamont.

  E3 Wilfred MacLeod,1914-1975, served in Germany in WWII, m. Catherine Clare <u>MacLeod</u>, daughter of Hector of Orwell Cove and Plenty, Saskatchewan. They lived in Edmonton, Alberta. Their children were:

    F1 Dr. Bruce Hector MacLeod, m. Brenda Colleen <u>Bunyan</u>, with issue:

      G1 Genevieve Sara MacLeod, born in Bangor, Wales.

      G2 Alexander Thomas MacLeod, born in Edmonton.

    F2 James Blair MacLeod, born in Edmonton, Alberta, m. Maureen Louise <u>Andrews</u>, with issue:

      G1 Andrew Blair MacLeod, born in Edmonton, Alberta.

      G2 Christine Louise MacLeod, born in Edmonton.

    F3 Donald Alexander MacLeod, born in Edmonton, m. L. Jean <u>Gore</u>, born in Edmonton, Alberta.

  E4 Hazel MacLeod, m. Emil <u>Lamereau</u>, in Yellowknife, N.W.T.

    F1 Patricia Lamereau.

D7 Alexander "Og" MacLeod, born May 27, 1862, m. in San Diego, California, with one daughter.

C8 Euphemia MacLeod, unmarried in Santa Barbara, California.

C9 Kate MacLeod, lived in Colorado Springs.

C10 Catherine MacLeod, died young and is buried in the Kirk Cemetery, Kinross.

C11 Malcolm MacLeod, 1830-1877, m. Christine <u>Martin</u>, 1832-1904, on Nov. 1, 1856, with issue:

D1 Charles MacLeod, born Oct. 3, 1857, at Murray Harbour Road.
D2 Isabella MacLeod, born Sept. 20, 1859, at Sparrows Road.
D3 Mary MacLeod, born Aug. 22, 1861, at Sparrows Road, m. Samuel McLeod (see Point Prim), with issue:
    E1 Alex MacLeod, m. Zelda MacBeth, they lived in Point Prim.
    E2 Sunny MacLeod.
    E3 John James MacLeod, m. Grace Stewart.
    E4 Bessie MacLeod, m. Charles Gillis, with issue:
        F1 Laughlin Gillis, m. Alberta Nicholson.
    E5 Christine MacLeod, m. Channing Deacon. They had children.
D4 Flora Ann MacLeod, m. John Allan MacDonald.
D5 Alexander MacLeod.
D6 Catherine MacLeod, born 1868, m. Angus Bruce, Grandview.
D7 Samuel Martin MacLeod, m. Catherine (Katie) MacLeod, with issue:
    E1 Christine A. MacLeod, born Oct. 4, 1899, m. Fred Larkin of Summerside in Sept. 1927, with issue:
        F1 Jean Larkin, m. Harvey McCoo, with issue:
            G1 Khristine McCoo.
            G2 Susan McCoo.
            G3 Debbie McCoo.
        F2 Robert Larkin.
        F3 William Larkin.
    E2 Mary MacLeod, born 1901, m. Gordon Blackett in Feb. 1924.
        F1 Donald Blackett.
        F2 Alvin Blackett.
    E3 Malcolm Alexander MacLeod, unmarried.
    E4 Jean Margaret MacLeod, m. Herb Poche on Aug. 12, 1926, they had no family.
    E5 Mabel Irene MacLeod, m. Sam D. Ivester, with issue:
        F1 Thelma Ivester.
        F2 Dorothy (Dotty) Ivester.
    E6 Olive Irene MacLeod, 1908-1949, m. Paul Cogswell, no family.
    E7 Annie Florence MacLeod, m. Cameron MacLure, with issue:
        F1 Lorraine MacLure, m. _____, with issue:
            G1 Brenda.
            G2 Douglas.
        F2 William "Billy" MacLure, m. Barbara Griffin, with issue:
            G1 Mark MacLure.
            G2 John MacLure.
        F3 David MacLure, m. Sandy Lee Nicholson, with issue:
            G1 Aaron MacLure.
            G2 Sara MacLure.
        F4 Brian MacLure.
    E8 Donald Wright MacLeod, born Sept. 24, 1914, m. Dorothy MacKinnon on June 25, 1938, with issue:
        F1 Beverly MacLeod, m. Sharon Amass, with issue:

G1   Lisa MacLeod.
G2   David MacLeod.
F2   Jean Audrey MacLeod, m. Morley Annear, Montague, with issue:
G1   Scott Annear.
G2   Lori Annear.
G3   Brian Annear.
G4   Stephen Annear.
F3   Donald Leigh MacLeod, m. Ann MacLeod Darrach.
G1   Amanda MacLeod.
F4   Kenneth Lorne MacLeod.
F5   Glenda Anne MacLeod, m. Billy Roberts.
E9   John Colin MacLeod, m. Margaret Webster, with issue:
F1   Gloria, m. and deceased.
F2   Velma MacLeod.
F3   Lynn MacLeod.
F4   Faye MacLeod.
F5   Nancy MacLeod.
D8   Donald William MacLeod, 1872-1895.
D9   Marjorie Catherine MacLeod, m. Murdock D. MacLeod (see Cardross).
D10 Infant, who died 1874.
B3   John "Sandy John" MacLeod, 1797-1873, m. Isobella Ross, 1809-1886, daughter of Lauchlin Ross, with issue:
C1   Mary MacLeod, born Jan. 2, 1834, m. Jacob Judson, Alexandra, P.E.I.
D1   John Judson, M.D., m. in Newark. They live in New Jersey and had four children, one named Joyce.
D2   _____, lived in Newark New Jersey, had a family.
D3   Walter Judson, m. in Newark, New Jersey, died in Toronto, Ontario, had one son.
D4   Isabel Judson.
D5   Isaac Judson, m. ____ Robertson. Family not known.
D6   Katherine Judson, m. Albert Jenkins, with issue:
E1   Clifford Jenkins.
E2   Lillian Jenkins.
C2   Margaret MacLeod (Mary II), born Oct. 7, 1835, m. Lauchlin Angus MacLeod, Kinross, with issue:
D1   Mary Ann MacLeod, m. Donald Livingstone, High Bank, with issue:
E1   Walter Livingston, never married.
E2   Milton Livingston, m. Anna Rankin, Pictou Island.
E3   Stanley Livingston, m. Nella MacDonald, they had a family.
D2   Isabel MacLeod, m. Murdock Fred MacDonald, Bellevue, with issue:
E1   Milton MacDonald, never married.
E2   Mabel MacDonald, m. ____ MacEachern, Mermaid, P.E.I.
E3   Wallace MacDonald, married in New Brunswick.
D3   Angus Alexander MacLeod, m. Mary Campbell, Uigg, P.E.I. Lived in Kinross, with issue:
E1   Gordon MacLeod, m. Mabel MacLeod, Arlington, Massachusetts.

F1 Wayne MacLeod.

F2 Elaine MacLeod.

E2 Willard MacLeod, m. Muriel <u>Martin</u>, with issue:

    F1 Donald MacLeod, m. Lorna <u>MacDonald</u>, with issue:

        G1 Jeffrey MacLeod.

        G2 Andrew MacLeod.

        G3 Timothy MacLeod.

        G4 John MacLeod.

    F2 Elva MacLeod, m. Donald <u>Nicholson</u>, with issue:

        G1 Gordon Nicholson.

        G2 Douglas Nicholson.

        G3 Lea Nicholson.

    F3 Keith MacLeod, m. Kay <u>Brehaut</u>, with issue:

        G1 Richard Keith MacLeod.

        G2 Janice Helen MacLeod.

    F4 Robert MacLeod, m. Sally <u>Stewart</u>.

    F5 Eleanor MacLeod, m. Munroe <u>Wheeler</u>, with issue:

        G1 Susan Wheeler, m. Mac <u>Dixon</u>.

        G2 Stephen Wheeler.

        G3 Wendy Wheeler.

        G4 Paul Wheeler.

        G5 Leslie Wheeler.

    F6 Walton MacLeod, m. Heather <u>Gillis</u>.

E3 Alistair MacLeod, m. Constance <u>Belyea</u>, St. John, New Brunswick. Alistair was in WWII. They had a boy:

    F1 David MacLeod.

E4 Everett MacLeod, m. Margaret ____, with issue:

    F1 Madeline MacLeod.

E5 Sinclair MacLeod, m. Elsie <u>MacGregor</u>.

D4 John Walter MacLeod, m. Grace_____, Newark, New Jersey, with issue:

E1 Walter MacLeod, married.

E2 Elva MacLeod, died.

E3 Dorothy MacLeod.

E4 Robert MacLeod.

C3 "Sandy" Alexander J. MacLeod, born in 1837, m. Mary <u>MacLeod</u>, 1844-1924, of Kinross. She was a sister of Laughlin Angus MacLeod, with issue:

D1 John Walter MacLeod, 1877-1958, m. Margaret <u>Edgerton</u>, in Vancouver, British Columbia, with issue:

E1 James Alexander MacLeod, m. June <u>Jamieson</u>, with issue:

    F1 David Alexander MacLeod, m. _____, with issue:

        G1 Fraser.

        G2 Connor.

        G3 ____.

    F2 Sandra Jean MacLeod, m. David <u>Berryman</u>, with issue:

        G1 Trinity Berryman.

        G2 A daughter.

E2 Jean MacLeod, m. John David <u>Beaty</u>, with issue:

    F1 John Leonard Beaty, m. Jean <u>Fisher</u>, with issue:

        G1 Ian David Beaty.

G2   Mark William Beaty.
G3   Karen Margaret Beaty.
G4   Andrew John Beaty.
F2   Ross James Beaty, m. Patricia Fockler, with issue:
G1   Carolyn Elizabeth Beaty.
G2   John Nicholas Beaty.
G3   Heather Danielle Beaty.
G4   Shannon Julia Beaty, twin to Heather.
G5   Fiona Louise Beaty.
F3   Phillip William Beaty, m. Nancy McGeer, with issue:
G1   Emma Jean Beaty.
G2   Angus Ian Beaty.
G3   Conner Michael Beaty, twin of Angus.
F4   Allyson Jean Beaty, deceased.
D2   Mary Catherine MacLeod, 1878-1924.
D3   Isabella MacLeod, 1879-1918, m. Malcolm MacLeod (her cousin).
E1   Mary Catherine MacLeod, unmarried.
E2   Blair MacLeod, died young.
E3   Hazel MacLeod, m. Emil Lemereau of Yellowknife, N.W.T.
F1   Patricia Lamoureau.
E4   Alexander MacLeod, m. Kay _____.
E5   Wilfred MacLeod, died in Edmonton, was married to Catherine MacLeod, daughter of Hector MacLeod of Orwell Cove and Plenty, Saskatchewan. Their family were:
F1   Dr. Bruce Hector MacLeod, m. Brenda Colleen Bunyan.
G1   Genevieve Sarah MacLeod, born in Bangor, North Wales.
G2   Alexander Thomas MacLeod, born in Edmonton, Alberta.
F2   James Blair MacLeod, m. Maureen Louise Andrews. They live in Edmonton, with two children:
G1   Andrew Blair MacLeod.
G2   Christine Louise MacLeod.
F3   Donald Alexander MacLeod, m. L. Jean Gore, they live in Edmonton, Alberta.
D4   Angus Alexander "Angus Sandy" MacLeod, born April 26, 1882, in Kinross and died on March 12, 1967, in Orwell Head. He married Mary Catherine Lamont, born March 30, 1890, in Dundee and died April 10, 1975, in Orwell Head.
E1   Alexander Wesley MacLeod, m. Gail Larkin, with issue:
F1   Linda MacLeod, m. John Mullin, with four daughters.
E2   David MacLeod, 1918-1949, m. Anne Bowles, no family.
E3   Dorothy "Isabel" MacLeod, m. Russell Furness, with issue:
F1   Donald Furness, m. Jean Wilson, with issue:
G1   Kathy Furness.
G2   Jason Furness.
G3   Lauren Furness.
F2   David Furness, m. Anne Marie Villa, with issue:
G1   Lee David Furness.
F3   Sheila Furness, m. Robin Barker.
E4   Ewen Lamont MacLeod, 1921-1992.

E5   Rhoda Maxine MacLeod, 1922-1923.

E6   Rev. John Walter MacLeod, m. Evangeline Rafuse, with issue:
- F1   David MacLeod.
- F2   Mark MacLeod.
- F3   Peter MacLeod.

E7   Harold Blair MacLeod, m. Laura Bennett, from Seal Rocks, Newfoundland.
- F1   Glen William MacLeod, m. Rosalyn Moore.
- F2   James MacLeod, m. Lauren Foster, with issue:
  - G1   Leland James Foster MacLeod,
- F3   John Michael MacLeod.
- F4   Robert Andrew MacLeod.

E8   Gladys MacLeod, m. George Freeze, Penobsquis, New Brunswick.
- F1   Catherine Freeze.
- F2   David Freeze.

E9   Mary MacLeod, m. Douglas Cameron, with issue:
- F1   Wayne Cameron, m. Suzanne ____.
- F2   Linda Cameron, m. Steve Wilson, with issue:
  - G1   Amanda Mary Wilson.

E10 Elinor MacLeod, January 9, 1932 - Feb. 8, 1932.

E11 Malcolm Kenneth MacLeod, m. Elsie Hickox, with issue:
- F1   Kenneth Martin MacLeod, m. Nancy McKenna, Iona.
  - G1   Kaley Melissa MacLeod.
  - G2   Jalen Taylor MacLeod.
- F2   Ina "Michelle" MacLeod, m. Gerald Muller, with issue:
  - G1   Kristie Melissa Muller.
  - G2   Stephanie Leigh Muller.
- F3   Pamela Anne MacLeod, m. Lance Roberts, with issue:
  - G1   Amelia Dawne Roberts.
  - G2   Brittany Skye Roberts.

C4 Catherine "Kate" MacLeod, 1840-1887, buried in Belfast Cemetery.

C5 Margaret MacLeod, 1843-1894, buried in the Belfast Cemetery.

C6 Alexander MacLeod, 1841-1914, m. Ann Martin, 1858-1943. They had a farm in Grandview and later moved to British Columbia to be near their son.

D1 John Walter MacLeod, 1880-1937, went to British Columbia at an early age to work at mining and lumbering. He had a homestead near Kamloops, which he developed as a dairy farm. He married Sarah Ann MacMillan, 1883-1959. She was from Glengary, Ontario. In 1912 they moved to Salmon Arm, British Columbia, where their farm is owned and operated by direct descendants. Their family are as follows:
- E1   Gladys Butcher.
- E2   Anne Woods.
- E3   Hugh McLeod.
- E4   Alexander Ross MacLeod, m. to _____ Winsome.
- E5   Evelyn Paterson.
- E6   Grace Panzer.
- E7   Lois Tinney.

> D2 Margaret MacLeod, 1882-1935, m. John <u>Kellington</u>, 1880-1924.
>> E1 Thomas Kellington, retired Lieut. Commander, living in Victoria, British Columbia.
>> E2 Alexander Kellington, 1919-1969.
> C7 Euphemia "Effy" MacLeod, 1848-1893, buried in Belfast Cemetery.

B4 Mary MacLeod, m. Peter Finlay <u>MacDonald</u>, nephew of Rev. Donald MacDonald.

> C1 Daniel MacDonald, Pine Hill Divinity Student, died of T.B. at a young age.
> C2 Murdock MacDonald, m. Dolly <u>Ross</u>, with issue:
>> D1 Mary MacDonald, m. Wilfred <u>Wood</u>, Pownal, three daughters.
>> D2 Clara MacDonald, m. _____ <u>Jardine</u>, Boston, Massachusetts, one daughter.
>> D3 Grace MacDonald, m. Stewart <u>MacDonald</u>, Arlington, one child.
>> D4 Ruby MacDonald, m. ____ <u>Olsen</u>. They have no family.
>> D5 Dorothy MacDonald.
>> D6 Donald MacDonald, on homestead in Orwell.
>> D7 David MacDonald, served in WWII.
> C3 John Finlay MacDonald, m. Sara <u>Gillis</u>, Orwell, with issue:
>> D1 Sadie MacDonald, m. ___ <u>Hurdle</u>. Sadie was an R.N. in WWII.
>> D2 Peter MacDonald, m. Helen _____, Massachusetts. They have no family.
> C4 Mary Ann MacDonald, m. Malcolm Hector <u>Campbell</u>, no family.
> C5 Mary Christy MacDonald, died in youth.

Children of Alexander "Tailleur" MacLeod and 2) wife Mary <u>MacLeod</u> of Skye:

B5 Roderick MacLeod.
B6 Flora MacLeod.

Information received from Mrs. Elsie (Kenneth) MacLeod, Kinross; Allan MacLeod, Charlottetown; A. Ross MacLeod, Salmon Arm, British Columbia; Lauren Foster MacLeod, Ottawa; and Kaye Nicholson, Whim Road.

MURDOCH "TAILOR" MACLEOD
MURDOCH "TAILOR" MACLEOD AND MARY MACLEOD OF ORWELL CROSSROADS

A   Murdoch "Tailor" MacLeod was born in Harris, Scotland. He joined the navy at an early age. Emigrating to P.E.I. in 1816, he later m. Mary MacLeod of Orwell Bridge. They were known as "Tailor" MacLeods to distinguish them from the many other MacLeods in the area. Murdoch died May 23, 1860, age 76. He and Mary are buried at Belfast. Their children were:

B1   Rachel MacLeod, m. William MacLeod of Lyndale. They had six daughters and one son. (See MacLeods of Orwell Cove.)

B2   Margaret MacLeod, m. Norman MacSwain, of Belfast. No children.

B3   Donald MacLeod, moved to U.S.A.

B4   John MacLeod, m. Miss Nicholson of Orwell Cove. No children.

B5   William MacLeod, of Dundee, m. Catherine Biggs of Newtown, with issue:

     C1   Neil MacLeod, of Orwell, m. Elizabeth Musick, of Kinross, with issue:

         D1   Percy MacLeod, 1897-1983, m. Margaret Bruce, with issue:

             E1   Lloyd MacLeod, m. Vivian Stewart, living in Charlottetown.

                 F1   Carl MacLeod.

                 F2   Ann MacLeod.

                 F3   Kathy MacLeod.

                 F4   Jennifer MacLeod.

             E2   Gerald MacLeod, m. Shirley Carver, living in Toronto, with issue:

                 F1   Bonnie MacLeod.

                 F2   Heather MacLeod.

             E3   Elspeth MacLeod, m. Robert Crane, living in Vernon, P.E.I.

         D2   Evelyn MacLeod, 1898-1946, m. Otis MacLeod. (See family of Norman MacLeod and Margaret MacPhee of Uigg and of "Old" Murdoch MacLeod of Uigg.)

             E1   Christine MacLeod.

             E2   Dorothy MacLeod, m. William Ratz, with issue:

                 F1   Evelyn Ratz.

                 F2   Susan Ratz.

                 F3   Elizabeth Ratz.

                 F4   Barbara Ratz.

             E3   Audrey MacLeod, m. Stan MacNair, with issue:

                 F1   Neil MacNair.

                 F2   Margot Christine MacNair.

                 F3   Andrea MacNair.

             E4   Shirley MacLeod, m. Charles Layton, with issue:

                 F1   Robin Layton.

                 F2   John Layton.

                 F3   Peter Layton.

                 F4   Charles Layton.

             E5   Norman MacLeod, 1927-1964.

             E6   Arnold MacLeod, m. Louise MacLeod. (See family of Donald Ban Oig MacLeod and Mary Martin of Murray Harbour Road.) Issue:

F1   Jean MacLeod.
F2   Robert MacLeod.
D3 Hilda MacLeod, m. Gordon Mills, with issue:
    E1   Robert Mills, m. Joyce Bernard, living in Montague.
    E2   Deanna MacDougall Mills.
    E3   David Mills, of Charlottetown.
    E4   Bonita Mills, lives in Halifax.
    E5   Douglas Mills, lives in Mermaid.
C2 Murdoch A. MacLeod, 1864-1927, m. Jessie Munro, with issue:
    D1 Alice MacLeod, m. Charles Stewart, with issue:
        E1   Joan Stewart.
    D2 Gwendoline MacLeod, m. Jack MacKay of Springfield, with issue:
        E1   James MacKay.
        E2   Stewart MacKay.
        E3   Doreen MacKay.
        E4   Morgan MacKay.
        E5   Gwen MacKay.
    D3 Munro MacLeod, m. Birdie Currie. No children.
    D4 Gladys MacLeod, m. Ernest Charlton, moved out West.
    D5 Margaret MacLeod, m. Windsor Campbell, with issue:
        E1   Eleanor Campbell, lives in California.
        E2   George Campbell.
    D6 Mary MacLeod, m. ____ Smith, living in U.S.A.
    D7 Ivan MacLeod, m. Irene Storey, living in Dartmouth, Nova Scotia.
    D8 Arthur MacLeod, m. Jessie MacLeod. (See family of Angus MacLeod and Mary of Valleyfield.)
        E1   David MacLeod.
        E2   Donald MacLeod.
        E3   Roger MacLeod.
C3 Annie MacLeod, m. Roderick MacLean, Dundee Road, with issue:
    D1 Laura MacLean, m. cousin Neil MacLeod, son of Annie's uncle Neil (B7).
        E1   Murdoch MacLeod, m. Ruth Furness, with issue:
            F1   George MacLeod, m. Grace Campbell, they live in Orwell.
                G1   Clayton MacLeod, m. Joan Hughes.
                G2   Valerie Anne MacLeod, m. Clifford Campbell, issue:
                    H1   Shanda Campbell.
                    H2   Crystal Campbell.
                G3   Susan MacLeod, m. Anthony McQuillan, issue:
                    H1   Anthony McQuillan.
                    H2   Michael McQuillan.
                G4   Victor MacLeod, m. Linda _____, with issue:
                    H1   Jolene MacLeod.
                F2   Joan MacLeod, m. Jim Harrigan, living in Vancouver, issue:
                G1   Geoffrey George Harrigan.
                G2   Shelley Anne Harrigan, university student.

> Shelley was one of a group of 22 Canadian students selected and sent for further studies in China in 1986.

- E2 Jessie MacLeod, m. MacLean <u>Drake</u>, Millview, living in Alberta.
- E3 Ora MacLeod, m. Wilfred <u>Drake</u>, Millview, with issue:
  - F1 Dorothy Drake, m. Gordon <u>Bears</u>.
  - F2 Eleanor Drake, m. George <u>Key</u>.
  - F3 Wendell Drake.
- E4 Mary MacLeod, m. Albert <u>MacLeod</u>, with issue:
  - F1 Stanley MacLeod.
  - F2 Virginia MacLeod.
- E5 Elsie MacLeod, moved to Alberta.
- E6 Leslie MacLeod, moved to U.S.
- E7 William MacLeod, m. Thelma <u>Behm</u>, with issue:
  - F1 Neil MacLeod, killed in car accident.
  - F2 Lynn MacLeod.
  - F3 Stephen MacLeod.
- E8 Irene MacLeod, m. Munro <u>MacLeod</u>. (See family of Alexander "Tailleur" MacLeod of Kinross.) They live in Toronto, with issue:
  - F1 Barry MacLeod.

C4 Mary MacLeod, m. Alexander <u>Anderson</u>.

C5 John Henry MacLeod, m. Jessie <u>MacDonald</u>, with issue:
- D1 Jack MacLeod, never married.
- D2 Wallace MacLeod, killed in WWI.
- D3 Jessie MacLeod, m. Shaw <u>MacMillan</u>, of Alberry Plains, with issue:
  - E1 Francis MacMillan, R.N.
  - E2 Jean MacMillan, m. Daryl <u>MacKenzie</u>.
  - E3 George MacMillan, engineer in Alberta.
  - E4 Edna MacMillan.
  - E5 Marina MacMillan.
  - E6 John MacMillan.
  - E7 Fred MacMillan.
  - E8 Florine MacMillan.

Also other children of William and Catherine who moved away from the Island.

B6 Bella MacLeod, died 1927, aged about 93. She m. Allan <u>Buchanan</u> of Mount Buchanan. They had children.

B7 Neil MacLeod, died 1910, aged 81, m. Isabella <u>MacDonald</u>, died March 13, 1892.
- C1 Neil MacLeod, m. cousin Laura, grand-daughter of William (B5). Their descendants are listed after Laura.
- C2 Murdoch MacLeod, never married.
- C3 Jessie MacLeod, never married.
- C4 Belle MacLeod, m. _____ <u>Moran</u>.
- C5 Christy MacLeod, never married. Lived in U.S.
- C6 Mary MacLeod.

B8 Catherine MacLeod, died 1903, m. Donald <u>MacLeod</u>, Orwell. They had, at least:

C1　Murdoch MacLeod, of Vancouver.

B9　Murdoch MacLeod, 1832-1917, m. Anne H. Enman, of Vernon River, with issue, among others:

C1　Lawrence MacLeod, farmed old homestead, Orwell.

C2　Frank MacLeod.

C3　Florence MacLeod ("Florrie").
　　　D1　Hazel.

C4　Mary MacLeod, m. William Greenwood.

B10　Norman MacLeod, died 1889, aged 63, of Dundee, m. Margaret Buchanan, of Point Prim. Norman and Margaret were both teachers. Their children were:

C1　Murdock MacLeod, born 1868.

C2　John Hammond MacLeod, born 1871.

C3　Mary Florence MacLeod, born 1873.

C4　Malcolm Lester MacLeod, born 1876, m. Isabella Stewart, Orwell Hill. They lived in Dundee on the original family homestead but separated around 1925 and Malcolm Lester moved to Saskatchewan. They had a son Russell who was adopted by a family by the name of Burgoyne of Stanley Bridge.
　　　D1　Russell Burgoyne, living in Ontario, m. Joan Montgomery, Calgary. She was descended from a family of Montgomerys who were United Empire Loyalists settling near St. John, New Brunswick. Issue:
　　　　　E1　Allan Russell Burgoyne, a dentist in Kitchener, Ontario, m. Dale Butcher, no family.
　　　　　E2　Nancy Burgoyne, Associate Director for Canada Council for the Arts, m. David Schutte, living in Ottawa, with issue:
　　　　　　　F1　Blair Russell Schutte, Ottawa.
　　　　　E3　Patricia Burgoyne, Bank Manager in Toronto, m. Richard Krajewski, a Chartered Accountant. They live in Mississauga.
　　　　　E4　Brian John Burgoyne.
　　　　　E5　Ross Montgomery Burgoyne, attending university.

B11　Anne MacLeod, born Jan. 1842, m. Richard Wood of Orwell. Among others:

C1　Cyrus Wood.

C2　Norman Wood, m. Miss MacPherson of Dundee. They had a family.

C3　Mary Jane Wood, m. Mr. MacInnis. They had a family.

B12　Alexander MacLeod, sea captain, ship owner and large land owner in Orwell Corner area of P.E.I., m. Jessie Campbell, born in Skye. Alexander died June 14, 1893, aged 70. Jessie died Jan. 18, 1893, aged 70. Their children were:

C1　Murdoch MacLeod, moved to Texas.

C2　Archibald MacLeod, M.D., died Oct. 1884, aged 25 years. Practised in British Columbia.

C3　Norman MacLeod, born 1852, m. Mary Ann MacSwain of Belfast, died 1927, aged 77. They lived in Vancouver, with issue:
　　　D1　Floretta MacLeod, m. Professor Lemuel Robertson, with issue:
　　　　　E1　Norman Robertson, a Rhodes Scholar and Canadian Ambassador to the U.S. during MacKenzie King's time, m. Henrietta J. Welling of The Hague, Netherlands, with issue:

F1   Florijohanna Robertson.

F2   Judith Robertson.

E2   Mary Robertson, m. John C. Oliver, with issue:

F1   Fergus Oliver.

F2   Craig Oliver.

E3   Barbara Robertson, m. W. Morton.

D2   Maxwell MacLeod, lived in Nanaimo, British Columbia, m. Henrietta MacLaren.

E1   Maxwell MacLaren MacLeod.

D3   Mary MacLeod, m. George Beveridge, with issue:

E1   James Beveridge.

D4   Samuel A. MacLeod, m. without issue.

C4   Hugh D. MacLeod, 1856-1917, m. 1) Katherine A. Munn of Orwell (died 1893, aged 37). He lived in British Columbia, with issue:

D1   Alex M. MacLeod,

D2   Jessie MacLeod, m. Oscar Neilson of Vancouver, with issue:

E1   Doris Neilson, m. Andrew Littlejohn.

D3   Mae MacLeod, m. Alexander Stevens.

Hugh m. 2) Jessie Munn, with issue:

D4   Mildred MacLeod, m. Ed Gilbert.

D5   Ada MacLeod, m. _____ Johnson.

C5   Alexander MacLeod, Jr., Master Mariner, 1858-1909, m. Kate Mac-Kinnon of Orwell North. Known as "Sandy Captain." He drowned at sea, issue:

D1   Alexander Daniel MacLeod, 1883-1954.

D2   Jessie R. MacLeod, 1885-1965, m. Malcolm Buchanan. They lived in Lynn, Massachusetts, with issue:

E1   George Buchanan.

E2   Leslie Buchanan.

D3   Stella MacLeod, 1890-1926, m. C. E. Rike.

D4   Annie K. MacLeod, 1892-1953, m. A. G. MacLeod, with issue:

E1   Arthur K. MacLeod, m. Beatrice Cooke, with issue:

F1   Anne MacLeod, m. David E. Park, with issue:

G1   Alan D. Park.

G2   Katherine A. Park.

D5   Leslie MacLeod, 1893-1965, m. Ethel M. Turner, 1893-1964, issue:

E1   Alexander L. MacLeod, m. Mildred Harris, with issue:

F1   Sandra MacLeod.

F2   Daniel G. MacLeod.

E2   Joan K. MacLeod, m. H. Hastings, with issue:

F1   Geoffrey Hastings.

F2   Carol Hastings.

F3   Gail Hastings.

E3   Gerald MacLeod, twin of Joan.

E4   Elizabeth Anne MacLeod, m. Victor Jones, with issue:

F1   Matthew Jones.

F2   Griffin Jones.

F3   Roberta Jones.

D6   Helen MacLeod, born 1889.

C6   John O. MacLeod, 1860-1935. Lived in Vancouver, m. Anne Mutlow of Orwell, with issue:

D1   William A. MacLeod.
D2   Jessie MacLeod, m. Frank <u>Donaghy</u>, with issue:
    E1   Jack Donaghy.
    E2   Catherine Donaghy.

Information provided by *Skye Pioneers*, Christine MacLeod of Uigg, Elizabeth Jones of Vancouver, Capt. Alex's will and cemetery transcripts.

ARCHIBALD MacLEOD
ARCHIBALD MacLEOD AND SARAH MacDONALD OF KINROSS

Three brothers Archibald, Angus, and Donald MacLeod, emigrated from Uig, Skye, in 1829 on the *Mary Kennedy*, and settled in Kinross, P.E.I.

A1   Archibald MacLeod, born c. 1792, died March 20, 1858, aged 66, buried in Uigg Church of Scotland Cemetery. He m. Sarah <u>MacDonald</u>, with issue:

B1   Duncan MacLeod, born c. 1839, died Feb. 1865, buried in Church of Scotland Cemetery, Uigg.

B2   William MacLeod, died young.

B3   Angus MacLeod, 1842-1873, aged 30. He was an M.D. in Cambridge, Massachusetts.

B4   John Archie MacLeod, died May 3, 1916, aged 83, m. Mary <u>MacLeod</u>, daughter of Alexander Og MacLeod, of Kinross. She died June 1, 1888, aged 53, issue:

C1   Sarah Ann MacLeod, July 15, 1856 - June 12, 1867.

C2   Daniel (Donald) MacLeod, born May 5, 1858, m. Esther (Emma) <u>Nelson</u> of China Point, they moved to Riverside, California, with issue:

D1   Lillian MacLeod.

D2   Verna MacLeod, m. Arnold <u>Shutter</u>. No family.

D3   Mildred MacLeod, m. William <u>Wiener</u>, with issue:

E1   William Wiener.

D4   Alice MacLeod, m. Clyde <u>Rex</u>, no children.

C3   Archibald MacLeod, born Nov. 1, 1860, m. 1) Annie <u>Robbins</u>, m. 2) Mary Belle <u>Pringle</u>.

D1   Mary Belle MacLeod, m. _____ <u>Cundy</u>, with issue:

E1   Carol Francis Cundy.

C4   Alexander J. MacLeod, 1862-1923, m. Christy <u>MacDonald</u>, 1866-1958, of Bellevue, buried in Orwell Head Church of Scotland Cemetery, with issue:

D1   John Cameron MacLeod, 1898-1918. Killed in WWI.

D2   Alexander Cameron MacLeod, born July 19, 1899. Died in infancy.

D3   Alexander Leavitt MacLeod, 1901-1953, Quincy, Massachusetts, m. Evelyn <u>Cahill</u>, 1901-1953, with issue:

E1   Alice MacLeod, m. Putnam <u>Borden</u>, with issue:

F1   Allison Borden.

F2   Kenneth Borden.

F3   Holly Borden.

F4   Neil Borden.

E2   Kathleen MacLeod, m. Paul <u>Lunetta</u>, with issue:

F1   Lynn Marie Lunetta.

F2   Paul Lunetta.

F3   Mark Lunetta.

F4   David Lunetta.

F5   Michael Lunetta.

E3   Joan Marie MacLeod, m. Joseph <u>Cicco</u>, of Windsor, Connecticut.

D4   Ewen Stanley MacLeod, 1902-1943, died in England in WWII.

D5   Mary Florence MacLeod, m. Wilfred <u>Furness</u>, Vernon, P.E.I., issue:

E1   Russell Furness, m. Dorothy Isobel <u>MacLeod</u>, with issue:
F1   Donald Furness, m. Jean <u>Wilson</u>, with issue:
G2   Jason Furness.
G3   Lauren Furness.
F2   David Furness, m. Ann Marie <u>Villa</u>, with issue:
G1   Lea David Furness.
F3   Sheila Furness, m. Robin <u>Barker</u>, with issue.

E2   Lloyd Furness, m. Kay <u>MacNeill</u> (MacDougall), with issue:
F1   Ralph Furness.
F2   John Furness.
F3   Gordon Furness.

E3   Marion Furness, m. William <u>Platts</u>, with issue:
F1   Susan Platts.
F2   David Platts.
F3   Douglas Platts.

D6   Angus Russell MacLeod, died in Quincy, Massachusetts, m. Marion <u>MacLaren</u>, Pittsfield, Massachusetts, with issue:
E1   Carol Jean MacLeod.
E2   Joyce MacLeod.
E3   Marion MacLeod, m. James <u>Early</u>, with issue:
F1   Matthew Early.
F2   Russell Early.
F3   Brooke Early.

D7   Christine MacLeod, m. Ernest <u>MacLeod</u>, son of Donald MacLeod and Catherine Enman, Orwell Cove. Their children were:
E1   Donald Beverly MacLeod, died in New York.
E2   John Clifford MacLeod, m. Shirley West <u>MacDonald</u>.
E3   Mildred Penelope MacLeod, m. Charles <u>Compton</u>.

D8   Kathleen MacLeod, R.N., Royal Victoria Hospital, Montreal.

D9   Alexander Edison MacLeod, m. Anne <u>MacLean</u>, Head of Montague.
E1   Judy MacLeod, adopted.

C5   Laughlin MacLeod, born March 24, 1864, m., wife's name unknown, issue:
D1   Lillian MacLeod, unmarried.
D2   Mary Annie MacLeod, unmarried.

C6   Isabella MacLeod, born 1866, m. Richard <u>Ward</u>, Haverhill, Massachusetts, issue:
D1   Saruna Mary "May" Ward.

C7   Catherine MacLeod, 1868-1905, m. James <u>Nicholson</u>, Seattle, Washington.

C8   Christine MacLeod, 1873-1963, m. Angus <u>MacLeod</u>, 1873-1963, of Bellevue and Oakland, California.
D1   Ward MacLeod, deceased.
D2   Margaret MacLeod, m. Carl <u>Holmgrain</u>, California.

C9   Margaret Euphemia MacLeod, 1875-1930, m. Frank <u>Leavitt</u>, Boston, Massachusetts.

C10 Angus John MacLeod, born March 28, 1878, m. May Manrill, Northampton, Massachusetts, with issue:

D1 Helen MacLeod, m. Francis St. John, Florida.

D2 Christine MacLeod, m. John Keith, Florida.

B5 Mary MacLeod, m. Angus Duncan MacDonald.

C1 Flora MacDonald, unmarried.

C2 Sarah MacDonald, m. Laughlin Bruce, Milltown.

C3 Christy MacDonald, m. Malcolm Matheson.

C4 Archibald MacDonald, unmarried.

C5 Duncan MacDonald, m. Margaret MacDonald, no family.

C6 Jessie MacDonald, m. Roderick Graham, Southport, with issue:

D1 Malcolm Graham.

D2 Flora Graham, m. George Warry, from England, lived in Southport.

E1 Margaret Warry, m. Wesley Buchanan.

E2 Sarah Warry, m. Douglas MacLeod, Darlington, with issue:

F1 Robert Graham MacLeod, m. Frances "Billy" Bourke, issue:

G1 George Douglas Henry MacLeod.

F2 Elizabeth MacLeod, m. Fred Cannon, with issue:

G1 Nancy Cannon.

G2 Stewart Cannon.

G3 Robert Cannon.

G4 Elizabeth Cannon, m. Gerrard Lachapelle.

F3 George MacLeod, killed WWII.

E3 Christine Warry.

E4 Annie Warry, m. George MacEachern, Cardigan.

E5 Charles Warry, lived in Charlottetown.

E6 John Warry, m. Elizabeth Hill, two children.

E7 Helena Warry, m.____ Barnes.

E8 Frederick Warry, died young.

B6 Sarah MacLeod, m. ____ Campbell, Head of Montague.

ANGUS MACLEOD
ANGUS MACLEOD AND MARY ROSS OF KINROSS

A2   Angus MacLeod, 1829 pioneer, m. Mary <u>Ross</u>, Grandview. They lived in Kinross.

   B1   Donald MacLeod, 1832-1909, m. Mary <u>Martin</u>, 1837-1914, daughter of William Martin of Valleyfield. They had four children born on P.E.I. before moving to Lucknow, Ontario, in 1867.

      C1   Mary MacLeod, born 1861, died in Cleveland, Ohio, m. Malcolm J. <u>MacLennan</u>, with issue:

         D1   Marguerite MacLennan.

         D2   John MacLennan.

         D3   Howard MacLennan.

         D4   Nina MacLennan, m. Marty <u>Andree</u>, no issue.

         D5   Vera MacLennan, m. Tom <u>Kirk</u>, with two children.

      C2   Catherine MacLeod, 1863-1885, buried in Kinloss, Ontario.

      C3   Angus MacLennan, 1864-1912, m. Margaret <u>Gollon</u>, Lucknow, Ontario. Angus was a merchant in Lucknow and had one son:

         D1   Kenneth MacLeod, who died in 1974.

      C4   Alexander MacLeod, 1868-1933, the last child of Donald and Mary to be born on P.E.I., operated a barber shop in Teeswater, Ontario, was m. but had no family and is buried in Kinloss, Ontario.

      C5   Rachel MacLeod, 1868-1946, born in Kinloss, Ontario, buried in Woodmere Cemetery, Detroit, Michigan, m. William <u>Gardam</u>, issue:

         D1   Russell G. Gardam, died in 1975.

         D2   Mary Martin Berniece Gardam.

         D3   Ethel Rae Gardam, m. Harvey H. <u>Lickley</u>.

      C6   Annie MacLeod, 1870-1905, buried in Kinloss Cemetery, m. Alexander <u>Fraser</u>, with issue:

         D1   Pearl Fraser, m. Fred <u>Doig</u>.

         D2   William Clarence Fraser.

         D3   Gordon L. Fraser.

         D4   Rena Fraser, m. Hector <u>Symons</u>.

      C7   William MacLeod, 1874-1974, buried in Woodland Cemetery, London, Ontario, m. Leona <u>Thompson</u> from Orillia, Ontario. They had no family. He was a Presbyterian minister, graduating from Knox College, Toronto.

      C8   Donald MacLeod, 1877-1935, m. Carolyn <u>Johnston</u>, of Ripely, Ontario. He farmed the homestead where he was born until his death, buried in Kinloss Cemetery. They had nine children:

         D1   Evelyn MacLeod, m. Dr. James E. <u>Little</u>.

         D2   Donalda MacLeod.

         D3   Ruth MacLeod.

         D4   Mary MacLeod, m. Lincoln <u>Martin</u>.

         D5   Johnston MacLeod.

         D6   Leonard MacLeod.

         D7   Murdean MacLeod.

         D8   Grace MacLeod, m. Ronald <u>Walker</u>.

         D9   Ronald MacLeod.

B2　Laughlin "Angus" MacLeod, m. Margaret <u>MacLeod</u>, sister of Sandy John MacLeod. The 1881 census lists Laughlin 52 years, Margaret 41, Mary 12, Isabella 10, Angus 7, John 2 years. Laughlin and Margaret's family were:

C1　Mary Anne MacLeod, m. Donald <u>Livingstone</u>, High Bank, P.E.I., with issue:

D1　Walter Livingstone, never married.

D2　Milton Livingstone, m. Anne <u>Rankin</u>, Pictou Island. They lived in Sarnia, Ontario, with issue:

E1　Donald Livingstone.

E2　Bruce Livingstone.

D3　Stanley Livingstone, m. Nella <u>MacDonald</u>, with issue:

E1　Ronald Livingstone, m. Joan <u>Campbell</u>, living in Montague.

F1　Merilee Dawn Livingstone, m. Brian <u>Trainor</u>.

F2　Stanley Livingstone.

F3　Lorena Livingstone.

E2　Joyce Livingstone, m. Jack <u>Kennedy</u>, with issue:

F1　Joel Kennedy, m. Monique <u>Boudreau</u>, with issue:

G1　Jordon Kennedy.

G2　Ashton Kennedy.

F2　Christopher Kennedy.

F3　Jonathan Kennedy.

F4　Nella Ann Kennedy.

F5　Ronald Kennedy.

E3　Wade Livingstone, m. Debbie <u>Dixon</u>, living in High Bank, issue:

F1　Joshua Livingstone.

F2　Veronica Livingstone.

E4　Velda Livingstone, m. Stephen <u>Wurts</u>, St. John, New Brunswick, with issue:

F1　Corrie Wurts.

F2　Derek Wurts.

F3　Sara Joy Wurts.

C2　Isabel MacLeod, m. Murdoch Fred <u>MacDonald</u>, Bellevue, with issue:

D1　Wallace MacDonald, married in New Brunswick.

D2　Milton MacDonald, never married.

D3　Mabel MacDonald, m. James <u>MacEachern</u>, Mermaid, they had four children.

C3　Angus Alexander MacLeod, 1872-1932, m. Mary <u>Campbell</u>, 1878-1974, they lived in Kinross, buried in Orwell Corner Cemetery, with issue:

D1　Gordon MacLeod, m. Mabel <u>MacLeod</u>, in Arlington, Massachusetts, with issue:

E1　Wayne MacLeod.

E2　Elaine MacLeod.

D2　Willard MacLeod, m. Muriel <u>Martin</u>, with issue:

E1　Donald MacLeod, m. Lorna <u>MacDonald</u>, with issue:

F1　Jeffrey MacLeod.

F2　Andrew MacLeod.

F3　Timothy MacLeod.

F4　John MacLeod.

E2　Elva MacLeod, m. Donald <u>Nicholson</u>, Head of Montague.

F1　Gordon Nicholson.

      F2 Douglas Nicholson.

      F3 Lea Nicholson.

    E3 Keith MacLeod, m. Kay <u>Brehaut</u>, living on old home in Kinross.

      F1 Richard Keith MacLeod, m. Pam (Clark) <u>Kays</u>.

      F2 Janice Helen MacLeod, m. Charles <u>Gillis</u>.

    E4 Robert MacLeod, m. Sally <u>Stewart</u>, they had a family.

    E5 Eleanor MacLeod, m. Munroe <u>Wheeler</u>, living near Montague.

      F1 Susan Wheeler, m. Mac <u>Dixon</u>.

      F2 Stephen Wheeler.

      F3 Wendy Wheeler.

      F4 Paul Wheeler.

      F5 Leslie Wheeler.

    E6 Walton MacLeod, m. Heather <u>Gillis</u>.

  D3 Allistair MacLeod, a lawyer in Halifax, m. Constance <u>Belyea</u>, St. John.

    E1 David MacLeod.

    E2 Ian MacLeod.

  D4 Everett MacLeod, m. Margaret _____, with issue:

    E1 Madeline MacLeod.

  D5 Sinclair MacLeod, m. Elsie <u>MacGregor</u>, from Montague, their family:

    E1 Mary MacLeod, m. Dr. Gordon <u>Callon</u>, Canning, Nova Scotia.

    E2 John Lee MacLeod, m. Catherine <u>MacKean</u>, living in Moncton.

      F1 Andrew MacLeod.

      F2 Colin MacLeod.

    E3 Gordon Bruce MacLeod, m. Cheryl <u>Brown</u>, with three children from a previous marriage.

      F1 Sonja Brown.

      F2 Tanya Brown.

      F3 La Lena Brown.

      F4 Aaron MacLeod.

    E4 Karen MacLeod, M.D., practising in Dryden, Ontario, where she is m. to Allen <u>Mazursky</u>, with issue:

      F1 Kathryn Mazurski.

      F2 Micheline Mazurski.

 C4 John Walter MacLeod, m. Grace _____, Newark, New Jersey, with issue:

  D1 Walter MacLeod, married.

  D2 Elva MacLeod, not living.

  D3 Dorothy MacLeod.

  D4 Robert MacLeod.

B3 Jessie MacLeod (daughter of Angus MacLeod and Mary Ross), m. Alexander <u>Bruce</u>, Valleyfield, they had 11 or 12 children, one of whom was Margaret Bruce, married to Simon <u>Campbell</u>, Uigg.

B4 Mary MacLeod, 1844-1924, m. Alexander John <u>MacLeod</u>, for their descendants see the family of Alexander "Tailleur" MacLeod.

B5 Rachel MacLeod, m. _____ <u>Martin</u>, Springton, P.E.I., with issue:

C1   Annie Martin.
C2   Alexander Martin.
C3   Laughlin Martin.
C4   Angus Martin.
C5   Christie Martin.
C6   Mary Martin.
C7   Cyrus Martin.
B6   Flora MacLeod, m. Angus <u>MacInnis</u>, Martinvale, P.E.I., with issue:
C1   Donald MacInnis.
C2   Angus MacInnis, m. Christie <u>MacDonald</u>.
C3   Mary MacInnis.
C4   Jessie MacInnis.
C5   James MacInnis, a clergyman in the U.S.A.
C6   Catherine MacInnis.

DONALD MACLEOD
DONALD MACLEOD AND MARY MACLEOD OF KINROSS

A3 Donald MacLeod, m. Mary <u>MacLeod</u> of Gallas Point. (See the "Horo" MacLeods of Orwell Cove and Earnscliffe for more details of their descendants.)

B1 Neil MacLeod, m. Mary <u>MacDonald</u> of Uigg.
    C1 Archibald MacLeod.
    C2 Samuel MacLeod.
    C3 James MacLeod.

B2 Malcolm MacLeod, m. Christy <u>Gillis</u>, Bellevue.
    C1 Mary MacLeod.
    C2 Donald MacLeod.
    C3 Rachel MacLeod.

B3 Norman MacLeod, unmarried.

B4 Alexander MacLeod, m. Susan E. <u>MacQueen</u> (cousin).
    C1 Stanhope MacLeod.
    C2 Victor MacLeod.

B5 Donald MacLeod, unmarried.

B6 Jessie MacLeod, m. John <u>MacBeth</u>, Bellevue, with issue:
    C1 Mary MacBeth, m. John <u>MacKinnon</u>, Lewes.
    C2 Margaret (Maggie) MacBeth, m. Mr. <u>MacLeod</u>, of Hartsville and Massachusetts.
    C3 Annie MacBeth, never married.
    C4 Bella MacBeth, m. Edwin <u>Perkess</u>, U.S.A.
    C5 Catherine MacBeth, died 1884, age 9 days.
    C6 Isabella MacBeth, died 1868, age 1 year.
    C7 Daniel Angus MacBeth, 1875-1950, never married.
    C8 Donald Alec MacBeth, m. Annie <u>Darrach</u>, 1886-1968, they lived in U.S.A.
    C9 Neil MacBeth, died 1954, age 77, m. Angusena <u>MacLeod</u>, no family.
    C10 Kenneth MacBeth, 1873-1955, m. Bessie <u>MacLeod</u>, from Hunter River. They farmed in Grandview, and had one daughter who died young.
    C11 John MacBeth, m. Mary Anne <u>Matheson</u>, Lewes. They farmed in Bellevue. (For their descendants see the Orwell Cove MacLeods.)

B7 Rachel MacLeod, m. Donald <u>MacPherson</u>.

B8 Catherine MacLeod, m. _____ <u>MacPhee</u>, Bellevue.

B9 Mary MacLeod, m. John "Sandy" <u>MacLeod</u>, Kinross, son of Alexander Og MacLeod, of Kinross, with issue:
    C1 Catherine MacLeod, m. Sam <u>Campbell</u>, Uigg.
    C2 Daniel MacLeod, m. Agnes <u>Cowan</u>.
    C3 Angus MacLeod, died in California.
    C4 Isabella MacLeod, m. Angus <u>Gillis</u>, Head of Montague.
    C5 John MacLeod, m. in Colorado Springs.
    C6 Malcolm MacLeod, m. Isabel <u>MacLeod</u>.

B10 Rachel MacLeod, m. _____ <u>Buchanan</u>.

Information provided by the late Matilda B. Ross, Kinross, and revised by Lauren Foster MacLeod, Ottawa, and Elsie MacLeod, Kinross.

Donald MacLeod
Donald MacLeod and Mary MacInnis of Montague

A   Donald MacLeod, was born in the Isle of Skye and settled in Montague, P.E.I., m. Mary Anne <u>MacInnis</u>, with issue:

B1   John MacLeod, 1853-1904, m. Jessie <u>MacMillan</u>, 1856-1927, with issue:

     C1   Donald MacLeod, m. Effie <u>Murchison</u>, with issue:

         D1   John Daniel MacLeod, 1910-1962, m. C. Margaret R. <u>Hockin</u>, issue:

            E1   Margaret Gail MacLeod, m. Donald John <u>Sear</u>, with issue:

                F1   Allan John Sear, m. Janice <u>Larsen</u>, with issue:

                   G1   Jaclyn Marlene Sear.

                F2   Donna June Sear, m. Gregory Winston <u>Kobitzach</u>, with issue:

                   G1   Daniel John Kobitzach.

                F3   Patty Ann Sear, m. Michael James <u>Sears</u>, with issue:

                   G1   Leslie Ann Sears.

                F4   Eric Donald Sear.

            E2   Catherine Dawn MacLeod, m. Robert <u>Loutit</u>, with issue:

                F1   Laurie Catherine Loutit.

         D2   Hector Murchison MacLeod, 1915-1979, m. Irene <u>Priest</u>, no family.

         D3   Donald Edwin MacLeod, 1920-1977, m. Bertha <u>Patterson</u>, issue:

            E1   Shirley MacLeod.

            E2   Sharon MacLeod, m. _____ <u>Ansari</u>, with issue:

                F1   Fez Ansari.

                F2   Sophia Ansari.

            E3   Donna MacLeod.

            E4   Daniel MacLeod, m. _____, with issue:

                F1   Scott MacLeod.

                F2   Anna MacLeod.

            E5   Auril MacLeod, twin to Betty.

            E6   Betty MacLeod.

            E7   Linda MacLeod.

     C2   John Malcolm MacLeod, 1888-1941, m. Emily <u>MacKay</u>, 1893-1967, with issue:

         D1   Margaret Ena MacLeod, m. Albert MacLean <u>Stevens</u>, no children.

         D2   Laura Jean MacLeod, m. Donald Edgar <u>MacLean</u>, 1922-1986, issue:

            E1   Judith Dawn MacLean, m. Jean-Marie <u>Ouellette</u>.

            E2   John Allan MacLean, m. Colleen H. <u>Hill</u>.

            E3   Heather Jean MacLean, m. Roderick Chester <u>Pratt</u>.

     C3   Vernon Hector MacLeod, born 1892, died 1938, unmarried.

     C4   Christina Currie MacLeod (Ena), m. Charles <u>Milton</u>, no family.

B2   Malcolm MacLeod, Avon, Massachusetts. Wife's name unknown, issue:

     C1   John MacLeod.

     C2   Malcolm MacLeod.

     C3   Frederick MacLeod.

     C4   Mary MacLeod.

     C5   Sylvia MacLeod.

C6   Donald MacLeod.

C7   Betty Ashley MacLeod.

C8   Mabel Bassett MacLeod.

B3   Mary MacLeod, m. Reginald <u>Stuart</u>, who died 1924. One son, died 1901, age 5 years.

B4   Flora MacLeod, m. _____ <u>Smith</u>.

C1   Harry Smith, died in the 1960s.

C2   Second son, killed in a train as a child.

B5   Annie MacLeod, lived in Massachusetts. Husband's name unknown.

C1   Louise, lived in Detroit, and m. _____ <u>Jagger</u>, with issue:

D1   Dr. Richard Jagger, lived in Ohio, died 1982, was married, wife's name unknown, they had a daughter:

E1   Janet Jagger, lives in Michigan.

D2   Annie Jagger, m. Milton <u>Cobb</u>. No family.

D3   Clarence Jagger, living in Pittsburgh, m. Fern _____, three children.

D4   Alice Jagger, m. Edwin <u>Shoults</u>, no children.

B6   Jennie MacLeod, 1869-1941. She was a nurse, never married.

B7   William MacLeod, born 1871, lived in San Jose, California, m. Ella _____, with issue:

C1   Donald MacLeod.

C2   Barbara MacLeod, m. Ralph <u>Ott</u>, with issue:

D1   Bartley Ott.

B8   Mary Ann MacLeod, 1873-1950, m. Malcolm <u>MacLeod</u>, with issue:

C1   John MacIntyre MacLeod, 1902-1903.

C2   Donald Heath MacLeod, 1903-1925.

C3   Alexander Roderick MacLeod, 1906-1981, m. Annie <u>MacKay</u>, issue:

D1   Elaine MacLeod, m. Clarence <u>McCarrison</u>.

D2   Alice MacLeod, lived in Sharon, Massachusetts, m. Earl <u>Falsom</u>, who was an undertaker. No children.

D3   Roderick Alexander MacLeod, Jr., worked with Delta Air Lines, m. Robin <u>Thorpe</u>, with issue:

E1   Heather MacLeod, m. William Henry <u>McClain</u>, lives in Swainboro, Georgia, where he is an Assistant District Attorney.

E2   Laurie MacLeod, m. William Lonnie <u>Bennett</u>.

E3   Judith MacLeod.

E4   Leslie MacLeod.

C4   Ella Adine MacLeod, 1910-1980, m. Walter <u>Levine</u>, no children.

C5   Anne MacLeod, born 1910.

C6   Jennie MacLeod, lived in Marion, Massachusetts, m. William <u>Jones</u>, with issue:

D1   William Dale Jones.

B9   Roderick MacLeod, left home when he was young. He was in Western Canada, then he went to sea. He was in England and Cape Town in 1894-1895, Rio De Janeiro in 1895, Valparaiso, Chile, Wales in 1896, Port Elizabeth, Africa, in 1896, North Eastern Rhodesia in 1900, Australia, Lake Victoria, Kampola, Uganda in 1902. He was ill with Black Water fever and last heard from in 1902.

Information was provided by Laura Jean MacLeod, Charlottetown.

JOHN MACLEOD
JOHN MACLEOD AND MARY MACKINNON OF PISQUID AND DROMORE

A   In the 1798 census there is an Alex MacLeod, Lot 37. This is assumed to be the father of John, he is thought to be the first settler of this family on P.E.I. John MacLeod died an old man on Jan. 20, 1878. He is buried in Fort Augustus Cemetery. His wife Mary MacKinnon was the daughter of John MacKinnon, and her mother was possibly a MacRae. Mary died in 1880.

B1   Alexander MacLeod, born in Dromore in 1835, m. ____ MacDonald, from Naufrage. They moved from P.E.I.

B2   Catherine MacLeod, born in Dromore, July 22, 1837, m. Alex Walker. Catherine and Alex had children but their names are unknown.

B3   Hugh MacLeod, born 1839, m. Catherine MacIntyre. They lived in Mt. Stewart.

     C1   John Alexander MacLeod, born Jan. 16, 1881.

B4   Elizabeth MacLeod, born in Dromore, 1841, m. a Noonan.

B5   Agnes Effie Nancy MacLeod, born 1843, m. John Walker. In 1866 Agnes lived in Red Point and later with Mary and Andy Hand.

B6   Mary MacLeod, m. Andy Hand. They had children, several of them died of diphtheria.

B7   John MacLeod, born 1855, baptized June 10, 1855, never married, moved from P.E.I.

B8   Angus MacLeod, 1851-1897, m. Bridget Hughes in 1881. She was born in 1865, died 1948, and is buried in Boston, Massachusetts. Angus is buried in Fort Augustus Cemetery. Their children were:

     C1   Mary Ann Josephine MacLeod, born May 1, 1883.

     C2   Catherine MacLeod (Lena), born May 16, 1885.

     C3   Lizzie MacLeod.

     C4   Nellie MacLeod.

     C5   Teresa MacLeod.

     C6   John Francis MacLeod, born May 10, 1884.

     C7   Joseph MacLeod.

     C8   George MacLeod.

     C9   Vincent MacLeod, baptized Dec. 4, 1887, m. Gertrude Kelly in 1916. She was born in Boston on July 16, 1895, and moved to the Island when she was six or seven years old. She died Feb. 11, 1971. Vincent died in 1929 and is buried in Fort Augustus Cemetery. They had issue:

         D1   Harold MacLeod, m. Evelyn Hughes.

         D2   Urban MacLeod, born in Dromore, m. Mary Callaghan, with issue:

             E1   Edna MacLeod, m. John Rogerson.

             E2   Janet MacLeod, m. Walter Bradley.

             E3   Vincent MacLeod.

             E4   Teresa MacLeod, m. Earl Hughes.

             E5   James MacLeod.

             E6   Jacqueline MacLeod.

D3   Leonard MacLeod, m. Ann <u>MacPhee</u>.

D4   Basil MacLeod, born 1921, m. Bernadette <u>MacDonald</u>.

D5   Emmett MacLeod, born in Dromore, died young.

D6   Fred MacLeod.

D7   Mary MacLeod, born in Dromore, m. Norman <u>Keoughan</u>.

D8   Joseph MacLeod, born in Dromore on May 2, 1917. He studied at St. Dunstan's University, Charlottetown. In 1942 he went to Halifax and studied theology at Holy Heart. He was ordained in 1948. His first commission was at St. Paul's Parish, Summerside, where he was first assistant for eight years. In 1956 he became priest at St. Margaret's Parish, near Souris, P.E.I. Father MacLeod served there for fifteen years until 1971. He is currently serving the Parish of St. James in Georgetown, P.E.I.

C10 Ambrose MacLeod.

C11 Allan MacLeod, died a young man.

All of Angus MacLeod's family moved to U.S.A. except for Vincent. The reason for this is not clear, but it may have been due to better work opportunities there, according to Father Joseph MacLeod.

This information was provided by Father Joseph MacLeod, Georgetown, dates taken from cemetery transcripts, and research at Beaconsfield.

John MacLeod
John MacLeod and Catherine Stewart of Glenwilliam

A   John MacLeod came to P.E.I. from the Isle of Skye as a young man. He m. Catherine Stewart of Heatherdale. They were both buried in Caledonia Cemetery. The dates on the stones read: John—died Feb. 27, 1913, at the age of 82 years, Catherine—died Feb. 16, 1912, at the age of 72 years. They had issue:

    B1   Alexander James MacLeod, born July 5, 1861, in Valleyfield, died in 1948, m. Margaret Belle MacPhee (Maggie), 1872-1961. They lived in Glenwilliam and are buried in Caledonia Cemetery. They had issue:

        C1   John MacLeod, born May 29, 1911. Never married.

        C2   Donald MacLeod, 1912-1984. He was the official piper for the Clan MacLeod in P.E.I., as well as a member of the pipe band overseas in WWII, and a piper at the Wood Islands Ferry terminal in P.E.I.

    B2   A brother.

This information was provided by John MacLeod, Glenwilliam.

NEIL MACLEOD
NEIL MACLEOD AND ELIZABETH CAVANAGH OF ORWELL HEAD, GRAND RIVER, AND CUMBERLAND HILL

A   Neil MacLeod, m. Elizabeth <u>Cavanagh</u>, 1813-1870. She is buried in St. George's Cemetery. Not much is known about Neil except that he bought land in Lot 55 in 1863 from Archibald Campbell, who had come to the Island as a United Empire Loyalist.

    B1   Mary Ann MacLeod, born 1837 in Belfast area, m. Thomas <u>Owen</u>, Feb. 15, 1860. He died 1869. He is buried in Georgetown Anglican Cemetery. She died in 1881 and is buried in Dundas. They had issue:

        C1   John Edward Owen, 1861-1881.

        C2   Thomas G. Owen, died 1863, 3 months old.

    B2   Archibald MacLeod, baptized Aug. 23, 1841, at Belfast, never married.

    B3   Kathryn MacLeod.

    B4   Margaret Jane MacLeod, m. Hughie <u>MacLean</u> of Albion Cross.

    B5   John Neil MacLeod, 1848-1921, m. Susan <u>Owen</u>, 1846-1932, with issue:

        C1   Neil J. MacLeod, 1873-1952, lived in Seattle, Washington, m. 1) Sophia <u>Miller</u>, who died in 1931, m. 2) Edna <u>Collins</u>, who died in 1970. Neil's children were:

            D1   Katherine MacLeod, 1902-1972, m. William P. <u>Dowie</u>. They lived in Tacoma, Washington, with issue:

                E1   Donald Neil Dowie, m. Betty L. <u>Leavitt</u>, with issue:

                    F1   Susan MacLeod Dowie.

                    F2   Laurie L. Dowie.

                    F3   Robbie L. Dowie.

                    F4   Donald Neil Dowie.

                E2   William P. Dowie, Jr., 1925-1926.

                E3   Mary K. Dowie, 1928-1988, m. Willis <u>Wheatley</u>, with issue:

                    F1   Kathy Wheatley.

                    F2   William Wheatley.

                    F3   Connie Wheatley.

                    F4   Mary Beth Wheatley.

            D2   John George MacLeod, 1906-1970, m. Avis <u>Hougan</u>. They lived in the Seattle area, with issue:

                E1   Roderick Neil MacLeod, m. Nelsie <u>Persson</u>, with issue:

                    F1   Scott Cameron MacLeod.

                    F2   David Neil MacLeod.

                    F3   Kathryn Elizabeth MacLeod.

                E2   Georgia Ellen MacLeod, m. Gerry <u>Goodmansen</u>, with issue:

                    F1   Kristie Beyh Goodmansen.

                    F2   Craig Douglas Goodmansen.

                    F3   Kelly Lynn Goodmansen.

        C2   Alexander MacLeod, moved to Western Canada, m., wife's name unknown.

        C3   Elizabeth MacLeod, m. Cyrus <u>Bruce</u> of Haverhill, Massachusetts, with issue:

            D1   Russel Bruce.

            D2   Hollis Bruce.

C4 Henry MacLeod, married and lived in Haverhill, Massachusetts.
C5 John MacLeod, m. Libby Robertson of East Point, lived in Bradford, Massachusetts.
    D1 Mildred MacLeod.
    D2 John MacLeod.
    D3 Eldra MacLeod.
C6 Emanuel MacLeod, died in infancy.
C7 Emma MacLeod, 1884-1925, m. Joseph Campbell, with issue:
    D1 Georgie Campbell, deceased.
        E1 Reginald Joseph Campbell, m. Jean Janzen, with issue:
            F1 Joe Campbell.
            F2 Christopher Campbell.
            F3 Sean Campbell.
    D2 Julia Campbell, m. Maurice Redmond, in Washington.
    D3 Ellen Campbell, m. Charles MacDonald, with issue:
        E1 Emma MacDonald, m. Frank McQuaid, with issue:
            F1 Monica McQuaid.
            F2 Stephen McQuaid.
            F3 Sean McQuaid.
        E2 Margaret MacDonald, m. 1) Gregory, 2) Campbell, with issue:
            F1 David.
            F2 Robert.
        E3 Patsy MacDonald.
    D4 John James Morris Campbell, 1919-1920.
    D5 Patricia Campbell, m. 1) John Donahue, with issue:
        E1 Daisy Donahue, m. Joe Brown, with issue:
            F1 Michael Brown.
            F2 Kathryn Brown.
            F3 Peter Brown.
            F4 Susan Brown.
        E2 Edward Donahue, m. Johannah VanDeBroek, with issue:
            F1 Genevieve Donahue.
            F2 Paul Donahue.
            F3 Mark Donahue.
        E4 Julia Donahue.
        Patricia, m. 2) Larry Doucette.
    D6 Emma Josephine Campbell, 1924-1925.
C8 Mary MacLeod, m. Waldo Daggett, Haverhill, Massachusetts, with issue:
    D1 Dorothy Daggett, m. ____ Randall, Haverhill.
    D2 Gladys Daggett, m. 1) Brown, 2) Sullivan, Haverhill, Massachusetts.
    D3 Helen Daggett, m. _____ West, South Carolina.
    D4 Ruth Daggett, m. _____ Chamberlain, Florida.
    D5 Ralph Daggett, Arizona.
    D6 Fern Daggett, m. _____ Cote, Arizona.
    D7 Arnold Daggett, Haverhill, Massachusetts.
    D8 Marguerite Daggett, m. _____ Hogan, Haverhill.
C9 Edward MacLeod, unmarried, died 1951.
C10 Herbert Gladstone MacLeod, 1889-1974, m. 1) Myrtle Hunter, 1894-1932.

D1   Ruth MacLeod, 1913-1926.
D2   Waldo MacLeod, m. Margaret MacKenzie, with issue:
    E1   Wayne MacLeod, m. Doris Hunter, with issue:
        F1   Vicki MacLeod.
        F2   Trevor MacLeod.
    E2   Keith MacLeod, m. Kathryn Garrett, with issue:
        F1   Kelli MacLeod.
        F2   Karla MacLeod.
    E3   Infant girl, died.
    E4   Infant girl, died.
D3   Marjorie MacLeod, m. Roderick MacKenzie, with issue:
    E1   Blair MacKenzie, m. Josephine Kickham, with issue:
        F1   Heidi MacKenzie.
    E2   Donald MacKenzie, m. Nancy Coronada, Guatemala, with issue:
        F1   Kristian MacKenzie.
        F2   Davin MacKenzie.
    E3   Roger MacKenzie, m. Mary MacDonald, with issue:
        F1   Troy MacKenzie.
        F2   Angela MacKenzie.
        F3   Tara MacKenzie.
        F4   Jeffrey MacKenzie.
    E4   Ruth MacKenzie, m. Robert Thorne, Newfoundland, with issue:
        F1   Wyatt Thorne.
        F2   Colin Thorne.
        F3   Roderick Thorne.
    E5   Daughter, died in infancy.
    E6   Daughter, died in infancy.
D4   Stewart MacLeod, m. Edith Turner, lived in Holliston, Massachusetts. Retired to Stratford, P.E.I., with issue:
    E1   Judith MacLeod, m. Peter Smith, Victoria, British Columbia.
    E2   Herbert MacLeod, single.
D5   Ann MacLeod, m. Clement Campbell, with issue:
    E1   Gary Campbell, m. Elaine Johnston, with issue:
        F1   Shelly Campbell.
        F2   Karen Campbell.
        F3   Shannon Campbell.
        F4   Jason Campbell.
    E2   Foster Campbell, m. Susan Harris, with issue:
        F1   Darcy Campbell.
        F2   Devon Campbell.
        F3   Colby Campbell.
        F4   Stacey Campbell.
        F5   Lindsey Campbell.
    E3   Debbie Campbell, m. Henry (Hank) Picard, Massachusetts.
    E4   Myrtle Campbell, m. Tommy McCormack, with issue:
        F1   Tyler McCormack.
    E5   Susan Campbell, single.
    E6   Julia Campbell.
Herbert Gladstone m. 2) Mary Josephine MacLeod.

C11 Elliot Roy MacLeod, 1891-1971, m. Hazel <u>Moore</u>, with issue:
- D1 William Moore MacLeod, m. Jane <u>Connolly</u>, with issue:
  - E1 Jane MacLeod, m. Robert L. <u>Wilson</u>, with issue:
    - F1 Bret David Wilson.
    - F2 Kelly MacLeod Wilson.
  - E2 Colleen Anne MacLeod, m. 1) David <u>Joslin</u>, 2) Michael A. <u>Javens</u>, with issue:
    - F1 Kylie Marie Javens.
    - F2 Lori Fae Javens.
- D2 Neil Moore MacLeod, 1918-1986 (twin to William), m. Helen <u>Waterman</u>, no family.

Information provided by Marjorie MacKenzie, Montague, P.E.I., and William Moore MacLeod, Oregon.

Angus MacLeod
Angus MacLeod and Christina of Bellevue

A   Angus MacLeod of Scotland emigrated to P.E.I. and settled in Green Marsh
(school district 1859 in Bellevue, Lot 58), m. Christina _____, with issue:

B1   Donald MacLeod, m. Catherine MacDonald, 1821-1883. She was the daughter of Alex MacDonald and Isabel MacDonald. Maternal grandfather was John of the Isle of Skye. They had the following children:

C1   Angus MacLeod, 1850-1881. He lived in "Rona" (today known as Mt. Vernon) with his wife Katherine Matheson, 1855-1900. Her father was Angus Matheson and they took the oath of Baptism together from the Wood Islands Presbyterian church by Rev. John Sutherland. They had issue:

D1   Angusena MacLeod, July 8, 1879 - Nov. 1958. Angusena knew her father Angus died when she was young but not sure of dates: they found on the bottom of her birth certificate the information that he was a corpse in the house at the time of her baptism, March 21, 1881. She m. John Robert Brown, of Pownal, son of Daniel Brown and Elizabeth Moore, with issue:

E1   Florence K. Brown, 1902-1971, m. in 1936 to Bennett J. Haywood, they had four children.

E2   Marjorie E. Brown, born 1905, m. 1) in 1946 to Walter Dunham, and 2) in 1977 to Albert Pugh, 1916-1983, no children.

E3   Robert D. Brown, born 1914, m. Oct. 1946 to Bertha Thompson, they had five children.

E4   Gordon MacLeod Brown, born 1919, m. Oct. 1948 to Rita Jenkins.

C2   Belle MacLeod, m. Dougall MacLeod.

D1   Isabelle, born March 27, 1853.

C3   Mae MacLeod, m. twice, no family.

Information was provided by Bertha Brown, Pownal.

MURDOCH MACLEOD
MURDOCH MACLEOD AND WIFE OF DUNDAS

A1 Murdoch MacLeod, wife's name unknown, came from Scotland about 1829, settling in the Dundas area, his children were:

B1 John Murdoch MacLeod, 1833-1909, buried in Dundas, m. Flora MacKenzie, 1848-1889, with issue:

C1 James A. MacLeod, 1879-1948, m. Sarah Jessie MacLeod, 1886-1968, daughter of Allan MacLeod and Sarah MacDonald, with issue:

D1 Alexander MacLeod, m. Jean Shepherdson, with issue:

E1 Kathy MacLeod, m. Kim Kennedy, with issue:

F1 Scott Kennedy.

F2 Kaitlin Kennedy.

D2 Sarah MacLeod, 1913-1941.

D3 Lawrence MacLeod, 1921-1978.

C2 John (Jack) MacLeod, m. Mary Josephine Bryan, with issue:

D1 John A. MacLeod, m. Alba MacKay, with issue:

E1 John MacLeod, m. Arlene Zepko, Augusta, Maine, with issue:

F1 Mary MacLeod.

F2 John MacLeod.

E2 Bill MacLeod, m. Robin Dunn, Wyoming, with issue:

F1 Manda MacLeod.

C3 Daniel MacLeod, 1881, worked on the railroad in Massachusetts, m. Sadie MacDonald, with issue:

D1 Flora MacLeod, never married.

D2 Martha MacLeod, never married.

D3 Elenor MacLeod, m. Jim Piepgrass, with issue:

E1 Lee Piepgrass.

E2 Daniel Piepgrass.

E3 Sarah Piepgrass.

C4 Christy Ann MacLeod, m. 1) John MacLeod, Point Prim, 2) Nathan Acorn, Dundas, no children.

C5 Rachel MacLeod, m. Frank Jenkins.

B2 Roderick Donald MacLeod, 1835-1923, m. Christy MacKenzie, 1840-1935, both buried in Dundas, with issue:

C1 Christina MacLeod, 1867-1922, m. Stewart Hunter of Dundas, they had ten children:

D1 Elmira Hunter, m. Rev. Alexander Firth, New Brunswick.

D2 Leslie Hunter, never married.

D3 John Hunter, m. 1) Marjorie Sutherland, 2) Josie Wood.

D4 Russel Hunter, m. Belle MacSwain, with issue:

E1 Borden Hunter, m. Ada MacDonald, Mt. Hope, they had five children.

E2 Heath Hunter, m. Betty _____, of Vancouver, British Columbia, they had three children.

E3 Norman Hunter, married a girl from Australia.

E4 Ernest Hunter, married in Washington.

D5 Walter Hunter, married a girl from Massachusetts. They had three girls.

D6 William Hunter, m. Katie Sutherland, sister of Marjorie, above. They had no family. They lived in Strathcona, P.E.I.

D7 Helen Hunter, m. Angus MacLean, Albion Cross, with issue:
　　E1 Beatrice MacLean, married in St. John, New Brunswick.
　　E2 Gloria MacLean, married in Townsend, Massachusetts.

D8 Janet Hunter, m. _____ Ricketson, Massachusetts, they had two sons.

D9 Myrtle Hunter, m. Herbert MacLeod. (See the family of Neil MacLeod of Cumberland Hill for a list of their descendants.)

D10 Fulton Hunter, m. 1) _____ Wood, from Fortune, 2) _____ Bryenton.
　　E1 A son.

C2 Annie MacLeod, 1870, daughter of Roderick Donald MacLeod and Christy MacKenzie, m. George White, with issue:
　D1 Roger White.
　D2 Norman White.
　D3 Sadie White, m. 1) Mr. Lincoln, 2) Mr. Barker.
　D4 Edna White, m. Clayton Briggs.

C3 Norman MacLeod, 1872-1901.

C4 Samuel MacLeod, 1874-1945.

C5 Gordon MacLeod, 1878-1920.

B3 James (Jim) MacLeod, lived in a soldiers' home in Maine at one time.

B4 Rachel MacLeod, married a captain and lived in New York.

B5 Kitty (Katie) MacLeod, m. Mr. Sutherland, with issue:
　C1 Belle Sutherland.
　C2 Marjorie Sutherland, m. John Hunter.
　C3 Katie Sutherland, m. William Hunter, brother of John.

B6 Annie MacLeod, 1844-1883, m. Darius David Clay, with issue:
　C1 Annie Laurie Emmeline Clay, 1869-1961, m. Frederick Andrew Shand from Windsor, Nova Scotia, with issue:
　　D1 Beatrice Eleanor Grace Shand, 1888-1976.
　　D2 Dorothy Elizabeth Shand, 1889-1980.
　　D3 Marjorie Gordon Shand, 1893-1980.
　　D4 Baby girl (stillborn), 1898.
　　D5 Florence Churchill Shand, 1900-1982, born in Windsor, Nova Scotia, died at Ajax, Ontario, m. Norman Winston Churchill of Windsor, Nova Scotia. He was Commanding Officer of the RCMP for the Province of P.E.I. from 1949 to 1953. They had four children, one of whom was Florence Virginia Churchill who m. William John Smith. They live in Ontario and have a daughter, Leslie Ellen Churchill Smith, who is married with a family.
　　D6 Katherine Anderson Shand, living in Windsor, Nova Scotia.
　C2 Grace Darling Clay, 1870-1966, Windsor, Nova Scotia, never married.

Information provided by Marjorie MacKenzie and Virginia Churchill Smith.

Murdoch MacLeod
Murdoch MacLeod and Jane Auld of Mermaid and Murray River

Murdoch MacLeod was listed as a "Claimant" (Loyalist or disbanded soldier) in the *Chronicle Herald* of May 1, 1841, and in "The Muster Roll" of disbanded and discharged soldiers who with their families arrived from Shelbourne to Charlottetown, Island of St. John, 26th July, 1784. Murdoch is described as a member of the 76th Regiment arriving by himself, age 27, and granted 100 acres in Lot 56. From the amount of land granted, it can be assumed he was a Private in the Army. In the "Warrant of Survey" for Lot 66, however, he is not listed among his shipmates as being allotted land in that area. However, in Lot 58 a Corporal Murdoch MacLeod is granted 200 acres and a map of the planned land division (Feb. 1784) shows a Murdoch allotted 100 acres bordering the Pinette River. Yet there is no trace of Murdoch ever settling in Pinette, and no land registry records of him either receiving or transferring land. We can only surmise that either there were two Murdochs, one of whom left P.E.I., or that, for some reason, Murdoch's grant was changed to a more desirable location. At any rate he eventually settled in Lot 48 overlooking the Hillsborough River.

There is a family tradition that Murdoch was a Major in the Army, but it seems very unlikely, as persons of higher rank received considerably larger land grants, and also there is no reference to any such rank until second- or third-hand sources. Perhaps the confusion came from Murdoch's daughter-in-law, Jessie MacLeod of the "Horo" MacLeods of Orwell Cove, who had a Major Murdoch in their family. We do know that Murdoch married Jane Auld of Covehead, Jan. 2, 1788, in Charlottetown, and they and six children (five boys, one girl) are listed in the 1798 census as residents of Lot 48. The only other MacLeods in that census are Alex of Lot 37 and Sergeant MacLeod of the Royalty of Charlottetown. It should also be noted that Murdoch and Jane's marriage licence shows Murdoch, farmer, and Jane Auld of Covehead. It does not state that they are both of Covehead, as do other licences. This is mentioned because another family tradition has Murdoch living in Covehead in 1788. Different accounts have Murdoch and Jane buried at Elm Ave. Cemetery, Charlottetown, or at Mermaid. We haven't been able to locate their graves at either site.

According to the family tradition of the Beach Point MacLeods, their ancestor John was also a son of Murdoch and Jane. They also claim that three of the five boys' names in the 1798 census were David, Norman and James. We know that William would have been a fourth as he was born in 1789. John's existence would fit in with the claim by William's descendant, Catherine Gelchrist, that there were eight boys and five girls.

We have had many sources of information on the family of Murdoch and Jane (Auld) MacLeod, most of which have not included David as a son. It seems very likely that he was, however, as in the 1861 census the family is listed as one born in a British Province and the rest in P.E.I. Since Barbara was born in New Brunswick, then David would have been born on Prince Edward Island prior to 1801. The 1798 census lists only three MacLeods: Alexander of Lot 37, Murdoch, Lot 48, and Sergeant MacLeod, Charlottetown. Consequently it is most likely that David is Murdoch's son. The Beach Point family tradition also serves to further verify this claim.

A   Murdoch MacLeod, apparently from Portree, Skye, born c. 1757, died 1813-14, m. Jane <u>Auld</u>, born c. 1768, died 1840. They were married on Jan 2, 1788, by Rev. DesBrisay in Charlottetown. Murdoch came to P.E.I. in 1784, having been in the British Army during the American Revolution. He received a land grant and was considered a United Empire Loyalist. Jane (or Jean) came to the Stanhope area with her family in 1770 on the ship *Falmouth*. (See the P.E.I. Heritage Foundation for more information on the Auld family). The list of children which follows may be incomplete, as one source claims that there were eight sons and five daughters. (Five boys and one girl were shown in the census of 1798.)

B1   William MacLeod, 1789-1873, lived on what was known as MacLeod's Point, Mermaid, m. Jessie <u>MacLeod</u>, 1799-1883, daughter of Roderick MacLeod, son of Donald, who emigrated from Kilmaluaig, Isle of Skye, to Orwell Cove in 1803. It was William and Jessie's home in which the pioneer Minister, the Rev. Donald MacDonald died in 1867. Their issue:

C1   Matilda MacLeod, died 1892, age 71, m. John <u>Ferguson</u>, Summerside, with issue:

D1   William Ferguson.

D2   Matilda Ferguson, m. George <u>Andrews</u>, St. Eleanors, one daughter:

E1   Ella Andrews.

D3   Jessie Ferguson, m. Phillip <u>Vanidsertine</u>, Summerside, with issue:

E1   Lorne Vanidsertine.

E2   Percy Vanidsertine.

E3   Florence Vanidsertine.

E4   Estelle Vanidsertine.

D4   John Ferguson.

D5   James Ferguson, died young.

C2   Mary MacLeod, died 1904, age 78, m. Angus <u>Stewart</u>, died 1901, aged 72, Culloden, with issue:

D1   Rebecca Jane Stewart, 1861-1936, m. John (Kinlock) <u>MacDonald</u>, 1857-1906, Orwell Cove, with issue:

E1   Stewart MacDonald, 1898-1961, m. Blanche <u>Matheson</u> of Cardigan, they lived in Massachusetts and he is buried in Cardigan Cemetery.

E2   Margaret MacDonald, 1895-1947, m. William <u>Brown</u>, 1878-1971, Pownal. They lived on the old MacDonald homestead in Orwell Cove, they had two children:

F1   Claudine Brown, m. Clifford <u>Brand</u>, they live in England and have one son:

G1   Garry Brand, m. with one daughter.

F2   Daniel Brown, m. in U.S.A. with a son and daughter.

D2   William Stewart, m. Catherine <u>Gilmore</u>. They lived in Belle River, with issue:

E1   Mae Stewart, m. Charles <u>Morrison</u>, died 1963, age 84, Roseberry, with issue:

F1   Anne Morrison, m. Colin <u>MacColl</u>, living in Eldon.

F2   John Morrison, m. Bessie <u>Larson</u>, living in Roseberry, issue:

G1   Linda Morrison, m. Lewis <u>Ross</u>, Flat River, issue:

H1   Jody Ross.

H2   Jenne Ross.
G2   Heidi Morrison.
G3   Anne Morrison, m. David <u>MacDonald</u>, son of Marcellus, Orwell, with issue:
  H1   Lori MacDonald.
  H2   Trevor MacDonald.
G4   Karen Morrison, m. John <u>Vantyghem</u>, Upper Newtown, with issue:
  H1   Trevor Vantyghem.
  H2   Tracy Vantyghem.
G5   Blair Morrison, m. Terry <u>Fontaine</u>, in Ottawa and have two daughters. He is in the Armed Forces.

F3   Laureston Morrison, living in Roseberry.
F4   Ernie Morrison, died 1971, age 45, m. Flora <u>Gillis</u>, died 1970, age 49. Their home was the Stewart home in Belle River, issue:
  G1   Laurie Morrison, m. Barbara <u>Knox</u>, living on the old home, with issue:
    H1   Michelle Morrison.
    H2   Melinda Morrison.
    H3   Bryan Morrison.
    H4   Blaine Morrison.
  G2   Betty Morrison, m. Wallace Morrison, they live in Cornwall, P.E.I., with issue:
    H1   Tara Morrison.
    H2   Shannon Morrison.
F5   William Morrison, died in Kamloops, British Columbia, May 25, 1986, never married.
F6   Murdoch Morrison, m. Doris <u>Cantelo</u>, living in Pinette, with issue:
  G1   Jeannie Morrison.
  G2   Barbara Anne Morrison, m. Wayne <u>Hambly</u>, living in Charlottetown, with issue:
    H1   Christa Hambly.
    H2   Leslie Hambly.
    H3   Andrew Hambly.
  G3   Glen Morrison.
E2   Laura Stewart, died 1972, age 84, m. James <u>Ross</u>. They lived in U.S.A. but retired to Belle River, with issue:
F1   Belle Ross, living in U.S.A.
F2   Catherine Ross, married in U.S.A.
F3   Colin Ross, married in U.S.A.
F4   Mae Ross, married in U.S.A.
F5   June Ross, married in U.S.A.
E3   Tom Stewart, married in Kamloops, British Columbia, no family.
E4   William Stewart, married in U.S.A.
E5   Angus Stewart, died 1960, age 72, m. Minnie <u>Lamont</u>, died 1983, age 91, issue:
F1   Vivian Stewart, m. Lloyd <u>MacLeod</u>, son of Percy, Orwell, with issue:

> > G1 Carl Stewart MacLeod, m. Debra <u>Cantwell</u>, living in Newfoundland, with issue:
> > H1 Matthew MacLeod.
> > G2 Cathy MacLeod, m. Bernard <u>Flanaghan</u>, with issue:
> > H1 Tyler Flanaghan.
> > G3 Anne MacLeod, m. Scott <u>MacDonald</u>.
> > G4 Jennifer MacLeod.
> > F2 Brenton Stewart, married in British Columbia. They have two children.
> D3 Alexander Stewart, son of Angus and Mary Stewart, m. Dorothy <u>Munn</u>, they lived in Oregon, with issue:
> > E1 Arthur Stewart, married in Seattle where he was County Clerk for many years, they had no family.
> > E2 Nathan Stewart was a noted singer.
> > E3 Mamie Stewart, married in the state of Washington.
> D4 Robert Stewart, never married.
> D5 Another son who died young.
> D6 Matilda Stewart.

C3 William MacLeod, died 1904, age 86, m. Christie <u>MacBeath</u>, died 1902, aged 75. They had no family and are buried in Marshfield.
C4 Roderick MacLeod, married in the Province of Quebec.
C5 Robert MacLeod, died 1893, age 65, m. Mary <u>MacEachern</u>, died 1903, aged 73, with issue:
> D1 Flora Ann MacLeod, 1863-1951, m. J. Henry <u>MacLean</u>, 1865-1939, Montague, who owned and operated the MacLean Carriage works at Montague.They had two daughters:
> > E1 Elsie MacLean, 1893-1971, m. Jim <u>Trainor</u>, son of the Peter Trainor who operated a store in Charlottetown and was murdered by two burglars about 1941. The two were convicted and hanged by the neck on the gallows next to and behind the present 1911 Jail. This was the last hanging in the Province. A board fence was built around the gallows for the purpose of screening the proceedings but the boards dried out in the sun, leaving spaces which provided a view for the crowd of people who gathered to witness the event. Elsie and Jim Trainor's children are:
> > > F1 Raymond Trainor, m. Jean <u>McAvoy</u>, they live in Ottawa with issue:
> > > > G1 Wayne Trainor, who lives in Charlottetown and works for the Post Office, m. 1) Miss <u>Dunphy</u>, from Cherry Valley, m. 2) Daphne <u>Stedman</u>.
> > > Raymond and Jean had three daughters as well.
> > > F2 Margaret Trainor, m. Len <u>Dewis</u>, Ottawa, with issue:
> > > > G1 Jim Dewis.
> > > > G2 Robert Dewis, both m. in Ottawa.
> > > F3 Larry Trainor, m. Marie <u>Jones</u>, in Sackville, New Brunswick. They live in Gibson, British Columbia, with issue:
> > > > G1 Diane Lyn Trainor, married in Ottawa.
> > > F4 Jack Trainor, was married, no family.

E2 Helen MacLean, 1896-1939, married in Detroit, no family and is buried in Lower Montague Cemetery.

D2 Elmira MacLeod, died 1948, age 77, m. Edgar White, died 1954, age 90, Montague and later Charlottetown. They had no family.

D3 Margaret MacLeod, m. Rev. A. D. MacDonald. He died in Calgary in 1946, aged 89 years.

D4 Robert MacLeod.

D5 John MacLeod.

C6 John MacLeod, Master Mariner, died 1901, age 68. He m. Mrs. Elizabeth (Ayers) Stewart. When he retired from the deep sea, he was captain of the ferry boat running between Charlottetown and Southport, before the bridge was built, later he owned and operated a grocery store on the corner of Prince and Sydney Streets, Charlottetown. This store was later taken over by his nephew Milton and his niece Addie, children of his brother David MacLeod, and was operated under the name of M. and A. MacLeod.

C7 Donald MacLeod, died 1901, aged 61, m. 1) Jane Ann MacBeath of Marshfield, died 1886, aged 55. They lived at Montague Bridge, with issue:

D1 Donald MacBeath MacLeod, who died in Winnipeg in 1947, aged 86. He married and left two sons.

E1 Clive Jeffrey MacLeod, Barrister, Winnipeg.

E2 Alexander John MacLeod, living in Manitoba.

D2 Alexander MacLeod.

D3 Gower MacLeod.

D4 William MacLeod, died 1863, aged 2 months.

D5 John Alexander MacLeod, died 1866, aged 2 years.

D6 Lizzie Adelle MacLeod, died 1878, 1 year.

D7 Lorne MacLeod, drowned Aug. 29, 1876, aged 6 years.

Donald m. 2) Phoebe MacDonald, with issue:

D8 Florence MacLeod.

D9 Jennie Estelle MacLeod.

D10 Mary MacLeod.

D11 Angus Kimble MacLeod.

C8 Christy Ann MacLeod, m. Neil MacKinnon, Canoe Cove, moved to Summerside, with issue:

D1 William Charles MacKinnon.

D2 Ellen Jane Ann MacKinnon.

D3 Cowan Rankin MacKinnon.

D4 Jessie MacKinnon.

D5 James Artemas MacKinnon, married with issue.

D6 Tillie Mae MacKinnon, never married.

D7 Christy Ann MacKinnon.

D8 Ethel Beatrice MacKinnon, m. _____ Degnan.

D9 Martha MacKinnon.

D10 John Neil Alexander MacKinnon, never married.

D11 Pearl Maude MacKinnon.

C9 David MacLeod, drowned June 6, 1885, age 45 years. He and two of his sons were lost during a storm off the coast of Newfoundland. He was married to Caroline Pippy, died Aug. 25, 1917, age 78, issue:

D1 William Hartley MacLeod, drowned with father, aged 22 years.

D2   John Edward MacLeod, drowned with father, aged 18 years.

D3   Cassie MacLeod, m. Angus MacRae, they lived in Wheatley River, with issue:

    E1   Marion MacRae.

D4   Milton MacLeod, m. Mae Barr, with issue:

    E1   Edison MacLeod.

    E2   Gordon MacLeod.

    E3   John MacLeod.

There may be others in this family, it is believed that they moved to U.S.A.

D5   Addie MacLeod, never married.

C10 Elizabeth MacLeod, m. Donald MacDonald, Winnipeg, Manitoba, with issue:

D1   Jeanette MacDonald.

D2   William MacDonald.

D3   John MacDonald.

D4   Angus MacDonald.

D5   Duncan MacDonald, killed in a mining accident in the Pas, Manitoba.

D6   Jacob MacDonald.

D7   Donald MacDonald.

C11 Jane MacLeod, m. Roderick MacKinnon, with issue:

D1   Isabella MacKinnon, who died April 11, 1940.

C12 James MacLeod, died 1932, aged 89, m. 1) Effie MacLeod, died Sept. 1880, aged 44, with issue:

D1   Jane Ann MacLeod, 1869-1935, m. Angus Beaton, 1861-1940, Melville, with issue:

    E1   Donald Beaton.

    E2   Louis Beaton.

    E3   John Beaton.

    E4   Mary Beaton, lived in Boston, Massachusetts.

    E5   Vernon Beaton, lived in New York.

    E6   Jean Auld Beaton, 1909-1956, buried in Belfast Cemetery.

D2   Roberta MacLeod, m. George Jenkins, as his 2nd wife. He had a daughter called Grace from a previous marriage, who was married in Peakes. Roberta and George died in California and had issue:

    E1   Ray Jenkins, married with a family in California.

    E2   Alma Jenkins, married with a family in California.

D3   Millicent MacLeod, died young.

James MacLeod m. 2) Emily Roberts, Murray River, she died in 1939, aged 79. They had one daughter.

D4   Millicent MacLeod, died 1973, aged 83, m. William S. MacEachern, died 1959, aged 83, Mermaid, with issue:

    E1   Jean MacEachern, m. Everett Lund, Bethel, with issue:

       F1   Ruth Lund, m. Brian Murray, living in New York.

       F2   Sterling Lund, publisher of the *Guardian Express* in Welland, Ontario, m. Gloria Ann Keresman, with issue:

          G1   Tania Lund.

       F3   Keith Lund, died Oct. 11, 1972, age 22.

F4   Eileen Lund, m. Dale <u>Lounsbury</u>, Charlottetown.

E2   Emily Marion MacEachern, m. Borden <u>Boswell</u>, Dunstaffnage, with issue:

F1   Evelyn Louise Boswell, died in infancy.

F2   William Earl Boswell, died in a tractor accident in
Dunstaffnage, Nov. 17, 1977.

F3   Linda Marlene Boswell, died in infancy.

F4   Ivan Boswell, m. Lucille <u>Brazil</u>, Johnston's River. They
live in Dunstaffnage, with issue:

G1   Melinda Boswell.

F5   Faye Boswell, m. Norman <u>Smith</u>, New Glasgow, P.E.I.,
issue:

G1   Roland Smith.

G2   Lana Smith.

G3   Amber Smith.

G4   Nelson Smith.

G5   Maria Smith.

F6   Ann Boswell, m. 1) _____ <u>Cooper</u>, with issue:

G1   Dean Cooper.

G2   Crystal Cooper.

Ann m. 2) John <u>Knox</u>, Belfast, with issue:

G3   John Earl Knox.

G4   Irwin Knox.

E3   Robert Earl MacEachern, died 1944, aged 13 years.

E4   Margaret Elva MacEachern, m. Fred <u>LeBlanc</u>, living in
Moncton, with issue:

F1   Wayne LeBlanc, m. Pamela _____, living in Western
Canada, with issue:

G1   Crystal LeBlanc.

B2   Norman MacLeod, born 1790s, m. Margaret <u>Smallwood</u>, from Mermaid.
In the 1841 census there was a Norman MacLeod living in Lot 64 with the
following children and ages: seven females and three males all under the
age of 16. There was one male and one female between the ages of 16-45.

C1   David MacLeod, died April 15, 1877, aged 49 years, m. Elizabeth
<u>MacLure</u>, she died Feb. 16, 1911, age 80 years. They are buried in
Murray River Wilmot Cemetery. They were married on Nov. 25,
1859, with issue:

D1   William Henry MacLeod, born Nov. 18, 1859, baptized Feb. 20,
1860. He was drowned at Matthew MacLure's Dam when he
slipped under moving logs. He is buried in Wilmot Cemetery,
Murray River.

D2   Matthew Morris MacLeod, 1862-1939, m. Letitia <u>Cook</u>, 1859-
1927. They are buried in Gladstone Cemetery, Murray River,
with issue:

E1   Isabell MacLeod, born Feb. 14, 1890, died 1960, unmarried.

E2   Margaret Russell MacLeod, 1895-1971, unmarried.

E3   William Francis MacLeod, born 1901, m. Marie Loretta
<u>Ferguson</u>, 1900-1975. They were married July 7, 1922, issue:

F1   Lowell Francis MacLeod, 1923-1946, served in WWII.

F2   Leila Joan MacLeod, m. Lloyd Henry <u>Tuttle</u>, they were
married Aug. 30, 1950, they live in Dallas, with issue:

G1   Lowell William Henry Tuttle.
G2   Joan Marie Tuttle, born March 21, 1953, died April 14, 1953.
G3   Lawrence Fuller Tuttle.
G4   Joan Alice Tuttle.

F3   Zelda Jean MacLeod, m. Noel <u>MacNevin</u> on Aug. 31, 1949. They lived their married life in Quebec until the summer of 1985, when they returned to homestead on P.E.I. and live with Zelda's father. They had issue:
G1   Nancy Lee MacNevin, m. Gerald <u>Godsoe</u>, living in Ottawa, with issue:
H1   William Henry Wayne Godsoe.
H2   Matthew Daniel Godsoe.
G2   Francis Scott MacNevin.

F4   Kenneth William MacLeod, m. Edith <u>LeLacheur</u>, with issue:
G1   Allan Francis MacLeod.
G2   David Keith MacLeod.
G3   Jean Elizabeth MacLeod.
G4   John Matthew MacLeod, m. Carla <u>Good</u> from Charlottetown.
G5   Kenneth Robert MacLeod.

F5   Allan Ferguson MacLeod, m. Margaret <u>Johnston</u>, from Georgetown, Allan is with RCAF in Summerside, issue:
G1   Lydia Susan MacLeod.
G2   Martha Jane MacLeod.

D3   Gavin MacLeod, 1867-1962, m. Louise Anne <u>Hawkins</u>, daughter of William Hawkins and Sarah MacLeod. Louise died April 13, 1912, aged 43 years. They had issue:
E1   William MacLeod, died at 1 1/2 years, buried in Wilmot Cemetery.
E2   Matthew MacLeod, 1892-1949, m. Emma <u>Phillips</u>, issue:
F1   Charles (Bert) Ethelbert MacLeod, 1914-1980, m. Marie <u>Kennedy</u>, from Peters Road, with issue:
G1   Neil Boyd MacLeod, 1940-1941, twin.
G2   Byron MacLeod, twin, m. Bernice <u>Billard</u>, issue:
H1   Phillip MacLeod.
H2   Daisy MacLeod.
F2   Anne MacLeod, m. Byron <u>Sharpe</u>, with issue:
G1   William Sharpe.
G2   Elizabeth Anne Sharpe, m. Richard <u>Collins</u>, Montague. They had a family.
F3   Carleton MacLeod, m. Katherine <u>MacQueen</u>, with issue:
G1   Caroline MacLeod.
G2   Brackley MacLeod, married a girl named Leslie.
G3   Linda MacLeod.
G4   Cynthia MacLeod, m. Norman <u>Stewart</u>, Murray River.
G5   Gail MacLeod.

F4   Basil MacLeod, m. Mina <u>MacLeod</u> from Murray River.
- G1   Boyd MacLeod, m. Jessie <u>Meney</u>, with issue:
  - H1   Christopher MacLeod.
  - H2   Kenneth MacLeod.
- G2   David MacLeod, m. Sheila <u>Bell</u>, with issue:
  - H1   Crystal MacLeod.

F5   Reagh MacLeod, m. Phyllis <u>Cantelo</u> from Eldon, issue:
- G1   Sam MacLeod, m. Joyce <u>Chapman</u>, Murray Harbour. They have children.
- G2   Beryl MacLeod, schoolteacher.

E3   Gavin MacLeod, died Nov. 3, 1984, m. Janet <u>MacLeod</u>, 1896-1969, buried in Gladstone Cemetery. Issue:
- F1   Lloyd MacLeod, lives in Dartmouth, has one daughter.
- F2   Joyce MacLeod, m. Gordon <u>Johnston</u>, living in Sturgeon.
- F3   Audrey MacLeod, m. Martin <u>MacKay</u>, living in Pictou.
- F4   Annie MacLeod, m. David <u>Soper</u>, living in Vermont.
- F5   Sadie MacLeod, 1925-1945, buried in Gladstone Cemetery.

E4   Billy Mitchell MacLeod, worked in mill in Murray River, never married.

E5   Sadie MacLeod, born Oct. 12, 1900, m. Austin <u>Bell</u>, 1894-1973. They lived in White Sands, with issue:
- F1   Gavin Bell, Jr.
- F2   Craig Bell, m. Esther <u>Williams</u>, they have a family.
- F3   Betty Lou Bell.
- F4   Pauline Bell.

D4 Margaret MacLeod, 1865-1868. Buried in Wilmot Cemetery.

D5 Jane Isabella MacLeod, born Aug. 20, 1869, m. David <u>Hawkins</u>, brother of Louise Ann, son of William and Sarah Hawkins.

D6 Margaret MacLeod, born Jan. 31, 1872, m. _____ <u>Carmichael</u> from Cape Breton or Boston.

C2 Jimmy (James) MacLeod, m. Catherine <u>Sanders</u>. In the Wilmot Cemetery there is a gravestone with James MacLeod, born 1831 — died 1878, and a Catherine, born 1835 — died 1929, these dates fit this generation, but as Catherine's last name is not stated we could not state this as definite, whereas a family member may well be able to verify this, knowing their burial place. Catherine m. 2) Harvey <u>Bishop</u>.

D1 James Evans MacLeod, 1861-1912, m. Mary Ann <u>Bishop</u>, 1863-1904. They are both buried in Gladstone Cemetery. Issue:
- E1   Ida MacLeod, single.
- E2   Clara Matilda MacLeod, 1886-1973, m. Ernest Arthur <u>Kirby</u>, 1878-1949. They are buried in Gladstone Cemetery.
  - F1   John W. Kirby, Charlottetown.
  - F2   Josephine Kirby, m. Ray <u>Stokes</u>.
- E3   Bessie Catherine MacLeod, m. William <u>MacPhee</u>, seven children.
- E4   Mary D. MacLeod (Mae), 1890-1980, m. Charles <u>Moore</u>, Murray River. She is buried in Gladstone Cemetery.
- E5   James Harvey MacLeod, 1891-1966, m. Muriel <u>Rafuse</u> from Martin's Point, Nova Scotia, with issue:

F1   Dorothy MacLeod, 1919-1981, m. Donald <u>Yadeson</u>, no family.

F2   Harvey MacLeod, m. Joan <u>Adshade</u>, Halifax, one son.
G1   Wayne James Harvey MacLeod, died at eleven years.

F3   Lorraine MacLeod, single.

E6   Minnie MacLeod, left P.E.I.

E7   Ethel MacLeod, m. Gordon <u>Kitchen</u> from New Brunswick.

E8   Cyrus Watson MacLeod, born Nov. 29, 1898, m. Ida Ada Marion <u>Johnston</u>, 1903-1942, buried in Gladstone Cemetery.

F1   Ralph MacLeod, married Peggy _____, from Cape Breton.

F2   Jean MacLeod, 1926-1968, m. William Wheaton <u>Gosbee</u>, 1910-1972, Beach Point. With issue:
G1   Ida Harriet Gosbee, m. Barry Paul <u>Ross</u>, issue:
H1   Vincent John Ross, m. Jarvin C. <u>Wang</u>, issue:
I1   Connor Ming-Jeng Ross.
H2   Velissa Jean Ross, m. David Ross <u>Dalton</u>.
G2   James William Gosbee, m. Beverly Mary <u>Miller</u>, with issue:
H1   Robert James Gosbee, m. Judi <u>Nantes</u>.
H2   Stacy Michelle Gosbee, m. Mark <u>Levy</u>.
G3   Marion Heather Gosbee, m. Ronald Ian <u>Matheson</u>, with issue:
H1   Timothy Ian Matheson.
H2   Kimberly Ann Matheson.
G4   Dennis Harold Gosbee, 1952-1968.
G5   Lester Murray Gosbee, m. Barbara E.A. <u>McGee</u>, with issue:
H1   Karen Ann Gosbee.

E9   Ernest MacLeod, m. Jennette Belle <u>MacLean</u>, from Pictou Island.
F1   John MacLeod, m. Helen <u>Glover</u>, Murray River, issue:
G1   Dale MacLeod.
G2   Debbie MacLeod.
F2   Ernest Marshall MacLeod, m. Olga <u>Beck</u> from Murray River. They have children, one of whom is named:
G1   Loyne MacLeod.
F3   Lavinia MacLeod, single.

D2   David Watson MacLeod, born Jan. 25, 1869, at Fullerton Marsh.

D3   Hannah MacLeod, born Dec. 26, 1874, at Lot 48.

D4   Norman MacLeod, born March 26, 1876, at Fullerton Marsh.

D5   Margaret MacLeod, 1871.

D6   Demaris Watts MacLeod, 1858-1936, m. Samuel <u>Hume</u> of Murray River. They had four children.

D7   Margaret Hannah MacLeod, 1878-1966, m. James H. <u>Cantelo</u>, 1872-1926. They had four children.

C3   Johnny Norman MacLeod, born 1844, in Murray River, m. Mary Ann <u>MacKenzie</u>, with issue:
D1   Frederick MacLeod, born 1867, m. Eliza <u>Penny</u>, with issue:
E1   Loretta MacLeod.

> E2 Frederick H. MacLeod, 1890-1957, m. Margaret Strickland, 1894-1977, with issue:
>> F1 Freda MacLeod.
>> F2 Margaret MacLeod, died in Boston, unmarried.
> D2 Hannah Francis MacLeod, born 1871 at Murray River, m. George MacKay, they lived in Trenton, Nova Scotia, with a large family.
> D3 Sarah MacLeod, born 1873 at Murray River, m. Jim Fraser. They lived in New Glasgow, Nova Scotia, with a large family.
> D4 Mary Ann MacLeod, born 1876 at Murray River, died 1953, m. Sewall Buchanan at Murray River, with issue:
>> E1 Ethel Buchanan, m. Stuart Adams.
>> E2 Ella Buchanan, m. John MacLeod, Victoria Cross.
>> E3 Warren Buchanan, m. Myrtle Acorn, lived in Belfast.
> D4 Amelia (Millie) MacLeod, born 1878 at Murray River, m. Will MacKay of Murray River, with issue:
>> E1 Gladys MacLeod, m. Jack Tom MacDonald. They had no family.
>> E2 Harry MacKay, m. Elsie Beck.
> D5 Ella Mae MacLeod, born May 1, 1881, at Murray River, died Oct. 9, 1927, in Spokane, Washington, m. Alexander Donald MacLeod, of High Bank, P.E.I. with issue and emigrated to Manhattan and Amsterdam, Montana. (See descendants of Norman MacLeod and Margaret MacKenzie of High Bank.)
> D6 Another daughter who died young.

C4 Jane MacLeod, m. William White.
C5 Elizabeth MacLeod, m. Charles White.
C6 Barbara MacLeod, m. Sam MacLeod.
C7 Margaret MacLeod, m. John Bears, with issue:
> D1 Elizabeth Bears, m. John Smart, living in the U.S.A.
C8 Fannie MacLeod, m. Vanidsertine.
C9 Mary MacLeod, m. William Bishop, with issue:
> D1 Caleb Bishop, 1872-1896.
C10 Hannah MacLeod, married John Roberts.
C11 Robert MacLeod, married a woman from Cape Breton.

B3 James MacLeod, born 1790s, was thought to have died as a young child.
B4 John MacLeod, there was possibly a son John. See Beach Point MacLeods.
B5 David MacLeod, born 1790s, was a miller in Murray River. He m. Barbara MacKay of New Brunswick. She died in July 1886 at age 82 and was said to have been survived by "Ten children, 74 grandchildren and 66 great-grandchildren" (*Daily Examiner*, July 28, 1886). The following is a partial list of their children. There has been a will found of David's and all the children that follow are listed:
> C1 Daniel MacLeod, 1826-1914, farmer in Lot 64, m. Mary Ann Bishop, 1828-1899, from Digby, Nova Scotia. Children are placed in order as estimated from the 1861 census (showing 3 females age 5-16; 3 males under 5 years) and the 1881 census which shows approximate ages.
>> D1 Mary Ann MacLeod, 1851-1938, m. Robert White, with issue:
>>> E1 Ella Jane White, m. 1) ____ Stewart, 2) Alex Harty.
>>>> F1 Ethel Harty, m. _____ Reynolds.
>> D2 Jane MacLeod, m. John Whiteway.
>> D3 Rosella MacLeod, born 1855 (called Drusella in 1881 census,

which must have been a mistake), m. Wallace <u>Duncan</u>. They had, at least, a daughter:

E1   Laura Annabel Duncan, m. William <u>MacLeod</u>, Calgary. (See William MacLeod, Wigmore Road.) Laura and William had two sons:
    F1   Sterling MacLeod, married in Oakville, Ontario.
    F2   Lloyd MacLeod.

D4   Daniel L. MacLeod, m. Clara Nenada <u>Stafford</u>, 1865-1943, lived in Oregon.

D5   William MacLeod.

D6   Calvin MacLeod, 1858-1939, m. 1) Margaret Catherine <u>Lowe</u>. She died Sept. 23, 1910, age 42. He m. 2) Lavinia C. Sanders White <u>Johnston</u>. Apparently when Calvin had a job cooking on a dredge one summer in Charlottetown, he would come home on weekends and he walked the 40 or 50 miles by the railroad track. His children were:

E1   Ella Blanche MacLeod, 1889-1982, m. Reginald Walter <u>Hollingshurst</u>, 1883-1945, with issue:
    F1   Jean Margaret Hollingshurst, m. Alexis William <u>Shumate</u>.
        G1   Alexis Michael Shumate, m. Mary <u>Patterson</u>.
        G2   Cathy MacLeod Shumate, not married.

E2   Victor MacLeod, 1893-1937, married a lady from Pennsylvania.

E3   George Howard MacLeod, 1896–1969, m. Charlotte Adelaide <u>Burgess</u>, 1895-1982, with issue:
    F1   Dorothy Alice Etta MacLeod, m. 1) Earl William <u>Lyda</u>, m. 2) Donovan Allan <u>McLean</u>, 1918-1987, m. 3) M/Sgt. Louis Ilo <u>Osina</u>, 1911-1987, with issue:
        G1   Regina Deloris Lyda, m. Robert William <u>Wheeler</u>.
            H1   Robinn Kim Wheeler, m. Gregory <u>McClain</u>.
                I1   Melownie Rose McClain.
            H2   Rolana Tracie Wheeler, m. Charles DeSantiago <u>Santisteven,</u> with issue:
                I1   Skye Champagne Wheeler-Santisteven.
            H3   Redawn Kellie Wheeler, m. David Eugene <u>Ward</u>.
                I1   Matthew David Ward.
        G2   Douglas Allan MacLean, m. Elena Marie <u>Manning</u>.
            H1   Donovan Allan MacLean.
            H2   Christopher Michael MacLean.

E4   Etta Elizabeth MacLeod, m. Heber <u>Bell</u>, with issue:
    F1   Shirley Bell.

D7   George MacLeod (Rev.), 1860-1947, m. Margaret <u>McRae</u>, died 1939.

E1   Arnold MacLeod (a Rhodes Scholar).

E2   Wilbur MacLeod.

E3   Russel MacLeod, died 1985.

E4   Preston MacLeod (Rev.).

D8   William David MacLeod, 1862-1944, m. Jessie <u>Bruce</u>, 1856-1906.

        E1   George Wallace MacLeod, 1888-1903.

        E2   John Calvin MacLeod, 1890-1976.

        E3   Ella May Scott MacLeod, born Nov. 5, 1893.

    D9   Oliver Cromwell MacLeod, born June 3, 1864, m. Florence May Potter.

    D10 John Eber MacLeod, 1866-1899.

    D11 James Harvey MacLeod (Doctor), 1869-1959, m. Clara Cuddy, died 1965, with issue:

        E1   Edison MacLeod.

        E2   Clair B. MacLeod, 1909-1968.

    D12 Irene Matilda MacLeod, 1872-1957, m. Edgar Giddings, 1865-1953.

        E1   Dwight Lyman Giddings (Rev.), 1901-1980.

        E2   Edgar Sterling Giddings, M.D., 1903-1971, m. Etta Cook, Murray River.

        E3   Gertrude Isabel Giddings, m. Geo. Oliver Whiteway, 1904-1987.

        E4   Bessie Irene Giddings, born 1907, m. George Tolmadge Philpot.

C2 Barbara MacLeod, 1828-1898, m. Robert Whiteway, 1830-1918, nine children.

C3 Hulda MacLeod, 1834, m. George MacKay, Murray River.

C4 James MacLeod, m. Isabel Weatherbie, of Vernon River.

C5 George MacLeod, 1842, m. Mary MacDonald.

C6 Mary MacLeod, m. John Murdoch.

C7 Matilda MacLeod, m. Calvin or William Bishop.

C8 Jane MacLeod, born Jan. 13, 1831, m. Philip Blake, son of James Blake and Catherine Sanders, they had six children.

C9 Elizabeth MacLeod, 1835-1916, m. Robert Sanders, 1837-1922, with a family of six.

C10 Sarah MacLeod, m. William Hawkins, with issue:

    D1   Louise Ann Hawkins m. Gavin MacLeod.

    D2   David Hawkins m. Jane Isabell MacLeod, Gavin's sister.

B6   Alexander MacLeod.

B7   George MacLeod.

B8   Robert MacLeod.

B9   Jane MacLeod.

B10 Mary MacLeod.

B11 James MacLeod, born Dec. 14, 1808, baptized at St. Paul's Church, Charlottetown. Died Nov. 5, 1884, and is buried in Mermaid Cemetery.

This information is from descendants of Murdoch and Jane MacLeod, and the files at Beaconsfield, Charlottetown.

GEORGE MACLEOD
GEORGE MACLEOD AND ANN MATHESON OF BEACH POINT

A1 George MacLeod was the son of John MacLeod and Sarah Currie. Sarah is believed to have come from Georgetown. George was born in 1840 and died in 1926. He married Ann <u>Matheson</u>. They had eleven children. See the family of Murdoch MacLeod and Jane Auld because John is believed to be the son of this family.

B1 Joseph MacLeod, 1873-1942, m. 1) Laura <u>Dunn</u>, and had three children:
    C1 Edda MacLeod.
    C2 Allan MacLeod, born 1905, married and had four boys.
    C3 Lois MacLeod, m. Wallace <u>Hume</u>, they had three boys:
        D1 Sheldon Hume.
        D2 Sterling Hume.
        D3 Alden Hume.
Laura died and Joseph m. 2) Mabel Gosbee <u>MacPherson</u>. They had twins but one died at birth.
        D4 Lloyd MacLeod, married a girl named Ann from the Belfast region.

B2 Jane MacLeod, 1874-1935, m. Levi <u>Stevens</u> in Boston. They had four children:
    C1 Clifford Stevens, was killed in a car accident in Portland.
    C2 Lois Stevens, lives in Boston.
    C3 Gladyee Stevens, lives in Boston.
    C4 Marion Stevens, lives in Boston.

B3 David Albert MacLeod, 1878-1955, m. Fayne <u>Harris</u>, they had one son.
    C1 Perley MacLeod, married a girl from Vancouver, they had no family.

B4 William Wallace MacLeod, born Jan. 22, 1876, died Sept. 23, 1876.

B5 Allan A. MacLeod, 1880-1949, m. Salome <u>Williams</u>, daughter of Abraham Williams and Elizabeth Herring. They were married July 12, 1909, by Rev. H. E. Thomas at the Trinity Church in Charlottetown. Salome was born Nov. 8, 1891, died March 28, 1981. Allan sailed all his life, which left Salome often alone. He worked on tug boats and later on the Wood Islands boat. Apparently he was a merchant marine out of Charlottetown at one time. They had five children.
    C1 John Francis MacLeod, born Aug. 16, 1910, m. Lillian <u>Waugh</u>. They had no children. Francis was killed in France in 1944.
    C2 Ernest Emerson MacLeod, born 1912, m. Irene <u>Adams</u> on Sept. 18, 1935. Irene was born June 23, 1914. She met Emerson while working in Beach Point. They had seven children:
        D1 Lincoln MacLeod, m. Karen <u>MacDonald</u> from Thorburn, Nova Scotia, with issue:
            E1 Kit MacLeod.
            E2 Sarah MacLeod.
        D2 Thelma (Tim) MacLeod, m. Joseph <u>MacDonald</u> from Morell, with issue:
            E1 Darlene Joanne MacDonald.
            E2 Karen Yvonne MacDonald.
            E3 Leah Charlene MacDonald.

D3 Carol MacLeod, m. Ken Nicolle from White Sands.
   E1 Allan Wayne Nicolle, m. Mary Lou Lowe from Murray
      River. They have one child:
      F1 Krystal Nicolle.
D4 George MacLeod, m. Vera Somers from Murray Harbour, with
   issue:
   E1 Derrick George MacLeod.
   E2 Anna Christine MacLeod.
D5 Jackie MacLeod, m. Maureen Bell from Charlottetown, with
   issue:
   E1 Trina Lynn MacLeod.
   E2 John Murray MacLeod.
D6 Brenda MacLeod, m. Finley Martin from Scranton, Pennsylvania,
   with issue:
   E1 Finley Michael Martin.
   E2 Arja Martin.
   E3 Robert Martin.
D7 Kevin MacLeod, m. Elaine Blue from Hopefield, with issue:
   E1 Kevin MacLeod.
C3 Helen Dorothy MacLeod, m. Harry White on Nov. 29, 1934, with
   issue. They had a number of children.
C4 Elizabeth Ann MacLeod (Beth), m. Clarence Jermyn, two children:
   D1 Douglas Jermyn.
   D2 Wendy Jermyn.
C5 Olive Grace MacLeod, m. Gerald Bell.
B6 Tryphena MacLeod, born Aug. 1882, died Oct. 17, 1929. Never married.
B7 Rhoda MacLeod, born March 7, 1885, died 1969. Single.
B8 Jessie Ann MacLeod, 1887-1963, m. Will C. Sencabaugh in Boston, with
   issue. They had six children who are all presently living in Boston.
   C1 Elmer Sencabaugh.
   C2 Lois Sencabaugh.
   C3 Albert Sencabaugh.
   C4 Hazel Sencabaugh.
   C5 Alden Sencabaugh.
   C6 Jean Sencabaugh.
B9 John William MacLeod, 1889-1949, m. Nettie MacLean of Peters Road,
   with issue:
   C1 Rhoda MacLeod, m. Harvey A. Veniot of Pictou. Harvey was the
      Speaker of the House for Nova Scotia Legislature and also a Provin-
      cial Court Judge. They have two adopted children:
      D1 James Stewart Veniot.
      D2 Susan Veniot.
   C2 Basil MacLeod, m. Genevieve Jamieson, Sturgeon. They have four
      children of whom only one lives in P.E.I.
      D1 John William MacLeod, Sturgeon, P.E.I.
      D2 Harvey Frederick MacLeod.
      D3 Vance Basil MacLeod.
      D4 Linda Mary Margaret MacLeod.
   C3 Fred MacLeod, m. Helen Herring from Murray Harbour, with four
      children:
      D1 John Martin MacLeod.

> > D2   Catherine MacLeod.
> > D3   Jane MacLeod.
> > D4   Rhoda MacLeod.
> > Rhoda, Basil, and Fred (C1, C2, C3) and their families all live in Stellarton, Nova Scotia.
> B10 Idella MacLeod, born June 1892, died March 9, 1939.
> B11 George MacLeod, 1896-1969, m. Hilda <u>Munn</u> of Murray River. They lived in Boston and had three children who are all in Boston.
> > C1   Ruth MacLeod.
> > C2   Betty Anne MacLeod.
> > C3   Ralph MacLeod.

A2   John MacLeod, born April 5, 1818, baptized on July 20, the following year.
A3   Jane MacLeod, born April 20, 1820. She was baptized July 20, 1820.
A4   James MacLeod, born May 24, 1822, baptized on July 3, 1822.
A5   Margaret MacLeod.
A6   Angus MacLeod.

Information provided by Brenda Martin and Emerson MacLeod of Beach Point and John William MacLeod of Sturgeon.

DONALD MOR MACLEOD
DONALD MOR MACLEOD AND FLORA NICHOLSON OF POINT PRIM

A   Donald Mor MacLeod of Garadh Fada, in Isle of Skye, came to P.E.I. in 1803
     and settled at Point Prim. Descendants still have the original warrant of land
     signed by Lord Selkirk. Donald m. Flora <u>Nicholson</u>. He must have died while
     still young—apparently by drowning, along with two neighbours named
     Murchison.
     B1   Mary MacLeod, m. _____ <u>Lechman</u> (or <u>Luachman</u>).
          C1   Malcolm Lechman.
          C2   Patrick Lechman, called himself "Peter Swift." He was a sea captain
               and made his home in Swansea, England.
     B2   Donald MacLeod, died Oct. 20, 1839, having strained himself while moving
          a boat. He m. Penelope <u>MacDonald</u> from Tupple Murry, Mull. She died in
          1880 at age 82. Donald's gravestone states that he died in 1849 at 38 years
          and was a native of Skye. This was a puzzle since his family emigrated
          in 1803. We were able to locate the 1841 census though, and it showed
          Penelope as a widow. Donald's death has been adjusted accordingly. (The
          grave marker was likely put up many years later, possibly at Pansy's death
          in 1880.) The census shows two males under 16 years (would fit Michael
          and John), two between 16 and 45 years, and one female under 16, and
          one 45-60 (presumably Penelope). Only one was born in Scotland. They
          had issue:
          C1   Michael MacLeod, 1834-1897, m. Jessie <u>MacRae</u>, 1829-1906, with
               issue:
               D1   Donald MacLeod, 1856-1885. Never married. A sea captain,
                    Donald caught a disease on ship and died in France and is
                    buried at Sette.
               D2   Murdoch MacLeod, 1857-1931, m. Alexandrina <u>Marshall</u> in New
                    Zealand. They moved extensively, as the children's birthplaces
                    will testify. Children's spouses' names are unknown to us.
                    E1   William MacLeod, born in New Zealand, married, with
                         issue:
                         F1   Nelson MacLeod.
                    E2   Jessie MacLeod, born in New Zealand, married, with issue:
                         F1   Opal.
                         F2   Beryl, married with children:
                              G1   Graham.
                              G2   Merle.
                         F3   Cudworth, married with children:
                              G1   Louise.
                              G2   Daryl.
                    E3   Alice MacLeod, born in New Zealand, married with issue:
                         F1   Richard, m. with two boys.
                    E4   Pansy MacLeod, born in P.E.I., married with issue:
                         F1   Flora, married, with issue:
                              G1   Cheryl.
                              G2   Lorrie.

    G3 Andrea.
    G4 Brett.
   F2 Betty (Roma), married, with issue:
    G1 Gary.
    G2 Colin.
    G3 Kevin.
    G4 Alan.
    G5 Daryn.
  E5 Zelda MacLeod, born Boston, Massachusetts, married, with issue:
   F1 Lichfield.
  E6 Donald MacLeod, born in Boston. Never married. He won a scholarship to Harvard from New Zealand in the 1920s, and became a prominent lawyer in New Zealand.
  E6 Charlie MacLeod, born in Boston. Never married. The family moved back to New Zealand sometime after his birth.
D3 Samuel MacLeod, 1858-1928, m. Mary <u>MacLeod</u>, 1862-1919. (See family of Malcolm MacLeod and Christine Martin, of Victoria Cross.)
  E1 Lauchlin MacLeod, killed in action 1917, at battle of Passchendaele. He was 28 years of age, never married.
  E2 Malcolm MacLeod, construction engineer in British Columbia, never married.
  E3 Daniel MacLeod, died 1950s. Lived on old homestead, m. Mary <u>Nicholson</u>, Orwell Cove, with issue:
   F1 Mary MacLeod, died as a young child.
   F2 Byrtus MacLeod, m. John <u>Hogg</u>. Living in Toronto.
   F3 Glen MacLeod, m. Betty ____. Lived in Toronto.
  E4 Bessy Piper MacLeod, m. Clarence <u>Gillis</u>, with issue:
   F1 Raymond Gillis, married in Pictou, with issue:
    G1 Zelda Gillis.
    G2 Robert Gillis.
    And others.
   F2 Laughlin Gillis, m. Alberta <u>Nicholson</u>. Living in Point Prim. Issue, four children.
   F3 Channing Gillis, lives in Nova Scotia, m. Mary ____, with children.
   F4 Mary Gillis, lives in Halifax, married with children.
   F5 Eric Gillis, lived in Point Prim. Killed in farm accident.
  E5 Alexander Daniel MacLeod, m. Zelda <u>MacBeth</u>. No children. A veteran of WWI, Alex farmed in Point Prim. Died 1983.
  E6 Christina Elizabeth MacLeod, m. Channing <u>Deacon</u>. Lived in Quincy, Massachusetts, with issue:
   F1 Mary Deacon, m. _____ <u>Clark</u>, Living in Los Almos, California, with boys.
   F2 Walter Deacon, lives in Quincy, Massachusetts, married with three boys and one girl.
   F3 Beverly Deacon, lives in Tustin, California, m. Russell <u>Bradley</u>, with issue:

G1 Janna Bradley.

G2 Christa Bradley.

E7 John James MacLeod, m. Grace Stewart, of Argyle Shore. They lived in Massachusetts where John worked 44 years for the New England Telephone Co. They retired to Point Prim. John James died in 1987. Their children are:

F1 John Alexander MacLeod, lives in Massachusetts, m. 1) Jacqueline Burke, with issue:

G1 Scott Micheil MacLeod.

F2 Nancy Ruth MacLeod, m. David Siddle, Massachusetts, with issue:

G1 Kristen Lee Siddle.

G2 Kevin James Siddle.

G3 Stephen John Siddle.

F3 Robert Channing MacLeod, m. Caroline Cronin, Pennsylvania.

G1 Cynthia "Cindy" MacLeod, m. Paul MacDonald.

G2 Steven MacLeod.

F4 Donna MacLeod, m. Larry Casler, California, issue:

G1 Sharilee Anne Casler.

G2 Mathew Stuart Casler.

D4 Mary Anne MacLeod, m. William Peach of Marble Head, Massachusetts, issue:

E1 May Peach, married with children.

E2 Flora Peach, never married.

E3 George Peach, m. ____ Goodwin, and had children.

E4 William Peach, never married.

D5 Lauchlin MacLeod, 1860-1889, died of pneumonia.

D6 Donald Alex MacLeod, Oct. 1861 - Jan. 9, 1888.

D7 Pansy (Penelope) MacLeod, m. George Stewart, Marble Head, Massachusetts.

E1 Jessie Stewart, m. Ezekiel Russell Peach (nephew of Mary Anne's husband, William), with issue:

F1 Ezekiel Russell Peach (known as Zeke).

F2 A girl.

D8 Flora Bella MacLeod, m. George Burton of Massachusetts and Los Angeles.

E1 George Burton, m. Mildred _____, with issue:

F1 Phyllis Burton, married with children. She is head of a department at the University of Chicago.

F2 A girl, lives in California.

E2 Wesley Burton, lives in California, married with children.

E3 Emeline Burton, m. Earle Swann, with issue:

F1 Donna Belle Swann, an artist. She has a family.

D9 Mary Elizabeth MacLeod, m. John Stuart, Point Prim, with issue:

E1 Edward Stuart, died young. Buried in Washington.

E2 Daniel Stuart, WWI veteran, navy, died in the thirties.

E3 George Stuart, died in early fifties, never married.

E4 Burton Stuart, m. Florrie ____, in California.

E5 Marjorie Stuart, m. Robert Nichol, lives in Beverly, Massachusetts,with three boys, one girl.

E6   Florence Stuart, never married. Lived in Vancouver. Worked for CNR.

C2   John MacLeod, m. Sophie Munroe of Nova Scotia. The 1881 census shows John as 54 and a farmer. Sophie was 42. They bought a house in Cambridge and moved it to where it is now situated and occupied by his grandson Harry. Their children were:

D1   Florence MacLeod, believed to be the oldest.

D2   Donald MacLeod, born July 23, 1857.

D3   Penelope Sophia (Pansy) MacLeod, born Oct. 17, 1861, married a MacFadyen.

D4   John J. MacLeod, born P.E.I. c. 1865.

D5   Liza or Elizabeth A. MacLeod, born in Nova Scotia c. 1869.

D6   Sam MacLeod, born Nova Scotia c. 1871.

D7   Etta MacLeod, m. George White, born c. 1873 in Nova Scotia, buried in "Floreita," U.S., in 1881 census,

D8   Archie MacLeod, killed in U.S. in a paper mill when a huge roll of paper fell on him. He was born in Nova Scotia c. 1875.

D9   Mary MacLeod, m. Leon MacLeod, date of birth unknown.

D10 Samuel MacLeod, buried in Murray Harbour North Cemetery.

D11 Maude MacLeod, 1880-1915, m. Fred Miller. Buried in Murray Harbour North Cemetery. Born in Nova Scotia.

D12 Albert MacLeod, born at Cambridge, May 25, 1883, m. Daisy Edith Higginbotham, married at Murray Harbour North Presbyterian Church on Jan. 28, 1909. Albert was a farmer and a fisherman. They celebrated their 68th wedding anniversary in 1977. Albert died March 19, 1978, Daisy died a few weeks later. Buried in Murray Harbour North Cemetery.

     E1   Archie MacLeod, born April 19, 1909, m. Gertrude Graham.

         F1   Glenn MacLeod.

         F2   Boyd MacLeod, m. Cindy Hicken.

         F3   Cheryl MacLeod, m. Ron Phillips, living in Oshawa.

         F4   Alana MacLeod, m. LeMoyne White.

         F5   Wendell MacLeod, m. Judy Hicken.

     E2   Janie May MacLeod, born Sept. 26, 1910, m. Clyde Kerwin. He died Oct. 11, 1985. Their children were:

         F1   Howard Kerwin, m. Mary Martin.

         F2   Blaine Kerwin, m. Sandra Graham.

         F3   Daryl Kerwin, m. Teresa Rice.

         F4   Louis Kerwin, m. Mary Jane ____, living in Ontario.

         F5   Basil Kerwin, m. Paula Good.

     E3   Albert Roland MacLeod, m. Myrtle Graham.

         F1   Joyce MacLeod, m. Raymond Machon.

         F2   Barry MacLeod, m. Dianne Gillis.

         F3   Myrtle (Binnie) MacLeod, m. Jackie MacLean.

         F4   Brenton MacLeod, m. Cynthia Graham.

         F5   Blair MacLeod, not married.

     E4   Samuel MacLeod, twin of Mary, died at birth, Nov. 15, 1916.

     E5   Mary MacLeod, twin of Samuel. Died at birth.

     E6   William Howard MacLeod, died at 4 years of age.

     E7   Howard William MacLeod, m. Gertrude MacDonald, issue:

        F1   Bonnie MacLeod, m. Donald <u>Morrison</u>.
        F2   Craig MacLeod.
        F3   Mark MacLeod.
        F4   John MacLeod.
    E8   Basil Roy MacLeod, m. Barbara <u>Sorrie</u>.
        F1   Carol MacLeod.
        F2   Van MacLeod, m. Carolyn <u>MacGregor</u>, living in Calgary.
    E9   Harry George MacLeod, m. Elaine <u>Vaniderstine</u>, with issue:
        F1   Patsy MacLeod, m. Gary <u>MacLure</u>, with issue:
            G1   Jason MacLure.
        F2   Sherry MacLeod.
    E10 Alicia Mae MacLeod, m. Chet <u>Irving</u>.
        F1   Tammy Irving, m. Stephen <u>MacLeod</u>.
        F2   Vicky Irving, m. Hal <u>Publicover</u>.
        F3   Nathan Irving.

Among Donald and Penelope's other children was a daughter who married a White of Massachusetts and a son who in turn had a son known as "Capt. Red Jack MacLeod." He was said to have been the first white man to ride the Whitehorse Rapids.

Information given by John James MacLeod of Point Prim. He had some early family documents, including the original land grant with Lord Selkirk's wax seal. Also from Harry and Elaine MacLeod of Cambridge, 1841 and 1881 censuses, cemetery transcripts and baptismal certificates.

Letter
Letter from John MacEachern to Michael MacLeod

There were two revivals during the pioneer Rev. Donald MacDonald's ministry on P.E.I., and some time before his death in 1867, he stated to his elders that another revival would occur following his own death.

This letter gives an account of the beginning of this revival, which later spread throughout all the churches which had been built under his ministry. Michael Mac-Leod, Point Prim, was one of a large number of elders ordained by Mr. MacDonald, and John MacEachern was a fellow elder from Millview, from where he writes to Michael regarding the church.

Cherry Valley, Dec. 17, 1891

Mr. Michael MacLeod

My Dear Sir,

I have no doubt you have heard an account of the Revival now going on in Rev. Mr. Goodwill's church at DeSable and the other churches under his charge. You will be pleased and no doubt surprised to hear that in extent and numbers it far exceeds the last revival under the late Mr. MacDonald's ministry. Last Sabbath being Mr. Goodwill's day at Birch Hill, he was unable to leave the people on the other side but sent two elders instead to hold meetings for a few days with us. In their account of the revival, they say they are amazed at the power with which he preaches the Word, and the extent of the awakening especially among the young children from eight years and upward, crying for mercy. The church at DeSable is packed full every night, all in motion, some in one stage and some in another, all apparently brought under the influence of the Spirit of God. The movement is not confined to our people alone, but numbers from other churches are brought under the influence of the Spirit. I will mention one case, a woman belonging to another church did not wish her family to be going, but could not keep them away. The mother followed and when she came into the church and saw her daughters among the rest under the Power, such as you have seen at former revivals, she stood for some time looking at them, when she broke down and was brought under the influence of the same Spirit. It is Mr. Goodwill's desire and prayer that the revival may extend to this side also. We are praying that this side may not be passed by when there is such an outpouring of the Spirit on the other side. May God bless yourself, wife and family, is the sincere desire of your friend.

John MacEachern

RODERICK MACLEOD
RODERICK MACLEOD AND MARGARET MARTIN OF GRANDVIEW

A1   Murdoch MacLeod, son of Murdoch and Margaret MacLeod who were from the Isle of Skye. Murdoch, his brothers John and Archibald (Archie) all left Skye, two emigrated to Australia and the other to New Zealand. Whereas their brother Roderick emigrated to Canada.

A2   John MacLeod.

A3   Archie MacLeod.

A4   Roderick MacLeod, 1814-1904, m. Margaret Martin, and lived in Grandview as a farmer. Roderick emigrated to Canada arriving in P.E.I. between 1828 and 1830 at age of 16-18 years, with the Belfast Settlers of Lord Selkirk. He was granted 100 acres of land in Grandview.

   B1   Murdoch Roderick MacLeod, 1839-1930, m. Isobella MacBeth, lived in Bellevue.

      C1   Roderick Alex MacLeod, born Sept. 6, 1876, m. Miss MacFarlane, no family.

      C2   Donald Ernest MacLeod, born May 25, 1878, m. Mary (Mamie) MacPherson, lived in Bellevue. Farmer. No descendants.

      C3   William Edgar MacLeod, 1880-1922, m. Mary (Martin) Schnelle, they lived in San Francisco and had no descendants.

      C4   Maggie Etta MacLeod, born 1884, m. William Cuthbertson, with issue:

         D1   William Murdoch Cuthbertson, born Dec. 7, 1912, m. Goldie Berg.

            E1   Barbara Margaret Cuthbertson, m. Christopher Deakin, they lived in Edmonton, with issue:

               F1   Randell Deakin, born Jan. 1967.

               F2   Bradford Deakin, born April 1971.

            E2   Thomas William Cuthbertson, born Feb. 20, 1956.

         D2   Clifford Cuthbertson, born April 14, 1914, married and had two children in Edmonton, Alberta.

         D3   James Cuthbertson, born July 7, 1915, m. Ruth Reid, living in Edmonton, and had two children.

         D4   Effie Cuthbertson, 1919-1965, m. Dr. Robert Anderson Brown, in British Columbia.

            E1   Michael Burton George Brown.

            E2   Robert Arthur Christopher Brown.

            E3   Stephen Herbert Alexander Brown.

      C5   Angus Murdoch MacLeod, 1885-1943, single.

      C6   Mary Bell (Mabel) MacLeod, born March 27, 1891, m. Jim MacBeth. They lived in Florida, with issue:

         D1   Catherine MacBeth, m. J.M. Richardson and lived in Palm Beach, Florida, with issue:

            E1   Rodney Lee Richardson, living in New Orleans, Louisiana.

   B2   Mary Isobella MacLeod, 1841-1906, m. Alexander N. MacPherson of Grandview.

      C1   Elizabeth MacPherson, 1877-1948, m. Malcolm MacPherson of Bellevue. He was a farmer and mail carrier. Their children were:

D1   Katherine MacPherson, born Aug. 18, 1894, m. Rev. James Irving Fletcher, with issue:
    E1   Gordon Fletcher, m. Doris MacLeod, with issue:
        F1   Donald Fletcher.
        F2   Lynn Fletcher.
        F3   Richard Fletcher.
    E2   Agnes Elizabeth Fletcher, m. John Peters, with issue:
        F1   Jack Peters.
        F2   James Peters.
        F3   Kenneth Peters.
        F4   Jeanne Peters.
D2   Minnie MacPherson, m. Angus L. MacPherson, with issue:
    E1   Robert MacPherson.
D3   Marie MacPherson, born April 6, 1901, m. Chester Martin of Caledonia, a merchant. No family.
D4   Angus Allen MacPherson, 1906-1956, m. Jennie Maynard, with issue:
    E1   Lloyd MacPherson, m. Eva _____.
    E2   Robert MacPherson, m. Willa Lorraine MacPherson, with issue:
        F1   Larry Gordon MacPherson.
        F2   Susan Lorraine MacPherson.
        F3   Bradley James MacPherson.
    E3   Kenneth MacPherson.
    E4   Russell MacPherson.
    E5   Raymond MacPherson.
D5   Ruth MacPherson, m. Callum Martin, of Bellevue, later of Charlottetown, who was a farmer and carpenter, with issue:
    E1   Kenneth Malcolm Martin, m. Constance Grant. Kenneth was an electrician and lived in Ashland, Massachusetts, with issue:
        F1   Kenneth Victor Martin.
        F2   Robert Callum Martin.
        F3   David Gregory Martin.
    E2   Bruce Irving Martin, m. Jennifer Levi. Bruce was an electrician and lived in Mermaid, P.E.I., with issue:
        F1   Derrek Dennis Bruce Martin.
        F2   Ryan Clifford Martin.
    E3   Faye Marie Martin, m. Wilbur Birt and lived in Mermaid, P.E.I.
C2   Roderick MacPherson, born Aug. 7, 1878, m. Kate Russell, with issue:
D1   Dorothy MacPherson.
D2   Ruth MacPherson.
C3   Angus Allen MacPherson, 1880-1901.
C4   John Willie MacPherson, born April 28, 1882.
C5   Dan Alex MacPherson, born March 10, 1884, m. Euphemia Munroe. They lived in Uigg. Dan was a general merchant. Their children were:
D1   Florence MacPherson, m. Mr. Fields from Ottawa.
D2   Walcott MacPherson, m. Flossie Hooper, Murray River. They lived in Ottawa, retired to P.E.I. They have one son.
D3   Cyril MacPherson, was a merchant marine seaman.

C6   Margaret MacPherson, 1886-1977, m. John Sandy <u>MacPhee</u>. They lived in Bellevue where John worked as a farmer.

    D1   Alex A. MacPhee, born Nov. 13, 1912, m. Marjorie <u>MacKinnon</u>. They lived in Grandview and had issue:

        E1   Jean MacPhee, m. Lloyd <u>MacDonald</u> of Kinross. He is a farmer.

            F1   David Lloyd MacDonald.

            F2   Baby MacDonald, born Jan. 10, 1956, stillborn.

        E2   Dorothy Mae MacPhee, m. Elmer <u>Squires</u>, with issue:

            F1   Brian Elmer Squires.

            F2   Judy Mae Squires.

            F3   Floyd Wayne Squires.

            F4   Paul Dwayne Squires.

            F5   David Wade Squires.

        E3   Baby MacPhee, died in infancy.

        E4   John Wayne MacPhee, m. Deborah Ann <u>Peardon</u>, with issue:

            F1   Melody Dawn MacPhee.

            F2   Stephen Wayne MacPhee.

    D2   Stanley MacPhee, born April 21, 1916, m. Cora Sanderson <u>Banks</u>. They lived in Bellevue where Stanley worked as a farmer. No family.

    D3   Mary MacPhee, born June 18, 1918, m. John <u>Sample</u>. They settled in Danvers, Massachusetts. John was a carpenter. They had issue:

        E1   John Robert Sample, m. Maryellen <u>Goodridge</u>, with issue:

            F1   Andrea Sample.

        E2   Kathryn Margaret Sample.

        E3   Stanley Richard Sample.

        E4   Carl Phillip Sample.

C7   Marina MacPherson, 1890-1934, m. John Angus <u>MacDonald</u>, of Lyndale, a farmer, they had no descendants.

B3   Margaret MacLeod, 1844-1929, m. John <u>MacLeod</u>, of Orwell. They settled in Garfield, P.E.I., with issue:

    C1   Margaret Belle MacLeod, m. Henry <u>Musick</u>, Kinross, with issue:

        D1   Ada Musick, born Feb. 11, 1910, m. Joe <u>Irving</u> and they lived in Manchester, Massachusetts, with issue:

            E1   Joanne Irving, m. Donald <u>Hunt</u> of Lynn, Massachusetts, with issue:

                F1   David Hunt, m. Karen_____.

                F2   Debbie Hunt.

                F3   Susan Hunt.

                F4   Lisa Hunt.

                F5   Peter Hunt, twin.

                F6   Cindy Hunt, twin.

            E2   Claire Irving, m. Leo <u>Speilberg</u>, lived in Manchester, Massachusetts.

                F1   Sherri Speilberg, settled in New York.

                F2   Jay Speilberg.

                F3   Karen Speilberg.

                F4   Leslie Speilberg.

D2   Hudson Musick, born Dec. 28, 1914, m. Elsie <u>MacKenzie</u>, lived in Kinross, with issue:
    E1   Edwin Musick, m. Anne <u>Murchison</u>, living in Pictou, Nova Scotia, issue:
        F1   Paul Musick.
        F2   Lisa Musick.
        F3   Allan Musick.
    E2   Roland Musick, m. Mary <u>Hewitt</u>, with issue:
        F1   David Musick.
    E3   Linda Musick, m. Ralph <u>Leard</u>, with issue:
        F1   Ronny Leard.
        F2   Cindy Leard.
    E4   Evelyn Musick, m. Bernard <u>MacDonald</u>, with issue:
        F1   Heidi MacDonald.
    E5   Lila Musick, m. Barry <u>Davidson</u> of Hamilton, Ontario, with issue:
        F1   Patricia Davidson.
        F2   Kimberly Davidson.
    E6   Brenda Musick, m. Angus <u>MacDonald</u>, Cape Breton, with issue:
        F1   Tyler MacDonald.
        F2   Lawrence Angus MacDonald.
        F3   Coady MacDonald.
    E7   Marlene Musick, m. David <u>Sark</u>, with issue:
        F1   Rachelle Sark.
D3   Roland Musick, born April 30, 1916, m. Evelyn <u>Scott</u>, they settled in Milton, Ontario. Roland served in WWII.
    E1   Xanne Musick, lived in Burlington, Ontario.

B4   Angus Roderick MacLeod, born 1849, m. Annie <u>MacLeod</u>, settled in Grandview. Angus was a farmer. Their children were:
C1   Angusina (Senie) MacLeod, m. Neil <u>MacBeth</u> of Grandview. No family.
C2   Isobell (Belle) MacLeod, single.
C3   Margaret A. MacLeod, 1880-1892.

B5   John Roderick MacLeod, 1851-1925, m. Christine <u>Bruce</u>, with issue:
C1   Margaret Sarah MacLeod, 1883-1974. Single, R.N.
C2   Angus Roderick MacLeod, 1885-1955. Single, operated a lumber mill.
C3   Laura May MacLeod, 1887-1905. Single, died of T.B. at 18 years.
C4   Angus Bruce MacLeod, born April 26, 1889, m. Mary Myrtle <u>Beck</u>. Served in WWI. Their children are:
    D1   Everett John MacLeod, m. Margaret <u>MacDougall</u>. They settled in Pierrefonds, Quebec, where Everett worked in electronics. Issue:
        E1   Ellen Margaret MacLeod.
        E2   Donald Bruce MacLeod.
        E3   Laura Beth MacLeod.
        E4   Everett Randall MacLeod.
    D2   Lloyd Beck MacLeod, m. Audrey Page <u>Lawrence</u>, with issue. They settled in Charlottetown where Lloyd worked as director at the research station.
        E1   Robert Bruce MacLeod, 1958-1958, buried in Amherst, Nova Scotia.

E2 Susan Margaret MacLeod.

E3 Kathryn Ann MacLeod.

E4 David Lloyd MacLeod.

D3 Willard Bruce MacLeod, m. Bernice <u>Francis</u> and settled in Calgary. Worked as an industrial accountant, with issue:

E1 Anna Francis MacLeod.

E2 Jeffrey Bruce MacLeod.

D4 Phyllis Christine MacLeod, m. Alexander <u>Dawson</u>, they lived in Uigg.

E1 Gwendelyn Anne Dawson, m. William <u>Kemp</u>, settled in Milltown.

E2 Hal Alexander Dawson, m. Helen <u>Brown</u>, lived in Uigg, with issue:

F1 Dennis Alexander Dawson, died March 1974 at birth.

F2 Denise Elizabeth Dawson.

E3 Gail Roberta Dawson, m. James Michael <u>Osborne</u>, Harrington.

F1 Patricia Marie Osborne.

E4 Karl Wallace Dawson.

E5 Myrna Faye Dawson.

E6 Richard Lee Dawson.

D5 Margaret June MacLeod, R.N., m. Malcolm Hugh <u>MacLeod</u>, Uigg.

E1 Barry Malcolm MacLeod.

E2 Shirley Margaret MacLeod.

E3 Donna Faye MacLeod.

D6 George Marfleet MacLeod, m. Betty Joyce <u>Bacon</u> and settled in Charlottetown, with issue:

E1 Valerie Joyce MacLeod.

E2 Michael George MacLeod.

E3 Brian Vincent MacLeod.

C5 John Daniel MacLeod, 1891-1912, single, died of T.B. at age 21.

C6 Everett MacLeod, 1893-1916. Single, killed in WWI in France.

C7 Annie Mae MacLeod, born April 17, 1895, m. Reginald Albert <u>Jenkins</u> and lived in Portland, Oregon. She was an R.N. and he was an engineer. Issue:

D1 Reginald Everett Jenkins, m. Mary Ellen <u>Sutton</u> and settled in Florida where he worked as a pilot in the U.S. Navy.

E1 Linda Lea Jenkins, m. Bruce Randall <u>McMurray</u> who was in the U.S. Army. They had issue:

F1 Maegan Lea McMurray.

E2 Bruce Albert Jenkins, m. Melissa <u>Rutland</u>, settled in Leesburg, Virginia, where he works as a paramedic, with issue:

F1 Jennifer Jenkins.

F2 Scottie Stephen Jenkins.

E3 Merry Kathleen Jenkins, m. Lynn <u>Smith</u>.

D2 Barbara Anne Jenkins, m. Roger Roy <u>Orem</u> and lives in Portland, Oregon, with issue:

E1 Randall Roy Orem.

E2 Lance Ernest Orem.

E3 Scott Preston Orem.

C8 Whitfield Kierstead MacLeod, m. Florence <u>Docherty</u>. They lived in Grandview on the old homestead, with issue:
- D1 Joan Margaret MacLeod, m. Gordon <u>MacDougall</u>, with issue:
  - E1 David MacDougall, m. Cynthia <u>Davis</u>.
  - E2 Nancy MacDougall.
  - E3 Linda MacDougall.
  - E4 Phillip MacDougall.
  - E5 Janet MacDougall.
- D2 John Wellington MacLeod, m. Mary <u>Masters</u>.

B6 Annie MacLeod, 1854-1936, m. Malcolm J. <u>MacDonald</u> and settled in Lyndale. Their children were:
- C1 John Angus MacDonald, never married.
- C2 Roderick MacDonald, died young.
- C3 Margaret MacDonald, had a son:
  - D1 Malcolm "Montie" MacDonald, never married.
- C4 Alexander Hector MacDonald, never married.
- C5 Elizabeth MacDonald, never married.
- C6 James MacDonald, served in WWII and later was killed in Oregon. His body was taken back to be interred in Orwell Head Cemetery.

A5 Margaret MacLeod.
A6 Another sister.
One sister married, bought the home farm and stayed on the Isle of Skye.

This information was provided by Dr. L. B. MacLeod of Charlottetown.

NORMAN MACLEOD
NORMAN MACLEOD AND MARY MACPHERSON OF VALLEYFIELD

A   Norman MacLeod, born c. 1818, m. Mary MacPherson, born c. 1825, both of
     Scotland. Norman had a sister, Mary, who married Malcolm MacPherson. No
     other siblings are known. Norman and Mary's children were:
B1   Peter MacLeod, born c. 1855, operated a store in Mt. Stewart.
B2   Catherine "Katie" MacLeod, 1856-1944, m. Angus Nicholson, 1856-1934.
B3   William Norman MacLeod, 1858-1933, m. 1) Sara Ployer, 1864-1909, m. 2)
     _____ MacLeod, and 3) Meriah _____. Issue:
  C1   John Ployer MacLeod, 1890-1978, m. Annie Jessie Bruce, 1892-1976.
       (See the family of Angus and Mary MacLeod of Valleyfield for a
       complete list of descendants.)
    D1   Helena Annie MacLeod, m. John Murdoch MacPherson, with
         issue:
      E1   Shirley MacPherson, m. Peter Madarin, with issue:
        F1   Patricia Madarin.
        F2   Sean Madarin.
      E2   Stanley MacPherson, m. Heather Clark, with issue:
        F1   Katherine MacPherson.
        F2   Suzanne MacPherson.
        F3   Gregory MacPherson.
        F4   Alex MacPherson.
      E3   Francis Irene MacPherson.
      E4   John David Bruce MacPherson.
    D2   Lillian MacLeod, twin to Helena, m. William (Billy) Hayden,
         Cherry Valley, with issue:
      E1   Lewis "Wayne" Hayden, farmer, m. Phyllis Knox, with
           issue:
        F1   Lewis Dean Hayden.
        F2   Jason Wayne Hayden.
        F3   Amy Elizabeth Hayden.
      E2   John Trueman Hayden, farmer, m. Sheila Anne Gill, with
           issue:
        F1   Marlene Anne Hayden.
        F2   April Dawn Hayden.
        F3   Bonnie Jean Hayden.
        F4   Heidi Marie Hayden.
        F5   Emily Kathleen Hayden.
      E3   Carole Jane Hayden, m. Kenneth Edison Wood, with issue:
        F1   James Edward Wood.
        F2   Ashley Hayden Wood.
        F3   Jo-Anne Estelle Delight Wood.
        F4   Scarlett Laureen Edna Wood.
      E4   Catherine Sareta Hayden, m. Daniel Raymond Ross, issue:
        F1   Margaret Anne Ross.
        F2   Donna Mae Ross.
        F3   Jewel Lynn Ross.
        F4   Willena Marie Ross.

        D3   Katherine Sareta MacLeod, 1922-1946, m. Wesley <u>Wallace</u> (Bud).
             E1   Harvey Wallace, m. Susan _____.
        D4   John William Bruce MacLeod, 1924-1948, unmarried.
        D5   George Sterling MacLeod, m. Agnes <u>Hewitt</u>, with issue:
             E1   Kathy MacLeod.
             E2   Bruce MacLeod.
    C2   Katie Lillie MacLeod, born Dec. 1891, died July 1892.
    C3   George P. MacLeod, 1892-1920, never married.
    C4   Norman MacLeod, born June 19, 1898, m. Florence <u>Morrison</u>.
    C5   Sara (Sadie) MacLeod, m. William <u>MacKenzie</u>.
B4   John Peter MacLeod, 1867-1917. Prominent scholar and lawyer in Victoria. Deputy General in British Columbia, 1910-1916, buried in Valleyfield.
B5   Norman MacLeod, born c. 1870, had a store in Amherst, Nova Scotia.
B6   Angus MacLeod, born Oct. 1848, lived in Shelburne, Nova Scotia, school principal.

There were other children, apparently 10 or 11 in all. Twins died in infancy and several died young.

The above information was provided by Lillian Hayden, Cherry Valley.

ANGUS MACLEOD
ANGUS MACLEOD AND SARAH NICHOLSON OF BELFAST

A   Angus MacLeod, born 1811, m. Sarah <u>Nicholson</u>, born 1823, daughter of John Nicholson and Mary MacLeod, Orwell Cove, buried in Belfast, with issue:

B1   Alexander MacLeod, 1846-1923, m. Alexina "Lexie" <u>Martin</u>, 1854-1920. Buried in Belfast. They had issue:

    C1   Angus MacLeod (Angus Mudfish), 1889-1971, m. Lexie <u>Nicholson</u>, 1887-1957. No family, they are buried in Belfast Cemetery.

    C2   Florence MacLeod, m. Harold <u>Whitlock</u>.

    C3   Sinclair MacLeod, 1891-1953.

B2   Rachel MacLeod, 1848-1931, m. Hugh <u>MacMillan</u>, 1834-1920, Wood Islands, issue:

        C1   Sarah Anne MacMillan, 1874-1947, m. Daniel Angus <u>Munn</u>, 1871-1941, of Little Sands, both buried in Little Sands.

        C2   Allan Angus MacMillan, born 1875.

        C3   Mary Elizabeth MacMillan, 1876-1876.

        C4   James (Daniel James) MacMillan, born 1877.

        C5   John (Jack Hughie) MacMillan, born 1881.

        C6   Janie MacMillan, born 1888, married in British Columbia to David <u>Stupich</u>, with issue:

        D1   David Stupich, M.L.A. in British Columbia.

        D2   Albert Stupich.

        D3   Violet Stupich, not living.

        D4   Alvin Stupich.

        D5   Marjorie Stupich.

        D6   Stanley Stupich, not living.

B3   Janet (Jessie) MacLeod, 1854-1933, m. John A. <u>Millman</u>, with issue:

    C1   Mary Elizabeth Millman, 1878-1966, m. William <u>Profitt</u>, with issue:

        D1   William Profitt, m. 1) Velda <u>Dunning</u>, she died one and one half years after their marriage, m. 2) Sophia <u>Simpson</u> and had two boys.

        E1   Harold Profitt, m. Eileen <u>Howard</u>.

        E2   Lloyd Profitt, m. Gwen <u>Court</u>, with issue:

            F1   Darrell Profitt.

        William m. 3) Gertrude <u>Sheen</u>.

        D2   Oliver Profitt, m. Margaret <u>Champion</u>, with issue:

        E1   Eileen Profitt, m. Roy <u>Clark</u>, with issue:

            F1   David Clark.

            F2   Sharon Clark.

            F3   Eric Clark.

            F4   Marlene Clark.

            F5   Roger Clark.

            F6   Sheila Clark.

            F7   Ivy Clark.

            F8   Michael Clark.

            F9   Sandra Clark.

            F10 Russell Clark.

            F11 Roy Clark.

E2 Audrey Profitt, m. Dan <u>Tinney</u>, with issue:
    F1 William Tinney.
    F2 Roger Tinney.
E3 Ralph Profitt, m. Helen <u>Heustis</u>, with issue:
    F1 Carla Profitt.
    F2 Lynn Profitt.
E4 Norma Profitt, m. William <u>Daley</u>, with issue:
    F1 Shanna Daley.
    F2 William Daley.
    F3 Scott Daley.
E5 Ronald Profitt, m. Norma <u>Craig</u>, with issue:
    F1 Tyler Profitt.
    F2 Aaron Profitt.
D3 Walter Profitt, twin of Oliver, died in infancy.
D4 Halsey Profitt, m. Charlotte <u>Bernard</u>, with issue:
E1 Jessie Profitt, m. Charles <u>Coles</u>, with issue:
    F1 Clarence Coles.
    F2 Bruce Coles.
    F3 Norman Coles.
    F4 Stewart Coles.
    F5 Grafton Coles.
    F6 Nancy Coles.
    F7 Glen Coles.
    F8 Wyman Coles.
    F9 Leland Coles.
E2 Ruth Profitt, m. Thomas <u>Hannah</u>, with issue:
    F1 Mary Hannah.
    F2 Beverly Hannah.
    F3 Debra Hannah.
    F4 Thomas Hannah.
    F5 Richard Hannah.
    F6 Cheryl Hannah.
    F7 Susan Hannah.
    F8 Paul Hannah.
    F9 James Hannah.
    F10 Carol Hannah.
E3 Claire Profitt, m. Marion <u>MacKay</u>, with issue:
    F1 Allan Profitt.
    F2 Kevin Profitt.
E4 Irene Profitt, m. Alvin <u>Bernard</u>, with issue:
    F1 Eleanor Bernard.
    F2 Sandra Bernard.
    F3 Blaine Bernard.
    F4 Darlene Bernard.
E5 Gerard Profitt, lives at home.
D5 Ruby Profitt, m. James <u>Bernard</u>, with issue:
E1 Doris Bernard, m. Clarence <u>Moase</u>, with issue:
    F1 David Moase.
    F2 Arnold Moase.
    F3 Linda Moase.
    F4 Marlene Moase.

E2   Hillard Bernard, m. Louise <u>Peterson</u>, with issue:
- F1   Jamie Lloyd Bernard.
- F2   Bonita Bernard.
- F3   Shawna Bernard.

D6 Herbert Profitt, m. Ella <u>Moase</u>, with issue:

E1   Wendell Profitt, m. Myrna <u>Docherty</u>, with issue:
- F1   Lynne Profitt.
- F2   Trevor Profitt.

E2   Mabel Profitt, m. James <u>Thompson</u>, with issue:
- F1   Kevin Thompson.
- F2   Steven Thompson.

E3   Alden Profitt, m. Marilyn <u>Campbell</u>, no family.

D7 Gladys Profitt, m. Robert <u>Stavert</u>, with issue:

E1   Donald Stavert, m. Judith <u>Woodside</u>, with issue:
- F1   Kelly Dawn Stavert.
- F2   Jeffery Douglas Stavert.
- F3   Aaron Robert Stavert.

E2   Lois Stavert, m. Wallace <u>MacLeod</u>, with issue:
- F1   Katherine MacLeod.
- F2   Cheryl MacLeod.
- F3   Glenna Mae MacLeod.
- F4   Stavert MacLeod.

E3   Bloyce Stavert, m. Janice <u>Colebrook</u>, with issue:
- F1   Allan Stavert.
- F2   Andrew Stavert.

D8 Arthur Profitt, m. Elva <u>Pickering</u>, with issue:

E1   Roland Profitt, m. Ruth <u>Johnson</u>, with issue:
- F1   Randy Profitt.
- F2   Sherri Profitt.

D9 Ernest Profitt, m. Irma <u>Parkin</u>.

D10 Kathleen Profitt, m. 1) Jack <u>Kemp</u>, he died in 1964. Issue:
- E1   Bruce Kemp.
- E2   Owen Kemp.
- E3   Mary Kemp.

Kathleen m. 2) Leaford <u>Bowes</u>.

D11 James Albert Profitt, died at 3 years old, in 1915.

C2 Margaret Millman, 1888-1965, m. Alexander <u>Campbell</u>, with issue:

D1 Hilda Campbell, m. Walter <u>Moase</u>, with issue:

E1   Eleanor Moase, m. Kenneth <u>Huestis</u>, with issue:
- F1   Coleen Huestis.
- F2   Marilyn Huestis.
- F3   Garth Huestis.

E2   Clarence Moase, m. Doris <u>Bernard</u>, with issue:
- F1   David Moase.
- F2   Arnold Moase, m. Joy <u>Meek</u>.
- F3   Linda Moase.
- F4   Marlene Moase.

E3   Francis Moase, m. Mary <u>Fyfe</u>, with issue:
- F1   Cynthia Moase.

D2 Alma Campbell, m. Wallace <u>Adams</u>, with issue:

E1   Earith Adams, m. Marvyn <u>Ramsay</u>.

D3   Jean Campbell, m. Clayton Stewart, with issue:
    E1   Wendell Stewart.
    E2   Joyce Stewart.
D4   Edith Campbell, died aged 13.
D5   Borden Campbell, m. Thelma Andrews, with issue:
    E1   Gwendy Campbell.
    E2   Gary Campbell.
    E3   Alexander Campbell.
    E4   Julie Campbell.
D6   Earl Campbell, m. Mary MacKay, with issue:
    E1   Carl Campbell.
    E2   Leigh Campbell.
    E3   Larry Campbell.
    E4   Lane Campbell.
D7   Marjory Campbell, m. Elmer Moase, with issue:
    E1   Roy Moase, m. Dianne Stewart.
    E2   Isabel Moase, m. Allan Paynter.
    E3   Olive Moase, single.
C3   Herbert Millman, 1880-1942, never married.
C4   Thomas Millman, 1882-1966, m. Lillian Whitney.
C5   Elbert Millman, 1890-1960, m. Mildred Johnson.
C6   Bertha Millman, 1894-1972, m. 1) Harry Brander, m. 2) Ben MacLeod, 1875-1970.
C7   Jessie Millman, m. Lawrence MacLeod, 1884-1969, Orwell.
B4   Elizabeth MacLeod, m. John MacKinnon, Charlottetown, with issue:
C1   Lottie MacKinnon, m. Edward Hammill.
C2   Myrtle MacKinnon, never married.
C3   Roderick MacKinnon.
C4   Huddard MacKinnon.
C5   Oliver MacKinnon.
B5   Mary Jane MacLeod.
B6   Katie Ann MacLeod.

This information provided by Herbert Profitt of Charlottetown, and information from the census and cemetery transcripts.

ARCHIE MACLEOD
ARCHIE MACLEOD AND JESSIE CAMPBELL OF WHIM ROAD

A   Archie MacLeod, died Dec. 15, 1884, age 82 years, m. Jessie Campbell, who died
     Dec. 22, 1879, age 69 years. They came to P.E.I. in 1858 on the ship *James Gibb*,
     and settled in the Whim Road area, where Archie was a farmer and known as
     "Big Archie." They came to P.E.I. with seven children. In the 1861 census there
     was an Archibald MacLeod living in Lot 59.
   B1   Catherine MacLeod, born 1831 in Kilmuir Parish, Isle of Skye, and died
        Jan. 10, 1926, lived all her life on the farm her father first settled on, buried
        in Valleyfield Cemetery.
   B2   James MacLeod (Captain Jim), 1851-1943, never married and sailed back
        and forth from the Island to Scotland taking over produce such as pota-
        toes. Later he went North during the gold rush and eventually settled
        in Dawson City, Yukon, where he worked in Customs. He is buried in
        Vancouver.
   B3   Alexander MacLeod.
   B4   Donald MacLeod, born c. 1845, m. Emily Yeoman from New Brunswick.
        Donald was on Lot 61 in the 1881 census. Donald married Emily at Vernon
        River on March 16, 1866, with issue:
      C1   George MacLeod.
      C2   Jessie MacLeod.
      C3   James MacLeod.
      C4   Archibald MacLeod, 1876-1926. Buried Lower Montague Cemetery.
           His stone was erected by Capt. James MacLeod.
      C5   John MacLeod, drowned at age 22.
      C6   William MacLeod, 1885-1964, m. Beatrice Publicover, born June 17,
           1904, died March 31, 1976. They are buried in Georgetown United
           Cemetery.
         D1   Eileen MacLeod, m. James Hunter, Ontario, with issue:
            E1   Jimmy Hunter.
            E2   Billy Hunter.
            E3   Carol Hunter.
         D2   Georgina MacLeod, m. Edward Clark, with issue:
            E1   Debbie Clark.
            E2   Jerry Clark.
         D3   Doris MacLeod, m. 1) Basil Gotell, with issue:
            E1   Kimbel Gotell.
            E2   Holly Gotell.
            E3   Faith Gotell.
            Doris m. 2) Arthur Lee Hemmelmin.
         D4   Margaret MacLeod, m. 1) Leslie Doughty, with issue:
            E1   Leslie Doughty.
            E2   Gordon Doughty m. 1) Sharron Perry, 2) Louise _____.
            E3   David Doughty.
            E4   Tye Doughty m. Donald Jeffery.
            E5   Sharon Doughty, m. Gerry Fiddis.
            Margaret m. 2) Kenneth MacDonald, St. George's, with issue:

      E6   Kenny MacDonald.

      E7   Emmett MacDonald.

D5   Ruby MacLeod, m. John Dalton, with issue:

      E1   John MacLeod, m. Karen MacDonald, Ontario.

      E2   Beatrice Dalton, m. Cyril Connors, Calgary.

      E3   Gail Dalton, m. Mickey MacDonald, from Georgetown.

      E4   Gay Dalton, Gail's twin, deceased and buried in Catholic Cemetery, Georgetown.

      E5   Margaret Marie Dalton, m. 1) Reginald Campbell, m. 2) Jim Revell, a lawyer in Charlottetown.

      E6   Brenda Lee Dalton, m. Donnie Graham, Murray Harbour North.

      E7   Scott Dalton, Montague.

D6   Everett MacLeod, m. 1) Louise Weatherbie. They live in Georgetown.

      E1   Allison MacLeod, m. Carol Ann Roche from Seven Mile Road.

      E2   Edna MacLeod, m. Clinton Chaisson, New Brunswick.

      E3   Billy MacLeod, m. Janet Sturgess from Georgetown.

      E4   James MacLeod, unmarried, living in Georgetown.

      Everett m. 2) Ethel Murphy from Montague.

      Everett m. 3) Alma Sonia from Georgetown.

      E5   Troy MacLeod.

      E6   Stephen MacLeod.

D7   Carl MacLeod, living in Georgetown.

D8   John Temple MacLeod, born Dec. 14, 1945, died 2 years old.

D9   Another infant who died.

Donald m. 2) Celia White, from Cape Bald, Shediac. They married Aug. 11, 1904, at St. David's United Church in Georgetown.

C7   Beatrice MacLeod, born Dec. 18, 1910, m. Willard Bernard, born Jan. 9, 1908. They live in Hunter River, with issue:

D1   Donald William Bernard, m. Eileen Keriens on Sept. 5, 1956.

      E1   Wendy Lee Bernard.

      E2   Kathy Robina Bernard.

      E3   Terry Donald Bernard.

D2   Clifford M. Bernard, m. 1) Alice Thoms on April 18, 1972, with issue:

      E1   Jason Lee Bernard.

      Clifford m. 2) Carol Phillips.

C8   Florence MacLeod, born May 13, 1905, m. Thomas Meney, Little Sands. Florence was adopted by Peter and Mary Ann (Conley) Johnston, Montague. She is buried in Montague Cemetery with Peter and Mary. After her death Thomas married again.

D1   Beatrice Meney, m. Bruce MacPherson, Little Sands, with issue:

      E1   Judy MacPherson, m. Alexander MacDonald, Belfast.

D2   Mae Meney, m. Alonzo Gamble, Wood Islands, with issue:

      E1   Ronald Gamble.

D3   Della Meney, m. Arthur Gillis. They are both deceased and are buried in Little Sands Cemetery. Their children are:

      E1   Robert Gillis, m. Lynda Compton, daughter of Douglas and Laura (Acorn) Compton, Wood Islands.

    E2 Clifford Gillis, living in Wood Islands.

    E3 Sterling Gillis.

    E4 Clarence Gillis, m. Donna <u>Creed</u>, Sturgeon.

  C9 Murdoch MacLeod, 1906-1975, m. Alma <u>Brehaut</u> from Murray Harbour.

    D1 Margaret MacLeod, m. Reggie <u>MacDonald</u>.

    D2 Susan MacLeod, m. Harvey <u>Sullivan</u>.

    D3 David MacLeod, m. Evelyn <u>MacGregor</u>. David is in the Air Force.

  C10 Catherine MacLeod, m. 1) Joe <u>Flood</u>, m. 2) Dave <u>Petrie</u>, from Sydney, Nova Scotia. They have two adopted children.

 B5 Robina MacLeod.

  C1 Murdoch MacLeod, born March 10, 1864, on the Whim Road and died in 1949, age 85 years. (The stone states born 1867, died 1951.) He married Ethel <u>MacFarlane</u> who died 1960, age 75. They lived in Lower Montague, with issue:

    D1 Leah Catherine MacLeod, m. Harvey <u>Ross</u>, Lower Montague, a cattle dealer and at one time had a fox ranch. They had issue:

      E1 Merrill Ross.

      E2 Donald Ross.

      E3 Leona Robina Ross, born and died May 19, 1942.

    D2 Robina Frances MacLeod, 1916-1967, m. Stewart <u>MacKenna</u>, Greenfield, they have three children.

    D3 James MacLeod, born 1918, m. Loretta <u>Reynolds</u>.

  C2 Jessie MacLeod, m. _____ <u>Whitman</u>, Orchard, Maine.

 B6 Unknown.

 B7 Unknown.

Information provided by Leah Ross, Lower Montague; Ruby Dalton, Montague; Beatrice MacPherson, Little Sands; Beatrice Bernard, Hunter River; research at P.E.I. Archives and Beaconsfield.

ANGUS MACLEOD
ANGUS MACLEOD AND MARY OF VALLEYFIELD

A   Angus MacLeod, born 1784, Isle of Skye, died 1871. Married Mary, born 1776, Isle of Skye, died Jan. 26, 1883, at 107 years of age. They had issue:

B1   Maggie MacLeod, m. Peter MacLeod of the other Valleyfield family, and settled in Dundas, with issue:
   C1   Annie MacLeod, m. Boyd____.
   C2   Sadie MacLeod.
   C3   Malcolm MacLeod.
   C4   John MacLeod.

B2   Mary MacLeod, single.

B3   John MacLeod, 1810-1883, m. Mary MacLeod, with issue:
   C1   Euphemia MacLeod, 1846-1867, single.
   C2   Margaret MacLeod, 1850-1947, m. Duncan Campbell, with issue:
      D1   Susan Campbell, 1878-1968, single.
      D2   Warren Campbell, 1880-1930, m. Etta Campbell, with issue:
         E1   Ruth Campbell, m. Wellington Nicholson, with issue:
            F1   Vera Nicholson, m. William Myshrall.
            F2   Russell Nicholson, m. Mary Robinson, with issue:
               G1   Robert Nicholson.
            F3   Joyce Nicholson, m. Fred Kirke.
      D3   Alexina Campbell.
      D4   Minnie Campbell, 1882-1974, m. Peter MacDonald.
      D5   Florence Campbell, born 1889, m. 1) Alex F. MacLeod and 2) Archie Stewart, with issue:
         E1   Preston MacLeod, married with children.
         E2   Lillian MacLeod, m. Calvin Hilchey.
         E3   Betty MacLeod.
   C3   John J. MacLeod, born Nov. 28, 1851, m. Lizzie MacPhee, with issue:
      D1   John MacLeod, born Aug. 25, 1886, died in WWI.
      D2   Mary Florence MacLeod, born Nov. 8, 1890, and baptized July 21, 1891, m. George MacLeod, with issue:
         E1   John MacLeod.
      D3   Willie MacLeod, born July 21, 1889, m. Margaret Morrison.
      D4   Katie Effie MacLeod, m. Kenny MacKenzie.
      D5   Jessie MacLeod, single.
      D6   Jennie MacLeod, R.N., single.
   C4   Jonathan MacLeod, 1853-1938, m. Catherine Matheson, 1854-1924, of Dover, on July 29, 1879, with issue:
      D1   Malcolm J. MacLeod, born Oct. 22, 1886, m. Martha _____.
      D2   Neil J. MacLeod, 1880-1971, m. Miss Stewart, three children.
      D3   John Matheson MacLeod, 1882-1974, m. Miss Stewart. They had children but their names are unknown.
      D4   John "Angus" MacLeod, born Dec. 23, 1884.
      D5   Mary "Florence" MacLeod, born July 29, 1888, m. William N. MacLeod of Valleyfield, with issue:
         E1   Foster MacLeod, m. with two children.

D6 Norman J. MacLeod, 1892-1964, m. Marion <u>Crockett</u>, with issue:
    E1 Arnold MacLeod, died at birth.
    E2 Alice MacLeod, born 1923, m. Murray <u>Lusher</u>.
D7 Murdoch "Addison" MacLeod, born Dec. 17, 1890. He m. Elizabeth <u>Munroe</u>, with issue:
    E1 Marie MacLeod.
    E2 Chester MacLeod.
    E3 Arthur MacLeod.
C5 Norman MacLeod, born Jan. 17, 1856.
C6 Flora MacLeod.
C7 Neil MacLeod, 1858-1880.
C8 Rev. Murdoch J. MacLeod,1861-1889.
C9 Angus MacLeod, 1862-1886.
C10 Kate MacLeod, m. Ronald <u>MacPherson</u> of Glen Martin, with issue:
    D1 Neil MacPherson, m. Miss <u>Murchison</u>.
    D2 Dan R. MacPherson, m. 1) Katie <u>MacKinnon</u>, daughter of John MacKinnon of Kilmuir. They had issue:
        E1 Hugh Alex MacPherson.
        E2 John MacPherson.
        E3 Malcolm MacPherson.
        E4 Ronnie MacPherson.
        Dan R. m. 2) Bessie <u>Walker</u>.
        E5 Catherine MacPherson, m. Russell <u>Jardine</u>.
        E6 Wallace MacPherson.
    D3 Peter MacPherson, single.
    D4 Alex MacPherson, single.
    D5 John MacPherson, m. Dorothy <u>MacLeod</u>, with issue:
        E1 Ronald MacPherson.
        E2 Catherine MacPherson.
    D6 Maggie MacPherson, m. John <u>Wedderbun</u>.
    D7 Effie MacPherson, m. John <u>Sutherland</u>, died in Quincy, Massachusetts, Feb. 1961, at age 84.
    D8 Mary MacPherson, single.
C11 Mary MacLeod, m. Ronald <u>Nicholson</u> of Glen Martin, with issue:
    D1 Angus Nicholson, married twice.
    D2 Kate Nicholson, m. Charlie <u>Martin</u> of Glen Martin, with issue:
        E1 Marion Martin, m. John <u>MacPherson</u>, with issue:
            F1 Martin MacPherson, died.
            F2 Angus MacPherson.
            F3 Katherine MacPherson, m. Ivan <u>MacPherson</u>.
        E2 Angus Martin, single, lives in Quincy, Massachusetts.
        E3 Chester Martin, m. Marie <u>MacPherson</u>, no family.
        E4 Marjorie Martin, m. Gordon <u>Scrimgeour</u>.
    D3 Lexie Nicholson, m. Malcolm <u>Gillis</u>, with issue:
        E1 Norman Gillis, died.
        E2 Lena Gillis, married.
        E3 Marion Gillis, m. Angus <u>MacDonald</u>.
    D4 Hannah Nicholson, m. Finley <u>Matheson</u>, with issue:
        E1 K. Rae Matheson, married.
        E2 Seymour Matheson, single.
        E3 Ansley Matheson, m. Betty _____, one child.

          E4   Mary Matheson, twin of Ansley.
     D5 John Dan Nicholson, single.
  C12 Effie MacLeod.
  C13 Lexie MacLeod, m. Norman Angus <u>MacPhee</u>, with issue:
     D1 Lizzie MacPhee, m. Billy <u>Campbell</u>, with issue:
          E1   Irene Campbell.
     D2 Billie Angus MacPhee, m. Myra <u>Vaniderstine</u>.
     D3 Maggie Belle MacPhee, m. John <u>Bruce</u>, with issue:
          E1   Murdoch Bruce, m. Olive <u>Lecco</u>.
          E2   Stanley Bruce, m. Anne <u>Thorbron</u>.
          E3   Norman Bruce.
          E4   Mary Bruce, m. Malcolm <u>MacKinnon</u>.
          E5   Ena Bruce, m. Vere <u>Beck</u>.
     D4 Angus MacPhee, m. Miss <u>MacKenna</u>.
     D5 Mary MacPhee, single.
     D6 Capt. Murdoch MacPhee, died WWI.
  C14 Addison MacLeod, single.
B4 Malcolm MacLeod, m. Jessie <u>MacDonald</u>, with issue:
   C1 John MacLeod, born April 15, 1857, m. Annie <u>MacPherson</u>. She was age 24 on April 28, 1891. They had issue:
     D1 Jessie MacLeod, m. Robert <u>Cook</u>. They had one daughter who did not marry.
     D2 Sadie MacLeod, m. Cyril <u>MacGregor</u>, with issue:
          E1   Eric MacGregor, single.
     D3 Belle MacLeod, m. William <u>Cook</u>, with one son.
     D4 Catherine MacLeod, m. Harry <u>Smith</u>.
     D5 Mamie MacLeod, m. _____ <u>Compton</u>.
     D6 Malcolm MacLeod, single.
     D7 Angus MacLeod, died 1922.
   C2 Alexander MacIntyre MacLeod (Sandy "Thresher"), m. Mary <u>MacDonald</u>. He ran a post office. He was born 1854. They had issue:
     D1 Jessie MacLeod, born July 17, 1871, m. Melville <u>Davis</u>.
     D2 Bessie MacLeod, born March 5, 1873, m. John <u>Brown</u>.
     D3 Malcolm MacLeod, born Feb. 20, 1875, m. Mary A. <u>MacLeod</u>.
          E1   Heath MacLeod.
          E2   Alex MacLeod.
          E3   Jennie MacLeod.
          E4   Ella MacLeod.
          E5   Annie MacLeod, twin of Ella.
     D4 Bella MacLeod, born May 16, 1878, m. George <u>Brown</u>.
     D5 Angus MacLeod, born Jan. 4, 1881, m. Lizzie <u>MacNevin</u>.
     D6 John Murdoch MacLeod, 1882-1902, never married, killed in Maine.
     D7 Christie MacLeod, born 1885, m. Alex <u>MacPherson</u> (Sandy Neil).
          E1   Evelyn MacPherson.
          E2   Catherine MacPherson, m. Cecil <u>LeLacheur</u>, with issue:
              F1   Ruth LeLacheur, M.D., m. Dr. <u>Craswell</u>, two children.
              F2   Jean LeLacheur, m. Mr. <u>Ward</u>.
              F3   Mary K. LeLacheur, m. Stan <u>Peardon</u>, with issue:
                  G1 David Peardon.
                  G2 A girl.

        E3   George MacPherson, m. Helen <u>MacPherson</u>, with issue:
            F1   Evelyn MacPherson.
            F2   Carol MacPherson, m. Harold <u>Hicken</u>.
        E4   Mary MacPherson, m. Merril <u>MacPhail</u>, with issue:
            F1   John MacPhail.
            F2   Judy MacPhail.
            F3   Joyce MacPhail.
            F4   Joan MacPhail.
    D8 Flora MacLeod, born Aug. 25, 1889, m. William <u>Hayes</u>.
    D9 Jessie MacLeod, born 1892, m. Leon <u>Janier</u>, from Lynn, Massachusetts.
    D10 Alex MacLeod, born 1893, m. Florence <u>Campbell</u>, with issue:
        E1   Preston MacLeod.
    D11 Roddie MacLeod, born July 1895, m. Isabelle <u>Walte</u>.
  C3 Christie MacLeod (possibly called Bella), single.
  C4 Maggie MacLeod, single.
  C5 Mary MacLeod, m. Mr. <u>Henry</u>.
B5 Alexander MacLeod, 1812-1895, m. Catherine <u>MacLeod</u>, 1819-1894. They were married in Skye and had issue:
  C1 Malcolm MacLeod, 1842-1894, m. Christie <u>Matheson</u>, 1881-1922, issue:
    D1 Christine MacLeod, m. John <u>MacMillan</u>, with issue:
        E1   Malcolm MacMillan.
        E2   Sterling MacMillan, m. Doris _____.
        E3   Doris Jean MacMillan, m. Dana <u>Beverly</u>, with issue:
            F1   Kenneth Beverly.
            F2   Bruce Beverly.
        E4   John MacMillan.
        E5   Twin boy that died in infancy.
    D2 Catherine MacLeod, m. Dan <u>Matheson</u>, with issue:
        E1   Lester Matheson.
        E2   Louise Matheson.
        E3   Edward Matheson.
    D3 Mary Louise MacLeod, m. Will <u>MacLean</u>, with issue:
        E1   Marion MacLean.
        E2   Nina MacLean.
        E3   Edna MacLean.
        E4   Bernice MacLean.
        E5   Charlie MacLean.
        E6   Mildred MacLean, m. Donald Stanley <u>Whiteford</u>, with issue:
            F1   Mary Lynn Whiteford, m. Hugh <u>Bruce</u>, with issue:
                G1   Tara Louise Bruce.
            F2   Willard Robert Whiteford.
            F3   Patricia Dawn Whiteford, m. Kenneth <u>Mitchell</u>.
            F4   Tanis Jean Whiteford, born March 8, 1955.
    D4 Florrie Jessie MacLeod, m. Jim <u>Darrach</u>, with issue:
        E1   Brad Darrach, m. Jackie _____.
        E2   Douglas Darrach, m. Mary _____, with issue:
            F1   Douglas Darrach, Jr.
        E3   Malcolm Darrach, m. Marion _____.
  C2 Angus MacLeod, c. 1846-1908, m. Jessie <u>MacDonald</u>, with issue:

D1   Alex MacLeod, m. Emily <u>Martin</u>, R.N., of Uigg, with issue:
    E1   Jessie MacLeod, m. Art <u>MacLeod</u>, son of Murdoch "Tailor" MacLeod, Orwell, with issue:
        F1   David MacLeod.
            G1   David MacLeod.
            G2   Susan MacLeod.
        F2   Donnie MacLeod.
        F3   Roger MacLeod, m. Elizabeth <u>Jamieson</u>.
    E2   John MacLeod.
D2   Maude MacLeod (adopted), m. Jonathan <u>MacLean</u>, of Edmonton.
    E1   Jessie MacLean, m. Earl <u>Wilcox</u>, with children.
D3   Malcolm MacLeod, died as a child.

C3   Sarah MacLeod, 1848-1932, m. Rod <u>MacLeod</u>, 1850-1923. They are buried in Valleyfield Cemetery. Their children were:
D1   Jessie A. MacLeod, 1880-1950, m. Charles <u>Perry</u>, 1865-1925, issue:
    E1   Marie Perry, born June 21, 1903, m. Robert <u>Moody</u>, with issue:
        F1   Robert Moody.
    E2   Stanley Perry, born 1905, m. Ella <u>McGlaughlin</u>, they had a family.
    E3   Roderick Perry, born July 22, 1907, m. Margie <u>Tyo</u>.
    E4   Minnie Perry, born Aug. 22, 1910, m. Ivan <u>Nelson</u>, with issue:
        F1   Sheila Nelson, born May 15, 1937, m. Joel <u>Franklin</u>.
    E5   Fred Perry, born March 7, 1913, m. Mary _____.
D2   Katie R. MacLeod, m. Lew <u>Hughes</u> of California.
D3   John R. MacLeod.
D4   Rod MacLeod, m. Florence ____. No family.
D5   Maggie MacLeod, m. Malcolm (Sandy Neil) <u>MacPherson</u>, brother to Alex, who m. cousin Christie (daughter of Alexander Mac-Intyre MacLeod), they had issue:
    E1   Catherine MacPherson.
    E2   Rita MacPherson.
D6   Minnie MacLeod.

C4   Mary MacLeod, born April 21, 1854 - 1880. Single.
C5   Annie MacLeod, 1857-1943, m. John D. <u>Bruce</u>, 1853-1935. They were married March 13, 1884, and had issue:
D1   Dan Bruce, m. Margaret <u>Schiller</u>, with issue:
    E1   Ester Bruce, m. Eugene <u>Hartnett</u>, with issue:
        F1   Shirley Hartnett.
        F2   Bob Hartnett.
        F3   Carol Hartnett, m. Dick _____, with issue:
            G1   Mark.
D2   Alexander John Bruce, born Jan. 9, 1886, died young.
D3   Alexander Munroe Bruce, born Jan. 15, 1888, drowned at age sixteen.
D4   Willie A. Bruce, born 1889, m. Mary <u>MacDonald</u> on Jan. 10, 1925. Mary's birth date was Nov. 10, 1899, they had issue:
    E1   Irene Bruce, m. Lloyd <u>Fraser</u>, Montague, with issue:
        F1   Faye Doreen Fraser, R.N.
        F2   Dawn Fraser.

F3　Marlene Fraser.

E2　Bessie Olive Bruce.

D5　Annie Jessie Bruce, 1892, m. John P. MacLeod (see family of Norman MacLeod and Mary MacPherson, Valleyfield), with issue:

E1　Helena MacLeod, m. John MacPherson, with issue:

F1　Shirley MacPherson, m. Peter Madarin, with issue:

G1　Patricia Madarin.

G2　Sean Madarin.

F2　Stanley MacPherson, m. Heather Clark, with issue:

G1　Kath MacPherson.

G2　Suzanne MacPherson.

G3　Gregory MacPherson.

G4　Alex MacPherson.

F3　Frances Irene MacPherson.

F4　John David Bruce MacPherson.

E2　Lillian MacLeod (twin of Helena), m. Bill Hayden, issue:

F1　Wayne Hayden, m. Phyllis Knox, R.N.

F2　John Hayden, m. 1) Wanda MacLeod, daughter of Alex MacLeod, Uigg, m. 2) Sheila Gill.

F3　Carol Hayden, m. Edison Wood, with issue:

G1　Jamie Wood.

G2　Jo-Anne Estelle Delight Wood..

F4　Rita Hayden, m. Danny Ross, with issue:

G1　Margaret Anne Ross.

G2　Donna May Ross.

G3　Lynn Ross.

E3　Rita MacLeod, m. Bud Wallace, with issue:

F1　Harvey Wallace, m. Susan ＿＿＿.

E4　Bruce MacLeod, born Feb. 22, 1924.

E5　Sterling MacLeod, m. Agnes Hewitt, with issue:

F1　Kathy MacLeod.

F2　Bruce MacLeod.

D6　Katherine Bruce, m. Jack MacLeod, Kinross, with issue:

E1　Louise MacLeod, m. Ralph Reynolds, with issue:

F1　Ronnie Reynolds, m. Sharon ＿＿＿.

F2　Gary Reynolds.

F3　Carol Reynolds, m. Derek Godsmark of London, England.

F4　Jackie Reynolds.

E2　Munroe MacLeod, m. Irene MacLeod, with issue:

F1　Barrie MacLeod, m. Brenda ＿＿＿, with issue:

G1　Steven MacLeod.

G2　Karen MacLeod.

E3　Ruth MacLeod, m. Mac Carver.

D7　John Samuel Bruce, born July 7, 1896, died age 16.

D8　Esther Bruce, m. Charles MacLeod, Alliston, with issue:

E1　Dorothy Helen MacLeod, m. Rollie Johnston, with issue:

F1　Merril Johnston, m. Beryl Shelfoon, with issue:

G1　Barbara Leanne Johnston.

G2　Heather Dawn Johnston.

      F2   Pauline Johnston.

      F3   Lynne Johnston.

      F4   Karen Johnston, m. Robert McIntee, RCMP, with issue:
           G1   Robert Todd McIntee.
           G2   Kirk McIntee.

E2   Alexander MacLeod, m. Sybil Estabrooks, with issue:

      F1   Alex MacLeod, m. Faye Drisdell, with issue:
           G1   Kathleen MacLeod.

      F2   Amy Ester MacLeod.

      F3   Jackie MacLeod.

      F4   Janice MacLeod.

      F5   Jill MacLeod.

      F6   Mark David MacLeod.

C6   Alexander John MacLeod, 1861-1940, m. Isabella (Bella) MacDonald, 1865-1961. Her brother was John N. MacDonald of Kilmuir and her niece Mary married Alex's nephew Willie A. (Annie's son). They had issue:

D1   Mary MacLeod, 1890-1969, m. Hugh Laurie, 1885-1955, issue:

E1   Jessie Laurie, born Feb. 8, 1915, m. George Crombie, 1914-1962.

      F1   Janet Crombie, m. Peter Dean.

      F2   Lorraine Crombie, m. Peter Smith, with issue:
           G1   Naomi Smith.

      F3   Margaret Crombie.

      F4   Christine Crombie.

E2   Jack Laurie, born 1918, m. Jean Pettypiece, born 1916.

      F1   Ellen Laurie.

      F2   Linda Laurie, m. Len Seguin.

D2   Christine MacLeod, R.N., 1892-1968, m. Dr. W. R. K. Beck, 1885-1941.

D3   Sally MacLeod (or Sadie), born 1893, m. D. C. Schurman, born 1885.

D4   Catherine MacLeod, born 1895, m. Russell Moore, born 1891.

E1   Isabel Moore, m. Ira Yeo, with issue:

      F1   Kenneth Yeo, m. Shirley Docherty, with issue:
           G1   Ruth Anne Yeo.
           G2   Jonathan Yeo.

      F2   Margaret Yeo, born Oct. 20, 1947, died March 7, 1957.

      F3   Judith Yeo.

      F4   Donald Yeo, m. Linda _____.

E2   Dell Moore, m. Delbert Johnson.

      F1   Catherine Anne Johnson.

E3   David Moore, m. June Beaton, with issue:

      F1   David Beaton Moore.

      F2   Catherine Elan Moore.

E4   Stanhope Moore, m. Eileen Annear, with issue:

      F1   Colleen Areta Moore.

      F2   Catherine Barbara Moore.

      F3   Janet Eileen Moore.

      F4   Alan Stanhope Moore.

      F5   Mary Beth Moore.

E5   Angus Moore, m. Gloria <u>Sencabaugh</u>, with issue:
      F1   Duane Moore.
      F2   Barry Moore.
      F3   Janice Moore.
      F4   Christine Moore.

D5 Rev. John A. MacLeod, 1896-1985, m. Jean <u>Wright</u>, with issue:
    E1   Angus MacLeod, m. Lorraine <u>Bell</u>, with issue:
      F1   Bruce MacLeod.
      F2   Heather MacLeod.
      F3   Angus MacLeod.
    E2   Lulu Irene MacLeod.
    E3   Isabell MacLeod, m. Doug <u>Southam</u>, with issue:
      F1   Gregory Southam.
      F2   Tracy Southam.
      F3   Sandra Southam.
    E4   Annie MacLeod, 1935-1936.
    E5   Ruth Margaret MacLeod, born 1937, died Oct. 29, 1937.
    E6   Christine MacLeod.
    E7   Dr. John MacLeod, m. Maureen <u>Stewart</u>, with issue:
      F1   Allison Anne MacLeod.
      F2   Robert Darryl MacLeod.

D6 Ruth MacLeod, born July 17, 1897, m. Charles <u>Pegg</u>, 1893-1968.
    E1   Christine Pegg, M.D., 1922-1972, m. Dr. David <u>Silverstein</u>.
      F1   Robert Silverstein.
      F2   Christopher Silverstein.
      F3   Peter Silverstein.
    E2   Alex Pegg.
    E3   Angus Pegg, m. Gwen <u>Barr</u>, with issue:
      F1   Neil Pegg.
      F2   William (Bill) Pegg.
      F3   Marion Pegg.

D7 Neil MacLeod, born Oct. 28, 1900, m. Dorrit <u>Paul</u>, born Oct. 28, 1906.

D8 Jessie MacLeod, R.N., born 1902, m. Dr. Carman <u>Rust</u>, born 1906.
    E1   Sandra Rust, m. Don <u>Gilchrist</u>, with issue:
      F1   Trevor Gilchrist.
      F2   Ian Gilchrist.
      F3   Andra Gilchrist.
    E2   Stanhope Rust, m. Judy <u>Murphy</u>, with issue:
      F1   Cameron Rust.
      F2   Dana Alexandra Rust.
      F3   Christine Rust.

D9 Angus Alexander MacLeod, 1903-1926.

D10 Florrie MacLeod, born June 12, 1905, m. 1) Ethan <u>Stewart</u>, born Dec. 11, 1901, and 2) Victor <u>Ling</u>. With issue:
    E1   Dr. David Stewart, m. Margaret <u>Matheson</u>, with issue:
      F1   Susan Stewart.
      F2   Pamela Stewart.
      F3   Jennifer Stewart.
      F4   Phillip Stewart.

E2 Sandra Stewart, m. 1) Harold <u>MacLean</u>, m. 2) Alden <u>Hume</u>. Issue:

F1 Christine Lynn MacLean.

F2 Harold David Stewart MacLean.

D11 Allan Stanhope MacLeod, 1907-1973, m. Dorothy <u>Thomson</u>, 1920-1971.

C7 John Alexander MacLeod, m. Mary <u>MacCormick</u>. They lived in California.

B6 Neil MacLeod, m. Janet <u>Nicholson</u>, lived in Belfast before moving to Valleyfield. He operated a store with his brother Donald. Neil and Janet had issue:

C1 Sarah MacLeod.

C2 Flora MacLeod, born Oct. 25, 1860.

C3 Angus MacLeod, born Nov. 20, 1858, m. Kate <u>Martin</u> on June 17, 1891.

D1 Jennie MacLeod, m. Dan <u>Smith</u>, Newtown, with issue:

E1 Everett Smith.

E2 Lee Smith, m. Marjorie <u>MacDonald</u>.

D2 Annie MacLeod, m. 1) Dan <u>Nicholson</u> and 2) Bob <u>Agnine</u>, with issue:

E1 Ellsworth Nicholson.

E2 Dorothy Nicholson.

D3 Alexander MacLeod, m. Margaret <u>Jacks</u>, with issue:

E1 Bruce MacLeod.

D4 Florrie MacLeod, m. Herb <u>MacKenzie</u>, with issue:

E1 John MacKenzie, died 1972.

E2 Jean MacKenzie, m. Kenneth <u>MacPhee</u>, with issue:

F1 Karen MacPhee.

F2 Heather MacPhee, m. Ricky <u>Campbell</u>.

F3 David MacPhee.

D5 Christine MacLeod, m. Alex <u>MacDonald</u>, with issue:

E1 Marylin MacDonald, m. Mr. <u>Bain</u>.

E2 Laurel MacDonald, m. Paul <u>Ash</u>.

F1 Linda Ash.

F2 Steve Ash.

E3 Robert MacDonald.

E4 Donald MacDonald.

C4 Donald MacLeod, born Dec. 16, 1856.

C5 Mary MacLeod, born July 28, 1855. Baptized Aug. 13, 1857.

C6 Neil MacLeod, m. Rachel <u>Matheson</u>, with issue:

D1 Jessie MacLeod.

D2 John William MacLeod, m. Annie <u>Matheson</u>.

D3 Matheson MacLeod.

D4 Catherine MacLeod.

D5 Stewart Neil MacLeod.

D6 Della MacLeod.

B7 Donald MacLeod, 1826-1868, m. Catherine <u>Nicholson</u>, 1823-1901, daughter of Samuel Nicholson and Mary MacDonald, Belfast, P.E.I., with issue. (All of their children were born in Belfast except Samuel and Marion.)

C1 Mary MacLeod, born 1845, m. Lysander <u>Snow</u>, died in Seattle, Washington.

C2 Flora MacLeod, 1847-1919, died in Gary, South Dakota, m. Donald
J. Bruce, Valleyfield, with issue:
  D1 Malcolm Fraser Bruce, 1865-1952, m. 1) Minnie Adele Border,
      m. 2) Viola Joos. He had five children and died in Jamestown,
      North Dakota.
  D2 Katherine Ann Bruce, 1867-1923, m. Myron Andrew Kenyon.
      They had six children, she died in Gary, South Dakota.
  D3 Barbara Elane Bruce, 1870-1953, m. Frank B. Gordon. They had
      seven children. She died in South Dakota or Portland, Oregon.
  D4 Daniel Raymond Bruce, 1877-1895, died in South Dakota.
  D5 Samuel James Bruce, 1880-1946, m. Rose Lynn Thompson, died
      in Watertown, South Dakota, leaving two children.
C3 Angus Alexander MacLeod, may have died young.
C4 Christina MacLeod, 1855-1944, m. 1) _____ MacWilliams, 2) Milton
Graham. She had two children from her first husband. She died in
Malta, Minnesota, and is buried in Balfor, North Dakota.
C5 James Jay MacLeod, 1856-1926.
C6 Margaret Harriet MacLeod, 1858-1965, m. 1) William Pennington,
from Wisconsin, 2) Stephen Calvin James, Sr. Margaret had five
children and died in California, age 107.
C7 Samuel James MacLeod, born 1860 in Valleyfield.
C8 Marion MacLeod, born 1867 in Valleyfield, m. Robert Lincoln.

This information was compiled by Mary Bruce, Montague; Florence Stewart, Montague; Sarah MacLeod, Maine; and Don and Arline Fifield, Marietta, Georgia.

SAMUEL MACLEOD
SAMUEL MACLEOD AND SELENA BLACKMORE OF MURRAY RIVER

A   Samuel MacLeod, 1829-1899, m. 1) Selena <u>Blackmore</u>, 1831-1866. They are buried in Wilmot Cemetery, Murray River. After Selena's death, Sam m. 2) Barbara <u>MacLean</u>. At the time of his death he was staying with his son Sam. (See Donald Ban's family, Murray Harbour Road.) They had issue:

B1   Donald Ban MacLeod, born 1849, m. Maria <u>Herring</u>,they moved to Kelvington in 1910, to be near his sons Neil and Wallace, who had homesteaded in that area. Donald and Maria's children were:

C1   Selena MacLeod, m. 1) Oliver <u>Beck</u>, 2) David <u>Beck.</u> They lived in Massachusetts.

C2   Neil MacLeod, m. Blanche _____, they lived in Kelvington.

C3   Belle MacLeod, m. Prentiss <u>Polly</u>, in the U.S.A.

C4   Elizabeth Catherine MacLeod, 1882-1951, m. Sandy <u>Graham</u>, they lived in Pilot Mound, Manitoba, and had at least:

D1   Grace Burke, living in London, Ontario.

C5   John MacLeod, died 1892.

C6   Wallace MacLeod, lived in Kelvington, never married.

C7   Silas MacLeod, m. Effie _____, living in Saskatoon at the time of his father's death, later perhaps in British Columbia.

B2   Elizabeth MacLeod, born 1851, m. ____ <u>Conway</u>, Washington, D.C., with issue:

C1   Ester Conway, New Hampshire.

C2   Alice Conway, New Hampshire.

B3   Selena MacLeod, born 1853, m. L. J. <u>Trudeau</u>.

B4   Mary Catherine MacLeod, born 1856, m. 1) William <u>Kemp</u>, m. 2) Hezekiah <u>Gifford</u>, Washington, with issue:

C1   Maude E. Kemp, 1883-1967, m. Donald J. <u>McDonald</u>, 1874-1967, Kelso, Washington, with issue:

D1   William McDonald, died 1904 in infancy.

D2   Allan A. McDonald, born 1906, m. Ruby <u>Primrose</u>, born 1916, Drain, Oregon. They had issue:

E1   Ruby McDonald, m. Percy L. <u>Clifton</u>, Jellico, Tennessee, with issue:

F1   Sharon L. Clifton, m. Steven <u>Torgerson</u>.

F2   Keith Clifton.

F3   Kendall Clifton.

F4   Tony Clifton.

E2   Allan McDonald, m. Joan <u>Wagner</u>, Los Angeles, California, with issue:

F1   Andrew McDonald.

F2   Justina McDonald.

E3   Dan R. McDonald, m. Rosela <u>Perez</u>, Los Angeles, California.

D3   William McDonald, born 1908, m. Grace <u>Eyer</u>, born 1909, Kelso, Washington, with issue:

E1   William McDonald, m. Delores <u>Jones</u>, Kelso, Washington, issue:

F1   Dan McDonald.
F2   Shawn McDonald.
F3   Ryan McDonald.

E2   Kenneth McDonald, m. Margaret <u>Pruitt</u>, Kelso, Washington.
    F1   Kenneth McDonald.
    F2   Bonnie McDonald.

E3   Janet McDonald, m. Lewis <u>Demarest</u>, Kelso, Washington, issue:
    F1   Aimel Demarest.
    F2   Steffanie Demarest.

D4 Donald McDonald, born 1910, m. Gladys <u>Jabusch</u>, born 1913, Kelso, Washington. They had issue:

E1   Larry McDonald, m. Nancy <u>White</u>, Kelso, Washington, with issue:
    F1   Libby McDonald.

E2   Judith McDonald, m. John <u>Stark</u>, Shelton, Washington, with issue:
    F1   Patrick Stark.
    F2   Carmen Stark.
    F3   Christopher Stark.

D5 Grace McDonald, born 1912, died in infancy.

D6 James McDonald, born 1914, m. Winnifred <u>Thomas</u>, born 1915, Phoenix, Arizona, with issue:

E1   Nancy McDonald, m. Thomas <u>Wolfe</u>, Portland, Oregon, with issue:
    F1   Debra Wolfe, m. Bret <u>Riot</u>.
    F2   Thomas Wolfe.
    F3   Timothy Wolfe.
    F4   Rachelle Wolfe.

E2   Rebecca McDonald, m. John <u>Larkin</u>, with issue:
    F1   Laura Larkin.
    F2   Jennifer Larkin.

E3   James McDonald, m. Caryn <u>Close</u>, Phoenix, Arizona, issue:
    F1   James McDonald.

D7 Robert McDonald, 1918-1943, m. Ann <u>Ford</u>, Kelso, Washington.

D8 Mary McDonald, born 1921, m. George <u>Fitchett</u>, Kelso, Washington.

E1   Monte Fitchett, m. Linda <u>Sturgis</u>, Redding, California, issue:
    F1   Megan Fitchett.

E2   Colleen Fitchett, m. Lawrence <u>Foster</u>, Longview, Washington.
    F1   Michelle Foster.
    F2   Trece Foster, born 1964.
    F3   Rae Ann Foster.
    F4   James Foster.
    F5   Anna Foster.

E3   Kathleen Fitchett, m. Harold <u>Fittro</u>, Longview, Washington.
    F1   David Fittro.
    F2   Michelle Fittro.
    F3   Jill Fittro.

E4   Kelly Fitchett.
E5   Mary Fitchett.

C2   Harriet Kemp, m. Otis <u>Innis</u>.
C3   William Kemp.
C4   Phoebe Gifford, m. Christopher <u>Peterson</u>.

B5   Samuel Martin MacLeod, 1859-1924, m. Maria M. <u>Sencabaugh</u>, 1859-1925.
     They are buried in the Murray Harbour South Cemetery. They had issue:
    C1   Mabel MacLeod, 1882-1941, buried in Murray Harbour South Cem-
     etery, m. to Arthur <u>White</u>, born 1887. They lived in Sydney, Nova
     Scotia, with issue:
        D1   Grace White, born 1913, m. Emerson <u>Cahoon</u>, Murray Harbour.
        D2   Pearl White, m. Harry <u>Angel</u>, Ontario.
        D3   Claude White, born 1921, m. Emily <u>Pie</u>, North Sydney, Nova
     Scotia.
        D4   Laura White, m. Parker <u>Lewis</u>, Pictou, Nova Scotia.
        D5   Mina May White, died 1913.
        D6   Nathan White, died 1916.
        D7   Twin, died 1917.
    C2   Ann MacLeod, born 1883, m. ___ <u>Babcock</u>, Watertown, with issue:
        D1   Margaret Babcock, m. Brian <u>Sinns</u>, Boston, Massachusetts.
        D2   Charles Babcock, lived in Boston, Massachusetts.
    C3   Minnie MacLeod, born c. 1884, never married, lived in New Glasgow.
    C4   Eber MacLeod, 1886-1967, m. Ida May <u>Beck</u>, 1894-1940. They are
     buried in Murray Harbour South Cemetery.
        D1   Hazel MacLeod, born 1915, m. Vere <u>Richards</u>, Murray Harbour.
        D2   Leon MacLeod, born 1924, lived in Murray Harbour.
        D3   Marguerite MacLeod, died at one year.
        D4   Windsor MacLeod, died at three weeks.
        D5   Maurice MacLeod, died at seven weeks.
    C5   Ernest MacLeod, born 1889, m. Ella ___, Kelvington, with issue:
        D1   Hazel MacLeod, m. Leonard <u>Rosenkes</u>, Battleford, Saskatchewan.
    C6   Malcolm MacLeod, born c. 1887, m. Mary <u>MacLennan</u>, Wood Islands.
        D1   Samuel MacLeod, lives in Nova Scotia.
        D2   Donald MacLeod.
        D3   George MacLeod, lives in Ontario.
        D4   John MacLeod, lives in Ontario.
        D5   Ester MacLeod, lives in Wood Islands.
        D6   Ethel MacLeod, lives in Massachusetts.
    C7   Frederick MacLeod, 1890-1957, m. Margaret J. <u>Strickland</u>, 1894-1977.
     They are buried in Murray Harbour South Cemetery.
        D1   Marshall MacLeod, m. Edith <u>White</u>, Murray River.
        D2   Doris MacLeod, m. John <u>Ferguson</u>, Murray River.
        D3   Lucille MacLeod, m. Benner <u>Mills</u>, Charlottetown.
        D4   Myna MacLeod, m. Basil <u>MacLeod</u>, Murray River.
        D5   Hope MacLeod, m. Clayton <u>Nicholle</u>, St. John.
        D6   Roy MacLeod, m. Dorothy <u>McLaughlin</u>, St. John.
        D7   Louis MacLeod, m. Doreen <u>Buell</u>, Murray Harbour.
        D8   Bruce MacLeod, m. Virginia <u>Jordan</u>, Murray Harbour.
    C8   Adelaide MacLeod, 1895-1962, m. William A. <u>MacDonald</u>, 1884-1957.
     They are buried in Murray Harbour Cemetery. They had issue:
        D1   John MacDonald, born 1924, m. Carrie _____, Halifax, Nova
     Scotia.
        D2   Murray (Bud) MacDonald, m. Carmen <u>Collier</u>, Murray Harbour.

      D3   Elizabeth MacDonald, m. Lloyd <u>Mellish</u>, Montague.

   C9   Daniel MacLeod, 1897-1966, m. Lucy Jane <u>Livingstone</u>. Daniel is buried in Murray Harbour South Cemetery. They had issue:

      D1   Ernest MacLeod, m. Olive <u>Richards</u>, Murray Harbour.

   C10 Jane MacLeod, 1889-1963, m. Elliot <u>Williams</u>, 1888-1965. They are buried in Beach Point Cemetery.

      D1   John Williams, m. Ann <u>Giddings</u>, Beach Point.

      D2   Fred Williams, 1922-1940, buried in Beach Point Cemetery.

      D3   Carrie Williams, m. Garnet <u>White</u>, Murray Harbour.

      D4   Eva Williams, m. Oliver <u>White</u>, Murray River.

      D5   Ester Williams, m. Craig <u>Bell</u>, White Sands.

      D6   Eber Williams, m. Pearl <u>Irving</u>, Beach Point.

      D7   Eileen Williams.

   C11 John MacLeod, 1902-1918. He was unmarried and is buried in Murray Harbour South Cemetery.

   C12 Daughter, 21 days old, buried in the Murray Harbour South Cemetery.

B6   Florence MacLeod, 1862-1920, m. Alvah M. <u>Jamieson</u>.

B7   Malcolm Rod MacLeod, b. 1866, m. Julia <u>LeLacheur</u>, Ft. Bragg.

Above information was compiled by Nick Wilburn, Murray Harbour, P.E.I., and Grace Burke, London, Ontario, and with dates from the cemetery transcripts at Beaconsfield.

MALCOLM MACLEOD

MALCOLM MACLEOD AND EFFIE MACDONALD OF PINETTE (GLASHVIN)

A   Malcolm MacLeod of Glashvin, Skye, and his wife Effie MacDonald, of Glen-
garry branch of the clan, arrived in Belfast on the *Polly* in 1803. They had issue:
B1   Christina MacLeod, born in Skye about 1782, died in Orwell about 1862,
m. Donald MacQueen. They had children.
B2   Anne MacLeod, m. Alexander MacLeod, from Skye, with issue:
    C1   John MacLeod, m. his cousin Christina MacQueen, with issue:
        D1   Donald MacLeod, of Orwell, died May 3, 1885, aged 53, m.
Catherine MacLeod, sister of Old Captain MacLeod, with issue:
            E1   Murdoch MacLeod, of Vancouver.
        Others unknown.
        D2   William MacLeod, of Sentie, Vernon River, m. his cousin Chris-
tina MacLeod, of Glashvin, with issue:
            E1   Margaret MacLeod, m. Lemuel Hayden.
            E2   Malcolm MacLeod.
            E3   Angus MacLeod.
            E4   Daniel MacLeod.
            E5   Bertha MacLeod.
            E6   Katherine MacLeod.
        Others unknown.
B3   Angus MacLeod (Big), of Glashvin, died Jan. 28, 1885, age 88, m. Margaret
Dockerty, of Skye, who died Dec. 11, 1863, aged 64. They had issue:
    C1   Katherine MacLeod, m. Ewen Martin and had children.
    C2   John MacLeod, of Sentie, Orwell River, died Jan. 13, 1908, aged 89,
m. Mary Martin of Wood Islands, who died July 13, 1888, aged 64.
        D1   John MacLeod, on the old homestead, m. Miss Jenkins of Seal
River. They had children:
            E1   Benjamin MacLeod, m. in British Columbia with a family.
            E2   Margaret MacLeod, m. James Murdoch Campbell, Uigg
and California.
            E3   John MacLeod, m. Mary Jenkins, with issue:
                F1   Malcolm MacLeod, m. Ruth Howlett, with issue:
                    G1   John Alexander MacLeod, m. Ruth Mutch, with
issue:
                        H1   Joyce MacLeod, m. in Cornwall, two children.
                        H2   Linda MacLeod, m. John Van[?], two children.
                        H3   Zelda MacLeod, m. Kevin Jenkins, son of
Clair, Crossroads. They have one child.
                F2   Mary MacLeod, m. 1) Capt. Leslie Murray.
                    G1   Leslie Murray, m. Helen Sullivan, Vernon, issue:
                        H1   Leslie Murray, m. in Fort Augustus.
                Mary m. 2) Sam Martin, Uigg. They had a large family,
among whom is Lloyd Martin, married, living in
Bunbury.
                F3   Gordon MacLeod, m. Florrie Martin, Uigg, with issue:
                    G1   Phemie MacLeod, married in U.S.A.

F4 Isabel MacLeod, m. Capt. Gault <u>Murray</u>, with issue:
  G1 Rev. Lewis Murray, m. Jean <u>Crawdice</u>, retired, living in Shelburne, Nova Scotia, with issue:
    H1 Jean Murray, m. to a <u>Brown</u> in Wood Islands.
    H2 Margaret Murray.
    H3 Gordon Murray, married.
  G2 Gordon Murray, m., died in 1942 in WWII, Air Force.
F5 John Dingwall MacLeod, m. Mary <u>Howlett</u>, with issue:
  G1 Isabel MacLeod, m. John <u>MacKinnon</u>, Kinross, issue:
    H1 Sandra MacKinnon.
    H2 Susan MacKinnon.
    H3 Johanna MacKinnon.
    H4 Hughena MacKinnon.
  G2 A brother.

C3 Mary MacLeod, m. Allan <u>Finlayson</u>, of Eldon, with issue:
  D1 Malcolm Finlayson, m. Belle <u>Anderson</u>, Orwell Cove, with issue:
    E1 Mina Finlayson, m. Charles <u>Nelson</u>.
    E2 Alene Finlayson, m. Frank <u>Reeves</u>, Lot 48, with issue:
      F1 Malcolm Reeves.
      F2 Francis Reeves.
    E3 William Finlayson, m. Miss <u>Ross</u>, with issue:
      F1 Mary Finlayson, m. John James <u>MacDonald</u>, of Glashvin. Other children not known.

C4 Donald A. MacLeod, 1826-1916, merchant by trade, m. Ann <u>MacKenzie</u>, from Flat River. She was born Oct. 1835, died March 1926. Issue:
  D1 Malcolm James MacLeod, D.D., of New York City, married and had children.
  D2 Daevina MacLeod, m. Dr. Harry K. <u>Johnston</u>, Charlottetown. They had children.
  D3 Hector A. MacLeod, was a banker in Hutchinson, Kansas. He was married and had children.
  D4 Ada MacLeod, m. Arthur <u>Putnam</u>, who was a banker in Sackville, New Brunswick. They had children.

C5 Anne MacLeod, m. Angus <u>Martin</u>, of Eldon.
C6 Christina MacLeod, 1828-1924, m. William <u>MacLeod</u> of Sentie, Orwell River, with children.
C7 Mary MacLeod, m. Hector <u>MacKenzie</u> of Flat River, with issue:
  D1 Margaret MacKenzie, m. John Francis <u>Martin</u>, M.D., of Eldon, issue:
    E1 Margaret Martin.
    E2 Elizabeth R. Martin.
    E3 Hector David Martin.
    E4 Mary Martin, m. Blair <u>MacMillan</u>, Calgary, with issue:
      F1 Aubrey MacMillan, barrister.
      F2 Francis MacMillan (B.Sc. University of Alberta).
      F3 Angus Malcolm MacMillan.
      F4 Christine MacMillan.

C8 Malcolm MacLeod, single.
C9 Margaret MacLeod, single.

C10 Angus MacLeod, of Glashvin, Pinette, m. Catherine MacRae of Point Prim.
  D1 Malcolm MacLeod, on old homestead, m. Alene MacPhee, with issue:
    E1 Jean MacLeod, died in infancy.
    E2 Kathryn MacLeod, m. Bill Foxton, Manitoba.
    E3 Florence MacLeod, m. Preston Gillis, Point Prim. Living in Dedham, Massachusetts, with four children.
  D2 Belle MacLeod, m. Rev. Mr. Cleave, United Church. They have three children in Sarnia.
  D3 Cyrus MacLeod, m. at age 80 to Mrs. Bernice MacWilliams. She was a cousin of Mrs. Damien Ross.
  D4 John William MacLeod, killed in 1917, WWI.
C11 Effie MacLeod, single.
C12 Sarah MacLeod, m. Robert MacWilliams of Eldon.
B4 Malcolm MacLeod, of West River, m. Miss MacLean, Point Prim.
B5 Donald MacLeod, of Surrey, m. Miss MacLeod. (See MacLeods of Surrey.)
B6 Catherine MacLeod, m. Mr. MacFadyen, of West River.
B7 Mary MacLeod, m. Findlay Dockerty of Glashvin, they had children.
B8 Catherine MacLeod, m. Angus Dockerty, with issue:
  C1 Donald Dockerty.
  C2 Malcolm Dockerty, of St. Peters Road, Cardigan.
B9 William MacLeod, Point Prim, died Feb. 5, 1885, age 85, m. Mary Lamont, had children, among others was:
  C1 Eunice MacLeod, m. Roderick MacLeod of Point Prim, they had children, among others was:
    D1 Essie or Jessie MacLeod.
B10 William MacLeod, born in Skye in 1783, died 1850, m. Catherine MacPherson, they emigrated to Uigg in 1831. They had issue:
  C1 Malcolm MacLeod.
  C2 John MacLeod.
  C3 Donald MacLeod (soldier in Civil War).
  C4 Angus MacLeod (see Lorne Valley family).
  C5 Alexander MacLeod.
  C6 Norman MacLeod.
  C7 Effie MacLeod.
  C8 Mary MacLeod.
  C9 Katherine MacLeod.
  C10 Jessie MacLeod, m. Angus R. MacSwain, Lorne Valley, with issue:
    D1 Christie A. MacSwain, m. H.E. Gurney.
    D2 Daniel MacSwain.
    D3 Mary MacSwain.
    D4 William MacSwain.
    Two others, names unknown.

Information obtained from *Skye Pioneers and the Island*, by Malcolm A. MacQueen, with some additions.

John Torquil MacLeod
John Torquil MacLeod and Jane Munro of Little Sands

A John Torquil MacLeod, of Raasay, and his wife Jane <u>Munro</u> had nine children who emigrated on the *Ocean*. John and Jane were deceased before emigration (1835).

B1 Son, name unknown, settled in Hartsville area.

B2 Donald MacLeod, settled in Hartsville area (see Hopedale family), issue:
    C1 John D. MacLeod, "The Sheriff," m. Christie Ann <u>MacKenzie</u>.
    C2 John E. MacLeod, m. Mary Ann <u>Nicholson</u>.
    C3 Angus MacLeod, unmarried, remained on the farm.

B3 John Torquil MacLeod, Jr., probably the eldest of the family, m. Sarah <u>MacLeod</u>. (See family of John MacLeod and Mary MacQueen of Rona.) They settled on a farm by the shore of Pictou Island. Sarah later lived in Little Sands where she lived to the age of 102. A widow for over forty years, she died in 1917.
    C1 Torquil MacLeod, 1856-1914, m. Christy <u>MacLean</u>, died July 6, 1936, at 80 years. Buried in Little Sands. They had issue:
        D1 Norman MacLeod, conductor on the New York Central Railways, Boston, Massachusetts.
        D2 Duncan MacLeod, engineer on the New York Central Railways, New York.
        D3 John Torquil MacLeod, died 1956, age 72, m. Effie Ann <u>MacLean</u>, who died 1942, aged 49. She was half sister of the Honourable J. D. MacLean, once Premier of British Columbia.
            E1 Ernest MacLeod, m. 1) Dora <u>Jones</u>, with issue, m. 2) Evelyn <u>Maxwell</u>. They retired to Little Sands.
                F1 Heather MacLeod, m. Kenneth <u>Dudyinski</u>, three children, Scarborough, Ontario.
            E2 Jean MacLeod, m. Ralph <u>Simpson</u>.
                F1 Donna Simpson, m. Bill <u>Ranahan</u>, New Glasgow, four living children.
                F2 David Simpson, m. Heather _____, no family, Alberta.
                F3 Janna Simpson, not married, Vancouver.
            E3 John Duncan MacLeod, m. Isabel <u>DeYoung</u>, Kitchener, Ontario.
                F1 John MacLeod, Jr.
                F2 Ernest MacLeod, m. Johanna <u>Green</u>, Kitchener, Ontario.
                F3 Gerald MacLeod.
            E4 Alexander MacLeod, m. Marie <u>Heinz</u>, with three adopted children, Sheraton Lake, British Columbia.
                F1 Ronald MacLeod.
                F2 Linda MacLeod, married in British Columbia, two children.
                F3 Laura MacLeod, married in British Columbia, two children.
            E5 Isabel MacLeod, m. Bill <u>Dayton</u>, Victoria, with issue:
                F1 John Dayton.

    F2 Thomas Dayton.

    F3 Kerry Dayton.

   E6 Murdoch MacLeod, m. Marguerite _____, Mesa, Arizona.

    F1 Gregory MacLeod.

    F2 Lynn MacLeod.

   E7 Anne MacLeod, m. Roy Simpson, brother of Ralph, Orono, Ontario.

    F1 Dennis Simpson.

    F2 Mark Simpson.

    F3 Stewart Simpson.

    F4 Paul Simpson.

  D4 Sarah MacLeod, 1879-1937, m. John Angus Blue, Hopefield, issue:

   E1 Tina Marion Blue, died at 8 months in 1919.

   E2 Sam Blue, m. Margaret Colpitts, Salisbury, New Brunswick. They had a family.

   E3 Alden Blue, m. Louise Stewart. They farm in Hopefield, issue:

    F1 Kevin Blue.

    F2 Elaine Blue.

   E4 James Blue, m. in Moncton, three children.

   E5 Jennie Blue, m. George Blue, Little Sands, with issue:

    F1 Laurie Blue, m. Bernice Stewart, with issue:

     G1 David Blue.

     G2 Heidi Blue.

     G3 Ronald Blue.

   E6 Evelyn Blue, m. Heath Larter, Hampshire, with issue:

    F1 Marilyn Larter, m. Keith Kennedy, Sherwood, issue:

     G1 Ruth Kennedy.

     G2 Sarah Kennedy.

     G3 Rizpah Kennedy.

    F2 Allison Larter.

    F3 Hilton Larter.

    F4 Wayne Larter.

    F5 Brian Larter.

    F6 Jennifer Larter.

  D5 Christina Ann MacLeod, died 1909, aged 17, buried in Little Sands.

B4 Ann Bhan MacLeod, m. John MacLeod (see Rona).

B5 Catherine MacLeod, m. John Livingstone, farmer of High Bank.

B6 Effie MacLeod, m. John Donald MacLennan, Fladday Island, Scotland. Issue:

  C1 Sandy MacLennan, m. Ann Martin, they lived in Peters Road, and had a large family, among whom was:

   D1 Charles, m. Mary Ferguson of Bethel, P.E.I.

B7 Mary MacLeod, m. Angus Stewart of Wood Islands. They had children.

B8 Betty MacLeod, m. John MacKenzie of Dundee, P.E.I. They had children.

B9 Jean MacLeod, m. John Beaton of Flat River, with issue:

  C1 Jack Beaton

  C2 Alex Beaton, m. Jessie MacDonald of Cape Breton.

Information provided by Rev. B. MacLeod, Montreal; Harold MacLeod, Montague; and cemetery transcriptions.

A Rona (Skye) Family in Canada
Articles by Father Bennet MacLeod

Rev. Father Bennet MacLeod was born in Ste. Teresa, Quebec, and made his first of several trips to Prince Edward Island about 1936. It was during this time he gathered information on his family and compiled a small booklet of family history. Unfortunately we were unable to locate a copy, but when in Edinburgh Library in 1982, I found the following articles, which he had submitted to the *Clan MacLeod Magazine*. There may be errors in the genealogy but we chose not to make any changes. (H.S.M.)

A Rona (Skye) Family in Canada

Some hundred and sixty years ago or more, an emigrating fever broke out in the Highlands of Scotland, and year after year hundreds of clansmen said good-bye to their native glens and bens, to seek new homes and life prospects across the ocean. In the nineteenth century alone, more than one hundred thousand Highlanders settled in Canada, where they increased so well that at last census of the Dominion in 1931, the Scotch population was 1,346,350; and for the sole French Province of Quebec, 35,778. No wonder then that the familiar Scottish clan names are found here, writ big everywhere and many a time in the place of Highest Honour.

The first migration of which we have record took place in 1772, when the ship *Alexander* landed in Scotchport, Prince Edward Island, with 210 passengers from South Uist. Thereafter sailings became more and more frequent; passage money was little, and the movement increased rapidly. Dr. MacCulloch (*Misty Isle of Skye*) tells us that: "Emigration had then the glamour of a new idea, and was palatable when the people resorted to it of their own free will. An emigrant ship would call into one of the lochs by night, and, the next morning, a whole township would be tenantless, its inhabitants having embarked to seek fortune beyond the seas." Numerous letters, which passed between the government and the Chief of MacLeods, beseeching him to take steps to prevent emigration if he could, still exist in the muniment room of Dunvegan Castle.

In 1803, at least five ships left the Highlands of Scotland for Canada alone. The *Favourite* from Ullapool landed 500 Highlanders at Pictou, Nova Scotia; the *Alexander* landed "a number" (not stated) at the same place, from Lewis. The *Polly*, the *Dykes* and the *Oughton* disembarked about 800 at Charlottetown, P.E.I., mostly from Skye.

The *Polly* was commanded by Captain Neil MacLeod of Glashvin and carried as Spiritual Advisor the Rev. Samuel MacLeod of Raasay. A monument still stands in the town of Belfast, P.E.I., marking the place where those early pioneers landed and on it are engraved the names of the leaders. As we may read in the interesting book of Malcolm MacQueen, *Skye Pioneers and the Island*, the *Polly* settlers were very successful, under the benevolent patronage of Lord Selkirk, and their success was a constant invitation for their clansfolk left in Skye to come and join them.

Passing over many intervening sailings, we come down to the year 1835. It was in that year, that our Rona family set forth on their pioneering enterprise. They sailed in a ship named *Ocean* (a very appropriate name for the journey before them) under the command of a relative of Captain Neil MacLeod, of the *Polly*, a young and audacious fisherman of Rona, Captain John MacLeod, who was not on his first trip to Canada. Most of the MacLeods were seamen, especially the new settlers of P.E.I. and frequently they sailed to Scotland , to load their ship with cattle (cows and sheep) for their new farms, exchanging them for fish and furs. It was certainly then the "Romance of Poaching in the Highlands." The folks of the two hemispheres were in surprisingly frequent relation. No wonder then, that the chief of the MacLeods was unable to stop emigration. The good race of the Norsemen was well awake in those early days.

The season was well chosen, for the *Ocean* arrived in Charlottetown on a bright summer day, August 1, 1835. How many were crowded in the ship we know not. We may assume, however, they were in goodly number, for in addition to the Captain's many relatives, were those of his wife, the MacLeods of Raasay, those of his mother, the Munros of Kilmuir (Skye), his grandmother's relatives, the MacQueens of Lochaber, his cousins Norman, Donald, James, Angus, John and Neil MacLeod: his clansfolks, the MacLennans of Fladday Isle, the MacKenzies, MacLeans, MacPhees, Gillies, Beatons, Martins, Mathesons, Morrisons, and Nicholsons, from Rona, Raasay and even from the Braes of Portree.

After several months of peregrinations east and west of Charlottetown, a couple of the Captain's wife's brothers settled with a party of the MacKenzies near Hartfield, P.E.I., in a very fertile district, which they named Hunter River, in remembrance of Hunter River in Australia, where a few years before a party of the MacLeods from Raasay had settled and from whom seductive letters had arrived at intervals, but they preferred to follow "Captean Ian Dubh." Another MacLeod from Raasay chose his land on the lovely shore of Little Sands, 40 miles south-east of Charlottetown. But Captain John MacLeod probably found the soil too good—too stoneless—nothing in it to remind him of the Rock Bound Isle of Rona from which he had originated. He chose his lands in Lots 60-62 of Queen's County, north of Wood Islands, in the highest and rockiest point of the Province, where fir and timber trees multiplied in their savage growth. He named this wild chosen land "Rona," in remembrance of the wee Scottish Isle, from which his family came.

In 1837 only these lots were granted to the Captain, to his two brothers, and to the greater part of the *Ocean* passengers. The forests were cleared out and the stony hills of Rona became a good farming district. Unfortunately, forty years ago, to please, I suppose, the American tourists, the name was changed to "Mount Vernon," although the home of the great Washington was certainly not in P.E.I., in the nests of the Loyalists, who stood against them.

"Ian Dubh," Captain John MacLeod, was the son of John MacLeod, fisherman of Rona (deceased before emigration) and his second wife, Mary Munro, and grandson of another John MacLeod (Raasay) and Mary MacQueen of Lochaber. Captain John and his two brothers lived a happy life in their new homes, surrounded by their clansfolks.

The transition from the sea to the fields was not a violent one. The settlers were sailors and fishermen for the first few years. Cods, lobsters, herrings, and oysters were in abundance. A few acres from their shore they could find an easy living from the sea, while the new lands were not yet ready for farming. In their spare time, most of the evenings were spent together around the fireplace, when the old folks would recall stories, songs, and dances of the past days in Skye, and so many beloved figures left behind. The clan spirit was so great in those days, that in order to pay a visit to their clansfolks, men and women walked from 20 to 60 miles (Little Sands, Hunter River, etc) through fields and forests, as if it were an ordinary trip.

When Captain John had cleared a large piece of land, he became a successful farmer. He died at the ripe old age of 86 (1897), without giving any previous signs of illness, while busily employed in feeding his cattle; his wife née Annie Bhan MacLeod (Raasay), died in 1907, at the age of 92—she had baked that same day. Two wonderful examples of an industrious "Hold Fast!" until the end. Now they rest in peace, near their Raasay people, in the beautiful country cemetery of Little Sands; but their memory is still alive throughout the East of the Province.

THE MUNROS

Captain John MacLeod was accompanied to Canada by his mother, née Mary Munro, and her three brothers, John, Alexander and Dan Munro, who settled at the Head of Montague, P.E.I. The Munros were closely related to the MacLeods, as we have said. Mary Munro was the widow of John MacLeod of Rona, Skye: her sister Jane was the wife of John Torquil MacLeod, Raasay, the Captain's brother-in-law; and her brother John married Mary MacLeod, the Captain's half sister. The Munros were certainly a strong race if we judge by their descendants, the Munro-MacLeans of P.E.I., all above six feet, one of them, at one time chief of Police in Vancouver, was the tallest man in Canada. Most of them are very successful; the very Honourable D. A. MacLean for example, Premier of B.C., and now President of the Federal Farm Loans in Ottawa: Harry MacLean, Superintendent of the Dominion Construction Co., Ottawa and Toronto; George Allan MacLean and his wife are both descendants of the Munros; Mr. G. A. MacLean is a Conservative Leader in Queen's County, where he has been several times candidate. He is a gentleman farmer in Lewes, P.E.I.; Donald Munro MacLean, brother of Mrs. G. A. MacLean, grandson of John Munro and Mary MacLeod is on one of the best farms of Wood Islands.

THE MACLEODS

Now begins the great puzzle: the enumeration of the MacLeods from Rona and Raasay who accompanied Captain John to Canada, and a nomenclature of their actual descendants as they are known.

PART FIRST
THE MACLEODS FROM RONA (SKYE)

The late John MacLeod of Rona Isle had three children by his first wife (name unknown):

1. Roddie, married in Scotland to Jean Gillies. He took a farm in Rona, P.E.I., next to his brothers', but a few years later he left the Island with his family. He has not been traced as yet.

2.   Catherine, who died unmarried.
3.   Mary, who married John Munro, the Captain's uncle, and settled in Montague, P.E.I., where a few of their descendants may still be met.

By his second wife, Mary Munro, he had nine children, who landed in P.E.I.:

1.   "Ian Dubh," i.e. Captain John MacLeod.
2.   Alexander.
3.   Sarah.
4.   Ann.
5.   Effie.
6.   Beatrice.
7.   Catherine.
8.   Ann-Mary.
9.   Maggie, who did not come from Scotland with the others.

Captain John MacLeod and Annie Bhan MacLeod from Raasay, married in P.E.I., had two sons and two daughters.

1.   John "Dubh."
2.   John Bhan.
3.   Ann, all born in Rona, P.E.I.
4.   Mary.

John MacLeod, Ste. Thérèse, Quebec

John "Dubh," born in 1848, went to the local school until the age of 17. Here he acquired a fairly good learning from the well-known Rev. John Sutherland, the Presbyterian Spiritual Advisor of the Congregation, a native of Skye, who had been a missionary in Australia. John "Dubh" left the Island on a trip to Skye with his father's cargo. In 1870 he took up railway building in Nova Scotia, Ontario, and Quebec, where, alone among the French Canadians, he married Eleanor Sanche, a granddaughter of Don Jose Sanche, a nobleman of Castille, Spain. In 1879 he returned with his wife and first child to Rona, P.E.I., to the old farm where he built a new house and barn, which still stand. To please his wife, who could not get accustomed to Gaelic, he returned to Ste. Thérèse de Bainville, Que., 20 miles north of Montreal, where he was received by his father-in-law Mr. Sanche, a grand white-bearded, old gentleman, who loved his Scottish son-in-law as one of his own, and granted him a stock of cattle for his new farm, which he cleared from the woods as his father had done in Rona. John "Dubh" introduced in Quebec the "MacIntyre" potato seeds he had from P.E.I. and today a few French farmers still grow this variety and call them "MacLaudes." John MacLeod became a very successful farmer and gardener. 1885 was for him and his wife a very mournful year. An epidemic of diptheria spread around Montreal, and as no serum was yet known the disease emptied the home. In one month, John MacLeod lost his four children, John, Joseph, Angus, and Hector. Providence, however, later granted to John MacLeod three more sons: Simon, Mark, and Bennet, who are still strong and healthy. John "Dubh" knew Gaelic and English, but in this settlement he had to speak French outside his home. He was a very active farmer, but peaceful and quiet, as a seaman he was respected and loved by his French countrymen.

1n 1906, in a general exhibition for the counties of Terrebonne and Two Mountains, John MacLeod was the first on the prize-winning list for cattle and farming. In 1921, exhibitor at Wembly Exhibition (England) he won the first prize for honey. He died in Ste. Thérèse in 1930, at the ripe old age of 82, still "Dubh," dark-haired (a characteristic of the Rona MacLeods) and having the appearance of a man of 50. Ill only one day, to conquer his acute pain, he went out a few hours before his death to stimulate himself in chopping wood. He certainly "held fast" to the end. He rests in peace with his wife (deceased in 1931) in Ste Thérèse Catholic Cemetery.

The three sons of John "Dubh" are the nimrods of the Laurentians, their favourite sport is big-game hunting in the wild virgin forests of Northern Quebec:

1. Simon MacLeod (53), Ste. Thérèse, bridgeman on the C.P.R. who married Annie Filion.
2. Mark MacLeod (52), farmer and locomotive engineer, who married Adeline Chapleau, has one son Edward MacLeod (24), married to Jeanine Cardinal, with issue—four daughters.
3. The Rev. Bennet MacLeod (43), who had his B.A. in Ste. Thérèse College and completed his studies in France and Africa, held his functions as a Catholic Priest in different Parishes of Montreal and Glengarry, Ont. and is now curate in the oldest Irish Church of Montreal, St. Gabriel's. He is a fervent member of the clan society.

John "Ban" MacLeod, the Captain's second son, died at the age of 27.

The Mathesons

Ann MacLeod, the Captain's eldest daughter, born 1845, married Alexander Matheson, farmer of Whim Road, P.E.I., they are both buried in Valleyfield, P.E.I. and their children, Annie, Mary and John Alexander Matheson are living somewhere in Boston, U.S.A.

The Rosses

Mary "Bhan " MacLeod, the Captain's youngest daughter, born 1858, married John Ross, a native of Skye. They lived on the Captain's farm and spoke only Gaelic in their home. They are interred in Caledonia, P.E.I. She passed away in her home in 1932, after 16 years of acute sufferings, a marvel of patience and faith. Children, four sons:

1. John Ross, who died in Halifax in 1916, at the age of 25, while training in the 105th battalion of the Canadian Army.
2. Padruig Ross (48), farmer in Mt. Vernon, unmarried.
3. Willie Ross (45), farmer and fisherman, Culloden, P.E.I., who married Minnie Acorn, with issue:
    1. Lillian Ross (23), married to Clayton Buell (deceased), Hopefield, P.E.I., mother of three young children.
    2. Mary (21), married to Harry MacLeod, fisherman, Hopefield.
    3. Jessie (16) and John Robert (14).
4. John A. Ross (40), youngest son of Mary Bhan MacLeod, unmarried, lives on the old farm of Capt. John.

Alexander MacLeod, the Captain's young brother was only 16 when he left Scotland. He later married Mary Nicholson, a native of Scotland, daughter of Neil Nicholson of Orwell, P.E.I. They settled on a farm near their relatives in Rona, P.E.I., where they both died in the same year, 1895, and were buried in Caledonia with their children Neil and Annie. Only one of their children is still living, Mary MacLeod, Mount Vernon, the widow of Norman MacKenzie, who taught school in P.E.I. for over fifty years. Mrs. Norman MacKenzie, although 83 years of age, retains a wonderful memory. I am indebted to her for most of the information I collected on the Island. She transmitted them to me in her mother's Gaelic tongue which she speaks fluently. The researches were quite difficult, as in Scotland the records were not officially kept until 1850, and in P.E.I. only in 1916. I visited the old Presbyterian Churches, but I could not find half the family records, which most of the time consisted of traditions and those obtained from the old family Bible. As to my own family, the house at Rona (now Mt. Vernon), was burned last November, and the owner, Mr. John Ross, died in January. The old-time letters of my ancestors, both of Rona and Raasay, correspondence from Scotland and Australia, old frames and souvenirs were completely destroyed.

Mrs. Norman MacKenzie's three sons all served during the Great War.

1. Malcolm, the eldest, died a few years after his return.
2. Alexander, the second, now a merchant in Wood Islands, P.E.I., was badly gassed in the war and has only one lung. He married Ruth MacLean and has three children: Mary, Donald and Sarena.
3. Neil, the third son (40), who served four years at the front as a machine-gunner, returned home with his health ruined. When told to apply for the Returned Soldiers' Pension, he brusquely replied, "Never—I did not go to war for money, but—for my Country!" He lives with his old mother and his sister, Mrs. Saunders and several young nephews and nieces, Saunders, Wilsons, MacPhersons, and MacDonalds, among whom Mrs. Norman MacKenzie appears as a well loved chief.

Sarah MacLeod, the Captain's eldest sister, born in Rona (1816), who married her brother-in-law, John Torquil MacLeod of Raasay.

Ann MacLeod, who married Dan Gillies, of Rona, P.E.I. They lived till their death on the neighbouring farm, west of Captain John's. Their children: John, Roddie, Malcolm, and Sarah, settled in Glen-Ross, Ontario. The only son of Dan Gillies and Ann MacLeod I had the pleasure to meet is James Gillies (78), a stone cutter, a real globe-trotter, who at his old age returned to Rona, to a wee corner of the old estate, where he lives in all the merriment of his celtic wit. Jimmy is the most joyful fellow on the Island.

Effie MacLeod, who married Peter MacLean, a native of Skye, in Belle River, P.E.I. One of their daughters married John Blue and a few of their grandchildren live in Montague, P.E.I.

Beatrice MacLeod, who died unmarried.

Catherine MacLeod, who married Malcolm Nicholson, of Orwell, P.E.I. with issue.

Ann Mary MacLeod, who married Archie MacLean of Little Sands, P.E.I., with issue:

1. John Archie (70), ex-fireman of Vancouver, now at his Pension in Mount Pleasant, British Columbia.
2. John Donald (63), a fisherman, Little Sands, married to Jessie MacPhee, with issue:
3. Chester (31), electrician in Charlottetown.
4. Archie (29).
5. Leonard (27).
6. Mac (20), fisherman and lobster trappers with their father.
7. May, the only daughter (25).
8. Laughlin (59).

* Maggie MacLeod was left in Skye, where she married William Matheson, they came to Canada only in 1841. Mr. William Matheson, was the founder of Glen William, P.E.I., where his grandson Angus (40) is still a prosperous farmer.

Part Second
The MacLeods from Raasay

John Torquil MacLeod, Raasay, and his wife Jane Munro, both deceased before emigration, had nine children on the *Ocean*.

Two of their sons, settled in Hunter River, near Hartfield, P.E.I., one of them left three sons well known in the Maritimes:

1. The sheriff John D. who married Christie Ann MacKenzie, aunt of the distinguished Minister of Glengarry, the Rev. D. M. MacLeod of Alexandria, Ontario.
2. John E. MacLeod, the second, was also married. Both families are widely scattered, and I did not have an opportunity to meet any one of them.
3. The third son, Angus, was unmarried, and remained on the farm.

John Torquil MacLeod (Junior), probably the eldest of this family, married the Captain's eldest sister, Sarah. They settled on a farm by the seashore of Pictou Island, where on a stormy night, a few times in a decade, the "fiery ship" may be seen. Is it a tale? Is it a Fairy or Fiery ship? Is it the ship that carried the stolen treasures of the pirate Captain Kidd? Or the French ship that came to hide on the coast the jewels and the crown of France, when poor Louis XVI and Marie Antoinette were beheaded during the Revolution? On the same coast of Little Sands and Wood Island, the French, before leaving the country in 1760, are supposed to have buried their gold. It was in this romantic Little Sands which recalls the fairy coasts of the Western Islands of the Highlands, that Sarah MacLeod lived to the extraordinary age of 102. A widow since over 40 years, the chief of the family, dark-haired to the end like the Rona MacLeods, with no apparent infirmities, she quietly passed away in 1917.

* The descendants of William Matheson state that William's wife was Mary Martin. Maggie may have been his first wife.

MY QUEBEC COUSINS
ARTICLE BY CATHERINE MCLELLAN

My brother Angus met me at the railway station with the box sleigh and the red mare. It was an Easter week-end in March in the late 1930s and my first visit home since Christmas. Travelling conditions were different then—cars didn't run on country roads in winter, at least not in P.E.I., and the train trip was slow, thirty miles in three or four hours with stops every couple of miles to unload passengers, mail and freight.

The previous year I'd found a job in Charlottetown which paid a little more than school teaching and was just as interesting, but we had to be in the office on Saturday mornings and thus the weekends were short. Angus was home from Mount Allison University for the year, partly because his help was needed on the farm, but mostly because the funds to pay his college expenses were not available; for these were the depression years.

It was a mild evening but there was still enough snow to make a sleigh ride pleasant and, as the red mare jogged along, I asked Angus for news, although I always kept in close touch with home by my mother's weekly letters. "Well," said Angus, "we had a real interesting visitor this week, a cousin of Mom's, a Father MacLeod." "You mean Rev. Roderick MacLeod?" I asked referring to my mother's first cousin, a missionary. "No," said Angus, "I mean the Rev. Father MacLeod, the one with the French accent from the Province of Quebec." Father MacLeod was brought to our home by a bachelor cousin who knew we had a spare room, a downstairs bedroom off the parlour which was reserved for guests. Father MacLeod had stayed for several days and my father, who knew every family for miles around, had driven him to see his relatives. My father's opinion of Father MacLeod was that he was a very fine man and not a bit bigoted.

Later, in answer to my queries, my mother told me that Father MacLeod's father was a young cousin of hers from our Scottish community who, years before, had gone to Quebec to work in the lumber woods for the winter. In the spring he came back to the old home and community with a bride from Quebec. Imagine bringing a French-speaking bride into a home and community in which the preferred language was Gaelic. The young couple must each have known enough English to communicate in that language but, in MacLeod's home, as in all the homes in that district, the language spoken would have been Gaelic, although English was used in the schools; and in the only church, which was Presbyterian, both languages were used. My mother said friction apparently developed between the bride and her mother-in-law and this came to a climax when the daughter-in-law "set a hen on the Sabbath." I can understand the family reaction, although I can't approve of it. Even in my childhood our church "kept the Sabbath" very rigorously. No avoidable work was done on Sunday. On Saturday, shoes were shined, baths taken, the vegetables and desserts prepared for Sunday dinner, so that Sunday could be, as far as possible, a day of rest. On Sunday you went to church and Sunday school, took a walk, read a book, usually the Bible, set an ample table for family and guests, fed the stock, and milked the cows. Only works of necessity and mercy were permitted.

But setting a hen could be done any day of the week if the hen were broody or "clucky." Before the days of incubators, chickens were hatched by having a broody hen sit on twelve or thirteen eggs for three weeks. Hens, of course, had to be broody, or anxious to sit. The poor bride, no doubt trying to be helpful had set a broody hen on a nest of eggs on a Sunday. This caused such a row that the young couple moved back to her home and her people in Quebec and, as far as I know, never came back. When they died they left a large family and here was Father MacLeod back on the Island and looking for his roots.

I asked my mother if she had told Father MacLeod about the broody hen. She was shocked at my question. "Of course not," she said. "No doubt his parents told him all they should." Father MacLeod did tell my parents that his father had taken some *MacIntyre* potatoes from the Island for seed, and they became popular in the local area where they were known as MacLeod potatoes.

Angus finally got back to Mount Allison in time to graduate in 1939 and to enlist in the Air Force. During his training in Quebec, he again saw Father MacLeod. Later, after the Second World War, Angus went into politics and when he was Minister of Fisheries in the Diefenbaker Government, Father MacLeod visited him a couple of times. Angus planned to visit him in Quebec but, before this happened, Father MacLeod took sick and died. There has been no further contact but we know there is in Quebec a family of MacLeods who speak French rather than English or Gaelic, all because of a critical mother-in-law and a broody hen.

© Catherine McLellan, published in *Atlantic Advocate*, August, 1978.

JOHN MACLEOD
JOHN MACLEOD AND 1) SCOTTISH WIFE AND 2) MARGARET MACPHERSON OF EAST LINE ROAD

A   John MacLeod m. 1) a Scottish woman. They came to P.E.I. circa 1835 from the Isle of Raasay. They lived on East Line Road, Lot 22, with issue:

B1   Murdoch MacLeod was left in Scotland with his cousin John MacKenzie, with whom he learned the tailoring trade. He and MacKenzie emigrated to Montreal and Toronto where MacKenzie died, then he came to the Island and lived for a time with his brothers before finally settling in Bedeque. His wife's name unknown.

    C1   Maggie MacLeod, m. _____ Duncan, lived in Baievert, New Brunswick, with issue:

       D1   Mary Duncan.

       D2   William Duncan.

B2   Donald MacLeod.

B3   Roderick MacLeod, 1825-1865, m. Jane Nicholson, 1840-1960 [sic], lived on East Line Road, with issue:

    C1   John MacLeod, 1857-1879.

    C2   Donald MacLeod, born 1859.

    C3   Roderick MacLeod, 1866-1893.

B4   Christine MacLeod, died Feb. 29, 1868.

B5   Mary MacLeod, m. Alexander MacLeod, a catechist who preached to the Gaelic people in the back settlements (Peters Road, Lot 63), with issue:

    C1   Mary MacLeod, m. _____ Sinclair.

B6   Catherine MacLeod, 1821-1904, m. 1) Donald Gillis, 2) Allan Bethune, 1820-1891, with issue:

    C1   James John Bethune, 1861-1926, m. 1) Maggie Christine MacLeod, 1864-1902, with issue:

       D1   Margaret Jane Bethune, 1887-1986, m. William Thomas Veale, 1884-1920, with issue:

          E1   Jeanette Katherine Veale, retired school teacher, living in Calgary.

       D2   Alexander Douglas Bethune, 1890-1912.

       D3   Allan Ferguson Bethune, 1892-1904.

       D4   John Gillis Bethune, m. 1) Ada Olive Merrill, 1904-1971, issue:

          E1   Denise Margaret Bethune, m. Donald Keith Johnston, M.D.

             F1   Shelley Margaret Johnston, m. Walter Stansfield Duykers.

             F2   Noreen Patricia Johnston, m. David Douglas Jones, issue:

                G1   Douglas Keith Jones.

             F3   Donna Beth Johnston, m. David Victor Osteraas.

          E2   Doreen Luverne Bethune, m. Gilbert Hugh Binnington, issue:

             F1   Dawn Luverne Binnington, m. Peter Jackson.

             F2   David John Binnington.

             F3   Lloyd Binnington.

John Gillis Bethune m. 2) Amy Wright Heddle.

D5   Edward Clarke Bethune, 1897-1905.
D6   Mary Louise Bethune, 1898-1912.
D7   James Albert Bethune, died in infancy.
C2   Daniel Bethune, lived in Great Falls, Montana, and later farmed in
Red Deer, Alberta, until his death in 1940, m. Cassie <u>MacKenzie</u>, with
issue:
D1   Margaret (Peg) Bethune, R.N., born in Great Falls, died in Pedly,
Montana.
D2   Allan Bethune, 1891-1958, m. Sarah _____.
D3   Kathryn Bethune, m. Francis <u>Runcy</u>, with issue:
E1   Ruth Runcy, m. Donald <u>Edling</u>, with issue:
F1   John Edling, m. Laurie <u>Cannon</u>, with issue:
G1   Brandon Andrew Edling.
C3   Christine Bethune, died 1931, m. Alexander D. <u>MacKenzie</u>, died 1924.
D1   Gordon MacKenzie, 1887-1970, m. Katie <u>MacLeod</u>, 1900-1979.
E1   Jeanne MacKenzie, m. 1) Lloyd Hugh <u>Harris</u>, 1922-1977.
F1   David Harris, m. Charlene _____, with issue:
G1   Sean David Harris.
F2   Carol Jean Harris, m. Randy _____, with issue:
G1   Ryan.
F3   Diana Elizabeth Harris.
D2   Eldon Bethune MacKenzie, 1888-1971, m. Ruth <u>Field</u>, 1895-1967.
D3   Hugh Alexander MacKenzie, 1895-1954, m. Ina <u>Fead</u>, with issue:
E1   William Harold MacKenzie, m. Helen Elienne <u>Klappstein</u>,
issue:
F1   Hugh Alexander MacKenzie, 1955-1957.
F2   Kathryn Dianne MacKenzie, m. Romain <u>Gutter</u>, with
issue:
G1   Troy William Gutter.
F3   Donald Gordon MacKenzie, m. Barbara Joan <u>Knoll</u>,
issue:
G1   Lauren Donnell MacKenzie.
F4   Barbara Gail MacKenzie, m. David <u>Knight</u>.
D4   Marguerite Allena MacKenzie, 1890-1971, m. Walter <u>Shuh</u>,
1876-1942.
E1   Harold Shuh, m. Janet _____.
E2   Ethel Shuh, m. Wilbur <u>Lyman</u>, with issue:
F1   Douglas Lyman m. _____, with issue:
G1   Lasann Lyman.
Ethel m. 2) Tom R. <u>Nicholas</u>, with issue:
F2   Duane Nicholas, m. Doraleen <u>McCoy</u>, with issue:
G1   Michelle Ann Nicholas.
G2   Stephanie Erica Nicholas.
G3   Stacy Denise Nicholas.
G4   Darren Duane Nicholas.
D5   Carrie MacKenzie, 1893-1971, m. Claude <u>Bagley</u>, with issue:
E1   Ida Maude Bagley, m. Arthur <u>Rees</u>.
F1   Sandy Christine Rees, m. William Brian <u>Gunton</u>, issue:
G1   Sean Brian Gunton.
G2   Lisa Gunton.
G3   Jason Gunton.

E2   Dewey (Duke) Bagley, m. 1) Juanita Wall, 2) Jeanne Gerber.
    F1   Dewey Bagley, m. Julie MacPherson, with issue:
        G1   Linda Bagley, m. Jim Murphy, with issue:
            H1   Michelle Murphy.
            H2   James Dewey Murphy.
            H3   Lisa Sue Murphy.
        G2   Debra Bagley, m. Robert Jiles, with issue:
            H1   Ryan Jiles.
        G3   Steven Bagley, m. Anna _____, with issue:
            H1   Debbie Bagley.
E3   Donald Bagley.
E4   Douglas Dennis Bagley, m. Sandra Joan Halverson, with issue:
    F1   Allison Elaine Bagley.
    F2   Michelle Kay Bagley.

John MacLeod m. 2) Margaret MacPherson, born on P.E.I.

B7   Alexander MacLeod, 1840-1882, buried in Bute, Montana, m. Jane Mac-Neill, she is buried in Springton, P.E.I. They had issue:
    C1   Maggie Christine MacLeod, 1864-1902, m. her cousin James John Bethune, 1861-1926 (see above).
    C2   Katherine MacLeod, 1872-1974, m. George Dixon, 1868-1952, with issue:
        D1   Annie Dixon, 1890-1972, m. Briggs Kinney, with issue:
            E1   Janet Kinney, m. 1) Frank Sicilia, with issue:
                F1   Briggs Sicilia, 1938-1969, m. Audrey ____, with issue:
                    G1   Shari Ann Sicilia.
                Janet m. 2) Joe Dreyer, with issue:
                    G2   Carolyn Dreyer.
            E2   Len Dixon Kinney.
        D2   Howard Dixon, m. Jessie _____.
        D3   Hiram Dixon, m. Vera _____. They had issue:
            E1   Scott Dean Dixon.
            E2   David Dixon, married with a daughter at least.
            E3   Deidre Kate Dixon, m. Stuart Smively, with issue:
                F1   Sarah Smively.
    C3   Donald (Dan) MacLeod, born 1864.
    C4   John (Curly Jack) MacLeod.
    C5   Sarah MacLeod, m. 1) Henry Bolt, 2) John MacKenzie, 3) Donald Kennedy.
        D1   Mabel B. Bolt, 1891-1968, m. Edwin Hiller, with issue:
            E1   Raymond Hiller, m. Elizabeth Priest.
        D2   Emma Bolt.
        D3   Harry Bolt.
        D4   Belle MacKenzie, m. George Campbell, with issue:
            E1   Minnie Campbell, m. Alexander Martin, they lived in Valleyfield, P.E.I.,with issue:
                F1   Flora Martin, m. Ronald Jamieson, Montague, with issue:
                    G1   Rhonda Jamieson.
                    G2   Steven Jamieson.
                F2   George Martin, m. Marilyn King, with issue:

G1 Angela Martin.
G2 Julie Martin.
F3 Brenda Martin, m. Earl <u>McClare</u>, with issue:
G1 Gillian McClare.
G2 John Martin McClare.
G3 Ashley Caitlin McClare.
G4 Allison McClare.
F4 Janet Martin, m. Dennis <u>Devoe</u>, Cape Breton, with issue:
G1 Amanda Devoe.
G2 Jocelyn Devoe.
G3 Daniel Devoe.
G4 Bethany Devoe.
G5 Richard Devoe.
G6 Sarah Jane Devoe.
E2 Mabel Campbell, m. Lorne <u>Beaton</u>, with issue:
F1 Catherine Beaton.
F2 Sterling Beaton.
F3 Norma Beaton.
F4 Louise Beaton, m. Clayton <u>Coughlin</u>, two daughters.
F5 George Beaton.
E3 Florence Campbell, m. Maurice <u>Vaniderstine</u>, with issue:
F1 Myra Vaniderstine, m. 1) Roland <u>Kennedy</u>, 2) Stephen "Butch" <u>MacPherson</u>.
G1 Jacqueline.
F2 Shirley Vaniderstine, m. Gary <u>Scully</u>, with issue:
G1 Pamela Scully.
G2 Tammy Scully.
G3 Joseph Scully.
G4 Andarlene Scully.
F3 Linda Vaniderstine, m. David <u>Gillis</u>, with issue:
G1 Christopher Gillis.
G2 Lisa Gillis, died in infancy.
E4 Lloyd Campbell.
E5 George Howard Campbell, m. Daisy <u>Oatway</u>.
E6 John MacKenzie Campbell, m. 1) Wanda <u>Bertram</u>, 2) Edith <u>Craswell</u>, from Hunter River.
E7 Donald Norman Campbell, died young.
D5 Katie MacKenzie.
D6 Jack MacKenzie, m. Thelma _____, with issue:
E1 Winnie MacKenzie.
E2 Maybelle MacKenzie, m. Bill <u>Belty</u>, they had four children.
D7 Dan MacKenzie.
D8 Margaret MacKenzie.
D9 Eddie MacKenzie, m. Dorothy _____, with issue:
E1 Barbara MacKenzie, among others.
D10 Nelson Kennedy, m. Isabel _____. They had four or five children, two of whom were:
E1 Gay Kennedy.
E2 Darlene Kennedy.
D11 Goldie Kennedy, m. John <u>Easter</u>, with issue:

        E1   John Easter.
        E2   Helen Easter.
        E3   Marjorie Easter.

C6 Alexander D. MacLeod, 1873-1961, m. Grace ____.

C7 Mary Jane MacLeod, died 1925, m. Donald Munroe, died 1928, issue:

    D1   Alexander D. Munroe, 1901-1979, m. 1) Loraine Batchelor, 2) Beatrice _____, with issue:
        E1   Donald Munroe, married with children.
        E2   Judy Beatrice Munroe, m. Edward F. Wilson, with issue:
            F1   Sandra Wilson.
            F2   Scott Wilson.
        E3   Harold Munroe.
        E4   Junior (Alex) Munroe.
        E5   Bonnie Munroe, m. M. J. Ackles.

    D2   Jennie Munroe, 1903-1960, m. _____ Stewart, with issue:
        E1   John R. Stewart.

    D3   Marion Munroe, m. Leonard Trowsdale, with issue:
        E1   Ellsworth Trowsdale.
        E2   Jennie Trowsdale, m. Alda Cugini, with issue:
            F1   Douglas Cugini.
            F2   Marilyn Cugini.
        E3   Shirley Trowsdale, m. Louis Feckner, with issue:
            F1   Lou Feckner, m. Susan _____.
               G1   Jamie Louis Feckner.
            F2   Michael Feckner.
            F3   Bobby Feckner.
            F4   Susan Feckner, died in infancy.
            F5   Sandra Feckner.
        E4   Muriel Trowsdale.

    D4   Annabella Munroe, m. _____ Teal, with issue:
        E1   Marion Teal, m. Moshen Trabelsi, with issue:
            F1   Yasmina Trabelsi.

    D5   Frank Walter Munroe.

    D6   Laura Munroe, m. Ron Stevenson, with issue:
        E1   Shirley Stevenson, m. _____ Wilkins, with issue:
            F1   Christopher Wilkins.
        E2   Glen Stevenson, m. _____, with issue:
            F1   Robbie Stevenson.
            F2   Nina Stevenson.

    D7   Jack Munroe, m. Marjorie Eileen Pickett, with issue:
        E1   John Munroe, m. Ervine Laine.
        E2   Jeffrey Munroe.
        E3   Brittany Munroe.
        E4   Corinne Munroe, m. Graham Mathes, with issue:
            F1   Shilo Mathes.

    D8   Lillian Sadie Munroe, m. _____ Backstrom, with issue:
        E1   John Charles Backstrom.
        E2   Alfred Ernest Backstrom, m. Roberta Elizabeth Clark, with issue:
            F1   Eric Ian Backstrom.
            F2   Kim Louise Backstrom.

E3   Mary Elizabeth Backstrom.
E4   Sharon Backstrom.
E5   Dorothy Backstrom, m. Don Osborne, with issue:
F1   Jennifer Osborne.
F2   Derek Osborne.
F3   Jeremy Osborne.
D9   Harold Munroe, m. Gladys _____, with a large family.
D10 Christena Munroe.
D11 Roy Munroe.
D12 Emma Munroe.
B8   Donald MacLeod, 1843-1897, was a school teacher and Presbyterian Minister. His autobiography and journal will be found elsewhere in this book. He m. Lucy Isabella Cowan, 1848-1935, of Murray Harbour North, and she is buried in Calgary. He died in Priceville, Ontario. They had issue:
C1   Mary Gertrude MacLeod, 1875-1940. School Principal for many years.
C2   Norman Alfred MacLeod, 1884-1939, m. Louise Jane Lewis, 1888-1917.
D1   James Donald MacLeod, 1917-1962, m. Ethel Wallmark, with issue:
E1   Norman D. MacLeod.
C3   Donald MacLeod, died in Vancouver, m. Lillian Hill Tout.
C4   John A. MacLeod, M.D., m. Amy Sing Cameron of Meaford, Ontario, with issue:
D1   John MacLeod.
D2   Marjorie MacLeod, died in Wales, m. Philip Bently, with issue:
E1   Phyllis Bently.
C5   Roderick James MacLeod, 1883-1922, was a Great Lakes sailor. He died in Owen Sound and was married to Lilly Beattie, with issue:
D1   Donald Beattie MacLeod, lives in Owen Sound, Ontario.
C6   Margaret Christabel MacLeod, 1887-1967, m. James Townsend McKie, Calgary, Alberta, with issue:
D1   Kenneth Townsend McKie, m. Florence J. Danyluk.
E1   Heather Mary Ann McKie.
E2   Katherine Florence McKie.
E3   Dana Jean McKie.

This information provided by Jeannette Katherine Veale, Calgary, Alberta, and Minnie Campbell Martin, Valleyfield and Montague.

There are indications that John F. MacLeod, Orwell Mills, and his brother Donald J. MacLeod, at one time Superintendent of Education of P.E.I., may belong with this family. However, we could not establish the exact relationship, therefore we are adding what meagre information we have gleaned from Beaconsfield files, cemeteries and other sources regarding them.

Donald J. MacLeod, in 1881, was at age 30, a Professor at Prince of Wales College, a Presbyterian, and lived in the house of John Good, Charlottetown. In 1882, he was married at St. James Church, Charlottetown, to Maggie MacPherson, a daughter of John MacPherson, of P.E.I. Railway (*The Examiner*, Dec. 28). A daughter was born on Nov. 17, 1883. He was appointed Superintendent of Education in 1891 and resigned in 1901. We could find no other information or descendants, if any.

John F. MacLeod, 1845-1915, moved from Strathalbane to Uigg upon purchasing the Orwell Mills. He married Annie Nicholson, Orwell Cove, 1851-1925, and according to her obituary, their children were: Angus, killed in WWI; Sandy in Saskatchewan; Alexander and William in Alberta; and John at home. The daughters were: Mrs. K. M. Jenkins, New Glasgow, Nova Scotia; Mrs. B. F. Dingman, Calgary; Mrs. Nathaniel Gay, Pownal; Mrs. Callum Bruce, Vernon River; Mrs. A. L. Walker, Fernie, British Columbia (mother of Janet, m. to Pierre Berton); Mrs. Clarence MacLeod, Cambridge, Massachusetts (see MacLeods of Cardross); and Hazel, teaching in British Columbia..

Rev. Donald MacLeod
Autobiography and Journal of Rev. Donald MacLeod

I was born on the First Thursday of February, A.D. 1843, in Prince Edward Island, Queen's County, East Line Road, Lot 22. My father's name was John MacLeod, and my mother's maiden name was Margaret MacPherson. My father was a native of the Isle of Raasay, Scotland. My mother was a native of Skye. They both died when I was very young for I am unable to remember either of them. I was therefore left to the care of my brothers and sisters. My father was married twice. From his first wife he had three sons and three daughters. From my mother, my full brother and I only remain, one dying in infancy. My half-brothers are Donald, Roderick and Murdoch. Murdoch was left in Scotland with his cousin John MacKenzie, tailor, and with whom he learned the tailoring. MacKenzie and he went to Montreal and Toronto where MacKenzie died. Then Murdoch came to the Island, and lived for a time with his brothers, then settled in Bedeque. Two sisters, Mary the eldest and Catherine the youngest, were married, Mary to Alexander MacLeod, Esq., and Catherine to Donald Gillis. (She is m. the second time to Allan Bethune.) Christy kept house for her brothers till they all (the first family) got married. Roderick was left in the homestead and I lived with him till the spring of 1860. He sent me to school as much as he could but not enough to get an education so I resolved to get it somewhere else. I left him, went to work in the woods, chopping poles at Donald MacKay's, Strathalbyn, earned some clothing, and went to Bedeque. I went to school there about a year. I worked morning and evening for my board. My object was to become a teacher. Candidates for teacher had to attend the Normal School five months, and were examined before being admitted. When I presented myself first I was rejected. The next month I succeeded (fall of 1861). I returned to Bedeque not having the means to pay my board in Charlottetown for five months. I returned to Charlottetown, however, a month after, relying on Providence to direct and help me. I was not disappointed. I met a friend, John Beaton, teacher, who acted the part of a true friend. He first got me into a tavern to board, but a week after, he got me to the house of George Henderson, plasterer, a most respectable man, and an elder in the Free Church. He gave me time to pay my board after I should become a teacher (so also did Cameron, the tavern keeper).

I spent a pleasant and profitable winter in the Normal School of which Joseph Webster was Master. There were sixty-three students in that term.

Leaving the Normal School, after having obtained my Licence to teach 19th March 1862 (I passed the Board before my time was up in the Normal School and had to put it in), I returned to Bedeque.

I looked for a school for some time. I went to Malpeque Road, Freetown; and one day walked from Peter Sinclair's to Fermoy School to be disappointed, the school being occupied. At Sinclair's on the farm belonging to John lives Alex McLeod, the husband of Mary, my sister Mary's daughter. To McLeod's I returned weary and wet from Fermoy. John Sinclair came in shortly after me and asked if I wanted a school. "Yes." "Well ours is vacant, but I don't know that you would do, or that they would hire you, but you might go and see. They have a meeting of trustees in the schoolhouse tonight."

I pulled on my boots again and went. I found five trustees talking politics there. I sat along side of a long bearded man—Sam Haslam. I said "Are these the trustees?" "Yes." "Well you want a teacher." "About advertising for one." "What class?" "O, I suppose first class (lowest)." "Well, I am a licensed teacher of the first class." The others were then spoken to by Mr. Haslam. One gentleman, Mr. Ferguson, wanted my recommendation from another school as teacher. When I told him I never taught—"Ha, ha, we don't want the likes of you here then." Mr. Ferguson was John Sinclair's brother-in-law, and he wanted them to hire him again, although Mr. Sinclair had been in the school about 16 years. The other trustee wanted to try me, however, and they got him to agree to my engagement on condition that I would come and show them my method of teaching. I came on the day appointed and satisfied them. I found that the children were not so far advanced as Mr. Ferguson thought. I was engaged to commence the school the seventeenth day of April, 1862. I pleased everyone but Mr. Ferguson and MacDonald who were cautious rather on account of political prejudice to the Haslams with whom I associated more than the others.

The school act was changed this year so that instead of getting 55 pounds from government, a teacher only got 40 pounds from government and 15 from the people. At the end of my first year at one meeting the inhabitants (in the schoolhouse) made up 12 pounds for me, but I would not stay because Ferguson and MacDonald were opposed to me. I then engaged in my native settlement, East Line Road, Lot 22. Commenced 15th May 1863. I remained only six months, the school being new and small, I lost 7 pounds on account of low average. I petitioned the Board of Education to let me clear. They did so. I then engaged in Darnley School, Lot 18. Commenced Dec. 16, 1863.

I continued in Darnley for one year. I then taught at Bonshaw, Lot 30, for two years and a half. I opened the school for the second quarter in the third year on the third day of June 1867. I notified the trustees that I was to leave them on the thirtieth of August following. While at Bonshaw I was Lieutenant of a Company of Volunteers (R. B. Stewart was Captain) and also Drill Instructor for it and the South Shore Company of Volunteers, and also for the Militia Company.

Before I left Bonshaw I made up my mind to go immediately to P. W. College, having in view to study for the ministry. 21st August 1867, I went to Charlottetown with Captain Stew and our Company to a review. It was "Caledonia Club" day. I competed, under not very favourable circumstances, for the prize in Pipe music, and got third prize. The year before I got the first prize against heavier odds. Heard Kennedy the Scottish vocalist the same evening, and went to "Club Ball" at Mason Hall.

At Bonshaw I was intimate with R. B. Stewart, Esq., Strathgartney and his family who treated me with the greatest kindness.

I commenced to go to Prince of Wales College in Charlottetown on Monday, September 16th 1867. Began Euclid definitions, Latin grammar,1st Declension. The amount of money due me I could rely on was 40/8/3 pounds.

Charlottetown, Nov. 2nd, 1869. Attended the funeral of P. D. Stewart-Adj. General, Militia, died last Friday, aged 85.

February 29th, 1868

My dear sister Christina MacLeod died on the 29th day of February, in the year of our Lord, one thousand eight hundred sixty eight. My brother Roderick who died when I was teaching in Bonshaw was to me a father all his days.

I attended Prince of Wales College for two years. Had to borrow from John L. MacKinnon, Teacher, afterwards Editor of the Summerside *Pioneer*.

When I was done of Charlottetown I taught at Murray Harbour South for one year, paid all my debts, and prepared to go to Dalhousie College, Halifax.

While in Murray Harbour I enjoyed myself well. I commenced to teach there 6th Aug. 1869. I formed many valuable acquaintants; boarded at Mr. David Chrichton's. And fell in love with Lucy Isabella Cowan.

Extract from my journal there: Friday, December 31st, 1869. I spent this evening at Peter MacLeod's, tanner, Murray Harbour South, where the Templars had a tea party. Although I was not a member I was invited. We had dancing, singing, plays, and speeches. I made several new acquaintants, among [them] Miss Lucy I. Cowan, whom I accompanied home.

While here I used to go frequently to Peter's Road, Lot 63, and 61 Road to hear Alexander McLeod, Esq., Catechist, my sister Mary's husband, preaching to the Gaelic people in these back settlements.

While in this district (Murray Harbour South) I passed for Grammar Teacher, and was offered the Grammar School at Centreville Bedeque. But the people of Murray Harbour South made up 24/3 pounds for me which induced me to stay out the year.

Halifax, Nova Scotia, Dominion of Canada

November 28th, 1873

I arrived at Halifax on Saturday 31st October last. Came from Charlottetown, P.E.I. I spent the summer on the Island fishing and visiting my friends. This is my third winter at Dalhousie College, Halifax. The subjects studied this winter are: Latin, Ethics, and Political Economy, History, French and Astronomy.

Friday, November 28th

Attended classes in Ethics, Latin — *Tacite Annalorum*, and History. History lecture on Mohomet. After classes came home — 52 Creighton St. — and opened this book. My fellow lodgers are James C. Hindman, Edward Gordon, and Donald C. Martin, the last two of the second year, the first of the fourth. Attended debating society — the Kritosophian — opened the debate, returned home.

Saturday, Nov. 29th

Remained in the house all the forenoon; studied History. Went out to football about three o'clock, played till dark. Studied History. Last night I was appointed to write a short essay to be read next Friday before the Kritosophian Society, afterwards to be published in the *Dalhousie Gazette*. The subject I contemplate is the *The Last Conquest of the Dominion* meaning my Native Colony, Prince Edward Island.

Sabbath, Nov. 30th

Attended service at Chalmers Church. Rev. Mr. Pitblado preached. Taught a Sabbath School class at 3 o'clock p.m.; attended again at Chalmers Church. We adjourned to Fort Massey Church where Mr. _____ [left out] was ordained by the Halifax Presbytery (by the laying on of hands) for the church at Bermuda.

Monday, Dec. 1st

Attended classes in French, Ethics, and History. Study as usual.

Tuesday, 2nd

At classes.

Wednesday, 3rd

Studied, attended classes, prayer meeting.

Friday, 5th

Classes. Completed my essay, "The Last Conquest of the Dominion," and in the evening delivered it before the Kritosophian Society. It was received with much favour and ordered to be published.

Monday 8th

Classes—Ethics and History, received a letter dated Dec 1st from Miss Lucy I. Cowan, Murray Harbour South, and answered by writing and mailing one the next hour.

Thursday, 11th

Classes as usual. This evening there is to be a lecture by Mr. Jenkins on the Satyrists of England taking Butler as the representative. The lecture was a rare treat, well delivered, well written, well received.

Friday, 12th

Classes as usual. This evening there is to be a lecture by Jenkins at Temperance Hall on the England of today. There is also service at Chalmers Church preparatory to Sacrament of the Lord's Supper next Sabbath. I would like to hear the lecture, but the service of God is more important than all other. In this consideration I must go to church. There is also appointment made for Gaelic Service at the Session House of Chalmers Church.

Thursday, 16th of April, 1875

Last Friday the 9th of our classes in the Theological Hall were formally closed. Rev. Dr. Burns of Fort Massey delivered the speech, his subject "Modern Infidelity." It was a very able effort. Rev. Mr. Grant of St. Matthew's made a speech on Collegiate Education Embracing Arts and Theology.

During the winter I was troubled more than once with asthma. "Popham's Asthma Specific" gives me immediate relief, and I hope much from it.

My winter on the whole has been a most happy one. My life has been made happier by my wife than any other earthly thing could make it. We live in love and affection. No jar or cross has marred our past short history in wedlock. Her ardent love and constant affection know no bound. In my troubles she is my comfort. In sickness she has been an angel of love. May the spirit of God be in us more and more, that we may abound in love to Him, as He had kindly given us love to one another, that His glory may be advanced in me and by us.

The Home Mission Board has assigned to me a field of labour for the summer, Margaree, Cape Breton. It is difficult to get there, I intend to go next week if possible. My wife will likely be going to East Boston, Mass., to her sister's, Mrs. Charles L. Fraser, 110 Meridian St. (drug store)—the ice being still in the gulf, so that she can't go to P.E.I. Next Tuesday she intends to go by the *S.S. Alhambra*.

Monday, 24th May, 1876

Big interval. North East Margaree, Cape Breton. Here we meet again my good journal. You have had a long voyage of it since I left you in Halifax on the 20th April last. I shall now as soon as I can tell you some of what happened since we last met. Well, after packing you up in my old red chest I sent you off to W. Boak's Wharf, Halifax aboard the *Thoonci* [?] *Hawk*, Captain N. White, bound for Margaree Harbour. He arrived at the Harbour sometime week before last, I think Friday. The old red trunk and you were brought up by Mr. Wm. Murray last Monday 17th May, but I will resume and tell all in detail from a little diary I kept in your absence.

Copying:

Wednesday, 5th May 1875

Left Halifax this day two weeks. Travelled by train to New Glasgow. Got on horseback from Post Office to Geo. Murray's. It cost me in travelling from Geo. Murray's to N.E. Margaree $14.95 with only one meal a day. Travelled by stage to Forks of Margaree. The roads horrible. Had to walk by turns as the drivers changed four times between Glasgow and the Straight of Canso. At Charles MacLeod's I had no room to study in, there being only one stove in the house—in the kitchen stove.

In this Malcolm MacLeod's I have a neat little room with bedroom off it. The study contains a square box stove—quite comfortable. A large map of Palestine, before me, where I now sit, a large looking glass, some pictures, statute books, P. Office books and some religious and instructive books make up furniture of room. It is retired from the rest of the house, promises to be a cosy place for study.

Priceville, Ontario, County of Grey, Monday 31st day of March 1879

This is the first entry into my journal since I left Margaree. How negligent of my duty to my poor old journal. Well, I am now pastor of the St. Columbia Church Congregation—residing in the old St. Andrew's church manse with my wife and two children.

Friday, Aug. 26th, 1881

Since last entry I have gone through some important things:—Have been at meeting of Presbytery in Harristown, in July, and was elected Moderator. It was July 12th. Then presided a Presbytery meeting Aug. 5th there in Presbyterian Church, McIntyre's Corner, where we ordained and inducted Mr. John Chisholm, M.A., to the pastoral charge of the congregation. My address to the minister appeared in the *Markdale Standard*. Again in Markdale on Aug.16th, I presided at the meeting of Presbytery adjourned from spring to ordain and induct Mr. Andrew Wilson to the pastoral charge of Markdale and Flesherton. Have been to Toronto to preach in Leslieville for R. S. Sinclair while he preached in my place July 24th. I was visiting yesterday and the day before in the village. The work of a pastor is no small task. It is laborious—thankless, except in the presence of some and this does not hold true of the many, but it is wonderful how soon people forget their proper relation with their minister—and how easily they are turned against him by the false, deceitful, and covetous.

Monday, August 29, 1881

Preached yesterday from Heb.4:14—was sometimes hampered with the manuscript. Wrote notes of my sermon today. I find as usual my greatest difficulty in selecting a text. I need divine guidance. I have to go to Elora next Tuesday to give an address on Sabbath School music. This comes from my having given an address on the same subject the first of March last in Mount Forest—which address was printed in the *Mount Forest Advocate* of the 10th of March and again by the *Markdale Standard*.

October 4th, 1890

The day spent about the manse (Priceville). On the first of this month I commenced A. Wilford Hall's treatment for the cure of asthma without medicine. Used it on the 1st and 2nd with imperfect apparatus. Think obtained some benefit from it. Spent evening in study. Have been very much hindered with asthma since last June, but was much better these last three days.

In Priceville on Tuesday, March 9, 1897, Rev. Donald MacLeod, B.A., died at the age of 54 years. The announcement reads:

THE FUNERAL
will leave his late residence for the Priceville Cemetery,
On Thursday March 11, 1897, at 3 o'clock, P.M.
Friends and acquaintances will please accept this intimation.

March 10, 1897, Priceville.

These are selections from a 75-page handwritten journal now in the safekeeping of his grandson, Mr. Kenneth McKie, Edmonton, Alberta, which we have received from Jeanette Veale, Calgary, Alberta.

DONALD MACLEOD
DONALD MACLEOD AND CATHERINE OF LORNE VALLEY

A   Donald MacLeod, believed to have come from the Isle of Skye in 1840. All their family was born in Scotland. Some of the family members believe that the names of the settlers were Angus and Mary, but during research on the family, the only settlers to be found in this area on those dates were Donald and Catherine. Their children were:

B1   Neil MacLeod, 1814-1908, m. Christine <u>MacLeod</u>, 1831-1869, with issue:

    C1   Euphemia MacLeod, born 1851, m. Andrew <u>Finlayson</u>, with issue:
        D1   Peter Finlayson.

    C2   Donald Neil MacLeod, born 1853, m. Flora <u>MacLeod</u>, with issue:
        D1   Tilly MacLeod, m. George <u>Douglas</u>, with issue:
            E1   Pearl Douglas, m. Harry <u>Connolly</u>.
            E2   Eleanor Douglas, m. Lincoln <u>Kennedy</u>.
            E3   Freda Douglas, m. Earl <u>Kennedy</u>.
            E4   Margaret Douglas, m. Charles <u>MacLeod</u>.
            E5   Herb Douglas, m. Yvonne <u>Rolfe</u>.
            E6   Loveland Douglas m. 1) Roy <u>Abarell</u>, 2) George <u>Mullen</u> (deceased), 3) Dennis <u>Lewin</u>.
            E7   Winston Douglas, m. Marjorie <u>Hooley</u>.
            E8   Lloyd Douglas, deceased, twin to Winston.
            E9   Shirley Douglas, m. George <u>MacCannell</u>.
        D2   Murdoch MacLeod, single.
        D3   Angus MacLeod, m. Annie <u>MacInnis</u>, with issue:
            E1   Norma MacLeod.
            E2   Anna MacLeod.
            E3   Roy MacLeod.
            E4   Glenda MacLeod.
            E5   Jackie MacLeod.
        D4   Maggie MacLeod, m. William <u>Finlayson</u>, with issue:
            E1   Edna Finlayson.
            E2   Eugene Finlayson.
            E3   Sylvia Finlayson.
        D5   Jimmy MacLeod, m. Grace <u>MacDougall</u>, with issue:
            E1   Carol MacLeod.
            E2   Lynda MacLeod.
        D6   Walter MacLeod, m. Laura <u>James</u>.
        D7   Harry MacLeod, m. Tilly <u>Ferguson</u>, with issue:
            E1   Milford MacLeod.
            E2   Sheldon MacLeod.
            E3   Joyce MacLeod.
            E4   Margaret MacLeod.
            E5   Dawn MacLeod.
        D8   Dorothy MacLeod, m. Harry <u>MacKay</u>, with issue:
            E1   Basil MacKay.
        D9   Emma MacLeod, 1901-1911.
        D10 Allen MacLeod, 1892-1947, m. Bertha _____.

D11 Peter MacLeod, died at age 18.

D12 William MacLeod, died at 6 months.

C3 Alexander (Sandy Neil) MacLeod, born 1857. Single.

C4 Peter MacLeod, twin to Alexander. Single.

C5 Allan Albert MacLeod, m. Mary Igoe, with issue:
   D1 Anna Christine MacLeod, m. Victor Hogan.
   D2 Mary MacLeod, m. Timothy O'Sullivan.
   D3 Alexander J. MacLeod, m. Mary Fitzgerald.

C6 Catherine (Phoebe) MacLeod, m. _____ MacAusland, with issue:
   D1 Percy MacAusland.
   D2 George MacAusland.
   D3 Becky MacAusland.
   D4 William MacAusland.
   D5 Harry MacAusland.

C7 Christina MacLeod, died 1864 at 5 years of age.

C8 Annie MacLeod, m. Alexander MacInnis, with issue:
   D1 Christy MacInnis, m. Alexander MacLeod. Family is listed under Alexander MacLeod.
   D2 George MacInnis, m. Florence MacKay, with issue:
      E1 Irene MacInnis.
      E2 Freda MacInnis.
      E3 Marjory MacInnis.
   D3 Lawrence MacInnis, single, deceased by drowning.
   D4 Philip MacInnis, m. Beatrice Hickox, with issue:
      E1 Lawrence MacInnis.
      E2 Evelyn MacInnis.
      E3 Gordon MacInnis.
      E4 Lowell MacInnis.
      E5 Rita MacInnis.
      E6 Eleanor MacInnis.
      E7 Philip MacInnis.
   D5 Murdoch MacInnis, m. Mildred _____, with issue:
      E1 Natalie MacInnis.
   D6 Annie MacInnis, m. Angus MacLeod. Family is listed under Angus MacLeod.
   D7 Wendell MacInnis, m. 1) Lena Hickox, 2) Pearl Gillis.
   D8 Warren William MacInnis.
   D9 Euphemia MacInnis.
   D10 Elmer MacInnis, m. Mabel MacKenzie from Canso, Nova Scotia.
      E1 Wanda MacInnis.
      E2 Kelvin MacInnis.
      E3 Claude MacInnis.
      E4 Laverne MacInnis.
      E5 Ivan MacInnis.
      E6 Roger MacInnis.
      E7 Carrie Lee MacInnis, 1964-1975.
      E8 Twin boys, deceased.
   D11 Ella Mildred MacInnis, 1909-1910.

B2 Alexander MacLeod, 1819-1897, m. Mary MacLeod, 1838-1904. Alexander was born in Skye and Mary was born in Inverness Shire. All their family were born in Lorne Valley, P.E.I.

C1 Sandy MacLeod, born 1861. He is buried in Keating Summit, Pennsylvania. His wife's name is unknown.
    D1 Esther MacLeod, 1894-1942.
    D2 Mary MacLeod, born 1901.
    D3 Horace MacLeod, 1907-1966.
C2 Donald (Dan) MacLeod, 1862-1907, m. Catherine (Kitty) MacLeod, 1857-1938. They are buried in Lorne Valley.
C3 Allan MacLeod, born 1864.
C4 Angus A. MacLeod, 1864-1933, m. Barbara Mustard, 1857-1925. They are buried in Lorne Valley.
    D1 Jane MacLeod, m. Neil Nicholson, with issue:
        E1 Christina Nicholson, single, deceased.
        E2 Peter Nicholson, killed in WWII.
        E3 Angus Nicholson, m. Lola Schumacher.
        E4 Sarah Nicholson, m. Leslie Gillespie, with issue:
            F1 Heather Gillespie, single.
            F2 Anne Gillespie, m. Paul MacDougall, with issue:
                G1 Mark MacDougall.
                G2 Angela MacDougall.
                G3 Ellen MacDougall.
        E5 Inez Nicholson, m. Frank Gillespie.
        E6 George Nicholson.
        E7 Neil Fred Nicholson.
        E8 Joseph Nicholson, m. Betty Bellinger, with issue:
            F1 Shirley Nicholson, m. Peter Veenstra, with issue:
                G1 Timmy Veenstra.
                G2 Joey Veenstra.
            F2 Donald Nicholson, m. Rosemary Bondy.
            F3 Paul Nicholson, single.
            F4 Neil Angus Nicholson, m. Valerie Pickle, with issue:
                G1 Sara Mae Nicholson.
                G2 Mark Joseph Nicholson.
        E9 John James Nicholson.
        E10 Samuel Nicholson, m. Gwen Wilson.
        E11 Gerald Nicholson.
    D2 James MacLeod, m. Florence Cobb, with issue:
        E1 Barbara Ruth MacLeod, died in infancy.
        E2 Dr. Angus Alexander MacLeod, m. Anne Jenkins, Orwell Cove. He is practising in Bonshaw, with issue:
            F1 Dr. Alan Angus MacLeod, m. Elaine Talma, living in Halifax, with issue:
                G1 Allison Anne.
                G2 Logan Allen MacLeod.
            F2 Dr. Valerie Anne MacLeod, m. Dr. Patrick Conlon.
            F3 Bruce James MacLeod.
            F4 Dr. Clive Frederick MacLeod.
            F5 Gina Barbara MacLeod.
        E3 Bruce Brenton MacLeod, died in infancy.
        E4 Barbara Jane MacLeod, single. She was a school teacher in Charlottetown, and is a Charter Member of Clan MacLeod Society of P.E.I.

E5   James Malcolm MacLeod, died in infancy.
E6   Frederick Cobb MacLeod, single.
D3 Minnie MacLeod, m. Leigh Cobb, with issue:
   E1   Jean Cobb, m. Wellington MacKay, with issue:
      F1   Preston Leeland MacKay, died in infancy.
      F2   John MacKay, m. Judy Stewart, with issue:
         G1   Corrie MacKay.
      F3   Sheila MacKay, m. James Clifford, with issue:
         G1   Anne Clifford.
      F4   Colin MacKay, m. Marlene Douglas, with issue:
         G1   Douglas MacKay.
         G2   Sandy MacKay.
      F5   Sylvia MacKay, m. John William Pomeroy, with issue:
         G1   Andrew Pomeroy.
      F6   Ruth MacKay, single.
   E2   Arthur Cobb, born Aug. 21, 1921, died Dec. 9, 1922.
   E3   Alexander Cobb, m. Reah MacEwen, with issue:
      F1   Linda Cobb, m. Clayton Blackett, with issue:
         G1   Craig Blackett.
      F2   Betty Cobb, single.
      F3   David Cobb, m. Paula Feehan, with issue:
         G1   Lacy Cobb.
         G2   Justin Cobb.
      F4   Pauline Cobb, m. John Busgos, with issue:
         G1   Judy Busgos, single.
         G2   Sonya Lee Busgos, single.
   E4   Sterling Cobb, m. Helen MacEwen, with issue:
      F1   Jo-ann Cobb, single.
   E5   Heath Cobb, m. Annie Matheson, with issue:
      F1   Debbie Cobb, m. Hallie MacKinnon, with issue:
         G1   Kimberly Ann MacKinnon.
D4 Alexander MacLeod, m. Christy MacInnis. This family moved
   to Ontario. They had issue:
   E1   Gordon MacLeod, m. Inge Wachendorf, two children.
   E2   Vernon MacLeod, m. 1) Helena _____, 2) Mary Zimmerman.
   E3   Lorne MacLeod, m. Ethel MacKinnon, five children.
   E4   Aletha MacLeod, m. Leith Sanderson.
D5 John M. MacLeod, single.
D6 Gordon MacLeod, died age 11 months.
D7 Barbara MacLeod, single.
C5 John MacLeod, 1867-1897, single.
C6 Catherine (Kate) MacLeod, 1871-1900, m. Alexander Nicholson, with
   issue:
D1 Neil Nicholson, married and lived in Maine.
D2 Mary Nicholson, m. Dan Stewart, with issue:
   E1   Tenna Stewart, m. Albert MacLeod. (See the family from
      Abney.)
      F1   Charlie MacLeod.
      F2   Willard MacLeod.
      F3   Basil MacLeod.
      F4   Donnie MacLeod.

    F5 George MacLeod.
    F6 Joyce MacLeod.
    F7 Ethel MacLeod.
    F8 Etta MacLeod.
   E2 Annie May Stewart, m. Joe Cameron, with issue:
    F1 Heather Cameron.
    F2 Bertha Cameron.
    F3 Elizabeth Cameron.
    F4 Catherine Ann Cameron.
    F5 Barbara Cameron.
    F6 Margaret Cameron.
    F7 John Cameron.
  D3 Johnnie Nicholson, deceased.
  D4 Alexander Nicholson, m. Rose Striegler, with issue:
   E1 Bert Nicholson, m. Myrtle _____.
   E2 John Nicholson.
   E3 Betty Nicholson.
C7 Murdoch MacLeod, 1872-1931, never married, buried in Vanderhoof, British Columbia.
C8 Peter MacLeod, born 1874, never married, buried in Minot, North Dakota.
C9 Christy MacLeod, 1876-1909. She was married but the name of her husband is unknown. She is is buried in Keating Summit, Pennsylvania. Issue:
D1 Gordon.
D2 Mary.
C10 Hughie MacLeod, 1878-1944, never married, buried in Vanderhoof, British Columbia.
C11 Malcolm MacLeod 1880-1963, m. Annie Palmer, with issue:
  D1 R. Hughie MacLeod, m. Rita Jay, with issue:
   E1 Ruth MacLeod.
   E2 Lorna MacLeod.
   E3 Heather MacLeod.
  D2 Isobel MacLeod, m. Alexander MacDougall, with issue:
   E1 Audrey MacDougall.
   E2 Gerald MacDougall.
   E3 Kathleen MacDougall.
   E4 Roger MacDougall.
   E5 Ferne MacDougall.
   E6 Wendy MacDougall.
   E7 Infant, deceased.
  D3 Dorothy MacLeod, m. Morley Markell, with issue:
   E1 Wayne Markell.
   E2 Steve Markell.
   E3 Terry Anne Markell.
  D4 Theresa MacLeod, m. Hector Trotter, with issue:
   E1 Colin Trotter.
   E2 John Trotter.
   E3 Lynn Trotter.
   E4 Jill Trotter.
  D5 Palmer MacLeod, m. 1) Gwen Fox, deceased.

E1   Doris MacLeod.
E2   Dianne MacLeod.
E3   David MacLeod.
Palmer m. 2) Edna _____.
D6   Peter MacLeod, m. Glenda MacLeod.
E1   Judy MacLeod.
E2   Barry MacLeod.
E3   Donna MacLeod.
E4   Susan MacLeod.
D7   Kenneth MacLeod, m. Shirley Myers, living in Calgary, with issue:
E1   Brent MacLeod.
E2   Malcolm MacLeod.
E3   Peter MacLeod.
E4   Jonathan MacLeod.
C12 Janie MacLeod, 1882-1959, m. George Snell, 1876-1953. They are buried in Vanderhoof, British Columbia, with issue:
D1   Mary Snell, m. Howard Alexander.
D2   Louise Snell, m. Ray Devauld, with issue:
E1   Ross Devauld.
E2   George Devauld.
E3   Allan Devauld.
E4   Don Devauld, wife and two small daughters were killed in a highway accident in 1974.
D3   Esther Snell, m. Chuck Williams, with issue:
E1   Geraldine Williams.
E2   Constance Williams.
E3   Linda Williams.
D4   Catherine Snell, m. Jim Clark, with issue:
E1   Michael Clark.
E2   Marilyn Clark.
E3   Gary Clark.
E4   Catherine Clark.
D5   Olive Snell, m. Ted Williams, with issue:
E1   Elizabeth Williams.
E2   Barry Williams.
D6   Albert (Bert) Snell, m. Gwen Moss, with issue:
E1   Edward Snell.
E2   Cindy Snell.
D7   Richard (Dick) Snell, m. Jean Johnson, with issue:
E1   Richard Snell.
E2   Gene Snell.
E3   Daird Snell.
B3   John MacLeod, m. Margaret Shaw. They moved to U.S.A., with issue:
C1   Allan MacLeod, born April 1, 1850.
C2   John MacLeod, born May 20, 1852.
B4   Angus MacLeod, died 1909, m. Ann MacKay, with issue:
C1   Alexander MacLeod, 1850-1917, m. Rachael Martin, 1872-1939, with issue:
D1   Annie MacLeod, m. William Minchin, with issue:
E1   John Minchin, m. Lois Hunter, with issue:

           F1   David Minchin.
           F2   Robert Minchin.
      E2   Eleanor Minchin, m. Melville Ralston. No family.
      E3   Rachael Minchin, m. Peter Davies, deceased. Issue:
           F1   Susan Davies.
           F2   John Davies.
           Rachael m. 2) to Dr. Floyd MacDonald, with issue:
           F3   Duncan MacDonald.
           F4   Robert MacDonald.
   D2 Sterling MacLeod, m. Annie MacDonald, with issue:
      E1   Donna MacLeod.
   D3 Belle MacLeod, m. Martin Shaw, with issue:
      E1   Gordon Shaw, single.
      E2   Sterling Shaw, m. Angelina Gillis, with issue:
           F1   Darryl Shaw.
           F2   Irene Shaw.
           F3   Jean Shaw.
           F4   Neil Shaw.
      E3   Raymond Shaw, m. Audrey Jay, with issue:
           F1   Donna Shaw.
           F2   Sandra Shaw.
           F3   Kevin Shaw.
           F4   Scott Shaw.
      E4   Stewart Shaw, m. Valerie Crane, with issue:
           F1   Murray Shaw.
           F2   Steven Shaw.
           F3   Wade Shaw.
           F4   Sherilee Shaw.
      E5   Jeanette Shaw, m. Vernon MacLeod, with issue:
           F1   Kimberly MacLeod.
           F2   Donald MacLeod.
           F3   Dale MacLeod.
      E6   Edna Shaw, m. Gordon Leard, with issue:
           F1   Caralee Leard.
           F2   Kristen Leard.
      E7   Barry Shaw, m. Kay Gillis, with issue:
           F1   Susan Shaw.
   D4 Alec MacLeod, m. Ruth MacEachern, with issue:
      E1   Barbara MacLeod, m. Ronald Fletcher, with issue:
           F1   David Fletcher.
           F2   Cindy Fletcher.
      E2   Bruce MacLeod, m. Patricia Myshrall, with issue:
           F1   William MacLeod.
           F2   Jason MacLeod.
      E3   William MacLeod, deceased.
      E4   Elaine MacLeod, m. Milvin Estey, with issue:
           F1   Jessica Estey.
      E5   David MacLeod, single.
C2 Jane MacLeod, 1852-1880, m. Johnny Johnson, with issue:
   D1 John Johnson.
C3 Roderick MacLeod, born 1855.

C4 Catherine (Kitty) MacLeod, 1857-1938, m. Donald (Dan) <u>MacLeod</u>. No family.

C5 Mary MacLeod, born 1862, m. Murdoch <u>Nicholson</u>. No family.

C6 Maggie MacLeod, 1863-1939, m. Alexander C. <u>MacDonald</u>, 1863-1940.

    D1 Annie Jane (Nana) MacDonald, m. Herb <u>MacKenzie</u>, with issue:

        E1 Margaret MacKenzie, m. Grant <u>Thompson</u>, with issue:

            F1 Heather Thompson.

            F2 Anne Thompson.

            F3 Carol Thompson.

            F4 Andrew Thompson.

        E2 Kenneth MacKenzie, m. Elaine <u>Chisholm</u>, with issue:

            F1 Alan MacKenzie.

            F2 Scott MacKenzie.

            F3 Donald MacKenzie.

    D2 C. Vernon MacDonald, single.

    D3 Wilbur MacDonald, single.

    D4 Milton MacDonald, m. Levita <u>Dingwell</u>, with issue:

        E1 Marjorie MacDonald, m. Dean <u>Reid</u>, with issue:

            F1 James Reid.

            F2 Carolyn Reid.

            F3 Donna Reid.

    D5 Florence MacDonald, m. Douglas <u>MacLaren</u>, with issue:

        E1 Doris MacLaren, m. Wallace <u>Jenkins</u>, with issue:

            F1 Robert Jenkins, m. Claudia <u>Nicolle</u>, with issue:

                G1 Bradley Jenkins.

                G2 Cynthia Jenkins.

            F2 Kenneth Jenkins.

        E2 Anna MacLaren, m. Homer <u>Campbell</u>, with issue:

            F1 Ian Campbell, m. Heather _____.

            F2 Robert Campbell.

         Anna MacLaren, m. 2) Arthur <u>Hill</u>.

B5 Catherine MacLeod, born 1828, m. John <u>MacLeod</u>, they moved to Oregon.

B6 Margaret MacLeod, 1830-1903, m. Alexander <u>Sutherland</u>, 1823-1913.

    C1 Margaret Sutherland, m. _____ <u>Birt</u>, with issue:

        D1 Arthur Birt.

        D2 Howard Birt.

        D3 Jonathan Birt.

    C2 Jessie Sutherland, went to the U.S.A.

    C3 Daniel Sutherland, buried in the U.S.A.

    C4 George Sutherland, 1872-1954, m. Ida <u>MacEachern</u>, 1874-1965, with issue:

        D1 Elmer Sutherland.

        D2 Alma Sutherland, m. Almon <u>Wood</u>.

This information was provided by Barbara MacLeod, Charlottetown.

JAMES MACLEOD
JAMES MACLEOD AND MARY MURCHISON OF UIGG

A   James MacLeod came to P.E.I. in 1829 with his brothers, "Old Murdoch" MacLeod and Norman MacLeod, both of Uigg area. Their parents were Neil MacLeod and Sophia Nicholson, both from the Isle of Skye. James was born in 1757, died 1841, m. Mary <u>Murchison,</u> born 1758, died 1856.

B1   John J. MacLeod, 1806-1888, m. Ann, who was born in Skye in 1820 and died in 1895. They are buried in Uigg Cemetery.

     C1   Alexander MacLeod, Rev. He married but wife's name is unknown.

         D1   John MacLeod.

     C2   Annie MacLeod, 1851-1889.

     C3   William MacLeod.

     C4   Mary MacLeod, died 1858, aged 10 days.

     C5   Alexander MacLeod, died May 25, 1859, aged 12 years.

     C6   Roderick MacLeod, died June 15, 1861, aged 2 years. There was also a grandchild Kate who died Dec. 1886, aged 13 months.

James had other children, but their names are unknown.

This information was provided by Norman MacLeod, Charlottetown, and cemetery transcripts from Beaconsfield.

ARCHIBALD MACLEOD
ARCHIBALD MACLEOD AND WIFE OF BELLEVUE

A   Archibald MacLeod, m. _____. Lived in Bellevue, with issue:

    B1   Alexander MacLeod, m. Flora <u>Beaton</u> of Little Sands. They lived in Hopefield, with issue:

        C1   Samuel Peter MacLeod, born 1870, settled in New Hampshire in 1888. He farmed and worked in the paper mills. He married and his wife died shortly after the marriage. No issue. Samuel m. 2) Clara E. <u>Porter</u> of Groveton, New Hampshire, with issue:

            D1   Samuel Porter MacLeod, m. Ethel <u>Leighton</u>, with issue:

                E1   Karen MacLeod, a French teacher at Skowhegan, Maine.

            D2   Nelson Alexander MacLeod, m. Clymena <u>Colburn</u>.

                E1   Marlene MacLeod.

                E2   Colburn MacLeod.

                E3   Sandra MacLeod.

                E4   Gregory MacLeod.

            D3   Helen MacLeod, m. Reginald <u>Bearor</u>, with issue:

                E1   Ronald Bearor.

                E2   Catherine Bearor.

            D4   Donald Beaton MacLeod, m. Annie <u>Elias</u>, with issue:

                E1   Freda MacLeod.

        C2   Christine MacLeod, born 1872, m. Roderick <u>MacKay</u>, 1868-1942, of Bellevue and Hopefield, with issue:

            D1   Annie MacKay, m. Duncan <u>MacKay</u>.

            D2   Flora MacKay, m. G. H. <u>Lyle</u>.

            D3   Katie MacKay, m. Bruce <u>Whiteway</u>.

            D4   Emily MacKay, m. John <u>MacLeod</u>.

            D5   Daniel Alexander MacKay.

            D6   Stewart MacKay, m. Mary <u>MacLennan</u>, with issue:

                E1   Jean MacKay, m. Paul Ernest _____.

        C3   Mary MacLeod, 1874-1963, m. Finlay <u>MacLean</u>, Hopefield, with issue:

            D1   Peter MacLean, m. Murdina <u>MacLean</u>.

            D2   William MacLean.

            D3   Florence MacLean.

            D4   Alexander MacLean.

            D5   Angus MacLean.

            D6   Lester MacLean.

        C4   Catherine MacLeod, m. Ernest <u>Rosebrook</u> in U.S.A., with issue:

            D1   Elbridge Rosebrook.

            D2   Albert Rosebrook.

        C5   Daniel MacLeod, 1880-1972, m. Maude <u>MacDonald</u> of Belle River and Boston, no family. They adopted a girl who died in her thirties.

This information from *History of Hopefield* and Samuel Porter MacLeod, Madison, Maine.

LETTER
LETTER FROM JOHN MACLEOD OF CARDROSS TO DONALD MACLEOD

Prince Edward Island,
Wood Island Road,
North America.
June 12th, 1875.

To:
Donald MacLeod,
Holman, Raasay, Scotland.

Dear Brother and Dear Mary your Beloved,

I take this opportunity of writing you once more to let you know that I am living as yet, and also to let you know the difficulties I met with in my old age. The death of Murdoch which took place on the first of April, 1873, and the death of his mother in April, 1874, and also what happened [to] Alexander Senior in a moment by losing the motion of his left side and that six years ago and got no recovery yet. He was a good house carpenter and could make cart wheels and plough and every kind of work in that line. And Alexander Junior called after your brother. I gave him good learning and a good trade. He served his time learning the carriage making and when he was out of his time he left the Island unknown to me and got married to a Yankee girl. Now he has got two sons and a daughter. The eldest son is called after his brother's name and the other called Frank and the girl Mary, and as I told you before, John left the Island twenty years ago and have not heard any account of him since 18 years. He was not 20 years when he left and his height was 6 ft. 2 inches and as stout accordingly, and Alex. Jnr. and Murdoch were just as big.

We had a snug property, 160 acres of free land and eight head of cattle, 2 horses, and 27 head of sheep. They were all sold by auction and I may say for half price. They were not sold for debt. The day Murdoch died we did not owe a cent to anyone. Death was the cause of all this.

I was planning one time to send for your son but thought it would be rather unfair to take your son from you. I think if you had come to the Island when you sold your property you would be better off and I am sure it would be better for your son.

I am sorry to say that I heard you are bed-fast since three years and another story that you are blind but I hope neither of them are right and also I am sorry that my near relatives are called to Eternity.

There are none of my uncle Duncan's family living, only Norman and two Catherines and Murdoch MacLean's widow, and also my cousins, Murdoch MacPhrier's family are all dead, only Catherine alone. We had a very heavy snow on the Island this last winter, the heaviest I've seen since I came here. But coming on towards the spring it all went away without much rain or flood.

Dear brother, I must now conclude with my kind compliments to your wife Jane, Norman, not forgetting the rest of your family. My kind regards to Widow MacLean and the same to his _____. You will mind me to James MacKenzie also.

No more at present time. May the Lord be with you all. Amen.

Your truly brother,

John MacLeod,
Wood Island Road,
Prince Edward Island,
North America.
My age 83 years.

A copy of the above letter was kindly given to us by the Hon. Angus MacLean, Lewes, P.E.I., and refers to the family of John MacLeod and Christine MacIntyre of Cardross. (H.S.M.)

EXCERPTS FROM A LETTER
LETTER FROM MALCOLM MACLEOD, ISLE OF RAASAY, SCOTLAND

The following excerpts of a letter received from Malcolm MacLeod, Isle of Raasay, Scotland.

November 15, 1986

My great-grand uncle John MacLeod, his wife Marion Gillis and their son Hugh, went to P.E.I. at the time 1851-54 when Raasay was claimed for a sheep farm.

I traced that Hugh was afterwards a merchant at Burbank, Bradalbane, P.E.I. His grandson Donald R. MacLeod lives in Sidney, N.S.

I don't know where John MacLeod settled in P.E.I. nor the name of the ship on which he went.

Another family from here was Kenneth Graham and his wife Rachel MacLeod. They settled not far from Hugh MacLeod. As far as I know, Rachel was related to us.

Also evicted earlier than the above were several families—all my relatives: Nicholsons, MacLennans, Mathesons, etc. etc. These went to P.E.I. on the *Polly*. There were also MacLeods from here who went to New Zealand with Rev. Norman MacLeod. Possibly they were first on P.E.I.

I correspond with John MacLeod, Vancouver (ancestors from here went to P.E.I.). His father was the pilot of the first flying boat that landed in Skye in the 1920s. His father was Earl MacLeod.

JOHN MACLEOD
JOHN MACLEOD AND CHRISTINE MACINTYRE OF MELVILLE, MONTAGUE AND CARDROSS

Duncan MacLeod was born in 1775 in Scotland and died in Scotland. He was the father of a large family, most of whom settled in the Rona, Mellville and Montague River areas on P.E.I. Their children were:

A1   Margaret MacLeod, 1795-1882, m. Murdoch <u>MacLean</u> in Raasay and they later moved to Melville, P.E.I., in 1832. He was the son of Neil (Mor) MacLean, and his wife, believed to be Ann MacLeod, both of Raasay. They had issue:

B1   Jessie MacLean, born 1823 in Raasay, buried in Caledonia, P.E.I., in 1914, never married.

B2   Margaret MacLean, 1828-1918, m. her cousin Norman <u>MacLeod</u>, of whom more will be said afterwards.

B3   Duncan MacLean , born at Flat River, Sept. 25, 1832, died 1906, buried in Caledonia, m. Margaret <u>MacPherson</u>, daughter of George MacPherson and Christy Matheson who came out from Skye on the *James W. Gibb* in 1858. Margaret was nineteen years of age at the time. They were relatives of Sandy Neil MacPherson of Grandview. Duncan and Margaret's family were:

C1   Murdoch MacLean, M.D., 1864-1903, who practised in San Francisco, buried in Caledonia, never married.

C2   Christy MacLean, 1866-1902, m. James <u>MacLennan</u>.

C3   Margaret MacLean, 1868-1934, m. John <u>MacPherson</u>.

C4   Catherine MacLean, born 1872, m. 1) Donald J. <u>MacPherson</u>, 2) John <u>Wolff</u>.

C5   Mary Anne MacLean, 1874-1879.

C6   Effie MacLean, 1876-1878, she and Mary above died of diphtheria.

C7   Jessie MacLean, 1878-1951, m. David John <u>Buell</u> of Murray Harbour.

C8   George Allan MacLean, 1880-1966, m. Sarah <u>MacLean</u>, they lived in Lewes, with issue:

D1   Margaret Christine MacLean, m. John William <u>MacKenzie</u>.

D2   Catherine MacLean, m. Hendry Ogilvy <u>McLellan</u> (see "My Quebec Cousins"), with issue:

E1   Flora Christine McLellan.

F1   Paulajo McLellan.

F2   Randolph Arthur McLellan.

E3   Hugh Hendry McLellan, m. Judith Ruthanne <u>Parent</u>, issue:

F1   Catherine Susan McLellan.

F2   Lloyd Hendfy McLellan.

F3   Thomas Harold McLellan.

F4   Lunn Doris McLellan.

D3   Duncan Murdoch MacLean, 1906-1911.

D4   Mary Isabella MacLean, 1908-1953, m. Kenneth Samuel <u>Nicholson</u>.

D5   Effie Margaret MacLean, m. Raymond Stanfield <u>Smith</u>.

D6   Murdoch MacLean, m. Glennith <u>Burtt</u>.

D7   Hon. John Angus MacLean, who served many years as a Member of the House of Commons, Ottawa, representing his native

Province, and later as Premier of P.E.I., m. Gwendolyn E.M. Burwash. They now reside in Lewes, P.E.I. They had issue:

- E1   Jean MacLean.
- E2   Alan MacLean.
- E3   Mary MacLean.
- E4   Robert MacLean.

   D8   Malcolm Daniel MacLean, 1916-1917.

   C9   John Angus MacLean, born 1882, died in Oakland, California, in 1928.

A2   Christine MacLeod, m. Murdoch MacLeod, who had a sister Mary, who married Malcolm MacLean, Lower Culloden. They had at least two children named John and Alec, another sister was married to John Munroe, also a brother Donald and another brother, who had a son named Donald, who had a daughter married to John MacLean, Heatherdale. Christine and Murdoch had issue:

B1   Norman MacLeod, 1827-1907, m. Margaret MacLean, 1828-1918. They were living in Upper Belle River on Douse's Road in 1857, and moved to Cardross sometime after that date. They are both buried in Cardigan Presbyterian Cemetery. Their children were:

- C1   Mary MacLeod, born June 4, 1854, at Back Settlement of Belle Creek. She was married to Daniel Dewar.
- C2   Anne MacLeod, m. Daniel MacLean.
- C3   Jessie MacLeod, born Oct. 26, 1870, at Selkirk Road. She m. John Oliver of West Devon. He was lost at sea on Dec. 12, 1893.
- C4   Christine MacLeod.
- C5   Alexander MacLeod, 1859-1927, born on P.E.I., m. Helen Stocker in the U.S.A., with issue:
  - D1   Margaret MacLeod, m. John E. McQuiston.
  - D2   Hazel MacLeod, m. Walter L. Lehman.
  - D3   Edith MacLeod, m. Ray E. Hawkins , with a daughter.
    - E1   Edith R. Griffin.
  - D4   Norman MacLeod, died young.
- C6   Murdoch MacLeod, 1865-1933, m. Sarah MacDonald, 1887-1976.
  - D1   Ernest MacLeod, m. Althea Sherren, with issue:
    - E1   Janet MacLeod.
    - E2   David MacLeod.
    - E3   Dorothy MacLeod.
    - E4   Scott MacLeod.
  - D2   Sterling MacLeod, born 1924, m. Kay MacLeod, Mount Hope, issue:
    - E1   Darlene MacLeod, m. Allen Robinson.
    - E2   Cheryl MacLeod.
    - E3   Beverly MacLeod.
  - D3   Alexander MacLeod, born 1922.
  - D4   Christina "Tina" MacLeod, born 1920, m. Arthur Russell, issue:
    - E1   Loreen Russell, m. Steve Fuller, with issue:
      - F1   Paul Fuller.
      - F2   Sarah Fuller.
      - F3   Laura Fuller.
    - E2   Margaret Russell, m. Daniel Andronucci, with issue:
      - F1   Lisa Andronucci.
      - F2   Mark Andronucci.
    - E3   Ann Alexandria Russell, m. Fred Pedley.

E4   John Russell.

D5   Margaret MacLeod, born 1918, m. Newton Smith.

D6   Norman MacLeod, born 1916, m. Alice Kelly, with issue:

  E1   Alexandria "Sandy" Lou MacLeod.

  E2   Elizabeth Ann MacLeod.

B2   Mary MacLeod, 1833-1929, born in Scotland, m. John Cummings, 1833 - c. 1909, from Lot 22, he was also born in Scotland, they lived in Hopedale, with issue:

C1   Alexander Cummings, born 1861.

C2   Roderick Cummings, 1862-1953, m. Flora Matheson, 1863-1938, they lived in Langly, British Columbia, with issue:

  D1   Daniel Cummings, 1889-1989, m. Rizpah Selby-Hele, 1894-1982, both buried in Murraysville cemetery.

C3   Christie Cummings, born 1864, m. William Tanton.

C4   James Cummings, 1866-1920, buried in Uigg cemetery, m. 1) Mary Grace Bolt, she died in childbirth, 1902, in Quincy, Massachusetts. James m. 2) Lottie Nicholson, 1871-1953, they had four children:

  D1   Daniel Cummings, a merchant in Vernon, P.E.I., m. Marguerite Docherty, from Victoria Cross.

  D2   John Cummings, m. Margaret Currie, they lived in Vernon River.

  D3   Garfield Cummings, m. Kay MacLeod.

  D4   Mary Cummings, m. Stephen MacMillan, parents of Elizabeth, see B7-C1-D1-E4-F2.

C5   Murdoch Cummings, born 1868.

C6   John Cummings, 1870-1965, married, lived in Vancouver.

C7   Margaret Cummings, m. George Webber Harper. She is buried in the People's Cemetery, Charlottetown.

C8   Daniel Murdoch Cummings, 1877-1946, m. 1) Nettie Pearl Mitchell, 1883-1912, m. 2) Olive Anne Stewart, she died in childbirth at age 21, m. 3) Margaret MacDonald.

B3   Alexander MacLeod, m. Margaret MacPherson, Little Sands, with issue:

C1   Murdoch MacLeod, 1856-1942, m. Sarah Ann Gillis, 1874-1943, from Orwell Cove. They farmed in Head of Montague and had two children:

  D1   Margaret MacLeod, m. Willard MacPherson, Orwell Cove and U.S.A.

  D2   Clarence MacLeod, m. Violet Coffin, living in Brantford, Ontario.

    E1   Harvey MacLeod.

    E2   Garth MacLeod.

    E3   Marie MacLeod.

C2   Sarah MacLeod, m. _____ Bissell, U.S.A., died young, leaving two children:

  D1   A daughter, died young of diphtheria.

  D2   Clarence Bissell, lived in U.S.A.

C3   Christine MacLeod m._____ Bissell, U.S.A., no family.

C4   Margaret MacLeod, m. Angus MacKenzie, Rona, P.E.I., and New Hampshire.

  D1   Walter MacKenzie, married in U.S.A, five children.

  D2   Jack MacKenzie, married in U.S.A.

  D3   Sarah MacKenzie, m. an undertaker in Newburyport, no family.

C5   John MacLeod, lived in Tonapah, Nevada, U.S.A.

C6   Catherine MacLeod, 1859-1937, m. 1) James MacLeod, 1849-1897,

Rona, P.E.I., son of Donald and Catherine MacLeod, with issue:

D1   Dan MacLeod, m. _____ Bell.

    E1   James MacLeod, living in Braintree, Massachusetts.

D2   Dan Alec MacLeod, born 1880, married in U.S.A., with issue:

    E1   Lillian MacLeod.

    E2   John MacLeod, died in his early teens.

    E3   Bart MacLeod.

    E4   Bill MacLeod.

    E5   Stanley MacLeod.

D3   John Murdoch MacLeod, born 1885, m. Effie Morrison, U.S.A., issue:

    E1   James Stewart MacLeod.

    E2   Morrison MacLeod.

    E3   Ann MacLeod, m. Noel Bell.

D4   John Malcolm MacLeod, died 1895, aged 8 years, and John Daniel (below), died of scarlet fever a month apart.

D5   John Daniel MacLeod, died 1895, aged 6 years

D6   Clarence MacLeod, 1896, m. Ona MacLeod, 1896-1943, daughter of John F. MacLeod, of Uigg, and Annie Nicholson of Orwell Cove.

    E1   John E. MacLeod, living in California since 1949.

    E2   Barbara MacLeod, m. Freeman Reynolds, Montague, who was killed in 1960s, she remarried and is living in U.S.A.

D7   Jessie MacLeod, born 1883, m. Charles Tibbetts, U.S.A., issue:

    E1   Charles Tibbetts, Georgetown, Massachusetts.

    E2   Justin Tibbetts, Wolfeboro, New Hampshire.

Catherine m. 2) Murdoch Gillis. He was m. 1) Mary Ellen Stewart, a first cousin of Catherine's. Their mothers were sisters.

D8   Sarah Gillis, m. John J. Connell, U.S.A., with issue:

    E1   John R. Connell, Columbia, Maryland, U.S.A.

    E2   Katherine Connell, m. a Mr. Walsh, Scituate, Massachusetts.

B4   John MacLeod, m. Christina (first wife).

B5   Christine MacLeod, m. Murdoch MacIntyre.

B6   Duncan MacLeod, m. _____ Collins.

B7   Donald MacLeod, 1843-1924, m. Mary Nicholson, with issue:

  C1   Christine MacLeod,1867-1957, m. John MacLennan, 1859-1900, Hartsville, they had six children:

    D1   Margaret MacLennan, 1891-1974, m. John Duncan MacKenzie, 1883-1953, Hartsville, with issue:

      E1   Dorothy MacKenzie, m. Morrison MacLean, 1902-1973, they lived in North Wiltshire, with issue:

        F1   Gwenyth MacLean, m. James Cruichshank, Vancouver.

        F2   Donald MacLean, m. Catherine Curley, they live in Calgary, with issue:

          G1   Robert MacLean, m. Gabriel Boundreau.

          G2   Timothy MacLean.

          G3   Patricia MacLean.

        F3   Rodney MacLean,m. Karen Cruwys, they live in Darlington, with issue:

          G1   Jane MacLean.

          G2   Sandra MacLean.

G3   Krista MacLean.
F4   Nancy MacLean.
F5   Malcolm MacLean, m. Jacqueline MacLean, They live
     in Darlington, with issue:
     G1   John MacLean.
     G2   Amanda MacLean, 1981-1982.
     G3   Adam MacLean.
E2   Mary MacKenzie.
E3   Kenneth MacKenzie, 1920-1994, m. Margaret Shea. They
     lived in Sudbury, Ontario, with issue:
     F1   June MacKenzie, m. Ed Brouillard, with issue:
          G1   Michael Brouillard.
          G2   Neil Brouillard.
          G3   Andrew Brouillard.
     F2   Mary MacKenzie, m. Paul Rask, with issue:
          G1   John Rask.
          G2   Ryan Rask.
     F3   Catherine MacKenzie, m. Brent Rouse, with issue:
          G1   Lynn Rouse.
          G2   Crystal Rouse.
     F4   Donald MacKenzie, m. Sandy _____, with issue:
          G1   Cuyler MacKenzie.
     F5   Nancy MacKenzie.
E4   John MacKenzie, 1925-1995, m. Norma Stewart. They lived
     in Hartsville, with issue:
     F1   Gail MacKenzie, m. Roger Hall, they live in Alberta,
          with issue:
          G1   MacKenzie Hall.
     F2   Bruce MacKenzie, m. Elizabeth MacMillan Larter, as
          her second husband, she is a member of the Provincial
          Legislature, issue:
          G1   Vanessa Larter.
          G2   Heath Larter.
          G3   Cassandra MacKenzie.
     F3   Donna MacKenzie.
     F4   Kenneth MacKenzie,m. Janice Morrison, with issue:
          G1   Jessica MacKenzie.
          G2   Jennelle MacKenzie.
          G3   James MacKenzie.
     F5   Sandra Lee MacKenzie.
E5   Donald MacKenzie, m. Marion (Scott) MacEachern. They
     live in Fortune Cove, with issue:
     F1   Heather MacKenzie, m. Blair Allen, with issue:
          G1   Sarah MacKenzie Allen.
     F2   Janet MacKenzie, m. James Bliss, as his second wife,
          his children from first marriage were:
          G1   Michelle Bliss.
          G2   Collin Bliss.
     F3   Margaret MacKenzie, m. Duncan Harris, they live in
          Calgary, with issue:
          G1   Gregory Harris.

               G2   Tyler Harris.

E6   Cuyler MacKenzie, living in Hartsville.

E7   Robert MacKenzie, m. Betty MacLeod, they live in Hartsville, with issue:

     F1   David MacKenzie,m. Barbara Simpson, they live in Rothsay, New Brunswick, with issue:

          G1   Craig MacKenzie.

          G2   Darryl MacKenzie.

     F2   Richard MacKenzie, m. Bonnie Beliveau, they live in Hartsville, with issue:

          G1   Shauna MacKenzie.

          G2   Lloyd MacKenzie.

     F3   Janice MacKenzie, m. Kirk Allen, 1955-1997, she is living in Hartsville, with issue:

          G1   Cuyla Allen.

          G2   Samantha Allen.

     F4   Thane MacKenzie, m. Laura Allen, living in Port Colborne, Ontario, with issue:

          G1   Michelle MacKenzie.

          G2   John MacKenzie.

     F5   Judy MacKenzie, m. Tyler Wright, living in Kinkora.

D2   Donald MacLennan, 1893, died as an infant.

D3   Mary (Mamie) MacLennan, 1894-1902.

D4   Katherine MacLennan, 1896-1983, m. John A. MacInnis, 1894-1959, they lived in Hopedale, with issue:

     E1   Kenneth MacKenzie, m. Jean Gordon, living in Charlottetown, with issue:

          F1   Katherine MacKenzie.

          F2   Karen MacKenzie.

     E2   Christine MacKenzie, Hopedale.

     E2   Malcolm MacKenzie, Hopedale.

     E3   Donald MacKenzie, Hopedale.

     E4   Allan MacKenzie, 1937-1940.

D5   Clara MacLennan, 1898-1990, lived in Boston.

D6   John MacLennan,1900-1989, m. Katherine MacDonald, 1906-1995, with issue:

     E1   Marjorie MacLennan, m. Robert Cochrane, with issue:

          F1   Stephen Cochrane, m. Sandra Patten, Toronto, issue:

             G1   Stephanie Cochrane.

          F2   Dean Cochrane, m. Carol Johnson.

          F3   Lisa Cochrane, m. Joseph MacLaren.

     E2   Anna MacLennan, m. Stewart Reeves, Freetown.

     E3   Carol MacLennan, m. Richard Young, living in Lower Sackville.

     E4   Donald MacLennan, on the homestead in Hartsville.

C2   Murdoch D. MacLeod, born 1876, m. Marjorie Catherine MacLeod, born 1876 (see MacLeods of Kinross). They had issue:

     D1   Daniel MacLeod, m. Mary Barnhouse, with issue:

          E1   Gordon MacLeod, m. ____ .

          E2   Mary Katherine MacLeod, m. _____ .

          E3   Dorothy Ellen MacLeod, m. _____ .

D2 Christine MacLeod, m. John Colbert, with issue:
    E1 Arlene Colbert, m. Ol [sic] Bland, Massachusetts, issue:
        F1 Christopher Bland.
D3 Jenny MacLeod, m. Russell Jewell, Hartsville, with issue:
    E1 Alice Rita Jewell, born Oct. 26, 1930, died Oct 29, 1930.
    E2 Cuyler Jewell, born 1932, died Oct. 3, 1978.
    E3 Lloyd Jewell, born Nov. 28, 1933.
    E4 Florence Lois Jewell, m. Donnie Rowell, Bangor, P.E.I.
        F1 Sheila Darlene Rowell.
        F2 Donald Jeffery Rowell.
    E5 Phyllis Jewell, born Feb. 17, 1938, died March 26, 1945.
D4 Cassie MacLeod, never married.
D5 Melville MacLeod, m. Mary MacSwain, they lived in Head of Montague, with issue:
    E1 Phillip C. MacLeod, m. Effie Paton, with issue:
        F1 Lorna Jean MacLeod.
        F2 Gordon Phillip MacLeod.
    E2 Melville MacLeod, died at seven months old.
    E3 James M. MacLeod, m. Sheila O'Brien, with issue:
        F1 Shannon MacLeod.
        F2 Shane MacLeod.
        F3 Shawn MacLeod.
        F4 Stephen MacLeod.
        F5 Sheralea MacLeod.
    E4 Catherine C. MacLeod, m. Cecil Nicholson, with issue:
        F1 Lisa Nicholson.
        F2 Ronnie Nicholson.
        F3 Andrew Nicholson.
        F4 Trevor Nicholson.
        F5 Jennifer Nicholson.
        F6 Aaron Nicholson.
    E5 Linda MacLeod, m. Ralph Moore, with issue:
        F1 Kimberly Moore.
        F2 Kevin Moore.
        F3 Douglas Moore.
        F4 Jason Moore.
    E6 Elinor J. MacLeod.
D6 Margaret E. MacLeod, m. Ray Crosby.
D7 Lewis MacLeod, never married.
D8 Infant son, died at birth.
C3 Margaret MacLeod, m. Louis Dean.
C4 Catherine (Katie) MacLeod, m. Samuel Martin MacLeod (see Kinross MacLeods). They lived in Head of Montague.
C5 Jessie MacLeod, m. _____ Whalen.
C6 Mary MacLeod, m. Dan MacKenzie of Quincy, Massachusetts.

This information was provided by Kaye Nicholson, Whim Road; Norman MacLeod, Michigan; Hon. Angus MacLean, Lewes; Marion MacKenzie, O'Leary; and research at Beaconsfield.

DONALD MACLEOD
DONALD MACKAY AND SARAH CATHERINE JONES OF NEW LONDON AREA

A   There was a Donald MacKay MacLeod who was born Oct. 31, 1833, in New London. His father's name was unknown and his mother was a MacKay. He m. Sarah Catherine (Katie) Jones, born Mar. 22, 1839, in Yarmouth, Nova Scotia. They were married in Carleton, South Bay, St. John, New Brunswick, on the 15th of April 1857. Donald farmed in Canada for a while and then moved to Orange, Texas, about 1875-1880, he then moved to Los Angeles, California. He died Nov. 13, 1918, in Los Angeles. Sarah died Jan. 30, 1922, in Los Angeles. They are buried in Englewood Cemetery, California, and had issue:

B1   John E. MacLeod, born May 11, 1858, in South Bay, New Brunswick, died 1861, buried in New London.

B2   Hannah Amelia (Minnie) MacLeod, born Dec. 7, 1861, New London.

B3   John Edward (Eddie) MacLeod, born July 4, 1863, New London.

B4   Carrie A. MacLeod, born Oct. 14, 1865.

B5   Frederick Eldon MacLeod, born March 4, 1867, Carleton, New Brunswick.

B6   William Wallace MacLeod, born April 16, 1869, Carleton, New Brunswick.

B7   Albert S. MacLeod, born March 4, 1871, Carleton, New Brunswick.

B8   Donald Herbert MacLeod, born Jan. 11, 1874, Fredericton, New Brunswick.

B9   Hugh Franklin MacLeod, born Jan. 11, 1874, Fredericton, New Brunswick.

B10   Andrew Bertram ("A. B." or "Bert") MacLeod, born March 7, 1878, Fredericton, New Brunswick.

This information was provided by Marion Gilbert Hewitt, Hemet, California.

Donald McLeod
Donald McLeod and Christian McLeod of Hopedale

A   Donald McLeod, 1811-1889, is the son of John Torquil McLeod and Jane Munroe, of Raasay (see Little Sands family). Donald m. Christian MacLeod, 1817-1876, they had issue:

B1   Mary McLeod, 1838-1904, m. Alexander MacLeod, 1819-1897. Their family is listed under the MacLeods of Lorne Valley.

B2   Murdoch McLeod.

B3   Catherine McLeod, born 1848.

B4   John D. McLeod, 1849-1920, m. Christy Ann MacKenzie, 1860-1897, with issue:

     C1   Gordon McLeod, m. Jane Nicholson, with issue:
        D1   Wellington McLeod.
        D2   Irving McLeod.
     C2   Wellington McLeod.
     C3   Janie McLeod, m. Dr. MacPherson, with issue:
        D1   Gordon MacPherson.
     C4   John Alex McLeod, m. _____ Jardine.
     C5   Calvin McLeod, m. _____ Buchanan.
     C6   Campbell McLeod.
     C7   John S. McLeod, died Jan. 18, 1892, age 2 years.
     C8   Calvin McLeod, died Aug. 25, 1894, age 6 months.

B5   Jane McLeod, 1850-1877, m. John Arthur.

B6   John E. McLeod, 1853-1939, m. Mary Ann Nicholson, 1867-1936.
     C1   George McLeod.
     C2   Duncan McLeod.
     C3   Christy McLeod, m. Reigh Barrett, with issue:
        D1   Thelma Barrett.
        D2   Betty Barrett.
        D3   Gertrude Barrett.
        D4   John Barrett.

B7   Angus McLeod, 1858-1927.

B8   Anne McLeod, born 1861.

Information provided by Barbara MacLeod, Charlottetown.

DONALD MACLEOD
DONALD MACLEOD AND CATHERINE OF IRIS AND HOPEFIELD

A   Donald MacLeod, died 1887. Apparently he came from Skye, emigrating to Belfast on the *Polly*. He married a woman named Christy in his will, known as Catherine to one set of descendants and known as Mary to another set of descendants. Her last name may have been <u>Martin</u>. They had issue:

B1   Roderick MacLeod.

B2   John MacLeod.

B3   Dougald MacLeod, born Dec. 28, 1840, at Kinross, died 1928. He m. Isabelle <u>MacLeod</u>, born April 8, 1853, in Mt. Vernon. She was the daughter of Donald and Mary MacLeod, and sister of Alex, Annie, Roderick, Christie, Margaret, Mary, and John. Dougald and Isabelle had issue:

C1   Donald Alexander MacLeod, known as "D. A." was born in Iris on Sept. 1877 and died Jan. 1966. He married Rachel <u>Matheson</u> in 1905 and they celebrated a 60th wedding anniversary. She was born in Dover in April 1881 and died April 1974. Her parents were Donald Matheson and Katie MacLeod. Katie was born in Mt. Vernon and had sisters Effie, Isabella MacRae, Catherine MacKenzie. Donald and Rachel lived in Massachusetts for several years before returning to Iris where D. A. worked as a section man for the CNR for thirty years. They had issue:

D1   James William MacLeod, lived in Massachusetts. He served 7 years in the U.S. Marines, worked 35 years in United Machine Corp., m. Marian <u>Peabody</u> of Massachusetts, with issue:

E1   June MacLeod.

E2   Lois MacLeod.

D2   Daniel Harris MacLeod, born in Massachusetts. He moved back to Massachusetts as a young man, but returned to Iris where he m. 1) Mary <u>Morrow</u>. She died in 1941.They had issue:

E1   Verna Catherine MacLeod, m. Robert <u>Delahint</u>, Moncton, issue:

F1   Daniel Robert Delahint.

F2   Kimberly Anne Delahint.

E2   Leaman Daniel MacLeod, m. Florence <u>Gosley</u>, living in Burlington, Ontario, with issue:

F1   Gary Daniel MacLeod.

F2   Roberta Mae MacLeod.

F3   Mark Lee MacLeod.

F4   Brenda Rose MacLeod.

F5   Catherine Verna MacLeod.

Danny worked at many jobs including operating a sawmill and a woodworking shop and as a carpenter at Beach Grove for 23 years. He m. 2) Roberta Phyllis <u>Campbell</u>, of O'Leary.

E3   Gerald Archibald MacLeod, m. Sharon <u>Hemphill</u>, of Covehead.

F1   Mathew Harris MacLeod.

F2   Ryan John MacLeod, twin of Mathew.

F3   Hayley Phyllis MacLeod.

D3 Kate Belle MacLeod, born in Massachusetts, m. 1) Herman Martin of Hopefield, with issue:

   E1 Edison Earl Martin, m. Marie MacLean, with issue:
      F1 Darlene Martin.
      F2 Cassie Martin.
      F3 Douglas Martin.
      F4 Donna Martin.
      F5 Dwayne Martin.
      F6 Lori Anne Martin.

   Katie m. 2) Clifford Newman.

   E2 Wayne Newman, m. Leslie Mousis of Toronto, with issue:
      F1 John Newman.
      F2 Wayne Newman.
      F3 Steven Newman.
      F4 Another son.

D4 Harry Tuttle MacLeod, born in Massachusetts, m. Mary Ross of Iris. He ran the general store in Hopefield. They had issue:

   E1 Marion Mae MacLeod, died in infancy.
   E2 Miriam Mae MacLeod, m. Cleveland Hancock, with issue:
      F1 Diane Hancock, m. Robert Panting.
      F2 Roger Hancock, single.
      F3 Barry Hancock, m. Robyn Richards.
   E3 Daniel William MacLeod, m. Mary Martin, Caledonia. They live in Eureka, Nova Scotia, with issue:
      F1 Robert MacLeod.
      F2 Mark MacLeod.
      F3 Melanie MacLeod.
   E4 Marvin Lorne MacLeod, m. Susan White, Murray Harbour.
      F1 Christopher MacLeod.

D5 Nellie Mae MacLeod, died in infancy.

D6 Christy Janet MacLeod, m. James Gosley. Both died in 1953 in a propane fire. They had issue:

   E1 Gordon Gosley, m. 1) Jean Kelly, m. 2) Karen MacLeod, daughter of Edison Earle MacLeod and Nanette Cook. They live in Hunter River, with issue:
      F1 Jennifer Gosley.
      F2 Angela Gosley.

D7 Simon Douglas MacLeod, born in Iris, m. Lillian White, of Little Sands. They live in Murray River, no family.

D8 Zelda MacLeod, m. Albert Perry, RAF Officer, whom she met when he was stationed in P.E.I. during WWII. They live in England. Issue:

   E1 Valerie Perry.
   E2 Ronald Perry.

D9 Edison Earle MacLeod, born in Iris, died 1967, m. Nanette Cook.

   E1 Karen MacLeod, m. Gordon Gosley, with issue:
      F1 Jennifer Gosley.
      F2 Angela Gosley.
   E2 Thomas MacLeod, m. Cathy Whiteway, with issue:
      F1 Rebecca MacLeod.
      F2 Kirk MacLeod.

E3   Wendy MacLeod, m. Lindsay Juniper, with issue:
 F1   James Juniper.
C2   Angus Murdoch MacLeod, married and died in Massachusetts.
C3   Catherine Mary MacLeod, m. Simon Buell, with issue:
 D1   Clayton Buell.
 D2   Sadie Buell.
 D3   Lizzie Buell.
 D4   Emily Buell.
 D5   Herman Buell.
 D6   Ethel Buell.
 D7   Daniel Buell.
 D8   Charlotte Buell.
 D9   Leon Buell.
 D10 Garnet Buell.
 D11 Dorothy Buell.
 D12 Doreen Buell.
C4   Henry Frank MacLeod, m. Edith Peabody, with issue:
 D1   Everett MacLeod.
 D2   Claire MacLeod, m. Norman Osborne.
 D3   Bruce MacLeod.
B4   Donald MacLeod.
B5   Margaret "Peggy" MacLeod.
B6   Christine "Christy" Margaret MacLeod, 1831-1927, m. Murdoch Beaton, 1824-1896, in 1850. They had issue:
C1   Angus Beaton, born 1852.
C2   John Beaton, born 1854.
C3   Alexander Beaton, m. ___, with issue:
 D1   Marion Beaton, m. Murdoch Hume (her cousin).
C4   Mary Ann Beaton, born 1858.
C5   Donald Beaton, born 1861.
C6   Murdoch Beaton, 1863-1945, never married.
C7   Catherine Beaton, born 1865, m. Peter G. Hume, Iris, with issue:
 D1   Donald Hume, married in U.S.A. with a son and daughter.
 D2   James Hume, m. 1) Myrtle Keenan, with issue:
  E1   Daniel "Don" Hume, married in Calgary, with a family.
  E2   Freeman Hume, m. Emily Buell, living in Orillia, Ontario, with a family.
  E3   A daughter, died young.
 James m. 2) Catherine Stewart, with issue:
  E4   Jean Hume, m. Andrew O'Connor, living in Ontario with a family.
  E5   Zelda Hume, m. William O'Neill, living in Iris, they had ten children.
  E6   Edison Hume, m. Clara MacLeod, deceased, Iris, they had five children.
 D3   Murdoch Hume, m. Marion Beaton, his cousin, with issue:
  E1   Donald Ernest Hume, died in Australia, 1984, m. Sheila Salter, they lived in England and had one daughter.
  E2   James Lawrence Hume, married in U.S.A., with a family.
  E3   Edwin Beaton Hume, living in Takoma Park, Maryland, single.

E4   Catherine Clarie Hume, m. 1) Sam <u>Giddings</u>, they lived in Summerside, with two children. She m. 2) Sylvestre <u>Gallant</u>.

E5   Marion Iris Hume, m. Tom <u>Gorman</u>, Maryland, eleven children.

E6   Murdoch Hume, m. Lorna <u>MacDonald</u>, living in Montague, with children:

      F1   Kevin Hume.

      F2   Lisa Hume.

E7   Margaret Rose Hume, living in Ontario. Unmarried.

C8 Mary Jessie Beaton, 1867-1872.

C9 Roderick Beaton, 1870-1965, unmarried.

C10 Sarah Beaton, 1872-1976. No family.

C11 James Beaton, 1875-1900, unmarried.

C12 Christine Beaton, born 1878.

B7   Marine MacLeod, m. _____ <u>Jordan</u>.

B8   Catherine MacLeod, 1834-1914, m. Alexander <u>Stewart</u>, 1832-1906, with issue:

    C1   Katie Ann Stewart, 1876-1972.

    C2   John Stewart.

B9   Jessie MacLeod, m. John <u>Hume</u>, with issue:

    C1   Peter Hume, m. Catherine <u>Beaton</u>, Christie's daughter.

Information was provided by Danny and Phyllis MacLeod, Betty Barnhill, Donald's will, Murdoch Hume, Montague, and cemetery stones.

Donald Ban Oig MacLeod
Donald Ban Oig MacLeod and Mary Martin of Murray Harbour Road

A   Donald Ban Oig MacLeod, of Valtos, Skye, emigrated in 1829. His wife was
      Mary Martin, also from Skye, they had issue:
  B1 Donald MacLeod, 1818-1896, school teacher, m. Mary Noble at Linwick,
      Quebec. They moved to Nairn, Ontario, and had issue:
    C1 Emma MacLeod, m. William Thompson of Windsor, Ontario, with
      issue:
      D1 Stewart Thompson, killed in WWI.
    C2 Martha MacLeod, m. Peter Stewart of Calgary, with issue:
      D1 Neil Stewart, Dunblane, Saskatchewan.
      D2 Gordon Stewart, Calgary.
      D3 Stanley Stewart, killed in action WWI.
    C3 David Noble MacLeod, m. Jean Waters. They lived in Edmonton,
      Alberta.
      D1 Douglas MacLeod, killed in action WWI.
      D2 George MacLeod.
      D3 Helen MacLeod, m. Gordon Crozier.
      D4 Agnes MacLeod.
    C4 Mary Priscilla MacLeod, m. Colin MacNiven of Minnesota, with
      issue:
      D1 Mary MacNiven.
    C5 Matilda MacLeod, lived in Winnipeg.
    C6 Frederick MacLeod, of Los Angeles, m. Anna Kinnisten, with issue:
      D1 Donald Keith MacLeod.
    C7 Edward Alexander MacLeod, m. Clara Holt, with issue:
      D1 Murray MacLeod.
    C8 Katalena MacLeod, Minneapolis.
  B2 John MacLeod, married with issue.
  B3 Malcolm MacLeod, died in Nebraska, m. 1) Anne MacPhee, died 1866.
      She was from Brown's Creek, P.E.I. They had issue:
    C1 Malcolm MacLeod, born Dec. 1844.
    C2 Jessie MacLeod, born April 1847, m. _____ Wight, of Quincy,
      Massachusetts.
    C3 Donald MacLeod, born Sept. 1849, married with a family.
    C4 John J. MacLeod, born 1851, m. Mary Finlayson, of Leith, Scotland.
      They lived in Uigg, with issue:
      D1 Louise MacLeod, m. John D. MacDonald of Kinross, no issue.
      D2 Malcolm MacLeod, m. Marion Hugh of Murray Harbour. They
      lived in Uigg, with issue:
        E1 Louise MacLeod, R.N., m. Arnold MacLeod (see the fam-
      ilies of Norman and "Old" Murdoch, both of Uigg, and
      Murdoch "Tailor" of Orwell Corner). Louise and Arnold
      have two children:
          F1 Jean MacLeod.
          F2 Robert MacLeod.
        E2 Malcolm MacLeod, m. Margaret MacLeod, R.N., with issue:
          F1 Barry MacLeod.

   F2 Shirley MacLeod.

   F3 Donna Faye MacLeod.

  E3 Clara MacLeod, R.N., m. 1) Robert Shaw, with issue:

   F1 Graeme MacLeod Shaw.

   F2 James Robert Shaw.

  Clara m. 2) Bobby MacLeod, Kinross.

C5 Donald Ban MacLeod, Rev., 1854-1918, m. 1) Elizabeth Dyer, with issue, m. 2) Mary J. MacLeod, Kinross.

 D1 Elizabeth MacLeod, m. Rev. William C. Wauchope.

C6 Charles MacLeod, born 1856, married with a family.

C7 Angus Charles MacLeod, born 1859. He lived in Langley, Washington.

C8 Roderick MacLeod, born 1861, married with a family.

C9 Hugh MacLeod, born 1863, a lawyer, he lived in Langley, Washington.

C10 Murdoch William MacLeod, born April 1866. He lived in Langley, Washington, married with a family.

B4 Roderick MacLeod, 1822-1896, m. Marjory Martin, daughter of his first cousin Charles. Their children were:

C1 Flora MacLeod, born 1848, m. Alexander Gillis, Orwell Cove and Grandview, with issue:

 D1 John Alexander Gillis, m. Elizabeth MacLeod of Valleyfield. They inherited his grandfather Roderick MacLeod's farm at Orwell Head.

  E1 Florence Gillis, R.N., Massachusetts.

  E2 Margaret Gillis, R.N., Massachusetts.

  E3 Donald John "J" Gillis, m. Mary Nicholson, Orwell Cove. They farmed in Lyndale, with issue:

   F1 Elizabeth Gillis, m. Arnold MacLean, Wheatley River. They farm in Kinross and have a family.

   F2 Florence Gillis, married in U.S.A.

   F3 Roger Gillis, m. Betty Howlett, with children.

  E4 Wilfred Gillis, m. Margaret Scott, with three daughters.

 D2 Roderick Gillis, m. a Waldorff, in Eureka, California.

 D3 Marjory Gillis, m. Charles Hammond Nelson, U.S.A.

 D4 Catherine Gillis, m. Fred Cheesman, Quebec.

 D5 Charles Gillis, m. Ann MacDonald, Eureka, California.

 D6 Elizabeth Gillis, lived in Vancouver, never married.

 D7 Mary Jane "Minnie" Gillis, m. Scott Stewart, Charlottetown. Issue:

  E1 Earl Stewart, m. Ruth Garnhum. They had a family.

 D8 Alexander Gillis, m. Adele Jane Ings, they lived in Detroit and had a family.

 D9 Sadie Gillis, m. Ray Bassett, Oakland, California.

 D10 Marjory Gillis, died age five.

 D11 Catherine Gillis, died in infancy.

C2 Marjory MacLeod, m. Malcolm Gillis of Lyndale, a brother of Alexander, who married her sister.

C3 Charles MacLeod, went to Australia.

C4 Christy MacLeod, m. Capt. Neil Campbell, Oakland, California.

C5 Donald C. MacLeod, born 1859, was a broker in Washington State.

C6 Malcolm MacLeod.

C7 Mary MacLeod, m. _____ Livingstone.

C8   Another daughter, m. John <u>MacPherson</u>, Kinross, with issue:
- D1   Malcolm MacPherson, m. Jessie <u>Murchison</u>, daughter of Sandy, Orwell Head, with issue:
  - E1   Mary MacPherson, m. Alec <u>Barrett</u>, Ottawa, with issue, Malcolm and others.
  - E2   Alexander MacPherson, lived in Kinross, single.
  - E3   John MacPherson, died in Toronto, aged 62, never married.
- D2   Christy MacPherson, m. John <u>Livingstone</u>, Hopefield, where they have descendants living.
- D3   Kate MacPherson, m. John "Stonehouse" <u>MacLeod</u>. (See family of "Tailleur" MacLeod.)
- D4   Died young.
- D5   Died young.

B5   Samuel MacLeod, lived in Murray River. (See family of Samuel and Selena Blackmore.)

B6   Nancy MacLeod.

B7   Margaret MacLeod, m. John <u>Livingstone</u> of High Bank. They are buried in Belle River.

B8   Catherine MacLeod, m. Malcolm <u>Martin</u> of Brown's Creek, with issue:
- C1   Charles Martin, married in Belmont, Manitoba, with issue:
  - D1   Emily Martin.
  - D2   May Martin.
  - D3   Ellen Martin of Winnipeg.
- C2   Samuel Martin, married in Belmont, Manitoba, with issue:
  - D1   Catherine Martin, m. Dr. <u>Stevenson</u>.
- C3   John Martin, of Los Angeles, California.
- C4   Daniel Martin, of Los Angeles, California.

This information from book *Skye Pioneers and The Island*, with additions.

JOHN MACLEOD
JOHN MACLEOD AND ANNIE ACORN OF CALEDONIA AND IRIS

A   John MacLeod, died in 1870, when his son Joseph was only eight years old. He married Annie Acorn of Peters Road. Both were buried on P.E.I. They had issue:

B1 Joseph MacLeod, 1878-1950, m. Effie MacLeod, 1883-1967, who was the daughter of John MacLeod and Isabella Matheson, who were both born on the Isle of Skye and first went to Nova Scotia. She had three sisters: Flora, went to the States; Mary, went to Nova Scotia and married a McNeil; and Christie. She had three brothers: John and Hugh went to the States; and a brother Duncan. Joseph and Effie married on March 16, 1904, in Caledonia. The dates for Joseph and Effie were found on the stones in Caledonia Cemetery. They had issue:

C1 Annie MacLeod, 1905-1971, m. Angus Matheson, 1892-1972, they are buried in Caledonia Cemetery. Annie had two boys:
   D1 Fulton, married in Summerside and had two or three boys.
   D2 Amiel, no family. He was in the Korean War, he died in Montague in 1982 and is buried in Caledonia.

C2 John Lawrence (Jack) MacLeod, born Aug. 11, 1906, in Caledonia, m. Ethel Campbell from Alliston. Jack joined the Armed Services in September of 1939. After spending two years in England, they farmed in Alliston. They retired to Montague where Jack died on May 22, 1966. Issue:
   D1 Lawrence Wallace MacLeod, born in Alliston.
   D2 Alethia June MacLeod, born June 26, 1931, in Iris. She drowned on Feb. 28, 1962, and is buried in Caledonia Cemetery.
   D3 Elwood Sydney MacLeod, born in Iris, m. Elva Gillis, from Point Pleasant, with issue:
      E1 George Henry MacLeod.
      E2 David William MacLeod.
      E3 Gordon Samuel MacLeod.
      E4 Linda June MacLeod.
   D4 Edward Joseph MacLeod, born in Iris, m. Shirley Stewart from Wood Islands, with issue:
      E1 John Edward Bruce MacLeod, m. Lynn Matheson from Hopefield.
      E2 Brian Darryl MacLeod.
   D5 John Lawrence MacLeod, died 2003, m. Rhoda Sanderson from Launching.

C3 Isabelle MacLeod, died as an infant in a house fire.
C4 Sadie MacLeod, born Nov. 5, 1909, died 1933, never married.
C5 Stanley MacLeod, born Aug. 25, 1910, in Caledonia. Farming was his occupation, m. Elizabeth Mae Hume, from Brooklyn, with issue:
   D1 Haughton MacLeod, born in Brooklyn, m. Dorothy LePan, with issue:
      E1 Jeff MacLeod.
      E2 Kenny MacLeod.

      D2   Elizabeth Louise (Beth) MacLeod, m. Alan <u>Wong</u>, with issue:
          E1   Jamie Wong.
          E2   Aimil Wong.

Joseph and Effie and children moved to Iris from Caledonia when Stanley was three months old.

   C6 Stewart MacLeod, born Nov. 21, 1913, m. Dolena <u>MacKay</u>, with issue:
      D1   Duncan MacLeod.
   C7 Christie MacLeod, m. Freddie <u>MacRae</u>.
   C8 Earl MacLeod, m. Bonnie <u>Blacquiere</u>. They had three or four boys:
      D1   Barry MacLeod, Southport.
      D2   John MacLeod, Ontario.
      D3   Dwight MacLeod, Ontario.
   C9 Eileen MacLeod, m. Carl <u>MacKenzie</u>, moved to Vancouver, one daughter.
   C10 Lois MacLeod, m. 1) Elgin <u>Buell</u>, with issue:
      D1   Sharon Buell.
      D2   Jimmy Buell.
      Lois m. 2) Eddie <u>Gay</u>.

B2   James MacLeod, m. _____ <u>MacDonald</u>, with issue:
   C1 Mary MacLeod, m. Reggie <u>Buell</u>.
   C2 John R. MacLeod.
   C3 Jessie MacLeod, m. Wilmot <u>MacLeod</u> (Barbara's son).
   C4 Frances MacLeod, m. Joseph <u>Kennedy</u>.

B3   Barbara Isabella MacLeod, born Jan. 1, 1878, had issue:
   C1 Lester MacLeod, Montague, m. Lois <u>Smith</u>, with issue:
      D1   Dianne MacLeod, m. Barry <u>White</u>.
   C2 Wilmot MacLeod, m. Jessie <u>MacLeod</u> (James' daughter). They lived in Hopefield, with issue:
      D1   Sylvia MacLeod, m. John <u>Stewart</u>, with issue:
          E1   Larry Stewart.
          E2   Brenda Stewart.
          E3   Dana Stewart.
          E4   Terry Stewart.
          E5   Jacqueline Stewart.
   C3 Benny MacLeod, was in WWI, killed in action.
   C4 Amelia MacLeod, m. Malcolm <u>MacDonald</u>.

B4   Mary Jane MacLeod, m. Peter <u>MacKinnon</u>, with issue:
   C1 Judson MacKinnon.
   C2 Harold MacKinnon, born 1911, m. Hannah <u>Campbell</u>, 1914-1986. She was a sister of Ethel Campbell, Jack's wife. They lived in Murray River, issue:
      D1   Helen MacKinnon, m. Edward <u>Young</u>. They live on Peters Road.
          E1   Ernest Young.
          E2   Mona Young.
          E3   Beverly Young.
          E4   Joan Young (twin).
          E5   June Young (twin).
      D2   John MacKinnon, m. Ethel <u>Crossman</u>, with issue:
          E1   Hannah MacKinnon, m. Thomas <u>Dougas</u>, with issue:
             F1   Tanya Dougas.
             F2   John Dougas.

   E2 Harold MacKinnon.
   E3 Kevin MacKinnon.
   E4 Linda MacKinnon.
   E5 Heather MacKinnon.
   E6 Barbara MacKinnon.
   E7 Roger MacKinnon.
  D3 Peter MacKinnon, m. Lois Singleton, with issue:
   E1 Carla MacKinnon.
   E2 Lorraine MacKinnon.
   E3 Cynthia MacKinnon.
   E4 James MacKinnon.
  D4 Beryl MacKinnon, m. Alvin Singleton, with issue:
   E1 Julie Singleton.
   E2 Anne Singleton.
   E3 Annabelle Singleton.
   E4 Lorne Singleton.
   E5 Darlene Singleton.
  D5 Nadine MacKinnon, m. Stirling Crossman, with issue:
   E1 Judson Crossman.
   E2 Tammy Crossman.
 C3 Pearl MacKinnon, m. Lee Nicolle, Murray River, with issue:
  D1 James Nicolle, died age 13.
  D2 Evelyn Nicolle, m. Emerson Johnston, Murray River, with issue:
   E1 Garry Johnston, m. Glenda Stewart, daughter of Alec and Elsie Stewart, with issue:
    F1 Janna Johnston.
    F2 Tara Johnston.
  D3 Audrey Nicolle, m. Howard Rafuse.
  D4 Norma Nicolle, m. Allen Prime.
  D5 Judson Nicolle, m. Mary Butler from Sheet Harbour, Nova Scotia.
  D6 Lois Nicolle, m. 1) Louis Jenkins, 2) Don MacLeod, Halifax.
  D7 Jo-Anne Nicolle, m. Lloyd Higgins, from Musquodoboit, Nova Scotia.
  D8 Hammond Nicolle, m. Eva Bears, daughter of John, Brooklyn.
  D9 Anne Nicolle, m. Timmy Fraser.
  D10 Blain Nicolle, m. Susanna Reid.
  D11 Darlene Nicolle, m. Bud Lowe, Murray River, with four children.
 C4 Kate MacKinnon, m. John Currie MacLean, they lived in New Brunswick.
 C5 Josie MacKinnon, m. _____ Stockfort, Murray River.
 C6 Devon MacKinnon, was married but the name of her husband is unknown.

This information provided by Ethel MacLeod, Montague, and Stanley MacLeod, Heatherdale.

ALLAN MACLEOD
ALLAN MACLEOD AND EUPHEMIA OF MELVILLE

A   Allan and Euphemia Macleod emigrated from the Island of Rona, in 1840. They, with Allan's brother Donald, settled in Melville, Lot 60. Their brothers John, and Malcolm settled in Dundas and their sister Christy MacLeod married Peter MacIntyre. Allan and Euphemia's family were:

B1   Donald MacLeod, came from Rona, Scotland, to P.E.I. in 1840. It seems likely that he is the son of Allan and Euphemia MacLeod. Donald m. Jessie Bruce, who died of measles on Jan. 12, 1906, age 54 years. She was a daughter of Sandy Bruce, Lyndale, and is buried at Valleyfield Cemetery. They had seven children, the order of birth is uncertain.

C1   Effie MacLeod, went to the U.S.A.

C2   Sarah MacLeod.

C3   Christie MacLeod, m. Isaac Acorn and had three boys. The only known name is Seymour, who married a woman named Sandra.

C4   Murdoch MacLeod, never married. He was a contractor in U.S.A.

C5   Katherine (Kate) MacLeod, m. Mr. Renault, and moved to U.S.A.

C6   Dan MacLeod.

C7   Allan MacLeod, 1874-1956, born in Alliston, m. Hannah Moore from Abney, born 1889, died at 92 years. They had three children. Allan was a stone mason.

D1   Albert MacLeod, born April 29, 1913, in Abney, m. Christine Stewart (Tina), from Brudenell. They had eight children:

E1   Charlie Albert MacLeod, m. Audrey MacDonald, with issue:

F1   Brenda Lee MacLeod.
G1   Jacinta MacLeod.

F2   Anita Ann MacLeod.
G1   Jennifer.
G2   Samantha.
G3   James.

F3   Charlene Marie MacLeod, m. Peter Ginson, New Brunswick.
G1   Natasha Ginson.

F4   Basil Sterling MacLeod, m. Hazel MacMaster, living in Dundas.
G1   Justin MacLeod.

F5   Alice Mae MacLeod.
G1   Matthew MacLeod.
G2   Nakita MacLeod.

F6   Stephen MacLeod, died in infancy.

F7   Kimberly Ann MacLeod.

E2   Willard James MacLeod, m. Carolyn Preper, with four children:

F1   Christine Marie MacLeod.

F2   Gordon William MacLeod.

F3   Tina Elizabeth MacLeod.

F4   Allan James MacLeod.

E3 Joyce Christine MacLeod, m. Chester Johnston, with issue:
    F1 David Chester Johnston.
    F2 Kevin Wayne Johnston.
    F3 Kenny Blair Johnston.
    F4 Blair Robert Johnston.
E4 Basil MacLeod, m. Diane McGillivary, with issue:
    E1 Mark MacLeod.
E5 Ethel May MacLeod, m. Elwood Kennedy, with issue:
    E1 Wayne Lewis Kennedy.
E6 Donnie MacLeod, m. Coleen MacDonald.
E7 George MacLeod, m. Carol Ann MacDonald.
E8 Etta Catherine MacLeod, m. Daniel McInnis, St. Peters.

D2 Annie MacLeod, born Sept. 4, 1917, m. 1) John MacLean, with issue:
    E1 John MacLean.
    E2 Blanche MacLean, m. Mr. Howard from Annandale.
    Annie m. 2) name unknown and had:
    E3 Donnie.
    E4 Sandra.
    Annie lives in Nova Scotia.

D3 Mary MacLeod, living in Nova Scotia. She married twice and had two children by the second marriage.

B2 Anna MacLeod, m. Archie MacLeod.
B3 Rachel MacLeod, m._____ MacLeod.
B4 Sarah MacLeod, m. _____ MacIntyre.
B5 Catherine MacLeod, m. Finlay MacLennan, Lot 60.
B6 Christy MacLeod, m. Neil MacLeod.
B7 John MacLeod, m. Catherine MacLeod, a sister of Angus Neil, John and Alex of Lorne Valley, they moved to Oregon.

Information on Donald MacLeod (B1) and his descendants was provided by Albert and Tina MacLeod. Information on Allan and Euphemia MacLeod (A) and on their children other than Donald (B2 through B7) was an addendum to this genealogy by Harold S. MacLeod and incorporated into the family tree by the publisher of this edition.

MALCOLM MACLEOD
MALCOLM MACLEOD AND EUPHEMIA MACDONALD OF VALLEYFIELD

A   Angus MacLeod, presumably of the Isle of Skye, but quite certainly of Scotland, had as far as can be learned two sons, William and Malcolm. The 1861 census lists Malcolm's family as: over 60, 1 male and 1 female; age 21-45, 1 male and 2 females; under 5 years old, 2 females and 1 male. Seven of the eight were born in Scotland therefore the family arrived in P.E.I. sometime after 1856.

B1   William MacLeod, wife's name unknown, with issue:
    C1   Norman MacLeod.
    C2   Murdock MacLeod.
    C3   Angus MacLeod.
    C4   Douglas MacLeod.
    The descendants live in New York State.

B2   Malcolm MacLeod, of Portree, Skye, Scotland, 1775-1876, m. Euphemia MacDonald, 1789-1878, with issue:
    C1   Donald MacLeod, wife's name unknown, with issue:
        D1   Mary Ann MacLeod, married Mr. Anderson.
        D2   Mary MacLeod, m. a MacLeod. Mrs. Mary MacLeod was living in Vancouver in 1923, she had one daughter.
            E1   Annie MacLeod, m. a MacLean, and in 1923 she was a widow with three grown children.
    C2   Angus MacLeod, wife's name unknown, with issue:
        D1   Rev. A. A. MacLeod, was a Baptist missionary, who retired to Vancouver.
        D2   Effie MacLeod, m. a MacDougall, and lived in Vancouver in the early days of the city. By 1923 she was widowed and thought to be wealthy. They had six children.
        D3   Margaret MacLeod, m. a Robertson and lived on P.E.I. Margaret had only one child who lived, she had others who died as infants. They moved to Vancouver's mild climate in an attempt to save their last child, May.
            E1   May Robertson, died 1961, m. Albert Fish, died 1974, they had two daughters:
                F1   Hilda May Fish, m. _____ Ronquist, with issue:
                    G1   Warren Ronquist, m. Patricia Ruth, with issue:
                        H1   Douglas Ronquist.
                F2   Violet Irene Fish, m. Mr. Blair, with issue:
                    G1   Donna Blair.
        D4   Elizabeth MacLeod, m. William Riley, no children.
        D5   Minnie MacLeod, m. an Allen. They had three children.
    C3   Peter MacLeod, m. Maggie MacLeod, daughter of Angus and Mary MacLeod, Valleyfield (see other Valleyfield family), with issue:
        D1   Annie MacLeod, m. _____ Boyd.
        D2   Sadie MacLeod.
        D3   Malcolm MacLeod.
        D4   John MacLeod.
    C4   John MacLeod.

C5   Alexander MacLeod ("Yankee Sandy"), 1827-1902, m. Margaret
     Matheson, 1833-1901. They were married c. 1856. They had issue:
     D1   Mary Margaret MacLeod, 1857-1950, m. Cuthbert Montgomery.
          He died 1892 and was an uncle of Lucy Maude Montgomery.
          Issue:
          E1   Donald Cuthbert Montgomery, 1892-1968, m. Margaret
               Cousins, died 1938, after the birth of her youngest child,
               Beulah. Issue:
               F1   Muriel Montgomery.
               F2   Hodge Montgomery.
               F3   Ruth Montgomery.
               F4   Sutherland Montgomery.
               F5   Margaret Montgomery.
               F6   Beulah Montgomery.
               Donald had a second wife whose name was Ethel.
     D2   Archibald James MacLeod, 1858-1935 m. Janie McEwen,
          1872-1924.
          E1   Cassie MacLeod, died Feb. 4, 1912.
          E2   Ruth MacLeod, 1892-1959.
          E3   Laura MacLeod, born July 24, 1894, m. Archibald Johnstone
               in Nov. 1920. He died in 1976. They had issue:
               F1   Wendell Johnstone, died June 7, 1951.
          E4   Maude MacLeod, 1898-1982, m. Herbert McEwen in Nov.
               1921. He died in 1986. They had issue:
               F1   Sterling Ross McEwen, m. Juanita Campbell, with
                    issue:
                    G1   Beverly Ann McEwen.
                    G2   Barry Campbell McEwen.
               F2   Archibald Stewart McEwen, m. Helen _____. They
                    lived in Stanley Bridge.
               F3   Janie Margaret McEwen, m. _____ Green, two
                    daughters.
          E5   Daniel MacLeod, born Feb. 1900, m. Irene Murray, issue:
               F1   Joy Victoria MacLeod, m. Lloyd Johnson, one child.
               F2   Janie Caroline MacLeod.
               F3   Alexander Donald MacLeod, m. Jean _____, with
                    issue:
                    G1   Donnie MacLeod.
                    G2   Kenneth MacLeod.
               F4   Scott Archibald MacLeod.
          E6   Vera MacLeod, m. Rupert Simpson, with issue:
               F1   Mary Elizabeth Simpson, m. Byron Houston.
               F2   Claude Simpson.
               F3   Beverly Edwin Simpson.
               F4   Herbert Simpson.
     D3   John Matheson MacLeod, 1860-1939, m. Alice Matheson in 1915.
          He was a minister of the Presbyterian Church and later of the
          United Church of Canada.
     D4   Alexander Daniel MacLeod, 1863-1956, m. Laura Hannah Rob-
          erts, 1872-1957. Alex was a minister of the Methodist Church
          and later of the United Church of Canada. They had issue:

E1 Nellie May MacLeod, 1897-1987, m. William Francis <u>Townsend</u>, 1891-1982, who was born in Albingdon, Illinois. They were married on March 29, 1924, in Calgary, Alberta, with issue:

    F1 Alice Louise Townsend, from first wife of William Townsend, m. Robert Donald <u>MacDonald</u>, Edmonton, issue:

        G1 Donna Louise MacDonald.

        G2 Robert William MacDonald.

    F2 Laura May Townsend, born in Stattler, Alberta, m. John Frederick <u>Perrot</u>, with issue:

        G1 Beverly John Perrot.

        G2 Donald Frederick Perrot, 1954-1956.

        G3 Nellie Perrot, 1957-1957.

E2 George Alexander MacLeod, 1900-1981, m. 1) Ruth <u>Turnbull</u>, 1898-1950, with issue:

    F1 Donald Lorne MacLeod, 1924-1987, born in St. John, New Brunswick, m. Leona <u>Clark</u> on Aug. 27, 1951, in St. John's, Newfoundland, issue:

        G1 Marilyn Ruth MacLeod, m. Alfred <u>Bailey</u>.

        G2 Carolyn Anne MacLeod.

        G3 Sally Elizabeth MacLeod, m. Carl <u>Willis</u>, issue:

           H1 Kyle Willis.

    Donald m. 2) Elizabeth Riley <u>Roesgen</u>, in Kitchener, Ontario, in 1979.

  George Alexander, m. 2) Doris <u>Fairweather</u>, m. 3) Ida <u>Hagerman</u>.

E3 Carmen Stewart MacLeod, 1905-1984, m. Edna Jean <u>MacPherson</u>, in 1953 in Moncton, they lived in Yuma, Arizona, and Edmonton, retiring to Victoria, British Columbia, in 1971.

E4 Edith Laura Margaret MacLeod, 1909-1963, lived most of her life in St. John, New Brunswick where she looked after her parents in their old age.

D5 Margaret Ann Belle MacLeod, 18651-1923, m. William <u>Ramsay</u>. They had no children but raised a girl named Alice around 1911 or 1912, legal adoption unlikely. She has now lost trace of her family.

D6 Katie Ann MacLeod, born July 20, 1868, died May 27, 1888.

D7 Malcolm Angus MacLeod, 1870-1942, lived on original MacLeod farm in Valleyfield, m. Rachel <u>Ross</u>, 1884-1968, with issue:

    E1 Alexander Daniel MacLeod, 1905-1981, was a banker, retired to Saskatoon in 1968, m. Ellen <u>Hodge</u>, born Oct. 12, 1906. They were married on Sept. 6, 1935, and had issue:

        F1 Roderick John MacLeod, born in 1940, m. Joan _____.

           G1 Christopher Ross MacLeod.

           G2 Paul Andre MacLeod.

           G3 Ann Rachelle MacLeod.

        F2 Helen Jean MacLeod (Wendy), m. G. Edward <u>Callahan</u>.

    E2 Maisie Margaret MacLeod, born Dec. 24, 1906, worked for the Federal Civil Service, retired to Charlottetown.

E3   Bessie Catherine MacLeod, born April 1909, m. Albert <u>Robertson</u>. She was a schoolteacher, living in Charlottetown.
    F1   Catherine Robertson.
    F2   Ian Robertson.

E4   Milton Ross MacLeod, born Dec. 2, 1910, m. Isobel <u>Dutton</u>, born Nov. 16, 1903. They had issue:
    F1   James Malcolm MacLeod, 1942-1982. His wife's name was Caroline, they had issue:
        G1   David MacLeod.
        G2   Ross MacLeod.
    F2   John Alexander MacLeod, m. Carol <u>Phene</u>, Valleyfield, Quebec.
        G1   Leesa MacLeod.
        G2   Peter MacLeod.
    F3   Marilyn Rae MacLeod, m. Gary <u>Rose</u>, with issue:
        G1   Angela Rose.
        G2   Stephen Rose.

E5   John Malcolm MacLeod, m. Ellie <u>Harnish</u> on Oct. 2, 1954, he was a minister of the United Church of Canada.

D8   Elizabeth Penelope MacLeod, 1873-1907, m. John <u>Gillis</u>, Orwell Head.
    E1   Florence Gillis.
    E2   Margaret Gillis.
    E3   Daniel J. Gillis, m. Mary <u>Nicholson</u>, with issue:
        F1   Elizabeth Gillis.
        F2   Florence Gillis.
        F3   Roger Gillis.
    E4   Wilfred Gillis, 1905 - c. 1971, m. Margaret <u>Scott</u>. They had three girls.

D9   Daniel John MacLeod, 1876-1901, died while a student in Theology at Dalhousie University, Halifax.

C6   Ann MacLeod.
C7   Another girl who remained in Skye.

This information submitted by Carol MacLeod, Valleyfield.

GEORGE MACLEOD
GEORGE MACLEOD AND ANN HENDERSON OF LONG CREEK

A   George MacLeod, 1840-1912, m. Ann <u>Henderson</u>, she died Jan. 27, 1929, age 87.
        George's father's name is unknown and his mother's name was Grace Piper
        (her parents were from England). Grace and her son George lived with her
        uncle Henry Knight in Long Creek, P.E.I. When Henry Knight died, George
        inherited his farm. They are buried in Long Creek Baptist Church Cemetery.
        They had issue:
B1   Archibald MacLeod, 1866-1952, m. Margaret <u>MacPhee</u>, 1868-1960. They
        lived in the U.S.A. Archibald was a carpenter and helped build the St.
        Thomas Anglican Church, Long Creek, now converted to a home in Canoe
        Cove. They are buried in Shaw's Pioneer Cemetery, St. Catherine's, P.E.I.
        They had issue:
        C1   Benjamin MacLeod, 1888-1947.
        C2   Lois MacLeod, died Jan. 24, 1896, age 5 years.
B2   Joseph MacLeod, m. Minnie <u>Gass</u>. They lived in Victoria, P.E.I. Joseph
        was a blacksmith and fisherman. They had issue:
        C1   William MacLeod.
        C2   Louis MacLeod.
        C3   Annie MacLeod.
        C4   David MacLeod.
        C5   George MacLeod.
        C6   James MacLeod.
        C7   Florence MacLeod.
B3   George MacLeod, Jr.
B4   Elizabeth MacLeod.
B5   John MacLeod, 1876-1959, m. Priscilla <u>MacNeill</u>, 1879-1950. Priscilla was
        from St. Catherine's, P.E.I. They lived in Long Creek, P.E.I. John was a
        farmer. They are buried in Long Creek United Baptist Church Cemetery.
        They had issue:
        C1   George MacLeod.
        C2   Roderick MacLeod.
        C3   Eveline MacLeod.
        C4   Robert MacLeod.
        C5   Marguerite MacLeod.
        C6   Leslie MacLeod.
B6   Alexander MacLeod, 1877-1967, m. Sarah <u>MacFadyen</u>, 1887-1966. They
        lived in Long Creek, P.E.I. He was a farmer and fisherman. They are
        buried in Canoe Cove Presbyterian Church Cemetery. They had issue:
        C1   Della MacLeod.
        C2   Myrtle MacLeod.
B7   Hector MacLeod, 1880-1953, m. Mary Jane <u>MacFadyen</u>, 1888-1921, from
        St. Catherine's, P.E.I. They lived in Fairview, P.E.I. The Donollie Travel
        Park is now on Hector's property. They are buried in Long Creek Baptist
        Cemetery. They had issue:
        C1   Annie MacLeod.
        C2   Garfield MacLeod, 1910-1944, killed in action Nov. 23, 1944, in WWII.
        C3   John MacLeod.

C4   Margaret MacLeod.

C5   Pearl Jane MacLeod, 1921-1922.

B8   Thomas MacLeod, 1881-1933, m. Eleanor Jane <u>Alchorn</u> (Nellie) from Fairview, P.E.I. They lived in Long Creek on Thomas' father's farm. Thomas was a farmer, carpenter and oyster fisherman. He was a sergeant in WWI. He died at the age of 52 leaving Roy his eldest son with the responsibilities of the household. Thomas is buried in Long Creek United Baptist Cemetery.

    C1   Roy MacLeod, 1914-1983, m. Irene <u>MacEachern</u>, born in St. Catherine's. They lived in New Argyle, P.E.I. He is buried in Shaw's Pioneer Cemetery, St. Catherine's. They had issue:

        D1   Clinton MacLeod, m. Elsie <u>Jones</u> from Glace Bay, Nova Scotia. They live in Cape Breton, Nova Scotia. Clinton is a carpenter and carpet layer. Issue:

            E1   Laverne MacLeod.

            E2   Bridgett MacLeod.

        D2   Joan MacLeod, m. Glendon <u>Kerr</u> from Springfield, New Brunswick, with issue:

            E1   Sherri Kerr.

            E2   Tracey Kerr.

        D3   Winfield MacLeod, m. Beth <u>Currie</u> from Fairview. Winfield is a carpenter. He now lives in the Yukon.

        D4   Angela MacLeod, living at home in New Argyle.

    C2   Mary MacLeod, 1917-1948. She died shortly after giving birth to twins. She married Richard <u>Dobbin</u>, and is buried in Kingston United Church Cemetery. After her death her husband took her daughter to Nova Scotia. to live with him and his mother. No one has heard from him since.

        D1   Donna Mae Dobbin.

        D2   Infant, twin at birth.

    C3   Louis MacLeod, born Sept. 29, 1918, in Long Creek, m. Ria <u>Marshall</u> from Glengarry, Nova Scotia. They made their home in Niagara Falls, Ontario. His early years were spent farming and fishing and in 1940 he joined the RCNVR. Their children were:

        D1   William MacLeod, m. Linda <u>Farrow</u> from Ontario, where they live. William is a welder. They had issue:

            E1   Adam MacLeod.

            E2   Mark MacLeod.

        D2   Douglas MacLeod, born July 25, 1962, died Oct. 1962

        D3   Linda MacLeod.

    C4   James Wendell MacLeod, born in Long Creek, m. Ria <u>Marshall</u> from Glengarry, Nova Scotia. He farmed and fished and spent his winters in Nova Scotia, where he had his own trucking business. Six weeks after his marriage he was killed in a truck and train accident on Nov. 20, 1951. He is buried in the Birchill Cemetery, Rocklin, Nova Scotia.

B9   Maude MacLeod, 1889-1917. She is buried in the United Baptist Church Cemetery, Long Creek.

Information received from Angela I. MacLeod, New Argyle, P.E.I., and cemetery transcripts.

MURDOCH MACLEOD
MURDOCH MACLEOD AND PHOEBE MACDONALD OF STRATHALBYN

A   Murdoch MacLeod, was born in Scotland c. 1807, the son of Murdoch MacLeod. He m. Phoebe MacDonald, 1808-1901. They spoke Gaelic. He left his wife and three children behind in Scotland and came to P.E.I. with his two brothers Angus and Sandy around 1830. Nine years later he sent for his wife and three children: Murdoch Jr., Ann, and Christie I. They had five children born in P.E.I.

B1   Murdoch MacLeod, Jr., born in Scotland.

B2   Ann MacLeod, born in Scotland.

B3   Christie I. MacLeod, born in Scotland.

B4   Margaret MacLeod, born in Strathalbyn, P.E.I.

B5   John MacLeod, born in Strathalbyn, P.E.I.

B6   Kate MacLeod, born in Strathalbyn, P.E.I.

B7   Christy MacLeod, born in Strathalbyn, P.E.I. Christie I. MacLeod had died.

B8   Donald MacLeod, born c. 1839 or 1841 in Strathalbyn. He died in St. Eleanor's, P.E.I., on Jan 19, 1914, when he fell from a roof to his death. He is shown in the 1880 atlas to hold 100 acres of land. He was married on July 12, 1867, at Charlottetown to Johanna Buchanan. She was born April 9, 1850, at Hunter River and died May 9, 1946, at Spalding, Saskatchewan. They had issue:

    C1   Christy Ann MacLeod, born Oct. 31, 1869, at Strathalbyn, m. a LaBrech. Baptized Dec. 20, 1868, by Rev. James MacCall. [Unclear who was baptized.]

    C2   Lawrence MacLeod, born Oct. 27, 1872, in Central Lot 16. He married Oct. 1902 in Stamford, Connecticut, to Mary Matthews, who was born Nov. 16, 1882, in Moulton, North Hamptonshire, England. Lawrence died May 28, 1956, and is buried in the "Alpine Cemetery," Perth Amboy, New Jersey. He was a fisherman and then on maintenance at R. & H., which later became E. I. Dupont. Mary died Oct. 16, 1964, and is buried in "Alpine Cemetery," Perth Amboy, New Jersey. Their family were:

        D1   Lawrence MacLeod, born 1903 in Perth Amboy, New Jersey, died 1908, buried in "Alpine Cemetery."

        D2   Mary MacLeod.

        D3   Harry Woolley MacLeod.

        D4   George Henry MacLeod, 1907-1984, born at Perth Amboy, m. Alma Violet Darke, born Nov. 8, 1914, in Bancroft, Maine. They had issue:

            E1   Lawrence John MacLeod.

            E2   Ellen Kay MacLeod.

            E3   George Henry MacLeod, Jr., m. 1) Veronica Pearl Hiatt. She was born at Nottingham, Nottinghamshire, England, with issue:

                F1   Stephen Paul MacLeod, born in Nottinghamshire, England, and was adopted by George in 1962, in New Brunswick, New Jersey.

                F2   Rebecca Alma Hannah MacLeod.

F3   George Henry MacLeod, III.
George Henry, Jr., m. 2) Juanita Louise <u>Bemarkt</u>. No children from this marriage.

C3   Phoebe Jane MacLeod, died in 1956 in Summerside, m. Alfred <u>Cahill</u>.

C4   Alice Jane MacLeod, born Feb. 3, 1875, in Wheatley River. Baptized Dec. 7, 1878, m. _____ <u>Corney</u>.

C5   John Edgar MacLeod, born Feb. 7, 1877.

C6   Laura Edith MacLeod, born Sept. 27, 1878, died Nov. 27 of the same year.

C7   Maggie Laura MacLeod, born June 27, 1879, died 1880.

C8   Bessie MacLeod, born Aug. 24, 1882, m. Ira <u>Carter</u>.

C9   May Ella MacLeod, born March 3, 1884, m. Gresham Russell <u>Wiles</u>, they lived in Archewill, Saskatchewan. She died on Feb. 26, 1984.

C10   Charles Fraser MacLeod, born Dec 25, 1886, died Nov. 7, 1914.

The above information was received from George H. MacLeod, Jr., Kernersville, North Carolina.

MURDOCH MACLEOD
MURDOCH MACLEOD AND SARAH MACINNIS OF GLASGOW ROAD

A   Murdoch MacLeod, died 1905, aged 41, buried in Portage Cemetery, m. Sarah <u>MacInnis</u>, died Sept. 30, 1938. They were both from Glasgow Road. He had one brother, John C. MacLeod, 1866-1958, buried in Portage, also two sisters, Cassie Anderson and Mrs. Godfrey. Murdoch and Sarah's children were:

B1   Gordon Malcolm MacLeod, 1900-1958, buried in Cardigan, m. Jessie Mae <u>MacInnis</u>, with issue:

     C1   Myrna Sadie Ann MacLeod, m. Wendell <u>Jenkins</u>, with issue:

         D1   Harvey Wendell Jenkins , m. Marie <u>Kelly</u>, with issue:

            E1   Amanda Dawn Jenkins.

            E2   Kelli Alicia Jenkins.

         D2   Shirley Anne Jenkins.

     C2   Vernon Donald Gordon MacLeod, m. Jeanette <u>Shaw</u>, with issue:

         D1   Kenneth Dale MacLeod.

         D2   Donald Gordon MacLeod.

         D3   Kimberly Ann MacLeod.

     C3   Kenneth John James MacLeod, m. 1) Judy <u>Campbell</u>, with issue:

         D1   Connie Jean MacLeod.

     Kenneth m. 2) Susan <u>Thompson</u>.

B2   Stanley Magnus MacLeod, 1903-1933, buried in Portage.

B3   John Leslie MacLeod, m. Hazel Rebecca <u>Ford</u>, with issue:

     C1   Ina Arlene MacLeod, m. Joseph <u>Hambly</u>, Jr. , with issue:

         D1   John Stephen Paul Hambly.

         D2   Darren Joseph Hambly.

Submitted by Susan Thompson MacLeod, Montague.

NEIL HUGH MACLEOD
NEIL HUGH MACLEOD AND ANNIE MARTIN OF GLEN MARTIN AND VALLEYFIELD

A   Neil Hugh MacLeod, of Glen Martin, m. Annie <u>Martin</u> of Valleyfield, P.E.I. After the death of his first wife and two of his children, who all died from T.B., Neil went to work in the mines near Sydney, Nova Scotia. He married a widow by the name of Mrs. <u>Berthiaune</u>. She had a daughter by her first husband whose name was Christina. After retiring, Neil and his wife and stepdaughter moved to U.S.A. An old envelope dated Oct. 30, 1933, shows the address of Gare Road, Webster, Massachusetts. He died during WWII.

B1   John MacLeod, did not marry. He died in 1909.

B2   Christina MacLeod (Tina), did not marry. She died in 1908.

B3   Alexander Robert MacLeod, 1892-1934, m. in Vancouver to Elizabeth <u>Woods</u> on June 17, 1915. She was born on March 18, 1895, in Comax, British Columbia.

    C1   Neil Melvin MacLeod, born Aug. 5, 1916, m. Florence <u>Vey</u> in 1939.

        D1   Robert Gayland MacLeod, born in Victoria.

        D2   Neil Courtenay MacLeod, born in Vancouver, m. June Louise <u>Martin</u>, with issue:

            E1   Tracy Louise MacLeod.

    C2   Robert Roy MacLeod, born in Comax, British Columbia, on March 18, 1919, m. Eileen Margaret L. <u>Costello</u> on Oct. 22, 1943, with issue:

        D1   Geoffrey Alexander MacLeod, m. Brenda <u>Ayers</u>, with issue:

            E1   Kirsten MacLeod.

            E2   Cara MacLeod.

            E3   Kori-Anne MacLeod.

            E4   Megan MacLeod.

        D2   Jacqueline Elizabeth MacLeod, born in Vancouver, m. Thomas <u>Richenson</u>, with issue:

            E1   Christopher Ray Richenson.

            E2   Mary Elizabeth Richenson.

        D3   Ian Robert MacLeod, born in Vancouver, m. Donna Louise <u>Walker</u>.

            E1   William Alexander MacLeod.

            E2   Margaret Lillian MacLeod.

        D4   Elizabeth Jean MacLeod, born in Dawson Creek, m. Jack <u>Lopatinsky</u>.

            E1   Eric Alexander Lopatinsky.

            E2   Grant William Lopatinsky.

        D5   Robert Michael MacLeod, born in Victoria.

    C5   Arthur Gilbert MacLeod, m. Connie <u>Koshure</u>, with issue:

        D1   Anne Elizabeth MacLeod.

        D2   Gavin MacLeod.

This information was provided by R. R. MacLeod, Victoria, British Columbia, and Chester Martin, Caledonia, P.E.I.

DONALD MACLEOD
DONALD MACLEOD AND CHRISTIE OF CLYDE AND SPRINGTON

A   Donald MacLeod, born in Scotland c. 1836. His wife Christie was also born in Scotland c. 1833. They farmed in Clyde, with issue:

    B1   Kenneth MacLeod, 1861-1944, m. Flora <u>MacNeill</u>, 1861-1954. Kenneth worked in the gold mines in British Columbia and as a carpenter in the U.S.A. He later bought a farm in Springton, they had issue:

        C1   Kenneth MacLeod, born 1900, m. Flora Grace <u>Nicholson</u>, no children.

        C2   Daniel MacLeod, 1902-1976.

        C3   Gordon MacLeod, 1887-1907.

        C4   Mary MacLeod, m. _____ <u>Harper</u>.

        C5   Belle MacLeod, m. Ray <u>Coles</u>.

        C6   Janett MacLeod, m. _____ <u>Pratt</u>.

        C7   Florence MacLeod, 1898-1912.

        C8   Blanche MacLeod, died 1928, m. _____ <u>Buchanan</u>, with issue:

           D1   Elmer Buchanan.

        C9   Christina MacLeod, 1889-1907.

        C10 Katherine May MacLeod (Katie), m. _____ <u>Dell</u>.

    B2   Daniel MacLeod, born c. 1863.

    B3   Flora J. MacLeod, born c. 1865.

    B4   Bella MacLeod, born c. 1866.

    B5   John MacLeod, born c. 1867.

    B6   Theophilus MacLeod, born c. 1868, m. Liza <u>MacNeill</u> (sister of Flora). She died a young woman, with issue:

        C1   Florrie MacLeod, m. _____ <u>Frizzell</u>.

    B7   James MacLeod, born c. 1870.

    B8   John A. MacLeod, born c. 1873.

    B9   Daniel MacLeod, born c. 1875, with issue.

Information provided by Kenneth MacLeod, Mrs. Neil Dan MacLeod, 1881 census, and C1 Kenneth's will.

SOUTH GRANVILLE
THE PIONEERS OF SOUTH GRANVILLE

Some families in 1841, others in 1843, left the land of history, crossed the Atlantic and finally settled in a vacant section, now called South Granville, which was not exactly the most desirable plot in Lot 21. Aided wholly by their unbending perseverance, they took land there under circumstances altogether different, without money and without assistance of agent or government. They changed the forest into fruitful fields at a time when winter was longer and more severe than it is in Prince Edward Island now.

The names of the pioneers were: MacKenzie Gunn, William Gunn, Benjamin Gunn, Angus MacKay, William MacKay, a certain Mrs. Isabelle (MacLeod) MacKay whose husband's name is now unknown, Murdoch Corbett, James Corbett, Robert Corbett, Hugh Morrison, Donald Morrison, Roderick MacLeod, Mrs. George MacLeod, Hugh MacKenzie, Charles MacKenzie, Hector Falconer, Cathel Keir, Angus Campbell, Neil Smith, and John MacMillan. All were from Sutherlandshire, Scotland, except John MacMillan, who was a native of the Isle of Lewis.

They all had respect to the ordinance of religion, and some of them were men of note. Hector Falconer, a man among a thousand, was a blessing to any community. A man of few, well chosen words, he was gifted with grace and education, and had a knack of holding his own in an argument without giving offence. They were often without a preacher, [but] a place of meeting was closed neither summer nor winter. The Sabbath, the weekly prayer meeting, the week of prayer, and the monthly meetings were never neglected by him, during the years of his activity, and that without human reward. Donald MacLeod, his right-hand man, had very clear and decided views in the ways of life and holiness as set forth in the Westminster Standards. His great gift (let us mention it with reverence) was a wonderful admittance into the secrets of God. In this respect, perhaps he was alone in his day; yet his manner was so decidedly self-dishonouring that but few of his fellow-worshippers knew of his real genius. There were others, but it is sufficient to say that in the closing years of the nineteenth century it was possible in a two-mile walk to pass at least twelve homes where the head of the family was an exemplary man of prayer.

This small community cast in its lot with the old and respectable Presbyterian Church at Clifton whose preacher afterwards was the Rev. Alexander Sutherland of sacred memory, followed by the Rev. Mr. Morrison. Then a Mr. MacMillan, a student pastor, and a Mr. MacQuirrey, another student pastor, followed by the Rev. Mr. MacDougall. There is no record available, and we cannot give reliable dates, but as far as we can gather, they commenced to build a church in 1863 which was finished two years later, and was opened for worship by the Rev. Mr. MacNeill. Although not a very palatial building in comparison to present-day structures, nevertheless, to the few who are still spared who worshipped God there with our patriarchal forefathers and ministers, it is hallowed ground, encompassed with memories dearer than architecture.

About the year 1871, the Rev. John Murray was inducted into the church. He later called for three elders at Granville. Hector Falconer and Donald MacLeod were unanimously appointed, but John MacMillan and Hugh MacKenzie shared honours for the third. Thus, all four were ordained elders. About twenty-five years afterwards, Alexander Falconer and John R. Corbett, of the second generation, were ordained elders by Rev. Alexander Sterling. Then, they also passed away, and the present standard-bearers, Hugh Corbett and Peter MacLeod, of the third generation, were ordained by the Rev. John Sterling a short time before Union. Although our number is very much diminished, there were none who voted to leave the church of their forefathers when the vote was taken.

During the ministry of the Rev. Alexander Sterling, a true copy of the old Covenanter, the communion season was an event of the summer looked forward to with desire. A number of God-fearing men and women from Hartsville, Rose Valley and the North side would attend. The Rev. John MacLeod from Hartsville would assist. Some seasons the Rev. Mr. MacLean from Valleyfield assisted. The labours of the field were laid aside Wednesday, not to be taken up until the following Monday afternoon. There would be three services Thursday, three Friday, a fellowship meeting in the forenoon, and on Saturday the Rev. Alexander Sterling would preach for over three hours in the forenoon.

This does not mean that he always preached long sermons, but since there was no service Saturday evening, his object, evidently, was to spend the whole season in the service of his Great Master, because His service was his chief delight. It is said that he spent the entire following night on his knees. Yet the Rev. John MacLeod went one better. On a certain communion Sabbath in the old church at Clifton when unassisted he commenced service at eleven o'clock and pronounced benediction in a very solemn manner after four o'clock in the afternoon.

These days are passed, to our sorrow, and with them their generation. Only Hector MacKenzie, one of nine brothers all of whom grew to manhood, is spared of the second generation. It becomes us to take up the poet's lament:

> They throng the silence of the breast,
> We see them as of Yore,
> The kind, the brave, the true, the sweet,
>
> Who walk with us no more.
> 'Tis hard to take the burden up
> When these have laid it down;
> They brightened all the joy of life,
>
> They softened every frown.
> But, oh, 'tis good to think of them
> When we are troubled sore;
> Thanks be to God that such have been
> Although they are no more.

Written by Robert MacKay shortly before he died at his home near Stanley Bridge on February 20, 1940, at the age of 92.

RODERICK MACLEOD
RODERICK MACLEOD OF SOUTH GRANVILLE

A   Roderick MacLeod came to South Granville area in 1843 with his six sons. Four
     of the brothers settled in the area, where they each had a 50 acre farm. The
     family was from Sutherlandshire, Scotland.

B1   Donald MacLeod, born in Sutherlandshire c. 1810, m. Mary MacLeod also
     of Scotland (aged 65 in 1881 census). Her father is unknown, mother was
     Mary O'Hara. Donald died April 12, 1897. He was the first elder in South
     Granville Presbyterian Church, where he and most of his relatives are
     buried. Issue:

     C1   Mary MacLeod, born in Nova Scotia c. 1854, died in South Granville,
          1912.
     C2   George MacLeod, 1834-1912, 8 years old when family emigrated to
          P.E.I., m. Sophia Blue of Wallace, Nova Scotia, 1846-1893, with issue:
          D1   John MacLeod, 1871-1917, lived in Wallace, Nova Scotia, m.,
               wife's name unknown, with issue:
               E1   Lorraine MacLeod, m. Elmer Donnelly, of Seattle, Wash-
                    ington.
               E2   Gretel MacLeod, m. Fred Goddard, Edmonton.
               E3   Laeta MacLeod, m. Percy Goddard, brother of Fred,
                    Vancouver.
          D2   Donald (Daniel) MacLeod, m. Jane Annie MacLennan, lived in
               Wallace, Nova Scotia, with issue:
               E1   Harold MacLeod.
               E2   Bert MacLeod.
               E3   Percy MacLeod.
               E4   Eva MacLeod, m. Gillis Sponberg.
               E5   Doris MacLeod, m. Wilfred Wickie.
          D3   Mary Sophia MacLeod, 1881-1970, Wallace, Nova Scotia, m.
               Joseph Miller Corbett, 1866-1953, with issue:
               E1   George Corbett.
               E2   Leslie Joseph Corbett.
               E3   William Corbett, 1906-1907.
               E4   Sophia "Eleanor" Corbett.
               E5   Esther Catherine Corbett, born Nanaimo, British Columbia.
               E6   Lawrence Daniel Corbett.
               E7   Ethel Mary Corbett.
               E8   Rose Adele Corbett.
               E9   Grace Margaret Corbett.
               E10 Estelle Corbett.
     C3   Roderick MacLeod, born Nova Scotia c. 1852, never m., died in South
          Granville.
     C4   Elizabeth MacLeod, born P.E.I. c. 1857, m. 1) George Chappell, 2)
          Max Genereux. Died in Banff, Alberta.
     C5   Annie MacLeod, born P.E.I. c. 1855, m. James MacLennan. Died in
          Nova Scotia.
     C6   Hugh MacLeod, born April 7, 1859, m. Mary Ann Corbett in 1897.
          Died Dec. 30, 1942, in South Granville, with issue:

D1   Elizabeth Alma MacLeod, m. David Archibald <u>MacLeod</u>, also of South Granville. His father was John MacLeod, apparently a cousin of Alma's grandfather. His mother was a Stewart. Brothers and sisters were: Dan (never m.), Hugh John (never m.), Elizabeth (m. a Callaghan and lived in Minnesota), and Lucy (m. Alvin Stensin). Alma and Archie lived in Boston for many years and Alma retired to a house built on the old farm.

D2   Donald Calvin MacLeod, 1900-1909. Died of scarlet fever.

D3   Rhoda May MacLeod, 1902-1958, m. Wallace <u>Moreside</u>.

D4   A daughter died in infancy.

D5   John Haig MacLeod, m. Lillian <u>Matheson</u>, she died 1980.
     E1   Chrissie Joan MacLeod, m. Leigh <u>Simmons</u>. They live in Kensington, with issue:
         F1   Marshall John Simmons.
     E2   Mary Irene MacLeod, lives in Darnley.
     E3   Donald Calvin MacLeod, m. Annie Beryl <u>MacLeod</u>, of French River (parents John and Ellen MacLeod). Donald and his son are the fourth and fifth generations to farm the original family land. His father, John Haig [D5], bought back into his family all the original 50 acre plots save for John's.
         F1   Heather Beryl MacLeod.
         F2   Donna Elaine MacLeod, m. Gerald <u>Arsenault</u>, Summerside.
         F3   Donald Mark MacLeod.
         F4   Dwight Hugh MacLeod.
     E4   Marshall Jean MacLeod, m. Roscoe <u>Pendleton</u>, Kensington.
         F1   Roscoe Kent Pendleton.
         F2   John Daniel Pendleton.
         F3   Donald Leslie Pendleton.

B2   John MacLeod, 1814-1881, in South Granville, m. Mary "Jane" <u>Gunn</u>. In the 1881 census, John and Jane are found living in Lot 21 with Roderick, 26, and MacKenzie, 22, both born in P.E.I. John is listed as 60 and Jane 48, both born in Scotland. Married March 9, 1853, with issue:

C1   Margaret MacLeod, born Dec. 23, 1856, in Kensington.

C2   MacKenzie MacLeod, baptized Dec. 20, 1868, in Kensington.

C3   John MacLeod.

C4   Roderick MacLeod, born c. 1855, died March 4, 1927, m. Agnes <u>MacDowell</u>, 1868-1929, buried in Mt. Pleasant Cemetery. They first farmed in North Granville-Rose Valley, then moved to Knutsford near O'Leary. From this farm they moved to Mt. Pleasant. They had issue:
     D1   Margaret Jane MacLeod, 1886-1973, m. Garfield <u>Green</u>, 1882-1950.
         E1   Ira Green, Springhill, P.E.I.
         E2   Ella Green, m. Gordon <u>Cotton</u>, Charlottetown.
         E3   Mae Green, m. _____ <u>Slock</u>, Trenton, Nova Scotia.
         E4   Roland Green, Sicamouse, British Columbia.
         E5   Edith Green, m. _____ <u>Ryan</u>, Bunbury.
         E6   Lennie Green, m. ___ <u>Vincent</u>, St.Eleanor's.
     Margaret m. 2) Lloyd <u>Rayner</u>, no children.
     D2   John William MacLeod, 1888-19—, m. 1) Inez _____, issue:

E1   John MacLeod, Massachusetts.
E2   Norma MacLeod, m. _____ Perodis, Connecticut.
John m. 2) name unknown, with issue:
E3   John MacLeod, Massachusetts.
E4   Pattie MacLeod, Massachusetts.
John m. 3) Agnes Stewart, no children.

D3   Alexander R. MacLeod, born March 4, 1890, died at birth.
D4   Thomas Hessel MacLeod, 1891-1972, m. Myrtle Adams, 1900-
      1969, buried in Foxley River Anglican Cemetery. Their family
      are:
E1   Cecil MacLeod, m. Blanche Craig, three sons.
E2   Doris MacLeod, m. Charles Casely, Coleman.
E3   Kenneth MacLeod, Milo, P.E.I., m. Blanche Craig, widow
      of Cecil.

D5   Samuel Howard MacLeod, 1893-1970, m. Phoebe Hately. Samuel
      was a carpenter and printer. They had issue:
E1   Maude MacLeod, m. ____ Shackleton, Massachusetts.
E2   Pearl MacLeod, m. Gordon Costain, St. Eleanor's.
E3   Ellen MacLeod, m. _____ Pye, Summerside.
E4   Wallace MacLeod, m. Syble Green, with issue:
      F1   Dale MacLeod.
      F2   Carl MacLeod.
      F3   Ann MacLeod.
      F4   Norma MacLeod.
      F5   Mary Lou MacLeod.
      F6   David MacLeod.
      F7   Sharon MacLeod.

D6   Robert Wallace MacLeod, 1893-1971, a carpenter and a war vet-
      eran, lived in Enmore, Lot 10, and Northam, Lot 13, m. 1) Rotha
      MacEachern, with issue:
E1   Robert Clinton MacLeod, m. Mildred Ramsay, Summerside.
      F1   Clinton "Junior" MacLeod, m. Wanda Buchanan, R.N.
            Lived in O'Leary until his death 1986, aged 41.
      F2   Blain MacLeod, Rev., m. Carol MacDonald, legal sec-
            retary. He is a pastor in Barrie, Ontario.
            G1   Andrew MacLeod.
            G2   David MacLeod.
      F3   Wensell H. MacLeod, m. Donna Morrison, studying
            for the ministry in Winnipeg, Manitoba, with issue:
            G1   Todd MacLeod.
            G2   Glen MacLeod.
      F4   Trudi Beryl MacLeod, m. Richard Steele, with issue:
            G1   Matthew Steele.
      F5   Grenville W. MacLeod, m. Nancy Hardy, with issue:
            G1   Trent MacLeod.
      F6   Jackie Dale MacLeod.
      F7   Susan MacLeod, m. Talbot Gaudet, with issue:
            G1   Joshua Gaudet.
            G2   Aaron Gaudet.
            G3   Katie Sue Gaudet.
      F8   Melody MacLeod.

E2   Sadie MacLeod, m. Roy <u>Ramsay</u>, Springhill, P.E.I., with issue:
  F1   Horace Ramsay, m. Sheila <u>Currie</u>, with issue:
    G1   Cindy Ramsay.
    G2   Scott Ramsay.
  F2   Louis Ramsay, m. Darlene <u>Graham</u>, with issue:
    G1   April Ramsay.
    G2   Laurie Ramsay.
    G3   Cheryl Ramsay.
  F3   Patricia Ramsay, m. Robert <u>Noye</u>, with issue:
    G1   Trevor Noye.
    G2   Kirk Noye.
  F4   Marsha Ramsay, m. David <u>Reid</u>.
  F5   Herman Ramsay, m. Marilyn <u>Ramsay</u>, with issue:
    G1   Charles Ramsay.
    G2   Linda Ramsay.
  F6   Bonnie Ramsay, m. Michell <u>Doiron</u>, with issue:
    G1   Andrea Doiron.
    G2   Christopher Doiron.
    G3   Nicholas Doiron.
  F7   Rueben Ramsay, m. Margaret <u>Chisholm</u>, with issue:
    G1   Brian Ramsay.
    G2   Andrew Ramsay.
  F8   Kevin Ramsay.
E3   Jean MacLeod, born 1927, died at birth.
Robert Wallace m. 2) Deborah <u>Pauptit</u>, from Bussum, Holland.
E4   Herman MacLeod, m. Blanche <u>Baglole</u>, with issue:
  F1   Dianne MacLeod, m. James <u>VanBuskirk</u>, St. Eleanor's.
  F2   Barry MacLeod, m. Shelley <u>Boekema</u>, with issue:
    G1   Jantina Elizabeth MacLeod.
E5   Julia Mary MacLeod, m. Clare <u>Dennis</u>, Port Dover, Ontario, issue:
  F1   Graham Dennis.
  F2   Gregory Dennis.
  F3   Angela Dennis.
  F4   Phillip Dennis.
E6   Victor Wallace MacLeod, m. Audrey <u>Armsworthy</u>, Northam, P.E.I.
  F1   Jody MacLeod.
  F2   Klasina MacLeod.
  F3   Benjamin MacLeod.
  F4   Jeffrey MacLeod.
E7   Charles John MacLeod, m. Sylvia <u>Noye</u>, with issue:
  F1   Kimberly MacLeod.
  F2   Debbie MacLeod.
D7   Alexander MacLeod, m. Eva Grigg <u>MacCaul</u>, lived in Mt. Pleasant.
E1   Reginald MacLeod .
E2   Georgie MacLeod, m. _____ <u>Barvley</u>, Trenton, Ontario.
D8   Annie Euta MacLeod, died 1986, m. Herbert <u>Hutcheson</u>, Ellerslie.
E1   Hubert Hutcheson.

E2   Emmett Hutcheson.
E3   Sherman Hutcheson.
E4   Ferne Hutcheson, died 1986, m. Fred Profitt, Spring Valley.
D9 David (Daniel) MacLeod, born 1898, m. Clara Phillips, issue:
E1   Charles MacLeod, Toronto, Ontario, m. 1) Stella LaDrew, died 1967, m. 2) Edna _____.
E2   Jenny MacLeod, m. Shippit Osoyous, British Columbia.
D10 Elizabeth Lottie MacLeod, m. William Trowsdale, Borden and Ellerslie, with issue:
E1   Gordon Trowsdale, Port Hill, P.E.I.
E2   Clinton Trowsdale, Ellerslie, P.E.I.
E3   Wayne Trowsdale, Ellerslie, P.E.I.
E4   Mary Trowsdale, Scarborough, Ontario.
E5   Verna Trowsdale, m. _____ Gillis, Streetsville, Ontario.
E6   Helen Trowsdale, m. _____ Arp, Borden.
D11 James MacLeod, 1902-1983, m. Pearl Biggar, with issue:
E1   Kenneth Aubrey MacLeod, m. Helen Champion, living in Kensington, P.E.I.
E2   Velma MacLeod, m. Robert Norton, McAdam, New Brunswick, with issue:
F1   Richard Norton.
F2   Pauline Norton.
F3   Robert Norton.
E3   Vernon MacLeod, m. Carol Chaisse, living in Toronto, Ontario.
F1   Kenneth MacLeod.
F2   David MacLeod.
F3   Pauline MacLeod.
F4   Kimberly MacLeod.
F5   Sidney MacLeod.
F6   Frank MacLeod.
F7   Jessie MacLeod.
E4   Erva (Dolly) MacLeod, m. George Nicholson, living in Toronto.
F1   Pauline Nicholson.
F2   Jean Nicholson.
E5   David MacLeod, living in Summerside.
E6   Pauline MacLeod,1938-1947, died in a car accident.
E7   Bernice MacLeod, living in Summerside.
E8   Dale MacLeod, living in Toronto, Ontario.
D12 Luella Pearl MacLeod, 1904-1969, m. Parker Stone, lived in Maine.
D13 Ira D. Sankey MacLeod, 1906-1957, m. Mary ___ , with issue:
E1   Dewey MacLeod, Charlottetown, P.E.I.
E2   John MacLeod, London, Ontario.
E3   James MacLeod, Brookfield, P.E.I.
E4   Verna MacLeod, m. _____ Cameron, Dartmouth, Nova Scotia.
E5   Carol MacLeod, m. ___ LeClair, Calgary.
E6   Bertha MacLeod, m. ___ Richards, Etobicoke, Ontario.
E7   Roderick MacLeod, Charlottetown, P.E.I.
E8   Blair MacLeod, Dartmouth, Nova Scotia.

E9   Brenda MacLeod, m. _____ Stokes, Southport.
D14 Mary Catherine MacLeod, 1908-1964, m. William A. Vye, Maine. No children.
D15 Bertha Agnes MacLeod, 1910-1984, m. Dewey Irving, died 1943.
    E1   George Irving.
    E2   Lila Irving.
    E3   Norma Irving.
    E4   Roy Irving.
    E5   Wilfred Irving.
    E6   Franklin Irving.
    E7   Ian Irving.
    E8   Parker Irving (Sonny).
    Bertha m. 2) Jens Hansen, with issue:
    E9   Tina Hansen, m. Anthony Macina.
    E10 Ronnie Hansen.

B3   Murdoch MacLeod, 1829-1885, buried in South Granville, m. Barbara Keir, also born in Scotland, 1840-1925.
    C1   Peter MacLeod, 1880-1969, m. Ethel MacLeod, 1886-1959, daughter of Donald, Vernon River, buried in South Granville, with issue:
        D1   Keir MacLeod, m. _____, with issue:
            E1   Judy MacLeod.
            E2   Maureen MacLeod.
        D2   Robert MacLeod.
        D3   Dennis MacLeod.
    C2   Robert MacLeod, 1868-1943, m. Elizabeth Ann Corbett, 1877-1912.
        D1   Wesley MacLeod.
        D2   Annie MacLeod.
        D3   Lillian MacLeod.
        D4   Mary MacLeod.
        D5   Robert MacLeod.
    C3   Mary Anne MacLeod, born 1863, m. Albert Parker, with issue:
        D1   Shirley Parker.
        D2   Merlin Parker.
        D3   Ruby Parker.
        D4   Ethel Parker.
    C4   Marie B. MacLeod, m. Malcolm Alexander MacLeod, her cousin.
        D1   Anabella MacLeod, m. Frank Brown.
        D2   John A. MacLeod.
    C5   Cathel MacLeod, 1871-1956, m. Euphemia MacLellan, 1875-1958, no children.
    C6   Roderick MacLeod, 1864-1917, m. 1) Annabelle, 2) Ruth Weeks Davies, 1893-1974, with issue:
        D1   Wesley MacLeod, 1904-1942.
        D2   Betty MacLeod.
    C7   Catherine MacLeod, born 1869, m. 1) George Morrison, 2) ____ Breault, New Haven, Connecticut.
    C8   Hughena MacLeod, born 1875, m. Isaac Thorpe, lived in Nova Scotia.
        D1   John Thorpe, m. Helen Smith, with issue:
            E1   Elaine Thorpe, m. Stanley Parker.
            E2   Ralph Thorpe, m. Diane Morrisey.
            E3   Doris Thorpe, m. Robert Kopp.

      D2 Gerald Thorpe, m. Helen <u>Russell</u>, with issue:
          E1 Lionel Thorpe.
          E2 Charles Thorpe.
          E3 Patricia Thorpe.
      D3 Timothy William Thorpe, m. Edna Elizabeth <u>Galley</u>, with issue:
          E1 Ronald Thorpe, m. Mary <u>Briand</u>.
          E2 Randolph Thorpe, m. Diana Ruth <u>Hatfield</u>.
          E3 Faye Thorpe, m. Wayne <u>Doyle</u>.
      D4 Murdoch MacLeod Thorpe, m. Helen Winnifred <u>Collicutt</u>, issue:
          E1 Patricia Rosalie Thorpe, died aged one year.
          E2 Betty Joan Thorpe, m. William Garth <u>Cochrane</u>.
   C9 Martha MacLeod, died of T.B.
   C10 Barbara MacLeod.
   C11 Annabelle MacLeod, born 1873.
B4 Hugh MacLeod, 1825-1888, m. Barbara <u>Campbell</u>. Hugh died when hit by a tree limb while working in the woods. They had issue:
   C1 Kate MacLeod, born 1879, m. Charles <u>Todd</u>, with issue:
      D1 Eliza Todd, m. Sheldon <u>Abbott</u>.
          E1 Edwin Abbott.
          E2 Robert Abbott.
          E3 Waldo Abbott.
          E4 Lois Abbott.
      D2 Earl Todd.
      D3 Ethel Todd.
   C2 Christy MacLeod, born c. 1881.
   C3 John Robert MacLeod.
   C4 Neil MacLeod, m. Margaret <u>Casely</u>, with issue:
      D1 Harry MacLeod, m. Ethel ____, with issue:
          E1 Harry MacLeod, m. Claudette ____, with issue:
              F1 Neil MacLeod, lives in New Hampshire.
          E2 Kevin MacLeod, married, with issue:
              F1 Christen MacLeod.
      D2 Clarice MacLeod, m. Harry <u>Yoken</u>, Portsmouth, New Hampshire, with issue:
          E1 Daniel Yoken, m. Janet <u>Konitz</u>, with issue:
              F1 Kim Yoken.
              F2 Michael Yoken.
B5 William MacLeod, went to live in Nova Scotia, died in Halifax and had six daughters.
B6 Robert MacLeod, also lived in Nova Scotia.

The above information was provided by Clinton and Mildred MacLeod, Summerside; Herman MacLeod, St. Eleanor's; Charles MacLeod, Lower Sackville, New Brunswick; Helen MacLeod, Kensington; Shelley MacLeod, St.Eleanor's; John and Alma MacLeod, South Granville; and Betty Thorpe, of Nova Scotia.

DONALD MACLEOD
DONALD MACLEOD AND SARAH OF MEADOWBANK

A Donald MacLeod, died 1890, aged 87, came to P.E.I. from Raasay, Scotland, in the year 1839 with one son Murdoch and a half brother, Mr. MacLean, who died of a rupture at 20 years of age. A letter from John MacLeod, Raasay, dated May 1, 1839, commends Donald stating: "Servant as ploughman for six years and I have always found him a good and faithful one, he was." He was m. to Sarah _____, died 1900, aged 87, they had ten children born on P.E.I., of whom eight died young in an epidemic, and were buried in St. Catherine's Cemetery.

B1 Murdoch MacLeod, died 1917, age 81, came with his parents from Scotland and m. Margaret Darrach, died 1935, aged 82. He was one of the charter members of the Orange Lodge at Long Creek. Their children were:

    C1 John MacLeod, died Dec. 9, 1879, aged 2 years, 11 months.

    C2 Sarah J. MacLeod, died Dec. 10, 1879, aged 1 year, 5 months.

B2 Ewen MacLeod, m. _____ Buchanan, and moved to Pennsylvania, where he worked as a private secretary to a health organization. Their children were:

    C1 Rev. George Daniel MacLeod, who spent fifty years of his ministry in the Toronto area. He was m. to Miss Steele, a sister of Dr. Steele, former Principal of Prince of Wales College, Charlottetown, issue:

        D1 Elizabeth MacLeod.

        D2 Margaret MacLeod.

        D3 Donald MacLeod.

        D4 Dorothy MacLeod, twin of Donald.

    C2 William MacLeod, m. Rosella MacDonald. He went to the U.S.A. in 1924, but moved back to P.E.I. in his retirement years. They had issue:

        D1 A daughter.

        D2 Frances MacLeod.

        D3 A son.

B3 George S. MacLeod, m. Jane McCubrey. They operated a grocery store in Hunter River. Their children were:

    C1 Mae MacLeod, married in western Canada, she had three children:

        D1 Helen, married twice and had two boys and a girl.

        D2 Beatrice, married, no family.

        D3 Allison, married with a family.

    C2 Phoebe Beatrice MacLeod, 1882-1899.

    C3 Elizabeth Alice Maude MacLeod, 1888-1890.

    C4 Louis MacLeod, m. Ruth Simpson, they lived in U.S.A., with issue:

        D1 George MacLeod, married, their children are:

            E1 Ruth Ellen MacLeod.

            E2 Allan MacLeod.

            E3 Miriam MacLeod.

            E4 Stewart MacLeod.

    C5 Daniel MacLeod, was an undertaker and also operated a store in Hunter River, m. Georgia Lawson, with issue:

D1 Chappie MacLeod, married Alice C. Jacob, with children:
- E1 David MacLeod, married with five children.
- E2 Dianne MacLeod, married with a son and a daughter.

D2 Sutherland MacLeod, m. Gail VanDermoot, no family.

D3 Eulalie MacLeod, m. Maurice Weeks, no family.

D4 Beatrice MacLeod, m. George Reed, no family.

D5 Ersel MacLeod, died in infancy.

C6 Vernon MacLeod, was a veteran of WWI. He operated a grocery store in Albany, P.E.I., m. Elsie Howatt, Victoria, P.E.I. Their family is:

D1 A son, died in infancy.

D2 Elizabeth MacLeod, m. Alfred Ramsay, they had four children:
- E1 Susan Ramsay, m. in Toronto, with two boys:
  - F1 Mark.
  - F2 Jasatha.
- E2 Linda Ramsay, m. Bentley Stoddart, Nova Scotia, with issue:
  - F1 Melissa Stoddart.
  - F2 Vanessa Stoddart.
- E3 Ewen Ramsay, m. Micheline _____, living in Ontario.
  - F1 Bonnie Ramsay.
- E4 Clare Ramsay, living in Nova Scotia, m. Alice ____, with four children.

D3 Alaister MacLeod, m. Ferne Howatt, they live in Albany, P.E.I., and had ten children:
- E1 Danny MacLeod, born 1953, died in a tragic car accident in 1979.
- E2 Cynthia MacLeod, m. David Buell, with issue:
  - F1 Danny Buell.
  - F2 Charlotte Anne Buell.
- E3 Imogene MacLeod.
- E4 Grant MacLeod, m. Jo-Anne Affleck.
- E5 Ronnalee MacLeod, m. Murray McAvinn.
- E6 A son, died in infancy.
- E7 Kent MacLeod.
- E8 Vernon MacLeod.
- E9 Harleigh MacLeod.
- E10 Corrie Ann MacLeod.

D4 Douglas MacLeod, m. Sheila Good, with issue:
- E1 Scott MacLeod.
- E2 Mark MacLeod.

D5 David MacLeod, twin to Douglas, operates a law firm in Charlottetown, m. Glenda Jamieson, with issue:
- E1 Alan MacLeod, 1961-1985, died in a tragic car accident.
- E2 Barbara MacLeod.
- E3 Stephen MacLeod.

This information supplied by Alaister and Ferne MacLeod, Albany, P.E.I.

JOHN MACLEOD.
JOHN MACLEOD AND WIFE OF LYNDALE

A   "Red" John MacLeod settled in Lyndale sometime after 1829, and it is understood that he was of the same family as the Sentia MacLeods of Vernon. He
had at least four sons and a daughter, of whom were:

B1   "Red" Donald MacLeod, 1852-1930, m. Sarah Gillis, Belfast, 1856-1926.
He farmed in Vernon River on the Murray Harbour Road at the top of
Hayden's Hill. Donald and Sarah had the following children:

    C1   Ernest MacLeod, m. Myrtle Ross, daughter of Albert Ross, of Vernon
River.

    C2   Cyrus MacLeod, m. _____ Nicholson, from Belfast. They lived in
U.S.A., no family.

    C3   Daniel MacLeod, m. Myrtle MacLeod, from west of Charlottetown,
they had a daughter.

    C4   Ethel MacLeod, m. Peter MacLeod, Breadalbane, with issue:

        D1   Keir MacLeod.

        D2   Robert MacLeod.

        D3   Doris MacLeod.

    C5   Jessie MacLeod, m. John MacQueen, Uigg, no family.

    C6   Mary MacLeod, m. _____ MacDonald, living in U.S.A. with two boys
and a girl.

B2   Angus MacLeod, lived in U.S.A.

B3   Murdoch MacLeod, lived in U.S.A.

B4   Annie MacLeod, m. a Gillis from Flat River and was the grandmother of
the late Dr. John Gillis, Eldon.

B5   John J. MacLeod, 1853-1929, lived in Lyndale, and was married to Flora
Anne Docherty, 1856-1943, whose family first settled in Lake Ainsley,
Cape Breton, later moved to P.E.I. and settled in the Southern Queens
area. Her sister Christy m. John Dan MacPherson, who was a descendant
of MacPhersons who settled originally in Earnscliffe. They lived on the
adjacent farm. John J. And Flora Anne's family all moved to U.S.A. They
were:

    C1   Mrs. Harry Haines, Massachusetts.

    C2   Mrs. Samuel Lewis, Massachusetts.

    C3   Mrs. M. Cummings, Massachusetts.

    C4   Mrs. Stella MacLeod, Massachusetts.

    C5   Mrs. Warren Penny, Massachusetts.

    C6   John N. MacLeod, New York.

    C7   M. D. MacLeod, Massachusetts.

    C8   Alexander MacLeod, Massachusetts.

    C9   Monty MacLeod, killed in WWI.

Information supplied by Harold S. MacLeod, Montague.

GORDON MACLEOD
GORDON MACLEOD AND MARY DOUGHERTY OF LONG RIVER AND BRAE

A   Gordon MacLeod, m. Mary Dougherty, with issue:

B1   John Doughart MacLeod, 1879-1944, m. Ida Casely, 1871-1946. John moved from Long River to Brae, and they are both buried in the Brae United Church Cemetery. Issue:

   C1   Rowena MacLeod, m. Harry Cannon. He was a fruit and vegetable inspector with the government. Issue:

      D1   Dorothy Cannon, m. Robert Maynard.

   C2   Louise MacLeod, m. Alva Jeffrey. He worked for the Island Telephone Company and died in 1977. They lived in Summerside and had no family.

   C3   Fred MacLeod, 1898-1982, m. May Boulter, with issue:

      D1   Joyce MacLeod, m. Seaman Bell.

      D2   Elaine MacLeod, m. Blair Ballum.

      D3   Errison MacLeod, m. Anna Ramsay, with issue:

         E1   Douglas MacLeod, m. Ellen Rennie, with issue:

            F1   Jerrie Kim MacLeod.

            F2   Sally MacLeod.

         E2   Terry MacLeod, m. Marlene Warren.

B2   Lou MacLeod, died young of T.B.

B3   Major MacLeod, went to U.S.A.

B4   Robert MacLeod, m. Kate Hogan.

B5   Lucy MacLeod, m. Allan ____, with issue:

   C1   Hazel _____, in the U.S.A.

   C2   Stamford _____, in the U.S.A.

B6   Chester MacLeod, m. Janie MacKay, with issue:

   C1   Rhoda MacLeod.

   C2   Eileen MacLeod.

   C3   Elmer MacLeod.

B7   Nelson MacLeod, m. Elizabeth "Bessie" Dunning, with issue:

   C1   Child died in infancy.

   C2   Grant MacLeod, m. Bernice Ferguson, with issue:

      D1   Debbie MacLeod.

      D2   Beverly MacLeod.

      D3   Earith MacLeod.

      D4   Carol MacLeod.

   C3   Jennie MacLeod, m. Elwood Campbell, with issue:

      D1   Eric Campbell, m. Myrt Bernard, with issue:

         E1   Diane Campbell.

         E2   Daryl Campbell.

         E3   Pat Campbell.

         E4   Helen Campbell.

         E5   Kathy Campbell.

         E6   Marilyn Campbell.

         E7   Dean Campbell.

         E8   Terry Lynn Campbell.

         E9   Kim Campbell.

          E10 Greg Campbell.
    D2 Norma Campbell, m. Jim <u>McAskill</u> from Manitoba, with issue:
          E1   Brian McAskill.
          E2   David McAskill.

Source: Elaine Ballum, Errison MacLeod, *A History of Brae*, and other family members.

HUGH MACLEOD
HUGH MACLEOD AND WIFE FROM SCOTLAND AND PRINCE EDWARD ISLAND

A   Hugh MacLeod and his wife were born in Scotland and emigrated to P.E.I. early in the 1800s as he had a son who was born in P.E.I. in 1825, and later lived in Prescott, Wisconsin, where he worked as a ship's carpenter.

B1   Donald MacLeod, 1825-1901, m. Marion <u>Smith</u> of Columbus, Ohio. She was the widow of ___ Masten, and had a son from that marriage whom Donald raised.

    C1   Hugh MacLeod, born in Hastings, Minnesota, 1870, died in Minneapolis, 1937, m. Hallie <u>Latham</u>, 1875-1963, with issue:

        D1   Donald Latham MacLeod, born 1900, died in California, 1971, m. Mildred <u>Peterson</u>, with issue:

            E1   George Douglas MacLeod, m. Joana <u>Myers</u>, with issue:

                F1   Anne Marie MacLeod.

                F2   Pamela Lorn MacLeod.

                F3   David C. MacLeod.

            E2   James D. MacLeod, m. Joan <u>Hovelsrud</u>, with issue:

                F1   Douglas MacLeod.

                F2   Donald John MacLeod.

                F3   Hallie Louise MacLeod.

                F4   Lisa MacLeod.

        D2   Gordon MacLeod, married, with issue:

            E1   Bob MacLeod.

            E2   Marion MacLeod.

            E3   Bruce MacLeod.

            E4   Margaret MacLeod.

        D3   Stanley Ralph MacLeod, a policeman in Minneapolis, m. Marvyl <u>Ostrander</u>, their children were:

            E1   William Ralph MacLeod, m. Clarabell (CeeBee) <u>Schweppe</u> from Wisconsin, with issue:

                F1   Heidi MacLeod, m. James <u>Sherer</u>.

                F2   Ronald Ralph MacLeod.

            E2   Michael Stanley MacLeod, m. Theresa <u>Roche</u>, with issue:

                F1   Hallie Ann MacLeod.

                F2   Robb MacLeod.

Information received from a family member in U.S.A.

DONALD MACLEOD
DONALD MACLEOD AND CATHERINE MACDONALD OF ORWELL COVE AND
EARNSCLIFFE

Donald MacLeod of Kendram in the Kilmaluaig district of Trotternish, Isle of Skye, emigrated to Belfast, Prince Edward Island, on the ship *Polly* in 1803. His wife, Catherine MacDonald, died in Skye. She was a sister of Margaret MacDonald, who was the wife of John "Kinlock" MacDonald of Orwell Cove. Her brother, Allan Mac-Donald, emigrated from Kilmuir Parish, Skye, to Lyndale, P.E.I., in 1829. Donald was accompanied by his four sons: Malcolm, Murdoch, Roderick, and Alexander, who were known on Prince Edward Island as the "Horo" MacLeods. This name no doubt was derived from the river Horo which emptied into the Kilmaluaig River which formed the western boundary of their croft in Kendram. Another son of Donald MacLeod remained on the croft in Skye and one of his descendants, Peter MacLeod, who m. Peggy MacPhee from Kilmuir, Skye, together with their two sons Lachlan and Angus live on the ancestral croft.

Malcolm, the elder son of Donald the Pioneer, bought a farm in Gallows Point, later called Earnscliffe, that was partially improved, the other three brothers settled on adjoining farms in Orwell Cove. The proximity of their farms enabled them to work together in clearing and improving their land. They also shipped their produce cooperatively, loading vessels at Brush Wharf with oats, which was the main cash crop, bound for European ports of call. Oats was the fuel of transportation before the days of the gasoline engine. In every town there were livery stables where a horse could be rented by the hour, by the day, or longer. There were large stables of truck horses used for inter-city transportation of goods. Consequently, the supplying of feed for these animals created a continuous and lucrative market for the oats grown by the early settlers. The soil of Orwell Cove and Earnscliffe was rich and productive. The beds of "mussel mud" that would supply lime and other trace elements to further enrich the land was nearby and cost nothing beyond the labour and the meagre equipment used to bring it to shore. Millions of bushels of oats were shipped over the years from wharves on both sides of Orwell Bay.

Poverty was not one of their worries. Hector MacDonald, who was married to Flora Nicholson, a sister of Murdoch's wife, arrived twenty-six years after the group and settled on the Murray Harbour Road. He used to speak of his amazement, when he arrived in Orwell Cove, to find prosperous-looking farms with large granaries and barns stocked with cattle, where he expected a wilderness.

The families of the first generation of settlers in the Belfast area were also comparatively healthy. They didn't seem to experience the devastating affects of childhood diseases such as diphtheria, scarlet fever, and other plagues which sometimes wiped out whole families in later generations.

All in all, the move to the New World was a good one. There was plenty of virgin territory nearby for their children and although they would shed many a nostalgic tear for the mountains of Skye, they recognized that Prince Edward Island was now their permanent home.

MALCOLM MACLEOD
MALCOLM MACLEOD AND RACHEL MACQUEEN OF EARNSCLIFFE

A   Malcolm MacLeod, son of Donald the pioneer, was married in Skye to Rachel MacQueen. They settled in Earnscliffe, with issue:

B1   Donald MacLeod, m. Marion Gillis, daughter of John Gillis and Catherine Nicholson of Orwell Cove. Donald and Marion lived in Earnscliffe where most, if not all, their children were born. They afterwards lived at Sparrows Road on a farm originally owned by a man named Doran, consequently he was known as Donald "Doran" to distinguish him from other Donald MacLeods in the area. Their children were:

C1   John MacLeod, died 1919, age 70, m. Flora Bruce, died 1927, age 77, of Lyndale, they lived in Charlottetown, with issue:

D1   John D. MacLeod, born 1872, died young.

D2   Jessie MacLeod, born 1873, died young.

D3   Wellington MacLeod, born 1874, died young.

D4   John Wesley MacLeod, born 1875, was a Master Mariner, sailing out of New York and later from the Pacific coast to the Orient, on passenger liners. When he retired from the sea because of failing eyesight, he built and owned the "Grand Hotel" in Ningpo, China. It is not known if he left any descendants.

D5   Wellington MacLeod, 1877-1896.

D6   Jessie MacLeod, 1879-1930, m. James D. Offer, 1877-1938, who was the son of George Offer, Charlottetown and his wife Katherine Bell of Wood Islands. Jessie and James owned and operated the "Royal Oak" hotel in Charlottetown, their children were:

E1   Georgie Maude Offer, 1906-1970, m. Robert Harold Cameron, 1899-1983. He worked for the Post Office in Charlottetown, they had one son:

F1   James Cameron, m. Alice Perry, Charlottetown. They live in Windsor, Nova Scotia, with issue:

G1   Robert George Cameron.

G2   Susan Elizabeth Cameron.

G3   Heather Frances Cameron.

G4   Joanne Carol Cameron.

E2   Kathleen Offer, 1908-1913.

E3   Elmer George Offer, m. Frances Dorothy Robertson, issue:

F1   Tom George Offer, m. Rita O'Callaghan, Cape Breton. Tom and Rita live in Summerside where they own and operate "Ideal Dairy." They have one son:

G1   Thomas J. Offer.

F2   Paul Offer, m. Leila Jean (Currie) Sands, they live in Tyne Valley where they operate a tourist home called "The Doctor's Inn." They have three children.

E4   Arthur James Offer, 1912-1912.

C2   Donald MacLeod, born 1848, m. Euphemia MacPherson of Grandview, sister of Alex "Spike" MacPherson, with issue:

D1   Mina MacLeod, m. John MacKinnon of Canoe Cove and U.S.A. She died young leaving a young daughter:

E1 Bertha MacKinnon, m. Mr. Hall, Massachusetts. They had a family.

D2 John D. MacLeod, single, school teacher.

D3 Margaret MacLeod, single, both she and John and two others died young of T.B.

C3 Malcolm MacLeod, born 1838, never married.

C4 Rachel MacLeod, 1839-1908, m. Malcolm Gillis, died 1926, age 89, of Head of Montague, with issue:

D1 Daniel Gillis, married in the U.S.A. with two children.

D2 Malcolm Gillis, m. Christy Gillis of Orwell, they had four children.

D3 Alexander Gillis, 1882-1964, m. Mary Gillis, 1885-1961, daughter of Donald Gillis of Orwell and his wife Sarah Lamont, who was a daughter of Ewen Lamont of Lyndale, Skye and P.E.I. They lived in Upper Montague, with issue:

E1 Sadie Gillis, 1914-1934, m. Gordon Ross, of Vernon River, no issue.

E2 Donald Gillis, m. Bobby Ross, sister of Harvey of Lower Montague, they lived in Charlottetown, with children:

F1 Ross Gillis, m. Eileen Hayter, of High Bank, they live in Charlottetown, with issue:

G1 Dwayne Gillis.

G2 Grant Gillis.

F2 Donna Gillis, m. Eddie Cudmore, Charlottetown, issue:

G1 Donald Cudmore.

G2 Kevin Cudmore.

G3 Karen Cudmore, m. Greg MacIsaac, with issue:

H1 Alexander MacIsaac.

E3 Archie Gillis, m. Ann Cameron, of Charlottetown, they live in Pictou, with issue:

F1 Dorothy Gillis, R.N., m. Jim MacConnel, Scotsburn. Jim operates the Scotsburn Creamery, they have four daughters:

G1 Dianne MacConnel, m. Arnold Cameron, issue:

H1 Katelyn Cameron.

H2 Samuel Cameron.

G2 Kim MacConnel, m. Gregory Duncan, with issue:

H1 Hannah Duncan.

H2 _____.

G3 Nancy MacConnel, m. Charles Manner.

G4 Susan MacConnel, in her 4th year in Dalhousie.

F2 Gordon Gillis, graduated from Dalhousie law school, and is Deputy Minister of Justice with the Nova Scotia Government. He married Rosie Price, from Louisburg, living in Dartmouth with a family.

G1 Gordon James Gillis.

E4 John Gillis, m. Kay MacPherson, Malcolm "George's" daughter from Belfast, they live in Montreal and have four daughters.

E5 William Gillis, m. Isabel Shaw, from Uigg. They lived in British Columbia where he was killed in a road accident leaving three daughters and a son.

F1 Carol Gillis.
F2 Betty Gillis.
F3 Pamela Gillis.
F4 David Gillis.
E6 Roy Gillis, m. Ann <u>MacLeod</u>, from Glen William, they live in Montague, no family.
E7 Gordon Gillis, was severely wounded in Italy during WWII, and died soon after returning to P.E.I.
D4 John Gillis, unmarried, was a carpenter in U.S.A.
D5 Sarah Gillis, m. Mr. <u>Stewart</u>, living in Florida, no family.
D6 Catherine Gillis, died 1892, age 20, never married.
D7 Euphemia Gillis, 1869-1932, m. Jerry <u>Beers</u>, 1862-1934, of Murray River, no family.
D8 Maggie Gillis, died 1879, age 4 years.
C5 Catherine MacLeod, m. Neil <u>MacDonald</u> of Belfast.
D1 Florence MacDonald, m. Alex <u>Gillis</u>, brother of Angus, lived in Head of Montague and later Butte, Montana, no family.
D2 Catherine MacDonald, m. Hector <u>MacDonald</u>, son of Allen MacDonald of Orwell Head.
E1 Daughter, m. Mr. <u>Edmunds</u> of Charlottetown and had children.
D3 Daniel MacDonald, M.D., m., lived in New York.
D4 Gordon MacDonald, single, lived in Boston, Massachusetts.
C6 Euphemia MacLeod, died 1867, aged 23, first wife of Jim <u>Kelly</u> of Uigg, with issue:
D1 Archibald Kelly, died 1891, age 26, unmarried.
D2 Margaret Kelly, died 1887, age 22, unmarried.
C7 Isabella MacLeod, never married.
C8 Flora MacLeod, 1845-1897, m. Roderick <u>MacKenzie</u>, of Dundas, issue:
D1 Jonathan MacKenzie, m. a French woman and lived in Dundas, with issue:
E1 Gertrude MacKenzie, m. a <u>Weller</u> and lived in St. John, New Brunswick, with three or four children.
E2 Roderick MacKenzie, died young.
D2 Dan MacKenzie, 1872-1914, m. Annie _____, 1880-1915, from Michigan, they lived in Dundas, where she was killed after being hit by the wagon shafts of a run-away horse as she was walking by the side of the road. They had a family of two girls, and since her husband had died previous to the time of her accident, her family in Michigan took charge of the daughters.
D3 Sarah MacKenzie, born 1880, m. a <u>Hibbard</u>, they lived in U.S.A., with issue:
E1 Elsie Hibbard, m. ____ <u>Appleton</u>, Massachusetts, no family.
E2 William Hibbard, never married, lived in the U.S.A.
D4 Alex MacKenzie, never married, buried in Dundas.
D5 Malcolm MacKenzie, married and lived in Rowley, Massachusetts.
D6 Mary MacKenzie, never married, U.S.A.
D7 Annie MacKenzie, 1889-1915, m. Erskine <u>Tremere</u> from Wiltshire, P.E.I., they lived in Massachusetts, with issue:
E1 Mabel Tremere, m. in New Hampshire, with a son and daughter.

E2   Virginia Tremere, m. Mac MacClaine, a druggist in Massachusetts. They had two girls and a boy.

E3   Wesley Tremere, m. Gladys _____, living in Massachusetts, with four daughters.

D8 Sam MacKenzie, 1886-1918, m. Ida Turner, they lived in Dundas and had no family.

D9 Florence MacKenzie, 1888-1980, m. 1) Dan MacDonald from Loch Lomond, Nova Scotia, m. 2) James MacKinnon, Gabarous, Nova Scotia, no family.

D10 Wallace MacKenzie, 1889-1968, m. 1) Rose Miller, Halifax. They later lived in Dundas, issue:

E1   Myrtle MacKenzie, m. Norman MacLeod, Strathcona. They live in Charlottetown where Norman taught school for many years. They were also founding members of the Clan MacLeod Society of P.E.I. Their children are:

F1   Arnold MacLeod, m. Marilyn MacKenzie, they live in Charlottetown, with issue:

G1   Tracy MacLeod.

G2   Jeff MacLeod.

G3   Nancy MacLeod.

F2   Kathryn MacLeod, m. Boyd White, Charlottetown, with issue:

G1   Paul White.

G2   Dawn White, m. John MacDonald, Charlottetown, with two children.

G3   Scott White.

Norman and Myrtle also had two children who died in infancy.

E2   Roderick MacKenzie, m. Marjorie MacLeod, they live in Montague, both of whom are active members of the Clan MacLeod Society of P.E.I. He is retired from the Fruit and Vegetable Inspection branch of the Federal Government. They have four children:

F1   Waldo Blair MacKenzie, m. Josephine Kickham. They live in Charlottetown, with issue:

G1   Heidi MacKenzie

F2   Donald Roderick MacKenzie, m. Nancy Elizabeth Coroneda from Guatemala, they live in Sudbury, Ontario, with issue:

G1   Kristian MacKenzie.

G2   Davin MacKenzie.

F3   Roger Heath MacKenzie, m. Mary MacDonald, Annandale, with issue:

G1   Troy MacKenzie.

G2   Angela MacKenzie.

G3   Tara MacKenzie.

G4   Jeff MacKenzie.

F4   Myrtle Ruth MacKenzie, m. Robert Thorne, from Cornerbrook, Newfoundland, with issue:

G1   Wyatt Thorne.

G2   Colin Thorne.

G3 Roderick Thorne.

Roderick and Marjorie also had two children who died in infancy.

E3 Margaret Rose MacKenzie, m. Waldo <u>MacLeod</u>, Dundas and Charlottetown, with issue:

F1 Wayne MacLeod, m. Doris <u>Hunter</u> of Strathcona, they live in Crossroads, P.E.I., with issue:

G1 Vicki MacLeod.

G2 Trevor MacLeod.

F2 Keith MacLeod, m. Katherine <u>Garrett</u>, living in Cornwall with two children:

G1 Kelli MacLeod.

G2 Karla MacLeod.

Margaret and Waldo also had two children who died in infancy.

E4 Elsie MacKenzie, m. Charles <u>Taylor</u>, Upton, one girl:

F1 Marlene Taylor.

E5 Murray MacKenzie, m. Mildred <u>Garrett</u>, they live in Bridgetown, with issue:

F1 Shirley MacKenzie, m. Jackie <u>Garrett</u>, with issue:

G1 Rosemary Garrett.

G2 Shelley Garrett.

G3 Jonathon Garrett.

F2 Sheila MacKenzie, m. Arthur <u>Garrett</u>, Bridgetown, no family.

E6 Georgie MacKenzie, m. Everett <u>Garrett</u>, Bridgetown, issue:

F1 Henry Garrett, m. Claire <u>O'Hanley</u>, St. Peters, they live in Forest Hill.

F2 David Garrett, m. Valerie <u>Garrett</u>, living in Forest Hill, with issue.

F3 Sharon Garrett.

B2 John MacLeod, 1823-1875, m. Margaret <u>Gillis</u>, daughter of Alexander Gillis and his wife who was a daughter of John "Kinlock"MacDonald of Orwell Cove, with issue:

C1 Alexander MacLeod, died 1905, age 42. "Sandy Peggy" m. Mary <u>Murchison</u>, daughter of Sandy Murchison, blacksmith on Orwell Hill, with issue:

D1 John MacLeod, died 1947, age 56. "Jack Peggy" m. Isabel <u>MacTavish</u>, died 1985, age 95, of Newtown, they lived in Orwell Cove, with issue:

E1 Malcolm MacLeod, single, living in Orwell Cove.

E2 Jean MacLeod, 1924-1983, m. Eric <u>Larter</u>, Charlottetown, with issue:

F1 David Larter, a lawyer in Charlottetown, m. Maureen <u>MacLean</u>, daughter of Edison and Lucille MacLean, Orwell Cove.

E3 Lloyd MacLeod, m. Georgia <u>Lacey</u>, Tracadie, they live in Ontario.

E4 Kathleen MacLeod, m. David <u>Gillis</u>, Eldon, with issue:

F1 Barbara Jean Gillis, m. Ron <u>Drake</u>, Vernon, they have three children.

F2   Kenneth Gillis.

E5   Kenneth MacLeod, farming in Orwell Cove, single.

D2   Alexander MacLeod, 1893-1983, farmed in Orwell Cove, never married.

D3   Jessie MacLeod, m. Aubrey MacLennan, Newtown, no family.

C2   Malcolm MacLeod, lived in Chicago, single, died in 1938.

C3   John MacLeod, lived with and took care of Mrs. Alexander Doyle, Orwell Cove,when she was old. He was known as "Johnac" or "Shonac," and never married.

C4   Rachel MacLeod, never married.

B3   Mary MacLeod, m. Donald MacLeod, of Kinross (1829 emigrant). Issue:

C1   Neil MacLeod, died 1912, age 78, buried in Edmonton, Alberta, m. Mary MacDonald, died 1919, age 79, buried in Uigg, daughter of Archibald MacDonald, Uigg (1829 emigrant). They lived in Bellevue. Neil was a carpenter and it was he who built the spire on Orwell Head Church. When the work was completed, he stood on the top of the spire and crowed like a rooster. Issue:

D1   Archibald MacLeod, U.S.A. or Western Canada.

D2   Samuel MacLeod, died 1918 at 36, buried in Uigg.

D3   James MacLeod, in Western Canada.

C2   Malcolm MacLeod, died 1904, age 76, m. Christy Gillis, 1848-1936, Bellevue, with issue:

D1   Mary MacLeod, 1871-1957, never married.

D2   Donald MacLeod, 1872-1944, known as "Donald the Bush," never married.

D3   Rachel MacLeod, 1881-1974, never married. The above family lived in Uigg.

C3   Norman MacLeod, never married, drowned at sea.

C4   Alexander MacLeod, died 1907, age 65, m. Susan E. MacQueen, died 1939, age 97, his cousin from Scotland. Donald MacKinnon, the noted genealogist from the Isle of Skye, states that she was a daughter of Martin MacQueen and his wife Rachel Martin, aunt of Rev. Angus Martin of Snizort and of Martin Martin of Tote, Snizort. A cousin of Martin MacQueen was John MacQueen, Gaelic schoolmaster in Trotternish, who emigrated to P.E.I. leaving four brothers and sister in Kilmuir. John MacQueen's great grandson is the Rev. John Sutherland Bonnell, D.D., L.L.D., at one time minister of Fifth Avenue Presbyterian Church, New York. Another cousin was Rev. Adam MacQueen, born in Uigg, Skye, who ministered in several charges in Ontario and was married to Norma MacLeod, a granddaughter of Neil MacLeod, last of Gesto [sic]. The Rev. Adam's brother was the Rev. John MacQueen of Daviot, Invernessshire. These MacQueens belonged to the MacQueen family of Duntulm, a branch of the Skye MacQueens. Alexander and Susan had two boys:

D1   Stanhope MacLeod, died 1932, age 52, never married.

D2   Victor MacLeod, never married.

C5   Donald MacLeod, never married, lived in Orwell.

C6   Jessie MacLeod, died 1928, age 85, m. John MacBeth, died 1903, age 66, of Bellevue. This MacBeth family came from Ross Shire, Scotland. They spent a year in Cape Breton before crossing over to Pinette in 1837. They walked to Green Marsh, now Bellevue, where along with

a MacDonald family, who I believe was connected by marriage, were
the first settlers in that area. Their children are:
D1   Mary MacBeth, m. John <u>MacKinnon</u> of Lewes, issue.
     E1   John Dan MacKinnon, lived in Western Canada.
     E2   John Hughie MacKinnon, m. in Nova Scotia with a family.
     E3   Mary Alice MacKinnon, m. in Nova Scotia with a family.
     E4   Jessie MacKinnon, m. Mr. <u>Murray</u> and lives in Nova Scotia.
     E5   Neil MacKinnon, m. Jessie <u>Nicholson</u>, with a family.
D2   Maggie MacBeth, m. Mr. <u>MacLeod</u>, from Hartsville, P.E.I., and
     later Massachusetts, with issue:
     E1   Talmadge MacLeod, married in U.S.A.
     E2   Beecher MacLeod, married in U.S.A.
     E3   Wilfred MacLeod, married in U.S.A.
     E4   Irving MacLeod, married in U.S.A.
     E5   Edwin MacLeod, not married, lives in U.S.A.
D3   Annie MacBeth, never married.
D4   Bella MacBeth, m. Edwin <u>Perkess</u>, in U.S.A., no family.
D5   Catherine MacBeth, died 1884, age 9 days.
D6   Isabella MacBeth, died 1868, age 1 year.
D7   Daniel Angus MacBeth, 1875-1950, never married.
D8   Donald Alec MacBeth, m. Annie <u>Darrach</u>, 1886-1968, East Roy-
     alty. They lived in Quincy, with issue:
     E1   Lorna MacBeth, m. Dr. <u>MacPhee</u> from Kilmuir, P.E.I., and
          U.S.A., with issue:
          F1   Ariel MacPhee, m. Allan <u>MacLeod</u>, Massachusetts.
          F2   William MacPhee, M.D., San Diego, California.
          F3   Lynn MacPhee.
     E2   Verna MacBeth, m. Larry <u>Brown</u>, U.S.A., with issue:
     F1   Marion Brown.
     F2   Richard Brown.
     E3   Ruth MacBeth, m. Robert <u>Bradbury</u>, U.S.A.
     E4   Blanche MacBeth, died young.
     E5   Marion MacBeth, R.N., single, living in Quincy.
     E6   Edith MacBeth, single.
     E7   Alexander MacBeth, married in U.S.A.
D9   Neil MacBeth, died 1954, age 77, m. Angusena <u>MacLeod</u>, died
     1970, age 86, of Grandview, no family.
D10 Kenneth MacBeth, 1873-1955, m. Bessie <u>MacLeod</u>, 1876-1927,
     from Hunter River. They farmed in Grandview, with issue:
     E1   Jessie MacBeth, 1908-1927, never married.
D11 John MacBeth, m. Mary Anne <u>Matheson</u> from Lewes. John died
     1969, age 91, and Mary died 1948, age 70. Their family were:
     E1   John MacBeth, single, died age 26.
     E2   Mary Belle MacBeth, m. Tony <u>Marini</u>, U.S.A. with issue:
          F1   John Marini, m. Rose _____, one child.
          F2   Francis Marini, married with four children.
          F3   Billy Marini, m. Betty <u>Johnstone</u>, they have three
               children.
     E3   Hughie MacBeth, 1910-1985, m. 1) Rita <u>Weatherby</u>, born
          1918, with issue:
          F1   Effie MacBeth, m. Lloyd <u>Scott</u>, Charlottetown, issue:

G1   Dianne Scott.
G2   Sheila Scott.
F2   Neil MacBeth, m. Elizabeth Reeves, with issue:
G1   Shelly MacBeth, m. Sheldon MacDonald.
G2   Jeffrey MacBeth.
F3   John MacBeth, m. Elaine McGarry, with issue:
G1   John E. MacBeth.
G2   Sean MacBeth.
F4   Marvin MacBeth, twin, m. Rosemary MacLean, issue:
G1   Trevor MacBeth.
G2   Lesa MacBeth.
G3   Pamela MacBeth, all living in Alberta.
F5   Melvin MacBeth, twin, living in Charlottetown.
F6   Debbie MacBeth, m. Arnold Gallant, with issue:
G1   Jonathon Gallant.
F7   Lorna MacBeth, m. Robert Thistle, living in Charlotte-
town, with two children.
Hughie m. 2) Evelyn (Arthur) Haywood, no family.
E4   Jessie MacBeth, m. Wendell MacLeod, son of Roderick
Charles of Lyndale, with issue:
F1   Ernest MacLeod, m. Alfreda Bears, daughter of the
noted singer, John Bears, Brooklyn. They live in
Kinross, issue:
G1   Darren MacLeod, m. Joni Garnhum.
G2   Darrel MacLeod, twin , died in infancy.
F2   Mary MacLeod, m. Neil MacDonald, Brudenell. They
have three children:
G1   Jody MacDonald.
G2   Donnie MacDonald.
G3   Kimberly MacDonald.
F3   Ewen MacLeod, m. Anne Murnaghan, Fort Augustus,
with issue:
G1   Christa MacLeod.
G2   Ryan MacLeod.
G3   Shannon MacLeod
F4   Anne MacLeod, m. 1) Aubrey Darrach, New Domin-
ion, with issue:
G1   Melanie Darrach, m. Reuben Creed, from
Sturgeon.
G2   Christopher Darrach, m. Mari Lynn Lewis.
Anne m. 2) Don MacLeod, one daughter:
G3   Amanda MacLeod.
E5   Effie MacBeth, died 1986, age 73, m. 1) David Roberts, issue:
F1   Melvin Roberts, m. Donna Poulton, they have two
girls.
Effie m. 2) John Ford with issue:
F2   Jessie Belle Ford.
E6   Kenneth MacBeth, single, living in Montreal.
C7   Rachel MacLeod, 1848-1936, m. Donald MacPherson, 1850-1932, of
Bellevue, with issue:
D1   Florence MacPherson, 1885-1976, never married.

D2 Dan William MacPherson,1891-1940, never married.

D3 Norman MacPherson, 1901-1948, never married.

D4 Christina MacPherson, never married.

D5 Jessie MacPherson, never married.

C8 Catherine MacLeod, died age 78, m. Peter MacPhee, Bellevue. He died in 1888, aged 49, with issue:

D1 Daniel MacPhee, in British Columbia

D2 Fred MacPhee, in New Hampshire.

D3 Mrs. John Ross, in Dorchester, Massachusetts.

C9 Mary MacLeod.

C10 Angus MacLeod.

B4 Alexander MacLeod, 1822-1893, in 1847 m. Christina Nicholson, 1828-1885, daughter of Donald Nicholson, miller of Orwell River, with issue:

C1 Rachel Lavina MacLeod, 1853-1934, m. Waldo Walker, 1850-1910, in Westboro, Massachusetts, with issue:

D1 Annie Walker, m. Edward Loafing, Massachusetts, with issue:

E1 Margaret Loafing.

D2 Joseph Walker, m. Emily Lavender, with issue:

E1 Charles Edward Walker.

C2 Malcolm J. MacLeod, 1858-1931, m. Sarah Docherty, of Seal River. They lived in Earnscliffe, with issue:

D1 Gordon MacLeod, 1893-1935, m. Verna Gorveatt, 1912-1942, of Nine Mile Creek. They had one son:

E1 Vernon MacLeod, who lives on the old homestead, settled first by his great-great grandfather, Malcolm MacLeod of Skye and Earnscliffe.

D2 Sydney MacLeod, 1895-1939, m. Harriet Jane MacPhee, 1902-1937, New Dominion, with issue:

E1 Eva Ruth MacLeod, living in Aurora, Ontario, was married to Joe McBride, who died 1984. They had two boys:

F1 Kevin McBride.

F2 Robert McBride.

D3 David Sutherland MacLeod, who is a minister in the United Church, m. Helen Margaret Grace Barfoot of Chatham, Ontario. He is retired and they live in St. John, New Brunswick. Their children are:

E1 Margaret MacLeod, m. Robert Hawkes. They live in Fredericton, New Brunswick, with five children.

E2 Joyce MacLeod, m. Dr. Ian Gilchrist, Moncton, New Brunswick. They have three children.

E3 Elizabeth MacLeod, R.N., m. Dr. Don Gamble, Ontario. They have three children.

E4 Lillian MacLeod, m. Guy Cyr, Ontario. They have three children.

D4 Eva MacLeod, living in Earnscliffe with her nephew Vernon MacLeod on the homestead.

D5 George MacLeod, died age 10 in 1913.

C3 William MacLeod, 1849-1899, m. Margaret Ross, 1855-1945, daughter of Walter Ross of Eldon. They lived in Los Angeles, California, issue:

D1 Amy MacLeod, born 1884 on P.E.I., m. Orville Chadsey, and they lived in California, with issue:

E1   Elmer Chadsey, m. Vivian Hall, living in Honolulu, issue:
    F1   Betty Chadsey.
    F2   Jean Chadsey.
    F3   David Chadsey.
E2   Lois Chadsey, m. Rev. F. S. Dick Wichman, living in San Francisco, with issue:
    F1   Annie Wichman.
    F2   John Wichman.
E3   Betty Chadsey, m. Torrance Roumpf, living in Oregon, with issue:
    F1   Margaret Roumpf.
    F2   Judy Roumpf.
E4   Orville Chadsey, of Washington, D.C., a clergyman, m. Barbara Mahrt, with issue:
    F1   Mark Chadsey.
    F2   Karen Chadsey.
    F3   Krista Chadsey.
D2 Spenser MacLeod, born 1886, m. Florence Schrimp, California, with issue:
    E1   Ruth MacLeod, m. James Dieffenwierth, California, no family.
    E2   Gordon MacLeod, m. Frances Dara Heath, California, issue:
        F1   Gordon Ross MacLeod.
        F2   Donald MacLeod.
        F3   Bruce MacLeod.
        F4   Thomas MacLeod.
    E3   Naomi MacLeod, m. John Austin Bradfield, California, issue:
        F1   Jo Ann Bradfield.
        F2   Judy Bradfield.
        F3   Janet Bradfield.
        F4   Juliet Bradfield.
D3 Walter Ross MacLeod, born 1889, m. Sadie Bell Kindervatter, California, with issue:
    E1   Walter Ross MacLeod.
    E2   Elizabeth MacLeod.
    E3   David MacLeod.
    E4   Daniel MacLeod.
    E5   Polly MacLeod.
    E6   Rosemary MacLeod.
C4 Daniel MacLeod, died 1868, aged 17.
C5 Mary Jane MacLeod, died 1874, aged 18.
C6 Jessie MacLeod, died 1878, aged 16.
C7 Charlotte Eunice MacLeod, 1860-1915, m. Charles Ward, 1854-1928, Massachusetts, with issue:
D1 William Ward, 1901-1983, m. Irene Braley, Massachusetts, issue:
    E1   Barbara Ward, m. Norman Hjulstrom, Massachusetts, issue:
        F1   Roger Hjulstrom.
        F2   Eric Hjulstrom.
        F3   Sandra Hjulstrom.
    E2   Charlotte Eunice Ward, m. Herbert Prounty Holbrook.

E3 Charles William Ward, m. Nancy Ann <u>Cabnal</u>, Connecticut, with issue:
F1 Glen Ward.
F2 Betsey Jane Ward.
F3 Robert Ward.
F4 William Ward.
E4 Nancy Louise Ward, m. 1) John <u>MacKenna</u>, died 1968, issue:
F1 John MacKenna.
F2 Jacqueline MacKenna.
Nancy m. 2) Thomas <u>Kingston</u>, with issue:
F3 Catherine Ann Kingston.
B5 Rachel MacLeod, 1806-1901, m. Donald <u>Gillis</u>, died 1874, aged 74, son of John and Catherine (Nicholson) Gillis, Orwell Cove, with issue:
C1 Capt. John Gillis, died 1919, aged 93. His obituary states that during his seafaring experience "he commanded some of the largest ships afloat, made several voyages around the world, navigating in all kinds of dangerous weather with the seas running mountains high and sweeping over the decks which threatened him with a watery grave, yet against such odds he never lost a ship or even a sailor and was pronounced one of the best seafaring Captains that ever left his native Province." He married his cousin Catherine <u>MacLeod</u>, Orwell Cove, daughter of Murdoch and Flora MacLeod, with issue:
D1 Margaret Gillis, 1856-1905, m. Neil Angus <u>Gillis</u>, 1854-1943, son of Angus Gillis of Orwell Cove and his wife Catherine MacLeod, daughter of Malcolm and Rachel MacLeod, Earnscliffe. Sir Andrew MacPhail, in his book *The Master's Wife* refers to Neil Angus as "that most honest and best carpenter, who would make the replica of a Chippendale chair or replace sills under an old barn with[out] equal." Neil and Margaret lived in Orwell Cove, with issue:
E1 John Murdoch Gillis, Orwell Cove, never married, died 1966, aged 76.
E2 Grover Gillis, Orwell Cove, never married, died 1961, aged 73.
E3 Arthur Gillis, died 1934, m. Mary <u>Gillis</u>, Orwell Cove and U.S.A., no family.
E4 Angus Gillis, died 1884, 3 months.
E5 Sadie Gillis, died 1893, age 9 months.
E6 Christina Gillis, died 1918, aged 36, m. Dan <u>Bruce</u>, died 1944, aged 73, of Lyndale, with issue:
F1 Margaret Bruce, m. Percy (Neil Billy) <u>MacLeod</u>, Orwell, with issue:
G1 Lloyd MacLeod, m. Vivian <u>Stewart</u>, of Belfast, with issue:
H1 Carl MacLeod.
H2 Cathy MacLeod.
H3 Anne MacLeod.
H4 Jennifer MacLeod.
G2 Gerald MacLeod, m. Shirley <u>Carver</u>, of Lyndale. They live in Ontario, with issue:
H1 Bonnie MacLeod.

H2   Heather MacLeod.

G3   Elspeth MacLeod, m. Bobby <u>Crane</u>, Vernon.

F2   Katie Bruce, m. James <u>Martin</u>, died 1953, age 52, son of John Sam Martin, Uigg, with issue:

G1   Loren Martin, living in Charlottetown.

G2   Emily Martin, m. Hal <u>White</u>, Murray Harbour and Bunbury, with issue:

H1   Harold White, married.

H2   Patsy White, m. _____ <u>Hebert</u>, Montreal.

H3   Gail White, single.

G3   Marilyn Martin, married in Ontario.

F3   Willard Bruce, died 1974, age 65, m. Margaret <u>Burke</u>, they farmed in Lyndale, with issue:

G1   Reginald Bruce, single.

G2   Donald Bruce, m. Beatrice <u>Bourgeois</u>, with issue:

H1   Anne Bruce.

H2   Donnie Bruce.

G3   Christine Bruce, m. Harvey <u>MacKenzie</u>, Valleyfield, with issue:

H1   Wade MacKenzie, m. Karen MacDougall, daughter of Rev. E. E. MacDougall, Valleyfield.

H2   Kevin MacKenzie.

G4   Sylvia Bruce, m. Harry <u>MacLean</u>, son of John of Uigg, with issue:

H1   Robert MacLean.

G5   Linda Bruce, m. Marcus <u>Wilson</u>, Alberry Plains, with issue:

H1   Kimberly Wilson.

H2   Karen Wilson.

H3   Kent Wilson.

H4   Kathy Wilson.

G6   Albert Bruce, married in Alberta.

F4   Carlyle Bruce, Lyndale, single.

F5   Alfred Bruce, Lyndale, single.

F6   Mabel Bruce, m. Ernest <u>MacDonald</u>, who was "Cape Breton" Dan's son from Hopefield. They had a large family among whom was:

G1   Lorna MacDonald, m. Donald <u>MacLeod</u>, son of Willard, Kinross, with issue:

H1   Jeffrey MacLeod.

H2   Andrew MacLeod.

H3   Timmy MacLeod.

F7   Atwood Bruce, m. Helen <u>Campbell</u>, Victoria Cross, living in Ontario, with issue:

G1   Lorne Daniel Bruce, m. Karen <u>Steele</u>, with issue:

H1   Danielle Bruce.

H2   Stacy Bruce.

D2   Catherine Gillis, daughter of Capt. John, m. _____ <u>Jackson</u>, Lot 48, no issue.

D3   Sarah Gillis, m. _____ <u>Curtis</u>, U.S.A., no family.

D4   Rachel Gillis, died 1903, age 39, never married.
D5   Murdoch Gillis, First Mate, was granted a medal for heroism for saving the lives of his whole crew when the ship was driven aground on the Newfoundland coast in a snowstorm. He swam for shore with a rope when the ship was breaking on the rocks. He made two attempts and was driven back, but was successful on the third attempt. He never married and died of T.B. about 1900.

C2 Donald Gillis, m. Catherine MacKinnon, of Georgetown, with issue:
D1   Archibald Gillis, m. Miss MacNeill, Providence, Rhode Island.
D2   Alexander Gillis, never married.
D2   Donald Gillis, never married.
D4   Charles Gillis, never married.
D5   Margaret Gillis, died 1890, age 28, m. William Jamieson, in Massachusetts. He was from Aberdeenshire, Scotland, and died in 1891, age 31, and is buried in Aberdeenshire. They had one son:
    E1   William Jamieson, died in Providence, Rhode Island, age 29.

C3 Neil Gillis, Orwell Cove, never married.
C4 Malcolm Gillis, 1834-1920, m. Jane Bell, 1838-1914, daughter of Robert Bell, Wood Islands, with issue:
D1   Alfred Gillis, 1873-1939, m. Jane MacKeegan, Belfast, she was a daughter of Malcolm MacKeegan, formerly from Marion Bridge, Nova Scotia, and Catherine Buchanan, Belfast. Alfred and Jane lived in Montague where he was a carpenter, with issue:
    E1   Leonard Gillis, m. Edith Richards, of Murray Harbour. They live in Montague, with issue:
        F1   Marjorie Gillis, m. Colin Westaway, living in Harrington, with issue:
            G1   Allen Westaway.
            G2   David Westaway.
        F2   Alfred Gillis, single.
        F3   Diane Gillis, m. Barry MacLeod, Lower Montague, with issue:
            G1   Treena MacLeod.
            G2   Paula MacLeod.
        F4   Betty Lou Gillis, m. Fenton Pollard, White Sands, with issue:
            G1   Stephen Pollard.
            G2   Andrew Pollard.
            G3   Greg Pollard.
        F5   Ruth Gillis, m. Arthur McGarry, Iona, with issue:
            G1   Troy McGarry.
            G2   Tracy McGarry.
    E2   Harry Gillis, died 1972, age 62, m. Filomena Vuozzo, issue:
        F1   Laura Gillis, m. Gordon Thompson, living in Port Hawkesbury, with issue:
            G1   Barry Thompson.
            G2   Cathy Thompson.
        F2   Edith Gillis, died 1979, age 48, m. Vincent Bowe, they lived in Nassau, Bahamas, with issue:
            G1   Stephanie Bowe.

                G2   Gordon Bowe.

          F3   Jean Gillis, died 1972, age 38, m. Duncan Wilson, Millview, with issue:

                G1   Filomena Wilson.

                G2   Wendy Wilson.

     E3   Catherine Gillis, m. Byron Stewart, died in 1975, age 66, Kensington, they lived in Montague and had one son:

          F1   Donald Stewart, living in Fort St. John, British Columbia, m. 1) Mary Lojochuk, no family, m. 2) Leona Krysak, with issue:

                G1   Alexandria Stewart, died 1970, age 9 months.

                G2   Byron Peter Stewart.

                G3   David Ian Stewart.

     E4   Jean Gillis, m. John R. MacLean, Caledonia and Massachusetts, with issue:

          F1   William MacLean, m. 1) Sally Bowman, living in Massachusetts, with issue:

                G1   Sally Jean MacLean, m. Mark Dcuba, living in New Mexico.

                G2   Heather MacLean, living in California.

            William m. 2) Diane MacGinn, issue:

                G3   Sean MacLean.

                G4   Kimberly MacLean.

                G5   Brian MacLean.

                G6   Christy MacLean.

          F2   Etta MacLean, m. Joe MacNamara, living in Massachusetts, with issue:

                G1   Paige MacNamara.

                G2   Jason MacNamara.

C5   William Gillis, m. Margaret Bell, sister of Jane, with issue:

   D1   Gamaliel Gillis, M.D., died 1898, age 45, practised medicine in Dundas and Montague where he lived in the house later owned by Jim MacLean on Main St. He married Isabella Johnstone, died 1898, age 43, daughter of David Johnstone, with issue:

     E1   Peter MacLaren Gillis, killed at Passchendale, France, WWI.

     E2   Flora Rose Gillis, 1884-1920, was a school teacher, she went to live with her aunt, Mrs. Margaret Taylor in Walden, Colorado, in an attempt to improve her health, and died in her sleep.

     E3   Jean Gillis, died 1985, age 97, was also a school teacher and was married in Regina to George Miller, who had come from the Ottawa area. Their family was:

          F1   Dell Miller, m. Olive _____.

          F2   Joyce Miller, single.

          F3   Gillis Miller, a lawyer in Regina, he died age 40, never married.

     E4   Johnstone Gillis, living in the State of Washington, aged 95, single.

     E5   Gamaliel Gillis, 1894-1970, married in England during WWI and made his home there, however, he expressed a wish that he be buried back on P.E.I. Consequently when he died, his ashes were sent back to Canada and interred in Lower Montague Cemetery.

- D2 Margaret Gillis, m. William Taylor, they lived in Colorado and have descendants living in the American West.
- D3 Rachel Gillis, m. Andrew Miller, Bridgetown, with issue:
  - E1 Margaret Miller, m. Jack MacLure, Dundas, with issue:
    - F1 Miller MacLure, m. Evelyn Little, from MacAdam, New Brunswick. They live in Ontario, no family.
  - E2 Laura Miller, m. Archie MacLean, a brother of N. D. MacLean, Charlottetown, they operated a store in Raymore, Saskatchewan.
  - E3 Etta Miller, U.S.A., never married.
  - E4 Neil Miller, lived in Bridgetown, never married.
  - E5 William Miller, U.S.A., never married.
- D4 William Gillis, m. Bella MacDonald, Murray Harbour, issue:
  - E1 A son.
- D5 Alexander Gillis, died young, not married.
- D6 John Gillis, drowned when young, unmarried.
- C6 Catherine Gillis, daughter of Donald and Rachel Gillis, never married.
- C7 Rachel Gillis, m. John MacKinnon, with issue:
  - D1 Fanny MacKinnon.
- B6 William MacLeod, died 1906, age 91, settled in Lyndale, m. Rachel MacLeod, died 1891, age 70, sister of "Old" Captain Alexander MacLeod, master of survey steamer *Gulnare*, issue:
  - C1 Mary MacLeod, m. Angus MacEachern, of Belfast, with issue:
    - D1 Kate MacEachern, never married.
    - D2 Norman MacEachern, never married.
    - D3 Margaret MacEachern, m. Neil MacLeod, of Pinette, no family.
  - C2 Donald MacLeod, died 1933, age 80, m. Sarah Martin, died 1901, age 45, sister of Dr. Martin Martin of Grandview, with issue:
    - D1 Maggie Alice MacLeod, 1890-1933, never married.
    - D2 Angus MacLeod, 1895-1971, never married.
    - D3 Alexander MacLeod, never married, aged 92, 1986, living in Lyndale with Donald Nicholson.
  - C3 Kate MacLeod, never married.
  - C4 Jane MacLeod, never married, 1860-1929.
  - C5 Maggie MacLeod, m. Murdoch MacLeod of Glen William and Boston, with issue:
    - D1 Margaret MacLeod, m. Mr. Brown, U.S.A.
    - D2 William MacLeod.
    - D3 John MacLeod.
    - D4 Minard MacLeod, believed most, if not all of this family died young.
  - C6 Agnes MacLeod, m. Mr. Hersham in U.S.A. They had one son.
- B7 Neil MacLeod, 1816-1901, m. Catherine MacDonald, of Kilmuir, P.E.I., whose mother was Isabella MacQueen, a sister of Neil's mother Rachel (see "Musical" Allan MacDonald and his descendants by Hugh MacDonald). Neil and Catherine had no family, they lived in Victoria Cross and are buried in Valleyfield Cemetery.
- B8 Christy MacLeod, m. Martin Martin, a son of Sam Martin, Orwell Cove. Sam Martin came from Skye to P.E.I. in 1803 and lived to the age of 107

years. His obituary states that he was honest, industrious and a good neighbour, and was able to walk about until a few weeks of his death. He died in 1854, the Sam Martin who settled in Uigg in 1829 was a relative. The children of Christy MacLeod and Martin Martin are:

C1 Malcolm Martin, born 1836, a school teacher, lived in Ontario.

C2 John Martin, 1843-1934, m. Jessie MacLean, 1859-1926, they lived in Bangor and are buried in Lorne Valley, they had issue:

D1 Mary Martin, died 1964, age 80, m. Duncan MacDougall, died 1943, age 62. They lived in Bangor, with issue:
E1 Freeman MacDougall, never married.
E2 Violet MacDougall, married Clarence Myers, died 1985, age 72, of Riverton, with issue:
F1 Lorna Myers, m. Emmett MacInnis, Morell, with issue:
G1 Belinda MacInnis.
G2 Beryl MacInnis.
F2 Lila Myers, m. Eric Kenny, Morell and Kinlock, issue:
G1 Matthew Kenny.
D2 Christine Martin, m. Donald Grant, Bangor, no issue.
D3 Katie Martin, never married, now a resident of Beach Grove Home.

C3 Sam Martin, 1835-1903, m. Flora Nicholson, 1838-1916, of Dundas. They lived in the Dundas area, with issue:

D1 Malcolm Martin, 1873-1906, died in U.S.A., buried in Dundas, single.
D2 Samuel Martin, 1878-1894.
D3 Freeman Martin, 1880-1921, never married.
D4 Howard Martin, married, lived in Saskatchewan, no family.
D5 Laura Martin, 1884-1944, m. Dan Nicholson, Dundas Centre, with issue:
E1 Gladys Nicholson, died young.
E2 Marion Nicholson, m. Norman MacKenzie, Cardigan, issue:
F1 Ruth MacKenzie, m. Douglas MacDonald, living in Hamilton, Ontario.
F2 Norma MacKenzie, living in Hamilton, Ontario.
F3 Willard MacKenzie, living in Hamilton, Ontario.
F4 Garth MacKenzie, living in Hamilton, Ontario.
F5 Donald MacKenzie, m. Claire Fogarty, they live in Cardigan, with issue:
G1 Kim MacKenzie.
G2 Darcy MacKenzie.
E3 Catherine Nicholson, 1921-1947, m. Osborne Wood, Pownal, with issue:
F1 Elaine Wood, married in Hamilton, Ontario, with one child.
E4 Margaret Nicholson, died in 1927, age 11 years.
D6 Katie Martin, 1875-1959, m. John MacLeod, "California Jack," 1868-1958. His father went to California by ship around the South American continent, before the Panama Canal was built. He worked in that area a few years before returning to take up land in Primrose, there were a number of MacLeod families in that area, hence the name. John and Katie's family:

E1   Howard MacLeod, m. Marion <u>MacEachern</u>, they now live in Bridgetown, their children are:

F1   Martin MacLeod, m. Wanda <u>Molyneaux</u>, with issue:
G1   Kimberly MacLeod.
G2   Andrew MacLeod.

F2   Catherine MacLeod, m. 1) Larry <u>Robertson</u>, with issue:
G1   Roger Robertson.
Catherine m. 2) John <u>Peters</u>.

F3   Jeanie MacLeod.

F4   John Ross MacLeod.

E2   Alexander MacLeod, m. Almeda <u>Howlett</u>, living in Ontario with issue:

F1   Barrie MacLeod, m. Stephanie <u>Cherney</u>, living in Ontario with four children.

F2   Russell MacLeod, married in Ontario.

F3   Roy MacLeod, married in Ontario with a boy and girl.

F4   Darlene MacLeod, m. Gerry <u>Shulty</u>.

F5   Kim MacLeod, living in Ontario.

D7   Christine Martin, daughter of Sam and Flora Martin, m. Alfred <u>Pope</u>, Chepstow, they had two boys:

E1   Freeman Pope, never married.

E2   Henry Pope, never married.

C4   Mary Martin, 1857-1905, m. John "Sargent" <u>MacLeod</u>, Strathcona, with issue:

D1   Victor MacLeod, 1896-1930, never married.

D2   Alpha MacLeod, never married.

D3   Christine MacLeod, R.N., married a medical doctor in New York.

C5   Katie Martin, m. William <u>Robbins</u>, Morell, no family

C6   A son, drowned December, 1874, age 27, at the Georgetown wharf.

C7   Neil Martin, lived in Denver, Colorado.

C8   Martin Martin.

B9   Catherine MacLeod, m. Angus <u>Gillis</u>, Orwell Cove, who was the brother of Donald Gillis, married to her sister Rachel. They had issue:

C1   Donald Gillis, died 1930, age 76, m. Mary <u>Martin</u>, died 1933, age 78, Grandview, with issue:

D1   Alexander Gillis, died 1973, age 89, never married.

D2   Daniel Gillis, 1885-1979, m. Mary <u>MacKenzie</u>, 1889-1981, Orwell Cove. They lived in Grandview, with issue:

E1   Catherine Gillis, m. Eric <u>Scott</u>, Grandview, with issue:

F1   Ivan Scott, married and living in U.S.A. with one son:
G1   Robert Scott.

F2   Norma Scott, m. Allie <u>Murray</u>, Crossroads, with issue:
G1   Cheryl Murray.
G2   Darlene Murray, R.N., Calgary, Alberta.
G3   Debra Murray.
G4   Brian Murray.

F3   Merrill Scott, m. Lodi Rienties, living in Montague, with issue:
G1   Doran Scott.
G2   Opal Scott.

E2   Laura Gillis, m. Clarence <u>Gillis</u>, her cousin, living at Tea

Hill. Their children are:

- F1 Gail Gillis, married and living in Prince George, British Columbia.
- F2 Kimberly Gillis, living in Charlottetown.

E3 Elmer Gillis, m. Pearl <u>Stewart</u>, with issue:

- F1 Larry Gillis, m. and living in Squamish, British Columbia, with two children.
- F2 Brenda Gillis, m. Kevin <u>Kemp</u>, living in Milltown Cross, with three daughters.

E4 Florence Gillis, m. Clarence <u>Reynolds</u>, 1919-1973, with issue:

- F1 David Reynolds, m. Gloria <u>Hicken</u>, living in Lower Montague,with two children.
- F2 Roy Reynolds, m. Linda <u>Hicken</u>, with two children.

D3 John Malcolm Gillis, m. Jessie <u>Gillis</u>, they had two boys:

E1 Clarence Gillis, m. Laura <u>Gillis</u>, they live at Tea Hill, two children:

- F1 Gail.
- F2 Kimberly.

E2 Ivan Gillis, who was blind, was a noted musician and composer, died 1946, age 28.

C2 John Gillis, school teacher, 1844-1929, lived in Victoria Cross, m. 1) Margaret <u>MacLean</u>, 1848-1901, with issue:

D1 Mary Gillis, 1874-1876.

D2 Hiram Gillis, lived in Nova Scotia.

D3 William Warren Gillis, died in 1906 in Minnesota.

D4 Horace Gillis, lived in Ontario.

D5 James Gillis, 1885-1916, lived in Sydney, Nova Scotia.

D6 George R. Gillis, 1883-1906.

John m. 2) Kate <u>MacLean</u>, Lyndale, she had one son:

D1 Alexander MacLean, died 1967, age 71, m. Gladys <u>Vaniderstine</u>, Heatherdale. Gladys m. 1) Malcolm <u>Lamont</u>, Victoria Cross, who was descended from Malcolm Lamont, an 1829 emigrant from Bernisdale, Isle of Skye, to Lyndale, P.E.I., their issue were:

E1 Peggy Lamont, m. Douglas <u>Nicholson</u>, who was killed in the Korean War, 1954, age 34, leaving two sons:

F1 James Nicholson, m. Beverly <u>Oatway</u>, they live in Yellowknife and have two children:

- G1 Geordie Nicholson.
- G2 Sarah Nicholson.

F2 Randolph Nicholson, single, living in Yellowknife.

E2 Ruth Lamont, m. George <u>Bowley</u>, Midgell, with issue:

F1 Preston Bowley, m. Diane <u>MacDougall</u>, they live in Charlottetown, with a daughter.

- G1 Deanna Bowley.

F2 Wayne Bowley, m. Cathy <u>Jackson</u>, Midgell, with issue:

- G1 James Bowley.
- G2 Gregory Bowley.
- G3 Richard Bowley.

F3 Anna Bowley, m. Garfield <u>Anderson</u>, Charlottetown, with issue:

G1 Erin Anderson.

G2 Glen Anderson.

F4 Joan Bowley, single, living in Charlottetown.

F5 Eric Bowley, m. Donna _____, Midgell.

E3 Eleanor Lamont, m. Moody <u>MacDonald</u>, Roseneath, issue:

F1 Gladys MacDonald, m. Elwood <u>MacIntyre</u>, Montague, issue:

G1 Michel MacIntyre.

F2 Elizabeth MacDonald, killed in an auto accident 1960, age 14.

F3 Kenneth MacDonald, m. Glenda <u>Graham</u>, Roseneath, issue:

G1 Steven MacDonald.

G2 Craig MacDonald.

G3 Andrew MacDonald.

F4 Donald MacDonald, m. Debbie <u>White</u>, living in Roseneath with one daughter:

G1 Kari MacDonald.

E4 Donald Lamont, m. Margaret <u>Rattray</u>, they live in Roseneath, with issue:

F1 Debra Lamont, m. Darryl <u>MacLean</u>, New Perth. She teaches school in Vernon River.

F2 Douglas Lamont.

F3 Donna Lamont.

The family of Alexander MacLean and Gladys Vaniderstine Lamont (D1) are as follows:

E1 Chester MacLean, died in Ottawa about 1975, age 42. He m. Joyce <u>Barnhart</u>, with issue:

F1 Heather MacLean, m. in London, Ontario, with two girls.

F2 Leslie MacLean, single.

E2 Ralph MacLean, m. Jeanette <u>Chaput</u>, Ottawa. They live in Brudenell with two children:

F1 Sandra MacLean, m. Randy <u>Fraser</u>, Montague.

F2 Elizabeth MacLean, m. Murray <u>Campion</u>, living in Lyndale.

E3 Cassie MacLean, m. Walter <u>Yhrnick</u>, Stoney Creek, Ontario. They have no family.

E4 Alexander MacLean, m. Sybil <u>Duggan</u>, they live near Alberton, P.E.I. Sybil has a yarn shop in Alberton. Their family:

F1 Derril MacLean.

F2 Sharon MacLean.

F3 Rodney MacLean.

E5 James MacLean, m. Verna <u>MacLaren</u>, they live in Brudenell with two children:

F1 Sharon MacLean.

F2 Gordon MacLean.

E6 George MacLean, lived in Kilmuir, never married, died, age 38, buried in Valleyfield Cemetery.

E7 Irene MacLean, m. Eddie <u>Huskins</u>, they live in Nova Scotia with one daughter:

F1   Eleanor Huskins.
E8   One child died in infancy.
C3   Malcolm Gillis, "Shy Malcolm," 1856-1944, m. 1) Isabella S. MacRae, died 1912, age 63, at Grandview. They had issue:
D1   Daniel Gillis, "Shy Dan," 1888-1952, never married, lived in Grandview.
D2   Margaret Bell Gillis, who lived in U.S.A.
Malcolm m. 2) Catherine MacDonald, daughter of Donald Duncan MacDonald, they had no family.
C4   Sarah Gillis, married in the U.S.A. with one daughter.
C5   Catherine Gillis, never married.
C6   John Gillis, never married.
C7   Malcolm Gillis, m. Jane MacLeod, Valleyfield, with issue:
D1   Malcolm Gillis, lived in Charlottetown, m. Lottie Smallwood.
D2   Isaac Gillis, who was married in Boston with two children.
C8   Neil Angus Gillis, 1854-1943, m. Margaret Gillis, daughter of Capt. John, Orwell Cove. For their descendants see under Rachel, daughter of Malcolm MacLeod and Rachel MacQueen, Earnscliffe.

Murdoch MacLeod
Murdoch MacLeod and Flora Nicholson of Orwell Cove

A2   Murdoch MacLeod, died July 7, 1859, age 84, son of Donald the Pioneer, settled in Orwell Cove and in 1804 married Flora Nicholson, died April 15, 1859, age 76, the daughter of "Old" Donald Nicholson, who had come over on the *Polly* from Flodigarry, Skye, and settled in Orwell Cove. His wife was Catherine MacArthur from Skye, but she had died previous to 1803. Donald Nicholson died at Orwell Cove in 1832 at age 96. All of his family, which consisted of seven daughters and two sons, eventually settled in the Belfast area. They are as follows:

B1   Donald MacLeod, died 1881, age 74, m. Katherine Gillis, died 1902, age 76, Orwell Cove. He was a school teacher and they lived in Lyndale, on Queen's Road. They had no family.

B2   Roderick MacLeod, lived on the homestead in Orwell Cove, never married.

B3   William MacLeod, m. Mary MacPherson, died 1895, age 67, of Murray Harbour Rd. She was the daughter of Malcolm and sister of "Old" John MacPherson. William and Mary had 100 acres on the Murray Harbour Rd., now called Kinross. William died 1894, age 73. Their children were:

C1   Flora MacLeod, 1855-1941, m. Donald Campbell, 1856-1938, Uigg, their children were:

D1   Hector Campbell, m. 1) May Ferguson, she died from a tubal pregnancy, m. 2) Laura Clark, they had no family.

D2   Mary Campbell, m. Angus MacLeod, for their descendants see the MacLeods of Kinross.

D3   Janet Campbell, m. William Dempsey, a policeman in Dorchester, Massachusetts, with issue:

E1   William Dempsey, married in U.S.A., no family.

E2   Francis Dempsey, never married, living in U.S.A.

E3   Florence Dempsey, m. Mr. Pruzzi, Massachusetts, with four children.

D4   Euphemia Campbell, m. Owen Crouse, they lived in Dorchester, Massachusetts, with issue:

E1   Walter Crouse, married.

E2   Everett Crouse, married.

E3   Florence Crouse, married.

D5   Stella Campbell, m. 1) William Cummings, from West Virginia. They lived in Massachusetts and had two children:

E1   Donald Cummings, married.

E2   Beatrice Cummings, married.

D6   Evelyn Campbell, m. Albert Murphy, U.S.A., with a son:

E1   Albert Murphy, married with four girls and a boy.

D7   Laura Campbell, died 1922, age 29, m. Alec Martin, 1891-1978, son of Dr. Martin, Grandview, no family.

D8   Billy Campbell, 1881-1957, lived in Charlottetown, never married.

D9   Edith Campbell, m. Sam Hume, he died May 2, 1967. They lived in Uigg on the farm formerly in possession of her father. They had one son:

E1   Donald Hume, who was killed in an air crash in Labrador during WWII. Donald m. Katherine Shaw, of Uigg, issue:

    F1   John Hume, m. Linda Bierens. They live in Uigg with two children:

        G1   Cathy Hume.

        G2   Donald Hume.

C2   Malcolm MacLeod, married in Vancouver, British Columbia, he owned more than one hotel in British Columbia and left no descendants.

C3   Daniel MacLeod, also lived in Vancouver and never married.

C4   Christy MacLeod, 1858-1947, lived in Charlottetown, never married.

C5   Rachel MacLeod, 1868-1949, m. VonClure Gay, 1858-1960, Pownal, they lived in Charlottetown and operated a nursery, with issue:

    D1   Russell Gay, m. Mary Jenkins, one son:

        E1   Lomer Gay, married.

    D2   May Gay, married a school teacher in Massachusetts, with issue:

        E1   Rachel, married.

        E2   Madeline, married.

    D3   Grace Gay, m. J. Harold McCabe, as his second wife, no family.

    D4   Wilfred Gay, m. Miss Jay, Mt. Stewart, they lived in New York, with issue:

        E1   Paul Gay.

        E2   _____.

C6   Murdoch William MacLeod, 1861-1936, lived on the farm home in Kinross, m. Annie Shaw, 1864-1944, they retired to Charlottetown when older, and are buried in the People's Cemetery, Charlottetown. No family.

B4   Malcolm MacLeod, died 1894, age 84, lived in Orwell Cove on the road to Brush Wharf, m. his cousin Flora Gillis, daughter of John and Catherine (Nicholson) Gillis of Orwell Cove. They had one daughter:

C1   Flora MacLeod, died 1895, age 39, m. Charles Nicholson, died 1901, age 55, son of Angus of Orwell Cove, with issue:

    D1   Catherine Nicholson, was second wife of Malcolm MacQueen, Orwell, who was a stone cutter. They lived in Fredericton, issue:

        E1   Willard MacQueen, m. Mabel Burgoyne, Plaster Rock, New Brunswick, with issue:

            F1   Gayland MacQueen, a United Church Minister who is married in Ontario with at least one son.

            F2   Louise MacQueen, m. Clayton Colpitts, New Brunswick and Boston, with issue:

                G1   Fred Colpitts, m. Anne Crowe, they have four children.

                G2   Clayton Colpitts, Jr., married, living in Tennessee with four daughters.

    D2   Sadie Nicholson, m. Newman Furness, Vernon and Vancouver, issue:

        E1   Gwendolyn Furness, m. Morgan Clarke, Vancouver, issue:

            F1   Marilyn Clarke, married in Vancouver with four children.

        E2   Margaret Furness, m. Mr. Ford. They had two daughters and a son.

        E3   Leslie Furness, died 1984, m. Agnes _____, lived in

Vancouver with two sons.

D3 Anne Nicholson, m. Milton <u>Furness</u>, Vernon, with issue:

E1 Ruth Furness, m. Murdoch <u>MacLeod</u>, 1907-1977, son of Neil, Orwell, with issue:

F1 George MacLeod, m. Grace <u>Campbell</u>, they live in Orwell, with issue:

G1 Clayton MacLeod, m. Joan <u>Hughes</u>.

G2 Valerie Anne MacLeod, m. Clifford <u>Campbell</u>, issue:

H1 Shanda Campbell.

H2 Crystal Campbell.

G3 Susan MacLeod, m. Anthony <u>McQuillan</u>, issue:

H1 Anthony McQuillan.

H2 Michael McQuillan.

G4 Victor MacLeod, m. Linda _____, with issue:

H1 Jolene MacLeod.

F2 Joan MacLeod, m. Jim <u>Harrigan</u>, living in Vancouver, with issue:

G1 Geofrey George Harrigan.

G2 Shelly Anne Harrigan. Shelley was one of a group of 22 Canadian students selected and sent for further studies in China in 1986.

E2 Dorothy Furness, m. Bernard <u>Tebeau</u>, U.S.A. with issue:

F1 Frances Tebeau, married in U.S.A., two children.

F2 Rosemary Tebeau, married in U.S.A., three children.

F3 Kenneth Tebeau, died age 37, married in U.S.A., with three children.

F4 Richard Tebeau, married in U.S.A., with three children.

F5 Carolyn Tebeau, married in U.S.A., with one child.

F6 Dorothy Tebeau, married in U.S.A.,with three children.

F7 Robert Tebeau, not married, living in U.S.A.

F8 Nancy Ruth Tebeau, married in U.S.A., two children.

E3 Fred Furness, m. Alice <u>Wilson</u>, living in Vernon River, issue:

F1 Elwood Furness, killed in car accident, age nineteen.

F2 Shirley Furness, m. Carl <u>Wilson</u>, with issue:

G1 Jamie Wilson.

G2 Cindy Wilson.

G3 Michael Wilson.

F3 Milton Furness.

F4 Margaret Furness, m. David <u>MacLeod</u>, Vernon.

F5 Douglas Furness.

F6 Marlene Furness.

F7 Sharon Furness, m. Ben <u>Voss</u>, Vernon, with issue:

G1 Shelly Voss.

G2 Christine Voss.

G3 Benjamin Voss.

E4 Beryl Furness, m. Harold P. <u>Stewart</u>, M.D., Charlottetown, with issue:

F1 Robert Stewart, m. Rhonda <u>Dewland</u>, they live in St. Louis, Missouri, with issue:

G1 Scott Stewart.

            G2   Melissa Stewart.

       F2   Beryl Evelyn Stewart, R.N., m. Allan <u>Chandler</u>, Charlottetown, with issue:

            G1   Gregory Chandler.

       F3   Joyce Stewart, m. Ricky <u>Vaive</u>, hockey player with Toronto Maple Leafs, they have one son:

            G1   Jeffrey Vaive.

       F4   Gordon Stewart, attending university in San Diego.

   E5   Anne Furness, m. 1) Vernon <u>Coles</u>, Charlottetown, issue:

       F1   Marilyn Coles, married in Fort Wayne, Indiana, with two children.

       F2   Gary Coles, married in Ontario with one child.

       F3   Wayne Coles, married in Ontario, with two children.

       Anne m. 2) Carl <u>Stewart</u>, with issue:

       F4   Carl Stewart, working in Mexico. Anne is now living in Santa Ana, California.

   E6   Phyllis Furness, m. Ray <u>Peters</u>, living in California, issue:

       F1   Leslie Peters, m. in California, with two children.

  D4   Angus Joseph Nicholson, m. Annie <u>Nicholson</u>, Orwell Cove. Their children were:

   E1   Christy Nicholson, was second wife of Edison <u>Taylor</u>, Lyndale. She had one son:

       F1   James Nicholson, married in U.S.A., with a family.

   E2   Donald Nicholson, single in U.S.A.

   E3   Muriel Nicholson, not living.

B5   Charles MacLeod, 1824-1903, m. 1) Catherine <u>Gillis</u>, daughter of William, Orwell Cove. She died young, no issue. He m. 2) Rachel <u>MacDonald</u>, died 1926, age 86, daughter of John "Kinlock" MacDonald and his wife Margaret MacDonald, Orwell Cove. This family of MacDonalds were from Kinlock, Isle of Skye, emigrating to this country with the Selkirk group in 1803, settling first at a place near Charlottetown which they named after their old home district in Scotland. They afterwards bought a large block of land in Orwell Cove in the Brush Wharf area and moved to be near their friends and relatives who were settled all along the shore from Orwell to Flat River. Charles MacLeod was a merchant for many years in Orwell Cove. His store was across the road from what in later years was known as D. D. MacLeod's store. His account book can be seen at Beaconsfield. About 1870 Charles traded his store and several acres of land with Alexander Doyle, in the Back Settlement, later named Lyndale. Doyle was a retired British Army Sergeant from the North of Ireland who was married to Mary Gillis, 1829-1923, of Orwell Cove, a relative of the MacLeods. The Doyles are both buried in Orwell Head Cemetery. The reason for the trade of properties was because of a tavern operating across the road from Charles in Orwell Cove. His family, at that time being young, he did not want to bring them up close to a liquor outlet. Since the Doyles had no family, it may have been a case of one person wanting to get away, and the other closer, to the tavern. Alexander Doyle was one of the leading forces in the formation of Lyon Orange Lodge in Uigg. This Lodge was one of the first, if not the first, on P.E.I. and was named after Doyle's dog Lyon. Apparently he had two dogs, one named Lyon and the other Major. Charles and Rachel's family were:

C1   Murdoch MacLeod, m. Etta <u>Carver</u>, sister of Mark Carver of Lyndale. They had no family and were separated some time before the turn of the century. It is understood she afterwards married in California. In 1895 Murdoch went to the State of Montana where he worked for the Fleury Ranch. This was a large spread of thousands of acres in the Choteau area, the foreman was Jesse Taylor and a number of Islanders had worked for them over the years. In 1910, according to an old newspaper clipping, Murdoch, with this Jesse Taylor, left Choteau early in the spring with 10,000 sheep for Calgary, Alberta. Calgary was a rail point and they would reach there in the fall to dispose of the animals to buyers in that area. He died about 1945, age 80, and is buried in Choteau, Montana.

C2   Margaret MacLeod, 1868-1943, m. Finlay <u>MacBeth</u>, Milltown, issue:

    D1   Margaret MacBeth, m. William <u>Fraser</u>, died 1980, age 88, Whim Road, with issue:

        E1   Mary Fraser, m. Stanley <u>Hicken</u>, Lower Montague, issue:

            F1   Carl Hicken, m. Peggy <u>Curran</u>, they have two children.

            F2   David Hicken, m. Sherry <u>Worth</u>, they have three children.

        E2   John Fraser, m. Barbara <u>Campbell</u>, issue:

            F1   Debbie Fraser.

            F2   Anne Fraser, m. Mario <u>Pater</u>.

        E3   Finlay Fraser, m. Nadine <u>Deighan</u>, living in Charlottetown, with issue:

            F1   Dalbert Fraser.

            F2   Darren Fraser.

            F3   Dean Fraser.

        E4   Anna Fraser, m. Russell <u>Hicken</u>, brother of Stanley above, with issue:

            F1   Linda Hicken, m. Roy <u>Reynolds</u>, with issue:

                G1   Tania Reynolds.

                G2   Tracy Reynolds.

            F2   Brian Hicken.

            F3   Murray Hicken.

    D2   Florence MacBeth, m. Edison <u>MacIntyre</u>, Brudenell, one daughter:

        E1   Jean MacIntyre, m. Al <u>Crooks</u>, died Nov 10, 1983, no family.

    D3   Mary MacBeth, died 1919, age about 24, m. Jess <u>Tarzian</u>, U.S.A., they had one boy:

        E1   George Tarzian, married in Illinois.

    D4   Charles MacBeth, killed in WWI, in the U.S. Army.

    D5   Sadie MacBeth, m. Milton <u>Fraser</u>, a brother of William married to her sister Margaret. They farmed in Brudenell, their children are:

        E1   Charles Fraser, m. Ruth <u>Johnstone</u>, living in Montague, with issue:

            F1   Scott Fraser.

            F2   Charlene Fraser, m. 1) Ross <u>Kempster</u>, 2) Garry <u>Martin</u>, one daughter.

            F3   Lorne Fraser, m. Harlene <u>Robbins</u>.

            F4   Randy Fraser, m. Sandra <u>MacLean</u>, with one daughter.

            F5   Garry Fraser.

        F6   Dannie Fraser, m. Anne <u>Sanderson</u>, with two boys.

    E2   Milton Fraser, m. Margaret <u>Dewar</u>, Montague, two children:

        F1   Heather Fraser.

        F2   William Fraser.

    E3   Kenneth Fraser, Brudenell.

C3 John MacLeod, died 1950, age 80, m. Margaret <u>MacDonald</u>, daughter of John ("The Point") MacDonald, Orwell Cove, his first cousin. They had the Lamont farm in Lyndale, but in 1925 their house burned to the ground and they moved to Massachusetts, they had issue:

D1 Charles MacLeod, never married, U.S.A.

D2 Catherine MacLeod, m. Mr. <u>Steele</u>, no family, U.S.A.

C4 Roderick Charles MacLeod, died 1956, age 80, m. Margaret <u>MacNeill</u>, Little Sands, daughter of Murdoch MacNeill and his wife Rebecca Lamont, daughter of Ewen Lamont, Lyndale. Margaret died Oct. 17, 1990, age 106 years and two days. They lived in Lyndale with the following family:

    D1   Ella MacLeod, died 1957, age 41, m. Edison <u>Taylor</u>, Millview, they lived in Lyndale, with issue:

        E1   Margaret Taylor, m. Dennis <u>Campion</u> of Birmingham, England. They live in Lyndale, with issue:

            F1   Julie Campion, m. Bruce <u>Blackett</u>, Georgetown, with two children:

                G1   Aaron Blackett.

                G2   Valen Rose Blackett.

            F2   Andrew Campion.

            F3   Ava Campion, m. James <u>Robinson</u>, Pugwash, Nova Scotia.

            F4   Murray Campion, m. Elizabeth <u>MacLean</u>, Brudenell. They live in Lyndale.

            F5   David Campion, m. Shanea <u>Bauer</u>, from British Columbia, they live in Mt. Vernon, P.E.I. and have two children:

    D1   Hannah Lynn Campion.

    D2   Rachel Campion.

        E2   Marion Taylor, m. 1) William <u>Ross</u>, Eldon, with issue:

            F1   Kent Ross, Toronto.

            F2   Joel Ross, Toronto.

            Marion m. 2) George <u>Grant</u>, they live in Saskatoon.

        E3   Prudence Taylor, m. Mark <u>MacDonald</u>, from Country Harbour Crossroads, Nova Scotia, and Massachusetts. His mother was Isabel MacGillivary from the Cardigan area, They have three daughters:

            F1   Michelle MacDonald, m. Michael <u>Keefe</u>, U.S.A.

            F2   Kimberly MacDonald, m. _____, U.S.A.

            F3   Stacy MacDonald, m. Randy <u>Deeran</u>, U.S.A.

        E4   William Taylor, m. Shirley <u>Penny</u>, Ontario, with issue:

            F1   Ronald Taylor.

            F2   Michael Taylor.

            F3   A girl, died at birth.

            F4   Brian Taylor.

        E5   Roderick Taylor, a successful businessman in Charlottetown,

m. Elizabeth <u>Keenan</u>, R.N., a noted singer and musician from Hamilton, Ontario. They live in Bethel, P.E.I. Their children are:

    F1   Chantelle Taylor, m. Darren <u>Wood</u>, Mt. Herbert, they live in Guelph, Ontario.

    F2   Matthew Taylor.

    F3   Daniel Taylor.

E6   Elsa Taylor, died June 5, 1991, aged 42 years.

E7   Sam Taylor, m. Sandra <u>Oldfield</u>, living in Ontario, one child.

E8   Harold Taylor, m. Wendy <u>Knowsley</u>, living in Ontario, with two children:

    F1   Amber Dawn Taylor.

    F2   Aaron Taylor.

E9   Wendell Taylor, a Charlottetown businessman, m. Pauline <u>DesRoche</u>, who holds an important position with Island Telephone Co., they have one child:

    F1   Christopher Ryan Taylor.

D2   Reginald MacLeod, m. Hazel <u>MacKinnon</u>, from Kilmuir, daughter of Carl MacKinnon. They lived in Halifax where he was a building contractor, they had issue:

E1   Margaret Anne MacLeod, R.N., M.A., m. John <u>Westlie</u>, Wisconsin, living in Meadowbank, P.E.I. Margaret is the author of a number of novels set on P.E.I.

E2   Florence MacLeod, m. Harley <u>Harper</u>, they both taught school in Charlottetown and live in Tea Hill, with issue:

    F1   Jonathan Harper.

    F2   Adam Harper, living in Ottawa.

E3   Roderick MacLeod, m. Jean <u>MacLellan</u> from Noel Shore, Nova Scotia, living in Bedford, Nova Scotia, with issue:

    F1   Janet Rebecca MacLeod, m. Brent <u>Butcher</u>, living in Kitchener, Ontario.

    F2   Ian MacLeod, living in Terrace, British Columbia.

D3   Wendell MacLeod, m. Jessie <u>MacBeth</u> (see under Malcolm MacLeod, Earnscliffe), with issue:

E1   Ernest MacLeod, m. Alfreda <u>Bears</u>, with issue:

    F1   Darren MacLeod, m. Joni <u>Garnhum</u>, living in Kinross.

    F2   Darrell MacLeod, a twin, not living.

E2   Mary MacLeod, m. Neil <u>MacDonald</u>, Brudenell, with three children:

    F1   Jody MacDonald.

    F2   Dannie MacDonald.

    F3   Kimberly MacDonald.

E3   Anne MacLeod, m. 1) Aubrey <u>Darrach</u>, New Dominion, issue:

    F1   Melanie Darrach, m. Reuben <u>Creed</u>, from Sturgeon.

    F2   Christopher Darrach, m. Mari Lynn <u>Lewis</u>.

    Anne m. 2) Donald <u>MacLeod</u>, Montague, with issue:

    F3   Amanda MacLeod.

E4   Ewen MacLeod, m. Anne <u>Murnaghan</u>, R.N., Fort Augustus, with issue:

    F1   Christa MacLeod.

F2   Ryan MacLeod.
F3   Shannon MacLeod.
D4   Hector MacLeod, m. Lily <u>Belsen</u>, London, England. They live in Nanoose Bay, Vancouver Island and have ten children, all living on the Pacific Coast:
E1   Joan Miriam MacLeod, m. Reuben <u>Jasper</u>, with issue:
F1   Shelly Jasper, m. Brian <u>Kuhn</u>.
F2   Angela Jasper.
F3   Kenneth Jasper.
F4   Michael Jasper.
E2   Judith Margaret MacLeod, m. Donald <u>Willett</u>, with issue:
F1   Wendy Willett.
F2   Timothy Willett.
E3   Paul Roderick MacLeod, m. Margaret <u>Vickers</u>, with issue:
F1   Jonathan MacLeod.
F2   Linda MacLeod.
F3   Andrea MacLeod.
E4   Wendy Lynn MacLeod, m. Robert <u>Graham</u>, issue:
F1   Deana Graham.
F2   Keith Graham.
E5   Matthew Barnet MacLeod, m. Candice <u>Bates</u>, with issue:
F1   Jolyn MacLeod.
E6   Daniel Peter MacLeod, m. Bonnie <u>Gale</u>, with issue:
F1   Lisa MacLeod.
F2   Brittany MacLeod.
E7   Roderick Charles MacLeod, m. Noreen <u>Miller</u>, with issue:
F1   Rebecca MacLeod.
F2   Curtis MacLeod.
E8   Timothy Roger MacLeod, m. Bonnie <u>O'Dresgal</u>.
E9   Jennifer Joy MacLeod.
E10   Dean Thomas MacLeod.
D5   Marion MacLeod, m. Ian S. <u>Leafe</u>, Birmingham, England. They live in Willowdale, Ontario, with issue:
E1   Francesca Leafe, a graduate from the Royal Conservatory of Music. She teaches music in Toronto. She m. William <u>Wright</u>, Stoufville, Ontario, with issue:
F1   Laura Emily Wright.
F2   Nicholas Charles Wright.
E2   Mary Leafe, m. Calvin <u>Weeks</u>, Ontario, with issue:
F1   Carson Alexander Vary Weeks.
D6   Ewen MacLeod (see soldier's last letter). He was killed in the Battle of Caen, France, in WWII.
D7   Harold S. MacLeod, m. Tilly <u>Compton</u>, living in Montague, where he was former Mayor and was Administrator of Riverview Manor. Their children are:
E1   Stephen Ross MacLeod, m. Barbara <u>Lamb</u>, living in Calgary, with issue:
F1   Cody Stephen Francis MacLeod.
E2   Janis Lynn MacLeod, m. John <u>Roberts</u>, with issue:
F1   Timothy Roberts.
F2   Mathew Roberts.

F3   Amy Lynn Roberts.
C5   Florence MacLeod, lived most of her life in U.S.A., m. 1) Herbert Wood, who was formerly from the Annapolis Valley. They separated and she m. 2) Mr. Donnelly, and lived in East Hempstead, New York. She had two children, at least, from Donnelly:
  D1   A daughter who married a Mr. Hefner.
  D2   A son.
B6   Donald "Beag" MacLeod, m. Katherine MacDonald, Belfast. They lived in Orwell Cove, with issue:
  C1   Capt. Murdoch MacLeod, 1853-1885, lost at sea, never married. *The Examiner* of June 1, 1885, reported that Capt. Murdoch MacLeod was commander and part owner of the Barque *Jessie Nickerson*. "She left San Francisco on the 21st of April and when four days out encountered a heavy storm. Capt. MacLeod was struck with the main boom, knocked overboard and was seen never more. His brother who was mate of the vessel returned with her to San Francisco, and sent the sad intelligence to his parents, he was thirty-two years of age."
  C2   Flora Anne MacLeod,1855-1933, m. James Molyneaux, 1854-1946, Dundas, with issue:
    D1   Dan Molyneaux, died 1971, age 84, school teacher, never married.
    D2   Etta Molyneaux, died 1972, age 79, m. Jim MacDonald, died 1973, age 92, Dundee and later Cumberland Hill, issue:
      E1   Woodrow MacDonald, living in Victoria Cross, single.
      E2   Marguerite MacDonald, m. Winston Wood, Mt. Herbert, with issue:
        F1   Gloria Wood, a home economist in Summerside.
        F2   Mary Lou Wood, a radiologist, m. Steve Wilson, living in Charlottetown, one child.
        F3   Barry Wood, living in Manitoba.
        F4   Wayne Wood, an agricultural engineer in Ontario.
        F5   Scott Wood, m. Beverly Miller, R.N., living in Halifax, two children.
        F6   Ian Wood.
    D3   Ida Molyneaux, m. Allen MacSwain, died 1972, Upton, issue:
      E1   Gordon MacSwain, never married.
      E2   Florence MacSwain, died young, m. Ara Farajan, California, they had three children.
      E3   Mildred MacSwain, m. Cyrus Docherty, died 1983, age 68, Cardigan, with issue:
        F1   Malcolm Docherty.
        F2   Marjory Docherty, nursing at Wedgewood Manor, Summerside.
        F3   Jean Docherty, dietitian at Wedgewood Manor, Summerside, m. Brian Ellis, they have two children.
        F4   Allan Docherty, m. Susan Brown.
        F5   Eileen Docherty, m. Craig Morrison, Halifax.
        F6   Stuart Docherty.
        F7   Heather Docherty, died young.
        F8   Wendell Docherty.
    D4   Gordon Molyneaux, m. Rachel MacKay, from Orangedale, Nova Scotia. He was a carpenter in Quincy, Massachusetts, with issue:

        E1   Wilfred Molyneaux, a clergyman, married with two children in U.S.A.

        E2   Leslie Molyneaux, not married, in the U.S.A.

   D5   Henry Molyneaux, died 1971, age 71, never married.

   D6   Lena Molyneaux, m. Chester <u>Dingwell</u>, Little Pond, with issue:

        E1   John Dingwell, m. Alice <u>Crockett</u>, from back of Town, issue:

             F1   Betty Dingwell, m. Jack <u>Higgans</u>, Charlottetown.

             F2   Lynn Dingwell, m. Damien <u>MacDonald</u>, Little Pond.

             F3   Lillian Dingwell, m. Lee <u>Garnham</u>, Montague.

             F4   June Dingwell, m. Harold <u>MacDonald</u>, living in Nova Scotia.

        E2   Bernice Dingwell, m. Alec <u>MacFarlane</u>. They had a store in Annandale, and had issue:

             F1   Emma MacFarlane, works for the Dept. of Highways, Charlottetown.

             F2   Linda MacFarlane, works for Dept. of Education, m. _____ <u>Cameron</u>, they live in Charlottetown, one child.

        E3   Ada Dingwell, lived in U.S.A., retired to Annandale.

C3   Margaret MacLeod, 1859-1893, m. Capt. James <u>MacLean</u>, 1839-1915, Orwell Cove, their children are:

   D1   Wilfred MacLean, m. Katie <u>Mutlow</u>, died 1975, age 82, Millview, they lived in Orwell Cove, with issue:

        E1   Edison MacLean, m. Lucille <u>MacDonald</u>, R.N., Flat River. They live in Orwell Cove, with issue:

             F1   Clair MacLean, living in Charlottetown.

             F2   Floyd MacLean.

             F3   David MacLean.

             F4   Maureen MacLean, R.N., m. David <u>Larter</u>, a lawyer in Charlottetown, one child:

                 G1   Jessica Jean Larter.

        E2   Alfred MacLean, m. Kitty <u>Christianson</u> from Nova Scotia, they have two sons.

        E3   Reginald MacLean, m. Sybil <u>Campbell</u> from Whim Road and have one son, an engineer in Western Canada.

             F1   Donald Kerr MacLean, m. Marlene <u>Molyneaux</u>.

   D2   James MacLean, m. _____ <u>Rattray</u>. She was from P.E.I. They live in Saskatchewan, with issue:

        E1   James MacLean.

        E2   George MacLean.

        E3   John MacLean.

        E4   Elsie MacLean .

        E5   Maybelle MacLean.

        E6   Louise MacLean.

        E7   Kay MacLean.

   D3   Capt. Murdoch MacLean, 1879-1951, m. Mamie <u>Stack</u>, St. John, New Brunswick, no family.

   D4   John MacLean, m. Edith <u>MacDougall</u>. They lived in Western Canada and later in Argyle Shore, with issue:

        E1   Margaret MacLean, m. Harold <u>MacKinnon</u>, Argyle Shore, with issue:

             F1   Harry MacKinnon, m. Rhoda <u>Boyle</u>, with two children.

E2 Arthur MacLean, m. 1) Helen <u>Keenan</u>, 2) Marjory (Curley) <u>Chapelle</u>.

E3 John Wesley MacLean, married, retired from Brantford, Ontario, Police Force, now living in Morell.

E4 Jimmy MacLean, drowned in Ontario.

E5 Edison MacLean, m. Shirley <u>Biggar</u>. He was burned to death in a motel fire in Ontario.

D5 Dan MacLean, lived in Western Canada, never married.

D6 Priscilla MacLean, died 1970, age 91, m. Nat <u>Molyneaux</u>, died 1946, brother of James, Crossroads, with issue:

E1 Ernest Molyneaux, m. Myrtle (Llewellyn) <u>Graham</u>, Southport, with issue:
F1 Douglas Molyneaux, married.
F2 Donna Molyneaux, m. Constable William <u>Dewsnap</u>.
F3 _____.

E2 Lloyd Molyneaux, m. Greta <u>Stackhouse</u>, with issue:
F1 Sheila Molyneaux.
F2 Ruth Molyneaux, married in Crapaud.

E3 Elsie Molyneaux, m. Jack <u>Degrace</u>, New Brunswick and U.S.A., with two children.

E4 Rita Molyneaux, m. Charles <u>MacGregor</u>, Charlottetown, with two children.

E5 Helen Molyneaux, m. Paul <u>Eton</u>, Truro, Nova Scotia. They have one child.

E6 Eleanor Molyneaux, m. Robert <u>Bovyer</u>, Mt. Herbert, issue:
F1 David Bovyer, killed on farm tractor.
F2 Steven Bovyer, not married.
F3 John Bovyer, not married.
F4 Nancy Bovyer, m. David <u>Holland</u>, one child.
F5 Wayne Bovyer.
F6 Lowell Bovyer.

E7 Katie Molyneaux, m. Cliff <u>Crouse</u>, Truro, Nova Scotia. They have one child.

E8 Murdoch "Buddy" Molyneaux, m. Anne _____, New Glasgow, Nova Scotia.

D7 Margaret MacLean, never married, lived in Cambridge, Massachusetts.

C4 John MacLeod, died 1932, age 63, m. Catherine <u>Murchison</u>, died 1914, age 53, with issue:

D1 Angus MacLeod, died of typhoid fever in Western Canada, 1919, aged 18 years.

D2 Hettie Belle MacLeod, died 1919, aged 22 years.

D3 John Oliver MacLeod, married with two children, living in U.S.A.

D4 Murdena MacLeod, m. Ernest <u>Shaw</u>, Uigg, issue:

E1 John Shaw, died 1969, aged 52, m. Anne <u>MacLean</u>, R.N., living in Uigg, with issue:
F1 Ian Shaw, m. _____, farming in Uigg on the Shaw homestead.
F2 Paul Shaw.
F3 Beth Shaw, R.N.

E2   Catherine Shaw, died 1986, aged 68, m. 1) Donald <u>Hume</u>, Uigg, who was killed in an air crash in Labrador during the Second World War. They had one son:

     F1   John Hume, m. Linda <u>Bierens</u>, living in Uigg, issue:

         G1   Cathy Hume, R.N., married in Summerside.

         G2   Donald Hume.

     Catherine Shaw m. 2) Harry <u>Lavers</u>, of Georgetown. He worked on the railroad, Murray Harbour line, with issue:

     F2   Debbie Lavers, m. Kevin <u>Quinn</u>, Charlottetown, they have two boys.

     F3   Gordon Lavers, m. Karen <u>MacKinnon</u>, St. Peters, with two children.

     F4   Helen Lavers, m. Robert <u>Enman</u>, Vernon, they have two boys.

E3   Isabel Shaw, m. 1) William <u>Gillis</u>, Head of Montague and British Columbia, with issue:

     F1   Carol Gillis, married in British Columbia.

     F2   Betty Gillis, married in British Columbia.

     F3   Pamela Gillis, married in British Columbia.

     F4   David Gillis.

     William Gillis was killed in a car accident in British Columbia. Isabel m. 2) her cousin John <u>MacLeod</u>, Nanaimo, British Columbia, no issue.

E4   Virginia Shaw, m. Harold <u>Enman</u>, Vernon, with issue:

     F1   William Enman, m. Norma <u>Ross</u>, Vernon.

         G1   Kelly Enman.

         G2   Bentley Enman.

     F2   Barry Enman.

     F3   Linda Enman, m. John <u>Shea</u>, living in Lake Verde, with issue:

         G1   Karrie-Anne Shea.

         G2   Tanya Shea.

         G3   Angele Shea.

     F4   Darlene Enman, m. Garry <u>Hunt</u>, living in Ontario.

     F5   Marilyn Enman.

     F6   Margaret Enman.

     F7   Kimberly Enman.

E5   Helen Shaw, R.N., m. John <u>Wheatly</u>, Charlottetown, issue:

     F1   John Milton Wheatly.

     F2   Carylon Anne Wheatly, m. Stephen <u>Hughes</u>.

     F3   Patti Helen Wheatly.

D5   Edith MacLeod, died 1973, m. Haywood <u>MacLean</u>, died 1983, aged 86, with issue:

     E1   Oliver MacLean, m. Hattie <u>Brown</u>, living in Oromocto, New Brunswick, their children are:

         F1   Theresa MacLean, m. Ralph <u>Conrad</u>, Sturgeon, two children.

         F2   Wayne MacLean, m. Carlyn <u>Brehaut</u>, living in Abney, P.E.I.

         F3   Charles MacLean, m. Cathy <u>Campbell</u>, Abney.

         F4   Sherren MacLean, m. Marvin <u>Gordon</u>, Abney, one boy.

F5   Linda MacLean, m. Elmer Gorveatt of Charlottetown.

F6   Catherine MacLean, m. Darrell Shaw, Eldon.

F7   Wanda MacLean, m. Harvey Gordon, brother to Marvin, two children.

E2   Haywood MacLean, m. Flo Robbins, living near Montague, with issue:

F1   Sterling MacLean, m. Mary Ellen Ramsay, Lot 16.

F2   Lester MacLean.

E3   John Laughlin MacLean, m. Lily Knox, they live in Heatherdale, with issue:

F1   John MacLean.

F2   Elwin MacLean.

F3   Esther MacLean.

F4   Carl MacLean, m. Phyllis Cook, in New Brunswick.

F5   Arnold MacLean.

E4   Angus MacLean, m. Alice Simmonds, from St. Peters, issue:

F1   Floyd MacLean, m. Helen Henneberry, living in Alberta with three children.

F2   Diane MacLean, married in Fredericton three children.

F3   Winston MacLean, in Alberta.

F4   Ferne MacLean, m. _____ McGuigan, Cable Head West, with three girls.

F5   Merrill MacLean, living in Alberta.

E5   Lester MacLean, married in Fredericton, with six children.

E6   Florence MacLean, m. Alec Darrach, Cornwall, P.E.I., issue:

F1   Wayne Darrach, m. Patsy MacPhail, R.N., daughter of Doug and Joan MacPhail, Argyle Shore, living in Argyle Shore, with children.

F2   Shirley Darrach.

F3   Blair Darrach.

F4   Lee Darrach, m. Norma MacIsaac, living in Cornwall, two children.

F5   Donald Darrach, m. Ruth MacNevin, daughter of Leonard. They live in Meadowbank, with issue:

G1   Dawn Darrach.

G2   Danny Darrach.

E7   Laura MacLean, m. Chester Lake, Borden, P.E.I., with issue:

F1   Robert Lake, m. Kim Miller, Toronto, one child.

F2   Gerald Lake, single.

F3   Darlene Lake, m. Paul Noonan, Summerside, with two children.

F4   Kenneth Lake, m. Janet MacPhee, Guelph, Ontario, with one child.

F5   Edith Lake.

F6   Donna Lake.

E8   Anna MacLean, m. Merrill Godsoe, Keppoch, with issue:

F1   David Godsoe.

F2   Nancy Godsoe, m. Dan Drost, New Brunswick.

F3   Merlynn Godsoe.

E9   Lawrence MacLean, m. Lois Bergeron, from Waterloo, Quebec. They live in Valleyfield East, with issue:

F1   Kevin MacLean, m. Rena Cook.
F2   Robert MacLean, m. Sheila Anderson.
F3   Timothy MacLean.
F4   Darlene MacLean, m. Kevin Byers, Strathroy, Ontario, one child.
F5   Bonnie MacLean.
E10 Arnold MacLean, m. Katie Patton, from Newfoundland. They live in Greenvale, P.E.I., with four children:
F1   Junior MacLean.
F2   Lornie MacLean.
F3   Kendra MacLean.
F4   Kerry MacLean.
D6   D. W. MacLeod, died 1985, m. Katie MacKenzie. They lived in Lower Newtown and had one son:
E1   John MacLeod, living in Newtown.
D7   Katie MacLeod, died aged 19, a school teacher.
C5   William MacLeod, died 1947, aged 77, Orwell Cove, m. Margaret Munroe, of Lyndale. She died in 1950. Their children were:
D1   Wellington MacLeod, who farmed in Uigg, m. Hannah Shaw, Lorne Valley, no family.
D2   Maxwell MacLeod, m. Priscilla Davey, Guernsey Cove, they live in U.S.A., with issue:
E1   Beverly MacLeod, m. Tony Varrone, they have two children.
E2   Nancy MacLeod, m. Ernie Jacobson, one child.
D3   Irene MacLeod, m. Earl Tufts, Massachusetts.
D4   Walter MacLeod, m. Marion MacLeod, daughter of Sam E. MacLeod, Uigg,who was a grandson of Rev. Sam MacLeod, 1829 emigrant. Walter and Marion farmed in Orwell Cove. Their children are:
E1   Winston MacLeod, not living.
E2   Mabel MacLeod, m. Ronald Barrett, living in New York, they have three girls and a boy.
E3   Byron MacLeod, m. Wanda Edwards, living in Kinlock. They have two children.
D5   Florence MacLeod, m. Al Lawrence, U.S.A., with one son:
E1   Kenneth Lawrence.
D6   Hazel MacLeod, m. Ralph Conrad, living in Halifax. She m. 1) Jack Griffiths, son of Rev. Griffiths, Belfast. Hazel has a family of three:
E1   Margaret Griffiths m. 1) Mirko Halozan, Halifax, m. 2) Harold Moss, Dartmouth, Nova Scotia, with issue:
F1   Stephen Halozan.
F2   David Halozan, twin of Stephen.
F3   Sonia Halozan.
E2   David Griffiths, m. Faye Diannne Thompson, with issue:
F1   Leanne Griffiths.
F2   Bradley Griffiths.
C6   Daniel MacLeod, 1863-1927, m. Flora Murchison, 1869-1956, sister of Donald Neil Murchison of Point Prim and also sister of his brother John's wife. Daniel and Flora farmed in Point Prim. They had a large family of eight girls and five boys. Their names are:

D1 Belle MacLeod, m. Murdoch "Red John" <u>MacLeod</u>, Dundee and Quincy, with issue:
- E1 Earl MacLeod, m. Shirley <u>Parry</u>, they live in Quincy, Massachusetts, and had five children.
- E2 Edison MacLeod, not living, was married and had a family of three
- E3 Sinclair MacLeod, married, one child, living in Washington.
- E4 John MacLeod, died at 6 years of age.

D2 Katherine MacLeod, m. Neil <u>MacDonald</u>, from the Kingston area on P.E.I. They lived in Quincy, Massachusetts, and had a family of nine children. Neil died when the youngest was six months old, and the eldest about fifteen years. The names of the children are:
- E1 Kenneth MacDonald.
- E2 Donald MacDonald.
- E3 Florence MacDonald.
- E4 June MacDonald.
- E5 Myles MacDonald, a clergyman living in Florida.
- E6 John MacDonald.
- E7 George MacDonald.
- E8 Francis MacDonald.
- E9 Richard MacDonald.

D3 Miriam MacLeod, was working in Quincy, but came home for health reasons and died suddenly at Point Prim, age 25.

D4 Margaret MacLeod, m. Neil <u>Nicholson</u>, Hartsville, brother of Rev. Donald Nicholson. They lived in Quincy, and had one daughter:
- E1 Irene Nicholson, m. Gordon <u>Parry</u>, brother of Shirley Parry, they live in Quincy and have five girls.

D5 Donald MacLeod, died 1969, age 70, m. 1) Mary <u>Mahoney</u>, they lived in Quincy, with issue:
- E1 Donald MacLeod, a Roman Catholic Priest, living in California.
- E2 William MacLeod, married in Quincy, three children.
- E3 Charlotte MacLeod, m. _____ <u>Flatly</u>, they have five children.

Donald m. 2) Alice <u>Allen</u>, from Cape Tormentine, New Brunswick, they lived in Quincy and had one son:
- E4 Allen MacLeod, married with two children.

D6 John MacLeod, died 1984, age 82, m. Myrtle <u>Lowe</u>, died 1985, age 83, daughter of Jim Lowe of Murray River and Grandview, P.E.I. They lived in Quincy, with issue:
- E1 Eileen MacLeod, m. Philip <u>Bourne</u>, they live in Pennsylvania, with issue:
  - F1 Beverly Bourne, married in Quincy.
  - F2 James Bourne, married in Washington, D.C.
  - F3 Patricia Bourne, single.

D7 Sinclair MacLeod, m. Sadie <u>Lowe</u>, a sister of Myrtle, with issue:
- E1 Miriam MacLeod, m. Wayne <u>Fraser</u>, a clergyman in Maine.
- E2 Dorothy MacLeod, m. Robert <u>Hannon</u>, a clergyman in Florida.
- E3 Lloyd MacLeod, killed in the war, U.S. Army, May 1951.

   E4 Robert MacLeod, married and living in Quincy.

  D8 Hector MacLeod, died 1979, age 73, m. Janetta Jardine, Brooklyn. They lived in Point Prim, with issue:

   E1 Joan MacLeod, m. 1) Alexander Stewart, with issue:

    F1 Terry Stewart, lives in Charlottetown.

    F2 Jerry Stewart, works on Wood Islands Ferry.

    Joan m. 2) Allen MacMill, living in Wood Islands.

   E2 Florence MacLeod, m. William Hambly, Charlottetown, they live in Thornhill, Ontario, issue:

    F1 Jennifer Hambly.

  D9 Ethel MacLeod, never married, living in Quincy.

  D10 Gertrude MacLeod, m. Francis Bligh, living in Wallacetown, Massachusetts, with issue:

   E1 James Bligh, married with three children.

  D11 Angusena MacLeod, m. Sam Frizzell, they lived in Eldon, issue

   E1 Kathleen Frizzell, m. Barry Nicholson, Flat River, living in Cornwall, P.E.I., with issue:

    F1 Kelli Nicholson.

    F2 _____.

   E2 Miriam Frizzell, m. Emmett Murphy, living in Charlottetown, with issue:

    F1 Dawn Murphy.

    F2 Christopher Murphy.

  D12 Walter MacLeod, m. Jean MacGrath, living in Massachusetts, with issue:

   E1 Susan MacLeod, m. Kenny White, living in Brockton, Massachusetts.

   E2 Ross MacLeod, married in Brockton, Massachusetts.

  D13 Kathleen MacLeod, living in Wallacetown, Massachuetts, not married.

B7 Margaret MacLeod, died 1892, Orwell Cove, m. Archie Matheson, died 1878, age 70, who operated a saw mill on his farm in Lyndale, with issue:

 C1 Murdoch Matheson, died 1911, age 70, never married, lived in Lyndale.

 C2 Flora Matheson, died at age 86, m. 1) John H. Stephens, with issue:

  D1 Johanna Stephens, 1878-1946, m. Adam Hicken, 1872-1954, issue:

   E1 Hazel Hicken, m. Bill Longridge, U.S.A. with one son:

    F1 Bill Longridge, married in U.S.A., with two children

   E2 Stephen Hicken, died 1976, age 75, m. Myrtle Nicholson, died 1982, age 79. They lived in Lower Montague, issue:

    F1 Stanley Hicken, m. Mary Fraser, issue:

     G1 Carl Hicken, m. Peggy Curran, with two children.

     G2 David Hicken, m. Sherry Worth, with three children.

    F2 Russell Hicken, m. Anne Fraser, sister of Mary, above. They live on the Whim Road, with issue:

     G1 Linda Hicken, m. Roy Reynolds, Whim Road, with issue:

      H1 Tania Reynolds

      H2 Tracy Reynolds.

     G2 Brian Hicken.

     G3 Murray Hicken.

F3 Hazel Hicken, m. Stillman <u>MacKinnon</u>, Lower Montague, with two children.

F4 Peggy Hicken, died 1981, m. Stuart <u>Dewar</u>, Montague, they had five children.

F5 Cecil Hicken, m. June <u>Graham</u>, two children.

F6 Harold Hicken, m. 1) Brenda <u>Praught</u>, with five children, m. 2) Carol <u>MacPherson</u>, no family.

F7 Lee Hicken, m. Marion <u>Crossman</u>, with three children.

F8 Gloria Hicken, m. David <u>Reynolds</u>, with two children.

F9 Diane Hicken, m. Blair <u>Sencabaugh</u>, with two children.

F10 William Hicken, m. Betty <u>Haneveld</u>, with one child.

E3 Reta Hicken, m. Ernest <u>Martin</u>, died 1981, age 80, Uigg, with issue:

F1 Margaret Martin, R.N., m. 1) Millard <u>MacDonald</u>, Charlottetown, with issue:

G1 Ian MacDonald, m. Debbie <u>Beaton</u>, daughter of Earl Beaton, Charlottetown, with issue:

H1 Joel MacDonald.

G2 Susan MacDonald, m. Joe <u>Mouris</u>, Deep River, issue:

H1 Katie Mouris.

G3 Kirsten MacDonald.

Margaret m. 2) Ninian <u>LeBlanc</u>, no issue.

F2 George Martin, m. Marjorie <u>Volk</u>, both engineers, working for Bendix in Baltimore, Maryland, issue:

G1 David Martin.

G2 Cathy Martin, married.

G3 Karen Martin.

F3 Muriel Martin, m. Bill <u>Davis</u>, he is a teacher in Toronto. They have four children.

F4 John Martin, not married, living in Uigg, works for Canada Employment in Montague.

E4 Etta Hicken, m. Certo <u>Minahan</u>, U.S.A., with one girl.

E5 Pearl Hicken, m. Ted <u>Kobel</u>, U.S.A, with one boy.

E6 William Hicken, m. Kathleen <u>Campbell</u>, Victoria Cross, with issue:

F1 Reagh J. Hicken, m. Marina <u>Graham</u>, from Smithville, Ontario. He is a Chartered Accountant, they live in Keppoch, with issue:

G1 Deidre Sarah Hicken.

G2 James William Hicken.

F2 William Blair Hicken, M.D., Director of Mental Health for P.E.I., not married.

Flora [C2] m. 2) Laughlin <u>MacLaughlin</u>, no issue.

C3 Sandy Matheson, Lyndale, m. Peggy <u>Bruce</u>, died age 75, sister of Archie Bruce, Victoria Cross. They lived in Milltown with the following children:

D1 Malcolm Matheson, m. Norma <u>MacPhee</u>, Kilmuir. Malcolm was a clergyman and had a pastorate at one time in Washington, D.C.

D2 Donald Alexander Matheson, married in Waterville, Maine.

D3 Neil Matheson, m. Maretta <u>Moore</u>, sister of Russell, Albion. She died in childbirth, there was no other family.

D4   Archie Matheson, never married, lived in Milltown.

D5   Alexander Matheson, married with two boys at least.
- E1   Peter Matheson, m. Mildred _____, living in U.S.A., with one daughter:
  - F1   Sally Matheson.
- E2   Burns Matheson, m. Edith _____, living in U.S.A., issue:
  - F1   Margaret Matheson.

D6   Clara Matheson, died 1918, age 38, m. William <u>Bruce</u>, Milltown. She had three daughters:
- E1   Margaret Bruce, m. Jim <u>King</u>, Milltown, no family.
- E2   Christie Bruce, married in U.S.A.
- E3   Maretta Bruce, in the U.S.A.

D7   Mary Jane Matheson, m. Charles J. <u>MacDonald</u>, Albion, issue:
- E1   Neil MacDonald, died 1969, age 73, married in Spokane, Washington, one son:
  - F1   Stanley Neil MacDonald, married in Washington State. He has five children.
- E2   Stanley MacDonald, died 1964, age about 67, m. Jennie <u>Balcolm</u>, Massachusetts, issue:
  - F1   Wilma MacDonald, m. 1) Dwane <u>Herring</u>, one child:
    - G1   Cheryl Herring, m. David <u>Galliger</u>, Cambridge, Massachusetts.
    - Wilma m. 2) Peter <u>Balduc</u>, with issue:
    - G2   Wilma Balduc, age 21, 1986.
    - G3   Peter Balduc, age 19, 1986.
- E3   Charlie MacDonald, m. Lucy <u>Phillips</u>, from Murray Harbour, living in Montague, no family.
- E4   Florence MacDonald, died 1983, age 68, m. Fred <u>Jeffries</u>, U.S.A., with issue:
  - F1   William Jeffries, m. 1) Louise____, with issue:
    - G1   Scott.
    - William m. 2) Jo-Anne _____, with two children.
  - F2   Robert Jeffries, m. Madeline _____, with two children.
- E5   Anna MacDonald, m. Stephen <u>Rundlett</u>, living in Santa Barbara, California, with issue:
  - F1   Nathan Rundlett, m. Judy _____, with about five children.
- E6   Dan Willie MacDonald, died 1921 aged 16.

D8   Peter Matheson, m. Margaret <u>Matheson</u>, Dundas, they lived in Waterville, Maine, with issue:
- E1   Alvin Matheson, died 1985, never married.
- E2   Neil Matheson, m. Dorothy _____, with four children.
  - F1   Mary Matheson, married.
  - F2   Lisa Matheson, married.
  - F3   Jim Matheson, married.
  - F4   Dale Matheson, married.
- E3   Fred Matheson, m. Lucille _____, with children.
- E4   Donald Matheson, m. Margaret _____, no family.
- E5   Peter Matheson, died young.

C4   Johanna Matheson, Lyndale, m. Donald <u>MacLean</u> of Lyndale and

Charlottetown, with issue:

D1 Aben MacLean, merchant in Charlottetown, m. Hettie Wood, Southport, they had no family.

D2 Lillian MacLean, m. George Tweedy as his second wife. He was a distant relative of Judge Tweedy, they had no family.

D3 Alexander MacLean, was a sailor, lost at sea at a young age.

C5 Kate Matheson, Lyndale, m. Henry Campbell, with issue:

D1 William Campbell, died young.

D2 Archie Campbell, died young.

D3 Cyrus Campbell, died young.

D4 Maggie Campbell, died young.

C6 Sarah Matheson, m. Lemuel Acorn, they had two children:

D1 George Acorn, m. Edna Creed, they had one son:

E1 Bentley Acorn, died young.

D2 Katie Annie Acorn, died 1984, m. Wilbert MacKinnon, Albion, with issue:

E1 Violet MacKinnon, married in St. John, New Brunswick, with one child at least.

E2 Olive MacKinnon, living in New Brunswick.

E3 Sadie MacKinnon, married in New Brunswick.

E4 Winnie MacKinnon, died young.

E5 Mary MacKinnon, m. Charles MacKay, in New Brunswick, with issue:

F1 Ivan MacKay, killed in WWII.

B8 Catherine MacLeod, m. Capt. John Gillis, Orwell Cove. His mother was Rachel, daughter of Malcolm MacLeod and Rachel MacQueen of Gallows Point, consequently his wife was first cousin to his mother. Their descendants are listed under Malcolm and Rachel (MacQueen) MacLeod, Earnscliffe.

B9 Mary MacLeod, m. Alexander MacDonald, Grandview. This family of MacDonalds apparently were from Mull and came over on the ship *Rambler*. They settled first in Point Prim on the farm later owned by Capt. Roderick Cameron. From there they moved to Sample Hill in Grandview. Mary and Alexander's family:

C1 Flora MacDonald, m. Donald MacKenzie, Grandview and later Orwell Cove, where they took over the farm of William Martin, son of Sam. William's wife was Catherine MacLeod, a sister of Flora's mother Mary. Flora and Donald had issue:

D1 Duncan MacKenzie, lived in Orwell Cove, never married.

D2 Donald John MacKenzie, m. Annie MacTavish, they lived in Orwell Cove, with issue:

E1 Lincoln MacKenzie, living in Orwell Cove.

D3 Katie MacKenzie, m. Alexander "Red Sandy" Martin, M.P., Valleyfield. She died at childbirth or soon after, leaving a daughter:

E1 Annabel Martin, 1910-1945, m. Merrill Craswell, Charlottetown, Annabel died at the birth of her son:

F1 Gordon Craswell, m. Shirley Stewart, Montague, issue:

G1 Jeffrey Craswell, Charlottetown.

G2 Sherry Craswell, Charlottetown.

D4 Mary MacKenzie, m. Dan Gillis, Grandview. For descendants see under Malcolm MacLeod and Rachel MacQueen, Earnscliffe.

D5   Dan MacKenzie, died young.

C2   Donald MacDonald, lived in Grandview, never married.

C3   Alexander MacDonald, lived in Duluth, Minnesota.

C4   Mary MacDonald, 1855-1929, m. Neil <u>Matheson</u>, 1849-1924, Heatherdale, with issue:

    D1   Dan Matheson, m. Mrs. Doris <u>Dawson</u>. He was a blacksmith in Heatherdale, they had no family.

    D2   Hughie Matheson, 1894-1960, m. Mary "Rory" Nicholson, Grandview, daughter of Roderick Nicholson, Orwell Cove, and his first wife, Jessie Morrison from Newfoundland. Mary was married first to Mr. Lowe in the U.S.A. and they had a daughter Irene who married and lived in California, also a son Henry Lowe who lived in U.S.A., never married. Hugh Matheson and Mary had no family.

    D3   Murdoch Matheson, lived on the Pacific Coast, never married.

    D4   Mary Matheson, 1890-1896.

    D5   Florence Matheson, 1892-1896.

    D6   Mamie Matheson, 1899-1905.

C5   Annie MacDonald, m. Archie <u>MacKenzie</u>. They lived at Mitchell River, he was a brother of Donald in Orwell Cove, married to his wife's sister. Murdoch MacKenzie, Lyndale, was another brother. Annie and Archie's family were:

    D1   William MacKenzie, m. Nellie <u>Williams</u>, he was drowned at Geoff's mill dam in Launching when making repairs to the waste gate. He left two small children and expecting a third, they are:

        E1   Hattie MacKenzie, died 1971, age 50, m. Lowell <u>Poole</u>, died 1983, age 73, Montague, issue:

            F1   Elaine Poole, m. Francis <u>Duffy</u>, Charlottetown. She works at Holland College, with issue:

                G1   Sally Anne Duffy.

                G2   Paul Duffy.

                G3   Karen Duffy.

            F2   Earl Poole, killed in truck accident in Toronto, Ontario, 1973, age 32, m. Janis <u>Scott</u>, New Brunswick, no family.

            F3   Merrill Poole, m. Marie <u>Scott</u>, living in Toronto, no family.

        E2   Earl MacKenzie, never married, was a sailor and was killed in an automobile accident in St. John, New Brunswick, about 1955. He was in his late forties when he died.

        E3   Lloyd MacKenzie, was married to a girl from New Glasgow, Nova Scotia. He was in WWII and died from the effects of wounds shortly after returning to Canada. He left two children.

    D2   Dan MacKenzie, married, no children.

    D3   Mary Anne MacKenzie, m. Josh <u>Williams</u>, with issue:

        E1   William Williams, m. Margaret <u>MacAuley</u>.

Annie [C5] m. 2) Allan <u>Shaw</u>, no family.

    D4   Christy MacKenzie, m. 1) Harold <u>MacGregor</u>, with issue, m. 2) Lawrence <u>Zorella</u>, Massachusetts.

        E1   Harold MacGregor, m. Elva <u>MacKenzie</u>, they lived in

Halifax and Massachusetts, with issue:

F1   Arthur MacGregor, died 1979, age 68, m. 1) Helen Parlee in Massachusetts, with issue:

    G1   Lawrence MacGregor, married in the American West.

    G2   Robert MacGregor, married in the American West.

    Arthur m. 2) _____, no family.

F2   Marie MacGregor, m. Walter Woodward, they live in Florida, with issue:

    G1   Joan Woodward, m. Arthur Hill, with three children.

    G2   Kenneth Woodward, married in New Hampshire, three children.

    G3   Pamela Woodward, married in Florida with one child.

F3   Harold Woodrow MacGregor, m. Marion Bradford of West Virginia. They lived in Massachusetts, but now in Seal River, with issue:

    G1   Sandra Jean MacGregor, m. Carl Hakkarainen, Holden, Massachusetts, with issue:

        H1   Michael Hakkarainen.

        H2   Adam Hakkarainen.

    G2   John Russell MacGregor, m. Linda Dalton, Boston, Massachusetts, with one child:

        H1   Laurie MacGregor.

    G3   Barbara Elaine MacGregor, m. Craig Ball, Cape Cod, U.S.A., with issue:

        H1   Timothy Ball.

        H2   Matthew Ball.

    G4   Robert Scott MacGregor, not married, in California.

D5   Malcolm MacKenzie, m. Mae MacRae. They had a family of four or five, among whom is:

    E1   Christine MacKenzie, R.N., working in St. John.

D6   Flora MacKenzie, m. Percy MacRae.They lived in New Glasgow, Nova Scotia

C6   Christy MacDonald, m. 1) Mr. Robinson in the U.S.A. They had two children:

D1   George Robinson.

D2   Sadie Robinson, they both lived in U.S.A.

Christy m. 2) Roderick Nicholson, born 1834, son of John "Stencholl" Nicholson and Mary MacLeod of Orwell Cove, with issue:

D3   Florrie Nicholson, 1889-1931, m. 1) James Thompson Ridge, who was killed in the American Army in WWI. They had a son James Ridge who is married with a family in the State of Maine. Florrie m. 2) Roderick Nicholson, son of Donald, Victoria Cross, with issue:

    E1   John Nicholson, died 1983, age 60, m. May Peardon, they lived in Montague, with issue:

        F1   Clinton Nicholson, m. 1) a German girl, two children:

G1   Mark Nicholson.
G2   Sandy Nicholson.
Clinton m. 2) Virginia <u>Burley</u>, living in British Columbia.

F2   Kimble Nicholson, m. Irene <u>Murray</u>, living in Orangeville, Ontario, with two boys:
G1   Jason Nicholson.
G2   John Nicholson.

F3   Carl Nicholson, m. 1) Valerie <u>Boudreau</u>, m. 2) Darlene <u>Bray</u>, they live in Toronto and have two children:
G1   Gillian Nicholson.
G2   Ryan Nicholson.

F4   Roger Nicholson, m. Velda <u>MacKenzie</u>, daughter of Duncan, Victoria Cross. They live in Southport, with two children:
G1   Cindy Nicholson.
G2   Keith Nicholson.

F5   Wade Nicholson, m. Emily <u>Cook</u>, daughter of Charlie Cook, Wood Islands. They live in Wood Islands, with two children:
G1   Justin Nicholson.
G2   Tyler Nicholson.

F6   Randy Nicholson, Montague.
F7   Lola May Nicholson, Montague.

E2   Bertha Nicholson, m. Cecil <u>Bell</u>, Montague, with issue:
F1   Victor Bell, m. Helen <u>Constains</u>, Montreal, with issue:
G1   Leonidas Bell.

F2   Sandra Bell, m. Alden <u>Gordon</u>, Murray Harbour, issue:
G1   John Gordon.
G2   Stacy Gordon.

F3   John Bell, m. Cindy <u>Harris</u>, Murray Harbour. Cindy comes from a singing family and is a noted singer and musician as well, their children are:
G1   Toby Bell.
G2   Zachary Bell.
G3   Thatcher Bell.

F4   Jerry Bell, m. Elizabeth <u>MacKinnon</u>, daughter of Jack, Brooklyn and Montague. They live in Port Hawkesbury, Nova Scotia, with issue:
G1   Heidi Bell.
G2   Cara Bell.
G3   Cory Bell, Cory and Cara are twins.

F5   Scott Bell, m. Brenda <u>O'Connor</u>, daughter of Flora O'Connor, Montague, Brenda works at the Montague Post Office, they have one child:
G1   Derek Bell.

E3   George Nicholson, m. Erma <u>MacLeod</u>, Springhill, issue:
F1   Pauline Nicholson, m. Eldon <u>Goutreau</u>, living in Scarborough, Ontario, with issue:
G1   Christopher Goutreau.
G2   Corrie Goutreau.

E4 Christine Nicholson, m. Robert <u>Lints</u>, Quincy, Massachusetts, with issue:
　　F1 Laurie Lints, married in Quincy.
　　F2 Nancy Lints, living in Quincy.
　　F3 Dianne Lints, living in San Diego, California.
E5 Daniel Nicholson, died age six.
E6 Florence Nicholson, died young.

D2 Sandy Nicholson, m. Margaret <u>Davey</u>, Quincy, Massachusetts, with issue:
E1 Alexander Nicholson, married with a family in California.
E2 Florence Nicholson, married with a family in California.
E3 Marjory Nicholson.
E4 Jean Nicholson, married with a family in New York.
E5 Robert Nicholson.
E6 A daughter.

D3 Sarah Nicholson, m. Joe <u>Mullins</u>, Quincy, Massachusetts, issue:
E1 Irma Mullins, married in California.
E2 Elwood Mullins, married in California.
E3 Janice Mullins, married in Quincy, Massachusetts.

D4 Jack "Rory" Nicholson, was killed in a car accident on the Pictou Causeway about 1968.

D5 Mamie Nicholson, she and her daughter Phemie were killed in an auto accident October 22, 1966, at age 60, m. Alexander <u>Gillis</u>, 1903-1953, Newtown, with issue:
E1 Joyce Gillis, m. Joseph <u>Kenny</u>, living in Massachusetts, with issue:
　　F1 James Kenny.
　　F2 Michael Kenny.
E2 Bennett Gillis, died 1966, age 35, m. Alma <u>MacPherson</u>, they lived in Lower Newtown, with issue:
　　F1 Merril Gillis, m. Robert <u>Cummings</u>, living in Southport, with issue:
　　　　G1 Jamie Cummings.
　　　　G2 Jeffrey Cummings.
　　F2 Bonnie Jean Gillis, m. Aaron <u>Rolson</u>, Eldon, with issue:
　　　　G1 Katelyn Rolson.
　　F3 Janet Gillis.
　　F4 Blair Gillis, m. Carol _____.
　　F5 Wayne Gillis, m. Enid <u>Brown</u>, Pownal, living in Newtown, with issue:
　　　　G1 Kelly Gillis.
　　　　G2 Lynn Gillis.
　　F6 Arlene Gillis, m. Wade <u>Buell</u>.
E3 Joan Gillis, m. Dougal <u>MacWilliams</u>, living in Labrador, with issue:
　　F1 Joanne MacWilliams.
　　F2 Pamela MacWilliams.
　　F3 Patricia MacWilliams.
　　F4 Scott MacWilliams.
　　F5 Paul MacWilliams.

E4   Phemie Gillis, killed along with her mother in a car accident, October 22, 1966.

E5   Miriam Gillis, m. John Nicholson, son of Raymond, Head of Montague. He and his brother Bruce drowned in the Pinette River in 1978, their children are:
F1   Joyce Nicholson.
F2   David Nicholson.
F3   Brenda Nicholson, m. Kenny Campbell, Montague, with issue:
G1   Troy Campbell.
G2   John Campbell.
G3   Naomi Campbell.
G4   Pamela Campbell.
F4   Shirley Nicholson, m. Larry Irving, Montague.
F5   Sadie Nicholson.

E6   Sadie Gillis, m. "Buster" Walter Bell, Belle River, with issue:
F1   Linda Bell, m. Paul MacKenzie.
F2   Larry Bell, m. Karen Sullivan.
F3   Derek Bell, m. Brenda Cantelo, daughter of Aubrey Cantelo and Beverly Beck, Montague.
F4   Sheila Bell.
F5   Sara Jane Bell.

B10 Catherine MacLeod, m. William Martin, son of Sam, Orwell Cove. They had two daughters at least:
C1   Christy Martin, never married.
C2   Margaret Martin, never married.
Donald MacKenzie, Grandview, was married to a niece of Catherine's and he moved in with the Martins and eventually inherited the farm.

B11 Christy MacLeod, never married, lived with brother Roderick, Orwell Cove.

Roderick MacLeod
Roderick MacLeod and _____ MacKenzie

A3 Roderick MacLeod, son of Donald MacLeod, the Pioneer, married in Skye, Miss MacKenzie (a relative of the Flat River MacKenzies), with issue:

B1 Jessie MacLeod, 1799-1883, m. William MacLeod, 1789-1873, Mermaid, a son of Murdoch MacLeod, who was originally from Portree, Isle of Skye, and came to Canada about 1784. Murdoch had married, after arriving, Jessie Auld, who had emigrated from Ayreshire, Scotland, about 1770. She died 1840 and Murdoch died 1814, both buried in Elm Ave. Cemetery, Charlottetown. Their son William and his wife Jessie MacLeod lived on what was known as MacLeod's Point in Mermaid and it was their home in which the pioneer minister, the Rev. Donald MacDonald died in 1867. For their descendants see the family of Murdoch and Jane (Auld) MacLeod.

B2 Christy MacLeod, m. William Gillis, son of John Gillis and his wife Catherine Nicholson. They had a family of eight:

C1 James Gillis, was a tailor and also operated the Post Office at Kinross for a number of years. He m. Ann Gillis, daughter of William Gillis, Lyndale, who was an 1829 immigrant. Ann's brother was Rev. John Gillis, who died about 1918 and is buried in Dundas Cemetery. James died in Vancouver, their children were:

D1 William Gillis, married in Vancouver with a family.

D2 James Gillis, who was a tailor married in Seattle.

D3 John Gillis, who was a school teacher married in Seattle.

D4 Christy Ann Gillis, m. Johnson Brundage, Boston, with issue:

E1 Gladys Brundage, m. Robert Greenwood, Los Angeles, with issue:

F1 Betty Jane Greenwood.

E2 Jean Brundage, m. Robert Gardyne, Massachusetts, issue:

F1 Robert Gardyne.

E3 Doris Brundage, m. Arthur Perkins, Illinois, issue:

F1 Sally Perkins.

F2 Polly Perkins.

E4 James Brundage, Cambridge, Massachusetts.

D5 Minnie Gillis, first wife of William Burch, Alberton, with issue:

E1 Hazel Burch, m. Victor Careu, Bermuda, with one son.

D6 Isabel Gillis, died young.

C2 Donald Gillis, m. his cousin Margaret MacLeod, daughter of William "Horo" MacLeod, with issue:

D1 William Gillis, died 1945, age 67, m. Euphemia Larabee, 1881-1978, Eldon, no family.

D2 Christy Ann Gillis, m. William J. Anderson, Boston, with four children.

D3 Mary Gillis, m. Arthur Gillis, son of Neil Angus Gillis, no family.

C3 Malcolm Gillis, died 1916, aged 68, m. Euphemia Murchison, died 1942, aged 95, daughter of Malcolm Murchison and his wife Jessie MacDonald, Point Prim, their children:

D1 Catherine Gillis, m. 1) Alexander MacEachern, Newtown, they had one son:

E1   Archie MacEachern, married and living in Washington
     State. They operated the Big Tree Inn in Seattle, Washington.
Catherine m. 2) Andrew <u>Swanson</u>, Seattle, no issue.
D2   Nellie Gillis, m. William <u>Rennie</u>, Quincy, with issue:
     E1   Euphemia Rennie, m. Dr. John <u>MacGowan</u>, Kilmuir and
          Quincy, Massachusetts, with issue:
          F1   John MacGowan, barrister, married in the U.S.A.
          F2   David MacGowan, married in the U.S.A.
D3   Christy Gillis, m. Jack <u>Jardine</u>, lived in Massachusetts, issue:
     E1   John Jardine, married in Florida with four or five children.
D4   Jessie Gillis, m. Peter <u>Penny</u>, Eldon, with issue:
     E1   William Penny, m. Beryl <u>Vaniderstine</u>, living in Eldon, no
          family.
     E2   Malcolm Penny, m. Joan <u>Crabtree</u>, living in Hamilton,
          Ontario, with issue:
          F1   Malcolm Penny, m. Catherine <u>Muirhead</u>.
     E3   John Penny, m. Ethel <u>Bezanson</u>, Ottawa, with issue:
          F1   Kenneth Penny, m. Yum <u>Hyse</u>.
     E4   Hampton Penny, m. Margaret <u>Gillis</u>, a sister of Rev. Ray-
          mond Gillis, former minister of Belfast. They live in Eldon,
          with issue:
          F1   John Penny, m. Muriel <u>Stewart</u>, daughter of Charles,
               Caledonia. They live in Crossroads, and had one son:
               G1   John Mark Penny, killed at the age of 6 years by a
                    snowplow while waiting for the school bus, near
                    Charlottetown, in April, 1985
          F2   Audrey Penny, m. David <u>MacLeod</u>, son of Allison,
               Charlotteotwn, with issue:
               G1   Penny MacLeod.
               G2   Carolyn MacLeod.
          F3   Peter Penny.
          F4   Lynda Penny.
     E5   Newton Penny, m. Kay <u>Eldridge</u>, living in Hamilton,
          Ontario, with issue:
          F1   Brian Penny, m. Susan <u>Thornborrow</u>.
          F2   Jeffrey Penny.
D5   William Gillis, m. Sadie <u>MacPherson</u>, lived in Quincy, Massa-
     chuetts, with issue:
     E1   Stanley Gillis.
     E2   Nellie Jean Gillis.
     E3   Eleanor Gillis.
     E4   Montie Gillis.
C4   John Gillis, lived in Orwell Cove, was a tailor and m. Sarah <u>MacDon-
     ald</u>, daughter of Hector MacDonald, Point Prim, no family.
C5   William Gillis, 1844-1931, m. Elizabeth <u>Duncan</u>, daughter of John
     Duncan and his wife Catherine MacLaren, Vernon River, with issue:
     D1   Christina Gillis, died young 1883-1901.
     D2   Isobel Gillis, died young.
     D3   William Gillis, 1887-1895.
     D4   Katie Gillis, m. Malcolm D. <u>MacDonald</u>, 1870-1962, son of
          Donald Hector MacDonald of Lyndale, they had one son:

E1 Lloyd MacDonald, who is farming on the old homestead, settled first by his great grandfather, Hector MacDonald, who was married in Skye to a daughter of "Old" Donald Nicholson of Orwell Cove. Hector and his family were 1829 immigrants. Lloyd m. Jean MacPhee, they have one son:
    F1 David MacDonald.

D5 Jessie Gillis, m. John M. Gillis, Grandview. They lived in Halifax, Nova Scotia, and had two sons:
    E1 Ivan Gillis, never married, was a noted musician and composer, died at a comparatively young age.
    E2 Clarence Gillis, m. Laura Gillis, his cousin, from Grandview, they live at Tea Hill, their children are:
        F1 Gail Gillis, married and living in Prince George, British Columbia.
        F2 Kimberly Gillis, living in Charlottetown.

D6 Emma Gillis, m. Edward Hackett, 1891-1971, they lived in Kinross, with issue:
    E1 Sterling Hackett, m. Margaret MacKenzie, Wood Islands, they live in Mt. Albion and their children are:
        F1 Sterling Alexander Hackett, not married in Charlottetown.
        F2 Edward Blair Hackett, m. Ann Walker, Alberry Plains. They live in Crossroads with a daughter:
            G1 Laurie Ann Hackett.
        F3 Ruth Emma Hackett, not married.
        F4 Donald Norman Hackett, living in Calgary.
        F5 Darlene Delores Hackett, at nursing school in Charlottetown.
        F6 Blaine Neil Hackett, living in Mt. Albion.
    E2 Blair Hackett, m. Erma MacPhail, Argyle Shore, they live in Charlottetown, no family.
    E3 Mildred Hackett, m. Wendell Robertson, Kingsboro, issue:
        F1 Diane Robertson, married in Kingsboro with two children.
        F2 Wendy Robertson.

D7 Duncan Gillis, lived on homestead on Orwell Hill, never married.

C6 Jessie Gillis, died 1938 age 88, m. Malcolm Lamont, 1847-1928, son of Ewen, of Skye and Lyndale, with issue:
D1 Christy Sarah Lamont, died in 1987 at the age of 107 years and 4 months. She m. Lauchlin "Donald Ban" MacPherson, 1863-1951, Lyndale. They raised a family of nine, all born at home. Christy Sarah had the unique record of never having spent a night in any hospital. Their family:
    E1 Donald MacPherson, m. Doris Dawe, lived in Toronto, Ontario, no family.
    E2 Christine MacPherson, m. Alex MacKinnon, 1892-1966, Strathlorne, Cape Breton and Massachusetts. They retired to P.E.I., no family.
    E3 Jessie MacPherson, died at age 20.
    E4 Lamont MacPherson, m. Ruth _____, no family, living in British Columbia.

E5   Duncan MacPherson, m. Viola <u>Gillespie</u>, Charlottetown, with one son:
  F1   Archibald MacPherson, m. Heather <u>Bigelow</u>, living in Halifax with two children.
E6   Arthur MacPherson, m. Jessie <u>Lord</u>, Tryon. They farmed in Grandview but retired to Charlottetown. Their family:
  F1   Charles MacPherson, m. Jean <u>MacKenzie</u>, living in Uigg, with two children:
  F2   Leah MacPherson, married, living in Charlottetown with one son:
    G1   George.
E7   Evelyn MacPherson, m. Walter <u>Banfil</u>, living in Massachusetts, with issue:
  F1   Roger Banfil, married in the U.S.A., with two children.
  F2   Wendy Banfil, married in the U.S.A., with one child
  F3   Douglas Banfil, not married in the U.S.A.
E8   John MacPherson, not married, living in Charlottetown.
E9   Martin MacPherson, m. Jennie <u>Beck</u>, Murray River, they lived in Vancouver with three children:
  F1   Geraldine MacPherson, m. James <u>David</u>, with three children, living in British Columbia.
  F2   Shirley MacPherson, married with family in British Columbia.
  F3   Kimble MacPherson, married in British Columbia.
D2 Catherine Lamont, 1880-1975, m. Angus A. A. J. <u>MacLeod</u>, 1882-1967, Kinross. They farmed at Kinross and raised a family of nine whose names will appear elsewhere in the book under the Kinross MacLeods.
D3 Elizabeth Lamont, died 1980, aged 87, m. David <u>Compton</u>, died 1930, aged 40, Brooklyn and Charlottetown, with issue:
E1   Malcolm Henry Compton, died 1936, aged 20.
E2   Ewen MacDougall Compton, died 1918 at 8 months, buried in Trenton, Nova Scotia.
E3   Esther Compton, died 1980, aged 60, m. Robert <u>Thurston</u>, Toronto. Their children are:
  F1   Lila Thurston, m. Timothy <u>Bain</u>, living in Musselman's Lake, Ontario, with issue:
    G1   Brandon Bain.
    G2   Jessica Bain.
  F2   Rodney Thurston, married Chantal <u>LaRue</u>, living in Haliburton, Ontario, with issue:
    G1   Chase Thurston.
    G2   Molly Thurston.
  F3   Irene Thurston, married Alex <u>Ghazarossian</u>, Ontario.
  F4   Trevor Thurston, living in Haliburton, Ontario.
E4   James Wellington Compton, m. Lorna <u>MacIsaac</u>, Dunblane, P.E.I. They live in Willowdale, Ontario, with issue:
  F1   Ronald Compton, m. Frances <u>Stead</u>, living in British Columbia with two children:
    G1   Christopher John Compton.
    G2   Daniel James Compton.

F2 Wendy Compton, died 1989, aged 42, m. George Provost of Montreal and Oakville, Ontario, their children:
   G1 Laurie Provost.
   G2 Mark Provost.
   G3 Ryan Provost.

F3 Judy Compton, m. Roger Slawson, living in Schomberg, Ontario, with one daughter:
   G1 Melany Slawson.

F4 James Compton, m. Bonnie Munro, who is descended from the Munros of Inverness Shire, Scotland, issue:
   G1 Travis James Compton.
   G2 Tyler Franklin Compton.

E5 Philip Compton, killed in plane crash on Tea Hill on January 12, 1942, aged 16 years.

E6 Tilly Compton, m. Harold MacLeod, great grandson of Murdoch "Horo" MacLeod, their children are:
   F1 Stephen Ross MacLeod, m. Barbara Lamb, living in Calgary with one child:
      G1 Cody Stephen Francis MacLeod.
   F2 Janis MacLeod, m. John Roberts. She is living in Calgary, with three children:
      G1 Timothy Roberts.
      G2 Mathew Roberts.
      G3 Amy Lynn Roberts.

E7 David Compton, Clergyman in the Free Church of Scotland, Ontario, m. 1) Peggy Ann Morrison, Detroit, they had two children:
   F1 Philip Kevin Compton, m. Betty Geddes, living in Florida, with two children:
      G1 Kevin Compton.
      G2 Heather Compton.
   F2 Cathy Compton, m. Marlo Oosterhuis, living in Ontario, with issue:
      G1 Margaret Susan Leigh Oosterhuis.

David m. 2) Flora MacKenzie, Loch Carron, Scotland. They have the following children:
   F3 Paul Compton.
   F4 Rhona Compton.
   F5 Steven Compton, m. Samantha Irons, living in Jasper, Ontario, with issue:
      G1 Kayleigh Compton.
   F6 Lisa Compton.

B3 Elizabeth MacLeod, died 1865 age 61, m. Neil Munn, died 1869, age 71, Mermaid, with issue:
   C1 Dollie Munn, lived in U.S.A.
   C2 Sarah Munn, 1831-1881, m. Hector Munn, 1826-1876, Wood Islands. Their children were:
      D1 Duncan Munn, 1853-1876, never married.
      D2 Elizabeth Ann Munn, 1855-1927, m. Daniel Munn, 1852-1911. They had a large family of seven children, some of their descendants live in the Murray River area.

D3   Mary Sarah Munn, 1857-1935, m. William <u>Needham</u>. They had a family of eight, none of whom, as far as is known, live on the Island.

D4   Flora Grace Munn, 1859-1945, m. John Henry <u>Compton</u>, 1854-1928.

   E1   Hector Compton, 1879-1970, m. Elizabeth Mae <u>Hume</u>, they lived in Belle River, 1888-1957, with their family:

      F1   Helen Dorothy Compton, died 1962, m. William <u>Matheson</u>, Belle River, they had two children:

         G1   Brenda Matheson, m. Leonard <u>Nylund</u>, Winnipeg, they have one boy.

         G2   Wayne Matheson, living in Southport.

      F2   Elmer Hume Compton, m. Lillian <u>Fredericks</u>, from Lloydminster, British Columbia. They live in British Columbia with one son:

         G1   Hamey Daniel Compton, who died at age 20.

      F3   Emily Florence Compton, m. Jack <u>MacKay</u>, Wood Islands, with issue:

         G1   Judy MacKay, m. Eric <u>Goodwin</u>, Charlottetown, with issue:

            H1   Christopher Goodwin.

            H2   Ian Goodwin.

         G2   Anne MacKay, m. Graham <u>Tweedie</u>, from Saskatchewan. They live in Halifax, with two children.

         G3   Mary MacKay, m. David <u>Gillis</u>, son of Dr. John Gillis, Eldon. They live in Point Claire, Quebec, with issue:

            H1   Jonathon Gillis.

            H2   Carley Anne Gillis.

         G4   Jean MacKay, m. Allan <u>Brown</u>, California.

            H1   Rebecca Brown.

      F4   George Hector Compton, m. Sybil <u>MacDonald</u>, Heatherdale. They live in in Pinette, with issue:

         G1   Robert Compton, m. Doris <u>MacDonald</u>, daughter of Marcellus MacDonald, Orwell, three children:

            H1   Robert Compton.

            H2   Kerri Anne Compton.

            H3   Benjamin Compton.

         G2   Kevin Compton, Charlottetown.

         G3   Dennis Compton, Charlottetown.

      F5   Russell Compton, lives in Belle River and is a builder of schooners and other seagoing vessels, following in the footsteps of his forbearers, some of whom were famous ship builders on the New England coast and on the south coast of Nova Scotia. He married Kathryn (Ky) <u>MacKenzie</u>, R.N., their family are:

         G1   Glen Compton, who was killed by an automobile Oct. 1, 1958, on his way to school.

         G2   Karen Compton, m. Scott <u>Miller</u>, Southport, issue:

            H1   Michael Miller, killed in 1991 by an automobile near U.P.E.I., Charlottetown.

            H2   Meggan Miller.

G3 Kenneth Compton, m. Diane <u>Tate</u>, with issue.
    H1 Leanne Compton.
    H2 Jackelene Compton.
G4 Barbara Compton, Charlottetown,
G5 Russell Compton, m. Darlene <u>MacRae</u>, Pinette, with issue:
    H1 Katie Anne Compton.
    H2 Glen Roy Compton.

F6 Grover Compton, m. Edna <u>Wilson</u>, they live in Leduc, Alberta, with three children:
    G1 Donald Compton, married in Leduc.
    G2 Daniel Compton, married in Leduc.
    G3 Gael Compton, married in Leduc.

F7 John Compton, m. Carol <u>Carrington</u>, New Brunswick, three children.

F8 Joyce Compton, m. Waldo <u>Taylor</u>, Wood Islands. He is a descendant of Donald Taylor who came over from Skipness, Argyleshire, Scotland, on the ship *Alexander* in 1820 and settled first in Rustico, Lot 26. He was a wheelwright by trade and moved to Wood Islands in 1825. Joyce and Waldo's children are:
    G1 Elizabeth Taylor, m. Reg <u>Samis</u>, Alma, Ontario. They have two girls.
    G2 Dianne Taylor, Charlottetown.
    G3 Cathy Taylor, Charlottetown.

E2 Elizabeth Compton, 1883-1986, m. Benjamin <u>Compton</u>, Belle River, with issue:
F1 Grace Compton, 1909-1973, m. Wilhelm <u>Madsen</u>, issue:
    G1 Daniel Madsen, m. in Toronto, with children.
    G2 Betty Madsen, m. Freeman <u>Herring</u>, Murray River. They live in Charlottetown.
    G3 Elmer Madsen, died young.
    G4 Olga Madsen, m. Mr. <u>Nicholson</u>, U.S.A., issue:
        H1 Keith Nicholson.

F2 Evelyn Compton, m. Axel <u>Rasmussen</u>, with issue:
    G1 Alice Rasmussen, is a widow.
    G2 Ellen Rasmussen, married, living in Nova Scotia.
    G3 Harold Rasmussen.
    G4 Carl Rasmussen, was married and drowned in Florida, leaving a young family.
    G5 Robert Rasmussen.
    G6 Roy Rasmussen.
    G7 Jean Rasmussen.
    G8 Axel Rasmussen.

F3 Alice Compton, m. Kenneth <u>MacKenzie</u>, Belle River, with issue:
    G1 Carol MacKenzie, m. Jerry <u>Johnson</u>, Charlottetown, with issue:
        H1 Ryan Johnson.
        H2 Tyler Johnson.
        H3 Mark Johnson.

G2 Marilyn MacKenzie, died young.
G3 Gael MacKenzie, m. Bill <u>MacPherson</u>, Charlotte-
town, with issue:
H1 Shane MacPherson.
H2 Allyson MacPherson.
G4 Scott MacKenzie, m. Miss <u>Nicholson</u>. He is in
the RCMP, stationed in Nova Scotia. They have
two children.
G5 Donna MacKenzie, m. Fraser <u>Inman</u>, Montague.
He is in the RCMP and they have two children.
G6 Bonnie MacKenzie.
G7 Wendell MacKenzie, m. Margaret <u>Power</u>, daugh-
ter of Rev. George Power, Charlottetown.
F4 Hon. Daniel Compton, M.L.A. and former Speaker
of the House, lived in Belle River where he carried
on a thriving business exporting lumber and pulp
along with a general store in Belle River. Dan m. Mary
<u>Compton</u>, daughter of James and Bessie Compton,
U.S.A. They have two children:
G5 Daniel Compton, a clergyman in the United
Church of Canada, m. 1) Sandy <u>Rutherford</u>, issue:
H1 Ellen Compton.
H2 Daniel Compton.
H3 Katie Compton.
H4 Sarah Compton.
Daniel married 2) Marsha _____.
G6 Susan Compton, married George <u>Julian</u>. They
have two boys and live in Kingston, Ontario.
H1 Peter Julien.
H2 Robert Julien.
F5 Elizabeth Compton, died young.
E3 James Compton, 1889-1979, m. 1) Lydia <u>Compton</u>, issue:
F1 Gladys Compton, m. Alfred <u>Lewis</u>, with three children
in Western Canada.
F2 Margaret Compton, m. Borge <u>Madeson</u>, not living.
They have four boys in Alberta.
James m. 2) Jane <u>Hume</u>, no family .
E4 Capt. Oliver Compton, 1897-1936, was lost at sea off the
coast of Nova Scotia, unmarried.
E5 John Compton, 1893-1972, m. 1) Cassie (Compton) <u>Bears</u>
as her second husband. She had two children (a) William
Bears, who is a piper, is married and lives in Maine; (b)
Benjamin Bears is married and lives in Orwell Cove. John
and Cassie's family are:
F1 Margaret Compton, m. Hank <u>VanOwerkirk</u>, died 1978,
age 47, with issue:
G1 Gerald VanOwerkirk, m. Sheila <u>Williams</u>. He is
in the RCMP. They have a son:
H1 Steven Robert Vanouwerkirk
G2 John VanOwerkirk, m. Patricia <u>Hall</u>, R.N. They
live at Crossroads with two children.

G3   Paul VanOwerkirk, m. Heather <u>Johnston</u> from
      Peters Road. They have two children:
      H1   Jason VanOwerkirk.
      H2   Ryan VanOwerkirk.
G4   Robert VanOwerkirk, m. Darlene <u>Knox</u>, daughter
      of Richard and Janet Knox, Montague. He is in
      the Armed Forces stationed at Calgary.
G5   Yvonne VanOwerkirk.

F2   Edith Compton, m. 1) Ralph <u>Young</u>, with issue:
      G1   Beverly Young, m. Dan <u>Kirk</u>, they have five
            children.
      G2   Ralph Young, married and living in Nova Scotia.
            He has five children.
      G3   John Young, living in Halifax, unmarried.
      Edith, m. 2) John <u>Gilmore</u>, Charlottetown.
F3   Catherine Compton, m. 1) Wendell <u>MacKenzie</u>. They
      had one boy:
      G1   Grant MacKenzie, living in Barrie, Ontario.
      Catherine m. 2) Walter <u>Richards</u>, they have two girls.
F4   Everett Compton, m. Corrie <u>VanOwerkirk</u>, sister of
      Hank. He is not living, they have no family, but Corrie
      has children from a previous marriage.

E6   Mary Grace Compton, 1885-1925, m. William <u>Jardine</u>, 1880-
      1937, with issue:
      F1   George William Jardine, died at two years.
      F2   Hector Jardine, married.
      F3   Lucy Jardine, m. Earl <u>Hume</u>.
      F4   James Jardine, m. Marie <u>VanOwerkirk</u>.
      F5   Ethel Jardine.
      F6   Mary Jardine.
      F7   Everett Jardine, died young.

E7   George William Compton, 1887-1966, married twice, no
      issue:

E8   Margaret Compton, 1891-1926, m. William <u>Compton</u>,
      Bangor, 1887-1969, with issue:
      F1   Olive Compton, m. Edward <u>Rowell</u>.
      F2   Mary Compton, m. Donald <u>MacPherson</u>.
      F3   Rose Compton, m. Roy <u>Rasmussen</u>.

E9   Ellen Compton, 1900-1982, m. 1) John <u>Compton</u>, m. 2)
      Donald <u>Compton</u>. Ellen and John had the following family:
      F1   Lloyd Compton, died 1980, age 59, was married, no
            family.
      F2   Emma Compton, m. Bill <u>Lewis</u>, living in Ontario with
            two children.
      F3   Arthur Compton, m. Alice <u>MacNutt</u>, living in Ontario
            with one child.
      F4   John Compton, died young.
      F5   Jean Compton, m. Tom <u>Johanson</u>, living in Ontario
            with three children.
      F6   Ben Compton, m. Hazel <u>MacKenzie</u>, they had two
            children in U.S.A.

F7   Flora Grace Compton, m. Fred <u>Cobb</u>, Bangor, issue:
G1   Lynn Cobb, died in 1983, aged 19 years.

F8   Patricia Compton, m. Fred <u>Hayman</u>. Pat lives in Woodstock, she has a son:
G1   Mark Hayman, married with a child.

F9   Mary Compton, m. Leonard <u>Cormier</u>, lived in Ontario, but now retired in British Columbia. They have three children

F10   Oliver Compton, m. Elva <u>Trainor</u>, they lived in Bangor, P.E.I. with the following children:
G1   Brian Oliver Compton, m. Doreen <u>MacEwen</u>. Their children are:
H1   Kyle Douglas Compton.
H2   Shawnda Lauren Compton.
G2   Herbert John Compton, married Donna <u>Johanson</u>, daughter of Tom Johanson and Jean Compton. Herbert and Donna live in Toronto.
G3   Glen Robert Compton, married Penny <u>MacLean</u>. Their children are:
H1   Kelsey Compton.
H2   Justin Compton.
G4   Lisa Marie Compton, m. 1) Peter <u>Runighan</u>, issue:
H1   Sarah Elizabeth Runighan.
H2   Helen Runighan.
Lisa m. 2)_____, living in Cape Breton.
G5   Rev. Kent Irwin Compton, minister in the Free Church of Scotland with a charge in Edmonton, Alberta, m. Isobel <u>Campbell</u>, from the Isle of Lewis, Scotland, they have one child.
G6   Scott Arthur Compton.

F11   George Compton, m. Eleanor <u>Ployer</u>, they live Sherwood and have two children:
G1   Laurie Compton.
G2   Lloyd Compton.

E10 Ben Compton, m. 1) Lydia <u>Jardine</u>, 1905-1971, and 2) Jessie Mae (MacInnis) <u>MacLeod</u>. Ben and Lydia's family are:
F1   Elizabeth Compton, m. Glen <u>MacKenzie</u>, in Toronto, with three children.
F2   Simon Compton, m. Jean <u>Hendry</u>. He is head of Cablevision Ltd., they have five children.
F3   Isabel Compton, m. Ken <u>Dingwell</u>, living in Morell with five children.
F4   Sophia Compton, m. Keith <u>MacLaren</u>. He was killed in an auto accident in Toronto in 1963. They had four children.
F5   Henry Compton, m. Ada <u>MacDonald</u>. Henry and Ada live in Bangor where they have a large farming operation, specializing in potatoes. They have three children:
G1   Donald Compton.
G2   David Compton.

G3   Davida Compton, married with one child.

F6   David Compton, m. Doris Swan, living in Windsor, Ontario, with two children.

F7   Ralph Compton, m. Pamela Hatton, living in Bangor. Pamela is a dedicated genealogist and has collected a massive amount of information which she has compiled into a Compton family history. Ralph and Pamela's children:
G1   Valerie Jane Compton.
G2   Ralph "Benjamin" Compton.
G3   Diana Jill Compton.

F8   Ruth Compton, m. Gerry Brouwer, living in Toronto with two children.

F9   Hope Compton, m. Larry Lutes. They live in Smithers, British Columbia, with two children.

F10 John Compton, m. Christine Hatton, living in Bangor with three children:
G1   Grant William Compton.
G2   Stephen Allan Compton.
G3   Angela Mavis Compton.

F11 Anne Compton, m. Richard Papenhausen, in St. John with two children.

E11 Mary Compton, died in 1881, age 11 months.

D5   Dorothy Munn, born 1861, m. Alex Stewart, they lived in the State of Washington, with three children.

D6   James Hector Munn, 1863-1926, m. 1) Margaret MacLeod, 1863-1886, m. 2) Ana Mae Edwards, 1871-1955.

D7   Jessie Munn, 1865-1890, m. Edward Roberts, they had one child, died young.

D8   Neil Alexander Munn, 1867-1889.

D9   John Daniel Munn, 1868-1939, m. Sarah A. Stephens, 1869-1945. John and Sarah had a family of ten children, one of whom, Edgar Munn, lived in Belle River.

C3   Donald Munn, 1833-1917, m. Jane Smith, 1838-1879.

C4   Roderick Munn, 1835-1927.

C5   Alexander Munn, born 1838.

C6   Mary Munn, born 1839.

C7   Anne Munn, 1841-1927, m. William MacKenzie, they had at least one son:
D1   Charles Munn MacKenzie, married in U.S.A., with a son:
E1   William R. MacKenzie, who lives in Marion, Massachusetts.

C8   Charles Munn, 1843-1932.

C9   William Munn, 1848-1937.

C10 James Munn, 1851-1927.

B4   Another daughter but no information could be found on her.

B5   Mary MacLeod, died 1886, age 88, m. John "Stenchol" Nicholson, died 1866, age 74, Orwell Cove, with issue:
C1   Malcolm Nicholson, born 1818, m. Jessie MacKinnon, born c. 1827. They lived in Orwell Cove and their children were:
D1   John Nicholson, born 1848, was a seaman.
D2   Simon Nicholson, born 1854, married and had four daughters.

D3 Margaret Jane Nicholson, born 1857.
D4 Charles Nicholson, born 1859.
D5 Elizabeth Nicholson, born 1862.
D6 Jessie Nicholson, born c. 1864.
D7 Malcolm Nicholson, born c. 1867.
D8 Sarah Nicholson, born c. 1866.
C2 John Nicholson, born 1820.
C3 Sarah or Marion Nicholson, born 1823, m. Angus MacLeod (see the family of Angus MacLeod and Sarah MacLeod, Surrey).
C4 John Nicholson, born 1825, m. Sarah MacEachern, with issue:
D1 John Nicholson, born 1866.
D2 Annie Nicholson, born 1867.
D3 Christine Nicholson, born 1872.
D4 Infant, born 1873.
D5 Catherine Nicholson, born 1877.
D6 William Nicholson, born 1880.
C5 Elizabeth Nicholson, born 1828.
C6 Jane Nicholson, born 1831, lived in Orwell Cove, never married.
C7 Roderick "Rory Hock" Nicholson, born 1834, m. 1) Jessie Morrison from Nova Scotia, with issue:
D1 Murdoch Nicholson, born 1866 in Newfoundland.
D2 John Nicholson, born 1868 in Newfoundland, married in U.S.A.
D3 Isabella Nicholson, born 1873 in P.E.I.
D4 Angus Nicholson, born 1876 in P.E.I., married in U.S.A.
D5 Mary Nicholson, born 1882, m. 1) Mr. Lowe, U.S.A., with issue:
E1 Irene Lowe, married in California.
E2 Henry Lowe, U.S.A. never married.
Mary m. 2) Hughie Matheson, Heatherdale, no issue.
D6 Jessie Margaret Nicholson, born 1886.
Roderick Nicholson m. 2) Christy MacDonald, Grandview. (For their descendants, see under Murdoch MacLeod, Orwell Cove.)
C8 Isabella Nicholson, born 1836, lived in Orwell Cove, never married.
C9 Margaret Nicholson (Peggy), m. John MacLeod.
C10 Donald Nicholson, born 1838, m. Sarah MacMillan, they lived in Orwell Cove, with issue:
D1 Daniel Nicholson.
D2 Angus Nicholson, died age 19 in 1892.
D3 George Nicholson, lived in U.S.A., never married.
D4 James Nicholson, lived in Orwell Cove, m. Annie MacPhee, sister of Rev. Sam MacPhee, with issue:
E1 Donald Nicholson, m. Della Young, they lived in the U.S.A. with a family.
E2 Sam Nicholson, married in the U.S.A., no family.
E3 Marion Nicholson, m. Dan Murdock, living in New York, with issue:
F1 Lloyd Murdock.
F2 Roger Murdock.
E4 Mary Nicholson, m. 1) John Hartnett, New York, they had one son:
F1 John Hartnett, living in U.S.A.
Mary m. 2) Sam Carr, no issue.

E5   Marjorie Nicholson, m. Philip Scully, New York, no issue.

E6   Jean Nicholson, m. Richard Jenkins, Pownal, with issue:

     F1   Floyd Jenkins, m. Helen _____, living in Ontario with two children:

          G1   Joanne Jenkins.

          G2   Melissa Jenkins.

     F2   Richard Jenkins, m. Gail Sheidow, living in Pownal, with issue:

          G1   Douglas Jenkins.

          G2   Randy Jenkins.

          G3   Robert Jenkins.

          G4   Susan Jenkins.

     F3   Darrel Jenkins, m. Janis Ranahan, living in Cherry Valley, with issue:

          G1   Stacey Jenkins.

          G2   Allison Jenkins.

          G3   Jonathan Jenkins.

     F4   Gregory Jenkins, m. Marion Geisc, living in U.S.A.

     F5   Brian Jenkins, m. Betty MacKenzie, living in Pownal.

     F6   Marjorie Jean Jenkins, m. Fred Richards, living in Pownal, with issue:

          G1   Steven Richards.

          G2   Lana Richards.

E7   Bertha Nicholson, m. John D. Bruce, High Bank, with issue:

     F1   Roland Bruce, single.

     F2   Earl Bruce, m. Enid Baldieu from Jamaica, living in Montague.

     F3   Annabelle Bruce, m. 1) Frank Grab, with issue:

          G1   Janice Grab, m. Kelly Kolke, Halifax.

          Annabelle m. 2) Bill Brehaut, Montague.

     F4   Marion Bruce, a journalist, was sometime editor of *Atlantic Insight*, now living in High Bank.

E8   Grace Nicholson, m. Ronald MacInnis, no family.

E9   George Nicholson, killed in Cape Breton in a road accident.

E10 John J. Nicholson, m. Lillian MacKenzie, living in Orwell Cove with a family.

D5 Mary Jane Nicholson, 1869-1916, m. Robert Emery, 1861-1935, Wood Islands, with issue:

E1   Daniel Emery, 1897-1925, never married.

E2   Katie Jane Emery, born 1900, m. George Taylor, she is living as a widow in St. John, New Brunswick, they had a large family.

E3   George Emery, 1903-1983, never married.

E4   Marion Emery, 1898-1927, m. Neil P. MacMillan, they lived in Wood Islands where he operated a flour mill, with issue:

     F1   Dan MacMillan, m. Yvonne _____, living in Wood Islands. They have one son:

          G1   Peter MacMillan.

     F2   Frank MacMillan, m. Bonnie ____, with issue:

          G1   Heather MacMillan.

          G2   Neil MacMillan.

G3   Ian MacMillan.

F3   Sally MacMillan, m. Keith Forsythe, living in Ontario with two children.

F4   Mary MacMillan, m. Ray MacPherson.

E5   James Allan Emery, m. Alvina Ferguson, living in Wood Islands, with issue:

F1   Kenneth Emery, m. Saundra Stewart, daughter of Alec and Elsie Stewart, with issue:

G1   Jane Emery, m. Joe McCaskill, living in Donagh.

G2   James Robert Stewart Emery.

G3   Gail Elsie Emery.

G4   Neil David Kenneth Emery.

G5   Darren Mark William Emery.

E6   Christina Emery, m. Hartford Stewart, Ellerslie and Boston, with a large family.

E7   Eveline Emery, m. Donald Crawford, Wood Islands, issue:

F1   William Crawford, m. 1) Bertha Ferguson, with issue:

G1   Donna Crawford, single.

G2   Robert Crawford, single.

William m. 2) Sharon Spice, Toronto, they live in Wood Islands.

E8   Mary Jane Emery, m. Hans Peterson, who died Nov. 1983, their children are:

F1   Harold Peterson, married west of Charlottetown.

F2   Ina Peterson, m. Norman Tweel, they have a family.

F3   Leigh Peterson, m. Shirley Drake, no family.

E9   Robert E. Emery, m. Jenny MacDonald from Antigonish. They had four children and lived in Massachusetts.

F1   Connie Emery.

F2   Janet Emery.

F3   Barbara Emery.

F4   Robert Emery, died in infancy.

B6   William MacLeod, died 1884, age 72, m. Mary MacInnis of Pinette. They had sixteen children, and five of their sons were Master Mariners:

C1   Roderick MacLeod, died at the age of two years.

C2   William MacLeod, died at the same age.

C3   Donald MacLeod, Master Mariner, who died in Liverpool, England, m. Margaret Gillis, of Point Prim, no family.

C4   Roderick MacLeod, died 1890, Master Mariner, who went to New Zealand in 1867 as mate on a brig commanded by his cousin Capt. Alexander Campbell, and settled there. He married in New Zealand to Hannah Sanky. They had three sons and a daughter:

D1   Roderick MacLeod, born 1876.

D2   William MacLeod, born 1878.

D3   A son, born 1880.

D4   Mary MacLeod, born 1883, m. Dr. Haseltine.

C5   John MacLeod, Master Mariner, died at home in 1890, never married.

C6   Mary MacLeod, m. to Mr. MacInnis, Caribou Island, Nova Scotia, no issue.

C7   Hector MacLeod, spent the greater part of his life in the great timber country of Humboldt in the northern part of the state of California.

There he held the office of County Supervisor for sixteen years. He died Dec. 31, 1910, aged 69 years, and is buried in Oakland, California. He never married.

C8 Margaret MacLeod, m. Donald Gillis, son of William, Orwell, with issue:

D1 William Gillis, m. Phemie Larabee, Eldon. They had no family.

D2 Christy Ann Gillis, m. William Anderson, Boston, with four children.

D3 Mary Gillis, m. Arthur Gillis, son of Neil Angus, Orwell Cove, they had no family.

C9 Jessie MacLeod, 1850-1931, m. John "the Rigger" MacDonald, 1841-1930, Pinette and Charlottetown. He operated a store in Charlottetown that supplied ships with sails, rigging and other needs, hence the name. Their children were:

D1 Janie MacDonald, born 1874, m. James Bishop, they lived in U.S.A. with issue:

E1 Alma Bishop.

E2 Mary Bishop, m. Eugene Robitaille, with issue:

F1 Eugene Robitaille, Jr., m. Doris _____, with issue:

G1 Martha Robitaille, m. Chris Galesta, one son.

E3 Ernest Bishop.

E4 Jessie Bishop, second wife of Eugene Robitaille, no issue.

D2 Florence MacDonald, 1875-1953, m. John Saunders, 1875-1940, from the Wood Islands area. They lived in Charlottetown, issue:

E1 Mary Saunders, m. _____ Arsenault, they live in Detroit with issue:

F1 Robert Arsenault, married in Detroit with a family.

E2 Harold Saunders, m. Ula Jenkins, they live in Charlottetown, with no family.

E3 Charles Saunders, died 1949, age 51, never married.

E4 Hibbert Saunders, m. Bobbie Wright, they live in Penticton, British Columbia, with issue:

F1 Douglas Saunders, m. Pauline Tadman, in British Columbia, with issue:

G1 Misty Carla Saunders.

G2 Michael Douglas Saunders.

F2 Joan Saunders, m. Mr. Moffet, British Columbia, with issue:

G1 Daniel Moffet.

G2 Patrick Moffet.

E5 Gladys Saunders, m. John Sweeny, Montreal, with issue:

F1 John Sweeny, married in Toronto.

F2 Sandra Sweeny, m. Mr. Hodgkin, Toronto, with issue:

G1 Sarah Lynn Hodgkin.

D3 Jessie MacDonald, never married.

D4 Mary MacDonald, born 1879, m. Robert Ward. They lived in the U.S.A., with issue:

E1 Mary Ward, U.S.A.

E2 Robert Ward, U.S.A.

E3 Beatrice Ward, m. Tom MacDonald, U.S.A., they have two boys and a girl.

E4   Elizabeth Ward, m. Mr. <u>Clark</u>, U.S.A.

D5   Duncan MacDonald, born 1880, died aged 14.

D6   John Angus MacDonald, 1884-1974, m. Elena Maud <u>Hill</u> from Richmond County, Cape Breton. They lived in Charlottetown, with issue:

       E1   Mary Carol MacDonald, m. Tom <u>Spencer</u>, from Blackpool, England. They live in Windsor, Ontario, no family.

       E2   John D. MacDonald, m. Amy Pearl <u>MacKenzie</u>, from Mt. Stewart. They live in Charlottetown, with issue:

           F1   Sheila Alena MacDonald.

           F2   Murray Hammond MacDonald.

D7   Bessie MacDonald, 1885-1964, m. Art <u>Nelson</u>, 1884-1972, from Charlottetown, no issue.

D8   Sarah MacDonald, 1887-1977, m. Howard <u>Murray</u>, 1880-1942, from Cape Breton, no family.

D9   Marie MacDonald, 1889-1952, never married.

D10 Maggie MacDonald, born 1890, died young.

D11 Robert MacDonald, 1892-1976, m. 1) Pearl <u>Howard</u>, with issue:

E1   Margaret MacDonald, never married.

Robert m. 2) Pearl _____.

D12 Howard MacDonald, 1894-1975, m. Euphemia <u>Keefe</u>, 1896-1971, from the Hartsville area. They lived in Charlottetown, issue:

E1   Jessie MacDonald, died in infancy.

C10 Donald MacLeod, m. Mary <u>Murchison</u>, daughter of Capt. James Murchison, Point Prim. They lived in Orwell Cove and later in Plenty, Saskatchewan, with issue:

D1   William MacLeod, Master Mariner, m. Winnifred <u>Wilson</u>, issue:

       E1   Elfreda MacLeod, m. Stanley <u>Palm</u>, with children. She died at a comparatively young age.

       E2   James MacLeod, was a school teacher, now living on Denman Island, British Columbia. His father, William, was Captain of a mine sweeper on the North Atlantic patrol during World War I. James, who was an infant at the time, was living with his mother and Elfreda in Halifax at the time of the Halifax Explosion. The house in which they were living was destroyed, but fortunately they escaped in the back of a buggy to the safety of a farm. James m. Norma Louise <u>Boake</u>. Their children are:

           F1   William Robert MacLeod, B.E.D., Prince George, British Columbia.

           F2   Daniel Kenneth MacLeod, L.L.B., Vancouver.

           F3   David James MacLeod, B.Sc., Calgary.

       E3   Lois MacLeod, died in infancy.

       E4   Margaret MacLeod, m. 1) W. <u>Bailey</u>, 2) W. <u>Kaines</u>.

       E5   Donna MacLeod, m. Albert <u>Scheffel</u>, Vancouver, British Columbia.

       E6   Winona MacLeod, a noted poetess with two books of poetry published, m. Arthur <u>Baker</u> of Nanaimo, British Columbia.

       E7   Iain MacLeod, D.D.S., practising in Vancouver, m. Margery_____.

       E8   Julia MacLeod, m. Mr. _____ <u>Nichol</u>.

D2 James MacLeod, never married. He farmed at Plenty, Saskatchewan, until retirement and died in Vancouver in 1956.

D3 Roderick MacLeod, M.D., practised in Vancouver. He taught
school in Orwell Cove at one time and later m. Elizabeth Jenkins, a sister of James, Orwell Cove. They had a homestead near
Plenty, Saskatchewan, and had a daughter Gertrude. At the birth
of her second child, Elizabeth and the baby both died. Roderick
then went back to school to study medicine and later m. Marion
Cato, and they had a family. Gertrude, daughter of Elizabeth,
when about age 20, was engaged to be married, took a violent
attack of polio which resulted in her death, consequently the
date set for her wedding was the day of her funeral.

D4 Hector MacLeod, born in Orwell Cove, moved to Plenty, Saskatchewan in 1906, m. Winnifred MacDougall in 1915. She was
also from the Orwell Cove area but at that time she was a ste-
nographer in Saskatoon. Their children were:

E1 Elizabeth Louise MacLeod, m. Archie Love, Windsor,
Ontario.

E2 Catherine MacLeod, m. Wilfred MacLeod (see Tailleur
MacLeod of Kinross). They lived in Edmonton, with issue:

F1 Bruce Hector MacLeod.
F2 Blair MacLeod.
F3 Donald MacLeod.

E3 Mary "Molly" MacLeod, m. Mr. Banks.

D5 Ewen MacLeod, M.D., practised in Vancouver. He m. Ella Per-
cival, with issue:

E1 Cameron P. MacLeod, m. _____.
E2 Douglas M. MacLeod, m. _____.

D6 Mary MacLeod, m. Dan MacIntosh, Plenty, Saskatchewan, issue:

E1 Walter MacIntosh.
E2 Alexander MacIntosh.
E3 Dorothy MacIntosh.
E4 Robert MacIntosh.

D7 Annie Louise MacLeod, m. Robert Mundell, Lemberg,
Saskatchewan.

C11 Alexander William MacLeod, Master Mariner, m. Elizabeth Nicholson,
daughter of Peter Nicholson, Orwell, with issue:

D1 William MacLeod, m. Alma Taylor, they had a family.
D2 Marion MacLeod, m. George Mutch, Earnscliffe, they had a
family.
D3 Mary MacLeod, m. Roger Cromsberry, Ottawa, with issue:
E1 Alexander Cromsberry and others.

C12 Murdoch MacLeod, died at the age of twelve.

C13 Angus MacLeod, died 1915, age 61, unmarried, at Orwell Cove.

C14 William MacLeod, was a twin brother of Angus and died in 1909,
age 55, unmarried at Orwell Cove.

C15 Elizabeth MacLeod, m. Mr. MacLagan, Caribou Island, Nova Scotia.
They had no family.

C16 John MacLeod, Master Mariner, New York, m. Jemima Murchison,
sister of Mary who was married to his brother Donald. They had
issue:

D1   Lillian MacLeod, living in New York.

D2   Maria MacLeod, m. Hammond <u>Bowman</u>, Attorney-at-law in New York.

D3   Nancy MacLeod, m. Frank <u>Hutcheson</u>, Charlottetown and U.S.A.

D4   John MacLeod, Attorney-at-law in New York.

MASTER MARINERS
LIST OF MASTER MARINERS

A list of the Master Mariners of the Belfast district appeared in the Charlottetown Guardian of April 22, 1922. Malcolm MacQueen republished this list with a few additions in the *Hebridean Pioneers*, 1957. Included were the following names:

MacLeod, Donald M., died at Point Prim.
MacLeod, Alexander, died at Point Prim.
MacLeod, Malcolm, died in Winnipeg.
MacLeod, Murdock "Beag," Orwell Cove, drowned in Pacific.
MacLeod, Alexander, Sr., Orwell, died Orwell, S.S. Gulnare.
MacLeod, Alexander, Jr., Orwell, drowned near Quebec.
MacLeod, John, Orwell, died sailing out of New York.
MacLeod, Neil, Orwell Bridge, died at sea, Pacific.
MacLeod, Roderick, Orwell Cove, died in New Zealand.
MacLeod, Donald, Orwell Cove, died of smallpox, Liverpool, England.
MacLeod, Alec William, Orwell Cove, died in Charlottetown, S.S. Northumberland.
MacLeod, John Sr., Orwell Cove, died in Orwell Cove.
MacLeod, John Jr., Orwell Cove, died in New York, 1934.

The last five named were brothers and sons of William "Horo" MacLeod, Orwell Cove.

ALEXANDER MACLEOD
ALEXANDER MACLEOD AND CATHERINE MACLEOD

A4   Alexander MacLeod, died age 87, son of Donald the Pioneer, was Captain in the militia and a school master in Skye before emigrating to Prince Edward Island. Donald MacKinnon, the Skye genealogist, stated that Alexander's wife was Catherine MacLeod, died 1876 age 86, daughter of Major MacLeod, a relative of Captain Murdoch MacLeod of Cuidreach, Snizort, Skye, whose wife was Marion, daughter of Major Alexander MacDonald of Cuirdeach and his wife Annabella, half sister of the "celebrated" Flora MacDonald. Alexander and Catherine's family were:

B1   Mary MacLeod, died 1847, age 38, buried in Belfast Cemetery, m. Donald "Ban" MacPherson, 1813-1890, who was born in the Isle of Skye, and emigrated to P.E.I. about 1829, taking up 100 acres of land in the Back Settlement, later called Lyndale. Donald and Mary's family were:

C1   Margaret MacPherson, born March 1, 1836, baptized the following day.

C2   Margaret MacPherson, born February 24, 1837.

C3   John MacPherson, 1838-1917, m. Ann MacLeod, 1849-1920, a sister of Malcolm "Grey Roderick" MacLeod of Lyndale, with issue:

D1   Florence MacPherson, m. Neil Sherwood, Coatsville, New Brunswick, with issue, John Sherwood and others.

D2   Archibald MacPherson, 1882-1956, carried on farming after the death of his father in Uigg, never married.

D3   Mary Catherine MacPherson, m. Captain Allen Gesner, Freeport, Texas, with a family.

D4   William MacPherson, born 1886, was killed at Britannia, British Columbia, in 1929.

D5   Katie MacPherson, lived at home, never married.

D6   Capt. John A. MacPherson, born 1882, was lost at sea, 1913.

C4   Sarah MacPherson, 1842-1915, never married, died in Waltham, Massachusetts, and is buried in Mount Feake Cemetery, Waltham.

C5   Donald MacPherson, born Oct. 24, 1844, went to New Zealand some time after 1881 and never returned to this country.

C6   Catherine MacPherson, 1840-1921, m. Malcolm Murchison, Point Prim, and according to the *Murchison Family History*, their children are:

D1   Mary Anne Murchison, m. Simon Alexander Murchison, Pinette, with issue, ten children.

D2   Mary Tena Murchison, lived in Oakland, California, never married.

D3   Catherine Alice Murchison, m. Norman Stewart, Little Sands. They lived in California, no family.

D4   Flora Margaret Murchison, m. Malcolm MacDonald, Caledonia, they lived in California, with issue:

E1   Elizabeth MacDonald.

E2   Alice MacDonald.

E3   Malcolm Neil MacDonald.

D5   Sarah Murchison, m. William MacDonald, Pinette, with issue:

E1 Finlay MacDonald, m. Martha ____, no family.
E2 Peter MacDonald, m. Donalda MacDonald, daughter of William and Mamie (MacTavish) MacDonald, Little Sands, with issue:
    F1 Daniel MacDonald, married in Vancouver, with a family.
    F2 Ida MacDonald, m. Garth MacLennan, five children.
    F3 Ronald MacDonald, m. Peggy ____, living in Charlottetown, one son.
    F4 Clifford MacDonald, m. Carol Campbell, one son:
        G1 Paul MacDonald.
    F5 Marilyn MacDonald, m. David McLarty, they live in Vancouver with one son:
        G1 Jason McLarty.
    F6 Dr. Allan MacDonald, m. Virginia MacDonald, daughter of Aloysius MacDonald, Panmure Island. Allan is practising dentistry in Crapaud, they have one child.
    F7 Dr. Stewart MacDonald, m. Judy MacMillan, Pownal. Stewart is practising in Montague, two children:
        G1 Mitchell MacDonald.
        G2 Vanessa MacDonald.

D6 Daniel Alexander Murchison, 1874-1963, m. Lena MacEachern, 1886-1975.
D7 William Archibald Murchison, m. Elizabeth Woodsworth, England. They lived in Atlantic City, New Jersey, and when Elizabeth died, he moved back to P.E.I., with issue:
    E1 Dan Murchison, died 1975, age 61, m. Eunice _____, New Jersey, with issue:
        F1 Elaine Murchison, m. Theodore Vanselous, New Jersey. They have three children.
    E2 Catherine Murchison, m. Arnold Ross, Bideford, P.E.I., with issue:
        F1 "Pat" Elizabeth Ross, m. William Dean, Summerside, with issue:
            G1 Shane William Dean.
            G2 Gregory Mark Dean.
        F2 Delbert Ross, m. Ila Kelly, living in Bideford issue:
            G1 Delbert Arnold Ross.
            G2 Shawna Ross.
            G3 Joanne Ross.
        F3 Vanessa Ross, m. Reginald Praught, living in St. John, New Brunswick, with issue:
            G1 Jason Praught.
            G2 Mary Ann Praught.
        F4 Robert William Ross, m. Trudy Reid, living in Charlottetown, with issue:
            G1 Michael Ross.
        F5 Roberta Ann Ross, m. John Bleumortier, living in Sussex, New Brunswick, with issue:
            G1 Sara Bleumortier.
D8 Peter Donald Murchison, 1872-1903, never married.

Donald "Ban" MacPherson [B1] m. 2) Sarah <u>MacDonald</u>, 1818-1900, daughter of Duncan (Hector) MacDonald, Grandview, with issue:

C7 Archibald MacPherson, 1853-1884, never married.

C8 Duncan MacPherson, 1856-1885, never married.

C9 Laughlan MacPherson, 1863-1951, m. Christy <u>Lamont</u>, daughter of Malcolm Lamont and his wife Jessie Gillis. She died in 1987 at the age of 107. She lived with her daughter Christine (MacPherson) MacKinnon in Charlottetown. Their family are listed elsewhere under Roderick, son of Donald of Skye and Orwell Cove.

C10 Anne MacPherson, born 1860, m. Angus John <u>MacPherson</u>, Brooklyn, with issue:

    D1 Sarah Catherine MacPherson, 1889-1969, m. Albert <u>Rivett</u>, one son, not living.

    D2 Sarah MacPherson, 1891-1892.

    D3 Donald MacPherson, died in England, in WWI.

    D4 Ewina MacPherson, 1895-1926.

    D5 Christine MacPherson, 1897-1992, lived in Massachusetts.

    D6 Sadie (Sally) MacPherson, 1899-1986, m. Clayton <u>Roberts</u>.

        E1 Clayton Roberts.

    D7 Anne MacPherson, 1903-1997, m. 1) Chessel <u>Annear</u>, Lower Montague, with issue:

        E1 Montie Annear, m. Doris <u>Green</u>, living in Calgary, no family.

        E2 Shirley Annear, m. William <u>MacDonald</u>, Sydney, Cape Breton. They live in Ottawa with four children.

        E3 Joyce Annear, m. Ian <u>Scrimgeour</u>, Cardigan. They live in Fredericton, New Brunswick, three children.

        E4 Norma Annear, living in Holland.

        E5 Dorothy Annear, m. Doug <u>Winters</u>, living in Liverpool, Nova Scotia, with three boys.

    Anne (MacPherson) Annear m. 2) Charles <u>MacLeod</u> of Alliston. They lived in Lower Montague.

C11 Catherine MacPherson, m. Reuban <u>Brehaut</u>, son of Robert of Lyndale, issue:

    D1 Robert Brehaut,m. Annie <u>Richards</u>, Alberry Plains. They lived in Lyndale with issue:

        E1 Mary Brehaut, m. Charles <u>MacEachern</u>, Belfast, with issue:

            F1 Floyd MacEachern, living in St. John, New Brunswick.

            F2 Blake MacEachern, married in Calgary.

            F3 Donna MacEachern, married in Calgary.

            F4 Gordon MacEachern, m. Linda <u>Walker</u>, Alberry Plains. They live in Belfast with one girl.

            F5 Ruth MacEachern, living in Charlottetown where she is a radio announcer.

        E2 Louise Brehaut, m. Bruce <u>Lecco</u>, Kilmuir, with one son:

            F1 Larry Lecco.

        E3 Clinton Brehaut, m. Beulah <u>Runions</u>, living in New Brunswick, with issue:

            F1 Helen Brehaut.

            F2 Robert Brehaut.

        E4 Kay Brehaut, m. Keith <u>MacLeod</u>, Kinross, with issue:

F1 Ricky MacLeod, married in Calgary.

F2 Janis MacLeod, married a son of Wilfred Gillis, Kilmuir.

D2 Sadie Brehaut, m. Harold Behm. They lived in Grandview with issue:

E1 Thelma Behm, m. William (son of Neil) MacLeod, Orwell, with issue:

F1 Neil MacLeod, killed in an auto accident, 1974, in Calgary, aged 20.

F2 Lynn MacLeod, m. John Holmes, living in Burlington, Ontario.

F3 Steven MacLeod, R.N., living in Charlottetown.

E2 Helen Behm, m. Hugh Robbins, son of Lloyd, Uigg, their issue:

F1 Ann Robbins, m. Harvey MacEwen, living in Alberton with four children.

F2 Teryl Robbins, m. Doris Neimer, with one girl.

F3 Donald Robbins, m. Frances Gormley, living in Uigg with three children.

F4 Leslie Robbins, living in Dawson City.

F5 Joyce Robbins, living in Ottawa.

F6 Philip Robbins.

E3 Teryl Behm, died young.

E4 Sheila Behm, m. 1) Donald Moran, Cobalt, Ontario, m. 2) Brian Kerr, St. John, New Brunswick. Sheila has two children:

F1 Cheryl.

F2 Victor.

E5 Sidney Harold Wynn Behm, m. Margaret Ratcliffe from England. Living in Fort MacMurray, they have three boys:

F1 Michael Behm.

F2 Lincoln Behm.

F3 Colin Behm.

D3 Ella Brehaut, m. Donald Latour, U.S.A.

D4 Mary Brehaut, died aged 21.

C12 Christine MacPherson, m. Mr. Green, Massachusetts, with one son:

D1 Donald Green.

B2 Mary MacLeod, died 1906, age 87, m. Alexander Anderson, died 1873, age 64, Orwell Cove, without issue.

B3 William MacLeod, died 1884, age 72, m. Christine MacDonald, died 1873, age 50, daughter of Finlay MacDonald, who was a brother of the Pioneer Minister, Rev. Donald MacDonald, without issue.

THE HIGHLANDERS
HIGHLAND SOLDIERS IN THE BRITISH AND CANADIAN ARMIES

The men from the Highlands of Scotland were outstanding as soldiers in the British wars. They could travel quickly over rough terrain and neither summer heat nor the snows of winter seemed to bother them. On long marches, they would wrap themselves in their plaids at night and sleep in the open, oblivious to snow or rain. According to one British General, who spoke admiringly of them, they could live off the land; all they required, in field supplies, were a few pounds of oatmeal with a little salt and they would march for miles over moor and mountain, and would fight the enemy with incredible courage and ferocity.

Roderick MacGowan in his account of the men of Skye tells of Norman MacLeod, of Minginish, Skye, who served in the 42nd Highlanders, who were sent down to drive the French out of Egypt. When they were almost overwhelmed by the French Cavalry, the British Commander ordered the Highlanders to drive them back, calling out, "My brave Highlanders, remember your country, remember your forefathers." The French Cavalry charged, but the Highlanders stood firm, first endeavouring to bring down the horse before the rider came within sword length, and then despatching the rider with the bayonet before he had time to recover his legs from the horse. The British gained a decisive victory that day and eventually retook all of Egypt and NorthAfrica.

Rev. Roderick MacLeod, Moderator of the Free Church of Scotland in 1863, in his address to the General Assembly stated that:

> During a period of not more than forty years, there were contributed to the armaments of Britain from the Isle of Skye: ten thousand foot soldiers, not fewer than twenty-one Lieutenant-Generals, or Major Generals, Captains and Subalterns, and, for various departments of the Civil Service, during the same period—besides no insignificant number of men and officers in the British Navy—Skye supplied four Governors of British Colonies, one acting Governor General of India, and one Lord Chief Baron of England, and one Judge of the Supreme Court of Scotland. We know not whether, of any equal extent of territory, and of no larger population any such statement could be made.

Francis Thompson in *Crofting Years* observed that:

> From 1740 to 1815 no less than fifty battalions of infantry had been raised mainly from the Highlands, besides many fencible or militia regiments. They fought in the Seven Years War when Britain gained India and Canada for her growing Empire. They fought in the American War of Independence, and in the Peninsular and Napoleonic Wars that followed. They distinguished themselves with Wolfe at Quebec, with Sir John Moore at Corunna, and Wellington at Waterloo. And it was the Highland Brigade and in particular the 93rd Highlanders, the "Thin Red Line," under the leadership of Sir Colin Campbell, which really saved the day at the Battle of Balaclava.

Canada, too, has benefited from the warrior skills of the Highlanders. It was Donald MacDonald, son of Randall MacDonald and Margaret MacLeod, of Berneray and South Uist, who having escaped the carnage of Culloden Moor, joined the French Army and it was he who was first pardoned, returned to England, joined the Army where he became fluent in that language. Eventually, he was pardoned and it was he who was first in scaling the Heights of Abraham in 1759, answering the French Sentry in excellent French, thereby enabling General Wolfe to assemble his army on the plains without alerting the enemy. He was killed later at the siege of Quebec in 1760. James MacLeod who was born in the Isle of Skye, had a distinguished career with the North West Mounted Police, maintaining law and order on the Great Western Plains of this country. His picture was on the 1986 34-cent Canadian postage stamp.

We remember also with justifiable pride, the sons and daughters of Highlanders born in Canada, who fought on the battlefields of Europe and other parts of the world, in several wars. They too have shown the courage that is born of Highland blood.

Private Ewen Angus MacLeod, who served with the North Nova Scotia Highlanders, was the son of Roderick Charles and Margaret (MacNeill) MacLeod of Lyndale, and was one of five brothers who wore the King's uniform during WWII. He took part in the Battle of Caen, France, where the full weight of the German Army was thrown against the North Novas, in a vain attempt to break through the Canadian lines. At one point the Canadians were forced to fall back in order to consolidate their position. Ewen Angus was among those who were assigned to cover the withdrawal and on July 25, 1944, he made the supreme sacrifice. A telegram was sent conveying the sad news to his parents. Two weeks after the telegram arrived, they also received the following letter which he had written and posted the evening before the battle. The Hector he referred to in the letter was his older brother who went overseas in 1941 and was serving somewhere in France. Alfred Bruce was a next door neighbour, also serving in the Canadian Army in France.

A Soldier's Letter
Letter from Ewen MacLeod to his Mother

The Salvation Army
"Keep in touch with the folks at home"
On Active Service
with the
Canadian Forces

July 20, 1944

Dear Mamma,

Just a few lines to let you know I am in the best of health and that I am getting along fine. I got a letter from you a few days ago that had come through Debert. I have not seen Hector yet. I was quite surprised a few days ago to see Alfred Bruce. I didn't have much time to talk to him but I was glad to see him. He didn't know what to say when I told him his father died. He did not know about it as he had not heard from home for some time he said. I suppose you are through haying by now. Well I haven't much news so I'll close for now and I want you to know that though I may be in danger from time to time I think of the verse in God's word which says *Be strong and of good courage. Be not afraid neither be thou dismayed. For the Lord thy God is with thee whithersoever thou goest* and I know also that you are praying for me. You can guess where I am when I say that I am writing this letter on a piece of a board in the field. I am hoping this letter finds you all well. Keep the letters coming.

Lovingly,

Ewen

My address is:

F82261 Pte E. A. MacLeod
N. N. S. H.
B.W. E. F.
R.C.A. A.

[Publisher's note: In previous editions, this letter appeared as a photocopy of the original handwritten letter.]

John MacLeod
John MacLeod and Margaret Nicholson from Glen William

A   John MacLeod, m. Margaret <u>Nicholson</u>, both believed to be from the Isle of Skye. They lived in Glen William and had issue:

B1 Roderick MacLeod, 1846-1909, m. Sarah <u>Bruce</u>, 1846-1921. They took over the Bruce farm in Glen William and had issue:

C1 Catherine MacLeod, died Nov. 26, 1899, age 26, m. John J. <u>MacDonald</u>, who was a miller, they had two daughters at least:
D1 Harriet MacLeod, died 1899, age 5 months.
D2 Sadie MacLeod, died at age 9 years.

C2 Margaret MacLeod, 1875-1936, m. John <u>Bruce</u>, 1867-1953, from Brooklyn, P.E.I., with issue:
D1 Christine Bruce, m. Claude <u>Wood</u>, they had no family.
D2 Catherine Bruce, m. Edward <u>MacCallum</u>, with issue:
E1 Donald MacCallum, m. Patricia Ann <u>MacPherson</u>.
E2 Anne MacCallum, m. David <u>Hyndman</u>.
E3 Carol MacCallum, m. Eugene Sterling <u>Lavers</u>.
E4 Gordon MacCallum, m. Marilyn Lynn <u>Robertson</u>, living in Charlottetown.
E5 Joan MacCallum.
D3 Rodney Bruce, m. Marion <u>Douglas</u>, from Georgetown, with issue:
E1 David Bruce.
E2 Ian Bruce, twin of David.
D4 Annie Bruce, was a school teacher and died in the Sanatorium.
D5 Willard Bruce, m. Margaret <u>MacKenzie</u>. They lived in Brooklyn, P.E.I. Their issue:
E1 Everett Bruce, deceased.
E2 Alexander Bruce, m. Catherine <u>Cain</u>.
E3 Mary Bruce.
E4 John Bruce.
D6 Sadie (Sally) Bruce, m. Wallace <u>Rodd</u>, Charlottetown, with issue:
E1 Margaret Rodd, m. Ivan <u>Duvar</u>.
E2 David Rodd, m. 1) Jean <u>Douglas</u>, 2) Linda _____.

C3 Mary Ann MacLeod, 1877-1941, m. John J. <u>Stewart</u>, 1873-1951, from High Bank, with issue:
D1 Flora Margaret Stewart, R.N., never married. She served in the U.S. Army Nurse Corps during WWII, shipping out to the Philippines in 1945 in preparation for the invasion of Japan and was on a hospital ship for 38 days from New York to Manila.
D2 Bruce Stewart, 1910-1968, farmed in High Bank, never married.
D3 Malcolm Stewart, 1912-1985, served overseas in the army from 1940-1945, m. Alexandria <u>MacLean</u> from Little Sands. They had no family.
D4 Sidney Stewart, 1914-1987, never married. He was a pilot in the RCAF during WWII.
D5 Sarah Stewart, m. Perley <u>Harris</u>, 1916-1997, from Guernsey Cove, P.E.I., no family.

C4 Mary MacLeod, m. Sidney <u>Davison</u>, they lived in Gloucester, Massachusetts, they had one daughter:
D1 Isobel Davison.
C5 Sarah MacLeod, m. Malcolm Alex <u>MacDonald</u>. They lived in Glen William and had issue:
D1 Bruce MacDonald, m. Florence <u>Paul</u>.
D2 Allister MacDonald, married.
D3 Catherine MacDonald, m. Robert <u>Jenkins</u>.
C6 Flora MacLeod, 1887-1923, m. Albert <u>Taylor</u>, who was a school teacher, they had one son.
D1 William Bruce Taylor, who was three years old when his mother died, was sent to live with his Aunt Margaret, married to John Bruce. When he was twelve years of age he went to live with his father in Saskatchewan. He later became a minister in the United Church, serving as a Chaplain in the Navy, later a prison Chaplain. He is now retired, living in Victoria, British Columbia. He married Frances _____, with issue:
E1 Craig Taylor, died young.
E2 Christopher Taylor.
B2 William MacLeod, never married.
B3 Murdoch MacLeod, m. Maggie <u>MacLeod</u>, daughter of William, Lyndale, they lived in Boston, with issue:
C1 Margaret MacLeod, m. Mr. <u>Brown</u>, U.S.A.
C2 William MacLeod.
C3 John MacLeod.
C4 Minard MacLeod, believed most, if not all of this family died young.
B4 Mary MacLeod, m. _____ <u>MacKenzie</u>.

Information source: Mary Dugas, Little Sands; Flora Stewart, High Bank; and Earle Bruce, Montague

NORMAN MACLEOD
NORMAN MACLEOD AND MARGARET MACPHEE OF UIGG

A1 Norman MacLeod, 1752-1837, m. Margaret MacPhee, 1778-1855, also m. Mary
_____. Norman, Murdoch and James, the three sons of Neil MacLeod and
Sophia Nicholson, came from Skye to Prince Edward Island in 1829 on the ship
Mary Kennedy. Norman is the first person listed in the Uigg Cemetery Book.

B1 Rev. Samuel MacLeod, 1796-1881, m. Margaret Currie, 1807-1902, issue:

C1 Norman S. MacLeod, 1838-1928, m. 1) Sarah MacLeod, daughter of
Ewen, farmed in Uigg, then moved to Montague to do carpenter
work. He m. 2) Mary MacNeill, of Little Sands. Norman and Sarah's
children were:

D1 Sarah MacLeod, 1876-1897.

D2 Hammond MacLeod.

D3 Samuel MacLeod.

D4 George R. MacLeod, assistant city engineer in Montreal, m.
Margaret Furness, a poetess, with issue:

E1 Elizabeth MacLeod, m. Cecil Davis, with issue:

F1 Susan Davis, m. Gerry Holstein, with three children.

F2 Tom Davis, m. Claudette Bellmore, lawyers in Quebec.

F3 Christopher Davis, married with one child.

D5 Rev. James D. MacLeod, a preacher in Rochester, New York,
died in 1927, m. _____, with issue:

E1 Fenwick MacLeod.

E2 Colleen MacLeod, married.

E3 George MacLeod.

C2 Mary MacLeod, known as Mary Sam, lived in Montague.

C3 Duncan MacLeod, known as Duncan the Lawyer, was a lawyer in
Charlottetown.

C4 James MacLeod, M.D., died 1927, m. Margaret Gates, with issue:

D1 James MacLeod, M.D., practised in Moose Jaw, was married.

D2 Bernice MacLeod, her nickname was Tutu, m. Frank Thomas,
with issue:

E1 MacLeod Thomas.

E2 Jack Thomas.

E3 Gordon Thomas.

E4 Sidney Thomas.

C5 Sarah MacLeod, 1843-1913, m. William MacLeod, 1841-1938, Bridgetown, shipbuilder, blacksmith and farmer, buried in Dundas, with
issue:

D1 Sam MacLeod, 1870-1940, m. Etta Bell, he was contractor in
British Columbia, with issue:

E1 Jean MacLeod, m. Eugene Dowl, with issue:

F1 Norma Dowl, m. David Hatcheson.

F2 Carolyn Dowl, m. George Ewing, with issue:

G1 Glenna Ewing.

E2 Norval MacLeod, m. Lena Long.

D2 Margaret MacLeod, 1872-1963, nursed many years in Grotton
School, Massachusetts. Never married, buried in Dundas.

D3   James MacLeod, 1877-1966, Sergeant in WWI. Lived after the war in British Columbia, never married, buried in Dundas.

D4   Edith MacLeod, 1880-1943, nursing sister in WWI, never married.

D5   Sadie MacLeod, 1884-1955, worked in Massachusetts, never married, buried in Dundas.

D6   Norman MacLeod, 1884-1964, m. Myrtle Jenkins. Farmer in Bridgetown, with issue:

E1   Lloyd MacLeod,m. Kay MacEachern, farmer in Bridgetown, later retired in Montague, issue:

F1   Billy MacLeod, m. Debbie Wood, he is a machinist, with issue:

G1   Scott MacLeod.

G2   Michelle MacLeod.

F2   Colin MacLeod, m. Maxine Gallant. Farmer in Bridgetown on the old home.

F3   Brenda MacLeod.

F4   Myrtle MacLeod.

F5   Heather MacLeod, m. Phillip Campbell, who is in the Canadian armed forces, issue:

G1   Anthony Campbell.

G2   Another child.

E2   Haddon MacLeod, m. Lexi MacDonald, he was a farmer and machinist, RCAF, WWII.

D7   Minnie MacLeod, 1886-1977, nursed in Massachusetts. Never married, buried in Dundas.

C6   Malcolm MacLeod, m. Esther Robertson, he was a farmer in Uigg, lived on old home. Their children were:

D1   Sam E. MacLeod, 1880-1959, m. Mabel Vaniderstine, he was a prominent farmer, lived on old home. He was active in community work and reared twelve children:

E1   Florence MacLeod, teacher, m. Floyd MacLean, in Kingsboro, with issue:

F1   Callum MacLean, m. Sylvia Bruce, with issue:

G1   Cynthea MacLean.

G2   Garth MacLean.

G3   Blane MacLean.

G4   Gail MacLean.

G5   Pamela MacLean.

G6   Kent MacLean.

G7   Holly MacLean.

G8   Craig MacLean.

F2   Haddon MacLean, m. Marilyn MacPhee, with issue:

G1   Andrea MacLean.

G2   Ian MacLean.

F3   Helen MacLean, m. Ross Young, with issue:

G1   Bonnie Lee Young.

G2   Linda Rae Young.

G3   Ross Young.

G4   Shelly Young.

E2   Edwin MacLeod, served in WWII, died in New Brunswick, never married.

E3   Margaret MacLeod, m. Sheldon <u>Hume</u>, Murray Harbour, issue:
    F1   David Hume, m. Marlene <u>MacNeill</u>, with issue:
        G1   Susan Hume.
        G2   Laura Hume.
E4   Malcolm MacLeod, m. 1) Elsie <u>Cranston</u>, 2) Marjorie <u>Judson</u>. He moved to British Columbia near Prince George and was in the lumber business, with issue:
    F1   Beverly MacLeod, m. Jack <u>Wilcox</u>.
    F2   Bruce MacLeod.
    F3   Norman MacLeod.
    F4   Laverne MacLeod.
    F5   Tracy MacLeod.
    F6   Lois MacLeod.
    F7   Glen MacLeod.
    F8   Gladys MacLeod.
    F9   Lori Jean MacLeod.
    F10 Dale MacLeod.
E5   Marion MacLeod, m. Walter <u>MacLeod</u>, they farmed in Orwell Cove, with issue:
    F1   Winston MacLeod.
    F2   Mabel MacLeod, m. Ronald <u>Barrett</u>, with issue:
        G1   Deane Barrett.
        G2   Carol Barrett.
        G3   Debbie Barrett.
        G4   Douglas Barrett.
    F3   Byron MacLeod, m. Wanda <u>Edwards</u>, with issue:
        G1   Brodie MacLeod.
E6   Gordon MacLeod, m. Myrtle <u>Wood</u>. Provincial Inspector with the Dept. of Agriculture. Lived in Charlottetown, with issue:
    F1   Douglas MacLeod, m. Norma <u>Scott</u>.
    F2   Ruby MacLeod, m. Wesley <u>Thompson</u>.
    F3   Raymond MacLeod, m. Joyce <u>Taylor</u>, with two children.
    F4   Vernon MacLeod, married.
    F5   Phyllis MacLeod, m. Harvey <u>Boswell</u>.
E7   Raymond MacLeod, m. Zita <u>Sullivan</u>. They lived in Oregon and California. He worked in the real estate business. Their children are:
    F1   Mildred MacLeod.
    F2   Jeannie MacLeod.
    F3   Debbie MacLeod.
    F4   Nadine MacLeod.
E8   Olive MacLeod, m. Ken <u>Arthur</u>, live in Del Rio, Texas, issue:
    F1   Heather Arthur, m. Warren <u>Pezold</u>.
    F2   Pamela Arthur m. Tom <u>Pezold</u>.
    F3   Kenneth Arthur, m. Priscilla <u>Croan</u>, with issue:
        G1   Sandra Arthur.
        G2   Kimberly Arthur.
        G3   Robert Arthur.
E9   Alex MacLeod, m. Florence <u>Cobb</u>, with issue:

F1   Wayne MacLeod, m. Katie <u>Herring</u>, with issue:
     G1   Lyla MacLeod.
     G2   Larry MacLeod.
     G3   Donna MacLeod.
     G4   Darlene MacLeod.
     G5   Garry MacLeod.
F2   Joyce MacLeod, m. Albert <u>Haslam</u>, with issue:
     G1   Albert Haslam.
     G2   Wayne Haslam.
F3   Roger MacLeod, m. Jean <u>Ford</u>, with issue:
     G1   Donnie MacLeod.
F4   Wanda MacLeod, m. 1) John <u>Hayden</u>, 2) Donald <u>Dawson</u>, with issue:
     G1   Mellissa Dawson.
F5   Barbara MacLeod, m. Ronald <u>O'Donnell</u>.

E10   James MacLeod, m. Winnifred <u>Fisher</u>. Lives in Ingleside, Ontario, with issue:
F1   Roy MacLeod, m. Patricia <u>Tinney</u>, with issue:
     G1   Donna MacLeod.
     G2   Lorrie MacLeod.
F2   Linda MacLeod, m. Edward <u>Periard</u>, with issue:
     G1   Joan Periard.
     G2   Jason Periard.
     G3   Stephen Periard.
F3   Gail MacLeod, m. Graham <u>MacDonald</u>, with issue:
     G1   Cynthia MacDonald.
F4   Sam MacLeod.
F5   Garry MacLeod.
F6   Nancy MacLeod.
F7   Russell MacLeod.
F8   Lloyd MacLeod.
F9   Mark MacLeod.

E11   Esther MacLeod, m. Ralph <u>Jeffords</u>, living in California, with issue:
F1   Malcolm Jeffords.
F2   Myra Jeffords .
F3   Elaine Jeffords.
F4   Kathy Jeffords.
F5   Harry Jeffords.
F6   Dorothy Jeffords.
F7   Wendy Jeffords.

E12   Harold MacLeod, m. Dorothy <u>Robinson</u>. They farm and operate Dunvegan Motel in Uigg on the old home. Their children are:
F1   Kier MacLeod, m. Wanda <u>Worth</u>, with issue:
     G1   Kirk MacLeod.
     G2   Amanda MacLeod.
     G3   Ellen MacLeod.
F2   Ian MacLeod, m. Faye <u>Quinn</u>, with issue:
     G1   Jeffrey MacLeod.
     G2   Justin MacLeod.

F3   Glen MacLeod.

F4   Heather MacLeod.

D2   Ella MacLeod, 1882-1960, R.N. Matron in a large hospital in Massachusetts, buried in Uigg.

D3   Margaret MacLeod, 1888-1967. Was private secretary for a Montreal judge. Buried in Uigg.

D4   Alex MacLeod, m. Hilda Heaton. He was a Rhodes Scholar, graduate of McGill and Oxford Universities, Lieutenant in WWII, Attorney for C.N.R. Practised law in Vancouver. Their issue:

E1   Elizabeth MacLeod, m. Richard Weldwood, with issue:

F1   Margot Weldwood.

F2   Susan Weldwood.

E2   Rosemary MacLeod, m. John Meyer, with issue:

F1   Lucas Meyer.

F2   Monica Meyer.

D5   Haddon MacLeod, m. Jessie MacIntyre. He had a B.Sc., served in WWI, after the war he was Chief Potato Inspector in British Columbia.

D6   Duncan MacLeod, m. 1) Margaret MacNaughton, m. 2) Dana Latimer. He was an engineer on C.N.R.

C7   Hannah MacLeod, died in infancy.

B2   A girl, m. Angus MacDonald, they left Uigg with their family.

B3   John MacLeod, 1820-1893, m. Rachel Gordon, 1818-1915, born in Skye, buried in Uigg.

B4   Catherine MacLeod, 1793-1883, m. Alex Cameron.

B5   Mary MacLeod, m. James MacDonald. Mary is a sister of Rev. Samuel and James is a brother of Angus. Both brothers are original settlers in Uigg. Mary and James settled in Bellevue, with issue:

C1   Norman MacDonald m. Annie MacLeod. Annie is a sister of Christy MacLeod, who is John's wife. John is son of Big Murdoch, with issue:

D1   Ola MacDonald, not married.

D2   Maynard MacDonald, m. Nellie Westaway.

D3   James MacDonald m. Elizabeth MacMillan.

D4   Eugene MacDonald m. Tillie MacLean, with issue:

E1   Roderick MacDonald, m. Adele MacNutt, with issue:

F1   Peter MacDonald, an adopted child.

F2   Barbara MacDonald, an adopted child.

E2   Phoebe MacDonald m. Frank Vaniderstine, with issue:

F1   Chester Vaniderstine, m. Faye Taylor, with issue:

G1   Donald Vaniderstine.

G2   Catherine Vaniderstine.

G3   Beverly Vaniderstine.

G4   Beryl Vaniderstine, m. John Nantha, with issue:

H1   Christopher Nantha.

C2   Mary MacDonald, m. Neil MacLeod, died in Edmonton, buried in Uigg, they had issue:

D1   Archibald MacLeod, 1881, died in Edmonton.

D2   Samuel MacLeod, died in 1918, buried in Uigg.

D3   James MacLeod.

C3   Donald MacDonald, m. Margaret Gordon, daughter of Donald Gordon, lived in Vancouver, with issue:

         D1   Rev. Donald MacDonald (Baptist), of Vancouver.

         D2   Malcolm MacDonald, a sea captain of Georgetown, P.E.I., married, with issue:

             E1   A daughter, m. H. A. Richardson, General Manager of the Bank of Nova Scotia.

B6   Roderick MacLeod, 1803-1888, m. Catherine MacLeod, 1807-1882, born in Skye, buried in Uigg, with issue:

         C1   Kate R. MacLeod, 1847-1890, lived in Montague.

         C2   Mary R. MacLeod, 1838-1914.

         C3   Christie MacLeod, 1844-1890.

         C4   John R. MacLeod, 1835-1913.

         C5   Malcolm MacLeod, 1840-1903, m. Barbara Rankin, he was a lawyer, and was first president of the Island Telephone Co., no family.

         C6   Ann MacLeod, 1842-1905, m. Alex Martin, 1842-1921, with issue:

             D1   Albert Martin, Dalhousie and Cornell graduate, C.E., not married.

             D2   Belle Martin, m. H. W. H. Knott, a lawyer in Montreal.

B7   Murdoch MacLeod, 1815-1899, m. Margaret Gunn, 1817-1916. Murdoch was born in Skye, his wife was born in Miramichi, New Brunswick. They lived in Uigg near the Baptist Church. He was known as "Big" Murdoch, with issue:

         C1   James MacLeod, 1840-1923, m. 1) Mrs. Robertson (nee Miss MacDonald), m. 2) Eva Bruce. James moved to Bridgetown where he was postmaster. Buried in Dundas, had issue:

             D1   Vernon MacLeod, was married and moved to Connecticut, where he was an insurance agent. He had two children.

             D2   Ada MacLeod, m. Mr. Robie, with one child.

         C2   Emma MacLeod, born 1834, m. William Burhoe, moved to Boston, where she raised her family of four:

             D1   Docia Burhoe, never married.

             D2   Margaret Burhoe, never married.

             D3   Stella Burhoe, m. Francis Price, with issue:

                 E1   William Price, married.

             D4   William Burhoe, married with one child.

         C3   Ben MacLeod, 1846-1931, m. 1) Mrs. Clay (nee Saville). They had one child:

             D1   Edgar MacLeod, never married.

         Ben worked at various occupations some of which were in Massachusetts, after marrying 2) Miss MacNeill, he moved to Crapaud.

         C4   John MacLeod, 1848-1937, m. Christy MacLeod, a sister of Neil MacLeod, a Summerside lawyer. John and Christy's issue were:

             D1   Otis MacLeod, 1890-1965, m. Evelyn MacLeod, 1898-1946. Otis was a successful farmer on the old home of "Big Murdoch," with issue:

                 E1   Christene MacLeod, school teacher, never married.

                 E2   Dorothy MacLeod, m. Bill Ratz, with issue:

                     F1   Evelyn Ratz, m. Dave Curphy, with issue:

                         G1   Riley Curphy.

                         G2   Jacqueline Curphy.

                     F2   Susan Ratz, m. Stephen Goldman, with issue:

                         G1   Sarah Goldman.

F3   Elizabeth Ratz, m. Dave <u>MacKay</u>.
F4   Barbara Ratz.
E3 Audrey MacLeod, m. Stanley <u>MacNair</u>, with issue:
F1   Neil MacNair.
F2   Margot MacNair, R.N., m. Jeff <u>Cooke</u>.
F3   Andrea MacNair.
E4 Shirley MacLeod, R.N., m. Charles <u>Leighton</u>, with issue:
F1   Robin Leighton, m. James <u>MacFadyen</u>, with issue:
G1   Leah Marie MacFadyen.
F2   John Leighton, m. Connie <u>Taggart</u>, with issue::
G1   Charles Leighton.
G2   Eric Leighton.
F3   Charles Leighton, m. Cathy <u>Wilder</u>.
F4   Peter Leighton, m. Sheila <u>Currie</u>.
E5 Norman MacLeod, never married.
E6 Arnold MacLeod, m. Louise <u>MacLeod</u>, R.N. Arnold farms the old farm after his father, grandfather and his great-grandfather, "Big Murdoch." Their issue:
F1   Jeannie MacLeod.
F2   Robert MacLeod, m. 1) Karen <u>Taylor</u>. m. 2) _____.

C5 Norman MacLeod, 1838-1880, m. Mary <u>Gillis</u>, 1831-1913. They moved to Strathcona. He worked in a shipyard, was killed in Maine, issue:
D1 Murdoch MacLeod, 1864-1945, carpenter, died in Bangor, Maine, never married.
D2 Hannah MacLeod, 1866-1962, m. Dr. Pearle <u>Copeland</u>, they lived in Boston, Massachusetts, with issue:
E1   Raymond Copeland, a dentist in Hyde Park, married.
E2   John Copeland, m. Eugenia T. <u>Copeland</u>, III, with issue:
F1   Eugenia T. Copeland, IV, m. 1) Albert H. <u>Porges</u>, 2) Paul W. <u>Bradshaw</u>, with issue:
G1   Scott L. C. Porges.
G2   Eugenia T. V Porges.
G3   Keith A. MacLeod Porges, married, with issue:
H1   Kyle A. Porges.
D3 Peter MacLeod, 1867-1952, was a prospector in British Columbia as well as other occupations, never married.
D4 Sam MacLeod, 1869-1951, carpenter and farmer in Strathcona, m. Annie <u>MacLeod</u>, 1865-1947, with issue:
E1   Lima MacLeod, forelady in Gillette's factory in Boston, Massachusetts, never married.
E2   Clarence MacLeod, worked in British Columbia, never married.
E3   Everett MacLeod, 1907-1962, m. Sarah <u>MacLeod</u>, 1921-1972. Everett farmed in Strathcona, with issue:
F1   Ernest MacLeod, m. Lynne <u>Britt</u>, with issue:
G1   Dawn MacLeod.
G2   Leah MacLeod.
F2   Charlotte MacLeod, m. Hans <u>Wisner</u>, with issue:
G1   Raquel Wisner.
G2   Kimberly Wisner.
F3   Raymond MacLeod, m. Ann <u>Madigan</u>, with issue:

G1 Colin MacLeod.

F4 Shirley MacLeod, m. Michael Kotspoals, with issue:
G1 Sarah Kotspoals.
G2 Michael Kotspoals.

F5 Phyllis MacLeod, m. Dennis Williams, with issue:
G1 Roderick Williams.
G2 Tara Williams.

F6 Claude MacLeod, 1946-1981, never married.

F7 Scott MacLeod, m. Rose Troken, with issue:
G1 Rose MacLeod.
G2 Eric MacLeod.

F8 Robert MacLeod, 1953-1974, killed in motor vehicle accident, never married.

D5 Malcolm MacLeod, 1871-1951, m. Catherine Hume, 1875-1972. He was a carpenter and farmer in Strathcona, with issue:

E1 Euphemia MacLeod, born in 1904, m. Lewis Rowland. Teacher in Florida.

E2 Katherine MacLeod, 1906-1971, m. Bill Hughes. She was a nurse in the U.S.A. and died in Florida.

E3 David MacLeod, 1907-1984, m. Pearle White. He served in WWII with American Forces, worked in Pasco fruit plant, buried in Florida.

E4 Elva MacLeod, m. George Mellish, farmer near Montague. Elva was teacher and good community worker.

E5 Norman MacLeod, m. Myrtle MacKenzie. Norman was a teacher and Vice-Principal at Queen Charlotte High School, with issue:
F1 Kathryn MacLeod, m. Boyd White, with issue:
G1 Paul White, m. Eileen Dingwell, with issue:
H1 Stacey White.
G2 Dawn White, m. John MacDonald, with issue:
H1 Melissa MacDonald.
H2 John Richard MacDonald.
G3 Scott White.
F2 Arnold MacLeod, m. Marilyn MacKenzie, with issue:
G1 Tracy MacLeod.
G2 Nancy MacLeod.
G3 Jeff MacLeod.

E6 John MacLeod, m. Nora Jackson, living in Strathcona.

D6 Margaret Jane MacLeod, 1873-1943, m. John MacDonald, died in Massachusetts, buried in Orwell Head, with issue:

E1 Millie MacDonald 1902-1983, nursed in Boston, never married.

E2 Addie MacDonald,1902-1983, nursed in Boston, never married.

E3 Alan MacDonald, 1903-1970, construction worker in Boston, never married.

E4 Pearle MacDonald, beautician in Boston, unmarried.

E5 Mary MacDonald, m. Carl Hiltz, lives in Malden, Massachusetts, with issue:
F1 Alan Hiltz.

C6 Murdoch MacLeod, 1832-1924, m. Miss <u>Currie</u>, with issue:
  D1 George MacLeod.
C7 Samuel MacLeod, 1844-1913, m. 1) Fannie <u>Joyce</u>, m. 2) _____.
    Samuel was a contractor in Omaha. He built the First National Bank
    in Omaha, Nebraska.
C8 Susan MacLeod, 1856-1954, m. Alex <u>Campbell</u>, 1858-1931, with issue:
  D1 Rita Campbell, born 1899, died of scarlet fever, never married.
  D2 Alma Campbell, 1896-1975, nursed in Boston, never married.
  D3 Donald Campbell, m. Mae <u>MacLeod</u>. Donald is a retired busi-
    nessman. Their issue:
    E1 Norman Campbell, 1940-1942.
    E2 Phyllis Campbell, m. John <u>Bernard</u>.
C9 Elizabeth MacLeod, 1834-1834, a twin sister of Susan. [Dates wrong?]
C10 William MacLeod, 1842-1938, m. Sarah <u>MacLeod</u>, 1843-1913. Sarah
    was the daughter of Rev. Sam MacLeod. William and Sarah's descen-
    dants are listed under A1, B1, C5.
C11 Mary Ann MacLeod, 1850-1930, m. Josiah <u>McVean</u>, 1845-1918. Josiah
    was a sea captain, they had issue:
  D1 Ethel McVean, never married.
  D2 Nettie McVean, 1883-1975, m. George <u>Beck</u>, with issue:
    E1 Robert Beck, m. Betty _____. Robert operated a shoe store.
    E2 Kenneth Beck, m. Eileen <u>Walker</u>. Kenneth was a salesman,
      with issue:
      F1 George Beck, m. Beth _____, with issue:
        G1 Kenneth Beck.
        G2 Holly Beck.
      F2 Marion Beck, m. Joe <u>Larabee</u>, with issue:
        G1 Melissa Larabee.
  D3 Harry McVean, m. Jean <u>Thompson</u>. Harry was a railroad con-
    ductor, with issue:
    E1 Harry McVean, m. Catherine <u>Stephenson</u>.
    E2 Betty McVean, m. 1) Hubert <u>Evans</u>, with issue:
      F1 Vallie Jean Evans, teacher, m. Clark <u>Bond</u>, school prin-
        cipal, with issue:
        G1 Gregg Bond.
        G2 Lisa Bond.
        G3 Amy Bond, m. Richard <u>Gibson</u>, with issue:
          H1 Brandon Gibson.
      F2 Bruce Evans, teacher and operations man-
        ager, Disney World, m. Alnetta <u>Hammond</u>,
        with issue:
        G1 Scott Evans.
      F3 Richard Evans, manager of Radio City Music Hall, m.
        Carla _____, with issue:
        G1 Eric Evans.
        G2 Jamie Evans.
    Betty m. 2) K. C. <u>Roberts</u>.
C12 Hughie Henry MacLeod, born 1838, died young.
C13 Robert MacLeod, 1839-1924, salesman, never married.
C14 Neil MacLeod, 1862-1917, moved to Minnesota, m. 1) _____, no issue,
    m. 2) Carry Seward <u>Young</u>, with issue:

D1 Jessie MacLeod, m. Arthur <u>Pratt</u>, they lived in Winchester, Massachusetts, with four children.
   E1 David Pratt, m. Cheryl ____, moved to Canandaiqua, New York, with issue:
      F1 Daniel Pratt.
      F2 Steven Pratt.
      F3 Gretchen Pratt.
   E2 Dorothy Pratt, m. Ralph M. <u>Packer</u>, they live in Vineyard Haven, Massachusetts, with issue:
      F1 John Russell Packer.
      F2 Elizabeth Morgan Packer.
      F3 Deborah Packer.
   E3 Marion Pratt.
   E4 John Pratt, m. Margery <u>Houlihan</u>, they live in Rockport, Maine, with issue:
      F1 Michelle Pratt.
D2 Donald MacLeod, m. 1) Dorothy <u>Quirk</u>, m. 2) Dorothy <u>Congdon</u>, m. 3) Louise <u>Congdon</u>, with issue from first wife:
   E1 John MacLeod.
D3 Neil Roderick MacLeod, Jr., 1904-1953, moved to Phoenix, m. Mary Louise <u>Bonthron</u>, with issue:
   E1 Carrie-Lou MacLeod, m. 1) ____ <u>Weir</u>, with issue:
      F1 Teodora Weir.
      Carrie-Lou m. 2) John <u>Howson</u>, Hyde Park, New York.
      F2 Charlotte Howson.
      F3 Susan Howson.
   E2 William MacLeod, m. Jean ____, moved to New Brunswick, with issue:
      F1 Adrianne MacLeod.
      F2 John T. MacLeod.
      F3 Kim Louise MacLeod.
      F4 Neil Roderick MacLeod.
B8 Neil MacLeod, m. Margaret <u>Vaniderstine</u>, with issue:
   C1 Norman MacLeod, m. Sarah <u>Glover</u>, with issue:
      D1 Neil MacLeod, died young.
      D2 Elsie MacLeod, never married.
      D3 Belle MacLeod, never married.
      D4 Mamie MacLeod, m. Ed <u>Saunders</u>, operated a meat market in Charlottetown, with issue:
         E1 Douglas Saunders, WWII, m. Pauline <u>Todd</u>, he was City Fire Marshall in Charlottetown, with issue:
            F1 Karen Saunders.
            F2 Sandra Saunders.
            F3 Roslyn Saunders.
            F4 Sarah Saunders.
            F5 Todd Saunders.
         E2 Norman Saunders, WWII, m. Florence <u>Baker</u>, with issue:
            F1 Catherine Saunders, m. Randy <u>Cook</u>, with issue:
               G1 Kevin Cook.
               G2 Danielle Cook.
         E3 Jack Saunders, WWII, manager Woolworth's in Sidney,

Nova Scotia, m. Joy Armstrong, with issue:

F1 Heather Saunders, m. Jim Eisenhower.

F2 John Saunders.

F3 Barry Saunders.

F4 Geoffrey Saunders.

F5 Mark Saunders.

F6 David Saunders.

F7 June Saunders.

F8 James Saunders.

E4 Heath Saunders, B.Sc., WWII, official with Quaker Oats, Saskatoon, m. Margaret Reeh.

C2 Peter MacLeod, called "Peter the Grit," m. Sophia Conrad, 1844-1928. Blacksmith, moved to Lorne Valley from Vernon River. They had a family of nine:

D1 Norman MacLeod, 1870-1930, operated the Dufferin House in St. John, New Brunswick, m. Ada MacKinnon, with issue:

E1 Violet MacLeod, never married.

E2 Roy MacLeod, m. 1) Anne Fraser, 2) Jean Crozier, nine children.

E3 Floyd MacLeod, never married.

E4 Valeda MacLeod, m. Stanley Meisner, with issue:

F1 Gloria Meisner, m. Arnold Coons, with issue:

G1 Arnold Coons, m. Maxine McNeely, with issue:

H1 Debbie Coons.

H2 Darla Coons.

H3 Twyla Coons.

G2 Robert Coons, m. Helen Popousek, with issue:

H1 Dallas Coons.

H2 Trevor Coons.

G3 Dennis Coons, m. Sharon Barrard, with issue:

H1 Jordon Coons.

H2 Michael Coons.

F2 Shirley Meisner, m. with three children.

E5 Winnifred MacLeod, m. Mr. Clark, with issue:

F1 Cynthia Clark, never married.

F2 _____.

F3 _____.

E6 Beryl MacLeod, R.N., m. Mr. Gooley, with issue:

F1 Grant Gooley.

F2 Craig Gooley.

F3 Glen Gooley.

E7 Olive MacLeod, died young.

E8 Leona MacLeod, never married.

D2 Margaret MacLeod, 1873-1962, m. Tom Conroy, with issue:

E1 Clarence Conroy, m. Ann Bowden, lived in U.S.A., issue:

F1 Helen Conroy, m. Francis Berry, U.S.A. with issue:

G1 Marjorie Berry, m. James Osgood, with issue:

H1 Erin Osgood.

G2 Scott Berry, m. Lauretta Wight, with issue:

H1 Jason Berry.

H2 Melody Berry.

G3   David Berry.

E2   Wilfred Conroy, m. 1) Florence <u>Griffin</u>, m. 2) Miss <u>Murdoch</u>, U.S.A., with issue:
  F1   Robert Conroy, m. Lois <u>Wannamaker</u>, with issue:
    G1   Leigh Conroy.
    G2   Marsha Conroy.

D3   Katherine MacLeod, born 1874, m. David <u>Massh</u>, lived in Philadelphia.

D4   Henry MacLeod, m. Belle <u>MacIntyre</u>, U.S.A, with issue:
  E1   Peter MacLeod, drowned at age 11.
  E2   Kenneth MacLeod, m. Barbara <u>Brown</u>, with issue:
    F1   Connie MacLeod.
    F2   Bonnie MacLeod.
    F3   Kenneth MacLeod.
  E3   Marcia MacLeod, m. Talbert <u>Currie</u>. They have a large family and live in West Virginia.

D5   Wesley MacLeod, m. Priscilla <u>Bambrick</u>, lived in Lorne Valley, with issue:
  E1   Charles MacLeod, m. Margaret <u>Douglas</u>, raised by Mabel MacLeod, with issue:
    F1   Gloria MacLeod, m. Sam _____.
    F2   Douglas MacLeod, m. _____.
    F3   _____.
    F4   _____.

D6   Matilda MacLeod, 1883-1963, m. Albert <u>Fennety</u>, with issue:
  E1   Edna Fennety, m. Raymond <u>Killegrew</u>, with issue:
    F1   Ann Killegrew, m. Ed <u>Hopkins</u>, with issue:
      G1   Cheryl Hopkins.
      G2   Edward Hopkins.
      G3   Mark Hopkins.
    F2   Barbara Killegrew, m. Joseph <u>Markel</u>.
    F3   Linda Killegrew, m. David <u>Turner</u>, with issue:
      G1   Jennifer Turner.
  E2   Dorothy Fennety, m. Harold <u>Jack</u>, live in Medford, Massachusetts.

D7   Bessie MacLeod, m. George <u>Fenwick</u>, Sussex, New Brunswick, with issue:
  E1   Elva Fenwick, m. Robert <u>Kinnear</u>, with issue:
    F1   Ritson Kinnear, m. Barbara <u>Fenwick</u>, Oromocto, New Brunswick, with issue:
      G1   Lacia Kinnear.
    F2   Elva Kinnear, m. Daniel <u>Powlenzuk</u>.
  E2   Vernon Fenwick, m. Martha <u>Wortman</u>, Sussex, New Brunswick, with issue:
    F1   George Fenwick, m. Debbie <u>Daigle</u>, with issue:
      G1   Jason Fenwick.
      G2   Angela Fenwick.
    F2   Barbara Fenwick, m. Ritson <u>Kinnear</u>.
    F3   Grace Fenwick m. Kent <u>Philpott</u>, with issue:
      G1   Roy Philpott.
    F4   Diane Fenwick, m. 1) Richard <u>Buchannan</u>, with issue:

G1   Crystal Buchannan.
Diane m. 2) Gordon <u>Coates</u>, with issue:
G2   Shane Coates.

F5   Katherine Fenwick, m. Bryant <u>O'Donnell</u>, with issue:
G1   Serrina O'Donnell.
G2   Leyan O'Donnell.
G3   Melissa O'Donnell.

F6   Avis Fenwick m. Leigh <u>Mullen</u>, live in New Brunswick, with issue:
G1   Stacey Mullen.

E3   Oscar Fenwick, m. 1) Marie <u>Graves</u>, no issue, m. 2) Iva <u>Fougere</u>. Iva was killed in car accident. Their issue:
F1   Joyce Fenwick, m. Rowland <u>Thorn</u>, with issue:
G1   Tania Thorn.
G2   Gina Thorn.

F2   Robert Fenwick, died young.

F3   Doreen Fenwick, m. John <u>Mason</u>, with issue:
G1   Joanne Mason.
G2   Cheryl Mason.
G3   Matthew Mason.

F4   Calvin Fenwick, m. Janet <u>Davis</u>, with issue:
G1   Wanda Fenwick.
G2   Rachel Fenwick.
G3   Rebecca Fenwick.
G4   Hannah Fenwick.
G5   Stephanie Fenwick.
G6   Ruth Fenwick.
G7   Jared Fenwick.

E4   Freda Fenwick, m. Vincent <u>Skely</u>, Kincardine, Ontario, with issue:
F1   Cheryl Skely, m. William <u>Subject</u>.
F2   Darrell Skely, m. Catherine <u>Vanderhout</u>.
G1   Jonathan Skely.
G2   Andrea Skely.
F3   Terry Skely, never married.

E5   Olive Fenwick, m. Peter <u>Dyker</u>, died in 1982, with issue:
F1   Gary Dyker, m. Janice <u>Whittard</u>, with issue:
G1   Melissa Dyker.
F2   Arnold Dyker, m. Barbara <u>Bradley</u>.
F3   Carolyn Dyker, m. Gary <u>Lane</u>, with issue:
G1   Geraldine Lane.
G2   Shawn Lane.

D8   Anna MacLeod, 1885-1968, m. Daniel <u>MacIntyre</u>, Peakes Road. Their children are:
E1   Bertha MacIntyre, m. Wilson <u>MacDonald</u>, with issue:
F1   Pearl MacDonald, m. Michael <u>McKenna</u>, with issue:
G1   David McKenna.
G2   Donna McKenna.
G3   Delight McKenna.
F2   Gordon MacDonald, m. 1) Frances <u>Chase</u>, m. 2) Verna <u>Smitanuik</u>, with issue:

> > > G1 Debbie MacDonald.
> > > G2 Stephen MacDonald.
> > > G3 Jody MacDonald.
> > F3 Kenneth MacDonald, m. Bonnie Publicover, issue:
> > > G1 Herbert MacDonald.
> > > G2 Timothy MacDonald.
> > F4 Stanley MacDonald, m. Carol MacDonald, with issue:
> > > G1 Alan MacDonald.
> > > G2 Dianna MacDonald.
> > F5 Carol MacDonald.
> E2 Isabella MacIntyre, m. Otis MacAssay, with issue:
> > F1 Mervyn MacAssay, m. Harold Blacquier, with issue:
> > > G1 Paula Blacquier.
> > > G2 Deborrah Blacquier.
> > > G3 Donna Blacquier.
> > F2 Judy MacAssay, m. Joe Cheverie, with issue:
> > > G1 Kimberly Cheverie, m. Fred VanDuikerken, with issue:
> > > > H1 Jennifer VanDuikerken.
> > > G2 Karrie Cheverie.
> > F3 Selvyn MacAssay, never married.
> E3 Wallace Allan MacIntyre, never married.
> D9 Mabel MacLeod, m. Murdoch MacDonald.

C3 Margaret MacLeod, died young.

C4 Neil MacLeod, died young.

C5 Annabelle MacLeod, went to Boston, lost contact.

C6 Katherine MacLeod, 1847-1921, m. John Jenkins, 1834-1921, with issue:

> D1 Margaret Elizabeth Jenkins, 1874-1935, m. 1) Milo French, with issue:
> > E1 Laura Catherine French, married in U.S.A. with at least two children.
>
> Margaret m. 2) Charles Frederick Walton.
>
> D2 Minnie Anna Gertrude Jenkins, 1879-1932, m. John Bradford Millman, 1870-1954. Their children are:
> > E1 Marion Orlo Millman.
> > E2 Anna Millman, m. Cyril Kennedy.
> > E3 Marie Millman, m. Ernest Westlake.
> > E4 Jean Millman, m. William Lawson.
> > E5 Joyce Millman, m. Harry Lapthorn.
>
> D3 Nellie Orlo Jenkins, 1882-1969, m. Frederick Dalrymple, issue:
> > E1 Henry John Dalrymple, married in U.S.A.
> > E2 Frederick Dalrymple, married in U.S.A.
>
> D4 Hilda Dobson Jenkins, m. Franklin Farrar Gould, 1878-1976, their children:
> > E1 John Thomas Gould, m. Dorothy Florence Wells.
> > E2 Louise Catherine Gould, m. Alden Howard Grant.
> > E3 Franklin Farrar Gould, m. 1) Marion Coe Wilcox, 2) Marion Steele.
> > E4 Kathryn MacLeod Gould, m. Andrew Thomas Ball.

C7 Mary MacLeod, m. Charles Sheido, issue:

D1   Herb Sheido, married in Boston.
D2   Margaret Sheido.
D3   Charles Sheido, m. Josephine <u>MacMillan</u>, with issue:
    E1   Leslie Sheido, m. _____ <u>Jenkins</u>, with issue:
        F1   Ralph Sheido.
    E2   Marie Sheido, m. Irving <u>Tweedy</u>, with issue:
        F1   Ann Tweedy.
        F2   George Tweedy.
    E3   Ralph Sheido, never married.
D4   Catherine Sheido, m. William <u>Redgeway</u>, live in Boston, issue:
    E1   Arthur Redgeway.
D5   Bessie Sheido, m. Henry <u>Vickerson</u>, Hermitage, with issue:
    E1   Charles Vickerson, never married.
    E2   Herb Vickerson, m. Catherine <u>MacPherson</u>, with two girls.
    E3   Harry Vickerson, never married.
D6   Norman Sheido, m. Martha <u>Wood</u>, with issue:
    E1   Evelyn Sheido, R.N., never married.
    E2   Myrtle Sheido, m. Gordon <u>MacKay</u>, with issue:
        F1   Harold MacKay, m. Jean <u>Stewart</u>, one boy and one girl.
        F2   Norman MacKay, m. Shirley <u>MacKay</u>.
        F3   Claude MacKay, m. Shirley _____, with two children.
    E3   Ella Sheido, died at age 18.
    E4   Mildred Sheido, m. Harry <u>Vaniderstine</u>, U.S.A., with issue:
        F1   Harry Vaniderstine.
        F2   Evelyn Vaniderstine.
    E5   Gordon Sheido, m. Florence <u>Smith</u>, with issue:
        F1   Norman Sheido, m. Ann <u>MacClaxey</u>, with issue:
            G1   Tom Sheido.
            G2   Jane Sheido.
        F2   Gail Sheido, m. Richard <u>Jenkins</u>, with issue:
            G1   Douglas Jenkins.
            G2   Randy Jenkins.
            G3   Richard Jenkins.
            G4   Susan Jenkins.
        F3   Douglas Sheido, m. Sandra <u>MacKenzie</u>, with issue:
            G1   Donald Sheido.
            G2   Jeffrey Sheido.
            G3   Joanne Sheido.
            G4   Laurie Sheido.
        F4   Russell Sheido, m. Patricia <u>Todare</u>, with issue:
            G1   Robert Sheido.
            G2   Richard Sheido.
            G3   Kathryn Sheido, m. Reuben <u>Roman</u>.
        F5   Annie Sheido, m. Cyril <u>Jones</u>, with issue:
            G1   Janet Jones.
            G2   Heather Jones.
            G3   Paulette Jones.
        F6   Kathryn Sheido, m. John <u>White</u>, with issue:
            G1   Karen White.
D7   Emerson Sheido, m. Margaret <u>MacIntyre</u>, with issue:
    E1   Harold Sheido.

      E2   Edison Sheido.

      E3   Ruth Sheido, m. Frank Huelin, with issue:
         F1   David Huelin.

 D8 George Sheido, m. Miss MacKenzie, no children.

 D9 Ernest Sheido, m. _____, with issue:
      E1   Margaret Sheido.
      E2   Edward Sheido.
      E3   Wilfred Sheido.
      E4   Harry Sheido.
      E5   Norman Sheido.
      E6   Ethel Sheido.

C8 Elizabeth MacLeod, 1850-1912, m. Thomas Furness, 1826-1917, issue:

 D1 Douce Furness, died at age 17 of ruptured appendix.

 D2 Arthur Furness, M.D., m. 1) Beryl Earle, who died early, m. 2) Lucy Toulon, a French professor at McGill, with issue:
      E1   Madeline Furness, m. Dr. Gallop, a teacher in Saskatchewan, with issue:
         F1   Michelle Gallop, m. Jane Jenkins.
      E2   Ann Marie Furness, a teacher in British Columbia, unmarried.

 D3 Alfred Newman Furness, m. Sadie Nicholson, who is a sister of Milton's wife, with issue:
      E1   Gwendolyn Furness, m. Morgan Clarke, with issue:
         F1   Marilyn Clarke, lived in Vancouver, m. _____, issue:
            G1 Robert.
            G2 Julie.
            G3 Sandra.
            G4 Keri, twin of Sandra.
      E2   Margaret Furness, m. Ross Ford, with issue:
         F1   Melva Ford, m. Marcelle Trucket, with issue:
            G1 Rory Trucket.
            G2 Bert Trucket. Rory and Bert are fifth cousins of Pierre Elliot Trudeau.
         F2   Velma Ford.
      E3   Leslie Furness, died 1984, m. Agnes Wharton, lived in Vancouver, with issue:
         F1   Robert Furness.
         F2   Stewart Furness.

 D4 Milton Furness, m. Annie Nicholson, Orwell, their children are:
      E1   Ruth Furness, m. 1) Murdoch MacLeod, with issue:
         F1   George MacLeod, m. Grace Campbell, with issue:
            G1 Clayton MacLeod, m. Joan Hughes.
            G2 Valerie MacLeod, m. Clifford Campbell, issue:
               H1   Shanda Campbell.
               H2   Crystal Campbell.
            G3 Susan MacLeod, m. Anthony MacQuillan, issue:
               H1   Anthony MacQuillan.
               H2   Michael MacQuillan.
         F2   Joan MacLeod, m. Jim Harrigan, Vancouver, issue:
            G1 Geoffrey Harrigan.
            G2 Shelly Harrigan, student, was selected to go to China for further studies.

Ruth m. 2) Earl <u>Vaniderstine</u>.

E2   Dorothy Furness, m. Bernard <u>Tebeau</u>, with issue:

    F1   Frances Tebeau, m. George <u>Bean</u>, with issue:

        G1   George Bean.

        G2   Steven Bean.

    F2   Rosemary Tebeau, m. 1) John <u>MacLean</u>, with issue:

        G1   Gail MacLean, m. David <u>Shaw</u>, with issue:

            H1   John Shaw.

            H2   David Shaw, married, with issue:

                I1   Michael Shaw.

            H3   Sarah Shaw.

        Rosemary m. 2) Fred <u>Eaton</u>, with issue:

        G2   Debbie Eaton.

    F3   Kenneth Tebeau, married, with issue:

        G1   Michelle Tebeau.

        G2   Kenneth Tebeau.

        G3   Wayne Tebeau.

        G4   Jeannie Tebeau.

    F4   Richard Tebeau, m. 1) Lauretta, 2) Ann, with issue:

        G1   Scott Tebeau.

        G2   Wendy Tebeau, married.

        G3   Richard Tebeau.

        G4   Kenneth Tebeau.

        G5   Eric Tebeau.

        G6   Sean Tebeau.

        G7   Elizabeth Tebeau.

    F5   Carolyn Tebeau, with issue:

        G1   Susan.

    F6   Robert Tebeau.

    F7   Dorothy Tebeau, m. Roger <u>Jenness</u>, with issue:

        G1   Todd Jenness.

        G2   Robert Jenness.

        G3   David Jenness.

        G4   Joey Jenness.

    F8   Margaret Tebeau.

    F9   Nancy Tebeau, with issue:

        G1   Jamey.

        G2   Michael.

E3   Fred Furness, m. Alice <u>Wilson</u>, Vernon, their children are:

    F1   Elwood Furness, deceased.

    F2   Shirley Furness, m. Carl <u>Wilson</u>, with issue:

        G1   James Wilson.

        G2   Cindy Wilson.

        G3   Michael Wilson.

    F3   Milton Furness.

    F4   Margaret Furness, m. David <u>MacLeod</u>.

    F5   Douglas Furness.

    F6   Marlene Furness.

    F7   Sharon Furness, m. Ben <u>Vos</u>, with issue:

        G1   Christine Vos.

        G2   Shelley Vos.

F8   Arthur Furness, m. Sheila <u>Cronin</u>, with issue:
    G1   Jonathon Furness.
    G2   Jason Furness.
    G3   Janelle Furness.
    G4   Jana Furness.

E4   Beryl Furness, m. H. P. <u>Stewart</u>, M.D, with issue:
    F1   Bobby Stewart, NHL hockey player, m. Rhonda <u>New-land</u>, St. Louis, Missouri, with issue:
        G1   Melissa Stewart.
        G2   Scott Stewart.
    F2   Beryl Stewart, R.N., m. Alan <u>Chandler</u>, with issue:
        G1   Gregory Chandler.
        G2   Robert Stuart Chandler.
        G3   Jonathon Chandler, died young.
    F3   Joyce Stewart, m. Rick <u>Vaive</u>, NHL player, Captain with Toronto Maple Leafs, with issue:
        G1   Jeffrey Vaive.
    F4   Gordon Stewart, student in San Diego.

E5   Anne Furness, m. 1) Vernon <u>Coles</u>, with issue:
    F1   Marilyn Coles, m. Robert <u>Irons</u>, Indiana, with issue:
        G1   Kevin Irons.
        G2   Danielle Irons.
    F2   Garry Coles, m. Dale _____, with issue:
        G1   Joanne Coles.
        G2   Luke Coles.
    F3   Wayne Coles, m. Gale _____, with issue:
        G1   Ryan Coles.
        G2   Jocelyn Coles.
   Anne, m. 2) Carl <u>Stewart</u>, living in California, with issue.
        G3   Carl Stewart, works in Mexico.

E6   Phyllis Furness, m. Roy <u>Peters</u>, California, with issue:
    F1   Leslie Peters, m. Kellie ____, with issue:
        G1   Crystal Peters.
        G2   Leslie Peters.

THE UIGG SCHOOLHOUSE
ARTICLE FROM *THE PATRIOT* DESCRIBING THE UIGG SCHOOL

We referred to this matter before. The schoolhouse is now finished. It is forty-five feet long and twenty-four broad—in fact the best country schoolhouse on the Island. The ceiling of the main room is twelve feet high, and there is a classroom attached which is eighteen by fifteen. In the second story is a hall with an arched ceiling, capable of holding four hundred people. It has also a platform for speakers, and is intended to be provided with settees for the auditors. The building reflects credit upon the contractor, Peter Martin, Esq., as well as on James McLeod, Esq., the Inspector. The teachers are at present D. McLeod and Miss McPhail.

This building is worthy of the educational reputation of Uigg. Point Prim has given us many successful sea captains, and this settlement occupies a first place for scholars and professional men. Among the latter may be mentioned Drs. Martin, Angus McLeod and James McLeod (now of this city); Malcolm McLeod, barrister, who is one of the leading minds of the bar; Neil McLeod, also fast on the way to winning a high place; and Duncan McLeod, a gold medalist of McGill University and also in the legal profession. To this fine array of educational talent we have the pleasure of adding Donald Ross, the winner of the Gilcrest Scholarship, and Alexander Nicholson, one of the first classical students at the old academy and the Prince of Wales College (and the son of Capt. MacLeod of the Gulnare) who is preparing to graduate at McGill.

Uigg has also given us the Revs. John Ross, J. B. MacDonald, D. G. MacDonald and John Gordon. To the teaching staff of the Island it has also given many members. To the settlement itself, and to its clever sons, may this schoolhouse be a creditable and useful monument and one upon which the people may be congratulated. To other districts we would say, "go and do likewise."

The Patriot, November 3, 1877

MURDOCH MACLEOD
MURDOCH MACLEOD AND WIFE OF UIGG

A2   Murdoch MacLeod, son of Neil MacLeod and Sophia Nicholson, came from Skye to Prince Edward Island in 1829 on the ship *Mary Kennedy*. Murdoch's family were:

B1   Roderick MacLeod, m. Flora MacDonald, with issue:

C1   Christine MacLeod, m. John MacLeod, Uigg, with issue:

D1   Otis MacLeod, his descendants are given under Norman, A1.

C2   Neil MacLeod, m. Belle Hayden. Neil was judge, lawyer and Premier of Prince Edward Island. His children were:

D1   Adele MacLeod, a teacher, never married.

D2   Marie MacLeod, m. Dr. MacKenzie, lived in British Columbia.

D3   Mary MacLeod, lived in British Columbia.

D4   A girl, mysteriously disappeared.

C3   Annie MacLeod, m. Norman MacDonald, with issue:

D1   Eugene MacDonald, m. Tilly MacLean, with issue:

E1   Roderick MacDonald, married with two children.

E2   James MacDonald, m. Elizabeth MacMillan, no issue.

E3   Maynard MacDonald, m. Neil Westaway.

E4   Ola MacDonald, never married.

C4   Margaret MacLeod, m. Rev. B. G. MacDonald, with issue:

D1   Mary MacDonald, m. _____ Avis, with issue:

E1   Margaret Avis, m. T. M. Rutherford, issue:

F1   Gordon Rutherford, married.

F2   Margaret Ann Rutherford, never married.

F3   Ina Mary Rutherford, teacher, never married.

F4   Elizabeth Rutherford, married.

C5   Belle MacLeod, m. George Rourke, with issue:

D1   Mima Rourke, m. Ham Myers.

C6   Priscilla MacLeod, m. William MacMillan, with issue:

D1   Gordon MacMillan, never married.

D2   Elizabeth MacMillan, teacher, never married.

D3   Norman MacMillan, m. Louise Bears, with issue:

E1   Gordon MacMillan (adopted), m. Dianne Perry, with issue:

F1   Cary MacMillan.

F2   Sarah MacMillan.

E2   Sandra MacMillan (adopted), m. Dennis Jamieson, issue:

F1   Tony Jamieson.

F2   Christopher Jamieson.

F3   Mitchell Jamieson.

C7   Murdoch E. MacLeod, m. 1) Elizabeth MacKinnon, with issue:

D1   Priscilla MacLeod, never married.

D2   Florence MacLeod, never married.

D3   William MacLeod, never married.

Murdoch E. m. 2) Georgie MacEachern, with issue::

D4   Edison MacLeod, m. Woodroe Tucker, live in Brookline, Massachusetts.

C8   John S. MacLeod, m. Sarah <u>MacLean</u>, with issue:
    D1   John MacLeod, m. Belle <u>Love</u>, with issue:
        E1   Jean MacLeod (adopted), m. Nelson <u>Morrison</u>, with issue:
            F1   Mark Morrison.
C9   Katie MacLeod, m. Dan <u>MacKinley</u>, with issue:
    D1   William MacKinley, a banker in U.S.A.
    D2   Albert MacKinley, a teacher.
    D3   Lois MacKinley, teacher, married.
C10 Sophia MacLeod, m. Fred <u>Vickerson</u>, Hermitage, with issue:
    D1   George Vickerson, never married.
    D2   Florence Vickerson, teacher, never married.
    D3   Marion Vickerson, R.N., m. David <u>Wright</u>, with issue:
        E1   George Wright, m. Velma <u>Wood</u>, with issue:
            F1   Debbie Wright, married.
            F2   Carol Wright, married.
            F3   Shirley Wright.
            F4   Valena Wright.
        E2   Helen Wright, m. Jack <u>Chambers</u>, with issue:
            F1   David Chambers.
            F2   Jacqueline Chambers.
            F3   Robert Chambers.
    D4   Neil MacLeod, married, went to Bolivia as a missionary and died there.
C11 Mary MacLeod, died young.
B2   Norman M. MacLeod, m. Miss <u>MacLean</u>, a grocer in Charlottetown with J. D. MacLeod, with issue:
    C1   Mary MacLeod, a musician, m. Dr. <u>MacDonald</u>, Calgary
    C2   Marion MacLeod, m. Dr. G. F. <u>Dewar</u>, Charlottetown, with issue:
        D1   Lloyd Dewar.
    C3   Maud MacLeod, m. Dr. Stewart <u>Carruthers</u>.
    C4   Catherine MacLeod, Charlottetown.
    C5   Murdoch MacLeod.
    C6   Sidney MacLeod, lived in Alberta.
    C7   Milton MacLeod, lived in Alberta.
B3   James MacLeod, never married, went to Australia, returned, died in Charlottetown, buried in Uigg.
B4   Ewen MacLeod, never married.
B5   Neil MacLeod, never married.
B6   Christine MacLeod, m. Malcolm <u>Gillis</u>, with issue:
    C1   Neil Gillis, buried in Belfast, m. Helen <u>Finlayson</u>, with issue:
        D1   John Gillis, married and moved to U.S.A.
        D2   James Gillis, m. Catherine, an Englishwoman, with issue:
            E1   Edna Gillis.
            E2   Irma Gillis.
            E3   Victor Gillis.
            E4   Douglas Gillis.
            E5   Billy Gillis.
        D3   Lewis Gillis, m. Mary, an Englishwoman, with issue:
            E1   Neil Gillis, and several others.
        D4   Kate Gillis, m. Hector <u>MacDonald</u>, with issue:
            E1   John MacDonald.

E2   Wesley MacDonald.
E3   Russell MacDonald.
E4   Helen MacDonald.
E5   Catherine MacDonald.
E6   Marion MacDonald.
D5   Christy Gillis, m. Malcolm Gillis, with issue:
E1   Douglas Gillis.
E2   Harold Gillis.
E3   Florence Gillis.
E4   Dorothy Gillis.
D6   Alex Gillis, moved to U.S.A., was married.
D7   Margaret Gillis, m. Mr. Young, had no family.
C2   Margaret Gillis, lived in U.S.A.
C3   Kate Gillis, m. Neil MacKenzie, worked on C.N.R. out of Charlotte-town, with issue:
D1   Ella MacKenzie, m. John Donald Martin, with issue:
E1   Harold Martin, never married.
E2   Marion Martin, m. Harold MacKie, with issue:
F1   Douglas Mackie, m. Jean Judson, with issue:
G1   David Harold Mackie.
F2   _____.
E3   Muriel Martin, m. Willard MacLeod, with issue:
F1   Donald MacLeod, m. Lorna MacDonald, with issue:
G1   Jeffrey MacLeod.
G2   Andrew MacLeod.
G3   Timothy MacLeod.
G4   John MacLeod.
F2   Elva MacLeod, m. Donald Nicholson, with issue:
G1   Gordon Nicholson.
G2   Douglas Nicholson.
G3   Leigh Nicholson.
F3   Keith MacLeod, m. Katherine Brehaut, with issue:
G1   Richard MacLeod.
G2   Janice MacLeod.
F4   Bobby MacLeod, m. Sally Stewart, with issue:
G1   Randy MacLeod.
G2   Robin MacLeod.
G3   Nancy MacLeod.
F5   Eleanor MacLeod, m. Munroe Wheeler, with issue:
G1   Susan Wheeler, m. Mac Dixon, with issue:
H1   John Dixon.
H2   Melinda Dixon.
G2   Stephen Wheeler.
G3   Wendy Wheeler.
G4   Paul Wheeler.
G5   Leslie Wheeler.
F6   Walton MacLeod, m. Heather Gillis, with issue:
G1   Gwendolyn MacLeod.
G2   Kevin MacLeod.
E4   Sam Martin, m. Mary Bozan, with issue:
F1   Brenda Martin, m. Bill Irwin, with issue:

G1 Jackie Irwin.
G2 Billy-Joe Irwin.
G3 Travis Irwin.
G4 Bobby-Sue Irwin.
G5 Jason Irwin.
G6 Adam Irwin.
F2 Ronald Martin, m. Wanda <u>Smith</u>, with issue:
G1 Julie Martin.
G2 Erin Martin.
E5 Lloyd Martin, m. Daisy <u>Alley</u>.
C4 Kate Gillis, not married. (There were two Kates in the family.)
C5 Flora Gillis, m. Donald Hector <u>MacDonald</u>, Grandview, with issue:
D1 Flora MacDonald.
D2 Annie MacDonald.
D3 Christine MacDonald.
D4 Malcolm MacDonald, m. Catherine <u>Gillis</u>, with issue:
E1 Lloyd MacDonald, m. Jean <u>MacPhee</u>, with issue:
F1 David MacDonald.
D5 Alexander MacDonald.
D6 Dolly MacDonald.

James MacLeod
James MacLeod and Mary MacKinnon of Uigg

A3   James MacLeod (brother of Old Norman), born in Skye, emigrated in 1829. Lived in Uigg, m. Mary <u>MacKinnon</u>. Buried in Uigg. All the family were six feet feet tall or more. Their children were:

     B1   James MacLeod.
     B2   Roderick MacLeod.
     B3   Alex MacLeod.
     B4   Christy MacLeod.
     B5   Mary MacLeod.
     B6   A girl.

This family were known as the MacHamish MacLeods.

Information received from Norman MacLeod, Charlottetown.

Donald MacLeod
Donald MacLeod and Mary Buchanan of Surrey

A1   Donald MacLeod, died March 28, 1907, age 92, m. Mary Buchanan, died Sept. 7, 1907, age 90. This information was found in the cemetery transcripts at Beaconsfield. They were both born in P.E.I. They had issue:

B1   Donald MacLeod, born Jan. 6, 1845, in Glashvin and baptized April 18, 1847, at Belfast Church.

B2   Murdoch MacLeod, born May 8, 1846, in Glashvin and baptized April 25, 1847, at Belfast Church.

B3   Jennet MacLeod (Jessie), 1848-1889. She was baptized Sept. 18, 1849, at Belfast Church. She married John MacLeod. He was the son of Donald MacLeod and Betsy MacLeod. He was born Aug. 14, 1834, and died 1922, baptized March 10, 1837. His nickname was "Little John." They had issue:

C1   John MacLeod, 1881-1938. Baptized Dec. 22, 1888. He married Mae Nicholson, who was born in 1881 in Surrey and died in 1967. John was a captain on the C.N. ferries out of Borden. They had issue:

D1   Everett Angus MacLeod, born in Borden, married twice. He had two sons from his first marriage:

E1   John MacLeod, living in Toronto.

E2   Colin MacLeod, living in Toronto.

Everett lived in Ontario for a number of years working for Shell. He returned to the Island with his second wife Denise Greenfield, formerly from Wales. They had a tourist home in Alliston for a number of years before moving to Montague.

D2   Jessie MacLeod, m. Mr. MacMillan, with issue:

E1   John MacMillan.

E2   Mark MacMillan.

E3   Scott MacMillan.

C2   George MacLeod, baptized Dec. 20, 1888. He married John's wife's sister, Katie Nicholson. They lived in Bridgewater, Nova Scotia.

C3   Angus MacLeod, baptized Dec. 20, 1888, not sure of birth date. He was a sailor, single.

C4   Mary MacLeod, m. Mr. Manchester, moved to the U.S.A., one son.

C5   Bessie MacLeod, baptized Dec. 20, 1888, m. Murril Peel, in British Columbia.

B4   Mary MacLeod, born May 20, 1850.

B5   Betsy MacLeod, born July 4, 1853, baptized Sept. 10, 1854.

B6   Rev. John MacLeod, 1856-1900, attended Queens College, Kingston, Ontario, graduated in Arts in 1883 and in Theology in 1886. He ministered in New York State, the Province of Quebec, and in 1892 he was called to Vankleek Hill, Ontario, where he lost his life when the end wall of the new stone church, then under construction, fell out, killing him and two workmen. He is buried in Gould, Quebec, was married to Melvina Ross from the Quebec Eastern Townships, with issue:

C1   J. Ross MacLeod, died in 1944, m. Wilhelmina Black from Huntington, Quebec, with issue:

D1   John William MacLeod, m. Joan Baxter from Toronto, living in Ottawa. Their children are:

        E1   John Ross MacLeod, Toronto.

        E2   Kenneth Haydn MacLeod, m. Madeline <u>DeWolfe</u>. They live in Fredericton, New Brunswick.

        E3   Margot MacLeod, m. Joel <u>Comeau</u>, with issue:

            F1   Justin John Comeau.

  C2 George MacLeod, at one time President of Algoma Oil Properties, died at Sault St. Marie, was married to Jessie _____, with issue:

        D1   Lucy Jean MacLeod, m. _____ <u>Johnson</u>, with issue:

            E1   A daughter.

        D2   Jessie Marion MacLeod, m. _____.

        D3   Heather MacLeod.

        D4   A son, died at birth.

  C3 Jean MacLeod, died in 1940, age 35, of a heart condition, m. Emile <u>Lods</u>, who taught at MacDonald College, Quebec. The E. A. Lods Building at the College was named after him. They had issue:

        D1   Margot Lods, living in Toronto.

B7   George MacLeod, born June 4, 1857, died May 13, 1883, age 26.

Information provided by Everett MacLeod, Montague, John W. MacLeod, Ottawa, and from research at Beaconsfield and P.E.I. Archives.

John MacLeod
John MacLeod and Margaret Scott of Colville Station and Charlottetown Royalty

A   John MacLeod, 1852-1931, son of John MacLeod from Skye, his mother's name unknown, m. Margaret Elizabeth <u>Scott</u>, 1859-1928. It is believed that her father was Rev. John Scott and her mother's maiden name was MacBeth. John and Margaret are buried in the Charlottetown People's Cemetery. John owned a farm at Colville Station, 10-12 miles northwest of Charlottetown. The farm was willed to David. John moved to Charlottetown and was a tailor and respected businessman there. He had a firm, known as *John MacLeod—Merchant Tailor* at 7 Euston Street. John and Margaret's children were:

B1   Winnifred G. MacLeod, born 1880, died April 6, 1936.

B2   Carlyle Sillars MacLeod, born 1881, died April 22, 1931.

B3   Jean W. MacLeod, born 1884, m. Will <u>Dalziel</u>, with issue:
    C1   J. W. Scott Dalziel, died 1977, m. Jean _____, with issue:
        D1   Margaret Dalziel.
        D2   Barbara Dalziel.
        D3   Katherine Dalziel.
    C2   Norman Dalziel.
    C3   Marnie Dalziel.

B4   Clair S. MacLeod, born 1888, died March 9, 1970.

B5   John Russell MacLeod, 1889-1950, m. Nancy <u>Strachan</u>, with issue:
    C1   Margaret Beverly MacLeod, m. Donald Clair <u>Beggs</u>, with issue:
        D1   Donna Laurie Beggs, m. James <u>Meier</u>, with issue:
            E1   Erin Leslie Meier.
            E2   Jeffrey James Meier.
        D2   Lorraine Margaret Beggs.
    C2   Winnifred Norma MacLeod, m. Denis P. <u>Boyle</u>, with issue:
        D1   Maureen Jane Boyle, m. Lorne <u>Walters</u>, with issue:
            E1   Jeremy Walters.
        D2   Jeffrey Brian Boyle, m. Sandie <u>Schmidt</u>, with issue:
            E1   Ryan Boyle.
        D3   Joanne Boyle.
    C3   John Keith MacLeod, m. June Lynne <u>Wolf</u>, with issue:
        D1   Lynne MacLeod.

B6   Arthur G. MacLeod, 1892-1954, m. Annie K. <u>MacLeod</u>, 1892-1953, issue:
    C1   Arthur Kelvin MacLeod, m. Beatrice M. <u>Cooke</u>, with issue:
        D1   Anne Beatrice MacLeod, m. David E. <u>Park</u>, with issue:
            E1   Alan David Park.
            E2   Katherine Anne Park.

B7   Keith Hamilton Shaw MacLeod, 1895-1920.

B8   Kenneth MacLeod, born 1899.

B9   David Sutherland MacLeod , 1899-1972, twin of Kenneth. David inherited the family farm.

Information provided by Beverly Beggs of North Battleford, Saskatchewan.

ANGUS MACLEOD
ANGUS MACLEOD AND SARAH CAMPBELL OF MALPEQUE

A   Angus MacLeod, 1805-1883, m. Sarah <u>Campbell</u>, 1800-1865, with issue:

B1   Margaret MacLeod, m. John <u>Beaton</u>.

B2   Christina MacLeod, m. Ronald <u>MacPherson</u>.

B3   Catherine MacLeod, 1843-1928, m. Hugh <u>MacInnis</u>, 1837-1902.

B4   Angus Norman MacLeod, 1849-1940, m. Sarah <u>MacKinnon</u>. Angus was baptized on May 26, 1860, on Malpeque Road. Their children were:

    C1   Ruth Evelyn MacLeod, m. Millar <u>MacPherson</u>.

    C2   Norman George Millar MacLeod, 1900-1901.

    C3   Marion Louise MacLeod, m. Jack <u>Large</u>.

    C4   John Finley MacLeod, m. Margaret <u>Sutherland</u>.

    C5   Neil MacLeod, m. 1) Lorine <u>French</u>, m. 2) Mildred ____, with issue:

        D1   Enid MacLeod, m. Art <u>Chandler</u>.

        D2   Barbara Ann MacLeod, m. Trevor <u>Campbell</u>.

        D3   Flora May MacLeod, m. Kenneth <u>Thompson</u>.

        D4   Angus Norman MacLeod, m. Nora <u>Heel</u>, with issue:

           E1   Bateson MacLeod.

        D5   Gayle Jean MacLeod, m. Frank <u>Murphy</u>.

        D6   Neil Samuel MacLeod.

    C6   Angus Malcolm MacLeod, m. Hilda <u>Pidgeon</u>.

    C7   Annie MacLeod, m. E. <u>Stalder</u>.

    C8   Angus Syme MacLeod, born and died 1890.

    C9   Sarah Margaret MacLeod, m. Neil <u>Simpson</u>.

    C10 Catherine Isabell MacLeod, m. Harold <u>Rogers</u>.

    C11 Ella May MacLeod.

    C12 Alexanderina MacLeod, m. Carl <u>French</u>.

B5   John Campbell MacLeod, 1847-1914, m. Margaret <u>Brown</u>, 1867-1958, issue:

    C1   Sadie MacLeod, died an infant.

    C2   Violet MacLeod, died an infant.

    C3   Sarah Campbell MacLeod, died 1958.

    C4   Margaret Alice MacLeod, died 1960, m. _____ <u>Cameron</u>.

    C5   John Campbell MacLeod.

This information was taken from a 1973 Centennial Project.

Letter
Letter from Donald MacLeod to Mrs. D. MacLeod

The following letter is copied from the original, now in the possession of Lorne Ramsay of Hamilton, P.E.I. It would appear to refer to a family settled in the Malpeque area.

St. John's, July 17th, 1803

My Dearest,

I wrote you from Murray Harbour to my sailing from there, which place I left the 7th and arrived here the 14th. I am now getting the cargo discharged and expect to sail from this place in 14 days straight for Charlottetown then I expect to have the pleasure of seeing you at Fox Head. Mr. Cambridge has an intention of selling the brig here but I do not think she will sell as the war discourages people at present, so that I expect coming immediately back here from the Island with another cargo of sawed lumber and towards fall to go to England except Mr. Cambridge alter his plans—I did not know of his intention of selling the vessel until I came to Murray Harbour and indeed if she had been sold I did not consider it a disappointment as I believe I should have been still kept in her and perhaps a better employ than Mr. Cambridge's. However, I believe she will not sell this time. The bearer Mr. Townsend will deliver you something that I have sent by him as I thought it better sending them by him than myself, as he goes straight to Princetown. There is a gown piece for Mrs. Will Murry at Bedeque and another for yourself, you will see the distinction between them as they are marked one Donald for you and the other for Wm. Murry. There are several other small things for which you will receive—I have bought you a ring but not so good as I could wish as there was hardly any such thing to be got. That I have kept myself—I have sent a pair of half boots to wear in winter and a pair of Morocco slippers also a pair of pattons. You will see all the rest of things yourself. There is a _____ for your mother and some for yourself. Also some tea. I would have sent you some sugar also but it being so very dear at present so I shall defer it until the next time I come here then perhaps it may be cheaper. Likewise the bed curtains I meant to buy but I could not find any to my liking, besides as I expect, please God, going to England I mean to refer it til then. Give my love to all brothers and sisters and every other connection young and old. I hope the shoes and boots will fit you—also thimble, the gold ring I have taken along myself as I hope to have the pleasure of putting it on your finger myself.

I remain my dearest, yours,

Donald MacLeod

P.S. Have sent you besides a kiss by the bearer, Mr. Townsend. Hope you shall receive the same.

[Addressed to:] Per favour Mrs. D. MacLeod, Capt. Townsend, Prince Town.

John MacLeod
John MacLeod and Catherine MacKay of Head of Montague

A1 John MacLeod, died 1866, aged 61, m. Catherine MacKay, died 1903, aged 88. They emigrated from the Isle of Skye or Raasay in 1839, and settled in Head of Montague, next to the County Line. There are indications he may be a son of Duncan MacLeod, who was an uncle of John MacLeod, Wood Island Road. (See letter to his brother Donald of Raasay.) John and Catherine had issue:

B1 Mary MacLeod, 1838-1891, m. Fred MacDonald, died 1873, aged 54, who emigrated from Ross Shire, Scotland, in 1837, settling in Green Marsh. For their descendants see the MacDonald family history.

B2 Catherine MacLeod, 1844, lived in U.S.A.

B3 John MacLeod, 1849.

B4 Murdoch MacLeod, 1852-1874.

B5 Malcolm J. MacLeod, 1847-1902, m. Annabella MacKenzie, died 1930, aged 78, from Baddeck, Cape BretonThey took over the homestead, with issue:

    C1 John A. MacLeod, married in California, no family.

    C2 Annie MacLeod, born 1879, m. Mr. MacPhail, Cape Breton and U.S.A., with issue:

        D1 John MacPhail.

        D2 Betty MacPhail.

        D3 _____.

    C3 Kate MacLeod, m. Ralph Card, U.S.A., with issue:

        D1 Freeman Card.

        D2 Wendell Card.

    C4 Barbara MacLeod, m. Lloyd Graham, U.S.A., with issue:

        D1 Edna Graham.

        D2 A son.

    C5 Mary MacLeod, m. Joseph Claflin, U.S.A., with issue:

        D1 Patricia Claflin, m. Roger Boyle, U.S.A., with issue:

            E1 Steven Boyle.

            E2 Ralph Boyle.

    C6 Josephine MacLeod, m. Clarence Freeman, U.S.A.

    C7 Malcolm J. MacLeod, died 1887, aged 6 years.

    C8 Daniel MacLeod, died 1896, aged 18 months.

    C9 Murdoch R. MacLeod, 1883-1973, m. Katherine Jessie MacKinnon, 1886-1973, daughter of Charles MacKinnon, Heatherdale. They farmed on the homestead in Head of Montague, with issue:

        D1 Wendell MacLeod, died 1986, aged 71, m. Claire Turgeon, no family.

        D2 Malcolm MacLeod, m. Doris Turgeon, sister of Claire, no family.

        D3 Jeanette MacLeod, U.S.A. and Meadowbank, P.E.I.

        D4 John MacLeod, m. Verda Allen, living in Cape Tormentine, issue:

            E1 Darlene MacLeod, m. Richard Moss, with issue:

                F1 Heidi Moss.

                F2 Catherine Moss.

                F3 Meggan Moss.

            E2 Gregory MacLeod.

        D5 Murdo MacLeod, living in Massachusetts.

Information: cemetery stones, baptismal records, and Malcolm and Doris MacLeod.

ALLAN MACLEOD
ALLAN MACLEOD AND EFFIE MACLEOD OF DARLINGTON

A   Allan MacLeod, died 1888, aged 63, born in Skye, m. Effie MacLeod, died 1906, aged 72, also born in Skye, and lived in Darlington. Their family:

B1   Effie MacLeod, never married.

B2   Jessie MacLeod, m. Angus Campbell, they lived in Darlington, with issue:
- C1   Norman Campbell, not married, lived out West.
- C2   Eldon Campbell, m. Jane Lynd, lived in Charlottetown, with issue:
  - D1   Vernon Campbell.
  - D2   Eleanor Campbell.
- C3   Annie Campbell m. Vernon Burke, Charlottetown, with issue:
  - D1   Velma Burke.
  - D2   Elwood Burke.
  - D3   Leigh Burke.
- C4   Lillian Campbell, m. Gordon MacCallum, Summerside, with issue:
  - D1   Joyce MacCallum, m. _____ MacArthur, living in Western Canada with two children.
- C5   Evelyn Campbell, m. Wilbur Younker, Kingston.
- C6   Marion Campbell, m. Arthur Garrett, Charlottetown.
- C7   Neil Campbell, m. Alvina Easter, Darlington, with issue:
  - D1   Errol Campbell.
  - D2   Blair Campbell.
  - D3   Roger Campbell.
- C8   Earl Campbell, m. Peg MacLean, Charlottetown, with issue:
  - D1   Boyd Campbell.
- C9   John A. Campbell, married with a family.
- C10   Jean Campbell, m. Neil Matheson, Framingham, Massachusetts, issue:
  - D1   Eugene Matheson.
  - D2   Gerald Matheson.
- C11   Leonard Campbell, m. Daisy Burke, living in Moncton, with issue:
  - D1   June Campbell.

B3   Mary MacLeod, died 1929, aged 73, m. Finlay Matheson, died 1930, aged 78, they lived in Darlington, no family.

B4   Isabella MacLeod, m. Mack Cummings, Darlington, with issue:
- C1   John Cummings, never married.
- C2   Alan Cummings, m. Florence MacInnis.
- C3   George Cummings, never married.
- C4   Flora Cummings, m. Jack Jardine, Freetown, with issue:
  - D1   Georgie Jardine, m. Don Seaman, with a family.
  - D2   Ruby Jardine, m. Dr. Lorne Bonnell, Murray River, with issue:
    - E1   Mark Bonnell, m. Ann MacGowan, with issue:
      - F1   Lorne Bonnell.
      - F2   Andrew Bonnell.
    - E2   Linda Bonnell, m. Steve Love, living in Ontario, with one boy:
      - F1   Norman Love.

B5   Katie MacLeod, m. George Morrison, Bradalbane, with issue:
- C1   Mary Morrison, m. Alan MacLean, lived in Moncton, with issue:

   D1 Winnifred MacLean.
   D2 Alan MacLean.
   D3 Sterling MacLean.
   D4 Eunice MacLean.
  C2 Miller Morrison, married in Western Canada, with a family.
  C3 Dan Morrison, married with a family.
  C4 George Morrison, married in Western Canada, with a family.
  C5 Ethel Morrison, married in Western Canada, with a family.
  C6 Alex Morrison, never married.
B6 John MacLeod.
B7 Dan MacLeod, never married, lived in Hartsville.
B8 Alex MacLeod, 1867-1933, m. Flora Graham, 1882-1953, lived in Hartsville.
  C1 Allan MacLeod, m. Luella Waite, in Cambridge, Massachusetts, issue:
   D1 Doris MacLeod, m. Louis Brown, with issue:
    E1 Jeffrey Brown.
    E2 Janet Brown.
    E3 Sharon Brown.
    E4 Timothy Brown.
   D2 Jean MacLeod, m. Gene Sanderman, with issue:
    E1 David Sanderman.
    E2 Martha Sanderman
   D3 Philip MacLeod.
   D4 Paul MacLeod.
  C2 Doris MacLeod, married in Michigan.
  C3 Jean MacLeod, m. _____ Sanderson, with issue:
   D1 David Sanderson.
   D2 Martha Sanderson.
   D3 Phillip Sanderson.
   D4 Paul Sanderson.
All of the above family in U.S.A.
  C4 Murdoch MacLeod, never married.
  C5 Bruce MacLeod, m. Florence Patterson, lived in Manitoba, with issue:
   D1 Sandra MacLeod, m. David Romano.
   D2 Heather MacLeod, married in British Columbia.
   D3 Cheryl MacLeod, m. Mr. ____ Pervis, Manitoba.
  C6 Earl MacLeod, m. Ethel Judin, in New Brunswick, with issue:
   D1 Graham MacLeod, married in Ontario.
  C7 Dan MacLeod, m. Jean MacDonald, living in Hunter River.
  C8 Mae MacLeod, m. Donald Campbell, Charlottetown, with issue:
   D1 Phyllis Campbell, m. John Bernard.
  C9 Everett MacLeod, m. Elda Clow, Summerside, with issue:
   D1 Arlyn MacLeod, m. Harold Leard, Summerside.
   D2 Jeffrey MacLeod.
   D3 Elizabeth MacLeod.
  C10 Elmer MacLeod, never married.
  C11 Catherine MacLeod, m. Dan Farquharson, with issue:
   D1 Ivan Farquharson.
   D2 Graham Farquharson.
  C12 Julia MacLeod, m. Major Waddell, Charlottetown, with issue:
   D1 Brian Wadell, m. Donna McGaugh, Charlottetown, with issue:
    E1 Jamie Waddell.

C13 Borden MacLeod, in Ottawa.
C14 Lillian MacLeod, m. Joseph <u>Gailbraith</u>, Ottawa, with issue:
    D1 Ronald Gailbraith, married in Ottawa.
    D2 Kenneth Gailbraith.
    D3 Eleanor Gailbraith.

Information received from Mae Campbell and Norman MacLeod of Charlottetown.

JOHN MACLEOD
JOHN MACLEOD AND MARY MACKAY OF HEATHERDALE

A   John Duncan MacLeod, 1824-1887, born in the Isle of Skye and came over on the ship *Hermione* in 1840, m. Mary <u>MacKay</u>, 1828-1900, who was also born in Skye and came over on the *George Washington* in 1841. They settled in Heatherdale. Their children were:

B1   Duncan McLeod, 1848-1938, m. Lizzie <u>MacPhee</u>, 1858-1932, from Heatherdale, they farmed in Dundas, with issue:

    C1   Mary McLeod, 1880-1964, m. Charles Eugene <u>Crawford</u>, 1878-1959, Greenfield, Massachusetts, with issue:

        D1   George Edward Crawford, 1905-1970, m. Elizabeth <u>Clement</u>, with issue:

            E1   Elizabeth Mary Crawford, born at Greenfield, Massachusetts, m. Carl <u>Whitcomb</u>, with issue:

                F1   Robert Carl Whitcomb.

                F2   Stephen Whitcomb.

        D2   Eugene McLeod Crawford, m. Alice May <u>Pierce</u>, with issue:

            E1   Duncan Pierce Crawford, m. Susan Elaine <u>Taylor</u>, issue:

                F1   Lori Beth Crawford.

                F2   Allison Sandra Crawford.

    C2   Angus McLeod, 1882–1967, born in Strathcona, lived in Vancouver, left for the Canadian Northwest in 1901, m. Ann Mae <u>Brotherton</u>, 1887-1939, she was born in Duluth, issue:

        D1   Kingsley Brotherton McLeod, 1909-1924.

    C3   John Allan McLeod, 1884–1962, buried in Rossland, British Columbia, m. Ruth <u>Petrie</u>, 1889-1922, who was born in Denver, Colorado, issue:

        D1   Allan McLeod, m. Margaret Wilhelmina <u>Hoeffer</u>, 1911-1977.

        D2   Lorne McLeod, 1919-1979, m. Jean <u>Gibson</u>, with issue:

            E1   Lorne Raymond McLeod, m. Ethel <u>Pepper</u>.

            E2   Robert John McLeod.

            E3   Allan James McLeod, m. Wanda Lynn <u>Hostetter</u>.

            E4   David Thomas McLeod, m. Patricia <u>Donnelly</u>, with one son.

        D3   Loretta Ruth McLeod, 1919-1996, twin to Lorne.

        D4   Raymond McLeod, 1922-1985, m. 1) Joan <u>Fairey</u>, 2) Linda <u>Harvell</u>.

            E1   Bruce McLeod.

            E2   Linda McLeod.

            E3   Douglas John McLeod.

            E4   Janet McLeod.

            E5   Donna McLeod.

    C4   William McLeod, 1886–1981, buried in Edmonton, m. Linda Evelyn <u>Flesher</u>, 1886-1977, with issue:

        D1   Harry Duncan McLeod, m. Yolande <u>Sylvester</u>, two children:

            E1   Duncan Allan McLeod, m. Darlene Marie <u>McGinnis</u>, issue:

                F1   Duncan Wilson McLeod.

                F2   Lincoln Allan McLeod.

                F3   Cameron Joseph McLeod.

             E2   Morgan William McLeod, m. Sharon Virginia <u>Larson</u>, issue:

                F1   Ryan William Morgan McLeod.

D2 Douglas Flesher McLeod, m. Nan Frances <u>Ballantyne</u>, issue:
 E1 Peggy Dianne McLeod, m. Larry <u>Ziegler</u>, with issue:
  F1 Jane Robin Ziegler.
  F2 Christian Douglas Ziegler.
 E2 Robin Susan McLeod, m. John <u>Fauquier</u>, with issue:
  F1 Claire Louise Fauquier.
  F2 Stephanie Catherine Fauquier.
D3 Gordon Allan McLeod, 1922-1926.
D4 Elizabeth Evelyn McLeod, 1919-1919.

C5 Daniel William McLeod, 1888-1983, buried in Edmonton, m. Elizabeth (Lillian) <u>Longmore</u>, 1896-1983, with issue, one daughter:
D1 Beatrice Maxine McLeod, m. Frank <u>Harrison</u>, living in Edmonton, Alberta, with issue:
 E1 Kenneth Frank Harrison, m. Gloria Marie <u>Bonikowsky</u>, issue:
  F1 Lindsay Marie Harrison.
  F2 Sara Ashley Harrison.
  F3 Taylor Kathleen Harrison.
 E2 Grant William Harrison.

C6 Annie Mae McLeod, born 1890, m. Neil <u>Shaw</u>, born 1884, from Georgetown, P.E.I.
D1 Allan Duncan Shaw, 1922-1925.
D2 Cyrus Kingsley Shaw, 1924-1986, m. Betty Elaine <u>Huestis</u>, issue:
 E1 Dorothy Ann Shaw.
D3 John Shaw, 1927-1986, m. Rhoma Catherine <u>Priest</u>, they lived in Montague, with issue:
 E1 Catherine Ann Shaw, married in Nova Scotia to Robert Vaughn <u>Lyons</u>, with issue:
  F1 Scott Vaughn Lyons.
 E2 Jo Ann Shaw, m. Craig Roderick <u>Walker</u>, with issue:
  F1 Joel Alexander Walker.
  F2 Nicholas Michael Walker.

C7 Malcolm Angus McLeod, 1893-1981, buried in Calgary, Alberta, m. Edith Clara <u>Parish</u>, 1898-1984, she was born in Barking, England, issue:
D1 William Duncan McLeod, born in Edmonton, m. Eileen Lorraine <u>Stibbards</u>, with issue:
 E1 Glen Duncan McLeod, m. Janine Marie <u>Rooney</u>, they live in Calgary, with issue:
  F1 Jason Duncan McLeod.
  F2 Paul James McLeod.
 E2 Deborah Jane McLeod, m. David Stuart <u>Brown</u>, they live in Calgary, with issue:
  F1 Monica Louise Brown.
  F2 Stuart Edward Brown.
 E3 Heather Lorraine McLeod, m. Richard Alan <u>Spencer</u>, issue:
  F1 Cameron Wade Spencer.
D2 Malcolm Ewen McLeod, m. 1) Alice Mary <u>Wrightson</u>, with issue:
 E1 Malcolm Charles Robert McLeod, m. Jo-Anne Michelle <u>Bund</u>, with issue:
  F1 Malcolm Douglas Paul McLeod.
Malcolm Ewen McLeod m. 2) Janet Louise <u>Carlson</u>.

C8   Alexander MacLeod, 1886-1978, buried in Brockton, Massachusetts, m. Deltha Almedia <u>MacFarlane</u>, 1899-1975.

C9   Ewen MacLeod, 1898-1957, m. Kathryn <u>Shaw</u>, 1897-1977, they lived in Strathcona, they had no family.

C10 Samuel MacLeod, 1901-1991, buried in Quincy, Massachusetts, m. Dorothy Veroqua <u>Coffin</u>, 1906-1966.

B2   Daniel McLeod, died in 1938 at Barrhead, Alberta.

B3   Jane MacLeod, married Malcolm <u>Gillis</u>, Grandview, with issue:

     C1   Malcolm Gillis, m. Lottie <u>Smallwood</u>, lived in Charlottetown, no family.

     C2   Isaac Gillis, married in Boston, with two children.

     C3   Angus Gillis, in British Columbia, never married.

B4   Margaret MacLeod, 1853-1934, died from injuries received when hit by an automobile in Massachuetts. She was married to John Malcolm <u>Gillis</u>, 1842-1904. They had the following children, all in the U.S.A.:

     C1   Malcolm John Gillis, 1876-1945, m. Mary G. <u>Murphy</u>, with issue:

         D1   Olive Gillis, m. 1) Walter <u>Leininger</u>, with issue:

             E1   Andre Leininger.

             E2   Carole Leininger.

             E3   Merrily Leininger.

         Olive married 2) Warren <u>Barr</u>.

         D2   Malcolm J. Gillis, Jr., m. Mary Elizabeth <u>Alexander</u>, with issue:

             E1   Fred Alexander Gillis.

             E2   Malcolm J. Gillis, III.

     C2   John William Gillis, 1878-1955, m. Dorothy Rose <u>Milner</u>, 1887-1980, in Edmonton, with issue:

         D1   John Edwin Gillis, 1913-1944, m. Margaret Maude <u>O'Dwyer</u>, lived in Vancouver.

         D2   Marjorie Ellen Gillis, m. Edward Wilson <u>Howard</u>, Edmonton, with issue:

             E1   Maureen Hazel Howard, married, living in Rhode Island, most if not all her children are married.

             E2   Allan Edward Howard, married with a family in Alberta.

         D3   Doris Katherine Gillis, 1916-1996, m. Wilmer Munro <u>Fawcett</u>, 1916-1988, they lived in Edmonton and British Columbia, issue:

             E1   Wilmer John Fawcett, m. Lucy Helen <u>Hominuke</u>, living in Vancouver, with issue:

                 F1   Anthony Simon Fawcett, in 1999 attending Queens University.

             E2   Michael Wayne Fawcett, m. 1) Angela <u>Whaley</u>, with issue:

                 F1   Shari Lynn Fawcett, married with children in British Columbia.

                 F2   Michael Steven Fawcett, living in Edmonton.

             Michael Wayne, m. 2) Carol Maureen <u>Wood</u>, living in Edmonton, with issue:

                 F3   Susan Janine Fawcett.

                 F4   Lisa Marie Fawcett.

             E3   Gerald Robert Fawcett, living in Calgary.

             E4   Donald Graeme Fawcett, living in Burnaby, British Columbia.

         D4   Donald James Gillis, m. Myrtle <u>Crowell</u>, living in Edmonton, with issue:

        E1   John William Gillis, Edmonton.

        E2   Robert James Gillis, married with a child in Alberta.

    D5   Theodore Gillis, 1920-1994, m. Shirley Marion Holland, they lived in Alberta, with issue:

        E1   Janis Lee Gillis, married with children.

        E2   Jamee-Lynn Gillis, married with children.

    D6   Harold William Gillis, 1922-1991, m. Richylda Rose Fenske, they lived in Alberta, with issue:

        E1   Judith Elizabeth Gillis, married with children, St. Albert, Alberta.

        E2   Jeffrey William Gillis, married with children, Kelowna, British Columbia.

        E3   Glen Harold Gillis, married with children, in Alberta.

    D7   Mary Josephine Gillis, m. Henry James Crawford, with children:

        E1   Nancy Lorraine Crawford, not living.

        E2   Douglas James Crawford.

    D8   Ruth Amy Gillis, m. John William New, 1927-1983, with issue:

        E1   Linda Noreen Braid, living in Vancouver.

        E2   Kathleen Diane Braid, living in Kelowna, British Columbia.

        E3   Catherine Ruth New, married with children.

        E4   Barbara Lynn New, married with children.

        E5   Dianne Dorothy New, married with children.

C3   Mary Gillis, born 1880, m. Finley MacNeill, with issue:

    D1   Margaret MacNeill.

    D2   Charles MacNeill.

    D3   Marie MacNeill.

C4   Katherine Ann Gillis, 1882-1959, took care of her mother, never married.

C5   Jean Evelyn Gillis, born 1887 (twin died at birth), m. Winfred Anderson Shattuck, born 1891, with issue:

    D1   Natalie Margaret Shattuck, m. 1) Andrew S. Lane, 2) Don M. Fay.

C6   Daniel Gillis, 1888-1969, married.

C7   Harry A. Gillis, 1891-1969, m. 1) D. Josephine L. Linton, 1891-1934, with issue:

    D1   Allan Gillis, 1921-1953, m. Patty Moran, with issue:

        E1   Christopher A. Gillis.

        E2   Gayle Gillis.

        E3   Nancy Gillis.

    After Allan's death, Patty Moran, m. Sidney Salkow, movie producer/director.

   Harry Gillis m. 2) Dorothy Delroy.

B5   Allan MacLeod, 1854-1930, m. Lexie MacDonald, 1872-1922, daughter of Sandy Allen MacDonald and his second wife _____ MacDonald, Lyndale. They moved to Dundas around the turn of the century. Their children were:

   C1   Garfield MacLeod, born June 30, 1894, m. Ada Hazel Matheson, born 1901, they lived in Dundas, with issue:

     D1   Lexie MacLeod, m. Robert Knosp, Long Island, New York. He was killed in a plane crash in Florida, they had a daughter:

        E1   Christine Knosp, married in Florida.

     D2   Wendell MacLeod, m. Betty MacDonald, Dundas, with issue:

E1   Merrill MacLeod.
E2   Wendy MacLeod.
E3   Wanda MacLeod.
D3   Leroy MacLeod, m. Joyce Holmes, they live in Charlottetown where he is a partner in M&M Furniture, with issue:
E1   Jill MacLeod.
E2   Allen MacLeod.
E3   Heidi MacLeod.
C2   Mary MacLeod, 1897-1953, m. Roy MacLean, 1893-1972, St. Peters, their children are:
D1   Peggy MacLean, m. Ralph Sanderson, with issue:
E1   David Sanderson, m. Michelle Dorsey, with issue:
F1   Gabriel Sanderson.
F2   Maria Sanderson.
D2   Flo MacLean, m. Ronald Morehouse.
D3   Lexie MacLean, m. 1) Grant MacLean, with issue:
E1   Mary MacLean, m. Bill MacEachern, Charlottetown, they had a large family.
E2   Heather MacLean, m. in St Peters, with issue:
F1   Daughter.
E3   Flora MacLean, not living.
E4   Peggy MacLean, married in Pictou, with three sons.
C3   Belle MacLeod, m. Edison Mutch, North River, with issue:
D1   Marjorie Mutch, m. Albert Boswell, living in Marshfield, issue:
E1   Eddie Boswell, m. Connie Dennis, they had three boys.
E2   Peter Boswell, m. Sandra MacKinnon, daughter of John MacKinnon, Kinross, they live in East Royalty.
E3   Wayne Boswell, m. Linda _____, living in Marshfield, they have two children.
D2   Lois Mutch, not married, living in Calgary.
D3   Jean Mutch, m. Fred Kitson, from North Wiltshire, with issue:
E1   Rhonda Kitson, m. Larry Broad, Fredericton.
E2   Karen Kitson, m. Guy Ferintosh, Toronto, with one child.
E3   Debbie Kitson, a lawyer in Halifax, married with two children.
E4   Donna Lee Kitson, m. Ed Harding, living in Peterborough, with three children.
E5   Kathy Kitson, m. Michael MacFarlane, living in New Brunswick, with two girls.
E6   Marsha Kitson, m. Brian Denver, Burlington, Ontario. They have three boys.
E7   Mark Kitson, m. Sharlene DeLong, living in Boughton, Ontario, they have two children.
D4   Isabel Mutch, m. Austin Bowman, Charlottetown, with issue:
E1   Lesa Bowman, living in Toronto.
E2   John Bowman, living in North Wiltshire.
C4   Malcolm MacLeod, farmed in Dundas, never married.
B6   Alexander MacLeod, baptized Jan, 24, 1857, died in the 1930s in New York State.
B7   John J. MacLeod, baptized Sept. 26, 1866, by the Rev. Alexander Munroe, Valleyfield, died in 1940 in the State of Montana.

Information from Alexina MacLean, Greenwich, P.E.I.; Alice Crawford, Greenfield Massachusetts; Isabel Bowman, Charlottetown; Wilmer Fawcett, Vancouver; and the records of William D.MacLeod, Calgary, Alberta.

MURDOCH MACLEOD
MURDOCH MACLEOD AND CHRISTIE MARTIN OF RAASAY, SCOTLAND

Murdoch MacLeod, Raasay, Scotland, had a brother John MacLeod, and also a brother Duncan (see Cardross MacLeods). Murdoch m. Christie <u>Martin</u>, with issue:

A1   Allan MacLeod, who may have settled in Hartsville.

A2   John MacLeod, who may have settled in Head of Montague.

A3   Donald MacLeod, who married and settled in Melville, P.E.I., with issue:
     B1   John MacLeod, m. Jessie <u>MacPhee</u>, with issue, at least:
         C1   William MacLeod, went to Western Canada.
         C2   A daughter who m.____ <u>MacRae</u>, in Point Prim.
         C3   Campbell MacLeod, was named after Rev. Malcolm Campbell, one time Pastor of Wood Islands Presbyterian Church, m. Cassie <u>MacKenzie</u>, from Belle River, they had no family.

A4   Malcolm MacLeod, died 1865, m. Maggie or Mary <u>Gillis</u>, daughter of John Gillis and Jessie MacLennan. They married in Scotland and settled in the Strathalbane area in 1830. Their children were:
     B1   Jessie MacLeod.
     B2   Murdoch MacLeod.
     B3   John G. MacLeod, born 1837 in P.E.I. and operated a sawmill in Wood Islands. He married in 1860, Sarah <u>MacSwain</u>, of Wolfville, Lot 60. They had children of whom was living at that time (c. 1905):
         C1   Donald Morrison MacLeod, m. in 1903, Miss Christie A. <u>MacLeod</u>, daughter of John and Rachel MacLeod.
     B4   Roderick MacLeod.
     B5   Alex MacLeod.
     B6   Allan MacLeod.
     B7   Norman MacLeod, m. Christie <u>MacIntyre</u>, with issue:
         C1   Margaret MacLeod.
         C2   Catherine MacLeod.
         C3   Jessie MacLeod.
         C4   Malcolm MacLeod.
         C5   John MacLeod.
         C6   Murdoch MacLeod.
         C7   Peter MacLeod.
         C8   Allan MacLeod.
         C9   Annie MacLeod.
         C10 Janie MacLeod, the only one of this large family living in 1967.

Information on this family was taken from the notes of J. Angus MacLean, Lewes, who also supplied the following:

Information from notes made by Catherine (MacLean) MacLellan, from information given her by her father George MacLean:

Ronnie Gillis' father, John Malcolm Gillis, Glen Martin, was George MacLean's second cousin, John Malcolm Gillis was the son of a MacLeod woman who was the daughter of Norman MacLeod, son of Duncan MacLeod. George MacLean was the son of Duncan MacLean, the son of Margaret MacLeod, the daughter of the above Duncan. Mabel MacDonald's father, in Bellevue, was also a second cousin of George Maclean, his mother also being a MacLeod.* Margaret MacLeod, daughter of Duncan, had a brother Norman. She also had a nephew Norman, married to her daughter. This last named couple lived in Cardross and her brother Norman lived in Rona.

* See the family of John MacLeod, Head of Montague.

ALEXANDER S. MACLEOD
ALEXANDER S. MACLEOD OF CALIFORNIA AND HAWAII

Alexander S. MacLeod was born on Prince Edward Island, Canada, of Scottish-Irish parentage. He spent his early years in Vancouver, British Columbia, where he attended the local schools. He took the engineering course at McGill University in Montreal, Quebec, and spent his summers working in logging camps, with survey crews and with the salmon fleets of Northern British Columbia.

He first went to California as a member of a rugby team and liked it so much that he returned the next year to study at the California School of Design, where he was an honour student and received a scholarship in his last year.

During the First World War he was in the 29th and 40th Engineers in France with the American Expeditionary Force. The fruit of that experience was a portfolio filled with sketches. Since 1921 Mr. MacLeod has lived in Hawaii. His paintings and lithographs have been exhibited all over the United States in such galleries as the National Gallery in Washington, the Museum of Modern Art and the National Academy in New York, the Pennsylvania Academy of Arts in Philadelphia and many others. He is the winner of numerous prizes for his water colours and lithographs and is the author and illustrator of many magazine articles. Mr. MacLeod was with the Engineering Corps in Honolulu on December 7, 1941 and he determined to make as complete a pictorial record as possible in Hawaii in war time.

This information was taken from the fly-leaf of a book he authored: *The Spirit of Hawaii–Before and after Pearl Harbour*, Harper & Brothers, New York, 1943.

Norman MacLeod
Norman MacLeod and Catherine Stewart of Culloden

A1   Norman MacLeod, who emigrated from Portree, Isle of Skye, was a son of
Murdoch MacLeod and Arabell MacDonald. Norman, with his brother Murdoch, settled in Culloden, P.E.I., where Murdoch died as a young man and
is buried in Valleyfield. They had another brother, Alexander, in Skye, who
later emigrated to Australia or New Zealand, and a sister, name unknown,
who married and had a family on P.E.I. Norman married Catherine Stewart,
daughter of John Stewart, and his wife Annie Matheson. The Stewart family
arrived in the same group as the MacLeod brothers, on the *James Gibb* in 1858.
They settled in Caledonia West. The family of Norman and Catherine were:

B1   Sarah MacLeod, m. Alexander MacLeod, they lived in Providence, Rhode
Island, with issue. (See the descendants of Angus MacLeod, Glen Martin.)
  C1   Marie MacLeod, who founded the MacLeod Optical Company, a large
business enterprise in the U.S.A., m. Wallace McKell, in Providence,
Rhode Island.
  C2   Norman MacLeod, m. Bertha _____, Rhode Island.
  C3   Edward MacLeod, m. Gladys _____, Rhode Island.
  C4   Austin MacLeod, married and had a daughter, Joyce MacLeod.
  C5   Florence MacLeod, m. Graham Smith, Connecticut.
  C6   Marion MacLeod, died young.
B2   Annie MacLeod, 1865-1947, m. Samuel J. MacLeod, 1870-1951, Strathcona,
P.E.I. (For their descendants, see the family of Norman MacLeod, Uigg.)
B3   Mary J. MacLeod, 1867-1964, m. Rev. D. B. MacLeod, 1867-1918. He was
of the family of Donald Ban Oig of the Murray Harbour Road.
B4   Annabella MacLeod, m. John Ross, Mt. Vernon and later Strathcona, with
issue:
  C1   Louise Ross, m. Samuel Woolridge, Cove Head, with issue:
    D1   Ross Woolridge, died young.
    D2   Margaret Woolridge, m. Alden Ellis, Charlottetown.
    D3   Marion Woolridge, married with a family.
    D4   Ellen Woolridge, twin of Marion, not married.
  C2   Katherine Ross, m. William MacEachern, Montague, with issue:
    D1   Ann MacEachern, m. Rev. Dr. John Cameron, Pastor of the Kirk
of St. James, Charlottetown.
    D2   Marion MacEachern, m. Howard MacLeod, Dundas.
  C3   Marion Ross, m. Chester Riley, Dundas, with issue:
    D1   John Riley, m. Audrey ____, Dundas.
    D2   Mary Riley, m. Chester Jenkins.
    D3   Thomas Riley, married in Ontario.
    D4   William Riley, married, living in Dundas.
  C4   Herbert Ross, m. Elsie Brown, living in Strathcona.
B5   Catherine MacLeod, m. Malcolm Bell of Belle River.
  C1   Annie Bell, m. John MacLean, P.E.I. and U.S.A., with issue:
    D1   Bernice MacLean, m. Ernest Gormley, they live in Florida.
  C2   Malcolm Bell, lived in British Columbia.
  C3   Edward Bell, m. Christine MacNeill, they lived in New York, with
issue:

D1   Carol Bell, m. Tom <u>Annicone</u>, with two daughters.
C4   Arthur Bell, lived in New York.
C5   Mary Bell, m. Raymond <u>Matthew</u>, living in Stoneham, Massachusetts, with issue:
D1   Lois Matthew, m. Eugene <u>Collings</u>, with five children.
D2   Alvin Matthew, never married, in Stoneham, Massachusetts.
C6   Loring Bell.
C7   Norman Bell, m. Christine <u>Beaton</u>, living in Belle River, with issue:
D1   Betty Bell, m. John <u>Livingstone</u>, Murray River.
E1   Kathryn Livingstone.
D2   Jean Bell, m. Wendell <u>Jenkins</u>, Millview, with issue:
E1   Wendy Jenkins, m. Archie <u>MacFadyen</u>, Meadowbank.
E2   Clayton Jenkins.
E3   Stacy Jenkins.
D3   Florrie Bell, lives in Halifax, Nova Scotia.
B6   Alexander S. MacLeod, 1865-1954, m. Mary <u>MacLean</u>, 1871-1960, with issue:
C1   Norman MacLeod, 1908-1922.
C2   Florence MacLeod, m. William <u>Cunningham</u>, U.S.A. She is now a widow, living with her sister Catherine in Charlottetown.
C3   Catherine MacLeod, m. Milton <u>Compton</u>, with issue:
D1   William H. Compton, m. Margaret <u>MacPherson</u>, they live in Massachusetts. Their issue:
E1   Child died in infancy.
E2   Gail Compton, m. Armond <u>Perron</u>, in U.S.A., with issue:
F1   Nicholas Armond Perron.
F2   Britanny Suzanne Perron.
F3   _____.
D2   Florence Compton, m. Gordon <u>Nicholson</u>, Belle River.
D3   Grace Compton, m. Roy <u>Foote</u>, living in Massachusetts, with issue:
E1   Jack Foote.
E2   Tammy Foote.
D4   Anna Compton, m. Lester <u>Dodsworth</u>, in Massachusetts, with issue:
E1   Susan Dodsworth.
E2   Charles Dodsworth.
C4   John Neil MacLeod, died in infancy, 1914.

This information received from Florence Cunningham, Charlottetown.

The above family was related in some way with the (Joiner) MacLeods of Kinross. We have no information on the Kinross family, other than was contained in an obituary to Dr. MacLeod, died 1918, aged 54 years, which appeared in local newspapers.

In Memoriam: Doctor Donald MacLeod

The death of Dr. D. MacLeod at Kinross on the 3rd inst. demands more than a passing notice. Dr. MacLeod, familiarly called "Dr. Dan," was born at Kinross about fifty-five years ago, the son of Donald (Joiner) and Flora MacLeod.

He was educated at Uigg school and at Prince of Wales College, and at the age of twenty became Principal of the above school, ably maintaining its high standard. After teaching there a few years, he entered Trinity Medical College, Toronto, and after four years study there, graduated from Trinity University with the degree of M.D., C.M.

He practised his profession for a short time at Pownal, P.E.I, .and then went to British Columbia where he practised at Donald and Nanaimo till the great Klondyke rush took place.

He was one of the first medical men who hit the trail for that Eldorado and remained there for seven years. After amassing a considerable fortune, he travelled extensively in Europe, visiting England, France, Italy and Germany. He also made several trips to China and finally settled at Vancouver, B.C., where he did a consultation practice for several years, when his health broke down and he came back to his old home.

 Since then he has been living in retirement doing gratis and urgent work that was required among his neighbours, whose highest respect and love he won both by his skill, and his kindly and unassuming disposition.

Dr. MacLeod, outside his professional attainments had a well stored mind. He was a great reader, a free English, Gaelic, and classical scholar, whom it was a delight to visit.

As a physician he was a good deal above average. As a man his kindly nature won for him the love and esteem of all with whom he came in contact, and it may be said of him, he died leaving behind him no enemies.

The end came instantaneously as he wished it to be in the midst of his duties.

He was one of a large family of whom there are only two sisters left, his only brother having died two years ago.

The sisters living at the time of Dr. MacLeod's death were:

   Mary, 1857-1923, and Christie, 1849-1926.

Others in the family were:

   Alexander, died 1917, aged 63 years.
   Annie, died 1876, aged 18 years.
   Catherine, died 1875, aged 22 years.
   The father, Donald MacLeod, died 1891, aged 74 years. Flora, the mother, died 1899, aged 78 years. Angus MacLeod, who was most likely a brother of Donald, died 1891, aged 87 years.

WILLIAM MACLEOD
WILLIAM AND MARY MACLEOD OF VALLEYFIELD

A   William MacLeod and Mary MacLeod, most likely born in the Isle of Skye, settled in Valleyfield on a farm later owned by John P. MacLeod. Their children were:

B1   Norman "William" MacLeod, born c. 1818, m. Mary MacPherson, born c. 1825, both born in Scotland and settled in Valleyfield. For a list of their descendants see under Norman and Mary MacLeod, Valleyfield.

B2   Mary MacLeod, m. Malcolm MacPherson, no information on their family, if any.

B3   Murdoch MacLeod, m. Catherine MacPherson, no information on their family.

B4   Douglas MacLeod, according to tradition either he or Murdoch or both, settled in or near Amherst, Nova Scotia.

B5   Angus William MacLeod, 1829-1916, m. Janet (Jessie) Nicholson, daughter of John Nicholson and Anne Montgomery, sister of Malcolm Montgomery who settled in Valleyfield. The family of Angus William and Janet were:

C1   Florence MacLeod, 1860-1930, m. in Colorado or Arizona, no family.

C2   Marion (Mary) MacLeod, 1862-1938, never married and lived in Massachusetts.

C3   John William MacLeod, 1863-1953, married in Chicago and lived in Bar Harbour, Maine. He had one son who was killed in a car accident.

C4   Katie MacLeod, 1865-1874.

C5   Annie MacLeod, 1867-1955, m. Rev. Angus Martin MacDonald, 1867-1927, son of Allan Alexander MacDonald and Marjorie Martin of Grandview, P.E.I., with issue:
   D1   Norman MacDonald.
   D2   Lowell MacDonald.
   D3   Marion MacDonald.

C6   William Alexander MacLeod, M.D., 1869-1945, m. Anna Marie Von Gordon, 1869-1952, they lived in Yarmouth, Nova Scotia, with issue:
   D1   Eleanor MacLeod, born 1900, died in infancy.
   D2   Herbert Douglas MacLeod, 1900-1968, m. Alice MacLean Kirk. They lived in Yarmouth, Nova Scotia, with issue:
      E1   John William MacLeod, m. _____, with issue:
         F1   Ian Herbert MacLeod.
         F2   Katherine Irene MacLeod, m. Robert Bedier, issue:
            G1   Jonathon Bedier.

C7   Alice MacLeod, 1872-1928, daughter of Angus William MacLeod and Janet Nicholson, m. Dr. J. Jones in Massachusetts, with issue:
   D1   Marion Jones, died age 6 months.
   D2   Muriel Jones, m. ____ Roache, with seven children.
   D3   Alice Jones, m. ____ Roache, with five children.
   D4   Flo Jones, died age 4 years.
   D5   John MacLeod Jones, died in infancy.

C8   Sara (Sadie) MacLeod, 1874-1890.

C9   Alexander MacLeod, born 1877, died same year.

C10 Murdoch Douglas MacLeod, M.D., 1877-1967, twin of Alexander, m. Barbara <u>Holzmann</u>, they lived in Yarmouth, Nova Scotia, with issue:
D1 Eleanor MacLeod.
D2 Marion MacLeod.
D3 Norman MacLeod, M.D.
D4 Barbara MacLeod.

Information from John W. MacLeod, Red Deer, Alberta, and Mary McGowan, Kilmuir, P.E.I.

JOHN MACLEOD
JOHN MACLEOD AND ANN MACRAE OF ISLE OF LEWIS AND CANADA

A   John MacLeod, 1846-1929, m. Ann <u>MacRae</u>, 1845-1938, with issue:

B1   Murdina MacLeod, died Jan. 13, 1919, m. John <u>MacLeod</u>, died May 11, 1924. They were married in 1912 and had issue:

    C1   Murdina MacLeod, m. _____, in 1940, with issue:
        D1   Jackie.

    C2   Mary Ann MacLeod, born Aug. 1, 1913, m. Murdo <u>MacLeod</u>, 1902-1972. They were married on Oct. 27, 1937, with issue:
        D1   Judith Ann MacLeod, born Sept. 13, 1944, m. Robert William <u>Baines</u>, born April 25, 1940. They were married Dec. 21, 1974, with issue:
           E1   Bonnie Jean Baines.
           E2   Brent Jerome Baines.
        D2   John MacLeod.

    C3   Donnie MacLeod, born Dec. 2, 1918, m. Olive <u>Brown</u>, with issue:
        D1   Donna MacLeod.
        D2   Norman MacLeod.

B2   Isabella MacLeod, died 1972, m. Norman <u>Thompson</u>, 1881-1948, with issue:

    C1   Murdo Thompson, 1913-1969, m. Maime _____, in 1940, with issue:
        D1   Norma Ann Thompson.
    C2   Alex Thompson, 1915-1958.

B3   Mary Ann MacLeod, 1880-1929, m. Murdo <u>MacLeod</u>, 1880-1963, with issue:

    C1   Roderick MacLeod, born Dec. 10, 1909, m. Evelyn Blanche <u>MacRae</u>, born July 15, 1915. They were married Jan. 3, 1943. Their children are:
        D1   Norman Rae MacLeod, m. Nancy E. E. <u>Gravel</u>, with issue:
           E1   Carolyn Heather MacLeod.
           E2   Michael Richard MacLeod, 1978, died same year.
           E3   Robert Andrew MacLeod.
        D2   Evelyn Ruth MacLeod, m. Ian Donald <u>MacLeod</u>, with issue:
           E1   Kirsteen Mairi A. MacLeod.
           E2   Shona Margaret MacLeod.
        D3   Kenneth Roderick MacLeod, m. Gertrude Elaine <u>Muschkat</u>, with issue:
           E1   Sarah Allyson MacLeod.
           E2   Timothy Albert Roderick MacLeod
        D4   Douglas Heath MacLeod, m. Leslie <u>Coggins</u>.

    C2   Mary Ann MacLeod, born April 7, 1911, m. Thomas <u>Parkinson</u>, 1889-1962.

    C3   Anne MacLeod, born Sept. 15, 1912, m. Robert E. <u>Knott</u>, born Feb. 10, 1911. They married July 11, 1938, with issue:
        D1   Claudia Anne Knott, m. Thomas Allen <u>Mays</u>, with issue:
           E1   Michael Mays.
           E2   Jeffrey Mays.
        D2   Doreen Lynn Knott, m. Jamy William <u>Carlson</u>, with issue:

E1   Theresa Lynn Carlson.
E2   Stacy Ann Carlson.
E3   Debra Kay Carlson.
D3   Donna Lee Knott, m. Charles M. Pierce, with issue:
E1   Christopher C. Pierce.
E2   Timothy Edward Pierce.
D4   Allan Knott.
C4 Kenneth Alex MacLeod, 1920-1972, m. Ruth Wagar, with issue:
D1   Alexander Murdo MacLeod, m. Joanne Miller.
D2   Jackie MacLeod.
D3   Sandra Twila MacLeod, m. _____ Bell, with issue:
E1   William Bell.
D4   Penny MacLeod.
D5   Wendy MacLeod.
C5 John MacLeod, m. Elsie Currie, their children were:
D1   Wayne MacLeod, m. Jeanette ____, with issue:
E1   Iain MacLeod.
E2   Cailin Shaughn MacLeod.
D2   Mavis Lynne MacLeod, m. Stewart John Henderson, with issue:
E1   Kaley Mavis Henderson.
C6 Christy Ann MacLeod, m. C. William Nelson, died May 23, 1971.
Their children were:
D1   Roy Nelson.
D2   Kathleen Nelson, m. Raymond Foster, with issue:
E1   Kimberly Foster.
E2   Heather Foster.
D3   Nancy Nelson.
B4 Chrissie Ann MacLeod, 1882-1916, m. Colin MacKenzie, with issue:
C1   Bellann MacKenzie, m. Duncan MacLeod.
B5 Donald MacRae MacLeod, 1881-1951, m. Christina Dolina McNab, 1885-
1937, with issue:
C1   Ina MacLeod, m. Leslie Gordon Davis, with issue:
D1   Leslie Donna Davis, m. Royce Coburn, with issue:
E1   Christopher Todd Coburn.
E2   Rebecca Coburn.
C2   Mary Muriel MacLeod, 1909-1978, m. Alvard D. F. Stearns, with
issue:
D1   Carole Ann Stearns, m. Carl Thomas Pfeuffer, with issue:
E1   Kelly Christina Pfeuffer.
E2   Andrew Carl Pfeuffer.
E3   Michele Jessica Pfeuffer.
D2   Nancy Jane Stearns, m. 1) T. J. Toronto, m. 2) Roger Hurney.
D3   Craig Bedford Stearns, m. Regina May Walkowski, with issue:
E1   Blair Colin Stearns.
C3   Anne MacLeod, died 1977, m. Roland Dumais, with issue:
D1   Connie Dumais, m. _____, issue:
E1   Michael, 1959-1975.
D2   Judy Dumais.

Information from Blanche MacLeod, Charlottetown.

PETER MACLEOD
PETER MACLEOD AND SARAH OF ALBION CROSS

A   Peter MacLeod, 1803-1877, m. Sarah ____, they settled in Albion Cross, Lot 55, on land purchased from a man named Campbell. They received the title in 1872. Their children were:

B1 Alexander MacLeod, 1834-1906, m. Isabel MacDonald, 1847-1923, with issue:

   C1 Sarah MacLeod, 1870-1938, m. Joseph Pope, 1862-1939.

      D1 Belle Pope, 1894-1964.

      D2 May Pope, 1896-1937.

      D3 Elizabeth Pope, 1898-1976.

      D4 John Pope, 1899-1975.

      D5 Alex Pope, 1901-1988.

      D6 Edward Pope, 1902-1949.

      D7 William Pope, 1904-1988.

      D8 Florence Pope, 1906, living in Charlottetown.

      D9 Duncan Pope, 1910, living in Toronto.

   C2 Florence MacLeod, 1872-1943, m. Fred Almedra. She is buried in Massachusetts, they had no family.

   C3 Margaret MacLeod, 1873-1945, never married, buried in Dundas.

   C4 Christy MacLeod, 1877-1906, never married, buried in Dundas.

   C5 Rebecca MacLeod, 1880-1918, m. Edward Crellin, with issue:

      D1 Enid Crellin, living in U.S.A.

      D2 Edward Crellin, not living.

      D3 Douglas Crellin, living in U.S.A.

   C6 Elizabeth MacLeod, 1881-1941, m. John Cahill, with issue:

      D1 Mary Cahill.

      D2 James Cahill, living in Massachusetts.

   C7 John Caleb MacLeod, 1882-1956, never married, buried in Dundas.

   C8 James Peter MacLeod, 1883-1943, m. Mary E. MacLean, 1895-1971, with issue:

      D1 Everett Frederick MacLeod, born in Waltham, Massachuetts, m. Adelaide Shirley Colpitts, with issue:

         E1 Karen Eileen MacLeod, m. Kent Donald MacLeod, Truro, Nova Scotia, issue:

         F1 Lindsay Rebecca MacLeod.

         F2 Sarah Ellen MacLeod.

         E2 Rev. Lorne Alexander MacLeod, Nova Scotia.

         E3 Grant Murray MacLeod, Moncton, New Brunswick.

      D2 Weston Alexander MacLeod, 1921-1935, born in Albion Cross.

      D3 Irwin James MacLeod, born in Mt. Hope, m. Ethel Robertson, they live in Charlottetown, with issue:

         E1 Lynn Karen MacLeod, m. Rodney Cudmore, they live in Pleasant Grove, with three children:

         F1 Weston Dewar Cudmore.

         F2 Ronald Aaron Cudmore.

         F3 Amy Joanne Cudmore.

         E2 Heather Elizabeth MacLeod, Charlottetown.

E3   Sandra Georgina MacLeod, m. Terrance Ian <u>Crombie</u>, Dartmouth, Nova Scotia, with issue:
- F1   Terrance James Crombie.
- F2   Tanya Marjorie Dawn Crombie.
- F3   Natasha Lee Crombie.

E4   Kevin James MacLeod, lives in New York.

E5   Pamela Lee MacLeod, Charlottetown.

D4   Hubert Angus MacLeod, born in Mt. Hope, never married.

D5   Christine Margaret MacLeod, born in Mt. Hope, m. 1) Thomas <u>Obea</u>, he died in 1974, leaving one son:
- E1   Robert Obea.

Christine Margaret m. 2) Donald <u>Gatchell</u>, they live in Townsend, Massachusetts.

D6   Elmer Edward MacLeod, single.

D7   Isabel Florence MacLeod, m. Adrian <u>Dekker</u>, Sherbrooke, P.E.I., issue:
- E1   Douglas Adrian Dekker, living in Summerside.

D8   Kathryn Rebecca MacLeod, born in Mt. Hope, m. Sterling <u>MacLeod</u> in 1956. They live in Sherwood, with issue:
- E1   Darlene Joy MacLeod, m. Alan <u>Robison</u>, they live in Parkdale, with issue:
  - F1   Christopher Leigh Robison.
  - F2   Michala Dawne Robison.
  - F3   Rebecca Kathryn Robison.
- E2   Cheryl Anne MacLeod, single, living in Cambridge, Ontario.
- E3   Beverly Dawn MacLeod, m. Elmer <u>Stavert</u>. They live in West Royalty, P.E.I.

B2   Malcolm MacLeod, 1840-1918, m. Mary <u>MacLeod</u>, 1831-1932. Three children died as infants. Birth dates of others are approximate, except for that of Peter.
- C1   Lydia MacLeod, born 1863, m. Warren <u>Gilman</u> of Boston, Massachusetts.
- C2   Christine MacLeod, born 1865, m. George P. <u>Urling</u> of Winthrop, Massachusetts. Died June 2, 1945.
- C3   Katie MacLeod, born 1867, m. C. H. <u>Urling</u>, of Cambridge, Massachusetts. Died Nov. 13, 1949.
- C4   Sarah Jane MacLeod, born 1869, m. John W. <u>MacKay</u>, lived in Kentville, Nova Scotia. Died Sept. 2, 1950.
- C5   Peter MacLeod, born 1871, m. Mary <u>Matheson</u> of Dundas, P.E.I. Died 1930.

B3   Margaret MacLeod, 1845-1879.

B4   William MacLeod, died young.

Information received from Everett Frederick MacLeod, Halifax, Nova Scotia.

JOHN OR NORMAN MACLEOD
JOHN OR NORMAN MACLEOD AND WIFE OF DARLINGTON AND ALLISTON

A   John or Norman MacLeod came to P.E.I. c. 1839, m. a woman from the Isle of Raasay. Their children were:

B1   John MacLeod.

B2   Norman MacLeod.

B3   Neil MacLeod.

B4   Alexander MacLeod, 1822-1909, m. Isabella MacLeod, 1822-1908. They farmed in Darlington but in their old age moved to Alliston to live with their son. Alexander and Isabella are buried in Caledonia Cemetery. Their children were:

C1   Alexander MacLeod, 1854-1938, m. Elizabeth MacDonald, 1855-1933, buried in Caledonia Cemetery. They had issue:

D1   Murdoch MacLeod, m. Georgia Foster from Moncton, New Brunswick. They lived in Western Canada, with issue:

E1   Vivian MacLeod, who died young.

When Murdoch's wife and daughter died, he moved to Murray River where he operated a tailor shop. He is buried in Peters Road Cemetery.

D2   Archibald MacLeod, died 1973, m. Gertrude Dixon, they lived in Malden, Massachusetts, with issue:

E1   Mary MacLeod, m. 1) _____ Ramsay, m. 2) Elmer Ogilvie.

D3   Alexander MacLeod, m. Ida Martin, they lived in California, no family.

D4   J. William MacLeod, m. Mae _____, a Scottish lady. They lived in Saskatchewan, with issue:

E1   Joyce MacLeod, who died young.

E2   Betty MacLeod, m. Ron Smith, in Saskatoon. They had two boys at least.

D5   Charles MacLeod, born 1895, m. 1) Esther Bruce, Valleyfield. They lived in Alliston, P.E.I. Issue:

E1   Dorothy Helen MacLeod, m. Rollie Johnston, with issue:

F1   Merril Johnston, m. Beryl Shelfoon, with issue:

G1   Barbara Leanne Johnston.

G2   Heather Dawn Johnston.

F2   Pauline Johnston.

F3   Lynne Johnston.

F4   Karen Johnston, m. Robert McIntee, RCMP, with issue:

G1   Robert Todd McIntee.

G2   Kirk McIntee.

E2   Alexander MacLeod, m. Sybil Estabrooks, with issue:

F1   Alex MacLeod, m. Faye Drisdell, with issue:

G1   Kathleen MacLeod.

F2   Amy Ester MacLeod.

F3   Jackie MacLeod.

F4   Janice MacLeod.

F5   Jill MacLeod.

F6   Mark David MacLeod.

Charles m. 2) Anne MacPherson <u>Annear</u>.

D6 Isabel MacLeod, 1879-1951, m. 1) David <u>Clow</u>, 1861-1905, m. 2) Thomas <u>Clow</u>. They had four or five children.

D7 Annie MacLeod, 1877-1891.

D8 Susan MacLeod, 1889-1890.

D9 Christie Anne MacLeod, 1891-1982, m. Fred <u>Johnston</u>, Murray River, with issue:

    E1 Archie Johnston, at one time Vice-President of Canadian General Electric, m. 1) Frances <u>Haunts</u>, with issue:

        F1 James Johnston.

        F2 Heather Johnston.

        F3 Alexander Johnston.

        F4 Margaret Johnston.

    Archie m. 2) Elizabeth <u>Parr</u>. They are now living in Halifax.

    E2 Sandra Johnston, m. Peter <u>Milburn</u>, no family

D10 Elizabeth MacLeod, m. Artemas <u>MacSwain</u>, Peters Road, with issue:

D11 Lucy MacLeod, 1897-1918.

D12 Maggie MacLeod, 1900-1901.

C2 Murdoch MacLeod, 1864-1931, a prominent Moncton businessman and councillor. He was elected alderman in 1907, 1908 and 1915. He was also elected alderman-at-large in 1916, and was an active promoter of Moncton's Bend View Park, renowned as an ideal vantage site for viewing the famous tidal bore of the Petitcodiac River. He married Lucy E. <u>Wran</u>, 1864-1914, with issue:

D1 Murdoch MacLeod, 1889-1927, m. Helen B. <u>Jamieson</u>, 1890-1962, of Hopewell Cape, New Brunswick, with issue:

    E1 Donald Murdoch MacLeod, m. Eileen J. <u>Blackburn</u>, with issue:

        F1 Ian Murdoch MacLeod.

        F2 Joan Helen MacLeod.

        F3 Deborah Lucie MacLeod.

        F4 Patricia Jamieson MacLeod.

    E2 E. Roberts MacLeod, 1918-1961, m. Helen _____, with issue:

        F1 Bruce Roberts MacLeod.

    E3 Lucy E. MacLeod, 1921-1987, m. Leonard <u>Huffman</u>, died 1958 (car accident). They had issue:

        F1 Leonard F. Huffman.

        F2 Michael J. Huffman.

D2 Emily MacLeod, died 1937, m. E. C. <u>Chapman</u>, and lived in Lacombe, Alberta, with issue:

    E1 Stewart MacLeod Chapman, m. 1) Mary E. <u>Wilkes</u>, 1920-1975, with issue, 2) Ethel M. <u>Cartwright</u>, no issue.

        F1 Terry MacLeod Chapman.

        F2 Donald Edmund Chapman.

        F3 Susan Elizabeth Chapman.

        F4 Frances Joan Chapman.

        F5 Sheila Mary Chapman.

    E2 Edmund O'Neal Chapman, 1919-1953.

    E3 Robert Andrew Chapman, 1924-1955.

    E4 Joan Elizabeth Chapman.

D3   Amy B. MacLeod, 1893-1941, m. Thomas H. Howard, no issue. They raised a niece, Lucy E. MacLeod.

D4   Harry W. MacLeod, 1897-1972, m. Mary Phyllis Lister, issue:

   E1   Millicent MacLeod, m. J. A. Roy Draper, with issue:

      F1   Mary Catherine Draper.

   E2   Leland MacLeod, m. Mary Joan Wilkins, with issue:

      F1   Cameron Bruce MacLeod.

      F2   Caren Alisa MacLeod.

D5   Edward Roberts MacLeod, 1899-1925, never married.

C3   John Norman MacLeod, 1859-1899, m. Carrie Martin, she died in 1900. John was a brass riveter by trade and lived in Buffalo, New York. He was killed in an industrial accident in 1899. They had issue:

D1   Norman Alexander MacLeod, 1893-1946, m. Lily McCartney Andrew, born 1893. She was from Prestwick, Ayrshire. Norman joined the Royal Newfoundland Regiment at the outbreak of war in 1914 and served overseas. They had issue:

   E1   John Norman MacLeod, born 1920, m. Phillis Munnings, 1918-1984. John was born in St. John's, Newfoundland. John joined the Royal Air Force in 1936 and retired in 1963. He and his family emigrated to Australia, with issue:

      F1   John Andrew MacLeod, m. Ruth Meyland, Australia, with issue:

         G1   David Oliver MacLeod.

         G2   Rebecca Ann MacLeod.

         G3   Elizabeth Lee MacLeod.

      F2   Stephen James MacLeod, m. Victoria Bate, Australia, issue:

         G1   Alastair James Neil MacLeod.

      F3   Alison Mary MacLeod, m. Daniel Johns, London, United Kingdom.

         G1   Emma Charlotte Johns.

      F4   Neil Philip MacLeod, 1953-1955, died in England.

   E2   Neil James MacLeod, m. Brenda Bancroft. They live in the United Kingdom.

D2   Neil Charles MacLeod, 1898-1916. He was killed in action on the Somme, France.

D3   Ernest Federick MacLeod, 1894-1955, m. Gladys Rita Cook. He joined the Royal Newfoundland Regiment at the outbreak of war in 1914 and served overseas. They had issue:

   E1   Ruby MacLeod, 1920-1968, m. Tasker Cook. They live in Newfoundland and have fourteen children.

   E2   Rita Joan MacLeod, born 1924, m. Angus Cook. They live in Newfoundland and have five children.

   E3   Ernest Federick MacLeod, m. Ethel Kersey. They live in Newfoundland, with seven children.

   E4   Gladys Marguerite MacLeod, m. Vernon King. They live in Newfoundland, with five children.

   E5   Helen Caroline MacLeod, m. Fred Bursey. They live in Newfoundland and have one child.

   E6   Barbara Neal MacLeod, born 1934, m. Thomas Dooley, living in Newfoundland with four children.

E7   Neil Charles MacLeod, m. Margaret <u>Fleming</u>. They live in Newfoundland with two children.

E8   Philip John MacLeod, m. Florence <u>Bowe</u>. They live in Newfoundland, with four children.

E9   Norman Mathew MacLeod, m. Sheila <u>Pollard</u>. Living in Newfoundland and have two children.

C4   Margaret MacLeod, m. Alex <u>MacLeod,</u> with one child.

C5   Christy MacLeod, m. John <u>Gillis</u>.

C6   Susan MacLeod,1850-1925, m. Mathew <u>Peckham</u>, 1850-1930. She raised John and Carrie's three children after their death, along with her own nine children.

C7   Neil Charles MacLeod, 1860-1937. A blacksmith by trade in Moncton, New Brunswick, m. Mary Isabelle <u>MacQueen</u>, 1862-1934. Issue:

D1   John William MacLeod, 1886-1961, resided in Shirley, Massachusetts, m. Margaret <u>Guthrie</u>, with issue:

E1   John Arthur MacLeod, 1916-1986. He lived in Philadelphia, m. Rosemary <u>DiSalvo</u>, with issue:

F1   Kenneth John MacLeod, born 1946. He lives in Los Angeles, California, m. Susan <u>Boyd</u>, with issue:

G1   Douglas Craig MacLeod.

G2   Megan Ann MacLeod.

E2   Margaret Bertha MacLeod, m. Randal <u>Brainard</u>, with issue:

F1   Bertha Brainard.

F2   John Brainard.

D2   Murdoch Neil MacLeod, 1888-1913. Never married.

D3   Neil Charles MacLeod, died in infancy, 1890.

D4   Rev. Archibald Alexander MacLeod, 1892-1953. Honourary Captain, Chaplain Services, WWII, m. 1) Elizabeth D. <u>Magee</u>, 1895-1926, with issue:

E1   Marion E. MacLeod, born 1915, m. Ralph L. <u>Burns</u>, with issue:

F1   Dr. Steven Burns.

F2   Colin Burns.

F3   Susanna Burns.

E2   Rev. Dr. Hinson A. MacLeod, a pilot in WWII, wounded flying a Hudson bomber over Bay of Biscay, m. Florence (Sue) <u>Curtis</u>, with issue:

F1   Bonnie E. MacLeod.

F2   Burns A. MacLeod.

Rev. Archibald A. MacLeod, m. 2) Barbara Grace <u>Murchison</u>, born 1904, daughter of Donald Neil Murchison, Point Prim, their children were:

E3   Colonel Wm. Bentley MacLeod, born 1928, m. Hugette <u>Bruneau</u>. He was awarded the Order of Military Merit by the Governor General of Canada for distinguished service with the United Nations peace-keeping forces. Issue:

F1   Wm. Bentley MacLeod.

F2   Ian MacLeod.

F3   Brian MacLeod.

E4   Mary Alexandra (Sandra) MacLeod, m. Rev. Kenneth <u>Thompson</u>, with issue:

F1   Rev. Paul Thompson.
F2   Paula Thompson.
F3   Mark Thompson.
F4   Elizabeth Thompson.
F5   Andrew Thompson.
E5   Barbara MacLeod, m. 1) David <u>Baxendale</u>, with issue:
F1   Robin Baxendale.
F2   Jennifer Baxendale.
Barbara m. 2) Arthur <u>Morgan</u>.
E6   Archibald A. MacLeod, m. Elaine <u>Tanton</u>, with issue:
F1   Mitchell MacLeod.
F2   Rachael MacLeod.
F3   A. Alexander MacLeod.
D5   Herbert Henry Booth MacLeod, born 1894, drowned in Hall's Creek, 1908.
D6   Mae Isabelle MacLeod, 1896-1973, m. Andrew <u>Blackmore</u>, with issue:
E1   Norman Blackmore, 1918-1985. Captured and imprisoned by German forces during air raids in WWII, m. Jean <u>Walker</u>. No children.
E2   Catherine Blackmore, m. George <u>Crawford</u>, with issue:
F1   Wanda Crawford.
F2   George Crawford.
F3   Linda Crawford.
E3   Jean Blackmore, born in Quebec City, m. John Edward <u>McKenna</u>, Toronto, with issue:
F1   John Edward McKenna, born in Toronto, m. Cindy <u>Cowan</u>, North Gower, Ontario, with issue:
G1   Meghan Elizabeth McKenna, born in Nova Scotia.
G2   Morag MacLeod McKenna, born in Nova Scotia.
F2   Bruce Andrew McKenna, living in Toronto, m. Deborah Mae <u>Smith</u>, Oakville, Ontario, with issue:
G1   Sean Andrew McKenna.
G2   Lindsey Anne McKenna.
G3   Ian Alexander McKenna.
F3   Katherine Mary Jean McKenna, m. Paul Leslie <u>Debenham</u>, Widness, England. They live in Kingston, Ontario.
F4   Graeme Norman McKenna, living in Los Angeles, m. Marcia <u>Forst</u>, Vancouver, British Columbia.
D7   Katie Dorothy MacLeod, 1898-1900.
D8   Bertha Jean MacLeod, 1900-1934, m. Robert <u>MacAleese</u>, with issue:
E1   Roberta Jean MacAleese, m. Lloyd <u>O'Brien</u>, with issue:
F1   Terrence O'Brien.
F2   Colin O'Brien.
F3   Derek O'Brien.
F4   Alan O'Brien.
E2   Daniel Neil MacAleese, m. Joy <u>Cousineau</u>, with issue:
F1   Debra MacAleese.
F2   Robert MacAleese.

   F3 Vicki MacAleese.

   F4 Angela MacAleese.

  E3 Inez Mae MacAleese, m. Ronald L. <u>Gaudet</u>.

   F1 Kevin Daniel Gaudet.

   F2 Karen Catherine Gaudet.

   F3 Paula Roberta Gaudet.

   F4 Brian Ronald Gaudet.

D9 Charles Robert MacLeod, 1903-1979. He was a blacksmith by trade in Moncton, New Brunswick, m. Mary Belle <u>Wells</u>, with issue:

  E1 Dorothy Jean MacLeod, m. Clarence A. <u>Thompson</u>, with issue:

   F1 Dr. Elizabeth Thompson.

   F2 Brent Thompson.

   F3 Bruce Thompson.

   F4 Nadine Thompson.

  E2 Donald Wells MacLeod, not married.

  E3 Evelyn Agnes MacLeod, m. George W. <u>Fowler</u>, with issue:

   F1 David John Fowler.

  E4 Sterling Amherst MacLeod, m. Albertine <u>Holmes</u>. No children.

This information is from John Norman MacLeod, Australia, and Donald MacLeod, Moncton, New Brunswick.

WILLIAM AND RONALD MACLEOD
WILLIAM AND RONALD MACLEOD OF POINT PRIM

William and Ronald emigrated from the Isle of Skye to Point Prim c. 1803 to join their older brother John who had previously emigrated to Canada.

A1 John MacLeod, m. Barbara _____. They had one son, William, born 1792.
A2 Ronald MacLeod, m. Jane MacDonald, with issue: William, born 1808.
A3 William MacLeod, m. Mary Lamont, with issue:
   B1 Janet MacLeod, born 1825.
   B2 John MacLeod, 1827-1904, m. 1) Christiana Murray, from Brookfield, Nova Scotia. They lived in Port Elgin, New Brunswick, where he was a blacksmith. Their children were:
      C1 William Malcolm MacLeod, 1855-1930, m. Augusta Carolyn Turner, Port Elgin, with issue:
         D1 Harold Ray MacLeod, 1887-1902, died as a result of a skating accident.
         D2 Russell MacLeod, 1889-1896, died of scarlet fever.
         D3 Christine Elizabeth MacLeod, 1893-1963, m. Wallace Smallwood, 1896-1973, of Newcastle, New Brunswick. They had one son:
            E1 Kenneth LeBaron MacLeod Smallwood.
         D4 William Kenneth MacLeod, 1895-1982, m. Marion Lamb Knight, Boston, with issue:
            E1 William Kenneth MacLeod, m. Judith Celia Hollett, Newfoundland. Issue:
               F1 William Kenneth MacLeod.
               F2 Robert Donald MacLeod.
               F3 Jane MacLeod.
               F4 Allison MacLeod.
         D5 Gordon Carette MacLeod, 1900-1980, m. 1) Lois Wry, Sackville, issue:
            E1 Betty MacLeod.
            E2 Gordon MacLeod.
         Gordon m. 2) Marjorie Oulton MacLeod, widow of Murray MacLeod, son of Floyd.
      C2 James Alexander MacLeod, 1858-1940, m. Belle McGlashing from Bayfield, they had a daughter:
         D1 Alice MacLeod.
      C3 John Mariner MacLeod, 1860-1907, m. Endora O'Brien. They had a daughter:
         D1 Mildred MacLeod, lived in U.S.A.
      C4 Clarence Lamont MacLeod, 1862-1948, m. Mary Jane Bell, with issue:
         D1 Constance MacLeod.
         D2 Helen Margaret MacLeod.
         D3 Jean MacLeod.
      C5 Alice Hatfield MacLeod, 1865-1957, m. Christopher Harper, Port Elgin. They had two children:
         D1 Herman Harper.
         D2 Blanche Harper.

Alice m. 2) Frank Raworth, Upper Cape, with two sons:

D3   John Raworth.

D4   Colin Raworth.

C6   Vessey Lina MacLeod, 1868-1904, m. Colin Matheson, with issue:

D1   Marjorie Matheson.

John MacLeod m. 2) Mary Murray, a sister of Christiana. Their children were:

C7   Floyd Elmore MacLeod, 1872-1964, m. Mary Emerson, of Dorchester, New Brunswick. They moved to Lacombe, Alberta, with issue:

D1   Norman MacLeod.

D2   Robert Arthur MacLeod.

D3   Mary Elizabeth MacLeod.

D4   Helen Grace MacLeod.

D5   Floyd Murray MacLeod, m. Marjorie Oulton, with a family.

C8   Arthur Lorne MacLeod, 1873-1947, m. Nellie Brown, St. John, New Brunswick, they had no family.

C9   Myrtle Rena MacLeod, 1877-1952, m. Fred Magee, Port Elgin. They had a daughter who died in infancy.

C10 Mabel Gracie MacLeod, 1879-1966, Port Elgin, never married.

B3   Alexander MacLeod, born 1829.

B4   Ann MacLeod, born 1831.

B5   Malcolm MacLeod, born 1833.

B6   James MacLeod, born 1836.

This information is from Marion Knight MacLeod, Port Elgin, New Brunswick.

ANGUS MACLEOD
ANGUS MACLEOD AND ANNIE MACDONALD OF LORNE VALLEY

A   Angus MacLeod, born in the Isle of Skye, died July 16, 1909, aged 82 years, m. Annie <u>MacDonald</u>, she died July 11, 1915, aged 89 years. They are buried in Lorne Valley. He was the son of William, who was the son of Malcolm and Effie MacLeod, Glashvin. Angus and Annie had issue:

B1   William Angus MacLeod, died April 1, 1916, m. Catherine <u>Matheson</u>. He is buried in Lorne Valley and had issue:

C1   Flora MacLeod, unmarried.

C2   Annie Mae MacLeod, m. Joe <u>O'Hara</u>.

C3   Lisa MacLeod, m. Joe <u>Hamilton</u>, with eight children:
    D1   Catherine Hamilton.
    D2   Florence Hamilton.
    D3   Annie Hamilton.
    D4   Joe Hamilton.
    D5   Muriel Hamilton.
    D6   William Hamilton.
    D7   Marjorie Hamilton.
    D8   Donald Hamilton.

C4   Donald MacLeod, born Sept. 5, 1882, m. Catherine <u>Yuth</u>.

C5   Archibald MacLeod, born Nov. 5, 1886, m. Emma <u>Myers</u>, they lived in South Boston, Massachusetts, with issue:
    D1   William MacLeod.
    D2   Florence MacLeod.
    D3   Donald MacLeod.
    D4   Robert MacLeod.

C6   Winnifred MacLeod, m. Lewis <u>Olmstead</u>. They had four children, lived in Lowell, Massachusetts:
    D1   Lewis Olmstead.
    D2   Catherine Olmstead.
    D3   Richard Olmstead.
    D4   Anne Olmstead.

C7   Hilda MacLeod, 1905-1943, m. Arthur <u>Myers</u>, Martinvale, P.E.I. Issue:
    D1   Lillian Victoria Myers, m. Armour <u>Weir</u>. Their children are:
        E1   Beverly Weir.
        E2   Anne Weir.
        E3   Douglas Weir.
    D2   Martin Bruce Myers, m. Doreen <u>Ellis</u>, they have three children:
        E1   Thane Martin Myers.
        E2   Doris Elaine Myers.
        E3   Norman Elliot Myers.
    D3   Muriel Catherine Myers, m. Heath <u>MacGrath</u>, with four children:
        E1   Heather MacGrath, m. Roger <u>Wightman</u>, with two sons:
            F1   Kyle Wightman.
            F2   Andrew Wightman.
        E2   David MacGrath.
        E3   Catherine MacGrath.
        E4   Alan MacGrath.

D4 Helen Winnifred Myers, m. Harold <u>Jackson</u>. They have three children:
    E1 Gordon Jackson, m. Karen <u>MacDonald</u>, with two sons.
    E2 Paul Jackson.
    E3 Lorraine Jackson.
C8 Christy Belle MacLeod, m. Athol <u>MacLeod</u>, living in Cambridge, Massachusetts.

Information from Martin Myers, Sherwood, and cemetery transcripts.

NORMAN MACLEOD
NORMAN MACLEOD AND MARGARET MACKENZIE OF HIGH BANK

A1   Norman (Tormod Bane) MacLeod, born at Eyre, Isle of Raasay, Scotland early in 1800. Said to descend from Lt. Norman MacLeod of the Royal Navy, Isle of Skye, and Margaret MacLeod of the MacLeods of Rigg (Lewis), granddaughter of Malcolm of Brea of the '45 through her father Norman. Tormod Bane was a carpenter and fisherman by trade and a minister of the gospel by avocation, who was educated in Biblical studies by the Gaelic Schools Society of Edinburgh and resided at Eyre, Isle of Raasay, until late summer 1830. At that time he sailed from Portree, with his pregnant wife Margaret MacKenzie of the MacKenzies of Applecross (Highfield) and daughter Mary Ann, for Prince Edward Island. After residing in Melville for some time, they moved to High Bank in 1835, where the family home still stands and the frontage road bears his name. They had issue:

B1   Mary Ann MacLeod, born at Eyre, Isle of Raasay, 1827, m. her cousin Donald MacKenzie of Iris, P.E.I.

B2   Alexander MacLeod (Blind Sandy) born on the Banks of Newfoundland in early September 1830 while his family was emigrating from Scotland to P.E.I. He was blinded in an accident while a sailor in the Far East and is reported to have married afterward and died in 1912 in Iris, P.E.I, with issue:

     C1   Mary MacLeod, died at Halifax, Nova Scotia.

     C2   Margaret MacLeod, died in Boston, Massachusetts.

B3   Donald Norman MacLeod, born May 25, 1833, at Melville, P.E.I., m. Janet MacLean, 1839 - Feb. 1912, of High Bank, P.E.I., granddaughter of Hector Mor MacLean (born c. 1775) of Hallaig, Isle of Raasay, died December 1911, at High Bank. They resided at High Bank where he was a farmer. Their children were:

     C1   John Donald MacLeod, born June 18, 1860, at High Bank, P.E.I., emigrated to the U.S.A. about 1883, settling in Helena, Montana. There he served as county surveyor, fire chief, city commissioner, and city engineer until his death, October 10, 1938, m. 1) Luella Shorquist (Larson), born May 28, 1870, died June 29, 1899 at Taylor Falls, Minnesota. They married at Bismark, North Dakota in 1888. Issue:

        D1   Beatrice MacLeod, born February 10, 1891, in Montana, m. Ross Allen, Sr., of Helena, with issue:

           E1   Ross Allen, Jr., born April 23, 1910, m. Helen Stadheim, born June 10, 1913, with issue:

              F1   Thomas J. Allen, born in Helena, m. Margot Roe, with issue:

                 G1   Bill Allen.

                 G2   Linda Allen.

                 G3   Laura Allen.

              F2   Lynn Allen, m. John Aaronen, with issue:

                 G1   Chad Aaronen.

              F3   Bonnie Allen, m. 1) Mr. Cochard, with issue:

                 G1   Matthew Cochard.

              Bonnie m. 2) Dee Pollack, with issue:

    G2 Helen Pollack.

   Bonnie also has three stepchildren:

    G3 Joann Pollack.

    G4 Catherine Pollack.

    G5 Robert Dee Pollack.

  E2 Ardis Allen, born May 13, 1912, in Helena, m. Walter Petersen, with issue:

   F1 Allen Petersen, m. Marcia _____, with issue:

    G1 Victoria Petersen.

    G2 Jeffrey Petersen.

    G3 Staci Petersen.

    G4 Steven Petersen.

    G5 Scott Petersen.

    G6 Jennifer Petersen.

    G7 Keri Petersen.

    G8 Jodi Petersen.

   F2 Arlene Petersen, m. James Welch, with issue:

    G1 David Welch.

    G2 LeAnne Welch.

    G3 James Welch, Jr.

   F3 Donald (Buddy) Petersen, m. LuAnn _____, with issue:

    G1 Brian Petersen.

    G2 Marlis Petersen.

    G3 Ronald Petersen.

    G4 Margot Petersen.

   F4 Toby Petersen, married with issue:

    G1 Christine.

    G2 David.

    G3 Jill.

    G4 Michael.

  E3 Donald Allen, born April 1915, in Helena, m. Mary Kelley, born October 1, 1915, with issue:

   F1 Ardis Jean Allen, m. Michael Voeller, with issue:

   F2 Judy Allen, m. Peter Burggraf, with issue:

    G1 Catherine Mary Burggraf.

    G2 Adolf Peter Burggraf.

    G3 Brett Allen Burggraf.

   F3 John Allen, m. Michelle Lovely, with issue:

    G1 Keith Allen.

    G2 Jerome Allen.

    G3 Khristy Allen.

D2 James Blaine MacLeod, born Helena, Montana, and died unmarried in New York City.

John Donald m. 2) Mattie Farquhar, died June 26, 1963, in Orange, Connecticut, with issue:

D3 Marjorie MacLeod, born July 10, 1903, in Helena, Montana, and died November 11, 1965, m. George A. Callahan in Orange, Connecticut, with issue:

E1 Robert Callahan.

E2 Michael Callahan.

E3 Timmy Callahan.

D4   Miriam MacLeod, born October 10, 1904, in Helena, Montana, m. Paul <u>Grant</u> of Fort Worth, Texas, with issue:
      E1   Judy Blaine Grant.
D5   Donald MacLeod, born 1905 in Helena, Montana, died of spinal meningitis in 1926, unmarried.

C2   William MacLeod, born 1862 at High Bank, P.E.I., was for a time assistant superintendent of a lead mine in Helena, Montana. He died unmarried at Tonopah, Nevada, about 1938.

C3   Malcolm MacLeod, born 1864 at High Bank and emigrated to Bozeman and Manhattan, Montana, in 1892, m. Julia <u>LeLacheur</u>, born January 1871, of Guernsey Cove, P.E.I., in 1896. Malcolm established the MacLeod Mercantile Company in Manhattan. His store, built in 1916, is still standing. He died in Montana in 1928. Issue:
D1   Florence MacLeod, m. Mr. <u>Elsenpeter</u> in Los Angeles, California.

C4   Norman MacLeod, born April 16, 1867, at High Bank. He was a merchant, ship owner, lobster cannery owner, and member of the Prince Edward Island Provincial Parliament. He died August 7, 1964, in Murray River, P.E.I., m. 1) Sarah <u>Bell</u>, 1878-1904, of White Sands, P.E.I., with issue:
D1   Alice MacLeod, born August 2, 1899, with issue:
      E1   Isabel MacLeod, who has taught at McGill University in Montreal and York University in Ontario, m. George <u>Sabapathy</u> in London in 1963. Residing in Charlottetown, they and their family are all accomplished musicians.
            F1   Norman Sabapathy.
            F2   David Sabapathy.
D2   Hastings MacLeod, born September 13, 1904, formerly lived in Murray River, now residing in Montague.
Norman m. 2) Alexina <u>MacSwain</u>, 1870-1954, without issue.

C5   Isabella MacLeod, born 1869 at High Bank and taught science in Boston, Massachusetts. She died in November 1918, and is buried at Little Sands.

C6   Mary Ann MacLeod, born 1872 at High Bank, a teacher who graduated from Prince of Wales College. She died in P.E.I., October 1954. She married Hammond <u>Nicolle</u> of Guernsey Cove, P.E.I., with issue:
D1   Leland "Lee" Nicolle, 1892-1988, Murray River, m. Pearl <u>MacKinnon</u>, with issue:
      E1   Evelyn Nicolle, m. Emerson <u>Johnson</u>.
      E2   Audrey Nicolle, m. Howard <u>Rafuse</u>.
      E3   Norma Nicolle, m. Alan <u>Pryne</u>.
      E4   Judson Nicolle, m. Mary <u>Butler</u>.
      E5   Lois Nicolle, m. 1) Louis <u>Jenkins</u>, 2) Don <u>MacLeod</u> of Halifax, Nova Scotia.
      E6   JoAnne Nicolle, m. Lloyd <u>Higgins</u>.
      E7   Hammond Nicolle, m. Eva <u>Bears</u>.
      E8   Anne Nicolle, m. Tim <u>Fraser</u>.
      E9   Blaine Nicolle, m. Susanne <u>Reid</u> of Murray River.
      E10 Darlene Nicolle, m. Clarence "Bud" <u>Lowe</u>.
D2   Clarence Nicolle, 1894-1988, m. Ella <u>Bears</u>, with issue:
      E1   Elbert Nicolle, m. Lois <u>Scott</u>, of Marshfield, with a family.
      E2   Lee Nicolle, m. Mary <u>Flyn</u>, with a family.

      E3   Joyce Nicolle, m. Earl <u>Renouf</u> of Halifax, Nova Scotia, with a family.

      E4   Clayton Nicolle, m. Hope <u>MacLeod</u> of Murray Harbour.

      E5   Lester Nicolle, m. Shirley <u>Blue</u> of Little Sands, with issue.

D3 James William Nicolle, born June 3, 1898, at High Bank, died young.

D4 Arnett Lowell Nicolle, born February 9, 1899, at High Bank, m. Sarah Isabel <u>Stewart</u>, 1911-1981, with issue:

      E1   Carol Anne Nicolle, m. Frank <u>Warsndorfer</u>, with issue:

            F1   Dennis Warsndorfer.

            F2   Lisa Warsndorfer.

            F3   Beth Warsndorfer.

            F4   Christine Warsndorfer.

            F5   Eric Warsndorfer.

      E2   Janet Elaine Nicolle, m. 1) Joseph <u>Furey</u>, with issue:

            F1   Janine Furey.

            F2   Steven Furey.

            F3   Lorraine Furey.

         Janet m. 2) Edwin <u>Kaiser</u>.

      E3   Betty Joy Nicolle, m. Donald <u>Harris</u>, with issue:

            F1   Shana Harris.

            F2   Tara Harris.

            F3   Tupper Harris.

            F4   Janel Harris.

            F5   Ayden Harris.

D5 Audrey Nicolle, born 1902 at High Bank, died unmarried in 1923.

D6 Isabel Nicolle, 1904-1982, m. Ray <u>Stewart</u>, 1903 - June, 1982, with issue:

      E1   Wendell Stewart.

      E2   Billy Stewart.

      E3   Arnett Stewart.

      E4   Ruth Stewart, m. Robert <u>Whiteway</u> of Charlottetown.

      E5   Lowell Carey Stewart, 1928-1929.

C7 Christina MacLeod, born August 17, 1874, at High Bank. After living some time in Boston, she moved to Montana and was a gold medal graduate of the Commercial College in Helena in 1912. She died in Oakland, California, c. 1958. She married Floyd <u>Hillyer</u>, with issue:

D1 Donald Floyd Hillyer, m. Mary Carina <u>Best</u>, with issue:

      E1   Christopher Malcolm Hillyer.

      E2   Bradley Charles Hillyer.

      E3   Cameron MacLeod Hillyer.

      E4   Edward James Hillyer.

C8 Alexander Donald MacLeod, born April 1877 at High Bank, died November 13, 1920, at Helena, Montana. He married Ella Mae <u>MacLeod</u> of Murray River, born May 1, 1881, at Murray River, P.E.I., died October 9, 1927, in Spokane, Washington. They emigrated to Manhattan, Montana, where Alexander was chief accountant for a cement plant at Bozeman and later manager of the Copeland Lumber Co. in Amsterdam. They had issue:

D1 Edna MacLeod, born in P.E.I. in 1901, died January 16, 1966, m. 1) George <u>Stevenson</u>, m. 2) Arthur <u>McGarry</u>, without issue.

D2 Ella Mae MacLeod, born October 1903 in Montana and died of spinal meningitis on February 18, 1909. Buried in Murray River, P.E.I.

D3 Eretha MacLeod, born July 16, 1905, in Manhattan, Montana, and died unmarried at Spokane, Washington, on March 5, 1930.

D4 Elwood Raymond MacLeod, born January 11, 1908, in Manhattan, Montana, and died November 23, 1978, in Woodburn, Oregon, m. Maebelle Margaret Sutton, with issue:

  E1 Donald MacLeod, married twice. Children of the first marriage were:

    F1 Melette MacLeod.

    F2 Darrin MacLeod.

D5 Ella Mae "Bonnie" MacLeod, born July 31, 1909, in Manhattan, Montana, m. 1) Grady Kelly, m. 2) Frank Melia, both without issue. She resides in San Francisco, California.

D6 Ernest Ross MacLeod, born 1911 in Amsterdam, Montana, and died July 24, 1940, in Baker, Montana, m. in 1935, Ethel _____ of Hinsdale, Montana, with issue:

  E1 John "Jackie" MacLeod.

  E2 Ella Mae MacLeod.

D7 Elton Ross MacLeod, born 1913 in Amsterdam, Montana, and died in a motorcycle accident in 1921.

D8 James Leland "Dickie" MacLeod (name later changed to Richard), born November 25, 1917, in Amsterdam, Montana, and died February 20, 1978, in Spokane, Washington. He was a technician for Pacific Northwest Bell Telephone for 41 years. He married Bernice Smith, 1918-1987, in Spokane, with issue:

  E1 James Richard MacLeod, born in Spokane, m. 1) Ellen G. Brockman, with issue:

    F1 James Brock MacLeod, born in Seattle, Washington.

    F2 Rory Richard MacLeod, born in Coeur d'Alene, Idaho. James Richard m. 2) Judith Osterberg Sylte, in 1982 in Athens, Greece, with stepchildren. He resides in Coeur d'Alene, Idaho, and is a professor at North Idaho College.

    F3 Anne Elisabeth Sylte.

    F4 John Christian Sylte.

  E2 Molly Jean MacLeod, born in Lewiston, Idaho, m. Robert Walsh, III, of Spokane, Washington, with issue. The family resides in Spokane, Washington.

    F1 Robert Dennis Walsh.

    F2 Ryan Walsh.

  E3 Patricia Elaine MacLeod, born in Spokane, Washington, m. Vernon Cooper, with issue. The family resides in Spokane, Washington.

    F1 Christopher Cooper.

    F2 Blake Cooper.

D9 Margorie (Helen) Hovde MacLeod, born 1920 in Helena, Montana, died May 4, 1973, in San Luis Obispo, California, m. Major Peter Mihelish of the U.S. Air Force, with issue:

  E1 Jeffrey Mihelish.

  E2 Jimmy Mihelish.

C9 John Dan MacLeod, born at High Bank, P.E.I., died April 2, 1972, at Montague, P.E.I. He was a civil servant and the family historian. He m. 1) Ethel <u>MacKenzie</u>, 1893-1930, of Pictou Island, Nova Scotia, with issue:

    D1 Mae Isobel MacLeod, m. Syd <u>Kerr</u> of Montague, with issue:

        E1 Blaine Kerr.

        E2 Ethel Kerr, m. James <u>Knox</u>.

    D2 Janet MacLeod, m. 1) Lowell <u>Reynolds</u>, with issue:

        E1 Freeman Reynolds, m. Barbara <u>MacLeod</u>.

        E2 Carl Reynolds.

        E3 A daughter who died young.

        Janet m. 2) _____ <u>Winter</u> without issue.

    D3 Harlan William MacLeod, 1912-1937, m. Florence <u>Murdock</u>, with issue:

        E1 Laurie MacLeod, m. Devona <u>Hewitt</u>.

        E2 Gloria MacLeod, m. Clifford <u>MacPherson</u>, with issue:

            F1 Catherine MacPherson, married, resides in Western Canada.

            F2 Linda MacPherson, married, resides in Western Canada.

    D4 Kenzie Murdock MacLeod, born 1914, died in infancy.

    John Dan m. 2) Ruth <u>Vickers</u> of Montague, P.E.I., with issue:

    D5 Maxine MacLeod, m. Jack <u>MacPherson</u>, with issue:

        E1 Donna Lee MacPherson.

        E2 Kerri Wynn MacPherson, m. Paul <u>MacLeod</u>.

    D6 Donna MacLeod, m. William <u>Pierce</u>, with issue:

        E1 Matthew Pierce.

Researched and submitted by James R. MacLeod, Idaho.

WILLIAM MACLEOD
WILLIAM MACLEOD OF WIGMORE ROAD

A1   William MacLeod, 1801-1885, and his wife (name not known), emigrated from Scotland to P.E.I., probably in 1840 as the 1861 census lists him and his wife as well as two of their children as born in Scotland. They settled on the Wigmore Road, taking a lease of land in 1841. Their children were:

B1   William MacLeod, died sometime before 1874, leaving two children who were mentioned in their grandfather's will.

    C1   Emma Janet MacLeod.
    C2   William MacLeod.

B2   Minnie MacLeod, born in 1832 in Scotland, m. John MacKay, with issue:

    C1   George MacKay, died in Montana.
    C2   Alex MacKay, died in California.
    C3   Lucy MacKay, died in Boston.
    C4   Jessie MacKay, died in California.
    C5   Jarvis MacKay, died in Oregon.
    C6   Jack MacKay.
    C7   Mary MacKay, died in Boston.

B3   George MacLeod, was also mentioned in his father's will dated 1874, but it is not known if he left any descendants. Apparently there was a son (it may have been George) who was a master mariner and upon retiring from the deep sea, took up land in the U.S.A., possibly Maryland, and when operating a plough struck an unexploded shell left from the Civil War. He was killed instantly. Some of his descendants visited P.E.I. a few years ago and met their relatives.

B4   Ann MacLeod, m. Richard Found, owner and operator of Fountain Mills on the Found River. Their children were:

    C1   Harlan Found, m. Janet MacLean, Hampton, with issue:

        D1   Dr. Eric Found, m. Marion Wilson, with issue
            E1   Mary Found.

        D2   Aubrey Found, m. I. Champion, Kensington. They live in Charlottetown with three children:

            E1   Gloria Jean Found, who was killed in an auto accident in 1965. She was married to Roger MacDonald, they had a daughter:

                F1   Tracy MacDonald, m. James Kenny, Charlottetown.
                    G1   Jamie Kenny.
                    G2   Craig Kenny.

            E2   Allen Found, m. Reta Faahey, they live in Pictou, with two children:

                F1   Patricia Found.
                F2   Leonard Found.

            E3   William Found, m. Darlene MacInnis, they live in Sherwood with three children:

                F1   Sheri Found.
                F2   Jennifer Found.
                F3   Erin Found.

C2 Walter Found, was married and living in California.

C3 George Found, married in Vancouver with two sons.

C4 William Found, was some time Deputy Minister of Fisheries and lived in Ottawa.

C5 Nettie Found, m. _____ Auld, Freetown, with issue:
  D1 Brewer Auld, m. Nettie MacKenzie, Freetown.
  D2 Walter Auld, was a Presbyterian minister, buried in Ontario.
  D3 Marguerite Auld, m. Everett Schurman, Freetown.
  D4 Annie Auld, was first wife of Rev. Waldron MacQuarrie.

B5 Alexander MacLeod, died 1918, aged 78, lived on the original homestead, m. 1) Mary MacLeod, who died in 1871, aged 30, sister of Malcolm who also lived on the Wigmore Road. They had two daughters:

C1 Janetta MacLeod, 1868-1950, m. James Morrison, they lived in the U.S.A.

C2 Mary MacLeod, married in the U.S.A.

Alexander m. 2) Christy Johnston, who died in 1899, aged 44, with issue:

C3 Kate MacLeod, 1872-1934, m. Alexander MacKay, living in Oregon.

C4 George MacLeod, 1875-1958, never married, lived in Vancouver.

C5 Ethel MacLeod, died 1894, aged 14.

C6 William McLeod, 1882-1966, died in Calgary, m. Laura A. Duncan, 1883-1981. She was from Vernon River, P.E.I. They had issue:
  D1 Lloyd Alexander McLeod, m. Victoria Odette Totton, with issue:
    E1 Roger Lloyd McLeod, m. Janice Mary Arthur, with issue:
      F1 Laura McLeod, born in Toronto, Ontario.
    E2 Richard Wayne McLeod, born in Ottawa, Ontario.
    E3 Patricia Carole McLeod, m. Bryan William Hebden, Hull, England.
    E4 Glen Alexander McLeod, m. Lisa Anna-Marie Levesque, issue:
      F1 Mason Alexander McLeod, born in Sydney, British Columbia.
  D2 William Stirling McLeod, 1912-1994, m. Freda Mary Lorraine Watts, with issue:
    E1 Ronald Stirling McLeod, m. Anna Elizabeth Woodward, with issue:
      F1 Andrew James McLeod, born in Toronto, Ontario.
    E2 Kenneth Gordon McLeod, m. Anita Louise Simmons, with issue:
      F1 David Stirling McLeod, m. Heather Anne Kirkvold, Sioux Falls, South Dakota.
    E3 Emily Anne McLeod, born in Ponca, Oklahoma.

C7 John J. MacLeod, 1884-1956, m. Florence Coppin, they lived in San Francisco, with issue:
  D1 Doris Eleanor MacLeod, 1914-1991, m. 1) Walter John Moeller, 1910-1975, lived in San Francisco, with issue:
    E1 Kenneth John Moeller.
    E2 Garry Edward Moeller.
    Doris m. 2) Eli C. Evon.

C8 Daniel MacLeod, 1887-1895.

C9 Ray Alexander MacLeod, 1883-1974, m. Gertrude Adele Bell, 1891-1967, with issue:

D1 Elmer MacLeod, killed in action in Italy, 1944, aged 31. He was married to Florrie Paynter, who later married Rev. Donald Campbell, one time minister of Zion Church in Charlottetown.

D2 Margaret Adele MacLeod, m. 1) Revel Dickieson, with two children:

 E1 Sheila Margaret Dickieson, 1938-1988, died in Ventura, California, m. Angus Bruce MacLaren, 1936-1994, son of Bruce, died in Santa Maria, California, their children are:

  F1 Ronald Bruce MacLaren.

  F2 Anthony Revel MacLaren.

  F3 Heather Dawn MacLaren.

 E2 Fred Dickieson, killed in an accident in the Barbados.

Margaret m. 2) Bryer Jones, living in Charlottetown, with two children:

 E3 John William Jones, m. Maria Dragone.

 E4 Fiona Jones, m. Randy MacDonald, their children are:

  F1 Jodi Margaret MacDonald.

  F2 Sara Judith MacDonald.

D3 David MacLeod, m. Pauline MacIsaac, living in Borden, P.E.I., with two children:

 E1 Barbara Joanne MacLeod, m. Preston Joseph Shea, living in U.S.A., with issue:

  F1 Erin Colleen Shea.

  F2 Connor Preston Shea.

 E2 David Elmer MacLeod, m. Katherine Mary Irene McNaughton, living in Halifax, with issue:

  F1 Michael David Gerald MacLeod.

  F2 Andrew Kenneth MacLeod.

D4 Louis MacLeod, m. Edith King from Cape Breton, they live on the original MacLeod homestead on the Wigmore Road, with issue:

 E1 Trudy MacLeod, teaching in Bluefield School.

 E2 Isabel MacLeod, a pharmacist, m. Dr. Fleming, living in Halifax. They had issue:

  F1 Peter Louis Fleming.

  F2 Carolyn Margaret Fleming.

  F3 Tricia Brown Fleming.

 E3 Donald MacLeod, m. Jane Hogg, living in Kensington, with issue:

  F1 Donald Ray MacLeod.

  F2 Kurt Denzil MacLeod.

C10 Laura MacLeod, 1890-1956, married William Johnson, lived in Vancouver.

C11 Elmer MacLeod, was drowned in 1911, aged 19, when skating near his home on the Stanley River.

C12 Archie McLeod, 1896-1987, m. Amy Johnstone, 1902-1985, daughter of David Johnstone, Long River. They lived in Calgary, with issue:

 D1 Donald Johnstone McLeod, 1931-1987, m. Brenda Mary Styan, in Toronto, with issue:

  E1 James Douglas McLeod.

  E2 Carol Ann McLeod.

        E3   David Bruce McLeod, m. Eve _____, with issue:
             F1   Sean Donald MacLeod.
    D2   Gordon Archibald McLeod, m. Shirley Ann <u>Barnett</u>, with issue:
        E1   Catherine Louise McLeod, m. Douglas <u>Baine</u>, with issue:
             F1   Jennnele Amanda Baine.
             F2   Jarryd Douglas Baine.
        E2   Kenneth Gordon McLeod, m. Lendy <u>Aiken</u>, with issue:
             F1   Katie McLeod, born in Hinton, Alberta.
             F2   Kendra McLeod, born in Hinton, Alberta.

B6   Donald MacLeod, 1852-1892, m. Annie <u>MacKinnon</u>, 1843-1936. Their children are:
    C1   William MacLeod, m. _____ <u>Heaney</u>, sister of Rev. Jacob Heaney, they had a family and lived in Oregon.
    C2   George O. MacLeod, 1873-1881.
    C3   John A. MacLeod, 1879-1880.
    C4   Harold S. MacLeod, 1881-1946, m. Catherine <u>Gillis</u>, they operated a very successful general store in Vernon River. Their children are :
        D1   Lloyd MacLeod, 1920-1997.
        D2   Donald MacLeod.
    C5   Matilda MacLeod, 1876-1958, m. George <u>Riley</u>, Clinton, with issue:
        D1   Willard Riley, m. Jean <u>MacEwen</u> from New London, with issue:
             E1   Frank Riley, was a banker, died in the Dominican Republic.
        D2   Anna Riley, m. Harold <u>Moakes</u>, with issue at least:
             E1   George Moakes.
    C6   Alice MacLeod, was second wife of Isaac <u>Bernard</u>, French River. They had one son:
        D1   Harold Bernard, m. Miriam <u>MacKay</u>, daughter of Albert, with issue:
             E1   Alan Bernard, m.____ <u>Carruthers</u>, living in French River, with a family.
             E2   Alice Bernard, married with a family.
             E3   Keith Bernard, married in French River, with a family.
             E4   Elva Bernard, m. James <u>Carruthers</u>, brother of Alan's wife, they live in Hamilton, P.E.I., with three children.

Information from Archives, Beaconsfield; Louis and Edith MacLeod, Wigmore Road; and Dr. L. A. McLeod, Oakville, Ontario.

JOHN MACLEOD
JOHN MACLEOD AND SARAH MACEWEN OF BONSHAW

A   John MacLeod, 1800-1865, was a sea captain and emigrated from the Isle of
      Skye in 1839, m. Sarah MacEwen, 1808-1895, from Edinburgh, Scotland. They
      settled on the Green Road in Bonshaw, and had the following children:
      B1   Colin MacLeod, 1830-1912, m. Christina MacLean, 1833-1897, with issue:
           C1   Daniel MacLeod, went to U.S.A.
           C2   Peter MacLeod, went to Alberta.
           C3   John MacLeod, went to Massachusetts.
           C4   Christine MacLeod, lived in U.S.A., buried in New Dominion.
           C5   Flora MacLeod, lived in Ontario, buried in Argyle Shore.
           C6   Sarah MacLeod, buried in People's Cemetery, Charlottetown.
           C7   Alexander B. MacLeod, 1870-1939, m. Winnifred MacKenzie, 1886-
                1974, their children were:
                D1   Lillian MacLeod, m. Arthur B. Curtis, Quincy, Massachusetts,
                     no family.
                D2   Myra MacLeod, m. Lauchie MacKinnon, no family.
                D3   Colin MacLeod, m. Isabel Crosby, with issue:
                     E1   Donald MacLeod, m. Heather MacPhee, with issue:
                          F1   Kenneth MacLeod.
                          F2   Jodi Lynn MacLeod.
                     E2   David MacLeod, m. Patricia DeCoste, with issue:
                          F1   William MacLeod.
                          F2   Robert MacLeod.
                          F3   James MacLeod.
                     E3   Shirley MacLeod, m. Thomas Inglis, they live in British
                          Columbia, no family.
                     E4   Gordon MacLeod, m. Nancy Jenkins, with issue:
                          F1   Angela MacLeod.
                          F2   Aaron MacLeod.
                     E5   Suzanne MacLeod, m. Lowell Oakes, with issue:
                          F1   Ellen Oakes.
                D4   Irene MacLeod, m. Roger Simpson, with issue:
                     E1   Dawn Simpson.
                     E2   Cam Simpson.
                D5   Ina MacLeod, m. Glen Nichol, with issue:
                     E1   Nora Nichol, m. Louis Belliveau.
                     E2   Mary Ann Nichol.
      B2   Donald MacLeod, 1831-1864, lived in U.S.A., buried in New Dominion.
      B3   Peter MacLeod, 1840-1874, lived in U.S.A., buried in New Dominion.
      B4   Neil MacLeod, buried in U.S.A.
      B5   Alexander MacLeod, buried in U.S.A.
      B6   Archibald MacLeod, buried in U.S.A.

Information from Barbara MacLeod, Charlottetown.

MURDOCH MACLEOD
MURDOCH MACLEOD AND WIFE OF HARTSVILLE AND PRIMROSE

A   Murdoch MacLeod, and his wife (name unknown) emigrated from Scotland
c. 1839 and settled in Hartsville, P.E.I. They had at least two children, Kate
MacLeod, who married somewhere in the Hartsville area, and Alexander.
Murdoch's children were:

B1 Alexander MacLeod, 1827-1924. He was age 12 years when leaving Scotland. He worked for a number of years in California during or shortly
after the gold rush of 1849. This was before the building of Panama Canal,
consequently, he went by boat around the South American continent. He
returned to P.E.I. and m. Mary MacLean, 1836-1901, who was also born in
Scotland, and was the daughter of Alexander MacLean and Kirsty MacKie,
who had settled in Long Creek. They left Hartsville in 1889, taking up
land in Primrose where they had to clear the stumps in order to plant
their crops. The farm in Primrose had the advantage of being close to the
"mussel mud" beds, which the farmers used to fertilize and lime their
land. Alexander and Mary's family were:

C1 John MacLeod, named "California Jack" because of his father's gold
rush days, and to distinguish him from other MacLeods in the area,
m. 1) Lottie Matheson from Hartsville, she died 1909, age 38. They
lived in Primrose with issue:

D1 Russell MacLeod, lived in U.S.A., never married.

D2 Annie MacLeod, m. Harry Moore, Milltown Cross. They lived
in Wilmington, Virginia, with issue:
E1 Charlotte Moore, m. Henry Stewart, U.S.A. They had five
children.
E2 Barbara Moore, m. Paul Carpenter, U.S.A. They had four
children.

D3 Mary MacLeod, m. Charles McGuire, U.S.A. issue:
E1 Shirley McGuire, married in California.
E2 Virginia McGuire, married in U.S.A.

D4 Katie MacLeod, m. Rudolph Wurlitzer, in U.S.A. no family.
"California Jack" m. 2) Catherine Martin, Dundas, with issue.

D5 Howard MacLeod, m. Marion MacEachern, farmed in Primrose
and are now retired and living in Bridgetown. Marion taught
school for 33 years. They had issue:
E1 Martin MacLeod, m. Wanda Molyneaux, with issue:
F1 Kimberly MacLeod.
F2 Andrew MacLeod.
E2 Catherine MacLeod, m. 1) Larry Robertson, with issue:
F1 Roger Robertson.
Catherine m. 2) John Peters. They had children.
E3 Jeanie MacLeod, single.
E4 John Ross MacLeod, single.

D6 Alexander MacLeod, m. Almeda Howlett, living in Ontario,
with issue.
E1 Barrie MacLeod, m. Stephanie Cherney, living in Ontario,
they have four children.

      E2   Russell MacLeod, married in Ontario.

      E3   Roy MacLeod, married in Ontario with a girl and boy.

      E4   Darlene MacLeod, m. Gerry Schultz, with a family.

      E5   Kim MacLeod, living in Ontario.

C2 David MacLeod, son of Alexander MacLeod and Mary MacLean, never married and is buried in California.

C3 Christy MacLeod, m. John Hodgins, living in California. They have descendants in the U.S.A.

C4 Effie MacLeod, lived in California.

C5 Kate MacLeod, m. William MacLean, Upton. They had one son.

      D1 John MacLean, married a girl from England and is living in Ontario.

Information provided by Howard MacLeod, Bridgetown.

John MacLeod
John MacLeod of the Isle of Skye

A   John MacLeod, of Isle of Skye (residence thought to have been Portree) had two daughters by his first marriage, wife's name unknown. He had three sons from his second wife, her name is also unknown.

B1   Mary MacLeod, 1820-1875, m. Malcolm <u>MacLeod</u>, 1813-1876. No information on Malcolm's family except that a niece, Mrs. Kate MacConnell (maiden name Bethune), lived in Brighton, near Quincy, Massachusetts, in 1910. She had a son Eben, born in 1891. Malcolm and Mary arrived at Hartsville, P.E.I., with their oldest son William in 1839. William was one and one-half years old at the time.

C1   William MacLeod, 1838-1917 (see Darlington File), m. Isabelle "Belle" <u>MacLeod</u>, died in 1935. They married Feb. 25, 1874. He fished with a fishing fleet off the Grand Banks for many years. According to one source he was the correspondent with the fleet for the Charlottetown Guardian. In 1910 they moved to Vancouver, British Columbia. They had issue:

D1   Mary MacLeod, born Jan. 7, 1876, m. Joseph "Joe" <u>Bishop</u>, 1864-1943. He was from Cornwall, England. They had issue:

E1   Leonard J. Bishop, 1904-1959, m. Ferne <u>MacDonald</u>, issue:

F1   James Stanley Bishop, 1938-1959.

F2   June Marie Bishop, m. Paul <u>Kyelgnard</u>. They had one son and one daughter.

E2   Isabelle Bishop, 1906-1907.

E3   William H. Bishop, 1908-1952, m. Detta <u>Miller</u> in Quincy, Massachusetts. They had no children.

E4   David L. Bishop, born 1913, m. Kathleen <u>Mulchay</u>, issue.

F1   Gail Bishop, was from second marriage to a ____ Lee.

E5   Stanley E. Bishop, 1914-1918.

D2   Catherine MacLeod, 1877-1959, m. 1) Ian <u>MacKeen</u>, m. 2) Rev. Robert <u>Roper</u>, he had one stepson. They lived in Vancouver.

D3   David MacLeod, 1881-1949, never married, lived in Vancouver.

D4   Roderick MacLeod, born 1884, went west as a young man.

D5   Malcolm MacLeod, 1886-1925, never married, served in the Vancouver Police Force.

D6   Alex Duff MacLeod, 1888-1909. He was killed in a mining accident in Wallace, Idaho, and is buried in Vancouver.

D7   Charles George Gordon MacLeod, 1889-1936, m. Katherine Pearle <u>MacDonald</u>, 1893-1962. They lived in Wiltshire, issue:

E1   Hope MacLeod, m. Leith <u>Easter</u>, with issue:

F1   Arnold Wayne Easter.

E2   William Ronald MacLeod, m. Elizabeth <u>Clark</u>, with issue:

F1   Joy Rebecca MacLeod.

F2   Ronald Hooper MacLeod.

F3   Brian Lincoln MacLeod.

F4   Jill Hope MacLeod.

E3   Sara Isabel MacLeod, m. William <u>Larter</u>, with issue:

F1   William Gordon Larter.

       F2   Karen Ann Larter.
       F3   Robert Gary Larter.
       F4   Paulette Nadine Larter.
       F5   Elmer Kent Larter.
       F6   Lincoln Francis Larter.

E4   Gordon Lincoln MacLeod, m. Isabel <u>Downe</u>, with issue:
       F1   Lynn Marion MacLeod.
       F2   Scott Gordon MacLeod.
       F3   Sandra Lee Dawn MacLeod.

E5   Katherine Pearle MacLeod, m. Lorne <u>Murray</u>, with issue:
       F1   Janice Margaret Murray.
       F2   Wade Gordon Murray.
       F3   Vickie Margaret Murray.

D8   Dr. John B. MacLeod, 1892-1958. Never married. He practised as an osteopath in New Westminster, British Columbia, and died there.

C2   John MacLeod, 1840-1917, was born at Strathalbyn, P.E.I., and lived most of his life in Quincy, Massachusetts, m. Effie <u>MacLeod</u>, issue:

D1   William B. MacLeod, m. Jessie <u>MacLeod</u>, in Quincy, Massachusetts. Issue:
       E1   Rita MacLeod, m. George <u>MacDonald</u>, three children.
       E2   Ruth MacLeod, m. Ed <u>Jenkins</u>, they had six children.
       E3   Chester Arthur MacLeod.
       E4   Jean MacLeod m. Ed <u>Gehrke</u>.
       E5   Catherine MacLeod, m. Joe <u>Bruton</u>, they had two daughters and one son.

D2   John Alexander "Alex" MacLeod, m. Mannie <u>Christian</u>. They lived in Lynn, Massachusetts.

D3   Dr. John Malcolm MacLeod, m. Ann <u>Cummings</u>, with issue:
       E1   Gordon MacLeod, m. Ann <u>Cochrane</u>, with issue:
           F1   Gordon Avery MacLeod.
           F2   Douglas Malcolm MacLeod.
           F3   William Bruce MacLeod.
           F4   James Redyard MacLeod.
       E2   John MacLeod, m. Amy <u>Ela</u>, with issue:
           F1   John Malcolm MacLeod.
           F2   Barbara Ann MacLeod.
           F3   Robert MacLeod.

D4   Flora MacLeod, 1874-1960, m. Rev. J. W. <u>MacKenzie,</u> Charlottetown, with issue:
       E1   Katherine MacKenzie, born 1905, m. Mr. Justice George <u>Tweedy</u>, with issue:
           F1   Gordon Tweedy, m. Carol <u>MacKenzie</u>.
           F2   Jean Tweedy, m. Roger <u>Perry</u>, with issue:
               G1   Jennifer Perry.
       E2   John MacKenzie, born 1908, m. Betty <u>Probert</u>, with issue:
           F1   Scott MacKenzie.
           F2   Linda MacKenzie.
       E3   Jean MacKenzie, born 1910, was a nurse in New York.
       E4   Evelyn MacKenzie, born 1912, m. Wilson <u>Becket</u>, issue:
           F1   Heather Becket, m. Gordon <u>MacLean</u>, one child.

F2 Joanne Becket.

F3 Wilson Becket.

E5 Anna Gordon MacKenzie, m. Don Rathbone, with issue:

F1 Gordon Rathbone.

F2 Debbie Rathbone.

D5 Mary MacLeod, 1873-1938, married in 1911 to Angus Martin, in Quincy, Massachusetts, with issue:

E1 Edna Martin, m. John Beeman.

E2 Florence Martin, m. Bob Sealy.

E3 John Martin, m. Laura _____.

E4 Ruth Martin, m. Richard Turner, with issue:

F1 Mary Ann Turner, married in Montague, with issue:

G1 Jennifer.

F2 Jane Bruce Turner.

F3 Richard Turner, Jr.

F4 Bruce Aerich Turner.

E5 Howard Martin.

E6 Marjorie Martin.

D6 Neil Murdoch "Murt" MacLeod, m. Belle MacFee (this is the way this name was spelled), Quincy, Massachusetts, with issue:

E1 June MacLeod.

E2 John MacLeod, married.

E3 Cuyler MacLeod, married.

E4 Gloria MacLeod, m. ___ Cline, four children.

D7 Catherine MacLeod, 1880-1964, m. Rev. Angus B. MacLeod, 1874-1952, with issue:

E1 Bessie Jean MacLeod, 1914-1987, lived in San Diego and retired to Vancouver where she lived with her sister Heather.

E2 Heather MacLeod, 1918-1990, m. Jack Gillies, 1917-1970. They lived in Vancouver, British Columbia, with issue:

F1 Bruce Gillies, works for the Dept. of External Affairs.

D8 Isaac Newton MacLeod, 1882-1950, m. Effie MacKenzie. They lived in Quincy, Massachusetts, with issue:

E1 Newton MacLeod, m. Peggy _____. They lived in Nashville, Tennessee.

E2 Eleanor MacLeod, m. Lincoln Foster in 1967, with issue:

F1 Caroline Anne Foster.

F2 Paula Jane Foster.

F3 Debra Drew Foster.

F4 James Lincoln Foster.

E3 Malcolm M. MacLeod, m. 1) _____ (name unknown) and had one child, possibly named June, m. 2) Shirley Green.

C3 Catherine MacLeod, m. Alex MacKenzie. They lived in Logan, Iowa, and also Woodbine, Iowa. She was born 1844, with issue:

D1 Daniel M. MacKenzie, [born?] 1869, was farming near Woodbine, Iowa, in 1934.

D2 Mary B. MacKenzie, born July 30, 1875, m. Sept. 28, 1905, to B. F. Messenger.

D3 Effie C. MacKenzie, born Oct. 24, 1877.

D4 Margaret MacKenzie, born Feb. 16, 1879. She taught school at Pottawattomie, Iowa. She did not marry.

D5   William M. MacKenzie, born Nov. 12, 1881, lived near Woodbine in 1914.

D6   John A. MacKenzie, born Dec. 23, 1883, of Omaha, died in the late 1930s.

D7   Gordon C. MacKenzie, born April 7, 1886.

D8   Bessie C. MacKenzie, born Oct. 15, 1888, taught school at Woodbine, Iowa, and did not marry.

D9   Mary Bella MacKenzie.

D10 _____.

C4 Mary MacLeod, 1844-1890, m. Murdoch MacKenzie, Tyne Valley, issue:

D1   Annie MacKenzie, m. Fred Lingley of Leavenworth, Washington.

D2   Katie MacKenzie, m. Arthur Waters.

D3   John MacKenzie.

D4   Mary MacKenzie.

D5   Lizzie MacKenzie.

D6   Dan MacKenzie.

D7   William MacKenzie.

D8   Maud MacKenzie.

D9   Tom Corbet MacKenzie.

D10 Alex MacKenzie.

The names listed above and order of age are uncertain. A Col. Jack Harris of Victoria, British Columbia, believes his aunt (C4) died in early 1890s. After her death, her son Alex (D10) came, at the age of about seven, to live with a Harris family at Cardigan, P.E.I. Alex later lived in Lorne Valley.

C5 Malcolm MacLeod, 1848-1900, m. Jane MacKay, on Dec. 25, 1876, at Summerside. He taught school at Cardigan from 1877 to 1880. He lived at Kensington from 1891-1892. He then taught at Sumas, British Columbia, from 1893 to 1897, also at East Langley, British Columbia, from 1897-1900. They had issue:

D1   Mary Jane MacLeod, 1877-1898.

D2   Rachel MacLeod, 1879-1936, was a nurse for many years in Vancouver.

D3   Charlotte MacLeod, 1880-1895, drowned during high tide on the way to church by rowboat at Sumas, British Columbia.

D4   Margaret Catherine MacLeod, 1885-1888.

D5   Lydia MacLeod, 1882-1895.

D6   Alexander Sterling MacLeod, 1887-1942, m. Anna MacDonald, with issue:

     E1   Allister MacLeod, m. Ila Fraser, they had two daughters. They live in Niagara Falls.

     E2   Flora MacLeod, born 1924, m. Mac Chute. They live in Thamesford, Ontario, and have three children.

     E3   John MacLeod, m. Lois MacCorquadale. They live in Embro, Ontario, and have four children.

D7   Hugh Malcolm MacLeod, 1889-1943.

D8   Catherine Emma MacLeod, born 1891, m. Alfred Tranmer in 1917. They had three children.

D9   Johannes Hope MacLeod, 1893-1920.

D10 Charlotte Lydia Dimple MacLeod, 1896-1940, m. Ed. Barnes, with three sons.

C6 Alexander MacLeod, died 1911, m. Emma Lusher, with issue:

D1 Harold MacLeod, died 1961, m. 1) Dorothy ____, m. 2) Virginia Lee Holbrook. They had one child.

D2 Lois MacLeod, 1890-1969, m. Tom Divine, with two stepchildren.

D3 Jean MacLeod, born 1901, m. R. L. Nickel. They had one son.

C7 Charles K. MacLeod, 1853-1922, m. Annie Beardsley, 1863-1945. They were married Dec. 25, 1890, with issue:

D1 Helen Margaret MacLeod, born Jan 14, 1893, m. Howard Ernest Foster on Sept. 11, 1913. They had three children.

D2 Charles Malcolm MacLeod, born Dec. 14, 1895, m. Lillian "Peggy" Porter on June 1, 1920. They had two children.

D3 Mary MacLeod, born Aug. 1900, did not marry. She was secretary to Bishop Lawrence in Cambridge, Massachusetts.

C8 Effie Christina MacLeod, 1859-1897, m. James Harris, 1846-1938. They lived in Cardigan Bay, and had eight children, all of whom moved away.

D1 Col. John J. "Jack" Harris, 1881-1965, m. Amy Scott in Quebec City in 1907. They lived in Victoria, British Columbia, eight daughters.

D2 William Harris, 1883-1956, m. Julia "Dot" Ward. They lived in Cranbrook, British Columbia, and had three sons.

D3 Emma Harris, born Feb. 1, 1886, m. Ray Bulpit in 1910. They had two sons.

D4 Margaret May "Peggy" Harris, born May 27, 1888, m. Albert R. Steacy, 1859-1926. They had one son.

D5 Charles Harris, born 1890, m. Mrs. Jenny Eisenhauer.

D6 Ketura Harris, 1892-1943, m. Duncan MacLaren.

D7 George Harris, 1894-1975, m. Mildred Logan. They had one son.

D8 Hilda Harris, 1897-1916. Her mother died a month after she was born. She was adopted as a baby by Capt. and Mrs. William MacLeod of Halifax. She died in her teens.

C9 John Alexander MacLeod, 1861-1938, m. Clara Joan Chadsey, 1867-1903. He taught in P.E.I. from 1879-1884, and then moved to British Columbia, issue:

D1 Malcolm Chadsey MacLeod, born 1888. He was killed in action on April 25, 1915, at St. Julien, near Ypres, Belgium, when Germans used poison gas for the first time.

D2 John Virgil MacLeod, 1890-1931, m. Muriel Shaw. They lived in North Vancouver, British Columbia, with issue:

E1 Ronald Alfred MacLeod, born 1920, m. Gladys ____, issue:

F1 Gavin Macleod.

F2 Christine MacLeod.

E2 John Shaw MacLeod, born 1911, m. Mary Sanderson, issue:

F1 Margaret Diane MacLeod, m. John Lyons.

F2 Bruce MacLeod.

E3 Joan MacLeod, born 1924, m. Jack Parrish, with issue:

F1 Kim Parrish.

F2 Grant Parrish.

F3 Michael Parrish.

F4 Robert Parrish.

D3 William Ray MacLeod, 1892-1934, m. Beulah Champion in 1921. They lived in Sardis, British Columbia, with issue:

> E1 Alexander Harvey MacLeod, 1924-1944, killed in action as RCAF bomber pilot in WWII.
> E2 Malcolm MacLeod, 1927-1952, m. Catherine Ellis. He was killed in an air crash at Comox, British Columbia, issue:
>> F1 Bruce MacLeod.

D4 Earl Leslie MacLeod, born 1894, m. Flora MacKechnie, issue:
> E1 John MacKechnie MacLeod, m. Jean Hickernell, with issue:
>> F1 Susan Diane MacLeod.
>> F2 David Leon MacLeod.
>> F3 Catherine Jean MacLeod.
> E2 Robert Virgil MacLeod.
> E3 Flora Margaret MacLeod, m. Albert C. Leisenring, with three children.

D5 Clarence Herbert MacLeod, 1897-1957.
D6 Effie Violet Eloise MacLeod, 1900-1925.
D7 Clara Mary "Manie" MacLeod, 1902-1926.

B2 A daughter of John MacLeod of Skye, m. _____ MacDonald and lived in Valleyfield, P.E.I. She died young and left a family.

B3 Alexander (Sandy) MacLeod, son of John MacLeod and his second wife, was a stone mason and went to Regina, m. Anne _____ with issue:
> C1 Norman MacLeod, never married, he lived in Vancouver where he taught school in the 1880s and 1890s. He later owned and operated saw mills and owned considerable real estate in boom days in Vancouver.
> C2 Dr. James MacLeod, m. Sadie MacLeod, they lived in Regina, Saskatchewan, and had at least one son:
>> D1 Dr. Gordon MacLeod, who was married and had four children.
> C3 Christie MacLeod.
> C4 Annie MacLeod, m. Dan Nicholson, with issue:
>> D1 Alexander Nicholson.
>> D2 Duncan Nicholson.
>> D3 A daughter.
> C5 Mary MacLeod, m. _____ MacLeod.

B4 Norman MacLeod, son of John of Skye and his second wife, m. _____ Miller, they lived in St. John, New Brunswick.

B5 John MacLeod, m. Christine MacKinnon, who was a daughter of Ian (Ban) MacKinnon, Kilmaluag, Skye. Her sister Catherine married William MacLeod, Kilmaluag, and were the grandparents of the late Rev. Dr. Ronald MacLeod, one time minister in Toronto. John and Christine came to P.E.I. in 1839 and settled in Springton, with issue.
> C1 Mary Ann MacLeod, m. _____ MacGinnes, lived in British Columbia, with issue:
>> D1 Bessie MacGinnes, m. John Vickerson.
>> D2 Florence MacGinnes, m. _____ Coombe, with issue:
>>> E1 Grace Coombe, m. Russel Frost, with issue:
>>>> F1 Jack Frost.
>>>> F2 Russel Frost.
>>> E2 Elinor Coombe.
>> D3 John MacGinnes, 1879-1972, m. Fanny MacKinnon from Cape Breton, with issue:
>>> E1 Dr. John D. MacGinnes, Prince George, m. Rosemary Carroll, with issue:

    F1 John D. MacGinnes.
    F2 Valerie MacGinnes.
    F3 Glen MacGinnes.
    F4 Jill MacGinnes.
   E2 Georgina MacGinnes, m. Percy <u>Williams</u>, Burnaby, British Columbia, issue:
    F1 Elaine Scott Williams.
    F2 Margo Williams.
    F3 Paul Williams.
   E3 Pearl MacGinnes, m. Cyril <u>Pope</u>, Coquitlam, British Columbia, with issue:
    F1 John Pope.
    F2 Peter Pope.
    F3 Jennifer Pope.
  D4 Donald MacGinnes, never married, retired to P.E.I.
  D5 Neil MacGinnes, deceased, lived in Montana.
  D6 Mary MacGinnes, m. ____ <u>Holt</u>, Belmont, Massachusetts.
  D7 Christine MacGinnes, m. _____ <u>MacMullen</u>.
  D8 Kenneth MacGinnes, deceased, lived in Idaho.
C2 Donald MacLeod, was a blacksmith in O'Leary, P.E.I., with a wife and family, no further information at this time.
C3 Bessie MacLeod, m. Ronald <u>MacDonald</u>, with issue:
  D1 Hugh MacDonald.
  D2 Annie MacDonald, m. ____ <u>Delaney</u>.
C4 Flora MacLeod, m. Donald <u>Nicholson</u>, with issue:
  D1 Bessie Nicholson.
  D2 Murdoch Nicholson.
  D3 Maggie Nicholson.
  D4 Allen Nicholson.
  D5 Hugh Nicholson.
  D6 John Nicholson.
C5 Hugh MacLeod, m. ____ <u>Haslam</u>, with issue:
  D1 John MacLeod, born 1871, m. Helen ____, born 1875, with issue.
   E1 Clarence MacLeod, 1896-1958, m. Margaret <u>Mitchell</u>, no family.
   E2 Grace MacLeod, born 1897, m. Eric <u>Smith</u>, born 1897, issue
    F1 Eric Smith.
    F2 Barbara Smith.
    F3 Kenneth Smith, married with children.
    F4 Ronald Smith, married with children.
   E3 Gladys Helen MacLeod, born 1899, m. William <u>Champion</u>, born 1898, Vancouver, British Columbia, with issue:
    F1 William Champion, m. Caroline <u>Howard</u>, with issue:
     G1 William Thomas Champion.
   E4 Hugh Allen MacLeod, 1900-1976, m. Laura <u>Macy</u>, no children.
   E5 Jean MacLeod, born 1904, m. Charles <u>Longley</u>, 1904-1976, with issue:
    F1 John Longley, m. Ann <u>Irwin</u>.
    F2 Helen Longley.
  D2 William MacLeod, born 1872, married but wife's name unknown, with three children.

          E1   Fred MacLeod.
          E2   Myrtle MacLeod.
          E3   Sadie MacLeod.
     D3   Laura MacLeod, born 1874, m. _____ Profitt, with issue:
          E1   Bessie Profitt.
          E2   Myrtle Profitt.
          E3   Fanny Profitt.
     D4   Ben MacLeod, born 1876, m. 1) ____, 2) Bertha Millman, issue:
          E1   Jean MacLeod, m. Blair Fraser.
          E2   _____.
          E3   _____.
     D5   Edith MacLeod, m. _____ Bernard, with issue:
          E1   Harold Bernard.
     D6   George MacLeod, m. 1) _____, 2) Lilla _____.
     D7   Hedley MacLeod, born 1892, m. _____, with issue:
          E1   Reginald MacLeod.
 C6 John K. MacLeod, 1837-1932, m. 1) Effie MacKenzie, 1847-1890, m. 2) Mary Ann MacLennan, 1852-1936, with issue:
     D1   Rev. Dr. Donald Morrison MacLeod, 1870-1941, m. 1) Elizabeth Irving, 1875-1910, a daughter of David Irving, Vernon, P.E.I., with issue:
          E1   David Irving MacLeod, m. Margaret Eddy McRoberts, they live in Oshawa, Ontario, with issue:
               F1   David MacLeod, m. Elizabeth Burton, with issue:
                    G1   Ian David MacLeod.
                    G2   James Abelson MacLeod.
               F2   Donald MacLeod.
     Rev. Donald Morrison MacLeod m. 2) Olive Usher, 1888-1972, with issue:
          E2   Mary Effie MacLeod, m. Rev. Dr. Hubert James Warnock McAvoy, with issue:
               F1   Rev. Ian M. McAvoy, m. Faye Hutchison.
               F2   Rev. Roderick Alan McAvoy.
          E3   Donald Morrison MacLeod, m. Catherine Shaw.
          E4   Dr. Gordon MacLeod, m. Cynthia Allison, with issue:
               F1   John Bruce Archibald MacLeod.
               F2   Alan James MacLeod.
          E5   Margaret Olive MacLeod, m. Robert Montgomery, issue:
               F1   Robert Fraser Montgomery, m. Lynda Megli.
               F2   Heather Margaret Montgomery, m. Hugh Sefton.
               F3   Scott Donald William Montgomery.
     D2   Rev. John B. MacLeod, 1872-1929, m. Helena Brodie, with issue:
          E1   Dr. J. Wendell MacLeod, Ottawa, m. 1) Margaret Wirple, m. 2) Jessie McGeachie, with issue:
               F1   Peter MacLeod, m. Margaret _____, with issue:
                    G1   Karen MacLeod.
                    G2   Kenneth MacLeod.
               F2   Wendy MacLeod, m. John MacDonald, with issue:
                    G1   Joan MacDonald.
                    G2   Sheila MacDonald.
                    G3   _____.

E2 Robert MacLeod, m. Bea <u>Beach</u>, issue:
    F1 Ian MacLeod, m. Alteles _____, with issue:
        G1 Gavin MacLeod.
    F2 Allison MacLeod.
E3 Kenneth MacLeod, m. Kay <u>Lamb</u>.
E4 Archie MacLeod, m. Betty _____, with issue:
    F1 Roderick MacLeod.

D3 Rev. Angus B. MacLeod, 1874-1952, m. Catherine <u>MacLeod</u>, 1880-1964. She was the daughter of John and Effie MacLeod, consequently second cousin to her husband. Issue:
E1 Bessie Jean MacLeod, lived in San Diego but retired to Vancouver to live with her sister Heather, she died in 1987.
E2 Heather MacLeod, 1918-1990, m. Jack <u>Gillies</u>, 1917-1970, they lived in Vancouver and had one son:
    F1 Bruce Gillies, with the Dept. of External Affairs.

D4 Bessie MacLeod, 1876-1913, m. Murdoch <u>MacLean</u>, 1872-1933, North Wiltshire, P.E.I. , with issue:
E1 Florence MacLean, 1896-1959, m. Rev. Wilfred <u>MacLeod</u>, issue:
    F1 Jean MacLeod, m. Robert <u>Schurman</u>.
    F2 Ian MacLeod.
E2 Sterling MacLean, 1898-1972, never married.
E3 Gordon MacLean, m. Marie_____, with issue:
    F1 Garth MacLean.
    F2 Heather MacLean.
    F3 Shirley MacLean.
    F4 Kenneth MacLean.
E4 Dr. Sheldon MacLean, never married, practised in New York City.
E5 Morrison MacLean, 1902-1973, m. Dorothy <u>MacKenzie</u>, issue:
    F1 Gwenneth MacLean.
    F2 Donald MacLean.
    F3 Malcolm MacLean.
    F4 Rodney MacLean.
    F5 Nancy MacLean.
E6 Dr. Lorne MacLean, m. Louise <u>Hurd</u>.
E7 Bessie MacLean, married with two children.

D5 Flora MacLeod, died Sept. 15, 1884, aged 2 years.

John K. MacLeod m. 2) Mary Ann <u>MacLennan</u>, with issue

D6 H. Chalmers MacLeod, 1894-1979, m. Amy <u>Frizzel</u>, 1907-1975. Buried in Hartsville Cemetery. They had issue:
E1 Mary Ida MacLeod, died in infancy.

Information received from Isobel MacLeod, Cornwall; David Irving MacLeod, Oshawa, Ontario; and Elena Cerrolaza, Montreal.

William McLeod
Obituary of William McLeod

There passed away to his eternal rest on May 28, at his home, Royal Oak Avenue, Burnaby, B.C., Mr. William McLeod in his seventy-sixth year.

The late Mr. McLeod was born in the Isle of Raasay, Inverness Shire, Scotland, in 1839, coming to Canada with his parents, Malcolm and Mary MacLeod, in September, 1840. They landed at Charlottetown, P.E.I., and in a short time moved to the district of Hartsville where they took up land in the green woods. Here he lived with his parents for over thirty years, assisting nobly in the hard task of transforming the standing forest into fertile and productive fields. In 1874 he married Isabelle McLeod, daughter of Roderick and Catherine McLeod of Darlington, and moved to his own home adjoining that of his father. Here he and his life partner with the bright hope of youth entered joyfully on the task of making a home. For thirty-six years they remained here and brought up a family of six sons and two daughters, courageously facing hardships and difficulties of life in the early years, in what is now known as the "Garden Province."

In the course of time the older members of their family left the parental home and entered on life's work in the "Great West." In 1910 the parents, anxious to join the absent members of the family, were constrained to let the old Island home pass into other hands.

For a year Mr. McLeod lived in Vancouver, but being a lover of the quieter and simple life he moved to the suburb of Burnaby, where he and Mrs. McLeod resided up to the time of his death.

By a host of friends in East and West, Mr. McLeod will be remembered as a man of sterling worth and steadfast loyalty to purity, honour and truth. In the home the guiding hand of a wise and good father and true husband will be missed more than words can tell.

Besides a sorrowing widow, the following children survive: David L., Malcolm, Rod, Gordon and John B., in British Columbia, Mrs. Joseph Bishop of Quincy, Massachusetts, and Mrs. John A. MacKeen, of Pasadena, California; also three brothers, John A. in British Columbia, and John and Charles in Massachusetts, and one sister, Mrs. A. McKenzie, in Iowa.

The above obituary, which has been slightly edited, appeared in the Charlottetown *Guardian*, July 16, 1915, page 6.

H.S.M.

John MacLeod
John MacLeod and Sarah Matheson of Dundas

A1   John MacLeod, born in Raasay in 1810. Came to P.E.I. in 1828-29. His father, name unknown, came also. It is not known if his mother came over; probably she did not. It is possible that Donald, who came with his wife Jane Nicholson, was a brother of John. The names of other members of the family, if any, are not known. John died in Dundas in June 1863. Buried in Belfast Cemetery. He m. Sarah Matheson, who was born in Skye in 1808. She came to P.E.I. in 1828 and died on March 16, 1884, in Little Sands. She is buried in Belfast Cemetery. Their children were:

B1   Mary MacLeod, 1831-1932. She is buried in Acorn Cemetery. Her husband was Malcolm MacLeod, 1840-1918, also buried in Acorn Cemetery, the dates of birth shown on their gravestones are incorrectly stated as Mary, 1857, and Malcolm, 1859. Three children died as infants. Birth dates of others are approximate, except for that of Peter.

    C1   Lydia MacLeod, born 1863, m. Warren Gilman, of Boston, Massachusetts.

    C2   Christine MacLeod, born 1865, m. George P. Urling, of Winthrop, Massachusetts. Died June 2, 1945.

    C3   Katie MacLeod, born 1867, m. C. H. Urling of Cambridge, Massachusetts. Died Nov. 13, 1949.

    C4   Sarah Jane MacLeod, born 1869, m. John W. MacKay. Lived in Kentville, Nova Scotia, died Sept. 2, 1950.

    C5   Peter MacLeod, born 1871, m. Mary Matheson of Dundas. Died 1930.

B2   Murdoch MacLeod, 1836-1923, buried in Dundas Cemetery. He m. Jane Acorn, 1839-1918, with issue:

    C1   Allan MacLeod, 1869-1931, m. Cassie Stewart, and had a son.

        D1   Harry MacLeod.

    C2   Geddy Murdoch MacLeod.

B3   Roderick MacLeod, 1837-1917, m. Flora MacLeod, 1822-1908. She was born in the Isle of Skye and was the daughter of Peter MacLeod who settled in Dundas in 1836. Flora's brother Malcolm was married to Mary, who was a sister of Roderick. Flora and Roderick's children were:

    C1   Sarah MacLeod, m. Joseph Mestico, Quincy, Massachusetts, issue:

        D1   Ray Mestico.

        D2   Raymond Mestico.

        D3   Florence Mestico.

    C2   Christy MacLeod, m. John MacPherson, Little Sands, one son:

        D1   Dan MacPherson, m. Kate Howe, whose maternal grandmother was Flora MacLeod, who married Angus Nicholson, both from the Isle of Skye and settled in High Bank. Flora and Angus had a son Roderick and a daughter named Flora, 1852-1945, who married 1) John Swan from Scotland who was drowned at sea. They had a daughter Jane Swan, 1880-1910, who married Captain Tom MacLure, Murray Harbour North. They lived in New York and had no family. Flora (Nicholson) Swan m. 2) John Howe from Murray Harbour. They had a daughter, Kate Howe, who m. 1) Joseph Ring of Jamaica Plains, Massachusetts, and they had a daughter who m. Leonard <u>Miles</u>, Salem, Massachusetts. Kate Howe m. 2) Dan <u>MacPherson</u>, Little Sands (D1). Their children were:

E1   Mary MacPherson, m. Carmen <u>Dugas</u>, Digby, Nova Scotia. They live in Little Sands.

E2   John Paul MacPherson, 1928-1930.

E3   Christy MacPherson, m. Arnold <u>Peters</u> from Mayfield, P.E.I. They live in Toronto, Ontario, with issue:
>   F1   Robert MacPherson, living in Moncton, New Brunswick.
>   F2   Keith MacPherson, m. Valerie <u>Stairs</u>, living in Mc-Adam, New Brunswick, with two children:
>   >   G1   Kathleen Elizabeth MacPherson.
>   >   G2   Fraser Alexander MacPherson.
>   F3   Carol Profitt, living in Toronto, Ontario.

E4   Joan MacPherson, m. Fred <u>Blakney</u>, Salisbury, New Brunswick, with children:
>   F1   Trent Blakney, m. Nancy <u>Richards</u>.
>   F2   Heather Blakney, living in Halifax.

E5   Paul MacPherson, m. Eleanor <u>Taylor</u>, living in Salisbury, New Brunswick, children:
>   F1   Brent MacPherson, m. Catherine <u>Alward</u>.
>   F2   Daniel MacPherson, m. Maureen <u>O'Hara</u>, with issue:
>   >   G1   Aaron Robert MacPherson.
>   >   G2   Johanna MacPherson.
>   >   G3   Justin Daniel MacPherson.
>   F3   Cathy MacPherson.
>   F4   Sherri MacPherson.

B4   John MacLeod, 1839-1914, m. Mary <u>Reilly</u> of Forest Hills, who died March 24, 1925, age 80. Buried in Dundas Cemetery, they lived in Mt. Hope, issue:

C1   Duncan Gavin MacLeod, died in Brittania Mine disaster in British Columbia, unmarried.

C2   Rev. Dr. Peter Allen MacLeod, m. Emma <u>Anderson</u>, Cable Head. He died in Ontario about 1937. Their children were:
>   D1   Blanche MacLeod, m. Professor <u>Hemphill</u>.
>   D2   Ernest MacLeod, married, no family.
>   D3   Muriel MacLeod, married Mr. <u>Hess</u>.
>   D4   A girl, died young.

C3   Christie MacLeod, m. George H. <u>Jones</u>, Harrington, with issue:
>   D1   George Jones, 1897-1988, m. May <u>Phillips</u>, Harrington, issue:
>   >   E1   Jeanne Phillips, died young.
>   >   E2   Pauline Phillips, married in Regina, three children.
>   >   E3   Joyce Phillips, married in Regina, two children.
>   >   E4   Douglas Phillips, married in Regina, four children.
>   D2   Mary Jones, born 1898, m. Albert E. <u>Phillips</u>, 1899-1980, issue:
>   >   E1   Herbert Phillips, m. Gladys <u>Wood</u>, four children.
>   >   E2   Mervin Phillips, m. Evelyn <u>Kerr</u>, three children.
>   >   E3   Christine Phillips, m. John <u>Allen</u>, three children.
>   D3   Katherine (Katie) Jones, 1900-1970, m. Lloyd <u>Jenkins</u>, 1898-1980, Dundas. Their children are:
>   >   E1   Hazel Jenkins, m. 1) Erwin <u>Jenkins</u>, m. 2) Ralph <u>Raynor</u>.

Hazel and Erwin had three children.
- E2 Evelyn Jenkins, single.
- E3 Cecil Jenkins, m. Marion Gratto, three children.
- E4 Bennett Jenkins, m. Gail Prowse, four children.
- E5 Beatrice Jenkins, m. Andrew Humphrey, two children.
- E6 Doris Jenkins, m. Donald Bowen, four children.
- E7 Alice Jenkins, m. Vincent White, two children.
- E8 Preston Jenkins, m. Eileen Henry, two children.
- E9 Pauline Jenkins, m. Jack Garnhum, four children.
- E10 Mary Elizabeth Jenkins (stillborn).
- D4 John Jones, 1902-1948, m. Mae Diamond, 1910-1988, with issue:
  - E1 Lois Jones, m. Alison Carr.
  - E2 Keir Jones, m. Evelyn Gregory.
- D5 Annie Jones, 1905-1995, m. John Pope, Chepstow and U.S.A.
  - E1 One child, stillborn.
- D6 Blanche Jones, 1910-1941, m. Earl Hughes, Cape Breton, one child.
- D7 Ida Christine Jones, died in infancy.
- C4 John W. MacLeod (Johnny the Schoolmaster), Upton, m. Sady Stead, with issue:
  - D1 George MacLeod.
  - D2 Marie MacLeod.
  - D3 Sterling MacLeod.
- C5 James Andrew MacLeod, 1872-1958, m. 1) Elizabeth MacLaren, 1886-1918, with issue:
  - D1 Herbert MacLeod.
  - D2 Florence MacLeod.
  - D3 John MacLeod, died young.
  - D4 Earle MacLeod, living in Charlottetown.
  - James Andrew m. 2) Christine MacLeod, 1887-1958, with issue:
  - D5 Mary MacLeod, 1922-1972, m. John DuPasquier, with issue:
    - E1 Sonia DuPasquier.
- C6 Finlay MacLeod, 1870-1896, married and had a son who died in infancy.
- C7 Daniel MacLeod, died 1905, aged 26.
- B5 Duncan MacLeod, 1840-1936, m. Sarah Hayden of St. Peter's Bay, 1845-1937. Buried in Dundas Cemetery. They were married Sept. 14, 1870, and lived in Dundas for over 60 years. They then moved to St. Peter's Bay. Issue:
- C1 John MacLeod, born July 1871, died March 1872.
- C2 John D. MacLeod, 1872-1958, m. Martha MacLaren, of Marshfield. They lived in Billerica, Massachusetts, and on P.E.I. Both are buried in Billerica, Massachusetts. Martha's mother Dorinda (Hayden) MacLaren was the sister of John's mother, Sarah. Their children were:
  - D1 Ernest MacLeod, 1898-1898.
  - D2 Robert MacLeod, 1899.
  - D3 James MacLeod, 1902.
  - D4 Sadie MacLeod, 1904-1915.
  - D5 John MacLeod, 1905-1915.
  - D6 Martha MacLeod, 1908-1960.
  - D7 Margaret MacLeod, 1910-1968.
  - D8 Walter MacLeod, 1912.
  - D9 Duncan MacLeod, 1915.
  - D10 Wallace MacLeod, 1917.

D11 Sarah MacLeod, 1921-1972.

C3 James D. MacLeod, 1874-1962, m. Christine MacKay, High Bank. They were divorced and had no children, m. 2) Emily Rose of Parkberg, Saskatchewan, and they adopted:

D1 Eleanor MacLeod.

James m. 3) Erma Murphy and had no children. They lived in New Perth and James is buried in People's Cemetery, Charlottetown.

C4 Robert Frank MacLeod, 1876-1880.

C5 Daniel Melvin MacLeod, 1878-1966, m. Ella MacIntyre, and lived in Brookline, Massachusetts, no children, m. 2) Esther MacDonald of Cape Breton and lived in Wakefield, New Hampshire. He and Ella are buried in Walnut Hills Cemetery, Brookline, Massachusetts. They had issue:

D1 Daniel MacLeod, Jr.

D2 Herbert MacLeod.

D3 Wesley Duncan MacLeod.

D4 Joel MacLeod.

C6 Robert Frank MacLeod, 1880-1963, m. Leona Dockendorff of North River. They lived in Brookline and Chatham, Massachusetts, and are buried in Walnut Hills Cemetery, Brookline, Massachusetts. They had issue:

D1 Gladys MacLeod, m. Shirley Souther.

D2 Frankie MacLeod, m. Arthur Healy.

C7 Wallace Freeman MacLeod, 1882-1956, m. Katherine A. MacLeod of Hartsville (daughter of Duncan and Jessie [MacLean] MacLeod). They lived in Dundas and in Brookline and Melrose, Massachusetts, and are buried in Puritan Lawn Cemetery, Peabody, Massachusetts. They had issue:

D1 Sarah Margaret MacLeod.

D2 Duncan Wesley MacLeod.

C8 Sarah Mary MacLeod, 1884-1969, m. Ira W. Martin, Eldon. They lived in Brookline, Massachusetts. Buried in Walnut Hills Cemetery, Brookline, Massachusetts. They had issue:

D1 Marion Mary Martin, died Oct. 28, 1911, shortly after birth. She is buried in Evergreen Cemetery, Boston, Massachusetts.

C9 Wycliffe Sterling MacLeod, 1886-1977, m. Alice Heyman of Wales. They lived in Billerica, and Cochicuate, Massachusetts. Her uncle Albert lived in Cochicuate. Her mother and brothers visited U.S.A., but returned to Wales. Alice is buried in Cochicuate, Massachusetts. They had a son:

D1 Ira MacLeod.

C10 Walter Scott MacLeod, 1888-1940, never married. He was a Methodist Minister and later a priest in the Anglican Church. He is buried in Walnut Hills Cemetery, Brookline, Massachusetts.

B6 Allan MacLeod, 1846-1907, m. Sarah MacDonald, 1846-1934. Sarah's parents were Alexander MacDonald and Mary Campbell. They came to Bellevue from Skye in 1840. They lived in California and Mt. Hope, and are buried in Dundas Cemetery. Allan and Sarah had issue:

C1 John Murdoch MacLeod, m. Ida MacDonald, with issue:

D1 Allan MacLeod, also a twin brother who died. He married Margaret Grace Taylor, with issue:

       E1   Rhoda Mae MacLeod, m. _____ Baker, with issue:
             F1   Nathan Earle Baker.
             F2   Kinza Mae Baker.
       E2   John Allan MacLeod, m. Sherry Jenkins, they had a family.
       E3   Valerie Grace MacLeod, m. Leslie MacEachern, with issue:
             F1   Keslie Grace MacEachern.
             F2   Katya Lynn MacEachern.
       E4   Margaret Dale MacLeod, m. Philip Claybourne, with issue:
             F1   Sarah Jean Claybourne.
             F2   Rebecca Katherine Claybourne.
       E5   Kathryn Ruth MacLeod, m. Brian O'Stroski.
       E6   Mark Taylor MacLeod.
       E7   Faith Maureen MacLeod.
  C2   Annie Laurie MacLeod, m. Elmer Hale, Middleboro, Massachusetts, with issue:
       D1   Judge Allan Hale, married with two boys and one girl.
  C3   Mary (Maizie) MacLeod, Plymouth, Massachusetts.
  C4   Sarah Jessie MacLeod, m. James A. MacLeod, of Mt. Hope, with issue:
       D1   Alexander MacLeod, m. Jean Shepherdson, with issue:
             E1   Kathy MacLeod, m. Kim Kennedy, with issue:
                   F1   Scott Kennedy.
                  F2   Kaitlin Kennedy.
       D2   Sarah MacLeod, 1913-1941.
       D3   Lawrence MacLeod, 1921-1978.
B7   Jessie MacLeod, date of birth unknown, died 1897. She was the second wife of John MacKay, of High Bank, with issue:
  C1   Sarah Ann MacKay, born Oct. 10, 1891, m. Norman Stewart, High Bank. With issue:
       D1   Evelyn Stewart, m. Ernest Machon, Murray Harbour. They have three children.
       D2   William Sweet Stewart, m. Sylvia Hooper Keenan, with issue:
             E1   Norman Stewart, m. Cynthia MacLeod (daughter of Carl MacLeod, Wood Islands), with issue:
       D3   Janet Stewart, living in Charlottetown.
       D4   Mary Stewart, m. 1) Clarence White, m. 2) Sandy MacDonald. They have three children.
       D5   Betty Stewart, m. Malcolm MacLean, six children.
       D6   Norman Stewart, m. Evelyn Swain, two children.
  C2   Willie MacKay, died in 1963, m. Christine MacDonald.
       D1   Stirling MacKay, m. Maureen Sullivan, born in Wales.
       D2   Leona MacKay, m. Oliver Giddings.
       D3   Jessie MacKay, m. Robert Dennison.
       D4   Catherine MacKay, married Basil Irving.
       D5   Donalda MacKay, married in Newfoundland.
       D6   Angus MacKay, m. Maisie Jewell.
       D7   Wayne MacKay, m. Lynn Emery.

Step-children by John's first wife, Annie MacLean: Mary E.; Catherine and Christine (Mrs. James MacLeod and Mrs. Peter MacLean, of High Bank); and John A., who died in childhood.

Information from Mary Dugas, Little Sands, and Sarah MacLeod, Kennebunk, Maine.

HECTOR MACLEOD
HECTOR MACLEOD AND LAVINIA WILLIAMS OF CHARLOTTETOWN

A1   Hector MacLeod, died 1939, aged 82, was perhaps from the Canoe Cove area, at least it is generally believed that his mother was Christine MacNevin from that area. It is also believed that Hector had two brothers, Charles and David, both married in U.S.A. Hector m. Lavinia Williams, she died 1935, aged 73. They lived a number of years in U.S.A. where some of their children were born. They returned to P.E.I. and lived in Charlottetown and are both buried in the People's Cemetery, Charlottetown. Their descendants are:

B1   David Nelson MacLeod, m. Mary E. Hayes, from Halifax, Nova Scotia, they lived in Limerick, Saskatchewan, with issue:

    C1   Wally MacLeod, m. 1) Hazel Tuplin, 2) a woman from Oxford, Nova Scotia, they live in Red Deer, Alberta, no family.

    C2   Gordon MacLeod, m. Sheila MacInnis. She died in1942. Their family:
        D1   David MacLeod.
        D2   Douglas MacLeod.
        D3   Janet MacLeod.

    C3   Marjorie MacLeod, m. Bruce Williams, with issue:
        D1   Gayle Williams, married in British Columbia.

    C4   Mabel MacLeod, m. Kassian Hylnka, with issue:
        D1   Adrian Gregory Hylnka.
        D2   Marven Hylnka.
        D3   Linda Catherine Hylnka.

    C5   Dorothea MacLeod, m. Art MacKenzie, Piapot, Saskatchewan, issue:
        D1   Robert MacKenzie.
        D2   Ruth MacKenzie.
        D3   A daughter.
        D4   A son.

    C6   Edith MacLeod, m. George McGill, Carmen, Manitoba, with issue:
        D1   Robert McGill, living in Winnipeg.

B2   Josiah MacLeod, born 1884, lived in Kentville, Nova Scotia, was married more than once and left eight children.

B3   Laura MacLeod, 1885-1955, m. Murdoch MacKenzie, 1877-1926, Bradalbane and Charlottetown, with issue:

    C1   Verna MacKenzie, m. Lawrence Rowe, with issue:
        D1   David Rowe, married in Charlottetown.

    C2   Eleanor MacKenzie, m. George Schleyer, with issue:
        D1   Wayne Schleyer, m. Gretchen ____.

    C3   Helen MacKenzie, m. Alex Corbett, Ontario, with two children.

    C4   Doris MacKenzie, m. Walter Duffy, Charlottetown, with a large family.

    C5   Joan MacKenzie, m. Donald Fagie, Quebec, two children.

    C6   Charles MacKenzie, died aged 24 in 1938.

    C7   Lawrence MacKenzie, married a girl from England, living in Quebec, with two boys.

B4   Neil Hudson MacLeod, 1887-1965, m. Maggie Wood, 1891-1942, from Southport. They lived in Charlottetown, with issue:

    C1   Hayden MacLeod, m. Gladys ____, from Nova Scotia, they live in Charlottetown, with issue:

D1 Robert MacLeod, married.
D2 Margaret MacLeod, married.
C2 Allison MacLeod, m. Eleanor Harvey, Charlottetown, three boys.
C3 Neil MacLeod, Camp Borden, single.
C4 Aben MacLeod, m. Marj Connick, North River Road, with issue:
D1 Brent MacLeod.
B5 Ethel Irene MacLeod, 1890-1971, m. Joseph MacDonald, 1888-1965, Charlottetown, with issue:
C1 Borden MacDonald, m. Vera Kirby, Charlottetown, with issue:
D1 Mardi MacDonald, married in Edmonton, with two daughters and a son.
D2 Ralph MacDonald, Ottawa.
C2 Norma MacDonald, m. Lawrence Edwards, Dartmouth, Nova Scotia, and Charlottetown. Their children are:
D1 Gloria Edwards, m. Thomas Echlin, Ontario, with two children.
D2 Reta Edwards, m. Lawrence Cudmore, Calgary, seven children.
D3 Vera Edwards, m. George MacDonald, Calgary, nine children.
D4 Borden Edwards, married in Calgary, no family.
D5 Tona Edwards, m. George Halliwell, Charlottetown, three children.
D6 Wilfred Edwards, m. Val Manning, no family.
D7 Catherine Edwards, m. Brian MacCallum, Crossroads, with three children.
D8 Leslie Edwards, died aged 19 in 1952.
B6 James Fullerton MacLeod, 1892-1978, m. Stella Vickerson, 1891-1977. They lived in Charlottetown, with issue:
C1 Ralph MacLeod, m. Helen Cameron, Charlottetown, with issue:
D1 Heather MacLeod, m. Paul Trewin, living in Halifax.
D2 James MacLeod, m. Debbie Stephenson, Charlottetown, issue:
E1 Carolyn MacLeod.
E2 Stephen MacLeod.
D3 Graham MacLeod, Charlottetown.
C2 Lois MacLeod, m. Jack Morris, Charlottetown, with issue:
D1 Donald Morris.
D2 Elizabeth Morris, m. _____ Steele, with issue:
E1 Jordon Steele.
C3 Marion MacLeod, living in Charlottetown, single.
B7 Harry Craswell MacLeod, 1896-1978, m. Florence Oakes, Breadalbane and Charlottetown. Their children are:
C1 Phyllis MacLeod, m. Albert Schleyer, brother of George, they live in Charlottetown, with issue:
D1 Frank Schleyer.
C2 Shirley MacLeod, 1925-1960, never married.
B8 Charles Albert MacLeod, 1898-1973, m. Catherine Jeffrey, Charlottetown, with issue:
C1 Alberta MacLeod, married in the North West Territories, two children.
C2 Irene MacLeod, married in Ottawa, two children.
C3 Joyce MacLeod, married in Calgary, two children.
C4 Robert MacLeod, married in Calgary, not living, one son.

The above information received from Norma Edwards, Charlottetown.

Mini Genealogies
Short Genealogies of MacLeod Families

A   Murdoch MacLeod, of Portree, Scotland.
     B1   Murdoch MacLeod, of Portree (?) and Culloden, P.E.I.
     B2   Alexander MacLeod, of Portree (?) and possibly Australia.
     B3   Norman MacLeod, of Portree and Culloden, P.E.I., came on the ship *James Gibb* in 1858.
         C1   Alexander S. MacLeod (Little Alex) of Culloden.

A   Norman MacLeod, born in Scotland, m. Mary <u>Gilbertson</u>, born 1825, Midyell, Raga, Shetland Islands, died July 4, 1894, in Chicago. Their children were:
     B1   Alexander MacLeod, born Nov. 27, 1850, P.E.I., died April 10, 1910, Chicago, Illinois. He married Sarah Jane <u>Dixon</u>.
     B2   Jane A. MacLeod, born Feb. 25, 1842, P.E.I., died July 29, 1922, Chicago, Illinois. Married Jacob D. <u>White</u>, born 1859, with issue:
         C1   Florence Adelaide White, born 1864, in Chicago, died July 13, 1893. Married Landon Taylor <u>Peck</u>, June 8, 1886, with issue:
             D1   Arthur Joseph Peck, born Nov. 22, 1891, died July 20, 1960. Married Ebba Maria <u>Svenason</u>, July 25, 1914.

A   Angus MacLeod, 1797-1885, lived in Bellevue, near Caledonia, m. 1) Belle <u>MacDonald</u>. They had issue:
     B1   Roderick MacLeod, went west and died there.
     B2   John MacLeod.
     B3   William MacLeod.
     B4   Annie MacLeod.
     B5   Mary MacLeod, m. Neil <u>Nicholson</u>.
   Angus m. 2) Margaret _____, with issue:
     B6   Roderick MacLeod.
     B7   Flora MacLeod.
     B8   Margaret MacLeod.
     B9   Katherine MacLeod.
     B10   Mabel MacLeod.

Donald MacLeod
Donald MacLeod and Christy Matheson of Darlington

A   Donald MacLeod, 1815-1898, born in Scotland. Emigrated to P.E.I. in 1840 and
m. Christy Matheson, 1826-1910. They farmed in Darlington. Their children
were:

B1 Captain Duncan MacLeod who was decorated by the King of Norway
and presented with an engraved telescope for an heroic rescue off the
coast of Norway.

B2 Alexander MacLeod, wife's name unknown, had at least two sons:
C1 Alexander MacLeod, Jr., m. Annie Miller whose first husband was
James Murray. They lived in Tignish.
C2 John MacLeod, born in Tignish, passed away at Beach Grove in the
1960s.

B3 John T. MacLeod, 1844-1923, m. 1) Christine Matheson, with issue:
C1 Duncan MacLeod, 1870-1906, killed in the San Francisco earthquake.
C2 Fred Alexander MacLeod, 1871-1970, m. Emma Mason. They lived
in Gorham, New Hampshire, with issue:
D1 Beatrice MacLeod, died age three years.
D2 Wilton W. MacLeod, 1900-1979, m. Dorothy McKechnie, they
lived in Gorham, with issue:
E1 Jean MacLeod, m. Corsan (Buddy) Lary, six children.
E2 Joan M. MacLeod, m. Edwin J. Adams. They live in Maine
with two children.
C3 Dan MacLeod, died at an early age with acute appendicitis, m. Jose-
phine Stone, with issue:
D1 Roderick S. MacLeod, 1912-1980, m. Emmy Lou Morrison. They
lived in Gorham, with issue:
E1 Gary Douglas MacLeod, m. Lorna Jean Smith. They live
in Pennsylvania, with issue:
F1 Aaron Douglas MacLeod.
F2 Megan Briar MacLeod.
E2 Greg Angus MacLeod, living in New Hampshire.
C4 John (Jack) MacLeod, 1877-1960, m. Pearl H. Stack, 1896-1980. They
lived in Calgary, with issue:
D1 Ian MacLeod, 1918-1986, m. Joanne Buterman, with issue:
E1 Jack MacLeod, m. Beverly Hougen, with issue:
F1 Cameron MacLeod.
F2 Allana MacLeod.
E2 Dianne MacLeod, m. Tom Brown, Red Deer, Alberta, issue:
F1 Bonnie Brown.
F2 Denise Brown.
D2 Mary Ramage MacLeod, m. Frank Studenka, with issue:
E1 Brian Studenka, living in Winnipeg.
D3 Agnes Lillian MacLeod, m. Wesley Finnon. They live in Win-
nipeg, with issue:
E1 Brenda Jean Finnon, m. Lorne Barske, with two children.

E2 Barbara Mary Finnon, m. Dick <u>Kuypers</u>, two children.
D4 Jean Helen MacLeod, living in Winnipeg.
C5 Lillian Ann MacLeod, 1880-1973, m. John Scott <u>Cairns</u>, Dunstaffnage, P.E.I. Their children were:
D1 Margaret Lillian Cairns, m. Lemuel Hicks <u>Webster</u>, 1902-1964. They lived in Boston, Massachusetts, with issue:
    E1 Beverly Ann Webster, m. George Miller <u>Olin</u>, with issue:
        F1 Heather Ann Olin, m. George Owen <u>Sweeney</u>.
        F2 Jo-Ann Elizabeth Olin, living in Connecticut.
    E2 Carol Minnie Webster, m. Stanley Allen <u>Hearn</u>, with issue:
        F1 Jason Peter Hearn.
        F2 Jonathon Andrew Hearn.
    E3 Roy Lemuel Webster, living in Massachusetts.
    E4 Shirley Elaine Webster, m. Fremont Lynwood <u>Bickford</u>, II, with issue:
        F1 Fremont Lynwood Bickford, III.
        F2 Robin Lynn Bickford.
        F3 Michael Lemuel Bickford.
        F4 Scott Lindsay Bickford.
    E5 Barbara Ruth Webster, living in Massachusetts.
D2 John William Cairns, 1911-1991, m. Margaret Jeanne <u>MacLeod</u> (daughter of Allison MacLeod). They lived in Dunstaffnage, P.E.I., with issue:
    E1 George MacLeod Cairns, living in Chatham, New Brunswick.
    E2 Donna Ruth Cairns, m. Allan <u>MacCormac</u>, living in Toronto.
    E3 John Robin Cairns, m. Lia Jane <u>Sewuster</u>, with issue:
        F1 Sean Gerald Cairns.
        F2 Mason William Cairns.
    E4 Donald Allison Cairns, m. Patricia Ann <u>Hunter</u>, with issue:
        F1 Robin Allison Cairns.
        F2 Mandi Dawn Cairns.
    E5 Jane Scott Cairns, m. Gary Rankin <u>McLaine</u>, with issue:
        F1 Sarah Grace McLaine.
        F2 Scott Rankin McLaine.
    E6 Robert Earle Cairns, m. Janet Doris <u>Baker</u>.
D3 Robert Carruthers Cairns, 1916-1987, m. Ethel Jean <u>Wilson</u>, issue:
    E1 Judith Jean Cairns.
D4 Ruth E. Cairns, m. Albert <u>Griffin</u>, 1910-1977, with issue:
    E1 Gordon Wain Griffin.
C6 Margaret Christy (Maude) MacLeod, 1882-1971, m. Alexander Donald <u>MacDonald</u>, 1860-1925, who was an uncle of John T.'s second wife. They lived near Dundas, with issue:
D1 Lillian MacDonald, 1907-1925.
D2 John Sterling MacDonald, born 1909, m. Annie Kathryn <u>MacDonald</u>.
D3 Muriel MacDonald, 1911-1930, buried in Dundas.
D4 Alexander MacDonald, 1913-1916.
D5 Douglas Dewer MacDonald, 1914-1964, m. Annie Kathryn <u>MacDonald</u>, with issue:
    E1 Cyril Dewer MacDonald, m. Debbie <u>Hoff</u>, with two children.

E2 Lloyd Arthur MacDonald, m. Audrey <u>MacDonald</u>, four children.

E3 Alexander Angus MacDonald, m. Woneta <u>Sanderson</u>, with three children.

E4 Sterling Douglas MacDonald, m. Betty <u>Hiltz</u>, with one son.

E5 Karen Alena MacDonald, m. Gordon <u>Jackson</u>, two children.

E6 Keith Blair MacDonald.

D6 Margaret Florence MacDonald, born 1917, m. Thomas (Ted) Edgar <u>Hoyle</u>, Stratford, Ontario, with issue:

E1 Barbara Anne Hoyle, m. Andrew Wilfred <u>Werner</u>.

D7 Allison MacDonald, 1919-1990, m. Dorothy Jean <u>Duncan</u> from Poplar Point, with issue:

E1 Kevin Alexander MacDonald.

E2 Kenneth Allison MacDonald.

D8 Alexina Freda (Lexie) MacDonald, 1922-1991, m. Norman Haddon <u>MacLeod</u>, they lived in Bridgetown, P.E.I., no family.

C7 Neil Archibald MacLeod, 1886-1944, m. Anne Coyle <u>Summers</u>, 1887-1979, born in Dundee, Scotland. They lived in Massachusets, one son:

D1 Neil Arnold MacLeod, m. Irene Floranne <u>Fancy</u>. They are living in Grandview, Texas, with issue:

E1 Sandy Stephen MacLeod, m. Nancy Jo <u>Harden</u>. They live in Euless, Texas.

E2 Lee Ann MacLeod, m. Keith Dwayne <u>Cox</u>, with issue:

F1 Joshua Keith Cox.

F2 Christopher Dwayne Cox.

E3 Scott Duncan MacLeod, m. Cathy Leigh <u>Brink</u>, living in Fort Worth, Texas, with issue:

F1 Katie Irene MacLeod.

F2 Ian Tanner MacLeod.

John T. MacLeod m. 2) Margaret Jane <u>MacDonald</u>, 1870-1968. Issue:

C8 Douglas Keir MacLeod, 1893-1963, m. Sarah Elizabeth <u>Warry</u>, 1897-1985, with issue:

D1 Douglas George MacLeod, 1921-1943, missing in action in Burma.

D2 Robert Graham MacLeod, 1925-1989, a lawyer in Charlottetown, m. Frances Isobel <u>Bourke</u>, 1926-1990, with issue:

E1 Glen Edward MacLeod, m. Sharon <u>MacAulay</u>, with issue:

F1 Craig Ronald Robert MacLeod.

F2 Kellie MacAulay MacLeod.

E2 Barbara Lynn MacLeod, m. James Malcolm <u>Phillips</u>, Charlottetown, with issue:

F1 Robbie Phillips.

F2 Jamie Lynn Phillips.

E3 George Douglas Henry MacLeod, living in Halifax.

D3 M. Elizabeth (Mickey) MacLeod, m. Fred Merriet <u>Cannon</u>, issue:

E1 Nancy Jeanne Cannon, m. John Gordon <u>Stewart</u>.

E2 Stewart Douglas Cannon, living in San Diego.

E3 Robert Frederick Cannon, living in Ottawa.

E4 Margaret Elizabeth Cannon, m. Gerard <u>Lachapelle</u>, living in Calgary, with issue:

F1 Sara Elizabeth Lachapelle.

F2 Rene Lauren Lachapelle.

C9 Allison MacLeod, 1895-1972, had a car dealership in Charlottetown, m. Ruth Sarah <u>Grady</u>, with issue:

    D1 Earle Grady MacLeod, 1921-1981, who was Chairman of the Civil Service Commission of P.E.I., m. 1) Eva <u>Irlam</u>, 2) Doris (Dode) <u>Howatt</u>, with issue:

        E1 Thomas Esmond MacLeod, m. Edith <u>Kelly</u>, with issue:

            F1 Jason Paul MacLeod.

            F2 Kelly MacLeod.

        E2 David Earle MacLeod, m. Audrey <u>Penny</u>, with issue:

            F1 Penny MacLeod.

            F2 Caroline Maud MacLeod.

        E3 Charlotte MacLeod, m. Robert <u>Thomsen</u>, with issue:

            F1 Karly Thomsen.

            F2 Logan Thomsen.

    D2 Margaret Jeanne MacLeod, m. John William <u>Cairns</u>, 1911-1991, Dunstaffnage, P.E.I. They had six children.

    D3 Donald Allison MacLeod, 1925-1957, m. Katherine <u>Williams</u>, issue:

        E1 James Allison MacLeod, 1948-1970.

        E2 Cathy Louise MacLeod, m. David Preston <u>MacDonald</u>, with issue:

            F1 Stacy Lee MacDonald.

                G1 Mikaela Dawn MacDonald.

            F2 Jeffrey Allison MacDonald.

            F3 David Christopher MacDonald.

        E3 Heather Jeanne MacLeod, 1955-1978.

C10 Jean MacLeod, 1906-1973, m. F. Rundell <u>Seaman</u>, with issue:

    D1 Rundell Upton Seaman, m. Adele <u>MacLeod</u>, Summerside, with issue:

        E1 A. Mark Seaman.

        E2 Suzanne J. Seaman.

B4 Flora MacLeod, m. _____ <u>Large</u>.

B5 Janet MacLeod, m. _____ <u>MacPherson</u>.

B6 Annie MacLeod, m. _____ Livingstone.

B7 Sarah MacLeod, was listed on the 1891 census as being a sister, 46 years of age and living with John T. MacLeod and family.

Researched by Beverly Ann Olin, Seekonk, Massachusetts, and Neil MacLeod, Grandview, Texas.

DONALD MACLEOD
DONALD MACLEOD AND MARY MACDONALD OF VICTORIA CROSS

A   Donald MacLeod, c. 1819-1890, m. Mary Macdonald, c. 1826-1883. Rev. J. H.
     Bishop states that Donald was a son of Murdoch MacLeod and Jane Auld,
     Mermaid. However, Earle Bruce says it is more likely to be Murdoch MacLeod,
     who was living in Little Sands in 1873 and was dead by 1880, leaving 97 acres
     in lot 51 to his son Donald. Donald and Mary's family were:
B1   James MacLeod, 1861-1944, m. Christy Ann Ross, 1869-1947. James was a
     farmer in Victoria Cross and also raised foxes. Christy was from Kinross.
     They are buried in Montague Community Cemetery. They had issue:
     C1   John "Milton" MacLeod, moved to Chicago, then to St. Louis, m. 1)
          Alice Hale, 1909-1979. Alice was from South Haven, Michigan. They
          were married in 1941 and had issue:
          D1   Carol Jean MacLeod, died at age five.
          D2   Mary Christine MacLeod, m. Roland Etzold, in California, issue:
               E1   Karen Etzold
               E2   Kristen Etzold
          John "Milton" MacLeod m. 2) Katherine Kouschuetzy, of Cincinnati,
          Ohio. She was a psychiatric social worker.
     C2   Alice MacLeod, m. Dr. Preston MacIntyre. They lived in Montague.
          She was an R.N. graduate from Mt. Sinai, New York. They were
          instrumental in establishing the first hospital in Montague area. They
          had issue:
          D1   Jack MacIntyre, D.D.S., Crossroads.
          D2   William MacIntyre, dentist in Montague.
          D3   Kenneth MacIntyre, M.D., shipwrecked and drowned off Ber-
               muda in 1967.
     C3   Beulah MacLeod, R.N., never married.
     C4   Blanche MacLeod, R.N., m. Harold Smith, a bank manager. They
          retired in Montague.
          D1   Ann Smith, married in Seattle, Washington.
     C5   Creta MacLeod, R.N., m. Edwin Cox from Maryland. They retired
          to Lower Montague, with issue:
          D1   James MacLeod Cox, M.D., practises in Lynchberry, Virginia.
          D2   Carolyn Cox, lived near Elmira, New York. She married Dr.
               McKane, they have four children.
     C6   Annie MacLeod, 1904-1906.
B2   Christy MacLeod, twin sister of James, 1861-1948, m. Angus Lamont,
     Victoria Cross, 1851-1947, with issue:
     C1   Silas Lamont, construction supervisor. He never married and was a
          veteran of WWI. He died in Edmonton.
     C2   James Lamont, owner of Pool Construction Co., Regina. He married
          late in life, no children.
     C3   Lizzie Lamont, died in her twenties. She is buried in Orwell Head.
     C4   Mary Lamont, 1890-1976. She worked for a bank in Charlottetown.
     C5   William Lamont, 1890-1952, twin of Mary. He was a farmer and
          never married.

B3 Mary MacLeod, m. Daniel <u>Fraser</u>, blacksmith in Kilmuir, with issue:
- C1 Ernest Fraser, killed in WWI, buried in Montague Cemetery.
- C2 Arthur Fraser, killed in WWI.
- C3 Artemas Fraser, died in Reno, Nevada. He never married.
- C4 Malcolm Fraser, teacher in British Columbia, he never married.
- C5 Mary Fraser, never married, died in Kilmuir.
- C6 Sarah Fraser, school teacher, never married.
- C7 Oswald Fraser, horse shoer and blacksmith in Kilmuir.
- C8 John Fraser, farmer in Kilmuir.

B4 Malcolm MacLeod, twin of Mary. He never married and settled in Ross-land, British Columbia. He was fire chief in the small mining town. He died in 1905, when still a young man.

B5 Priscilla MacLeod, m. Donald <u>MacLeod</u>, in Schuyler, Nebraska. They moved to San Diego where she died. They had issue:
- C1 Alice MacLeod.
- C2 Edith MacLeod.
- C3 William MacLeod.
- C4 Another son.

B6 Mary MacLeod (possibly her name), m. brother of Donald MacLeod, also in Nebraska, with issue:
- C1 Mary MacLeod, m. Father Jeremiah <u>Crowley</u>, an early reformer of the Roman Catholic Church. He was excommunicated.
- C2 Annie MacLeod, m. David <u>Reed</u>. She died during childbirth.

B7 "Red" Jack MacLeod, m. Ella <u>Annear</u>. They lived in Victoria Cross and had one son:
- C1 Hudson MacLeod, m. Lou _____, from Saskatchewan, with issue:
    - D1 Barbara MacLeod, married in Montreal.

Source of information: John "Milton" MacLeod, St. Louis, Missouri.

John MacLeod
John MacLeod and Flora Stewart of Hartsville

A1 John MacLeod, 1816-1891, on March 14, 1849, m. Flora Stewart, born 1825, both born in Scotland. John is buried in Hunter River Cemetery. Their family were:

B1 Flora MacLeod, 1854-1939, m. Mr. MacLeod, with issue:

C1 Richard MacLeod, 1878-1925, m. Matilda May Ford, 1889-1981, daughter of Richard Ford and Eliza Casford. Matilda May married in 1959 her second husband, who was Rev. Albert Wellington Lougheed, a United Church Minister, he died in Charlottetown, Dec. 1966, and was buried alongside his first wife on Manitoulin Island, Ontario. Matilda May was laid to rest beside Richard in the Portage Pioneer Cemetery. Richard and Matilda's children were:

D1 John Charles MacLeod, 1915-1990, m. in Liskeard, Ontario, Merle Winnifred Cornell, from that area, with issue:

E1 Janet May MacLeod, m. 1) Dennis MacKay, with issue:
F1 Jonathon MacKay.
F2 Richard MacKay.

E2 Marion Ann MacLeod, m. Eric Gordon Manuel, a bank manager in Charlottetown, with issue:
F1 Pennie Evelyn Manuel.
F2 Scott Stevenson Manuel.
F3 Kelly Lisa Manuel.
F4 Aaron John Manuel.

D2 Jennie May MacLeod, m. Jack Tollerton, with issue:
E1 Robert James Tollerton, born in Vancouver.
E2 Susan Jane Tollerton, born in Vancouver.

D3 Athol Richard MacLeod, m. Mona Isabel Bishop in Victoria, British Columbia, with issue:
E1 Frederick Allan MacLeod.
E2 Judy May MacLeod, m. Robert Campbell, Vancouver, issue:
F1 Matthew Robert Campbell, born at William's Lake, British Columbia.
F2 Christy Lisa Campbell.
E3 Joan Dianne MacLeod, m. Daniel John Derpak, Vancouver, with issue:
F1 James MacLeod Derpak.

D4 Clayton Alexander MacLeod, a housing inspector with the P.E.I. government, m. Muriel Toombs, Long River, P.E.I., who was employed with Addiction Services, both retired, they had issue:
E1 Sandra Louise MacLeod, m. Elmer Linus Cullen (son of Frank and Mildred [McKenna] Cullen of Charlottetown). They live in Charlottetown and have a son:
F1 Clayton Francis Cullen.
E2 Dianne Elizabeth MacLeod, m. Robert John Mundy, Toronto, Ontario (son of Ralph and Dorothy of Toronto), issue:
F1 Kimberly Anne Mundy.
F2 David Robert Mundy.
F3 Scott Matthew Mundy.

E3   Patricia Elaine MacLeod, m. John Kopeck, son of Thomas and Iris Kopeck of Colorado, they live in Wayne Co., Illinois, with issue:

   F1   Christopher John Kopeck.
   F2   Katrina Lynn Kopeck.

E4   Alanna Marie MacLeod, m. Irwin Wade Webster, son of Sterling and Edith (Hawbolt) Webster of the Bangor Road, P.E.I. Irwin and Alanna live on the Bangor Road with four children:

   F1   Justin Wade Webster (stillborn).
   F2   Krystn Cailey Webster.
   F3   Michael Irwin Webster.
   F4   Megan Emma Lee Webster.

B2   Malcolm MacLeod, born Oct. 1855, Hazel Grove, P.E.I.
B3   John MacLeod, born May 1, 1858.
B4   Ewen MacLeod, born Sept. 1, 1860, Upper Rustico, P.E.I.
B5   Janet MacLeod, born June 30, 1862, Rustico, P.E.I.
B6   Charles MacLeod, born Jan 1, 1868, died Jan. 11, 1922, Hunter River, P.E.I., buried Portage Cemetery, P.E.I.
B7   Margaret MacLeod, born Jan. 15, 1869, California Rd., P.E.I.
B8   Frederick Alexander MacLeod, born Feb. 15, 1871, Brookfield, P.E.I.

Information submitted by Sandra L. (MacLeod) Cullen, Charlottetown.

John MacLeod
John MacLeod and Wife of Hartsville

A   John MacLeod and his wife, originally from Scotland, emigrated to Hartsville, where they bought a farm. They are buried in Hartsville Cemetery.

   B1   Allan MacLeod, m. Catherine <u>MacLeod</u> of Springton.* They moved to Central Lot 16. Buried in Central Lot 16 Cemetery. Allan and Catherine had issue:

      C1   John MacLeod, m. Louisa <u>Ryder</u> from St. Nicholas. Buried in Central Lot 16 Cemetery. They had issue:

         D1   Oliver MacLeod, m. Leta <u>Campbell</u> from Irishtown. Moved to Breadalbane in 1952. Honourary life members of the New London Campbell Clan.

         D2   Major MacLeod, 1907-1971, m. Marillo <u>Daye</u> from Wellington, issue:

            E1   Carl MacLeod, m. Linda <u>Birch</u>, with issue:

               F1   Duston Ateesha MacLeod.

            E2   Edna MacLeod, m. Walter <u>Wadden</u>, with issue:

               F1   Rita Wadden, m. Robert <u>Campbell</u>.

         D3   Wilfred MacLeod, 1908-1986, buried in Central Lot 16 Cemetery, m. Dorothy <u>Hutchinson</u>, with issue:

            E1   Clarence MacLeod, died 1966, m. Sylvia <u>MacArthur</u>, issue:

               F1   Kelly MacLeod.

               F2   Kimberley MacLeod.

            E2   Joyce MacLeod, m. Floyd <u>MacKinnon</u>, Summerside, issue:

               F1   Finton MacKinnon.

               F2   Denise MacKinnon.

               F3   Keigon MacKinnon.

            E3   Lilly MacLeod, m. Ronald <u>Ronahan</u> of Summerside, with issue:

               F1   Patachia Ronahan.

               F2   Garth Ronahan.

               F3   Trevor Ronahan.

               F4   Palema Ronahan.

            E4   Ronald MacLeod, m. Gail <u>MacMillan</u> of Miscouche, issue:

               F1   Trudy MacLeod.

               F2   Catherine MacLeod.

         D4   John MacLeod 1909-1976.

         D5   Norman MacLeod, m. Lillian <u>Pye</u>, with issue

            E1   Allan MacLeod, m. Tilly <u>Rushton</u> of Miscouche, with issue:

               F1   Whitney MacLeod.

               F2   Jason MacLeod.

            E2   Auston MacLeod, m. Flora <u>Dougay</u>, living in St. Eleanors, issue:

               F1   Rodney MacLeod.

               F2   Dwayne MacLeod.

               F3   Kent MacLeod.

            E3   David MacLeod, m. Linda <u>Joughray</u>, they live in Philadelphia.

    D6   Lena MacLeod, m. Preston <u>Winchester</u>, with issue
          E1   Alma Winchester, m. David <u>Marrell</u>, with issue:
               F1   Davie Marrell.
               F2   Kevin Marrell.
               F3   Cheryl Marrell.
          E2   Gloria Winchester, m. Ernest <u>Inman</u>, with issue
               F1   John Inman.
               F2   Bryon Inman.
               F3   Dwayne Inman.
               F4   Lee Ann Inman.
          E3   Leigh Winchester.
          E4   Keith Winchester, m. Patricia <u>Gillis</u>, live in Miscouche, issue:
               F1   Daron Winchester.
               F2   Amanda Winchester.
          E5   Gordon Winchester, m. Janet <u>Myers</u>, with issue
               F1   Ivan Winchester.
               F2   April Winchester.
          E6   Lavinia Winchester, m. Eric <u>MacAusland</u> of Summerside.
    D7   Lavinia MacLeod, 1917-1933, buried in Central Lot 16 Cemetery.
  C2   Jessie MacLeod, m. ＿＿＿ <u>Daken</u> of Cambridge, Massachusetts, with issue:
    D1   Ruth Daken.
  C3   Phoebe MacLeod, m. ＿＿＿＿＿.
  C4   Christine MacLeod, m. Arthur <u>Gifford</u> of Brockton, Massachusetts.
  C5   Lavinia MacLeod, m. George <u>Snoy</u> of Brockton, Massachusetts.

* Catherine had a brother Donald who was married and had a family and lived in Belmont, Lot 16, for a few years, then they moved to St. Eleanors, from there to Western Canada. Some of their family stayed on P.E.I. She and Donald also had a sister married to a Walker from Charlottetown. They had two sons, Frank and James Walker. Frank was in WWI, came back to Charlottetown, and was made editor of the Charlottetown *Guardian* until his retirement.

John C. MacLeod
John C. MacLeod and Flora MacKenzie of Hopedale

A1 John C. MacLeod, 1823-1900, emigrated from Scotland, m. Flora MacKenzie, 1830-1911. They lived in Hopedale, P.E.I. Their children were:
 B1 John J. MacLeod, 1858-1937, m. Flora MacKay, 1861-1948, Bonshaw, issue:
  C1 John A. MacLeod, m. Arabell MacDougall.
  C2 Mary Ann MacLeod, 1886-1975, m. John Gordon, 1880-1938, Appin Road.
   D1 Lewis Gordon.
   D2 Cassie Gordon, m. _____ MacPhee.
   D3 John Gordon.
   D4 Murchison Gordon, 1920-1944, lost at sea, WWII.
   D5 Florence Gordon, m. _____ Gamble, with issue.
  C3 Louis D. MacLeod, m. Janet Gordon, they had a family.
   D1 Donald MacLeod, m. Mary MacPhail, with issue:
    E1 Verna Ruth MacLeod.
    E2 Donalda MacLeod, m. _____ Burda.
   D2 John Lester MacLeod.
   D3 Eva Myrtle MacLeod, m. _____ Curtis.
  C4 Norman MacLeod, 1889-1968, m. Grace Cudmore, born 1894, issue:
   D1 Guy MacLeod.
   D2 Oliver MacLeod.
   D3 Glennie MacLeod, m. Eric Ferguson, Bonshaw.
   D4 Dorothy MacLeod, m. _____ Hyde.
  C5 Florrie MacLeod, m. Harry Cudmore, with issue:
   D1 Nettie Cudmore, m. _____ Leard.
   D2 Ruby Cudmore, m. _____ Cannon.
   D3 Sheldon Cudmore.
   D4 Morris Cudmore.
   D5 Mildred Cudmore, m. _____ Ferguson.
   D6 Freeman Cudmore .
  C6 Cassie MacLeod, 1893-1909.
  C7 Geddie MacLeod, m. Janet Darrach, with issue:
   D1 Florence MacLeod, m. Carl Burke, Charlottetown.
   D2 Constance MacLeod, m. Ivan MacArthur.
   D3 Kaye MacLeod.
  C8 Ruth MacLeod, m. Clark Crosby, 1892-1960, with issue:
   D1 Marguerite Crosby, m. _____ Darrach.
   D2 Clayton Crosby.
   D3 Merrill Crosby.
   D4 Katherine Crosby, m. _____ Simmons.
   D5 Ray Crosby.
  C9 Elizabeth MacLeod, m. J. William MacDonald, Bonshaw, with issue:
   D1 Dr. Peter MacDonald.
   D2 Hollis MacDonald.
   D3 Mary MacDonald, m. _____ Blumell.
   D4 Carol MacDonald.
   D5 Betty MacDonald, m. _____ MacPhee.

C10 Lillian MacLeod, m. James W. Boyce, Bonshaw, with issue:
    D1 Keith Boyce.
C11 Annie MacLeod, m. George Milford, with issue:
    D1 Noel Milford.
    D2 Carl Milford.
    D3 Donald Milford.
    D4 Ferne Milford, m. _____ Johnson.
C12 Sterling MacLeod, m. Vina MacPhail, with issue:
    D1 Roma MacLeod, m. Neil MacDougall.
    D2 Christine MacLeod, m. Gordon MacNevin.
    D3 Joan MacLeod, m. _____ Trowsdale.
    D4 Heather MacLeod, m. _____ McCloskey.
    D5 Keir MacLeod.
C13 Elsie MacLeod, m. W. Reginald Jenkins, Charlottetown, with issue:
    D1 Bill Jenkins.
    D2 Kenneth Jenkins.
C14 Stephen MacLeod, m. Ruth Villet, Bonshaw, with issue:
    D1 John MacLeod.
    D2 Dr. Claire MacLeod.
B2 Murdoch MacLeod, 1854-1944, m. 1) Euphemia MacInnis, 1859-1915, issue:
C1 Mary Ann MacLeod, m. John Morrow, Arlington, Massachusetts, with five children.
C2 Florence MacLeod, 1881-1959, m. Warren Phinney, Massachusetts, three children:
    D1 Warren Phinney, m. Daisy ____, with issue:
        E1 Warren Lee Phinney.
        E2 James Phinney.
    D2 Grace Euphemia Phinney, m. Keith Johnston, from P.E.I. They lived in Charlottetown and Quincy, Massachusetts, with issue:
        E1 Sandra Johnston, m. ____ Pompeo.
        E2 Warren Johnston.
        E3 Wallace Johnston.
    D3 Neil Phinney, m. _____, with issue:
        E1 Richard Phinney.
        E2 Robert Phinney.
        E3 William Phinney.
C3 Alexander MacLeod, 1883-1937, m. Kate ____, Massachusetts, no family, buried in Belfast Cemetery, P.E.I.
C4 Katherine MacLeod, 1886-1895, buried in Hartsville.
C5 John MacLeod, 1889-1912, m. Laura ____, no family. Lived in Massachusetts.
C6 Rachel MacLeod, 1892-1985, m. Harold Matthews, lived in Massachusetts, one child:
    D1 Marjorie Matthews, m. Henry Bemont, with issue:
        E1 Stephen Bemont.
        E2 Pamela Bemont, m. Bruce Aberle, with issue:
            F1 Dwight Aberle.
            F2 Laura Aberle.
        E3 Matthew Bemont.
C7 Sarah Eliza MacLeod, 1893-1973, m. Ernest Graham, New York, with two children:

        D1   James Graham, married and living in Florida with a family.

        D2   Name unknown.

   C8   William MacLeod, 1895-1920, WWI Veteran (U.S. Army). He drowned in the West River while visiting P.E.I., buried in Hartsville. He had no family.

   C9   Walter Wixen MacLeod, born 1900, lived in Massachusetts, no family.

   C10 Gordon MacLeod, m. Agnes Broughall, in the U.S.A., with issue:

        D1   Barbara Ann MacLeod.

        D2   Madeline Rachel MacLeod.

        D3   Alice MacLeod.

        D4   Margaret MacLeod.

        D5   Agnes MacLeod.

        D6   William Gordon MacLeod.

   C11 Irving MacLeod, 1904-1953, a twin to Gordon, m. Gertrude MacLean, they lived in Massachusetts with two daughters:

        D1   Gertrude Evelyn MacLeod.

        D2   A daughter.

Murdoch m. 2) Louise Howlan, with issue:

   C12 Murdoch MacLeod.

B3   Christine MacLeod, died 1924, age 62, m. W. W. Wixen, U.S.A., with issue:

   C1   W. Wixen, died 1958, age 66, he and his mother buried in Hartsville.

B4   Kate MacLeod.

B5   Mary MacLeod, m. Eddie Arnold.

Information received from Dr. Peter MacDonald, Bonshaw; Barbara MacLeod, Charlottetown; and Marjorie Bemont, East Orleans, Massachusetts.

DONALD MACLEOD
DONALD MACLEOD AND FLORA MACNEILL OF SPRINGTON

A   Donald MacLeod came from the Isle of Skye to Springton where he m. Flora
     MacNeill. Donald built the first stone dike in the area and his family became
     known as the "Stone Dike MacLeods" to differentiate them from the many
     other MacLeods in the area. They are buried in Hartsville Cemetery. Their
     children were:
     B1   John "Stonedike" MacLeod, born 1836 in Hartsville, m. 1) Flora Stuart,
          issue:
          C1   Mary Margaret MacLeod, born Oct. 31, 1862, m. Robert MacKenzie
               and lived in Springfield, with issue:
               D1   Walter MacKenzie, M.L.A. [Member of Legislative Assembly]
                    at one time.
               D2   Laura MacKenzie, m. Fred Haslam.
               D3   Bessie MacKenzie, a school teacher, moved west.
          C2   Flora Ann MacLeod, born March 1, 1864, m. Henry Dixon, with issue:
               D1   George Dixon.
               D2   Herbert Dixon.
               D3   Grace Dixon, m. Wesley McNevin, with issue:
                    E1   Florence McNevin, m. Lorne Nicholson.
          C3   Alexander MacLeod, born Nov. 21, 1866, m. Sarah MacInnis. They
               moved to New Jersey. They had issue:
               D1   Velda Victoria MacLeod, m. A. A. Altien.
               D2   Florence "Irene" MacLeod, m. John Selah.
               D3   Ruth Winnifred MacLeod, R.N., died young.
          C4   Daniel MacLeod, m. 1) Annie Beaton. Moved to Gorham, Maine, m.
               2) Flora MacDonald. No children.
          C5   Christie Ann MacLeod, m. Donald MacLure. Moved to Alberta. No
               children.
          C6   Alan Stuart MacLeod, not married.
          C7   Catherine MacLeod, m. Franklin Hickox of Springfield, with issue:
               D1   Fred Hickox, moved to U.S.A.
               D2   Ella Hickox, moved to U.S.A.
               D3   Florrie Hickox, lives in North Granville.
               D4   Mildred Hickox, moved to U.S.A.
               D5   Eldon Hickox.
               D6   John Hickox, lives in Springfield.
               D7   Allan Hickox.
          C8   Mary MacLeod, m. Alfred Cameron, no children.
          C9   James Grant MacLeod, born Nov. 21, 1878, m. Mary S. Edwards, with
               issue:
               D1   Lois Jean MacLeod, not married.
          John m. 2) Effie MacKenzie. No children.
     B2   Neil MacLeod, m. Mary MacDonald.
     B3   James MacLeod, never married.
     B4   Janet MacLeod, m. Kenneth MacKenzie.
     B5   Flora MacLeod, m. Alex MacLellan.
     B6   Maggie MacLeod, born Sept. 1847, m. James MacLeod.

B7   Mary MacLeod, m. Thomas <u>Robinson</u>.
B8   Ann MacLeod, born 1855, m. Hector <u>MacDonald</u>.
B9   Kate MacLeod.
All children but John Stonedike moved to U.S.A.

Information provided by Lois MacLeod, Hampshire, and Hartsville Church records.

Belfast Settlers
Heads of Families, Belfast Church, 1811

The following is a list of the heads of families for the Belfast Church, 1811.

Rev. Dr. Angus MacAulay
Donald Stewart
Martin Martin
Donald Gillis
Charles Stewart
Malcolm Buchanan
Donald MacRae, Sr.
John MacPherson
Donald Buchanan
Donald MacRae
John Bell
Donald MacLeod
Evander MacRae, Elder
Lachlin MacLean
Donald MacQueen
Hector MacDoanld
Malcom Bell
Peter Murchison
Murdoch MacLean
Malcolm McMillan
Alexr McKinzie
Donald MacKinnon
James Cowrie
Hector Morrison
Donald Murchison, Elder
Donald McNeill
Donald McRae
Donald MacLeod
Malcolm Mun
Murdoch Buchanan
John Murchison
Jas. Currie
John MacQueen
Donald Murchison
Jas. Munn
Alexr Lamond
Alexr McLeod
Hector MacMillan
Ernest McKinzie
John MacDonald, Sr. Elder
James MacMillan
John Buchanan
John MacDonald, Jr.
Angus Mun

Donald MacRae
John Gillis
Allan MacMillan
Hector McQuary
Donald Nicholson, Elder
Archibald Blue
Roderick MacRae
Murdo MacLeod
Malcolm MacNeill
Donald Odochardy
Donald MacPherson
Dugald Bell
John MacRae
Harry MacLeod
John Mun
Angus Odarchy
Saml Martin
Angus Bell
John McLeod
John Nicholson
John MacPherson
Donald McPhee
Donald Nicholson
Finley MacRae
John McLeod
John MacKenzie
Duncan MacRae
Finly Odarty
John Campbell
Peter Campbell
Allen Shaw
John Ross
Angus Beaton, Sr.
Murdoch McDonald
Donald Beaton
Kenneth MacKenzie, Sr.
Angus MacDonald
John Beaton
John MacRae
Donald MacLeod
Donald Ross
Finlay MacRae
Donald MacInnes
Angus Beaton

Alex McArthur
Malcolm MacLeod
Angus Ross
Alexr McKenzie
Chas Stewart
Samuel Beaton
John McDonald
John McDonald
John Gillis
Alex McLeod
Donald McLeod
Angus MacMillan

Rory "Mor" MacLeod
Excerpt from *Skye Pioneers and the Island*

The task of clearing the forests, in order to plant their crops, was formidable. It was no job for a weakling, consequently, size and strength were respected. Malcolm MacQueen in *Skye Pioneers and the Island*, tells of Rory "Mor" MacLeod of Pinette, P.E.I.

"The strength of some of these Highlanders was prodigious. Rory MacLeod, of Pinette, father of Capt. Malcolm MacLeod, who died in Vancouver in 1924, was recognized as one of the strongest men in Canada. While yet a boy, he gave an exhibition of strength that won him a prize. In a grocery store in Charlottetown he was challenged to exhibit his prowess. He finally was offered a bedtick full of oatmeal as a gift if he could lift it. One of the homemade linen bedticks, manufactured in the hand looms on the farm from native flax, was produced. This was filled with oatmeal, and thus filled, weighed about twelve hundred pounds. Rory Mor, without hesitation, got under this huge, ungainly mass, and with it over his shoulders walked to the dock, from whence he took it by boat to his Belfast home.

"He was frequently compared with Angus MacAskill, one of the world's greatest giants. Born in Harris, Scotland, in 1825, when six years of age he emigrated with his parents, nine sisters, and three brothers, to St. Ann, Victoria Co., Cape Breton Island, N.S., where he was known as Gillie Mor St. Ann. Although his father was only five feet nine inches in height, and his mother an average size woman, he was seven feet nine inches in height. He was three feet eight inches across the shoulders. The palm of his hand was six inches wide and twelve inches long. He wore a shoe eighteen inches in length. His strength was enormous. In disengaging himself from an anchor of tremendous weight, which he lifted to his shoulder, he received an injury from the effects of which he ultimately died. This man only, would the Belfast people admit, was more powerful than the Rory MacLeod of Pinette, their hero."

STRATHALBYN
REMARKS BY THE HON. A. B. MACKENZIE IN JULY, 1895

The Hartsville Presbyterian Church observed its fiftieth anniversary in July of 1895. At this gathering the Hon. A. B. MacKenzie, who was formerly from the Strathalbyn area, gave a history of the early settlement and events leading up to that time.

This was reported fully in the *Daily Patriot* of July 4 and 5, 1895, and also compiled into a small booklet which can be viewed at the Provincial Archives, Charlottetown.

In his opening remarks, he recalls his happy childhood in Strathalbyn, and states that all of the aged sires and noble matrons of those early days are gone to their eternal home save and except two men, namely Alexander MacLeod, the nestor of the parish and Alexander McIntosh; and seven women, namely, Mrs. Donald MacDonald, Mrs. John Cameron, Mrs. Roderick McIntosh, Mrs. John McIntosh, Mrs. Donald McKinnon (little), Mrs. Murdoch MacLeod, and Mrs. Alexander McIntosh.

We would liked to have printed Mr. MacKenzie's most interesting address in its entirety, but unfortunately, because of its length we are forced to delete a large part. However, the following portions of the history will, no doubt, be of interest to the descendants of the people whom he mentions, and others as well.

"Early in the summer of 1831, a large band of stalwart young Highlanders, chiefly from the Isle of Skye, accompanied by their families, emigrated to Prince Edward Island, at that time sparsely settled with a population of about thirty-two thousand people, while Charlottetown was but a village, with a population of about twenty-five hundred people, some of whom settled in the Southern part of Queen's County, while some twenty families, induced by the prospect of purchasing land in fee simple, and on easy terms, decided to settle on Lot 67.

"The names of the first pioneers were Miles McInnis (Mulmoire), Donald McKinnon (Domnhal Mor), James Nicholson, Donald and Alexander Martin, John Ross, Peter Stewart and his son John, Malcolm MacDonald (Callum Ban)—a grand type of the old, venerable Highland Chieftain, and his three sons, Donald, John and Alexander, Malcolm (Callum Prior), John McLeod (Brebatar)—another type of Highland hero, and his son Donald, lately deceased, Lodwick McIntosh (Mul Donich)—a man of patriarchal bearing and appearance, and his four sons, Roderick, John, Alexander and Donald, and John Matheson and his father Jonathon (joiner), and his brother Alex who is still hale and hearty though over eighty years of age, he is the father of education in the settlement, and Donald and Angus Beaton. These were joined a year or two afterwards by Angus MacDonald (Ainmach Raighal), Angus and Ronald Stewart, John Cameron, George Cahill, Nathaniel Kelly, Robert Todd, Neil MacKinnon (Neal Ruagh), Donald MacKinnon (Donmhal Beag), Donald MacLeod (MacLachlan), Malcolm MacLeod (Callum Crubach) and his brother Alexander (Sampson), and John MacLeod (Tain Ban Soar).

"As all the northern parts of Lots 31, 65, 29 and 30 and all Lot 22, save a small portion at the north end—as well as the eastern ends of Lots 25, 26 and 27 were still, and for some years after, an unbroken wilderness, their nearest neighbours to the west were the Wrights of Middleton, on the south Victoria; on the east the McNeills of North River, and the Haslams and the Bagnalls on the north.

"Their effects had to be carried on their backs from Johnstons during the summer months, until the Anderson road was opened in the years 1833-34. Their first care was to clear a little patch of ground whereon to erect their first cabins, which consisted of small structures of round logs—twelve by sixteen feet covered with moss or clay with a small hole dug in the ground for a cellar and capacious chimney, the lower part of which was built of rough stones with a wooden mantle piece and the upper part or smoke-stack of cats, which consisted of parts of clay mixed with straw fastened on small round sticks, placed horizontally tier after tier until it reached about two feet above the roof.

"After getting well settled, their next care was to build a schoolhouse at Springton on a plot of land given to the settlement by their landlady for that purpose. Their first schoolhouse was a rather primitive and crude structure. It was a round log house twelve by sixteen, covered with bark or turf. It had one window of six panes, eight by ten. Their first teacher was Alexander MacLeod (Alaister Beag), who is still alive.

"During the first few years the people had no stated means of grace among them. Mr. James Nicholson, who was a bosom friend of the Rev. Dr. Roderick McLeod of Snizort, from the commencement of the settlement, and for some years afterward, held a prayer alternately in his own house, and Lodwick McIntosh, every Sabbath, where he read and expounded the Word to those who came to hear him.

"The Rev. Robert Patterson, of Bedeque, visited the settlement in the summer of 1836, and preached a sermon in the open air near James Nicholson's house, on which occasion he baptised several children. I am informed that Rev. John MacLennan of Belfast, visited the settlement the same summer, but held no public religious services. In the year 1837, the Rev. Donald MacDonald visited the settlement and preached then and occasionally for some years afterwards in Donald McLeod's house, until his people built a church in the year 1847. Many of his hearers came under the power of his preaching. Their old church was torn down about thirty years ago, but I understand his adherents have a new one in course of construction in Stanchel, a new school district, carved out of the Springton and Rose Valley school districts.

"In the year 1833-34, the new Bedeque Road, or as it was afterwards called for many years, 'The Anderson Road,' named after Hon. Alexander Anderson, of Bedeque, who surveyed the line, was opened, from McNeill's, North River, towards North Wiltshire, which was then an unbroken forest, thence through to what is now called Southwest, to Bedeque.

"The opening of the new road was a great boon to settlers as it not only gave them means of communication with the outer world, but also afforded them an opportunity of replenishing their exhausted exchequers, by earning money at building the road. About this time, some of them had so advanced in material property as to have a horse or a yoke of oxen, with which to haul their grist to the mills. Previous to this time, querns of hand-mills, taken from the old country, were used by some to convert their grain into meal.

"Their farming implements were chiefly made up of the following articles: a good Roger's or Weatherbie's narrow axe, a hoe, a reaping hook, a grubbing hoe, a flail, a frow, and spoke-shave. After a few years a yoke for the ox, a straw collar and wooden hames for the horse, a pair of cart wheels, a wood sleigh and slide car, a v-shaped harrow with wooden teeth, a hand rake and a big pot for the double purpose of making soap and boiling maple syrup were added.

"In the summer of 1839 another ship of emigrants from Scotland landed in Charlottetown, of whom some thirty or forty families cast in their lot with their fellow-countrymen in Scotch settlement. These late arrivals settled up in what is now called Hartsville, Johnston Road, Lot 22, Rose Valley, Lot 67. Though they had in a measure to contend against similar hardships with the first settlers, yet they had the advantage of the friendship, experience, and assistance of those who came first, as well as the advantage of the new road, opened some six years before. Among these people were a considerable number of earnest, pious and God-fearing men, who were converted under the preaching of such men as Dr. Roderick MacLeod (Maister Ruareadh) of Snizort, Skye, Dr. Kennedy of Red Castle (An Chaistel Ruadh), Rev. Mr. McRichard—recently deceased, and Dr. McDonald (of Ferintosh).

"Among these I might mention the names of Alexander McLeod, the Preacher, and his brother John, John Gillis (A Sheiram) and John Matheson, the father of the late Angus Matheson. Immediately after his arrival Alexander McLeod took an active lead in conducting religious meetings, not only in the Springton schoolhouse, but also in private houses in the different localities, in which his countrymen had settled. Often preaching during the summer months in the open air, or in a grove of woods. In the summers 1840-41 there were a further accession of some seventy families of emigrants from Scotland who joined their old neighbours in the new settlement; these settled in the western part of Rose Valley, Johnston Road (east) Brookfield, West Line Road, Hazel Grove, Junction Road, Colville Road, and Dock Road. Among these newcomers were also men of eminent piety, notably the late Allan McSwain of pious and immortal memory, afterwards an elder for forty-eight years; his brother Murdoch McSwain, Donald Buchannan and Murdoch Buchannan, who for three or four years had settled in Bonshaw, after which he removed to Springton and was one of the first three elders who composed the first session at the formation of Strathalbyn Congregation whose jubilee we are today celebrating. Although Mr. Buchannan could not read, I believe he could recite from memory the greater part of the Old and New Testaments; also John McLeod (Iain MacFaireadh Og) and Murdoch McLeod (Murachadh Beag) who settled in New London, but who from his arrival in the country closely identified himself with his countrymen, in the Scotch Settlement. He was a man of rare intelligence, a good Gaelic and English scholar, equally conversant with both languages, but above all, he was a true and earnest Christian in every sense of the word. He was an orator of no mean order. He was really the first evangelist to Strathalbyn, and was for many years engaged in catechizing and preaching the Word in the different settlements I have referred to. When he would be on the rounds both old and young would be in a flurry refreshing their memories on the questions of the shorter catechism. I believe he was instrumental in doing more real good in the place than perhaps any other man. Mr. John McNeil, a Gaelic and English teacher, sent to Cape Breton, by 'the Society for the propogation of Christian knowledge' in Glasgow, Scotland, in the year 1830, who, after remaining in Cape Breton for a few years in a place now called Orangedale, removed to this Island, and settled in Bannockburn. Under his able preaching of the Word as well as that of the forementioned Murdoch and Alexander McLeod, a wave of religious awakening passed over the place and scores of men and women who afterwards became pillars and shining lights in the congregation, of whom the most have since gone home to glory, ascribed their first awakening about their soul's salvation, to the faithful preaching of these lay preachers. Among these men I might recall the sacred memory of James McLeod, John Cameron, John McLeod (Ban Soar), who afterwards became one of the ruling elders, Murdoch McLennan (Ruadh), Roderick Gillis, Brookfield, John McInnis (Ean MacEoghan), Alexander McLennan, Malcolm McLeod (Callum Ruadh), elder, the late Angus Matheson, Malcolm, Murdoch, and Donald Gillis, Roderick McLeod (Roireadh Mor), and Donald Nicholson. Of the heads of the families of those who arrived in 1839-40-41, only the following are yet alive: Donald Nicholson, John McLeod and wife, Mrs. Allen McSwain, Alexander MacPherson and wife, Donald McDonald, Rose Valley; Mrs. Murdoch McKinley, Malcolm Gillis, West Line; and John Geo. McLeod, Bradalbyn; Mrs. John Matheson and Mrs. Murdoch Gillis, Rose Valley; and John McKay, Hartsville.

"About the year 1843, the year of the disruption of the Free Church from the Church of Scotland, the Quarterly question meetings, which, I understand, have been kept up in the congregation to the present time, were established. These meetings continued some days and were made the occasion for many years afterwards, of scores of pious men and women to assemble together from Cardigan, Dundas, Brown's Creek, Wood Islands, West River and New London. Among those dear fathers, from the different places referred to, who were wont to take part in discussing 'the Question' at these meetings, you will pardon me (as the religious history of the congregation would be incomplete without them) if I mention the names of McKay Campbell (Caie), Hector Falconer, William McIntosh, Alexander Sutherland, Angus McKenzie, William Ross, George McKay, James Henderson, James Morrison, and Donald McLeod, New London. The last three octogenarian elders are still alive: Alexander Munroe, Dundas, Martin McPherson (Maistain Beag), Donald Bruce (Sero), William Martin, Donald Montgomery (Ruadh), Donald MacBeth, Malcolm Bruce, Malcolm Matheson, Malcolm Campbell, Donald McRae and Sween-Campbell (Swaine), Brown's Creek; the last of whom was mighty in the Scriptures (in his native tongue, and greatly beloved by all). Angus McLeod, Kinross; James Munn, Wood Islands; Allan McSwain (Allain Eaghan), Long Creek; Donald McLeod (Domnhall Mac a Phrior) and John McLeod (Ian Mullear), Bonshaw; Alexander MacDonald (Alaister McUillham), Alexander McKinnon and Malcolm McDonald (elder), New Glasgow Road; the last of whom is still alive; Alex Campbell and Murdoch Bethune, Brookfield; Donald McKinnon (Torbuck); the Hon. Kenneth Henderson, Union Road; and Mungo MacFarlane, St. Peter's Road; and Donald Henderson, North Wiltshire. This practice was more closely attended to afterwards during communion seasons.

"In the summer of 1844 a public meeting was held at which it was unanimously agreed to commence the building of a church forthwith, and within a short time the contract was let to John McKenzie (Soar Mor), a native of Pictou, N.S., for a handsome amount, considering the scarcity of money at that stage of their history. He prepared the building material and commenced building early in the spring of 1845 and towards the first of July had so rapidly progressed with the work that the outside of the building was finished in that month fifty years ago. Before the floor was laid in it, a Mr. McMillan from Scotland preached a sermon therein, the people being seated on the floor beams.

"The sacrament of the Lord's Supper was disposed for the first time in the congregation in July 1845, by the Rev. Alexander Farquharson of Middle River, Cape Breton.

"Some eighty or a hundred people sat down to commemerate their Saviour's dying love. Three elders were ordained on this occasion, namely Alexander McLeod, Murdoch Buchannan, and Allan McSwain. Some fifty or sixty children were baptised on this occasion, many of whom were in their teens.

"The first regular ordained minister over the congregation was the Rev. Alexander Sutherland. He was settled over the congregation of New London. Clifton and Scotch Settlement in the fall of 1852. He preached Gaelic and English alternately every Sabbath in each place for seven years. He was an able preacher, full of zeal in the Master's service. He was instrumental in doing a great deal of good in the congregation. His name will be long remembered among them as one who did not give an uncertain sound when he blew the gospel trumpet.

"Before closing you will pardon me for referring to the noble band of Christian women, who fifty years ago, were real mothers in Israel whose lives shone like stars in darkness, but who have since gone home to glory, to bask in the refulgent rays of the Son of Righteousness.

"Without making dividuous distinction, I might mention among many other excellent women, who through faith obtained a good report in the Strathalbyn Congregation, the names of Mrs. John Mathewson (Bean Choir Eion Mich Eion), Mrs. James Nicholson, Mrs. Neil McKinnon (Bean N'Heil Ruadh) of hospitable fame, Mrs. John McDonald (Fion Galla Bean Oig), Isabel MacLeod (Nighean Domhail Gobh), Catherine MacLeod (Bantrach a'tailer), Mrs. Mary MacKay (Mary Og), Mrs. Malcolm Nicholson, Springton, Mrs. John MacLeod (Bean Ian Ban Soar), Mrs. Margaret MacLeod (Mereadh Ruadh), Christy MacLean, Rose Valley; Mrs. Murdoch MacKenzie (Bean Mureacheadh), Rose Valley; Mrs. Donald McInnis (Bean Dh'onal Og), and I think I might with becoming modesty include among these faithful ones, who though dead yet speak to us, by the example of their pure lives, as well as their unswerving devotion to the cause of pure and undefiled religion, my own dear mother (Catherine Nighean S'heoras). In those early days of fifty years ago the people in this parish lived like one large and happy family in sweet accord and harmony, each neighbour striving to help the other, bearing each other's burdens. Brotherly love and good will ruled supreme. They were always ready to forgive and forget each other's foibles and shortcomings. When one member suffered all the members suffered."

THE MACCRIMMON PIPERS
THE MACCRIMMON PIPERS BY MADELINE MACCRIMMON

As is the case with many Highland names, it is impossible to trace with certainty the origin of the name MacCrimmon, the locality where the founder of the family was born and the date when the MacCrimmons first became associated with the MacLeods of Dunvegan.

There are several accounts of the origin of the MacCrimmons but most of these seem to be tied to traditional lore and lack of documentary evidence. One of the most interesting tales relates that in the time of the Holy Wars, the MacLeod Chief of Dunvegan visited Cremona, Italy, and heard a piper. He brought him back to Dunvegan and this man became the first piper to MacLeod at Dunvegan and the first McCrimmon member. MacLeod gave to him the name "Cremonach" which became MacCremona (son of Cremona). Although there is a slight similarity in the name to Cremona, no true evidence supports this tale and it is well to remember that the bagpipes were a world-wide musical instrument. The Gaelic spelling of the name MacCruimmein bears no resemblance to Cremona at all.

It was also said that the MacCrimmons came of a royal Irish race but again there is no proof.

The account of the MacCrimmon origin which bears the best logic, places them on the south part of Harris in the 12th century. During the course of this 12th century, one Paul Balkison became the owner of several districts in Skye and the Outer Isles, and it is believed that he bequeathed his lands to Leod, the ancester of the Mac-Leods. It was stated that the MacCrimmons acknowledged Leod as their overlord and entered the service of the MacLeods in the capacity of musicians. Again it is difficult to substantiate this by by authorative evidence as information about the MacLeods is also lacking at this early period.

Black's dictionary of Scottish names states that MacCrimmon is derived from the old Norse HRO(th)MUND which due to changes in language and normal changes in names was reduced to ROMUN which later became to Mac (son of) RUMEN then to the Gaelic MacCrimmein. From the Norse origin of the name it would appear that the family were Norse, but intermarriage with the early Celts would certainly wipe out any clear genetic line.

The first member known to tradition is Fionniagh na Plaife Baine (Findlay of the plaid), who was supposed to be a contempory of Alasdair Crotach (1547), chief of the MacLeods. Alasdair's greatest distinction is the founding of the MacCrimmon School of Pipers at Borreraig and settling the MacCrimmons at Borreraig and Bore-dale (Skye). The school, which had thick walls, was divided into two parts at right angles, with one part forming the classroom and the other the sleeping apartments. The college was situated on a high stretch of land across the loch from Dunvegan Castle, the home of the MacLeod Chief.

To the MacCrimmons is conceded the credit of developing the Ceòlmhor (great music), the distinctive pipe music of the Highlanders, whether it be a lament or salute, a battle piece, a pastoral meditation or a spirited pibroch.The old Highland saying, that it takes seven years to make a piper, is not far from wrong. For generations these great MacCrimmon pipers were unequalled as tutors at their college at Borreraig and every student had to study seven years at least before the MacCrimmons would acknowledge him as one of their products.In the time period about 1500-1800, the MacCrimmons were simultaneously pipers to the MacLeods at Dunvegan, Glenelg and Harris. During this time, the MacCrimmons trained many pipers for other clans such as the MacIntyres, MacArthurs, MacKays and Campbells.Appreciation of the noble Ceòlmhor quickly spread over the Highlands until no self-respecting Chief was without his piper and frequently this piper had to receive his final training at the MacCrimmon School of Pipers.

The MacCrimmons were not only musician-teachers but also notable composers and enriched the pibroch music (great music) with many fine tunes. While the grass grows green today where the College stood, the memory of these master musicians is preserved in the compositions and in the names in the vicinity of the MacCrimmon homeland. Among the compositions that are preserved and played today are some of Donald Mor MacCrimmon's master pieces—"MacDonald's Salute" and "MacLeod's Controversity" or Patrick Mor's "Lament of the Children" which was composed after the piper lost seven of his eight sons through a fever. Another number is "Cha Till MacCruimmein" (never more MacCrimmon). This one was composed by Donald Ban MacCrimmon who predicted his own death at Inverness in 1745. Before long he met his death from a bullet as he was piping the MacLeods against Prince Charlie's forces. The early MacCrimmons were gifted, as documents at Dunvegan Castle contain a Notary Doqurt to the effect that Hector MacCrimmon signed a deed on behalf of Isabella, wife of Sir Rory Mor, 1595. "Sir" John MacCrimmon appears as one of the witnesses to a contract of friendship signed at Inverness in the 16th century, one of the contracting parties being MacLeod at Dunvegan. The use of the word "Sir" before the name MacCrimmon denotes not a title of honour but merely a person possessing a certain amount of scholarship and facility in writing. This ability was important to the MacCrimmons in recording their piping compositions. They were first to devise a system of putting pipe music on paper, the tunes having previously been passed on from generation to generation by ear and fingering only. Had this system not been developed, many tunes would have been lost. The end of the MacCrimmon pipers came with the Disarmament Act following 1745 and this had its effect of virtually eliminating the wearing of the kilt and other Highland dress and the playing of the pipes. This suppression of the music of the pipes had its effect not only on the Island and mainland but also destroyed the MacCrimmon School of Piping.

The 300-year period (1500-1800) was a troublesome time for the MacLeods, who were in strife with other clans, heavily in debt, and in difficulties with the Government, nevertheless, they maintained the MacCrimmons in their College. Since the MacCrimmons were in the service of the MacLeods in the capacity of musicians, they enjoyed certain privileges. They became the hereditary pipers to the MacLeods with at least seven of the greatest pipers following in line.The first was Donald Mor, who was a favourite with his chief Rory Mor, and the last known MacCrimmon Piper was Iain Dubh in or about 1842. By means of this musical service, the Mac-Crimmons became a Sept of the MacLeods.

On August 2, 1933, a Memorial Cairn to the MacCrimmons of Borreraig was unveiled by MacLeod of MacLeod, 27th Chief.

In 1966, Hugh MacCrimmon, Professor of Life Sciences at the University of Guelph, Ontario, bought a school and attached house near the cairn on the Isle of Skye. In this school he has opened a Piping Centre for pipers throughout the world. It is not a museum but a Mecca for pipers with a good reference library on piping, selections of MacCrimmon music on tapes, played by the world's best pipers and a spot for piping competitions open to the world.

THE HON. FREDERICK JOSEPH MACLEOD
EXTRACT FROM *THE CANADIAN MEN AND WOMEN OF THE TIMES*

MacLeod, Hon. Frederick Joseph, 1870-1920, a brilliant scholar, author, lawyer and statesman, was the son of the late Hector MacLeod of Charlottetown Royalty, Prince Edward Island, and was born there in the year 1870. He was educated in the public schools, Prince of Wales College, Charlottetown, Dalhousie University (B.A. 1890), Halifax, N.S., and Harvard University (A.B. 1891), Cambridge, Mass., U.S.A. In the year 1899 he received the degree of L.L.B. from Harvard as well. He was an instructor in Mercersburg College 1894-95, and in the Nebraska State University, 1895-1896.

He was admitted to the Massachusetts bar, as a counsellor-at-law law in 1899 and thereafter practised his profession in Boston, Mass. He ably assisted in drawing up the Business Corporation Law Act of that State. He was elected to the Senate of Massachusetts as a Democrat in 1905, and subsequently he was appointed Chairman of the State Railway Commission, Mass., in 1911.

He was the author of a treatise relating to the taxing of corporations in all the States of the Union (1903) and also contributed many articles on legal and political subjects to magazines. He was past president of the Canadian Club, Harvard University, and was chosen president of the Canadian Club, Boston, Mass., in 1908.

In June, 1910, he married Miss Elizabeth Gwendolen Conner, daughter of T. C. Conner, West Summerville, Mass.

The St. John Telegraph newspaper has written of Mr. MacLeod as follows:

"A man of unblemished character, fine intellectual attainments and great tact and judgment; he is a credit to the land of his birth."

Morgan, *The Canadian Men and Women of the Times*, Toronto, William Briggs, 1912

ROBERT MacLEOD AND JOHN MacKAY MacLEOD
LETTERS FROM DESCENDANTS OF ROBERT MacLEOD AND JOHN MacKAY MacLEOD

The following is an extract of a letter from Gladys Bronson, Attleboro, Massachusetts.

March 1, 1986

I have been unable to obtain any information about my great, great-grandfather Robert MacLeod while he was in P.E.I. I don't know whether he came from Scotland by himself or he was with his parents.

He was born 1789 and died in 1857 at Cape North, Cape Breton. He married Effie MacPherson in 1810 and their first born was Murdoch MacLeod (my great-grand-father). Effie came over from Scotland at age six with her parents from Skye. I believe they settled in the Belfast area.

In 1821 Robert MacLeod, his brother-in-law Norman (Noah) MacPherson, and his father-in-law Donald MacPherson went to Lake Ainslie, Cape Breton. They petitioned for land and it was granted. According to the Archives in Halifax, Robert MacLeod was 30 years old in 1821, was married and had three children. He was granted land at Lake Ainslie and the farm was called Loch Ban lot #12. Norman MacPherson was 29 years old in 1821, was married and had two children. His farm is called Loch Ban. There was no mention of Donald being granted any land but it says he was 50 years old in 1821, was married and had five children. I know that Donald MacPherson went back to P.E.I. with the rest of his family. He and his wife are buried in P.E.I. but I don't know where.

Robert MacLeod and his family and Norman MacPherson and his family moved to Pleasant Bay, Cape Breton, around 1826. They stayed there about a year or two then moved to Cape North, Cape Breton. There they made their permanent home.

The following is an extract of a letter received from Mrs. Janie MacLeod Oliver, Baltimore, Maryland.

February 23, 1986

My paternal grandfather was John MacKay McLeod (name spelling later changed to MacLeod). His birth date is believed to be April 20, 1865. (Different sources give different dates.) His parents were John McLeod, a shipbuilder, and Mary Jane Arthur. He was born in Summerside, P.E.I., and it is believed that he attended school in Irishtown. He had two sisters, Sophia and Mary. Sophia's married surname might be MacDonald, and Mary married Kane (or Crane). They (the sisters) moved to Massachusetts, U.S.A., possibly Boston. The reason why we know so little of grandfather's family is because he had a family quarrel and left home at the young age of thirteen to go to sea. He never returned to his family. Eventually he became a U.S. citizen, married my grandmother in Baltimore, Maryland, and built a house in Lansdowne, Maryland, which is near Baltimore. Grandmother reared nine children at this home, the youngest of whom is my father. Grandfather was away at sea most of his life and was a famous sea captain. He died August 13, 1928. Grandmother's name was Wilhemina (Minnie) Maria Christensen MacLeod. John and Minnie's children were: Jane, John, Harry, Freda, Mabel, Elmer, Inez, Osborne, and Wendall (my father). Only Inez and Wendall are still living.

FAMILIES OF RONA
MacLeod Families of Rona and Nearby Districts

There were a number of MacLeod families who settled in Rona and adjacent districts in Queen's County, many of whom left to put down roots in other parts of Canada and U.S.A.

It would be difficult, if not impossible, to trace these families today. However, the following is a list of children from this area whose baptisms were recorded, together with the parents' names and place of child's birth.

I must add a word of caution to future historians that this is not a complete list of the families mentioned. In most cases there are other children whose names were not available, perhaps having been baptized somewhere other than their home parish church, or else failing to record the baptism. This was compiled from the records from Beaconsfield.

Allen MacLeod and Effie <u>MacLeod</u>, Raasay.
> Murdo MacLeod, born 1840.

Allen MacLeod and Christy <u>MacSwain</u>, Mellville.
> John MacLeod, born 1873; John Allan MacLeod, born 1880.

Angus MacLeod and Catherine <u>Matheson</u>, Rona.
> Angusena MacLeod, born 1879.

Alexander MacLeod and Mary <u>Nicholson</u>, Rona.
> Mary MacLeod, born 1869.

Donald MacLeod and Catherine <u>MacLeod</u>, Rona.
> Isabella MacLeod, 1847; James MacLeod, 1849; Janet MacLeod, 1851; Mary MacLeod, 1853.

Farquhar MacLeod and Christy <u>Nicholson</u>, Rona.
> Donald MacLeod,1853; Malcolm MacLeod, 1855.

Farquhar MacLeod and Eunice <u>Shaw</u>, Rona.
> Allan MacLeod, 1869; Eunice MacLeod, 1869.

James MacLeod and Catherine <u>MacLeod</u>, Rona.
> Donald MacLeod, 1878; Daniel Alex MacLeod, 1880; Jessie Mary MacLeod, 1883; John Murdoch MacLeod, 1885.

John MacLeod and Jessie <u>MacPhee</u>, Mellville.
> Flora MacLeod,1869; Wm. Murdoch, 1884 (Wood Island Road)

John MacLeod and Anne <u>MacLeod</u>, Rona.
> Anne MacLeod, 1846; John MacLeod, 1852.

John MacLeod and Mary <u>Gunn</u>, Rona.
> Catherine MacLeod, 1872; Ann MacLeod, 1874; Peggie MacLeod, 1875; Christy MacLeod, 1877; Catherine MacLeod, 1879; Neil MacLeod, 1879.

John MacLeod and Marion <u>Matheson</u>, Raasay.
> John MacLeod, 1840.

Neil MacLeod and Margaret <u>MacLeod</u>, Rona.
> Malcolm MacLeod, 852; Angus MacLeod, 1854.

Norman MacLeod and Rachel <u>MacLeod</u>, Rona.
>   Janet MacLeod, 1848; Janet or Catherine MacLeod, 1850. Isabel
>   MacLeod, 1852; Effy MacLeod, 1866.

Roderick MacLeod and Flora <u>Matheson</u>, Mellville.
>   Allan MacLeod, 1870; Christina MacLeod, 1874.

Roderick MacLeod and Sarah <u>Bruce</u>, Rona.
>   Sarah Ann MacLeod, 1884.

Roderick MacLeod and Mary <u>Matheson</u>, Rona.
>   Catherine MacLeod, 1848; Christy MacLeod, 1846; Margaret MacLeod,
>   1851; James MacLeod, 1854.

RED JOHN MACLEOD
RED JOHN MACLEOD, JESSIE BRUCE AND MARGARET GILLIS

A1   John (Red John) MacLeod, born circa 1806, probably on Prince Edward Island. He resided on the Dundee Rd., Lyndale (Orwell Rear), Lot 50, and is believed to have m. 1) Jessie <u>Bruce</u> and, after the birth of several children, m. 2) Margaret <u>Gillis</u>, who gave birth to at least three children. Margaret died in 1874 at the age of 52 and is buried at the Orwell Head Cemetery. She is named as the mother of Annie, Angus, and Murdoch in two death certificates and by some descendants of the family. Her obituary states that she is survived by her husband and seven children. The 1881 census for Lot 50 lists John as a widower, age 74, living with Donald and his wife Sarah, John, Murdoch, Annie, and Angus. Another son, Malcolm has already moved or married and is not listed here, but will likely be listed in Caledonia or Valleyfield with his wife Margaret Stewart. Jessie Bruce is noted as the mother of Malcolm on his death certificate. The seventh child of John MacLeod has not yet been identified. John may have died in July 1885 when an entry in a neighbour's (Lamont) diary refers to attending "old Red John's funeral." The children of John (Red John) MacLeod are listed below:

B1   "Red" Donald MacLeod, 1852-1930, m. Sarah <u>Gillis</u>, 1856-1926, from Belfast. He farmed in Vernon River on the Murray Harbour Road. Donald and Sarah had the following children:

    C1   Jessie MacLeod, died 1879, m. John <u>McQueen</u>.
    C2   Mary MacLeod, m. James S. <u>MacDonald</u>.
    C3   Ethel MacLeod, died 1886, m. Peter <u>MacLeod</u>.
    C4   J. Ernest MacLeod, died 1888, m. Myrtle <u>Ross</u>.
    C5   Cyrus MacLeod, died 1890, m. Margaret <u>Nicholson</u>.
    C6   Daniel A .MacLeod, died 1892, m. Myrtle L. <u>Stewart</u>.

B2   John J. ("Red John") MacLeod, 1853-1929, lived in Lyndale, on the Dundee Road, m. Flora Anne <u>Docherty</u>, 1856-1943, from Lake Ainsley, Cape Breton. Their children all moved to the U.S.A.:

    C1   Margaret A. MacLeod, died 1884, m. Harvey <u>Haines</u> from Marblehead, Massachusetts.
    C2   Mary C. MacLeod, died 1886, m. Murdoch <u>Cummings</u> from Whycogomaugh, Cape Breton.
    C3   John N. MacLeod, died 1888, lived in Staten Island, New York, and worked as a ship's carpenter.
    C4   Monty J. MacLeod, 1890-1918, was not married. He was killed in WWI while serving in the 72nd Seaforth Highland Regiment of the Canadian Army as a corporal.
    C5   Florence MacLeod, died 1891, m. Samuel W. <u>Lewis</u> from St. John's, Newfoundland.
    C6   Murdoch D. MacLeod, died 1892, m. Isabelle J. <u>MacLeod</u> from Point Prim.
    C7   Catherine M. MacLeod, died 1896, m. Charles Warren <u>Penny</u> from Auburndale, Nova Scotia.
    C8   Stella MacLeod, died 1898, m. Arthur <u>Thaxter</u>.
    C9   Alex MacLeod, born circa 1900, was not married.

B3   Malcolm J. MacLeod, 1854-1921, m. Margaret <u>Stewart</u>, daughter of Malcolm Stewart and Sarah McKenzie. They lived in Caledonia, P.E.I., and in the 1890s moved to Rockport, Massachusetts, where Malcolm worked for a granite company. Their children were:

     C1   Mary Rachel MacLeod, died 1878 m. 1) John Malcolm <u>MacLeod</u>, m. 2) Herbert <u>Rankins</u>.

     C2   Margaret MacLeod.

B4   Murdoch J. MacLeod, c. 1859-1937, m. Charlotte <u>Moreshade</u> or <u>Mosher</u>. Murdoch worked as a carpenter and lived in Newton, Massachusetts. They had three sons and a daughter:

     C1   John MacLeod, died 1886, m. Maisie <u>Nickerson</u> from Cape Negro, Nova Scotia.

     C2   Harold MacLeod, died 1889, m. Catherine <u>Tomlin</u>.

     C3   Catherine MacLeod.

     C4   Richard MacLeod, died 1905. m. 1) Abigail <u>Pratt</u>, m. 2) Estelle <u>Daniels</u>.

B5   Annie MacLeod, 1861-1947, m. John <u>Gillis</u>, from Flat River. They lived in Flat River with children:

     C1   Christy Anne Gillis, died 1885, m. John A. <u>Clark</u>.

     C2   Margaret May Gillis, died 1887, m. Murdoch <u>Cameron</u> from Brooklyn, P.E.I.

     C3   John Herbert Gillis, died 1889, m. Annie Laura <u>Martin</u> from Valleyfield, P.E.I.

     C4   Mary Gillis, died 1891, m. John Robert <u>Ross</u>.

     C5   Hector Gillis, died 1894, m. Flostena A. <u>Nickerson</u> from Yarmouth, Nova Scotia.

B6   Angus MacLeod, 1865-1949, m. Christine <u>MacLeod</u>. He moved the family to the U.S.A. circa 1900. Angus was a boat builder. His wife, and many of the children, eventually settled in Quincy, Massachusetts. Angus lived in Ellsworth, Maine, for the last ten years of his life. Their children were:

     C1   Margaret MacLeod, died 1890, m. Fred <u>Alger</u>.

     C2   John S. MacLeod, died 1893, m. Grace <u>MacKinnon</u>.

     C3   Mary Jane MacLeod, died 1894, m. Charles <u>Pendleton</u>.

     C4   Annie MacLeod, died 1897, m. 1) George <u>Orr</u>, m. 2) John <u>Marini</u>.

     C5   Marion MacLeod, died 1899, m. Samuel <u>Carlino</u>.

     C6   Lillian MacLeod, died 1903.

     C7   Angus MacLeod, Jr., died1905.

     C8   Christine MacLeod (twin to Angus), died 1905 m. Clayton <u>Bickerstaff</u>.

     C9   Florence MacLeod, died 1906, m. John <u>MacPherson</u>.

     C10 Grace Fern MacLeod, died 1907, m. Walter <u>Hayden</u>.

B7   Unknown child.

Cemetery Transcriptions
Cemetery Transcriptions from the Files at Beaconsfield, Charlottetown, Compiled by Tilly MacLeod

The number to the left indicates the marker number within the cemetery.

Alberton, Hillcrest United Presbyterian

48 Hodgson—In loving memory of Katheryn A. MacLeod, beloved wife of Franklyn J. Hodgson, died Sept. 8, 1921.
58 Montague MacLeod—Nov. 18, 1871, March 31, 1957. Mary MacLeod—Nov. 14, 1873, Nov. 29, 1954, wife of Fred Dowse.

Alberton, Old Dock Cemetery

19 In memory of James Sinclair, son of James A. and Hannah McLeod, died Nov. 4, 1895, aged 17 yrs.

Alberton, St. Peter's Anglican Cemetery

106 Laura J. Wallace—wife of Alec MacLeod, died Nov. 16, 1884, aged 18 yrs. 10 mos.
108 Anne MacLeod—wife of Capt. Jas. Ireland, 1824-1892.

Alexandra Baptist

25 Cecil H., died Oct. 1879, age 3 yrs. 5 mos. Laura M., died Nov. 12, 1879, age 1 yr. 3 mos. Children of D. (M.?) and Mary McLeod.

Appin Road Cemetery

15 John Gordon, Nov. 9, 1880 - July 28, 1938. His wife, Mamie MacLeod, July 24, 1886 - Jan. 9, 1975. Their son Smn. L. Murchison, Dec. 19, 1920 - April 29, 1944. Lost at sea.
17 Norman MacLeod, Aug. 23, 1889 - Dec. 15, 1968. His wife Grace Cudmore, Dec. 21, 1894—.

Annandale (Presbyterian) United Church

45 Rachel MacLeod, wife of Frank Jenkins, 1884-1919.
74 Alfred Robertson, 1857-1939. Matilda Turner, his wife, 1853-1926. Their daughter, Mabel, wife of Donald McLeod, 1881-1910.

Argyle Shore Cemetery

24 Flora MacLeod, 1865-1949.
84 Donald Gordon, Dec. 12 - 25th, 1946. Infant son of Vina and Sterling MacLeod.
292 J. William MacDougall, Feb. 15, 1884 - May 18, 1962. His wife, Elizabeth C. MacLeod, Feb. 28, 1897 - Oct. 25, 1967.

BANGOR, FREE CHURCH OF SCOTLAND

7   Grace Emily MacLeod, died July 11, 1979, age 59 yrs.

BEACH POINT

10   Capt. Allan A. MacLeod, 1880-1949. Salome Williams, his wife, 1891-19—. John Francis, their son, 1910-1944. Killed in action at Caen, France.
37   George MacLeod, 1840-1926. Ann Matheson, his wife, 1853-1931. Tryphena, their daughter, 1882-1928. Idella, their daughter, 1893-1937.
47   Capt. John F. Williams, 1869-1912. Abraham Williams, 1841-1913. Elizabeth Herring, his wife, 1850-1929. Eileen Faye Williams, 1943—. Elliot L. Williams, 1888-1965. Katie Jane MacLeod, his wife, 1899-1963. Frederick M. Williams, 1922-1940.

BELFAST, ST. JOHN'S PRESBYTERIAN

208 Jessie, daughter of Norman and Mary Ann McLeod, died Aug. 20, 1877, age 1 year, 2 mos.
627 Donald A. MacLeod, born Feb. 26, 1826, died June 30, 1916. Ann MacKenzie, his wife, born Oct. 1835, died March, 1926. Maggie MacLeod, died 1864, age 3. Malcolm James MacLeod, born May 24, 1865, died Oct. 5, 1940. Henry Blakeley, son of Malcolm and Edith MacLeod, 1899-1920.
423 Allan G. MacLeod, died Aug. 14, 1893, age 43. Christy, his wife, died Nov. 22, 1898, age 50. Margaret A., died Sept. 15, 1882, age 11 years, Jessie M., died Nov. 27, 1908, age 30, their daughters.
277 Angus McLeod, died at Orwell, Feb. 23, 1862, age 63.
188 Angus MacLeod, died May 24, 1915, age 61. William, his brother, died May 1, 1909, age 55.
380 Benjamin McLeod, killed while with flying corps at Camp Borden, Nov. 21, 1921, age 24.
378 Catherine A. MacLeod, wife of J. W. MacLeod, died March 5, 1922, age 49. Annie May, daughter, died Aug. 4, 1919, age 10. John W. MacLeod, 1866-1946.
285 Donald McLeod, died at Orwell Head, April 15, 1875, age 80. Native of Isle of Skye, Scotland.
333 Donald MacLeod (Stonehouse), died Dec. 10, 1905, age 80.
284 Donald McLeod, died Aug. 18, 1870, age 41.
220 Donald McLeod, Catherine, wife of D. MacLeod, died May 5, 1882, age 52.
263 Donald J. McLeod, beloved husband of Louise E. McLeod, died Aug. 19, 1900, age 38.
190 Effie McLeod, died Oct. 4, 1893, age 42.
144 John McLeod, died April 3, 1864, age 91. Flora, his wife, died April 1, 1862, age 79.
192 Isabella, wife of John McLeod, died Oct. 3, 1886, age 76. Erected by daughter Maggie.
193 John McLeod, died Dec. 14, 1873, age 76.
248 John McLeod, Orwell Cove, died April 9, 1875, age 53. Also his son, an infant, died March 1, 1866.
125 John McLeod, a native of Cape John, Pictou, Nova Scotia. He was drowned in the St. of North on Aug. 3, 1867, age 46.
202 John McLeod, died Feb. 14, 1905, age 79.

418 John McLeod, 1847-1913. Hannah McLeod, 1830-1917. Douglas McLeod, 1840-1902.

261 John McLeod, died March 3, 1872, age 35.

106 John A. MacLeod, August 30, 1890 - April 24, 1947.

293 John D. MacLeod, 1832-1922. Jessie MacLeod, his wife, 1848-1889 (?).

330 John Robert, died March 22, 1887, age 18. Margaret, died Sept. 3, 1863, age 25. Children of John and Mary McLeod.

387 Junius A. MacLeod, 1887-1962. Isabel MacLeod, Feb. 12, 1918 - Oct. 22, 1919. John A. MacLeod, killed in action in France, Nov. 25, 1921 - Aug. 15, 1944.

191 Katie, daughter of John and Isabella McLeod, died Nov. 22, 1887, age 42. Erected by sister Annie.

143 Christy McLeod, died April 18, 1881, age 66. Donald McLeod, died April 17, 1884, age 79. John McLeod, died July 28, 1879, age 62.

169 Daniel, died July 19, 1868, age 17. Mary Jane, died Sept. 21, 1874, age 8. Jessie Margaret, died Aug. 24, 1878, age 16. Children of Alexander and Christie McLeod, China Point.

189 Margaret, daughter of John and Isabella McLeod, died Feb. 10, 1894, age 45.

283 Mary McLeod, died Dec. 17, 1876, age 35. Angus McLeod, lost at sea, July, 1862, age 28.

288 Murdoch MacLeod, died Sept. 13, 1920, age 74. Christy, his wife, died Feb. 28, 1925, age 81. Georgie, their daughter, died Sept. 8, 1934, age 54.

235 Neil, son of William and Margaret McLeod, died April 1, 1884, age 21.

300 Norman McLeod, died Nov. 18, 1897, age 58. Peter A., his son, died Sept. 25, 1893, age 16.

262 Sarah McLeod, died Jan. 13, 1854, age 59. Neil McLeod, her husband, died Nov. 5, 1861, age 60.

187 William McLeod, died July 17, 1862, age 61.

515 Daniel Smith, 1872-1951. Jennie MacLeod, his wife, 1892-1973. A. Everett Smith, their son, 1919-1966. Buried in Pinehill Cemetery, Toronto.

308 John Gillis, died April 3, 1911, age 50, of Flat River. Annie MacLeod, his wife, died Dec. 7, 1947, age 86. John Herbert Gillis, died Feb. 9, 1945, age 57.

395 Charles D. MacLeod, April 13, 1875 - June 9, 1961. Catherine Matheson, his wife, Nov. 22, 1879 - Oct. 31, 1961.

339 David McLeod, 1830-1917. Ann Morrison, his wife, 1828-1915.

344 Neil MacLean, 1847-1923. Katherine MacLeod, his wife, 1854-1935. Angus M. MacLean, 1877-1966.

306 Roderick MacRae, 1838-1926. Eunice MacLeod, his wife, 184?-1934. Alexander D. Smith, 1860-1942. Sarah MacRae, his wife, 1862-1946.

331 John McLeod, died July 12, 1908, age 81. Mary McDonald, his wife, died Nov. 23, 1912, age 84. Margaret, died Sept. 3, 1863, age 2. John Robert, died March 22, 1887, age 18. Catherine, died Sept. 12, 1935, age 69. Their children.

472 Frederick McDonald, died Aug. 7, 1873, age 54. Emigrated from Ross Shire, Scotland, A.D. 1837. Mary McLeod, his wife, died Nov. 3, 1891, age 53. Emigrated with her parents from Inverness Shire, Scotland, 1839. Mary G., died Dec. 8, 1890, age 10 mos. Maggie, died April 23, 1879, age 6 yrs. 8 mos. Their children.

462 Malcolm MacLean, died July 1866, age 68. Mary MacLeod, his wife, died 1876, age 80. Jessie, died Dec. 7, 1904, age 81. Christie, died March 29, 1905, age 73. Their children. John MacLean, Culloden, died Feb. 10, 1915, age 76. Annie MacLeod, his wife, died Dec. 11, 1927, age 85. Mary, their daughter, died Dec. 13, 1899, age 25.

14 Murdoch MacRae, 1908—. Margaret MacLeod, his beloved wife, 1922—. Norman Malcolm, their beloved son, 1951-1974.

36 Aubrey MacLellan, July 8, 1901 - Feb. 9, 1968. Jessie MacLeod, his wife, Jan. 2, 1897 - Aug. 5, 1974.

57 Daniel A. MacLeod, 1876-1958. Janetta Riley, his wife, 1883-1965.

81 John M. Martin, 1864-1950. Catherine MacLeod, his wife, 1872-1956.

96 Norman S. MacEachern, 1879-1951. Catherine MacEachern, 1876-1954. Margaret MacLeod, 1883-1971.

216 George R. MacKenzie, 1841-1934. Mary MacLeod, his wife, 1836-1921.

209 Christy Ann McLeod, wife of Donald MacEachern, died Feb. 12, 1887, age 28.

22 Campbell MacLeod, 1887-1974. Cassie MacKenzie, his wife, 1895—.

166 Margaret McLeod, wife of James Kelly, died Oct. 22, 1867, age 23. Margaret A., died Nov. 5, 1887, age 22. Archibald, died April 7, 1891, age 26. Their children.

203 John S. McEachern, died Jan. 23, 1907, age 63. Mary Isabel McLeod, wife of John, died Oct. 4, 1901, age 46. Norman McSwain, died Feb. 28, 1901, age 86. Margaret McLeod, his wife, died Feb. 21, 1899, age 77. William E., their son, died June 28, 1897, age 7 mos.

174 Malcolm Finlayson, died Sept. 15, 1871, age 84. Margaret, his wife, died April 19, 1850, age 73. Natives of Isle of Skye. James A., son of Allan and Mary Finlayson, died Feb. 14, 1884, age 23. Allan Finlayson, died July 13, 1894, age 80. Mary MacLeod, his wife, died Jan. 10, 1906, age 82.

182 Donald McLeod, Sr., died July 24, 1881, age 74. Catherine Gillis, his wife, died Oct. 17, 1902, age 76.

158 Christena, wife of Alexander McLeod, died June 20, 1885, age 60. Alexander McLeod, died Oct. 3, 1893, age 73. Jane Nicholson, born March 20, 1814, died March 28, 1899.

151 Annie B. Nicholson, wife of John MacLeod, 1867-1946.

161 Angus Beaton, died March 1, 1863, age 56. Ann, his wife, died March 5, l869, age 60. Angus Beaton, 1861-1940. Jane Ann MacLeod, his wife, 1869-1935. Jane Auld, 1909-1956.

l49 Archibald McRae, died July 2, 1905, age 84. Flora McLeod, his wife, died Feb. 20, 1911. Capt. Murdoch McRae, died March 16, 1892, age 60.

201 Samuel Nicholson, died May 19, 1861. Flora McLeod, his wife, died Feb. 1867, age 77.

157 Daniel McKinnon, born 1869, died 1911. Flora MacLeod, his wife, 1869-1944. John Earle, their son, 1909-1911. Donaldena Mary, their daughter, 1905-1920.

316 Ewen Ross, Flat River, died Aug. 18, 1895, age 68. Donald E. Ross, died Oct. 8, 1947, age 83. Christy C. MacLeod, his wife, died Sept. 19, 1948, age 82. Frank Martin, son of Donald E. and Christy C. Ross, died Sept. 15, 1896, age 1 yr. Annie MacLeod, wife of Ewen Ross, died June 7, 1915, age 84.

332 Robert McWilliams, born Oct. 1838, died Jan. 1908. Sarah McLeod, his wife, born Sept. 1843, died Aug. 1923. John R. McWilliams, born March 26, 1878, died July 9, 1949. Catherine Bruce, wife of J. R. McWilliams, born May 20, 1875, died Nov. 25, 1946.

459 Donald McLeod. died at Melville, Lot 60, March 22, 1865, age 74. Emigrated to P.E.I. from Scotland 1830 with his wife Jane Nicholson. Erected by his daughter Bella and grand-daughter.

132 Donald S. MacLeod, 1840-1903. Isabella MacDonald, 1849-1928. Erected by daughter Mary. Jackson MacLeod. Alice M. MacLeod, 1880-1957. James R. MacLeod, 1886-1964.

135 Charles MacLeod, 1837-1912. Jessie MacLeod, his wife, 1835-1875. Neil, their

son, 1868-1885.

134 Angus Stewart, died Nov. 17, 1901, age 72. Mary McLeod, his wife, died April 18, 1904, age 78.

128 Alexander Stewart, 1831-1906. Catherine MacLeod, his wife, 1834-1914. Katie Ann, their daughter, 1876-1972.

120 John MacKinnon, 1861-1938. Elizabeth MacLeod, his wife, 1859-1945. Mrs. Mabel A. Giddings, their daughter, 1829-1939. William C. Giddings, her husband, 1882-1939. Both buried at Dorcester, Mass.

379 Lexie Nicholson, wife of Angus N. MacLeod, 1881-1957. Angus N. MacLeod, 1889-1971. Alexena Martin, wife of Alexander MacLeod, 1854-1920. Alexander MacLeod, 1846-1923. Sinclair MacLeod, 1891-1953.

371 Thomas Ross, 1851-1925. Euphemia MacLeod, his wife, 1857-1920. Angus W. Ross, 1880-1887. Neil Ross, 1894-1918, killed in France. Their children.

460 John McLeod, died at Dundas, June 1863, age 52. A native of Raasay, Scotland. Sarah Matheson, his wife, died March 16, 1884, age 76. A native of Isle of Skye.

426 Angus MacLean, 1861-1938. Christine MacLeod, his wife, 1860-1949. Malcolm A., 1886-1888. Margaret J., 1888-1910. Their children.

396 John Angus Martin, Feb. 15, 1865 - Feb. 4, 1948. Christena Florence MacLeod, his wife, Nov. 18, 1871 - Feb. 4, 1968.

463 Kenneth MacBeth, died June 26, 1862, age 73. Isabella, his wife, died July 1, 1883, age 88. John MacBeth, died Oct. 29, 1903, age 66. Jessie MacLeod, his wife, died March 15, 1928, age 85. Bella, died Aug. 2, 1868, age 1 year. Catherine, died Feb. 12, 1884, age 9 days. Their daughters.

405 John A. MacLeod, born 1840 - died 1899. Anne Nicholson, his wife, born 1838 - died 1931. Samuel, their son, born 1880, died 1910.

512 Ann McLeod, wife of Donald F. Smith, died April 7, 1892, age 72. Native of Isle of Skye.

225 Ewen Gillis, died April 8, 1887, age 68. Elizabeth MacLeod, his wife, died Dec. 8, 1879, age 54. Elizabeth, their daughter, died Nov. 1, 1878, age 34. Angus, their son, died Jan. 1, 1884, age 24. Erected by their sisters Christy and Flora.

267 Christina MacLeod, wife of William Ross, died Jan. 15, 1890, age 62. William Ross, died Aug. 1, 1903, age 82. Children: Donald W., died Dec. 22, 1889, age 31. Kitty Jane, died Jan. 14, 1890, age 24. Samuel W., May 1862 - March 1943. Matilda MacLean, died Jan. 20, 1890, age 16.

264 John N. McLeod of Orwell, died Dec. 22, 1902, age 78. Elizabeth McDonald, his wife, died March 2, 1918, age 88. Alexander MacLeod, died Dec. 22, 1862, age 3 years. Margaret, died May 10, 1866, age 5 weeks. Neil McLeod, died at Portland, Oregon, U.S.A., Nov. 20, 1906, age 42.

290 Murdoch Beaton, 1824-1896. Christy McLeod, his wife, 1831-1927.

246 Donald Gillis, died October 3, 1874, age 74. Rachel McLeod, his wife, died Jan. 1, 1901, age 95.

294 Capt. John MacLeod, Dec. 3, 1891 - Nov. 9, 1938. Mary Nicholson, his wife, March 1, 1881 - March 13, 1967.

236 William N. MacLeod, 1829-1912. Margaret MacDonald, his wife, 1832-1914.

287 Alexander McKenzie, 1829-1921. Mary McLeod, his wife, 1833-1915.

871 Arthur Graham Putnam, 1876-1966. Ada MacLeod Putnam, 1878-1966.

628 Arthur Graham, son of Arthur G. and Ada MacLeod Putnam, died Dec. 5, 1919, age 11 years.

282 Capt. Alex McLeod, elder, native of Isle of Skye, Scotland, died Sept. 20, 1861, age 87. Catherine, his wife, died Feb. 19, 1876, age 86. Christina McLeod, died Oct. 20, 1873, age 50. William McLeod, died May 16, 1884, age 72. Mary McLeod,

wife of Donald McPherson, died Apr. 20, 1847, age 38.

250 Malcolm Gillis of Orwell, died Sept. 1, 1847, age 38. Christy McLeod, his wife, died April 5, 1881, age 73. John Gillis, died Dec. 14, 1850, age 21 years.

851 Alexander McLeod, died April 14, 1888, age 89. Mary Campbell, his wife, died Sept. 5, 1881, age 72. Alexander McLeod, died Aug. 1838, age 66. Mary McPherson, his wife, died March 1843, age 69. Emigrated from Skye, 1803. Catherine, died Aug. 22, 1869, age 25. Neil, died Oct. 1859, age 6. Children of Alexander and Mary McLeod.

646 Angus McLeod (Hill), died Dec. 23, 1894, age 86. Rev. Charles McLeod, his son, died at North Dakota, Sept. 18, 1913.

819 Angus McLeod Glasvin, died Jan. 28, 1885, age 88. Margaret, his wife, died Dec. 11, 1862, age 64.

986 V.R. 1360 A. B., Angus Neil McLeod, Royal Can. Navy, Oct. 22, 1919.

645 Angus McLeod, died April 12, 1923, age 74. Mary A. McLeod, died Dec. 24, 1929, age 68.

852 Annie McLeod, died July 28, 1966, age 74.

715 D. Wilber, son of Rev. George B. and Margaret McLeod, died April 11, 1900, age 4 years, 10 months.

809 Angus McLeod, Melville, died Sept. 7, 1920, age 69. Jessie MacLeod, his wife, died at New Bedford, Mass., March 16, 1922, age 87. Malcolm McLeod, died 1867, age 11. Christina Beaton, his wife, died 1864, age 63. Jessie McLeod, died 1874.

804 Neil Nicholson, died April 23, 1893, age 90. Ann McLeod, his wife, died March 5, 1879, age 71. Alexander, died 1837, age 4 years. Catherine, died 1855, age 19. Children of Neil and Ann.

647 Ann Martin, wife of Angus McLeod, died March 14, 1883, age 64.

587 Angus MacLeod, 1837-1915. Catherine MacRae, his wife, 1848-1926. Sgt. John W., their son, born 1886, killed in France, May 9, 1917. Malcolm A., their son, 1879-1951.

854 Catherine, wife of Roderick McLeod, died Oct. 12, 1875, age 76. Donald M., her son, age 6 years. Roderick MacLeod, born in Scotland, emigrated to P.E.I. 1821, died March 18, 1887, age 90.

994 Neil Haywood MacLean, Oct. 27, 1895—. Catherine Edith MacLeod, Nov. 21, 1893 - March 20, 1973, his wife. John Lauchlin, their infant son.

987 Catherine M. Murchison, wife of John D. McLeod, died April 25, 1914, age 53. John D. McLeod, died March 3, 1932, age 63. Hettie Bell, their daughter, 1897-1919. Angus Neil, their son, 1901-1919.

902 Christina C. Stewart, wife of Rev. A. A. McLeod of the Can. Baptist Mission, Ramachandra duram, India, died at Belle River, Nov. 16, 1897, age 40.

892 George, beloved son of Donald and Mary McLeod, died May 13, 1883, age 26.

985 Christy Ann McLeod, died April 5, 1931, age 70. Donald McLeod, died May 3, 1900, age 74. Katie MacDonald, his wife, died Nov. 13, 1920, age 92. Wm. D. McLeod, died March 6, 1947, age 76. Margaret A. Munroe, his wife, died Sept. 13, 1950, age 77.

893 Donald McLeod, died March 28, 1907, age 92. Mary Buchanan, his wife, died Sept. 7, 1907, age 90.

872 Donald McLeod, died Dec. 14, 1865, age 60. Elizabeth, his wife, died June 24, 1865, age 59. Jessie, their daughter, died May 16, 1870, age 38.

640 Ronald MacRae, Nov. 23, 1854 - March 8, 1932. Effie Ann MacLeod, his wife, Aug. 29, 1861 - June 29, 1952. Alexander Roderick, their son, Nov. 1, 1895, killed in action April 9, 1917.

988 Daniel D. MacLeod, 1863-1927. Flora Murchison, his wife, 1869-1956. Miriam MacLeod, 1897-1925.

970 Elizabeth A. MacLeod, wife of Alex W. Finlayson, 1870-1947. Nathaniel MacLeod, 1912-1926. Alexander W. Finlayson, 1864-1946.

810 James McLeod, son of Wm. and Mary McLeod, died April 17, 1858, age 21 yrs.

816 Janet, wife of John McLeod, died March 13, 1886, age 77. John McLeod, Point Prim, died Oct. 23, 1862, age 67.

583 Jean Isabelle, 8 mos., daughter of Malcolm A. and Allena M. MacLeod.

447 John D. MacLeod, 1841-1927. Jessie McPhee, his wife, 1844-1928. Mary W., 1880-1884. Katherine A., 1882-1886. Their daughters. Sister Isabella, 1837-1923. Hannah B., their daughter, 1871-1940.

824 John McLeod [remainder of stone sunken].

741 John McLeod, died Nov. 1, 1869, [illegible], age 35.

730 Joseph Millburn, son of Alex and Ida MacLeod, died at Orwell Mills, May 11, 1901, age 4 mos.

750 Alexander Ross, died April 2, 1937, age 73. Isabella McLeod, his wife, died June 23, 1915, age 57.

946 Charles Nicholson, died Nov. 5, 1901, age 55. Flora McLeod, his wife, died April 27, 1895, age 39. Malcolm F., their son, died in Klondike, April 21, 1902, age 22. Ezra A. died Feb. 1, 1972, age 79. Malcolm McLeod, died Jan. 23, 1894, age 84. Flora, his wife, died Feb. 4, 1899, age 78.

602 Malcolm James MacLeod, born May 24, 1865, died Oct. 5, 1940. Henry Blakeley MacLeod, June 27, 1899 - Sept. 2, 1920. Malcolm J. MacLeod, Jr., Aug. 23, 1916 - Nov. 22, 1944.

818 Margaret, daughter of Angus and Margaret McLeod, died April 24, 1858, age 18.

843 William Malkman, 1885-1965. Murdoch Buchanan, died 1917. Margaret MacLeod, his wife, died 1923.

1006 Clarence J. Panton, 1903—. Margaret MacLeod, his wife, 1913-1973. John C. Panton, their son, 1935—.

811 William McLeod of Point Prim, died Feb. 5, 1885, age 85.

895 William M. MacLeod, died Aug. 11, 1919, age 69. Mary McRae, his wife, died Dec. 25, 1920, age 70. Hilda C. MacLeod, their daughter, died Nov. 8, 1915, age 18.

621 Almira Nicholson, wife of Peter McLeod, died at Calgary, Aug. 11, 1911, age 28.

823 Sarah McLeod, died Aug. 9, 1885, age 22. Christina McLeod, died July 3, 1883, age 19. William Wallace McLeod, died 1871, age 1 year. Angelina McLeod, died 1858 in infancy.

684 Donald D. Ross, born Dec. 25, 1834, died Sept. 21, 1906. Margaret McLeod, his wife, born April 23, 1845, died March 8, 1939. Daniel, their son, born July 6, 1875, died Nov. 2, 1944. John R., their son, born Jan. 8, 1864, died Nov. 3, 1943. Florence Beaton, his wife, March 8, 1890 - July 20, 1973.

601 Sarah Hooper, wife of Norman R. McLeod, died June 2, 1906, age 62. Norman R. MacLeod, died Oct. 11, 1918. age 74. Lila D. W., their daughter, died Feb. 10, 1901, age 24.

779 James A. MacLean, 1839-1915. Margaret I. MacLeod, his wife, 1859-1893. Capt. Murdoch J., their son, 1879-1951. Margaret I. MacLean. Ann MacLean, 1838-1910.

878 Mary, late wife of Donald MacLeod and daughter of Samuel Murchison, died Nov. 6, 1855, age 37. Erected by her sons Capt's M. and A. MacLeod.

76 Daniel D. MacLeod, 1863-1927. Flora Murchison, his wife, 1869-1956. Miriam MacLeod, 1897-1925.

75 John D. MacLeod, March 3, 1932, age 69. Catherine M. Murchison, his wife,

April 25, 1914, age 53. Hettie Bell, their daughter, 1897-1918. Angus Neil, their son, 1901 - Oct. 22, 1919.

28   John M. Martin, 1864 - March 29, 1950. Catherine MacLeod, his wife, 1872 - Nov. 5, 1956.

26   Norman S. MacEachern, 1879-1951. Catherine MacEachern, 1876 - Oct. 5, 1954. Margaret MacLeod, 1883—.

74   Donald McLeod, May 3, 1900, age 74. Katie MacDonald, his wife, Nov. 13, 1920, age 92. Christy Ann, their daughter, April 5, 1931, age 70. William D. MacLeod, March 6, 1947, age 76. Margaret A. Munroe, his wife, Sept. 13, 1950, age 77.

112   Angus MacLeod, 1837-1915. Catherine MacRae, his wife, 1848-1926. Malcolm A. their son, 1879 - March 2, 1951. Sgt. John W., 1886 - May 9, 1917, killed in France. Jean Isabelle, daughter of Malcolm and Allena MacLeod, 8 mos.

705   Alex McRae, died July 25, 1892, age 82. Mary McLeod, his wife, died Jan. 22, 1899, age 82. Annie McRae, died Feb. 20, 1870, age 25. John McRae, died March 3, 1888, age 33. Children of Alex and Mary McRae.

576   Hector McKenzie, born April 25, 1830, died Sept. 2, 1916. Mary McLeod, his wife, born Oct. 10, 1831, died June 18, 1908. Angus, their son, died in Donville, Mass., Sept. 1, 1908, age 36. Hector D. McKenzie, born August 19, 1867, died Sept. 11, 1935. Katherine Lizzie McKenzie, born Dec. 19, 1865, died July 24, 1952. Christine McKenzie, born 1873, died Aug. 4, 1963.

9   John MacKinnon, 1861-1938. Elizabeth MacLeod, his wife, 1859-1945.

17   John A. MacLeod, Aug. 3, 1890 - April 24, 1947.

102   Norman R. MacLeod, died Oct. 17, 1918, age 74. Sarah Hooper, his wife, June 2, 1906, age 62. Lila D. W., their daughter, Feb. 10, 1907, age 24.

128   Hector MacKenzie. April 25, 1830 - Sept. 2, 1906, son of Hector McKenzie and Margaret McRae, brother of Capt. R. K. McKenzie. Mary MacLeod, his wife, Oct. 10, 1831- June 19, 1908, daughter of Angus MacLeod and Margaret Dockerty.

92   Nathaniel MacLeod, 1912-1926. Alexander W. Finlayson, 1864-1946. Elizabeth A. MacLeod, his wife, 1870 - Sept. 4, 1947.

152   John A. MacLeod, 1840-1899. Anne Nicholson, his wife, 1838-1931. Samuel, their son, 1880-1910.

BELLE RIVER

11   John Livingstone, native of Isle of Colonsay, Scotland, died Jan. 1, 1869, age 71. Margaret MacLeod, his wife, died April 24, 1903, age 88. Native of Isle of Skye.

24   Donald McLeod, died May 28, 1914, age 71. Letitia, wife of Donald McLeod, died Dec. 27, 1902, age 55. Angus, their son, died at sea, Dec. 20, 1902, age 24.

BELLE RIVER PIONEER CEMETERY

6   John Livingstone (same as Belle River, above). Margaret McLeod, his wife. Donald McLeod (same as Belle River, above). Letitia, his wife and son Angus.

BIDEFORD UNITED

120   Alexander MacLeod, Private 85th Battn. C.E.F., 28 April, 1956, aged 61.

BIRCH HILL, FREE CHURCH OF SCOTLAND

123 John Robert Brown, 1872-1950. His wife Angusena MacLeod, 1878-1958. Margaret H. Brown, 1869-1967.

71 Stephen Myers, born in England 1753, died in Charlottetown 1843. Flora MacLeod, his wife, and their daughter Lydia.

7 Howard Hazen MacLeod, Sept. 9, 1917, age 5 yrs. Hazel Margaret, Jan. 24, 1917, aged 4 days. Children of N. Hudson and Margaret MacLeod.

48 Wilfred Drake, 1901-1971. His wife, Ora MacLeod, –. Their son, Wilfred Drake, 1926-1928.

BRAE, IMMACULATE CONCEPTION CATHOLIC CEMETERY

108 In memory of Donald McLeod, died Dec. 2, 1908, aged 73—May his soul rest in peace. 2nd side—MacLeod, In memory of William McLeod, died Sept. 3, 1909, aged 28—May his soul rest in peace. 3rd side—In memory of Annie MacLeod, died Feb. 7, 1911, aged 30. R.I.P.

BRAE UNITED PRESBYTERIAN

58 MacLeod/Father/John D. MacLeod, 1870-1944. MacLeod/Mother/Ida L. Caseley, 1871-1946. "In God Have I Put My Trust."

BREADALBANE, ST. ELIZABETH'S ANGLICAN

44 William Todd, 1857-1938. Leonard Todd, 1887-1974. Jemima MacLeod, his wife, 1895—.

62 John A. McLeod, 1870-1951.

68 James F. MacLeod, 1848-1942. Mary Munroe, his wife, 1853-1938.

69 Rachel MacLeod Wilbur, 1893-1955.

72 John James MacLeod, April 13, 1895 - June, 5, 1960. Florence G. MacDougall, his wife, July 7, 1902 - Sept. 21, 1968.

80 Charles A. Todd, Oct. 25, 1881 - April 8, 1978. Catherine MacLeod, his wife, Sept. 25, 1880 - Sept. 8, 1958. Robert E. Todd, their son, Jan. 17, 1922 - May 18, 1970.

BROOKFIELD PRESBYTERIAN

114 Mary Ann MacPherson, wife of Finley Matheson, died Jan. 25, 1909, aged 55. Finley Matheson, died Sept. 4, 1930, aged 78, also his wife Mary MacLeod, died Aug. 6, 1929, aged 73.

5 C. G. Gordon MacLeod, Nov. 18, 1889 - Dec. 7, 1936. His wife, Katherine Pearl MacDonald, July 17, 1893 - Aug. 12, 1962.

11 MacLeod, Jean, infant 1919. Keith, died 1923, aged 5 mos. John A. MacLeod, 1884-1925.

110 John MacLeod, 1887-1949. His wife, Georgie Sentner, 1898-1951. His mother Mrs. Isabelle Russell.

78 Murdoch MacLeod, died June 10, 1890, aged 46. John MacLeod, died July 1, 1874, aged 63, and his wife Jane Sellars, died May 13, 1890, aged 78. Catherine MacLeod, wife of James MacDonald, died Oct. 1, 1890, aged 44. Jane Ann MacLeod, died May 9, 1923, aged 72.

84   John McLeod, died June 13, 1883, aged 75, also his wife Christ—na (?), died March 18, 1893, aged 73.

79   Margaret McInnis, wife of Roderick McLeod, died Feb. 20, 1899, aged 76. Roderick McLeod, died March 7, 1902, aged 89. Their son John, died Feb. 18, 1900, aged 47. Their daughter Catherine, 1846-1934.

66   Daniel J. MacInnis, 1884-1951. His wife Isabel MacKenzie, 1896-1964. Hugh MacInnis, 1837-1902. His wife, Catherine MacLeod, 1843-1928.

112 John T. MacLeod, 1844-1929. His wife Christie Matheson, 1846-1887.

70   William Henderson, died May 24, 1897, aged 77. His wife Flora MacLeod, died Oct. 20, 1877, aged 56. Children: John M., died March 21, 1878, aged 4 years. Isabella F., died March 1863, 1 year.

60   Angus MacLeod, died Dec. 10, 1934, aged 73. His wife Christine Campbell, died July 22, 1956, aged 89.

61   L.A.C. Roderick McLeod, R.C.A.F., April 1, 1945.

54   Angus N. MacLeod, 1849-1940. His wife Sarah MacKinnon, 1857-1939. Their children: Angus Synic, 1890-1890. Norman G. M., 1900-1901.

45   Donald S. Campbell. His wife Ethel M. MacLeod. Their son, Alexander Norman, 1940-1942.

43   G. Fenton MacLeod, May 27, 1938 - Jan. 12, 1968.

49   Alexander Campbell, 1858-1931. His wife Susan M. MacLeod of Uigg, 1856-1954.

57   John Campbell McLeod, one of the Pioneers of the Yukon, died Sept. 21, 1914, aged 67. His wife Margaret Brown, Nov. 15, 1867 - June 8, 1958. Also their children who died in infancy: Sadie, born Dec. 23, 1901. Violet Augusta, born Aug. 2, 1910. Sarah Campbell, Aug. 12, 1903 - Dec. 26, 1958. Margaret A. Cameron-Allie, Jan. 13, 1905 - Sept. 21, 1966.

46   Isabella MacLeod, wife of Hammond Crabbe, 1868-1914. Also Nellie and Bessie Crabbe. Hammond Crabbe, 1868-1953.

42   George W. MacLeod, 1876-1956. His wife Mary S. Johnston, 1875-1970. Son Frederick E., 1907-1969. Ella Katie, daughter of Murdoch and Jane MacLeod, born March 8, 1883, died May 18, 1891. Donald MacLeod, died July 30, 1898, a native of Scotland, emigrated to P.E.I. in 1840. Also his wife Christy Matheson, died May 22, 1910, aged 84. Murdoch MacLeod, 1848-1930. His wife Jane Tinney, 1846-1933.

19   Norman MacLeod, 1840-1924. His wife Margaret Drummond, 1848-1908. Their children: Sadie Belle, 1884-1922. Angus Leslie, 1886-1892.

22   Catherine McPherson, wife of L. H. McLeod, born Sept. 30, 1830, died Jan. 2, 1922.

20   Dougald MacPherson, 1848-1947, also his wife Janet MacLeod, 1860-1940, also three children: Hilda A. MacLeod, died Jan 3, 1958, aged 55. Roderick MacLeod, died Aug. 13, 1931, aged 67, also his wife Lucy Ann MacDuff, July 27, 1935, aged 60.

BROOKLYN CHURCH OF SCOTLAND (ANGLICAN)

17   W. Alexander Martin, 1856-1931. Annie MacLeod, his wife, 1857-1937. John, 1892-1894. Georgina, 1889-1900. Nora, 1885-1902. Annie Campbell, 1883-1904. Margaret, 1887-1904.

10   Nora, daughter of Angus and Mary MacLeod, died May 1, 1886, age 24.

BRUDENELL BAPTIST CEMETERY

98   John Alexander Gordon, died 1920, aged 73. His wives, Margaret J. Hender-
      son, died 1884, age 26. Margaret J. MacLeod, died 1944, aged 82. Kenneth H.
      Gordon, 1883-1949.
109   Annabella MacLeod, wife of George W. Rourke, died July 28, 1905, aged 49.

CALEDONIA PRESBYTERIAN

10   Alexander MacLeod, 1822-1909. Isabella MacLeod, his wife, 1822-1908.
57   Margaret, wife of Malcolm MacLeod, 1865-1912. Pte. John N. MacLeod, 1894-
      1916. Pte. Milton O. MacLeod, 1895-1920.
64   Peter William MacLeod, 1904-1976. John Dan MacLeod, 1907—.
99   Norman McLeod, died June 3, 1891, age 85.
102   John D. MacDonaid, 1862-1934. Jessie MacLeod, his wife, 1860-1958. Florence,
      their daughter, 1891-1923. Ewen, their son, 1895-1918. Neil M., their son, 1899,
      age 3 mos. Annie MacPherson, his wife, 1830-1919.
143   Angus Matheson, 1892-1972. Annie May MacLeod, his wife, 1904-1971.
105   Alexander D. MacLeod, 1854-1938. Elizabeth C. MacDonald, his wife, 1855-
      1933. Susan, 1889-1890. Annie, 1877-1891. Maggie, 1900-1901. Lucy, 1897-1918.
      Their children.
139   John N. MacLeod, 1841-1895. Mary A. Gunn, his wife, 1846-1935. Katie MacLeod,
      1879-1950. Neil MacLeod, 1813-1895. Margaret MacLeod, his wife, 1828-1910.
138   Christy MacLeod, wife of Timothy Young, died _____ 13, 1918, age 58. [Stone
      broken]
45   John Bruce, 1867-1953. Margaret MacLeod, his wife, 1875-1936. Annie, their
      daughter, 1909-1939.
18   Malcolm McKenzie, 1851-1931. Mary McLeod, his wife, 1860-1922.
9   Isaac S. Acorn, 1878-1963. Christena MacLeod, his wife, 1885-1973.
129   Catherine Stewart, wife of Norman MacLeod, 1837-1922. Norman, her grandson,
      1908-1922. John Neil, her grandson, 1914-1914. Alexander S. MacLeod, died
      Feb. 1, 1954, age 89. Mary MacLean, his wife, died March 25, 1960, age 89.
200   John A. MacLeod, 1868-1933. Catherine A. Matheson, his wife, 1870-1936.
195   Donald McPhee, died Dec. 24, 1899, age 77. Mary MacLeod, his wife, died
      Nov. 5, 1925, age 87.
158   Norman MacKenzie, 1830-1900. Mary MacLeod, his wife, 1856-1943. Mary
      Ann, 1892-1893. Christine Wilson, 1890-1931. Their daughters.
173   Mary Jane Stewart, died July 22, 1894, age 18. Eliza MacLeod, wife of Dougald
      Stewart, 1879-1915. Dougald Stewart, 1867-1951. Mary A. MacDonald, his wife,
      1879-1965.
156   Alexander McLeod, died at Rona, April 28, 1895, age 76. Mary Nicholson, his
      wife, died July 9, 1894, age 67. Natives of Scotland. Annie, died Nov. 8, 1893,
      age 29, their daughter.
147   John L. MacLeod, 1905-1966. Catherine E. Campbell, his wife, 1907—. Altheia
      J. MacLeod, their daughter, 1931-1962. John L. MacLeod, Gunner R.C.A., May
      23, 1966, age 60.
149   Alexander J. MacLeod, 1870-1948. Margaret Belle MacPhee, his wife, 1872-1961.
97   William McLennan, died Feb. 19, 1921, age 62. Annie MacLeod, his wife, born
      Dec. 11, 1873, died March 20, 1941. Donald McLennan, died June 7, 1947, age 47.
150   John MacLeod, died Feb. 27, 1913, age 82. Catherine Stewart, his wife, died
      Feb. 16, 1912, age 72.

63   Margaret Matheson, wife of Angus J. MacLeod, Jan. 8, 1869 - Nov. 18, 1944.

118   Donald Matheson, 1888-1926. Catherine MacLeod, his wife, 1851-1938.

109   Roderick MacLeod, 1846-1909. Sarah Bruce MacLeod, 1847-1921. Flora MacLeod Taylor, their daughter, 1887-1923.

120   Christy McLeod, wife of Neil McLean, died Jan. 11, 1914, age 71. Neil McLean, died May 8, 1918, age 78. John, their son, died July 21, 1910, age 35.

135   James McLeod, died Feb. 22, 1897, age 47. Catherine McLeod, his wife, died Oct. 31, 1937, age 77. Malcolm, died Aug. 20, 1895. John D., died Sept. 20, 1895. Sons of James and Catherine McLeod.

146   Altheia J. MacLeod, 1931-1962.

110   Annie McLaughlin, wife of M. J. McLeod, died March 17, 1920, age 59. Charles, their son, died April 6, 1893, age 6 yrs. John, their son, died May 3, 1895, age 1 yr., 10 mos. Murdoch J. McLeod, died June 16, 1940, age 80.

39   Donald A. MacDonald, Oct. 10, 1853, died Oct. 31, 1920. Catherine MacLeod, his wife, born April 4, 1860, died Jan. 10, 1933. Florence M. MacDonald, 1898-1922.

107   Catherine McLeod, wife of John J. McDonald, died Nov. 26, 1899, age 26. Harriet, their daughter, died June 9, 1899, age 5 mos.

66   Margaret, relict of Alexander McLeod, age 92. A native of Braes of Portree, Isle of Skye, Scotland.

125   Catherine McLeod, wife of the late Donald McLeod of Rona, P.E.I., died April 8, 1896, age 83.

148   Joseph A. MacLeod, 1878-1950. Effie MacLeod, his wife, 1883-1967. Sadie Jane MacLeod, their daughter, 1909-1933.

CANOE COVE PRESBYTERIAN

188   Euphemia McLeod, wife of John MacLean, died April 18, 1893, age 79.

203   Ann McLeod, wife of [? broken stone], died March 30, 1890, age 60.

231   Roderick MacKinnon, 1823-1891. Jane MacLeod, his wife, 1834-1908.

241   William L. MacLeod, 1892-1976. Rosillia M., 1890-1976.

301   Alexander MacLeod, June 17, 1877 - May 6, 1967. Sarah Ann MacFadyen, his wife, May 2, 1887 - Dec. 9, 1966. Myrtle Marie Darrach, granddaughter, Oct. 23-24, 1936.

CAPE TRAVERSE FREE CHURCH OF SCOTLAND

224   Thomas Bishop, died Dec. 6, 1919, aged 82. Also his wife Margaret McLeod, died Dec. 8, 1895, aged 55.

229   Neil McLeod, died Oct. 12, 1855, aged 59. Emigrated to P.E.I. 1806.

CARDIGAN ALL SAINTS ROMAN CATHOLIC CEMETERY

139   Dougald MacLeod, M.D., 1817-1886. His wife, Margaret J. MacIntyre, 1819-1912. Mary MacLeod, wife of Edward Reeves, 1848-1888.

CARDIGAN, ST. ANDREW'S PRESBYTERIAN

5   Neil Shaw, June 9, 1884 - Feb. 3, 1977. His wife, Annie MacLeod, Sept. 14, 1890 - March 21, 1972. Their sons: Allan Duncan, April 21, 1922 - Jan. 22, 1925. Allan D. (Joey), April 7, 1929 - Feb. 5. 1931.

81 Alex Sutherland, died March 30, 1913, aged 90. His wife, Margaret McLeod, died Nov. 29, 1903, age 73.
53 Ernest David MacLeod, died Feb. 23, 1975, age 48.
55 Sarah Loreen MacLeod, died Dec. 20, 1976, age 89.
90 Norman MacLeod, died April 8, 1907, age 80. His wife, Margaret MacLean, 1828-1918. Murdoch MacLeod, 1865-1933.
104 Annie M. MacLeod, 1906-1962, wife of William Minchin.
105 Sterling A. A. MacLeod, April 12, 1908 - Feb. 4, 1970.
106 Flora Catherine MacPherson, April 2, 1876 - Feb. 9, 1937. Murdoch McLeod, May 5, 1864 - Oct. 5, 1931. Charles Earle MacPherson, 1909-1969.
109 Gordon MacLeod, 1900-1958.

CAVENDISH UNITED

283 Cassie A. MacLeod, wife of James Simpson, died July 26, 1883, aged 29.
294 Leopold E. MacLeod, son of James and Mary MacLeod, died Dec. 23, 1865.
299 James T. MacLeod, died Sept. 30, 1892, aged 73. His daughter, Mary T., died July 31, 1899, aged 24. His son, Donald Wallace, died at Vancouver, B.C., July 28, 1897, aged 36.
300 Winnie MacLeod, wife of Allan Stewart, Dec. 1, 1872 - Feb. 24, 1903.
301 Winnifred, daughter of Winnie and W. A. Stewart, died Nov. 4, 1903, aged 8 mos.

CENTRAL LOT 16, UNITED CHURCH

37 Minnie MacLeod, died 1965.
51 Margaret H. MacLeod, 1889-1969.
113 Clarence John MacLeod, 1941-1966.
130 Levinia MacLeod, 1910-1976.
130 John MacLeod, 1883-1957.
131 John D. MacLeod, 1884-1957.
137 Allan MacLeod, died 1915, aged 70. Catherine MacLeod, died 1923.

CHARLOTTETOWN, ELM AVENUE, ST. PAUL'S ANGLICAN

33 Mary Ann, daughter of James and Ann McLeod, died April 21, 1832, aged 9 mos.
72 Hugh McLeod [rest of inscription lost].
79 Laughlan McCloud, died March 23, 1858 [?], aged 94 [?]. Martha E., daughter of Angus and Margaret McCloud.

CHARLOTTETOWN PEOPLE'S CEMETERY

A-1

40 Earl Thomas MacLeod, June 28, 1900 - June 13, 1968.
15 Elizabeth R. Wyatt, wife of S. A. MacLeod, died Jan. 10, 1944.
25 Margaret June MacDonald, wife of John T. MacLeod, May 5, 1870 - May 31, 1968. Douglas Keir MacLeod, Oct. 17, 1893 - Nov. 16, 1963.
47 Norman MacLeod, died at St. Avards, March 13, 1903, aged 73 yrs. Also his wife,

Mary MacLean, died Aug. 26, 1927, aged 87 yrs. Margaret Harriett MacLeod, born Sept. 14, 1862, died Oct. 9, 1929.

A-2

14   James A. McLeod, 1823-1913. His wife, Annie Mitchell, 1829-1898.

26   MacLeod—Beloved wife, Margaret Laura Brown, July 10, 1892 - Feb. 16, 1979.

55   Emilie Annie, wife of Daniel MacLeod, died May 16, 1892, aged 24.

75   Parkman—Jane MacLeod, wife of E. G. Parkman, 1852-1883. Seymour, 1877-1883. Estelle, 1881-1884. Gordon C., 1876-1900.

89   Ivan George MacLeod, 31 Dec., 1908 - 23 Dec., 1978.

93   Garrett—Janet MacLeod, died Apr. 27, 1943.

114   Caroline Pippy, wife of David MacLeod, died Aug. 25, 1917, aged 78. David MacLeod, aged 44, and their sons: Hartley, aged 21. Edward, aged 19, lost at sea, June 6, 1883. Also their daughter Addie MacLeod, 1873-1943. D. Milton MacLeod, 1880-1922. Ruth, daughter of Milton and May MacLeod, born Nov. 7, 1913, died Feb. 9, 1914.

184   Duncan C. McLeod, K.C., died Aug. 11, 1915, aged 64.

185   James MacLeod, M.D., died Dec. 22, 1900, aged 56. His wife, Margaret Alma Gates, 1855-1927.

238   Philip Blake, died Apr. 18, 1900, aged 70, also his wife, Jane McLeod, died Dec. 7, 1902, aged 72.

265   MacLeod—Flora Currie, wife of M. G. MacLeod, died at Omaha, Nebraska, March 28, 1888.

493   John MacLeod, 1852-1931, his wife, Margaret Elizabeth Scott, 1859-1928.

440   111311 Sapper Keith MacLeod, C.R.T.C.E.F., 6th Dec., 1920.

507   Edwards—Leslie Lawrence Edwards, June 5, 1933 - Nov. 22, 1952. Joseph H. MacDonald, 1888-1965. His wife, Irene E. MacLeod, 1891-1971.

529   Hansen—Jessie MacLeod, wife of John Hansen, 1874-1934.

534   MacKinnon—Laughlin P. Mackinnon, 1909—. His wife, Myra F. MacLeod, 1916-1974.

560   Herbert H. MacLeod, 1895-1972.

562   Murdoch H. MacKenzie, July 12, 1877 - Oct. 10, 1926. His wife, Laura E. MacLeod, Sept. 24, 1885 - March 24, 1955. Their son, Charles H., April 22, 1914 - May 9, 1938.

584   Elizabeth McLaren, wife of Murdoch N. MacLeod, 1856-1926. Murdoch N. MacLeod, 1859-1944.

592   Matheson—Roderick William, born March 27, 1851, died Oct. 18, 1918. Also his wife, Sarah McLeod, born Feb. 21, 1853, died Dec. 7, 1921. Eleanor G. Matheson, wife of John A. MacLeod, June 13, 1890 - Oct. 20, 1918.

639   Sarah J. MacLean, wife of John S. MacLeod, 1868-1936. John S. MacLeod, 1862-1937. John A. MacLeod, 1900-1972.

651   Murdock W. MacLeod, 1861-1936. Annie Shaw, his wife, 1864-1944.

699   Norman J. MacLeod, 1892-1964. Marion E. Crockett, his wife, 1890-1973. Arnold, their son, March 9-11, 1928.

710   Alexander S. MacLeod, died Feb. 3, 1931, age 91. Elizabeth Ann MacLeod, died Feb. 8, 1948, aged 87.

749   Edwin G. Saunders, 1881-1928. Mamie Katherine MacLeod, his wife, 1883-1976.

801   Charles Albert MacLeod, April 17, 1898 - Aug. 28, 1973. Catherine A. Jeffrey, his wife, July 14, 1902—.

838 Harry C. MacLeod, Aug. 14, 1896 - Feb. 5, 1978. Florence Oakes, his wife, April 25, 1896 —. Shirley M. MacLeod, daughter, Dec. 13, 1925 - April 5, 1960.

873 W. Robert Cook, 1882-1967. Jessie C. MacLeod, his wife, 1892 —.

901 Joseph Kaye MacLeod, 1927-1972, son of Mr. and Mrs. Geddie MacLeod.

1329 John MacLeod, died Jan. 6, 1919, aged 70. Flora Bruce, his wife, died Oct. 26, 1927, aged 77. Wellington McLeod, died Oct. 20, 1896, aged 19.

624 Rev. Alexander B. MacLeod, born March 17, 1853, ordained Oct. 21, 1882, died April 19, 1916. Annie Larkin, his wife, born Oct. 18, 1851, died Mar. 21, 1940.

874 Harry Arnett MacLeod, Nov. 24, 1925 - Sept. 3, 1966. Accidentally killed at work.

886 John Finley MacLeod, March 3, 1897 - Jan. 3, 1960. His wife, Margaret Montgomery Sutherland, Jan. 20, 1900 - July 24, 1970.

902 Geddie MacLeod, son of J. J. and Flora MacLeod, born in Riverdale, Dec. 15, 1894, died in Charlottetown, May 3, 1959.

915 Douglas Bruce MacLeod, Nov. 10, 1911 - Feb. 22, 1969. Mabel MacDougall, his wife.

937 James Fullerton MacLeod, Oct. 23, 1892 - Jan. 16, 1978. Stella M. Vickerson, his wife, Dec. 17, 1891 - Jan. 7, 1977.

949 Leith E. MacLeod, 1901-1966.

1023 Currie—William Victor, June 9, 1887 - July 16, 1962. Margaret MacLeod, his wife, May 17, 1887 - April 30, 1959.

1061 Sankey I. MacLeod, Private, D.F.C., Jan. 30, 1957, age 50.

1086 John Archibald MacLeod, May 30, 1890 - May 25, 1950.

1088 Const. Barry W. MacLeod, 26757, Feb. 24, 1947 - May 1, 1975.

1087 Frederick A. MacLeod, Sept. 26, 1917 - Aug. 9, 1966.

1124 William H. MacLeod, Nov. 8, 1884 - May 19, 1945. Amelia J. MacDonald, his wife, 1888 —. Norman L. MacLeod, son, 1918-1958.

1142 Alexander D. MacLeod, died May 30, 1907, aged 65. Elizabeth Susan MacQueen, wife of A. D., Poetess and Authoress, died Jan. 14, 1939, aged 97. Hugh Stanhope MacLeod, son, died April 16, 1932, aged 52.

1152 Harry D. Johnson, M.D., born June 28, 1863, died June 3, 1944. Davina MacLeod, his wife, born June 21, 1863, died Feb. 5, 1950.

1215 Offer—Jessie McLeod, wife of James D. Offer, Oct. 12, 1879 - Aug. 23, 1931. James D. Offer, 1877-1938.

H

1440 McLeod—Katherine McNevin, wife of Angus McLeod, 1856-1908. C. Oliver McLeod, 1879-1911.

1443 Dalziel—John, 1845-1940. His wife Fanny Jane Smith, 1847. Children: Arthur, 1884-1911. Mrs. Fannie MacLeod, 1881-1917, among others.

1491 Walker—George Walker, Aug. 28, 1826, April 2, 1907. His wife Christina MacLeod, died April 28, 1924, aged 74.

1501 Henry Sutherland, died Jan. 10, 1910, aged 72. His wife Margaret McLeod, died May 26, 1917, aged 78. Ethel G. Sutherland, 1879-1964.

1538 Wallace S. MacLeod, Sept. 23, 1899 - April 6, 1959.

1554 Rev. J. M. MacLeod, M.A., July 22, 1860 - Feb. 15, 1939. His wife, Alice M. Matheson, 1878-1940. Infant son, John Malcolm.

1557 William A. MacDonald, 1889-1944. His wife Catherine I. MacLeod, 1893-1929. Son, Gordon, 1921-1955.

1556 Rev. J. W. MacKenzie, 1852-1926. His wife, Flora MacLeod, 1874-1960. Kenneth Gordon, 1914-1916.

1572 George Forbes Dewar, M.D., 1865-1961. His wife, Marion I. MacLeod, 1874-1942. Daughter, Dorothy, 1903-1904. Son, Robert Lloyd, 1907-1946.

1643 James Joseph MacLeod, 1934-1979. Harry Milford, 1935-1960. Irene Laura, 1936-1937.

1698 Malcolm C. MacDonald, died June 22, 1922, aged 59. His wife, Annie McLeod, died June 19, 1919, aged 50.

1808 John MacDonald, 1843-1930. His wife Jessie MacLeod, 1850-1931. Their daughters: Maria, 1888-1952. Jessie, 1878-1958.

1831 Hector MacLeod, died Feb. 7, 1939, aged 82. His wife, Lavenia W. Williams, died April 30, 1935, aged 73.

1859 MacLeod—N. Hudson, 1887-1965. His wife, Maggie Wood, 1891-1942.

1876 VonClure Gay, Feb. 1858 - Feb. 1960, his wife, Rachel M. MacLeod, March 1868 - Jan. 1949. Christina MacLeod, March 1858 - Dec. 1947.

1981 Fletcher MacLeod, 1927-1978.

1987 J. M. Daniel MacLeod, Leading Stoker R.C.N.V.R., 28 Dec. 1974, aged 57.

1959 George H. Douglas, 1882-1963, his wife Matilda MacLeod, 1886—.

2016 Lloyd Allison MacLeod, Nov. 4, 1921 - Oct. 22, 1977.

2017 Neil MacLeod, Nov. 16, 1895 - Oct. 20, 1977. Served with 105th Batt. C.E.F.

1686 Jean MacLeod, died Mar. 26, 1919, aged 17 years. George S. MacLeod, died Nov. 10, 1938, aged 72 years. His wife, Isabel Small, died Nov. 29, 1960, aged 82 years.

1685 John Wallace MacLeod, born in Springvale, P.E.I., Oct. 13, 1877, died in Trinidad, Colo., Feb. 14, 1919. His daughter Evelyn Adele, 1917-1922. Florence E. MacLeod, 1874-1963.

1718 Samuel MacLeod, Private, 25th Batt. C.E.F., March 21, 1959, age 67.

1776 Murdoch A. MacLeod, June 15, 1906 - April 17, 1975. His wife, Alma Maude Brehaut, Jan. 21, 1909 - July 5, 1952.

CHARLOTTETOWN ROMAN CATHOLIC

2157 John P. S. MacLeod, Gunner, R.C.A., Nov. 27, 1959, aged 45.

1329 Andrew J. McLeod, Sergeant, R.C.A.S.C., July 10, 1977, aged 67.

1844 Ethel J. MacLeod, wife of J. Alfred Gallant, Oct. 9, 1919 - March 29, 1943.

2119 Gertrude D. MacLeod, 1908-1966, wife of Ivan Williams.

2057 Albert E. MacNeill, 1885-1967, His wife, Mary E. MacLeod, 1890-1972.

803 Allen Robert MacLeod, Aug. 29, 1942 - May 9, 1947, son of Robert and Winnifred MacLeod.

604 Everett Owen Beagan, 1901-1974. His wife, Margaret Mildred MacLeod, 1903-1942.

894 Martha M. MacKenzie, wife of Daniel W. MacLeod, Aug. 15, 1876 - Dec. 12, 1964.

CHERRY VALLEY, CHRIST CHURCH (ANGLICAN)

9   Shaw MacMillan, Jan. 14, 1882 - Nov. 1951. His wife, Jessie MacLeod, Feb. 13, 1901 - April 6, 1973.

CHERRY VALLEY UNITED (METHODIST)

54   MacLeod—Elsie Verna Gorveatt, 1912-1942, wife of Gordon MacLeod, 1893-1975.

55   MacLeod—Sidney D., 1895-1939. His wife, Harriette J. MacPhee, 1902-1937.

50   Sarah, daughter of D. P. and Ann Irving, Sept. 1868 - May, 1904. David Purdy Irving, 1841-1922. Anne Tweedy Irving, 1849-1917. Margaret Irving McRae, 1871-1923. Elizabeth Irving, wife of D. M. MacLeod, March 1875 - Sept. 1910.

32   John Hayden, 1849-1942. His wife, Elizabeth MacLeod, 1855-1939.

26   MacLeod—Malcolm A., 1879-1965. Ruth, 1906—.

CLYDE RIVER PRESBYTERIAN

125   Two infant sons of Wilfred and Florence MacLeod, Sept. 1920 - Sept. 1921.

37   Donald, 1821-1910 (?). Catherine, his wife, 1831-1898.

CLYDE RIVER RESTORED PIONEER CEMETERY

15   In memory of Ann Henderson, wife of Donald McLeod, died Oct. 1851, aged 31.

CORNWALL UNITED (METHODIST)

95   Catherine MacLeod, wife of D. G. MacKinlay, June 24, 1852 - Jan. 8, 1916. D. G. MacKinlay, 1853-1938. Jessie McKinlay, died Nov. 25, 1880, aged 52.

CRAPAUD, PEOPLE'S CEMETERY

118   George McLeod, son of Rev. C. M. and Lida Young, June 12, 1903 - Nov. 20, 1914.

6   Joseph MacLeod, died Oct. 19, 1952, aged 86. His wife, Minnie Gass, died Sept. 28, 1933, aged 59. Their son, James T. MacLeod, died July 29, 1971, aged 62.

CRAPAUD, ST. JOHN'S ANGLICAN

14   Mary Florence MacLeod, 1917-1970, wife of David Stewart Sherren, 1910-1973. Twin grandchildren, Laurie Ann and Carol Rose, 1971-1971.

138   McVittie, Clara Jane, wife of John MacLeod, 1861-1933.

198   E. Vernon MacLeod, Sept. 15, 1893 - Feb. 5, 1960. His widow, Elsie Howatt Hacker, Sept. 30, 1966.

324   Harry E. Cudmore, Aug. 16, 1891—. His wife, Florrie M. MacLeod, March 20, 1891 - July 10, 1977.

218   Louis Davis MacLeod, Jan. 19, 1888 - June 3, 1972. His wife, Janet Mary Gordon, Oct. 6, 1889 - Dec. 2, 1963. Donald MacLeod, 1908-1970.

CUMBERLAND, ST. MARTIN'S ROMAN CATHOLIC

10   Vanessa Veronica McLeod, 1977.

DUNDAS COMMUNITY CEMETERY, PROTESTANT

21   Allan J. MacLeod, 1854-1930. Alexina MacDonald, his wife, 1872-1922.

23   Garfield MacLeod, June 30, 1894. Ada Hazel Matheson, his beloved wife, April 15, 1901.

53   Seymour Taylor, July 21, 1889. Amanda MacLeod, his wife, July 13, 1893 - Dec. 25, 1970.

81   Malcolm McLeod, 1859-1918. Mary McLeod, his wife, 1857-1932. Peter McLeod,

their son, 1871-1930, also three infant children.

82　Murdoch MacLeod, 1836-1923. Jane Acorn, his wife, 1839-1915. Allan MacLeod, their son, 1869-1931. Cassie Stewart, his wife, 1865-1939.

123　Neil Nicholson, died April 20, 1919, age 66. Mary MacLeod, his wife, died June 25, 1928, age 73. Angus A. Nicholson, died Nov. 3, 1895, age 7 years. William Angus Nicholson, died Dec. 5, 1951, age 55.

128　Normena Lee Stewart, wife of Giddy MacLeod, 1875-1911. John Murdoch, their infant son.

131　John McKay, died Dec. 27, 1922, age 78. Mary McLeod, his wife, May 7, 1911, aged 65. Annie McKay, died March 17, 1876, age 6 years.

Dundas United Church (Presbyterian)

2　Alec C. MacLeod, 1827-1924. His wife Mary MacLean, 1833-1901. John A. MacLeod, 1868-1958. Also his wife, Katherine Martin, 1875-1959.

35　Alexander D. MacDonald, 1860-1925. His wife Christy M. MacLeod, 1882-1971. Their children: Lillian, 1907-1925. Muriel, 1911-1930. Douglas, 1914-1961.

146　Flora MacLeod, wife of Roderick McKenzie, 1845-1897. Dan McKenzie, 1872-1914. His wife, Annie, 1880-1915. Samuel McKenzie, 1886-1918. Roderick McKenzie, 1835-1923.

265　Wallace R. MacKenzie, Oct. 27, 1889 - Nov. 1, 1968. Rose Miller, his wife, April 14, 1892 - May 7, 1960.

41　Catherine, beloved wife of Neil McLeod, died Oct. 23, 1925, aged 73.

43　Margaret, daughter of Peter and Sarah McLeod, died Aug. 2, 1879, aged 34.

44　Peter McLeod, died Jan. 11, 1817, aged 74.

47　Lottie E. Matheson, wife of John A. MacLeod, died July 14, 1909, aged 38. Their son, Warren, died April 2, 1909, age 6 mos.

55　Sarah, wife of William C. MacLeod, born Dec. 9, 1843, died April 2, 1913. William C. MacLeod, born May 30, 1842, died Feb. 22, 1938. Margaret A., born April 19, 1810, died Aug. 16, 1871. Murdoch, born Oct. 4, 1814, died April 16, 1875. Joseph, born Feb. 10, 1819, died March 10, 1879.

57　David, son of Malcolm and Catherine MacLeod, March 25 - May 15, 1915. Norman N. son of Norman and Myrtle MacLeod, Dec. 22, 1941 - Sept. 24, 1942.

69　J. Andrew MacLeod, 1872-1958. His wife, Bessie MacLaren, 1886-1917. His second wife, Christena MacLeod, 1887-1958. His daughter, Mary C. Dupasquier, 1922-1972.

75　Euphemia MacLeod, wife of Murdoch Lamont, died Aug. 17, 1876, aged 55 yrs. Native of Isle of Skye, Scotland, emigrated to P.E.l., 1840.

78　Angus McLeod, Father, 1924-1881. Christy McDonald, Mother, 1830-1904. Erected by their daughter Effie.

79　Peter McLeod, died June 7, 1882, age 64. Native of Isle of Skye, Scotland.

85　Sarah Hayden MacLeod, 1845-1937, wife of Duncan MacLeod, 1840-1936. Their sons, John D., 1871-1872, Robert F., 1876-1880.

88　Florence McLeod, wife of D. P. McLeod, died Dec. 5, 1904, aged 28.

89　Allan McLeod, April 17, 1907, age 60.

90　Sarah MacDonald,1846-1932, wife of Allan MacLeod.

91　William J., son of John M. and Ida M. MacLeod, July 16, 1919 - Dec. 11, 1920.

133　John McLeod, died May 7, 1914, age 75, also his wife Mary Reilly, died March 24, 1925, age 80 yrs.

134　Daniel W. McLeod, died June 21, 1905, age 26.

135　Finlay D. McLeod, May 1, 1870 - April 25, 1896. Finlay J., his son, died in infancy.

145 In memory of Sarah, beloved wife of Donald McLeod. [Stone sunk into ground.]

161 Alexander MacLeod, died July 2, 1906, age 72. His wife, Isabel MacDonald, 1847-1923. Elizabeth Cahill, 1881-1941. Christy Hannah, his daughter, died May 24, 1906, age 29. Margaret Isabella, 1873-l945.

166 Flora McKenzie, wife of John M. McLeod, died Nov. 28, 1889, age 41.

167 John M. MacLeod, died Dec. 1, 1909, age 76.

168 James A. MacLeod, 1879-1948. Sarah J. MacLeod, 1886-1968. Sarah K. MacLeod, 1913-1941.

173 Claudia, 1946. Beverly, 1951. Infant daughters of Waldo and Margie Mac-Leod. Heather, 1950. Norma Jo, 1962. Infant daughters of Roddie and Marge MacKenzie.

175 Stewart Hunter, 1860-1922. His wife, Christina C. McLeod, 1867-1922, their daughter, Almira C., wife of Rev. Alexander Firth, 1891-1957.

176 MacLeod—1894 Myrtle Hunter, 1932—, wife of Herb MacLeod. Ruth, daughter, 1913-1926.

177 John N. MacLeod, 1848-1921. His wife, Susan Owen, 1846-1932.

178 MacLeod—Roderick MacLeod, 1835-1923. His wife, Christy MacKenzie, 1840-1935.

184 MacLeod, P. Alexander, died March 19, 1946, aged 60 yrs. John C. MacLeod, died June 6, 1956, aged 74 yrs. James H. Molyneaux, 1854-1946. His wife, Flora Ann MacLeod, 1855-1933.

190 Myrtle Ruth, May 21, 1953 - June 15, 1953, daughter of Myrtle and Norman S. MacLeod.

191 MacLeod, Malcolm O., 1871-1951. His wife, Catherine Hume, 1875-1972.

193 MacLeod, John M., Aug. 22, 1881 - Aug. 25, 1949.

199 MacLeod, 1889. Herbert G., 1974. His wife, Mary J., 1896.

201 MacLeod, James P., 1884-1943. His wife, Mary I. MacLean, 1895-1971.

202 MacLeod, Weston A., 1921-1935.

210 Duncan MacLeod, 1848-1938. His wife, Elizabeth MacPhee, 1858-1934.

211 MacLeod, Ewen, 1898-1957. His wife, Kathryn Shaw, 1896-1978.

245 Stewart, Erving A., 1909-1935. Charles Stewart, 1867-1955. His wife, Mary Ann MacLeod, 1875-1974.

249 John MacLeod, 1858-1935. His wife, Flora MacNeill, 1846-1934.

251 Mrs. Christy MacLeod, 1846-1929. Malcolm, her son, 1873-1927. Jessie, her daughter, 1871-1937. Isaac, her son, 1892-1946.

252 John A. Ross, 1865-1944. His wife, Annabella MacLeod, 1869-1959.

261 William N. MacLean, March 3, 1861 - Jan. 31, 1949. His wife, Katherine Mac-Leod, March 6, 1870 - Dec. 24, 1962.

267 Donald R., infant son of N. W. and Myrtle MacLeod, June 12, 1931.

268 Norman W. MacLeod, 1882-1964. Myrtle B. Jenkins, 1891-1967.

272 John W. MacLeod, 1868-1933.

273 Sterling William MacLeod, died June 4, 1978, aged 59.

274 James G. MacLeod, 1840-1923. Adam Roby, 1870-1926.

275 Sadie F. MacLeod, Nov. 19, 1884 - July 9, 1955. Edith E. MacLeod, R.N., Feb. 19, 1880 - June 26, 1943. Margaret A. MacLeod, R.N., Aug. 24, 1872 - May 10, 1963. Sgt. James F. MacLeod, 3 B.N. C.R.T. C.E.F., March 10, 1877 - March 13, 1966.

276 Minnie MacLeod, died July 16, 1977, aged 88.

282 Everett J. MacLeod, Sept. 22, 1907 - Aug. 22, 1962. His wife, Sarah Belle MacLeod, May 16, 1921 - Sept. 19, 1972.

283 Robert John MacLeod, June 28, 1953 - June 24, 1974, son of Everett and Sarah MacLeod.

284 Samuel J. MacLeod, 1870-1951. His wife, Annie MacLeod, 1865-1947.
297 Edna May MacLeod, 1879-1957. Ralph W. MacLeod, her son, 1924-1939.
298 John William MacLeod, died Jan. 12, 1977, aged 86.
302 Haddon MacLeod, died May 30, 1970, age 48.

Dunstaffnage Central United

39   Helen M. MacLeod, wife of H. Fenton Court, Sept. 7, 1905 - Oct. 6, 1947.

Flat River Presbyterian

8   Christina McLeod, wife of Malcolm Beaton, Flat River, died June 1, 1885, age 53. Mary McLeod, their mother, died June 26, 1827, age 72. Natives of Caithness, Scotland.
5   Donald McLeod, Jan. 20, 1900, age 61. Jessie Beaton, his wife, died Feb. 27, 1931, age 98.

Fort Augustus, St. Patrick's Roman Catholic

150 Mrs. Gertrude McLeod, nee Kelly, 1894-1971. Her husband, Vincent McLeod, 1887-1929.

Foxley River Anglican

1   MacLeod—Cecil J. MacLeod, Aug. 14, 1924, June 20, 1972—His·wife Blanche Craig, March 14, 1934—.
110 MacLeod, Hessie MacLeod, Aug. 4, 1891, April 4, 1969—His wife Myrtle Adams, Aug. 28, 1900, June 10, 1969.

Fredericton Community

5   W. Franklin Hickox, 1860-1956. Catherine MacLeod, 1874-1951.
65   Archibald Gillis, died March 13, 1888, age 78. Samuel, his son, died Oct. 28, 1877, age 14. Catherine Nicholson, his wife, died April 21, 1894, age 69. Archibald, died Sept. 12, 1903, age 58. Catherine MacLeod, died Aug. 23, 1913, age 68.
9   Alexander MacLeod, died March 17, 1915, age 57. Agnes G. Biggar, his wife, died May 21, 1923, age 69. Millage A. MacLeod, born Aug. 10, 1880, died Apr. 13, 1925.
12   Joy Darlene, Feb. 18, 1955 - Feb. 24, 1955, daughter of Millage and Hazel MacLeod.
22   Margaret P. Biggar, wife of Herbert Buchanan, died May 24, 1920, age 23. Blanche B. MacLeod, also his wife, 1904-1929. Herbert Buchanan, 1896-1968. Murdoch Buchanan, 1853-1931. Mary Nicholson, his wife, 1859-1936.
31   Parmenas Smith, 1852-1924. Millicent B. MacLeod, his wife, 1860-1941. Harry, their son, 1889-1942.
35   Richard Charles Smith, Aug. 8, 1875 - March 29, 1960. Mary Elizabeth MacLeod, his wife, June 16, 1889 - Jan. 2, 1968. Also two infants.
55   Euphemia J. Hill., wife of Robert McLeod, died Feb 1, 1916, age 39.
56   Jacob Ling Sellar, 1884-1925. Bertha M. MacLeod, his wife, 1888-1968 (also later wife of Carl Jewell).

FREELAND PRESBYTERIAN

55 Annie MacLeod, 1880-1942.
83 In memory of Catherine McLeod, wife of Robert Morrison, died Sept. 11, 1900, aged 64. Lord I come to Thee for rest. Morrison, Robert, died Jan. 28, 1915, aged 84.

FRENCH RIVER, YANKEE HILL CEMETERY

12 John MacLeod, native of Durniss, Southshire, Scotland, who departed this life June 21, 1836, aged 75.
13 In memory of Hugh McLeod, French River, died March 18, 1866, aged 71.
14 Kenneth McLeod, died July 15, 1844, aged 82. Also Ann Morrison, his wife, died June 29, 1841, aged 61, who emigrated to America 1805 from Parish of Durniss, Scotland.
15 In memory of Nancy, wife of Hugh McLeod, died May 15, 1869, aged 76.
16 Hugh McLeod, died July 25, 1845, aged 74.

GEORGETOWN UNITED

1 Effie C. MacLeod, 1859-1897.
169 Marjorie A. C. MacLeod, wife of John Hilchey, 1863-1925.
182 William A. MacLeod, Private 78 Batt. C.E.F., Feb. 1, 1964, aged 79.
183 William A. MacLeod, 1885-1963. His wife, Beatrice Florence, 1904-1976.
205 Daniel Skinner, 1815-1957. His wife, Katie MacLeod, 1871-1950. Son, J. Albert (Bert) Skinner, 1902-1972, daughter Elizabeth Skinner, 1898—.
231 Warren B. Hemphill, Jan. 9, 1900 - Aug. 19, 1968. His wife, Edna M. MacLeod, May 6, 1902 - Feb. 10, 1960.

HAMPSHIRE UNITED CEMETERY

34 John Watts, Jan. 14, 1846 - Dec. 31, 1940. His wife, Jeanette MacLeod, March 17, 1852 - Nov. 18, 1942. John Watts, May 26, 1885 - May 8, 1961.
39 Thomas Locke, 1844-1927. His wife, Margaret MacLeod, 1841-1919. Daughters: Frances, 1881-1920. Mary, 1884-1923. Interred at Halifax. John McLeod Locke, buried in B.C., 1872-1949. Richard W. Locke, 1868-1950.

HARTSVILLE CEMETERY

1 MacKenzie, Donald, 1844-1909. His wife Mary MacLeod, 1855-1925. Their children: John, 1872-1902. Christie A., 1882-1901. George, 1890-1907. Alexander, 1886-1910. Also two infant sons.
7 Allan McLeod, died Feb. 22, 1871, aged 78. Erected by son Duncan McLeod.
8 John McLeod, died May 8, 1850, aged 17. Euphemia McLeod, died Aug. 8, 1852, aged 26. Both children of M. and G. McLeod
12 James McLeod, died Dec. 18, 1872, aged 30 yrs.
13 Mary, daughter of Donald and Flora MacLeod, died Mar. 10, 1887, aged 43. Erected by her daughter Florence M. McLean.
16 In memory of Effie, wife of John K. McLeod, died Jan. 22, 1890, aged 43. Also their daughter.
18 MacLeod, John, 1837-1917. His wife Flora Stuart, 1838-1902. Their daughter

Mary C. MacLeod, 1876-1946.

21   Katherine McLeod, wife of Angus Gillis, 1846-1876. Angus Gillis, 1839-1935. Infant Daughter Christine, 1874-1874. John Gillis, 1872-1928.

22   In memory of Sarah McLeod, born Sept. 28, 1893, died Feb. 19, 1896.

23   Sarah Gillis, died May 25, 1894, aged 75, wife of John McLeod, died Jan 25, 1893, aged 81. A native of Rona, Scotland.

25   In memory of Jeanette, daughter of Hugh and Christina I. McLeod, died Nov. 30, 1917, aged 25.

26   In memory of Malcolm McLeod, died Nov. 25, 1882, aged 26 yrs., 8 mos.

27   In memory of John McLeod, died June 4, 1878, aged 24.

28   MacLeod, Hugh, 1847-1928. Native of Raasay, Scotland, and his wife Christine Isabel McDonald, 1859-1936.

29   In memory of Mary, beloved wife of Hugh McLeod, died May 19, 1878, aged 29 yrs.

38   In memory of Mary McLeod, wife of Neil McDonald, died April 29, 1847, aged 32. Christy McDonald, died Nov. 10, 1877, aged 34, daughter of Neil and Mary McDonald.

47   Roderick McLeod, born Mar. 8, 1825, died July 31, 1865, also his wife, Jane Nicholson, died May 24, 1900, aged 60. John, son of R. McLeod, born July 1, 1854, died Dec. 23, 1879. Roderick, son of R. McLeod, born Jan. 23, 1866, died Aug. 13, 1893.

49   Sarah McLeod, wife of [?] Nicholson, died Apr. 23, 1887, aged 67.

51   MacLeod—Murdoch Alexander MacLeod, Aug. 24, 1894 - Dec. 4, 1976.

53   MacLeod—1887 Neil Dan McLeod, 1972. His wife 1897 Eliza Almanda Ross.

56   MacLeod, John Duncan, 1894-1965. Veteran of two wars.

57   MacLeod, Sadie McKay, April 20, 1894 - July 27, 1967, wife of Everett G. MacLeod. Catherine (Cassie) MacLeod, R.N., Feb. 12, 1886 - Dec. 6, 1972.

60   MacLeod, Malcolm Lloyd. His wife Florence Jean Ward.

62   John J. MacLeod, 1844-1925. His wife Catherine, 1844-1924.

65   James McLeod, died Nov. 30, 1872, aged 58. Also his wife Flora, died June 8, 1891, aged 73. Their son Donald, died Oct. 30, 1886, aged 35.

70   Christy Ann McKenzie, wife of John D. McLeod, died Sept. 12, 1897, aged 37. John D. McLeod, died Aug. 27, 1922, aged 75. Their sons: John S., died Jan. 18, 1892, aged 2 yrs. Calvin, died Aug. 25, 1894, aged 6 mos.

73   Christy, beloved wife of Donald McLeod, died Feb. 25, 1876, aged 59.

74   Jane McLeod, wife of John Arthur, died Oct. 18, 1877, aged 27. Catherine, daughter of Donald and Christy McLeod, died Nov. 2, 1884, aged 38. John E. McLeod, died March 5, 1899, also Mary Ann Nicholson, wife of John E., died June 8, 1936, aged 69. Adline Arthur, aged 3 mos.

77   Christine MacLeod, wife of W. W. Wixen, died Oct. 1, 1924, aged 62. Their son, W. Wixen, died Dec. 26, 1958, aged 66.

78   MacLeod, 1858 John J. MacLeod, 1937. Also his wife 1861 Flora MacKay, 1948. Children: 1893 Cassie, 1909. Infant daughter.

82   MacLeod, 1908 Daniel S. MacLeod, 1972.

83   Flora McInnis, wife of John B. McLeod, died July 4, 1886, aged 58. Their daughter, Sarah, died April 6, 1891, aged 22.

84   John McLeod, died Dec. 26, 1902, aged 92. His wife Flora McLean, died May 23, 1873, aged 53. Natives of Inverary, Scotland. Their daughter Christie, died June 9, 1908, aged 62.

88   Mary Ann McLeod, wife of Kenneth McInnis, died Mar. 31, 1896, aged 43. Kenneth McInnis died Jan. 24, 1924, aged 90.

92 John MacLeod, born April 10, 1842, died Feb. 1, 1919. Effie MacLeod, born Jan. 19, 1844, died Dec. 2, 1926. Infant son Neil, 1878-1879.

93 McLeod, Maggie C., daughter of Malcolm and Jane McLeod, died Nov. 13, 1888, aged 3 yrs.

94 Malcolm McLeod, died May 3, 1876, aged 64. His wife Mary, died Sept. 22, 1875, aged 56.

95 Duncan Matheson, died July 23, 1908, aged 70. His wife Mary MacLeod, died Mar. 13, 1921. Daughters: Margaret A., died March 22, 1892, aged 20. Susie, died April 3, 1892, aged 18. Euphemia, died July 2, 1898, aged 17.

96 Catherine Matheson, wife of Neil MacLeod, died Aug. 11, 1903, aged 54.

97 Donald MacLeod, son of Roderick and Isabella, died at Victor, Col., Sept. 17, 1896, aged 25. Mary MacLeod, died Oct. 14, 1903, aged 23. Jessie Ann, died May 11, 1905, aged 21. Roderick MacLeod, died May 10, 1910, aged 69. His wife Isabella Nicholson, died Dec. 4, 1934, aged 89.

98 Allan MacLeod, born Aug. 9, 1872, drowned May 4, 1911.

99 John J. McLeod, killed at Montana, Feb. 17, 1895, aged 24, also Flora C., died Dec. 22, 1886, aged 3—Children of Duncan and Mary McLeod. Duncan McLeod, died Mar. 7, 1910, aged 66. His wife, Mary MacSwain, died Mar. 18, 1930, aged 89.

100 John C. MacLeod, died Jan. 23, 1900, aged 77. His wife, Flora, died May 27, 1911, aged 81.

105 Malcolm McLeod, died May 10, 1875, aged 67. Native of Inverness Shire, Scotland, and emigrated in 1840.

111 Malcolm McLeod, died March 1, 1890, aged 30. Erected by his brother Alexander.

112 Sarah McLeod, wife of John McLean, died Mar. 14, 1885, aged 28.

113 Effie MacLeod, wife of Donald L. MacLeod, 1858-1923. John R. MacLeod, 1843-1929. Angus R. MacLeod, 1854-1935.

114 Roderick McLeod, died Feb. 19, 1861, aged 44. His wife, Catherine, died Dec. 16, 1890, aged 71. Ann MacLeod, wife of Daniel MacDonald, died 1914, aged 67.

115 Donald James MacLeod, 44th Can. Inf., born Sept. 14, 1890. Killed in action, Cambrai, France, Sept. 28, 1918.

116 Donald R. MacLeod, died Sept. 28, 1914, aged 69. His wife Margaret Morrison, died Nov. 2, 1922, aged 76.

119 Norman E. McLeod, died Aug. 6, 1875, aged 21.

120 Alexander McLeod, died Mar. 6, 1872, aged 31 years. His wife Mary Matheson, died Mar. 30, 1873, aged 34 years.

121 Allan McLeod, died Nov. 24, 1888, aged 63. His wife Effie McLeod, died May 31, 1906, aged 72.

122 Flora MacKenzie, wife of Alexander McLeod, died March 7, 1885, aged 66. Alexander McLeod, died Nov. 2, 1905, aged 89. Catherine McLeod, died June 25, 1902, aged 71.

126 Norman McLeod, 1841-1914. His wife Janette Nicholson, 1851-1908.

130 Norman McLeod, died July 16, 1888, aged 44. His wife, Mary McKay, 1839-1925.

134 Donald McDonald, died June 11, 1832, aged 63. Native of Skye, Scotland. His wife, Catherine McLeod, died Jan. 9, 1895, aged 60. Native of Raasay, Scotland.

137 Margaret MacLeod, wife of J. J. Bethune, died Nov. 17, 1902, aged 36. Allan F., 1892-1904. Edward C., 1897-1905. Alex D., died Aug. 1, 1912, aged 22. Mary Louise, died Nov. 8, 1912, aged 14. J. J. Bethune, died July 4, 1926, aged 65. Lottie Gairet, wife of J. J., died Aug. 5, 1904, aged 21.

138 Allan Bethune, died Oct. 27, 1891, aged 71. His wife Catherine McLeod, died June 11, 1914, aged 83.

143 Malcolm McLeod, died April 4, 1888, aged 22.

144 Alexander MacLeod, 1819-1904. His wife Sarah Betsy MacKenzie, 1831-1911. Children: Sarah, wife of John Hill, 1858-1884. Malcolm, 1866-1888. Murdoch, 1863-1902. Mrs. Murdoch MacL., 1859-1937. Christy MacLeod, 1890-1963.

145 Murdoch MacLeod, 1854-1941. His wife, Euphemia MacInnis, 1859-1915. Their children: Catherine E., 1835-1889. John, 1889-1912. William, 1895-1920.

146 Alexander McLeod, died March 8, 1902, aged 82. His wife, Anne, died March 19, 1900, aged 72. Daughter, Christina, died May 15, 1949, aged 86.

159 Archibald McQueen, died Jan. 29, 1909, aged 76. His wife, Isabelle McLeod, died Aug. 2, 1917. John, died Feb. 13, 1900, aged 34. Annie, wife of Ora Kaye, died Apr. 19, 1901, aged 27. Jennie, died April 15, 1910, aged 38. Donald, died April 24, 1941, aged 74.

167 Malcolm Campbell, died May 11, 1870, aged 52. His wife, Jessie McLeod, died Nov. 27, 1880, aged 51. Daughter, Jessie Ann, died May 10, 1876, aged 11.

168 Margaret, daughter of the late Malcolm and Jessie Campbell, died May 13, 1903, aged 38.

170 Laughlin McLeod, died Nov. 19, 1889, aged 79. His wife, Ann, died Jan. 17, 1891, aged 74.

172 Norman McKenzie, born 1833, died April 21, 1905, aged 72. His wife Flora McLeod, died Aug. 24, 1913, aged 72.

173 Malcolm McKenzie, died March 31, 1918, aged 75. His wife Isabel McLeod, died Jan. 29, 1927, aged 79.

177 John MacKenzie, 1792-1881. His wife Catherine MacLeod, 1800-1873. Born in Scotland, came to Hartsville in 1838.

195 John K. MacLeod, 1837-1921. His wife Effie MacKenzie, 1847-1890. Also his wife, Mary Ann MacLennan, 1852-1936. H. Chalmers MacLeod, 1894-1979. His wife, Amy Frizzell, 1907-1973. Their daughter, Mary Ida, May 24, 1937 - May 24, 1937.

196 Duncan MacLeod, 1841-1922. His wife, Jessie MacLean, 1942. Their daughter, Margaret, 1888-1909. Their son, Lt. Col. Allan, 1881-1965. His wife, Flora MacLeod, 1887-1945.

197 2368539 Private John MacLeod, C.F.C.C.E.F., 15 Oct., 1925.

204 Neil R. MacLeod, 1878-1950. His wife Katherine M. Nicholson, 1884-1964.

205 Neil MacLeod, died Jan. 9, 1911, aged 73. Flora A., died Oct. 20, 1938, aged 90. Sons: James D., died March 10, 1923, aged 42. Neil J., died Sept. 8, 1944, aged 67. Ella M. McDonald, wife of Kenneth MacLeod, 1885-1931.

211 Alexander J. MacLeod, died Nov. 22, 1904, aged 56. His wife, Annie MacLean, 1858-1926. Minnie, died Oct. 14, 1918, aged 24. Harriet, died Aug. 6, 1917, aged 19.

213 Alexander B. MacLeod, 1867-1933. His wife Flora Ann Graham, 1882-1953.

214 Pte. Earl MacLeod, 1907-1970. Cape Breton Highlanders.

215 Sgt. Murdoch A. MacLeod, Aug. 8, 1904-Sept. 1, 1957.

216 MacLeod, Kenneth, 1861-1944. His wife, Flora MacNeill, 1861-1954. Christena, 1889-1907. A. Gordon, 1887-1907. Florrie, 1898-1912. Daniel A., 1902-1976. Kenneth, 1900—.

218 Alexander MacLeod, 1861-1925. His wife, Margaret MacDonald, 1866-1956.

224 MacLellan, Alexander J., died Oct. 3, 1948, aged 81. Catherine Jane MacLeod, died April 12, 1960, aged 82.

Hunter River Presbyterian Cemetery

3 George S. MacLeod, 1853-1934. His wife Jane McCoubrey, 1850-1934. Elizabeth A. Maud, daughter of George S. and Mary J. McLeod, died Nov. 27, 1890, aged 2 yrs. Phebe Beatrice died March 12, 1899, aged 16.

5 John McLeod, died April 2, 189[?], aged 75.

24 Lt. Col. T. S. MacLeod, died Jan. 22, 1902, aged 52. His wife, Martha Stevenson, died Nov. 12, 1938, aged 90.

25 Ewen S. McLeod, 1852-1932. His wife, Margaret J. Buchanan, 1862-1938.

26 Ida Louisa, daughter of Ewen and Margaret McLeod, died Sept. 26, 1896, aged 8 mos., 5 days.

48 George D. MacLeod, born Jan. 2, 1848, died March 5, 1919. His wife, Isabelle Cummings, born Oct. 3, 1855, died Jan. 11, 1947. Lieut. Elmer G. MacLeod, R.F.G., killed flying in Flanders, Nov. 23, 1917, aged 24.

63 Daniel L. MacLeod, 1886-1931. His wife, Georgie Lawson, 1889-1934.

87 George H. MacMillan, 1872-1946. Cassie MacLeod, wife of George H., 1879-1944.

106 John S. MacLeod, 1897-1952. His wife Bessie M. Barrett, 1899-1965.

132 Hickox—Daniel Hickox, May 9, 1892 - June 24, 1963. His wife, Annie Lillian MacLeod, May 12, 1900 - Feb. 6, 1975.

Kensington People's Cemetery

21 Margaret MacLeod, 1843-1913, wife of Hugh MacLeod. Their daughter, Mary Edith, wife of C. W. Bernard, 1879-1939.

23 MacLeod, Hugh Benjamin, 1877-1971, his wife, Bertha Millman Brander, 1894-1972.

222 W. C. MacLeod, 1879-1945. His wife, Amelia M. Profett, 1876-1968.

Kelly's Cross, St. Joseph's Roman Catholic

36 Harry A. MacLeod, Oct. 16, 1896 - Feb. 16, 1969. His wife, Laura Jane McCaughey, Oct. 28, 1894 - March 12, 1978.

Kingsboro United Baptist

221 In memory of Margory, wife of James C. MacLeod, died April 1, 1892, age 62. Melvina, their daughter, died April 19, 1871, age 2 yrs.

Little Sands

104 John Angus Blue, March 24, 1873 - March 7, 1951. Sarah MacLeod, his wife, Sept. 9, 1879 - July 5, 1957. Tina Marion, their daughter, March 21, 1919 - Nov. 18, 1919.

224 Donald Stewart, died May 5, 1888, age 53. Catherine MacLeod, his wife, died Jan. 11, 1915, age 76.

203 John J. MacLeod, died at Rona, Jan. 11, 1879, age 27.

212 Alexander McLeod, died Sept. 16, 1906, age 63. Flora McLeod, died Jan. 16, 1922, age 80.

240 James McLeod, born in Scotland in 1842, died at High Bank, April 17, 1907. Christina McDonald, his wife, born in Scotland 1838, died at Charlottetown, March 29, 1928.

225   Donald A. MacLeod, 1862-1928. Catherine Stewart, his wife, 1864-1948.

83   Donald MacLeod, 1833-1911. Janet MacLean, his wife, 1839-1912. Isabella, their daughter, 1869-1918. Sarah J. Bell, 1878-1904, wife of Norman MacLeod, 1830—. Alexander MacLeod, 1910—.

81   Alex J. McLeod, died on military duty May 22, 1916, age 40. John J. MacLeod, died April 24, 1914, age 40.

80   Rachel, wife of John McLeod, died March 7, 1885, age 51. Allen, died July 10, 1859, age 71 (?). Donald, died Dec. 28, 1859, age 21, their children. John Dan, died June 11, 1893, age 1 year, son of John and Jessie McLeod.

100   Barbara MacLeod, 1878-1952.

99   Donald A. MacLeod, 1877-1966. Rachel Matheson, his wife, 1881-1974.

73   Roderick MacLeod died Nov. 18, 1918, age 80. Flora MacLeod, his wife, born in Isle of Skye 1822, died March 15, 1908. Jessie, wife of John McKay, died Nov. 28, 1897, age 41. 4 infant children of John and Christina McPherson. John McPherson, 1870-1943, lived in Ashland, Oregon. Christina MacLeod, his wife, 1866-1948.

98   Catherine Morrow, wife of Daniel H. MacLeod, died April 2, 1941, age 30.

93   Sarah Gillis, wife of Arch MacLeod, died April 1, 1899, age 53. Malcolm, her son, died Feb. 16, 1908, age 27.

89   Harry T. MacLeod, March 31, 1913 - Dec. 11, 1968. Mary E. Ross, his wife, May 17, 1917—. Marion Mae, Sept. 20, 1934 - Oct. 31, 1935.

118   Finlay MacLean, 1849-1935. Mary E. MacLeod, his wife, 1874-1963.

71   Daniel D. Livingstone, died March 27, 1955, age 77. Rachel A. MacLeod, his wife, died July 13, 1966, age 75. Cpl. Clarence Livingstone, North Nova Scotia Highlanders, born 1919, died in France, Aug. 9, 1944.

65   Malcolm MacLeod, Sept. 2, 1923 - July 13, 1946, drowned at Port Credit, Ontario. Malcolm N. MacLeod, Nov. 6, 1887 - Oct. 2, 1957. Elizabeth MacPherson, his wife, June 21, 1888 - May 8, 1954.

94   Christina Ann, daughter of Torquil and Christy MacLeod, died Nov. 2, 1909, age 17. John MacLeod, died July 28, 1956, age 72. Effie Ann MacLean, wife of John MacLeod, died May 4, 1942, age 49. John MacLeod, died May 4, 1942, age 49. Torquil MacLeod, died Dec. 10, 1914, age 58. Christy MacLean, his wife, died July 2, 1936, age 80.

72   John G. MacKay, 1849-1929. Annie MacLean, his wife, 1847-1890. Jessie A. MacLeod, his wife, 1854-1897. Roderick MacKay, April 7, 1868 - May 16, 1942. Christie MacLeod, his wife, April 8, 1872 - Dec. 27, 1952. Stewart MacKay, 1915-1976.

53   Alex J. McDonald, born Dec. 29, 1864. Wilhemina McLeod, his wife, born Dec. 30, 1864, died Nov. 15, 1931.

42   John J. Stewart, 1873-1951. Mary A. MacLeod, his wife, 1877-1941. J. Bruce Stewart, 1910-1968.

28   James A. MacLeod, April 10, 1883 - May 16, 1962. Christy Ann MacDonald, his wife, July 26, 1884 - May 1, 1961.

43   Donald Livingstone, died May 12, 1917, age 63. In memory of Mary Munn, died July 12, 1899, age 34. Mary A. MacLeod, wife of Donald Livingstone, died Jan. 7, 1948, age 80.

27   Franklin B. MacLeod, 1947—. Claudia J., his wife, 1948—. Matthew C., their son, July 1975 - Oct. 1975.

21   Minnie MacLeod, Aug. 19, 1895 - Dec. 9, 1972.

22   Clifford Newman, 1911-1971. Katie Bell MacLeod, his wife, 1910-1978, also wife of Herman Martin.

4   Norman MacLeod, April 16, 1867 - Aug. 7, 1964. Alexina MacSwain, his wife, Aug. 10, 1870 - June 9, 1954.

Long Creek, United Baptist

59   Evelyn MacLeod, Nov. 13, 1908 - Apr. 3, 1962, wife of Frederick Bertram.

60   Lorne Murchison, Feb. 9, 1931 - July 10, 1962, son of Mary and George MacLeod.

46   Leonard A. MacNevin, May 29, 1917—. Myrtle R. MacLeod, Dec. 5, 1914—. Angus Kent, dearly loved twin son, March 9, 1955 - Oct. 22, 1977.

23   Hector MacLeod, 1880-1953. Mary Jane MacFadyen, his wife, 1888-1921. Their children: Pearle Jane, 1921-1922. Spr. G. Garfield, 1910-1944, killed in action Nov. 23, 1944.

42   George MacLeod, died Feb. 26, 1912, age 72. Annie Henderson, his wife, died Jan. 27, 1929, age 87. Ida Maud MacLeod,died Aug. 1, 1917, age 28.

53   John MacLeod, 1876-1959. Priscilla MacNeill, his wife, 1879-1950.

Lorne Valley

64   Neil McLeod, 1814-1908. His wife, Christina, died Aug. 1869, age 38. Their children: Christina, died 1864, aged 5. Infant son. Peter McLeod, 1858-1906. Alex McLeod, 1857-1925, also his wife, Christy, 1823-1921.

117   Catherine MacLeod, 1860-1940.

116   Florence MacLeod, 1889-1938.

112   Archibald D. MacLeod, May 11, 1896 - July 21, 1966.

111   Murdoch Aben MacDonald, 1881-1961. His wife, B. Mabel MacLeod, 1886-1963.

113   Hilda MacLeod, beloved wife of Arthur Myers, 1905-1943.

118   Father—In memory of Angus McLeod, died July 16, 1909, age 82. Mother—his wife, Annie McDonald, died July 11, 1915, aged 89. Son, William, died April 1, 1916.

73   Angus MacSwain, died Nov. 20, 1903, age 64. His wife, Jessie MacLeod, died Jan. 20, 1930, age 90. John MacLeod, died Oct. 20, 1905, age 81.

33   Neil P. Nicholson, 1875-1952. His wife Jane Gordon MacLeod, 1886-1923. Their children: Christena M., 1906-1929. Peter E., 1907-1943, Killed in W.W.II. Neil Frederick, 1916-1918. John James, 1920-1922. Gerald, 1923, age 3 weeks.

36   Alexander Martin, 1843-1924. His wife, Margaret MacLeod, 1842-1935.

37   Alex A. MacLeod, died Aug. 12, 1917, age 67. His wife, Rachel Martin, died Sept. 21, 1939, age 62.

38   Peter MacLeod, died May 18, 1917, aged 72. His wife, Sophia Conrad, died Oct. 23, 1928, age 84. N. W. Wesley C., died Sept. 23, 1918, age 46.

23   Alexander MacLeod, Feb. 21, 1895 - March 7, 1941.

93   Mary Martin, wife of John S. MacLeod, 1857-1905. Son, S. Victor, 1896-1930.

68   Daniel A. MacLeod, died Nov. 28, 1907, age 45. His wife, Catherine MacLeod, died Oct. 8, 1938, age 81.

69   Alexander MacLeod, born in Isle of Skye, Scotland, 1819, died 1897. His wife, Mary, born in Inverness Shire, Scotland, 1838, died 1904. John MacLeod, born 1867, died 1897. G. MacLeod, born 1878, died 1880.

71   McInnis—Alexander, June 1864 - Feb. 19, 1944. His wife, Annie M. MacLeod, Aug. 1868 - Feb. 19, 1935.

83   Shirley, daughter of Gordon and Jessie MacLeod, June 29, 1932 - Aug. 4, 1934.

2   Daniel McIntyre, July 9, 1868 - July 29, 1959. His wife, Annabelle MacLeod, March 15, 1885 - Dec. 17, 1968.

18 James Mustard MacLeod, Aug. 16, 1888 - July 14, 1955. His wife, Ethel Florence Cobb, June 9, 1889 - Aug. 7, 1962.

22 Alexander C. MacDonald, 1863-1942. His wife, Margaret MacLeod, 1869-1939.

17 Malcolm MacLeod, Feb. 7, 1880 - Dec. 2. 1963. His wife, Annie Palmer, born in Devonshire, Eng., Jan. 22, 1891 - June 9, 1975.

LOWER MONTAGUE, UNITED (METHODIST)

205 Harvey Ross, 1912—. Leah C. MacLeod, his wife, 1914—. Leona Rubina, their daughter, born and died May 19, 1942.

150 Angus McQueen, died April 12, 1900, age 60. Flora MacLeod, his wife, died July 1, 1927, age 75. An infant child.

354 J. Henry MacLean, born June 24, 1865, died Nov. 25, 1939. Flora Ann MacLeod, his wife, born July 17, 1863, died April 5, 1951. Helen Lewis Lowery, their daughter, born July 12, 1896, died May 18, 1939. Elsie May Trainor, their daughter, Aug. 6, 1893 - Aug. 6, 1971.

106 Sarah, wife of William White, died Sept. 23, 1894, age 72. Edgar C. White, died July 4, 1954, age 90. M. E. McLeod, wife of E. C. White, Dec. 27, 1948, age 77. Clarinda J. White, died Feb. 21, 1922, age 73. William White, died Nov. 11, 1904, age 90.

352 Archie MacLeod, 1876-1926. Erected by his uncle Capt. James MacLeod. Capt. James MacLeod, 1851-1943. Buried in Vancouver, B.C. Murdoch A. MacLeod, 1867-1951. Ethel MacFarlane, his wife, 1886-1960.

201 Norman J. MacDonald, died May 11, 1916, age 70. Annie MacLeod, his wife, died April 12, 1928, age 84.

199 Stewart D. McKenna, 1921—. Frances Rubina MacLeod, his wife, 1916-1967.

322 Angus MacKenzie (Sgt.), died in General Hospital, Vancouver, B.C., 1885-1920. Charles MacKenzie, 1845-1920. Catherine MacLeod, his wife, 1859-1933.

369 Daniel Fraser, Jan. 6, 1855 - Nov. 25, 1921. Mary MacLeod, his wife, Oct. 31, 1857 - Jan. 23, 1937.

323 Angus McLeod, and his wife Mary, died March 7, 1911, age 84.

294 Sarah Stead MacLeod, April 4, 1891 - Nov. 3, 1964, wife of Lemuel Robertson.

MARGATE UNITED

97 Barbara MacLeod, wife of John Parsons, died Aug. 1, 1881, aged 29 years, also 2 infant children, Anna and Joseph.

64 Hannah M. MacLeod, wife of Lewis J. Taylor, 1877-1909.

MARIE COMMUNITY

4 Gordon G. S. Sanderson, 1898-1978. His wife, Margaret F. MacLeod, 1903-1974.

MARSHFIELD, ST. COLUMBA PRESBYTERIAN

141 Sophia E. Godfrey, wife of George J. MacLeod, died Dec. 11, 1903, aged 52.

137 Hector MacLeod, died June 6, 1905, aged 67. His wife, Melinda Douglas, died May 19, 1921, aged 74.

140 George A. McLeod, died Aug. 5, 1905, aged 60.

142 Bovyer—Nelson R., M.D.C.M., Oct. 1869 - Feb. 1961. His wife, Mary Emily MacLeod, Oct. 1875 - Mar. 1951.

145 Mary J. MacLeod, wife of Hector A. Darrach, died Oct. 27, 1897, aged 24.

146 Donald McLeod, died Jan. 3, 1894, aged 53. His wife, Flora MacDougall, died June 17, 1874, aged 32. Florence A. MacLeod, 1890-1978, daughter of Donald McLeod and his wife Effie MacDonald.

147 John S. MacLeod, died Jan. 29, 1889, age 75. His wife, Mary, died Sept. 13, 1869, age 56. Their son, John, died April 19, 1877, age 37.

7 John Scott Cairns, July 2, 1873 - Jan. 9, 1959. His wife, Lillian Ann MacLeod, June 16, 1880 - June 12, 1973.

10 Jane, wife of Donald McLeod, died Dec. 25, 1977, age 46.

38 William Connolly, 1845-1928. His wife, Catherine MacLeod, 1857-1947. Beatrice, 1882-1911. Percy, 1892-1913. Mattie, 1879-1922.

50 Kenneth McLeod, died July 25, 1888, age 65.

94 Hannah MacLeod, wife of Peter McNair Robertson, died June 8, 1917, age 65. Peter McNair Robertson, 1851-1931. Their children: Robert Fergus, died Jan. 6, 1858, age 2. Isabella, died Jan. 24, 1858, age 24. James, died Oct. 30, 1893, age 55.

97 Alexander M. MacLeod, 1853-1921. His wife, Katherine Rodd, 1868-1965. John Eric MacLeod, Nov. 21, 1908 - Jan. 17, 1961.

100 William McLeod, died April 27, 1904, age 87. His wife Christina McBeath, died March 22, 1902, age 75.

103 Alberta Bessie, daughter of Henry and Sarah A. McLeod, died April 13, 1884, age 5 yrs. 4 mos.

104 Wallace S. McLeod, died Nov. 2, 1878, age 1 yr.

98 Edward J. Landry, Feb. 3, 1900 - Sept. 15, 1966. His wife Margaret E. MacLeod, March 16, 1911 - Dec. 23, 1968.

102 Herbert S. MacLeod, died Sept. 10, 1892, age 23. Sarah Anne Stewart, wife of Henry Meyseth McLeod, born May 12, 1836, died Jan. 20, 1910. Henry Meyseth MacLeod, died Jan. 29, 1899, age 62. Henry S. MacLeod, R.A. McGill, 1898, died Jan. 22, 1902, age 26. Rev. Ambrose McLeod, M.A., died at Cambridge, Mass., June 17, 1893, aged 29.

105 James Wyatt, born Aug. 1832, died April 13, 1908. His wife, Matilda G. MacLeod, born 1845, died Mar. 9, 1890. Matilda, J. Ambrose/James Bismark and Mary, children of Jas. and Matilda Wyatt.

57-1 Mary McLeod, wife of William Bishop, born March 18, 1835, died May 13, 1896.

MEADOWBANK, HYDE AND CROSBY PIONEER CEMETERY

19 A. Clark Crosby, 1892-1960. Ruth MacLeod, his wife—.

21 W. Roy Crosby, Aug. 4, 1907—. Margaret E. MacLeod, his beloved wife, May 22, 1911—.

MERMAID, CALVIN PRESBYTERIAN

104 George MacLeod, died Jan. 3, 1894, age 53. His wife, Jessie MacDonald, died Feb. 20, 1930, age 75. James M. McLeod, died Dec. 19, 1907, age 75. James M. McLeod, died Dec. 19, 1907, age 24.

113 James MacLeod, died March 5, 1884, age 75.

118 Daniel McLeod, died Nov. 11, 1875, age 76.

95 Donald MacDonald, died March 26, 1912, age 84. His wife, Jane McLeod, died Oct. 12, 1882, age 51.

57 Donald MacLeod, 1759-1835. His wife, Catherine MacLean, 1757-1853.

58 Capt. John MacLeod, died Oct. 16, 1901, age 70.

49   William MacLeod, 1779-1873. His wife, Jessie, 1799-1883 (F. Gorges). Effie, wife of James MacLeod, 1836-1880. James MacLeod, 1844-1932. His wife, Emily Roberts, 1860-1938. Mary Millicent born July 19, 1874, died August 27, 1875.

44   Walter C. Munn, April 29, 1877 - July 21, 1964. His wife, Annie S. MacLeod, Oct. 29, 1877 - Feb. 26, 1971.

50   Robert McLeod, died Feb. 19, 1893, age 64. His wife, Mary MacEachern, died Dec. 16, 1903, age 73. Ewen McLeod, died May 13, 1892, age 33.

10   William Smallwood MacEachern, 1876-1959. His wife, Millicent MacLeod. Their son, Earl, 1932-1944.

Midgell Cemetery

5   Leigh Cobb, Sept. 2, 1892 - Oct. 23, 1975. His wife, Minnie E. MacLeod, Jan. 9, 1892 - July 17, 1967.

29   Thomas Gordon, Jr., June 30, 1959 - May 31, 1974, son of Thomas and Eleanor.

126 Daniel P. MacLeod, 1875-1947. Minnie J., 1868-1948.

180 Mary J. MacLeod, Oct. 30, 1897 - June 6, 1953, wife of Roy MacLaine, Nov. 22, 1893 - Aug. 14, 1972.

337 Russell MacLaren, 1892-1975. His wife Etta MacLeod, 1892— .

Milton Anglican

251 C. Amos Rodd, Jan. 18, 1875 - May 8, 1937. Catherine Ann MacLeod, his wife, 1888-1966.

Montague Community Cemetery

13   Jean Marguerite MacLeod, wife of W. H. Poole, 1905-1927. Major William Herbert Poole, O.B.E., 1894-1959.

239 Lt. Col. Edwin Booth Cox, A.V.S., Jan. 20, 1910— . Creta MacLeod, R.N., his beloved wife, July 9, 1911 - July 2, 1974.

231 William Byron Sharpe, Nov. 6, 1910 - June 29, 1971. His wife, Louisa Ann MacLeod, May 15, 1916— .

242 Ethan H. Stewart, Dec. 11, 1901 - Oct. 31, 1974. His wife, Florrie J. MacLeod, June 12, 1905 - July, 1985.

186 Allan MacLeod, Feb. 3, 1876 - March 11, 1956.

205 John M. MacLeod, 1903-1952, Lance Bombardier P.C.A.

41   Cameron C. MacLure, Sept. 11, 1896 - March 27, 1947. His wife, Annie MacLeod, Oct. 4, 1910 - Jan. 14, 1964.

32   Angus Lamont, 1851-1947. His wife, Christy MacLeod, 1855-1948. Their son, William R. Lamont, 1890-1952. His twin sister, Mary Lamont, 1890-1976.

142 John D. MacLeod, 1864-1951. His wife, Ellen Janet Annear, 1876-1956.

156 Alexander J. MacLeod, 1861-1940. His wife, Isabel MacDonald, 1865-1961. Their sons: Angus Alexander MacLeod, 1903-1926. Commander A. Stanhope MacLeod, 1907-1973.

140 MacIntyre—Alice MacLeod, Sept. 21, 1900 - May 10, 1956. Son, Kenneth Ross McIntyre, M.D., born May 11, 1939, lost his life in shipwreck disaster off the coast of Bermuda, Dec. 3, 1967.

139 James D. MacLeod, 1861-1944. His wife, Christy Ann Ross, 1867-1947. Daughter Annie, 1904-1906.

141 Hudson MacLeod, 1906-1972.

Mt. Buchanan, Polly Cemetery

25 Capt. Donald H. MacDonald, 1812-1892. Flora Murchison, his wife, 1816-1904. Their children: Anne, 1844-1932. Donald, 1853-1924. Mrs. Catherine MacLeod, 1843-1899. Jessie MacLeod, 1850-1892.

28 Capt. J. Murchison, 1854-1928. Catherine Finlayson, his wife, 1856-1929. Their children: Effie J. MacLeod, 1885-1928. Angus Alexander, 1893-1929.

32 John McKinnon, 1853-1933. Flora C. MacLeod, his wife, 1853-1941. Isabella MacKinnon, 1844-1937.

37 Margaret B. Nicholson, wife of Daniel MacLeod, 1897-1926. Mary L., daughter, 1923-1925. Daniel MacLeod, 1892-1957.

44 Angus M. Murchison, 1860-1924. Agnes MacLeod, his wife, March 29, 1864 - Dec. 7, 1958.

61 John A. Stewart, 1868-1949. Mary E. MacLeod, his wife, 1870-1932. Daniel, son, 1897-1923, died at Vancouver, B.C. Charles Burton Stewart, 1903-1953. George Stewart, 1904-1958.

63 Allan Buchanan, died Dec. 6, 1919, age 86. Isabelle MacLeod, his wife, died Nov. 8, 1927, age 89. Angus A. Buchanan, died Jan. 19, 1920, age 40, buried at Nicaragua, S.A. Mrs. Frank Morrill, died March 2, 1922, age 40. Children of Allan and Isabelle Buchanan.

64 Clarence L. Gillis, 1891—. Bessie P. MacLeod, his wife, 1894-1962.

70 Mary MacLeod, wife of Samuel MacLeod, 1862-1919. Samuel MacLeod, 1859-1928. Laughlin, their son, killed in action, Oct. 30, 1917, age 28.

71 Michael McLeod, 1834-1887. Jessie, his wife, 1829 - March 30, 1906. Capt. Dan MacLeod, died March 4, 1884, age 28. D. Alexander, died at Sette, France, Jan. 9, 1888, age 27. Laughlin A., died Aug. 23, 1889, age 29.

74 Capt. Alex MacLeod, died Dec. 26, 1894, age 48. Margaret Murchison, his wife, died May 12, 1895, age 42. Their four infant children. Donald M. MacLeod, their son, died April 8, 1947, age 65.

102 Donald McLeod, died Oct. 20, 1849, age 38. A native of Isle of Skye, Scotland. Penelope, his wife, died Nov. 30, 1880, age 82. A native of Tupple Murray, Mull, Scotland.

107 Ewen Martin, died April 3, 1875, age 54. Catherine McLeod, his wife, died Dec. 26, 1895, age 73. Margaret Martin, wife of Rev. F. A. Kidson, died April 21, 1876, age 28. William Edward, died October 1, 1876, age 6 years, 3 months, son of Martin and Mary Martin.

Mt. Herbert United

1 Euphemia McDonald, wife of Angus McLeod, died Aug. 6, 1913, age 77.

Mt. Pleasant Cemetery, Church of The Nazarene

3 Pauline MacLeod, May, 1937 - May, 1945.

7 In loving memory of Roderick McLeod, died March 4, 1927, aged 72 yrs. His wife Agnes MacDowell, died June 22, 1929, aged 61. "The pains of death are past, labour and sorrow cease, and life's long warfare, closed at last. His soul is forever in peace."

8 MacLeod—Roderick, March 25, 1899, March 28, 1953. His wife Clara Mae Phillips, Sept. 20, 1902, April 4, 1975. Asleep in Jesus.

9 712168 Private Daniel MacLeod, 78th Battalion, C.E.F., 4th March, 1928.

10   Green—In loving memory of John Garfield Green, Feb. 10, 1882, April 7, 1950. His wife, Margaret Jane MacLeod, Oct. 31, 1886, Sept. 18, 1973. At Rest.

MT. STEWART PEOPLE'S CEMETERY

153   Minnie Louise, daughter of Rev. A. B. and Annie McLeod, died May 27, 1891, age 4 yrs. 2 mos.

226   Peter W. MacLeod, 1854-1923.

227   Frank J., son of Peter W. and Maggie MacLeod, died June 10, 1897, age 13 yrs.

121   Murdoch MacLeod, died Dec. 3, 1883, age 73. His wife Anna, died Sept. 19, 1886, age 50.

120   Alexander MacLeod, son of Murdoch and Annie MacLeod, drowned July 1, 1875, age 3.

9   William Lester MacLeod, May 22, 1887 - Feb. 29, 1956. His wife Etta May Pigott, June 8, 1889 - April 13, 1970.

MT. STEWART, ST. ANDREW'S ROMAN CATHOLIC

195   Laura MacLeod, 1884-1949.

267   Donald C. MacDonald, 1918-1953. His wife, Lilly MacLeod, 1912-1963.

MURRAY HARBOUR ENGLISH CHURCH CEMETERY

James MacLeod, killed in action, 1939-1945.

J. Frank MacLeod, died since the war.

Lloyd J. MacLeod.

MURRAY HARBOUR NORTH PRESBYTERIAN

179   Daniel A. McLeod, died Aug. 16, 1894, age 95.

17   Peter S. MacDonald, 1865-1920. Effie MacLeod, his wife, 1866-1925. Evelyn, their daughter, 1889-1901.

22   David B. Clow, 1861-1905. Isabelle MacLeod, his wife, 1879-1951. Lorena, their daughter, 1901-1931. Elizabeth Caroline, their daughter, 1903-1904.

133   Anne McLeod, wife of Malcolm Bethune, died Oct. 30, 1896, age 71.

MURRAY HARBOUR SOUTH

286   John McLeod, died Nov. 19, 1880, age 62. Ann, his daughter, died Feb. 1876, age 16.

287B   Elizabeth Ross, wife of John McLeod, died June 26, 1877, age 59.

321   Lillian Sarah Beck, R.N., wife of Murdoch MacLeod, Dec. 20, 1886 - Jan. 19, 1964.

346   Laura Mina, wife of Joseph MacLeod, died May 12, 1909, age 28.

452B   William Albert MacDonald, Oct. 7, 1884 - Aug. 12, 1957. Elizabeth Adelaide MacLeod, his wife, Jan. 17, 1895 - May 26, 1962.

486   James MacLeod, Pte. 105 Batt., C.E.F., 6 May 1962, age 61.

487   James MacLeod, Oct. 10, 1900 - May 6, 1962. Miriam Giddings, his wife, Jan. 1, 1898—.

61   Lloyd J, MacLeod, Pte. Cape Breton Highlanders, 25th Dec. 1974, age 55.

92B   Sheldon Wallace Hume, Dec. 29, 1927—. Margaret Alma MacLeod, his wife,

June 4, 1929—. Warren Glendon, their son, Nov. 19, 1949 - May 25, 1950.

93B Henry Wallace Hume, April 8, 1901 - April 28, 1972. Lois Florence MacLeod, his wife, Sept. 25, 1906—.

113A Ernest R. MacLeod, March 26, 1922. Olive Richards, his wife, Jan. 23, 1923. Daniel B. MacLeod, Aug. 18, 1897 - Aug. 10, 1966. Lucy Jane Livingstone, his wife, Dec. 27, 1900—.

119A Frederick H. MacLeod, Nov. 10, 1890 - May 11, 1957. Margaret J. Strickland, his wife, Aug. 8, 1894 - April 28, 1977.

123B William G. Gosbee, May 3, 1910 - Dec. 3, 1972. Jean B. MacLeod, his wife, July 1, 1926 - Dec. 14, 1968. H. Dennis Gosbee, their son, Nov. 14, 1952 - Oct. 6, 1968.

352B Hammond J. Nicolle. Mary Ann MacLeod, his wife, 1872-1954. Audrey, their daughter, 1902-1923. James Willie, their son, 1898-1910.

390A Samuel M. MacLeod, 1859-1924. Maria M. Sencabaugh, his wife, 1859-1925. John E. W., their son, died Feb. 18, 1918, age 16. Their infant daughter, age 21 days.

396B Lewis R. White, 1907-1956. Lauretta MacLeod, his wife, 1907—.

441 Eber MacLeod, 1886-1967. Ida Beck, his wife, 1894-1940. Marguerite, their daughter, age 1 year. Windsor, their son, age 3 weeks. Maurice, their son, age 7 weeks.

400A Mabel R. MacLeod, 1882-1941, wife of Arthur White. Their children: Mina, May, 1913. Nathan, 1916. Twins, 1917.

396 Austin B. Bell, May 8, 1894 - Dec. 11, 1973. Sadie I. MacLeod, his wife, Oct. 12, 1900—.

130B Harry Frederick White, April 21, 1909—. Helen Dorothy MacLeod, his wife, Nov. 19, 1915—.

28A Albert MacLeod, 1878-1953. Fayne Harris, his wife, 1883-1970.

141 Lemuel MacLeod, died Feb. 28, 1912, age 57. Mary E. MacLeod, his wife, 1861-1936.

140 Thyne, 1883-1892. Emerson, 1894-1902. Sons of Lemuel and Mary MacLeod.

143 Joseph MacLeod, March 24, 1874 - June 14, 1942. Maybelle MacPherson, his wife, Aug. 26, 1885 - Feb. 22, 1958.

161C Minnie F., daughter of D. and I. Machon, died Jan. 6, 1886, age 7 years. Reuben W. Machon, 1870-1937. Belle Hyde, his wife, 1874-1965. Daniel Machon, died April 20, 1911, age 78. Isabella McLeod, his wife, died Feb. 14, 1928, age 84.

187 William McLeod, died April 1, 1893, age 64.

188 Isabella, wife of William McLeod, died Jan. 10, 1899, age 68.

192B Perley T. Harris, Sept. 12, 1872 - July 2, 1942. Barbara MacLeod, his wife, Oct. 14, 1872 - May 23, 1943.

259C Warren B. Brehaut, 1879-1943. Effie MacInnis, 1886-1976. Joseph Brehaut, 1837-1901. Rebecca MacLeod, his wife, 1847-1892.

270A Maria MacLeod, wife of Charles Lelacheur, died Aug. 9, 1893, age 44.

MURRAY RIVER, GLADSTONE

1 Frederick R. MacLeod, 1908-1970. Mary Ann, his wife, 1915—. Infant daughter died 1954.

3 Ernest Arthur Kirby, Sept. 19, 1878 - Aug. 14, 1949. Clara Matilda McLeod, his wife, July 7, 1886 - Dec. 4, 1973.

245 Robert Sanders, died April 21, 1922, age 85. Elizabeth MacLeod, his wife, died July 23, 1915, age 80.

7 Capt. John A. Munn, 1873-1943. Christie MacLeod, his wife, 1888-1959.

13 Mary P., wife of John MacLeod, died June 29, 1911, age 72.
14 Harlan MacLeod, 1912-1937.
60 James Evans MacLeod, died Feb. 8, 1912, age 51. Mary Ann Bishop, his wife, died Sept. 5, 1904, age 41.
64 George MacLeod, 1878-1923.
61 Annie B., wife of Frederick W. McLeod, died March 10, 1905, age 32. Their son, born June 22, 1901, died July 10, 1901.
65 Sadie MacLure, 1880-1969, wife of George MacLeod.
66 Our darling Bessie May MacLeod, June 4, 1918 - Feb. 11, 1919.
67 G. Lester MacLeod, 1916-1952.
109 Cyrus Watson MacLeod, Nov. 29, 1898—. Ida Ada Marion Johnson, his wife, March 14, 1903 - Nov. 25, 1942.
123 George MacKay, 1845-1931. Huldy MacLeod, his wife, 1834-1905. John W., their son, 1876-1900.
128 Matthew MacLeod, 1862-1939. Letitia Cook, his wife, 1859-1927. Isabelle, their daughter, 1890-1960. Margaret, their daughter, 1895-1971.
129 A. B. Lowell Francis MacLeod, died Feb. 25, 1946, age 22. Served with R.C.N. in W.W.II.
133 Edgar G. Giddings, 1865-1953. Irene M. MacLeod, his wife, 1872-1957.
152 David MacLeod, died Oct. 23, 1914, age 88. Mary Ann Bishop, his wife, died Feb. 16, 1899, age 71. John Albert MacLeod, died July 23, 1899, age 53.
153 Faye Evelyn MacLeod, May 30, 1946 - Jan. 11, 1950, daughter of Walter and Lois MacLeod.
163 C. Janet MacLeod, Feb. 3, 1896 - June 2, 1969, wife of Gavin MacLeod. Sadie MacLeod, Dec. 10, 1925 - June 4, 1945.
166 Matilda MacLeod, died May 7, 1920, age 74.
169 George MacLeod, 1842-1905. Mary MacDonald, his wife, 1844-1906. Huldah, their daughter, 1869-1907. David John, their son, 1876-1948.
179 Alexander J. MacDonald, 1904—. Freda Marie MacLeod, his wife, 1910-1948.
184 Matthew M. MacLeod, July 1, 1892 - May 23, 1949.
200 Victor MacLeod, 1892-1937.
201 Margaret Catherine, wife of Calvin MacLeod, died Sept. 10, 1910, age 42. Calvin MacLeod, died Jan. 16, 1939, age 81.
202 Neil Boyd, son of Ethelbert and Marie MacLeod, Nov. 2, 1940 - March 26, 1941.
249 John D. MacLeod, Aug. 6, 1883 - April 2, 1972. Ethel A. MacKenzie, his wife, July 22, 1893 - Sept. 15, 1930. Kenzie Murdoch, infant son, 1914.
251 John Whiteway, 1851-1938. Jane MacLeod, his wife, 1849-1934.
256 Mary D. MacLeod, Feb. 26, 1890—, wife of Charles Moore.
264 William Francis MacLeod, 1901—. Marie Loretta Ferguson, his wife, 1900-1975.
269 William S. Buell, March 14, 1888 - Jan. 7, 1967. Catherine M. MacLeod, his wife, Oct. 11, 1893—.
278 Margaret MacLeod, June 6, 1912 - March 20, 1972, wife of Clifford Warren. Erected by her Aunt M. M. MacLeod.
296 J. Sewell Buchanan, 1877-1933. Mary A. MacLeod, his wife, 1877-1953.
307 Frederick W. Johnston, 1892-1969. Annie MacLeod, his wife, 1891—.

MURRAY RIVER (WILMOT)

1 James MacLeod, 1831-1878. Catherine, his wife, 1835-1929.
7 David McLeod, died April 15, 1877, age 49. Elizabeth MacLure, his wife, died Feb. 16, 1911, age 80. William McLeod, died Oct. 26, 1879, age 20. Margaret,

born March 28, 1865, died 1868. Son and daughter of David and Elizabeth MacLeod.

8   Gavin MacLeod, died July 1, 1962, age 95. Louisa Ann Hawkins, his wife, died April 13, 1912, age 43.

9   William, son of Gavin and Louisa MacLeod, died Nov. 20, 1890, age 1 yr. 6 mos.

34   Samuel McLeod, died Jan. 12, 1899, age 74. Selina Blackmore, his wife, died April 24, 1886, age 39.

34A Eliza R., died Dec. 4, 1892, age 3 years. John M., died Dec. 18, 1892, age 9 years. Children of Donald and Maria McLeod.

NEW DOMINION, PRESBYTERIAN

69   Christina MacLean, wife of Colin MacLeod, died May 6, 1897, age 64. Colin MacLeod, died Feb. 10, 1912, age 82.

97   Donald McLeod, died Feb. 3, 1890, age 87. Sarah S., died Jan. 10, 1900, age 87. Johnie D. MacLeod, died Dec. 9, 1879, age 2 years. Sarah J., died Dec. 10, 1879, age 1 year. Murdoch McLeod, died Aug. 26, 1917, age 81. Margaret Darrach, his wife, died Feb. 10, 1935, age 82.

162 John McLeod, died Feb. 1, 1863, age 76. Marion McDonald, his wife, died March 10, 1866, age 70. Natives of Isle of Harris, Scotland. Alexander MacLeod, died Sept. 23, 1892, age 67. John McLeod, died Oct. 1, 1882, age 44. Margaret McLeod, died Feb. 19, 1907, age 78. Murdoch McLeod, died Jan. 29, 1916, age 92.

233 Paula Anne, daughter of David and Patricia MacLeod, May 6, 1974.

67   Alexander B. MacLeod, 1870-1939. Winnifred E. MacKenzie, his wife, 1886-1974.

68   Christena McLeod, 1864-1925.

59   Peter McLeod, died March 12, 1874, age 34.

116 Martin L. MacDonald, Aug. 2, 1894 - July 3, 1972. Myrtle Buchanan MacLeod, his wife, March 23, 1900 - Dec. 14, 1966.

58   John McLeod, died Sept. 22, 1865, age 65. Sarah McEwen. his wife, died Feb. 21, 1895, age 87. Natives of Scotland. Donald, their son, died Jan. 2, 1864, age 33.

NEW GLASGOW CEMETERY

60   Rachel C. McLeod, wife of W. D. McCoubrey. 1846-1927/1848-1932. Annie Ausline, died Dec. 15, 1898, aged 15. Lucy Levina, died Aug. 5, 1899. aged 22, daughters of W. D. and Rachel McCoubrey.

74   Evelyn F., daughter of John and Mary McLeod, died July 8, 1897, aged 18. Also Marion E., died April 15, 1900, aged 3 yrs. George Melvin, born Aug. 22, 1882, died June 5, 1922. His wife, Cora A. White, 1876-1967. MacLeod, John T., 1855-1933. Also his wife Mary Smith, 1855-1929.

NEW LONDON, GEDDIE MEMORIAL

6   In memory of John McLeod who perished in the wreck of the Carrie R. Rich on North Cape Reef in the gale of Aug. 24, 1878, age 42 years, 6 mos., and his wife Sophronia Western Sime, born Aug. 16, 1864, died June 29, 1916. Also their son Hugh Cambridge, died June 13, 1864, age 1 yr. 9 mos.

55   In memory of George MacLeod, died May 21, 1874, aged 58. Barbara, his wife, died June 7, 1873, aged 54.

56   Hugh MacLeod, Dec. 12, 1829 - April 24, 1917. His wife Marion Wall, March 4, 1843 - July 17, 1881.

57   Henry S. MacLeod, died Aug. 11, 1885, aged 31. Also his son, William M., died Jan. 19, 1901, aged 20 yrs.

68   J. Artemus MacLeod, died Mar. 8, 1889, aged 42. Lucilla Matilda MacLeod, died Aug. 28, 1905, aged 62. Annabella Mackie, his wife, born Dec. 6, 1813, died Oct. 30, 1897. Leslie E. MacLeod, distinguished journalist, born March 27, 1862, died in New York, Oct. 18, 1899. John MacLeod of Durness, Scotland, 1761-1836. His wife, Mary MacPherson, arrived by Brig Polly 1805, buried at Yankee Hill. John MacLeod born Nov. 20, 1809, died Dec. 3, 1895. Lucy MacLeod born Oct. 15, 1855, died in Richmond, Virginia, Dec. 26, 1900. Henrietta Maria MacLeod, died Dec. 19, 1912, age 70 yrs. Louise Jane MacLeod, born Sept. 15, 1839, died March 21, 1924.

81   Newton MacLeod, 1848-1937. His wife Eliza J. MacLeod, 1853-1936.

82   Private John Fred MacLeod, 28th Battalion C.E.F., 18th Jan., 1943.

83   Harold Artemas MacLeod, 8th Canadian Siege Battery, June 10, 1897 - March 3, 1917, son of A. C. and Agnes MacLeod, buried at Aldershot, England. John Fred MacLeod, 1884-1943. A. Cuthbert MacLeod, 1852-1931, also his wife Agnes Ross MacLeod, 1855-1943.

92   James Lamont, 1825-1918, his wife Isabel MacLeod, 1830-1909. Their daughter Nancy, wife of D. MacKinnon, 1863-1936.

116   Nelson MacLeod, 1886-1965. Wife, Bessie Dunning, 1888—. Their infant son, 1919.

132   J. Kenneth MacLeod, 1903-1939.

133   Underhill—Hartle, 1863-1941, his wife Sarah Bernard MacLeod, 1856-1946.

134   Capt. Alfred D. MacLeod, 1860-1944. His wife Catherine E. Mountain, 1889—.

141   Elmer J. MacLeod, Gunner, C.F.A.C.E.F., 29 Aug., 1958, aged 65. [Also on 142.]

142   His wife Isabel MacLeod, Dec. 31, 1892 - Sept. 20, 1962. Annie MacLeod, Dec. 26, 1884 - March 16, 1959.

145   Wm. Hugh, son of Donald and Amelia. Born July 25, 1826, died Feb. 6, 1898.

146   Neil Fulton MacLeod, died Oct. 19, 1873, age 12. Also his cousin John Edward, died Oct. 19, 1862, age 5 yrs.

147   Emily Sims, wife of Benjamin McLeod, died April l, 1883, age 30 yrs. 4 mos.

148   John Franklin, son of John MacLeod, died May 19, 1857, aged 4 mos.

149   Mark the perfect man and behold the upright for the end of that man's peace. Sacred to the memory of Donald MacLeod who departed this life Sept. 17, 1858, in the 57th year of his age. He was a man of Christian simplicity and his manner, honest and upright, mighty with the fear of God, love to man, and labouring to manifest in all relations of life this two fold object, a kind and devoted husband, a tender and loving parent; he also gained for himself the esteem and confidence of neighbours and acquaintances and died in peace, it is hoped, with God and man. For the space of twenty-six years he discharged the duties of an elder in the Presbyterian Church and secured much influence with Pastors and people in this important office.

150   In memory of Amelia Harriet MacKay, relict of the late Donald MacLeod, died at French River, New London, Jan. 17, 1898, age 90.

213   In memory of Ada Blanch, daughter of Andrew and Priscilla McLeod, died June 25, 1906, age 17.

214   Father—In memory of Andrew MacLeod, died March 2, 1905, age 46. Mother— Priscella B. Bell, wife of Andrew MacLeod, Feb. 4, 1948, 80.

225   MacLeod—Gordon MacLeod, 1848-1929. His wife Mary Doughart, 1846-1928. Children—Annie S., 1872-1879; Louis F., 1880-1919; Chester G., 1892-1973; Jane J. MacKay, wife of Chester, 1882-1969.

239 Mary J. MacLeod, 1840-1905. Donald F., 1877-1901, John D., 1880-1899, sons of Benjamin and Emily MacLeod, at rest, Mary J. MacLeod and Barbara MacLeod, daughters of Donald and Amelia H. MacLeod.

244 Ella Maria, beloved daughter of Andrew and Elizabeth MacLeod, died March 19, 1900, aged 26. John Lemuel MacLeod, died March 3,1937, aged 62. Andrew MacLeod died April 7, 1914, aged 73, also his wife Elizabeth, died Dec. 22, 1923, aged 79.

247 Constable—John Murray, 1878-1955, his wife Annabel MacLeod, 1885-1973.

248 McLeod—Maggie Bell McKay, wife of Ira W. McLeod, born Nov. 28, 1883, died Apr. 24, 1921, also his wife Laura M. Dixon, born Dec. 25, 1892, died May 18, 1943. Ira W. MacLeod, born Dec. 20, 1883, died Dec. 26, 1967.

255 At rest, Ada, the loving wife of J. D. MacLeod who departed this life Feb. 7, 1909, youngest daughter of the late Joseph MacEwen, Cambellton, N.L. J. D. MacLeod, born Jan. 7, 1832, died Aug. 16, 1913. MacLeod—born 7-25, 1826.William H., died 2-20, 1882. Mary, 4-9, 1839. Mary Jane, 3-24, 1905. Penelope, 7-2, 1846. Hugh, 1882, 2-9, 1826. Ann. Children of D. and A. H. MacLeod, French River.

256 At rest, Alice, wife of Capt. G. A. MacLeod, born June 16, 1844, died Feb. 28, 1928. At rest—George A. MacLeod, born Feb. 9, 1843, died Aug. 20, 1905. MacLeod, Everett, 1876-1952, his wife, Johanna Stewart, 1878-1960.

258 McLeod, F/O Harold Willard MacLeod, D.S.O. 412 Sqdn. R.C.A.F., WWII, Nov. 2, 1918 - Aug. 25, 1972.

259 MacLeod—In loving memory of Capt. Wallace M. MacLeod, 1878-1958. Amelia A. Stewart, wife of Wallace MacLeod, 1879-1940.

260 Hugh M. Campbell, 1864-1928, his wife Margaret MacLeod, 1868-1955.

263 McLeod, Clara E. Stewart, wife of George B. McLeod, 1889-1926. George B. McLeod, 1888-1928.

264 In loving memory of Andrew MacLeod, 1856-1951, Joanna Profitt, wife of Andrew MacLeod, 1860-1943. Emeline, 1885-1964.

281 Margaret Ruth MacLeod, 1892-1957.

324 Lillia G., daughter of Neil and Hattie McLeod, died Jan. 13, 1891, aged 8 yrs. 7 mos.

325 Hattie M. Blackeney, wife of Neil MacLeod, 1853-1913. Capt. Neil MacLeod, 1856-1928. Also their daughter Lillia G., 1882-1891.

333 In memory of Murdoch McLeod, died May 31, 1885, age 77.

334 In memory of Ann Hardy, wife of Murdoch McLeod, died Aug. 20, 1898, aged 84.

335 In memory of John MacLeod, died March 5, 1911, aged 55.

336 MacLeod, William Preston, 1887-1953, his wife C. Belle Fife, 1885-19—.

340 Catherine Elizabeth, daughter of Kenneth and Catherine MacLeod, born 1853, died Nov. 5, 1905.

341 In memory of Kenneth McLeod, died Oct. 14, 1883, aged 80. Also his wife Catherine, died Mar. 13, 1902, aged 91.

343 In memory of William A., adopted son of Kenneth McLeod, died May 30, 1893, aged 11 years 4 mos.

344 In memory of Kenneth McLeod, died July 8, 1893, aged 66.

345 In memory of Margaret McPherson, wife of Kenneth McLeod, died Oct. 28, 1900, aged 66.

346 Infant son of George and Hannah McLeod.

347 In loving remembrance of Annie Leeta, daughter of George and Hannah McLeod, born Oct. 12, 1891, died July 18, 1907.

348 MacLeod—Hannah Bernard, wife of George MacLeod, 1859-1948. George MacLeod, 1858-1952.

371   Husband, John MacLeod, born Jan. 26, 1821, died Oct. 2, 1901. Margaret Stewart MacLeod, born Dec. 25, 1827, died May 12, 1911.

372   In memory of Kate A. Bernard, wife of Heath F. MacLeod, died June 27, 1907, aged 28. MacLeod—Amelia Harriet MacLeod, died April 6, 1967, aged 93. In memory of Heath F. MacLeod, died July 30, 1957, aged 79.

386   James Hugh McLeod, born Nov. 22, 1847, died Nov. 4, 1917. Also his wife Margaret Jane Sudsbury, born Dec. 7, 1860, died April 22, 1951.

387   MacLeod, Robert, 1875-1948. His wife Katie A. MacLeod, 1875-1962. Their son, Pte. Leslie Wm. MacLeod, 105th C.D.N., N.F. Batt. 1897-1917.

395   MacKay—Charles S. MacKay, 1874-1965. His wife, Rachel MacLeod, 1880-1935, their daughter, Mary Irene, 1915-1936.

404   Hugh M. Campbell, 1864-1928, his wife, Margaret MacLeod, 1865-1955.

413   MacLeod, K. Heath, 1891-1977, and Elizabeth R. MacLeod, 1890-1971.

414   Infant daughter of Heath K. and Elizabeth R. MacLeod, died Jan. 22, 1917.

417   McLeod—Murdoch McLeod, Dec. 20, 1884 - April 27, 1976, his wife, Elizabeth Johnstone, Jan. 21, 1891. Their daughter, Margaret, July, 1928 - July, 1928.

427   MacLeod, Ralph Stewart, drowned May 2, 1947, aged 37 yrs. His wife Mary Ellen Found.

468   MacLeod—Kenneth Cecil MacLeod, July 18, 1895 - Aug. 31, 1962. Hattie Ella Tuplin, Aug. 14, 1895 - July 31, 1962, wife of Kenneih Cecil MacLeod.

470   MacLeod, Charles Allison, Mar. 5, 1909 - July 9, 1965. His wife Hazel Gertrude Somers.

NEW LONDON PROTESTANT

8   MacLeod, James D., 1852-1937, also his wife Georgie A. Fyfe, 1872-1951.

10   MacLeod—Winnifred Vivian Baglole, wife of Duncan A. MacLeod, Dec. 11, 1921 - Nov. 29, 1960. Their son Kenneth Clair, May 8, 1942 - Sept. 19, 1963.

23   MacLeod, Ray Alexander MacLeod, 1883-1974, his wife, Gertrude Adele Bell, 1891-1967. MacLeod—Sgt. Elmer S., killed in action in Italy, Sept. 14, 1944, aged 31 yrs.

25   MacLeod—Harold S. MacLeod, 1881-1946.

78   Mother—In loving memory of Eleanor M. MacLeod, 1868-1920. James C. Frizzell, 1874-1925.

80   Murray—John T., 1860-1932, his wife, M. Caroline MacLeod, 1871-1955. Their son, George A., 1908-1947.

89   In memory of Christy Johnston, wife of Alex MacLeod, died June 6, 1899, aged 44. Their children: Ethel, died Nov. 18, 1894, aged 14. Daniel, died Jan. 6, 1895, aged 7 yrs. 9 mos. Elmer MacLeod, drowned Dec. 26, 1911, aged 19. Alexander MacLeod, died Aug. 28, 1918, aged 78.

92   In loving memory of Andrew MacLeod, 42nd Stanley, died Mar. 24, 1907, aged 82 yrs. Also his wife Euphemia MacKenzie, died June 21, 1924, aged 83 yrs. George, son of Andrew and Euphemia, died Apr. 3, 1909, aged 22. Charles E. MacLeod, died June 9, 1929, aged 58. Gertrude MacLeod Brown, 1880-1967. J. Gordon MacLeod, died June 17, 1914, aged 29.

93   To the memory of the inestimable departed worth—Annabella, beloved wife of Andrew McLeod, who departed this life the 16th day of December, 1850, aged 22 yrs.

94   McLeod—Margaret, daughter of Donald McLeod, Aug. 19, 1845, aged 38 yrs.

100   In memory of Donald McLeod, 42nd, died Oct. 21, 1874, A.E.S.S.

113 Malcolm McLeod, died Oct. 13, 1908, aged 74. Mary McKinnon, wife of Malcolm McLeod, died April 23, 1900, aged 59. Murdoch McLeod, died July 11, 1877, aged 79. Also his wife, Catherine, died March 11, 1883, aged 83.

122 To the memory of Roderick McLeod who departed this life March 11, 1859, aged 74, also to that of his spouse Catherine McLeod, who departed this life the 15th of July of the same year, aged 70 years. They were both natives of Sutherland County and emigrated to this country 1847.

124 MacLeod—John, died July 11, 1885, aged 68. His wife, Elizabeth Ross, died Dec. 17, 1889, aged 65. Their daughter, Elizabeth MacLeod, died June 9, 1941, aged 76.

126 In memory of William MacLeod, died June 24, 1885, aged 84, a native of Scotland.

127 In memory of Mary, beloved wife of Alexander McLeod, died Jan. 11, 1871, aged 30.

166 In memory of Christana McLeod, beloved wife of George McKay who departed this life Dec. 11th, 1856, aged 56.

249 Donald MacLeod, 1852-1892, also his wife, Annie MacKinnon, 1843-1936. George O., 1873-1881. John A., 1879-1880.

293 In memory of Barbara MacLeod, wife of Robert McKay, died Feb. 22, 1905, aged 72. Robert McKay died May 30, 1908, aged 79.

297 Duncan MacLeod, 1818-1887, his wife, Dolly MacKay, 1823-1912. Their daughter, Mary, 1858-1926.

300 Brown—John Andrew, 1869-1941. His wife, Edith Catherine McLeod, 1872-1945.

304 Roderick MacLeod, 1810-1889, his wife, Catherine MacInnis, 1815-1907. Son, Murdoch, 1844-1872. Daughter, Marion MacLeod, 1858-1933.

305 Lauchlin McLeod, died May 4, 1889, aged 49. His wife, Mary MacLean, died May 18, 1931, age 97. Margaret A. McLeod, died Aug. 26, 1906, age 25.

318 MacEwen _____, 1858-1942, also his wife Jessie McLeod, 1858-1949. Daughter, Ella B., 1887-1939.

319 Kenneth McLeod, died Oct. 2, 1897, aged 74. John W. McLeod, died Dec. 26, 1924, aged 60. Also his wife, Eliza F. MacKinnon, died March 23, 1951, aged 77. Also his wife, Sarah Whitehead, died Jan 20, 1912, aged 80.

329 Capt. John McLeod, died Sept. 20, 1897, aged 77, also his wife, Johanna, died Dec. 7, 1900, aged 87. In memory of Grace McKay, wife of James M. McLeod, died Nov. 18, 1927, aged 73. James M. McLeod, died Jan. 11, 1929, aged 75. John MacLeod, died Nov. 26, 1957, aged 72. His wife, Mary McRae, 1883-1961. Duncan, son of James M. and Grace McLeod, died Feb. 25, 1898, aged 8 yrs. 2 mos.

334 William McKay, died Mar. 29, 1893, aged 31. Also his wife, Mary McLeod, died Feb. 27, 1902, aged 31.

349 Margaret McLeod, wife of George McLeod, died Jan. 16, 1912, aged 75.

350 John McLeod, died Dec. 27, 1872, aged 78. Also his wife, Catherine McKay, April 9, 1879, aged 79.

New London, St. Thomas Anglican

10 In memory of Anne Pidgeon, child of Donald and Mary MacLeod, died March 11, 1859, aged 1 yr. 4 mos.

17 James D. Pidgeon, native of Honiton, Devonshire, England, died Dec. 18, 1886, age 84 yrs. His wife, Ann McLeod, died April 14, 1888, age 83 yrs. Native of Sutherlandshire, Scotland.

NORTH BEDEQUE, UNITED PRESBYTERIAN

267   Jessie MacLeod, 1866-1931. Edgard C. MacLeod, 1861-1939.

266   Mary Moyse, wife of Alexander McLeod, died Nov. 13, 1906, aged 80.

265   Mary Robbins, wife of Murdoch McLeod, died Feb. 13, 1875, aged 42.

214   George McLeod, 1847-1935, also his wife, Bella Gillis, 1866-1951.

171   Gerald E. MacLeod, Jan. 1, 1926 - July 7, 1963. John Mac MacLeod, 1889 - June 9, 1963.

174   Erected by their son Donald, Father, Philip McLeod, died Feb. 28, 1900, aged 63, also his Mother, Annie MacDonald, died Jan. 8, 1896, aged 51.

O'LEARY, ST. LUKE'S ANGLICAN CEMETERY

27   In memory of James Duncan, died Dec. 2, 1895, aged 64, also his wife, Flora. Annie MacLeod, died Aug. 1, 1925, aged 82.

ORWELL CORNER, UNITED PRESBYTERIAN

1   Murdoch A. MacLeod, 1871-1936. Jessie R. MacLeod, 1873-1938.

2   Neil MacLeod, died Aug. 25, 1910. Isabella McDonald, his wife, died March 13, 1892.

3   Norman McLeod, died July 5, 1889, age 43. Murdoch A., his son, died March 28, 1888, age 19.

4   Lawrence S. [?] MacLeod, 1877-1952. Jessie Millman, his wife, 1884-1969. Murdoch MacLeod, 1832-1917. Annie H. Enman, his wife, 1849-1893.

5   Murdoch Alfred, died Dec. 9, 1887, age 13 yrs. 3 mos, son of Murdoch and Annie MacLeod.

6   Archibald, died May 9, 1886, age 1 yr. 8 mos. Mary E., died Nov. 10, 1890, age 2 yrs. 7 mos Children of Hugh D. and Katie A. MacLeod. Hugh D. MacLeod, 1856-1927. Katie A. Munn, his wife, died Sept. 22, 1893, age 37. Jessie Munn, his wife, 1867-1958.

7   Archibald MacLeod, B.A. M.D., graduate of McGill College, Mtrl., and the New York Polyclinic, who died at New Westminister, B.C., Oct. 15, 1884, aged 25 yrs. 8 mos.

8   Alexander MacLeod, Master Mariner, died June 14, 1893, age 70. Jessie Campbell, his wife, died Jan 18, 1893, age 70. Alex R. M. MacLeod, died June 10, 1897, age 16.

9   Donald McLeod, died May 3, 1885, age 53.

11   Mary, wife of John McLeod, died July 13, 1888, age 64. John McLeod, died Jan. 13, 1908, age 89. John M. McLeod, died Dec. 8, 1945, age 82. Mary Jenkins, his wife, died Dec. 4, 1950, age 79.

12   W. Gordon MacLeod, died March 4, 1918, age 24. Erected by his wife.

13   Jessie, wife of John H. McLeod, died March 22, 1901, age 45. John H. McLeod, died Aug. 26, 1914, age 57. John W. McLeod, their son, died Aug. 30, 1940, age 41. In memory of Flora, wife of John H. McLeod, died Nov. 25, 1945, age 80.

6   Catherine Biggs, wife of William McLeod, died Jan. 14, 1897, age 66. Neil W. McLeod, died July 9, 1947, age 75. Bessie C. Musick, wife of Neil W. McLeod, died Dec. 26, 1943, age 70.

16   Capt. Murdoch A. MacLeod, 1864-1927. Jessie A. Munro, his wife, 1875-1949.

20   Mary Catherine MacLeod, wife of John Finley MacRae, Aug. 4, 1875 - Feb. 4, 1961. Bertha MacLeod, Oct. 2, 1873 - Jan. 6, 1966.

21 William MacLeod, 1827-1905. Christena MacLeod, his wife, 1828-1924.

23 Malcolm J. MacLeod, 1858-1931. Sarah M. Docherty, his wife, 1867-1953.

24 George Talmage, son of J. and Sarah McLeod, died Sept. 13, 1913, age 10 yrs.

25 Grace W. McLeod, died Feb. 20, 1901, aged 20.

6   William McLeod, died Oct. 3, 1907, age 79.

26 Mary MacLeod, 1871-1957. Rachel MacLeod, her sister, 1884-1974.

27 Donald M. MacLeod, 1872-1944.

28 Malcolm McLeod, died March 1, 1904, aged 76. Christine Gillis, his wife, 1848-1936.

29 George E. McLeod, born Aug. 26, 1883, died June 26, 1911. Catherine Mutch, his wife, later wife of E. S. Channell, 1881-1965.

30 Capt. Alex MacLeod, 1854-1919. Eliza, his wife, 1851-1923. Christiana M., died Aug. 17, 1904, age 15. Hector Russell, died May 23, 1907, age 19. Children of Capt. Alex and Eliza MacLeod.

31 John MacPherson, 1839-1917. Annie MacLeod, his wife, 1849-1920. William D. MacPherson, killed in Britannia, B.C., 1886-1929. Archie D. MacPherson, 1882-1956. John A. MacPherson, born 1880, drowned at sea 1913.

32 Alexander McLeod, died May 21, 1901, age 64. Mary McLeod, his wife, died May 15, 1924, age 85. Mary C. McLeod, died June 11, 1924, age 45.

33 Willard MacLeod, died July 13, 1978, age 70.

34 Angus Alistair MacLeod, April 25, 1912 - March 3, 1967.

35 Angus A. MacLeod, 1872-1932. Mary C. Campbell, his wife, 1878-1974.

42 Murdoch R. MacLeod, Oct. 6, 1907 - March 4, 1977.

45 Alexander Anderson, born 1846, died 1836. [Date obviously wrong. 1886?]

46 William-Greenwood, March 3, 1882 - Oct. 31, 1965. Mary MacLeod, his wife, March 1, 1882 - Jan. 2, 1969.

47 Capt. Alexander MacLeod, Jr., born 1857, died April 16, 1909.

48 Gay—Christena MacLeod, 1879-1962.

49 Ona C. MacLeod, wife of Clarence J. MacLeod, April 22, 1896- Dec. 12, 1943.

50 John F. MacLeod, 1845-1915. Annie Nicholson, his wife, 1851-1925. Angus, their son, killed in action in France, Sept. 15, 1916, age 41. Jeanette Emery, wife of John A. MacLeod, 1888-1926.

54 Donald J. MacLeod, 1875-1955. Catherine A. Gillis, his wife, 1878-1963.

51 John Alexander, beloved son of James and Jane McLeod, died Jan. 29, 1891, age 19.

52 James N. McLeod, died March 18, 1924, age 90. Jane Nicholson, wife of James N., born in Orwell Cove May 14, 1835, died June 30, 1917.

55 John D. MacDonald, Dec. 27, 1875 - Nov. 8, 1958. K. Louise MacLeod, his wife, Nov. 1, 1881 - March 10, 1968

59 Jessie Catherine McLeod, Oct. 2, 1881 - Aug. 8, 1959. Amos, May 10, 1892 - Dec. 27, 1965. Susan Elizabeth, Oct. 2, 1887 - Feb. 16, 1975. Maude, Nov., 1, 1889 - Sept. 25, 1975.

60 J. Ernest MacLeod, Nov. 20, 1888 - April 3, 1967. Myrtle M. Ross, his wife, Sept. 18, 1899—.

61 Donald McLeod, 1852-1930. Sarah Gillis, his wife, 1856-1926, and an infant daughter.

62 Neil Hugh MacLeod, March 2, 1875 - Nov. 26, 1968. Katie Lauretta MacLean, his wife, Sept. 22, 1885 - July 26, 1969.

63 Roderick MacLean, died March 9, 1947, age 93. Annie E. MacLeod, his wife, died Dec. 16, 1940, age 77.

64 Richard Wood, 1844-1928. Annie MacLeod, his wife, 1841-1935. Katie Erma, his

daughter, 1883-1896. Bertha Wilcox, his daughter, 1880-1912. Norman Wood, his son, 1876-1950. Katie MacPherson, his wife, 1886-19 —.

65 Capt. Gault R. Murray, Oct. 25, 1884 - Jan 14, 1967. Isabel MacLeod, his wife, Oct. 2, 1895 - Sept. 10, 1967. Ethel, Feb. 2, 1883 - Nov. 13, 1938.

57 Donald Malcolm MacLeod, July 11, 1933 - Feb. 11, 1967.

ORWELL HEAD, CHURCH OF SCOTLAND

1 WAR MONUMENT
E. Stanley MacLeod, 1902-1943.
Everett MacLeod, 1893-1916.
Ewen A. MacLeod, 1925-1944.
Wallace C. MacLeod, 1895-1918.
John C. McLeod, 1898-1918.
Monty J. MacLeod, 1890-1918.

2 Margaret S. MacLeod, R.N., 1883-1974.

3 Rev. D. B. MacLeod, M.A., 1854-1918. His wife, Mary J. MacLeod, 1867-1964.

5 Donald D. MacLeod, June 5, 1856 - April 15, 1939. His wife, Catherine Penelope Enman, April 10, 1859 - Sept. 28, 1940. Ernest MacLeod, Oct. 2, 1885 - Dec. 8, 1958. Infant daughter, Sept. 14, 1940.

8 Malcolm R. MacLeod, 1852-1929. His wife, Effie MacDonald, 1858-1909. Daughters: Christy Flora, 1902, age 8 mos. Infant, 1898. Roderick MacLeod, 1815-1891. His wife, Catherine MacDonald, 1826-1901. Also their son, Alexander MacLeod, 1890-1969.

9 Mildred Ruth, daughter of M. R. and Isabel MacLeod, died Nov. 14, 1907, aged 2 yrs. 4 mos.

10 John S. MacLeod, died Nov. 21, 1901, age 77. Mary MacLeod, his wife, died March 1, 1928, age 69. Malcolm R. MacLeod, 1879-1921. Belle MacLeod, died Sept. 25, 1918, aged 89. John Blair MacLeod, 1901-1929.

11 Alexander McLeod, died Jan. 7, 1910, age 78.

12 Malcolm Gillis, 1846-1901. Margary MacLeod, his wife, 1850-1908. Their daughters: Catherine A. Gillis, 1875-1876. Mary C. Gillis, 1877-1917. Their sons: John Gillis, 1881-1900. Alexander Gillis, 1885-1912. Margaret Gillis, 1890-1924 [or 1921].

14 Alexander Gillis, 1837-1906. Flora MacLeod, his wife, 1841-1931.

15 Artemas, son of D. D. and Penelope McLeod, died Aug. 20, 1884, age 2 mos.

20 John A. MacLeod, died May 8, 1916, aged 83. Mary MacLeod, his wife, died June 1, 1888, aged 53. Alexander C., son of A. J. and Christy MacLeod, died 1899, age 3 mos. Alex J. MacLeod, 1862-1923. Christie MacDonald, his wife, 1866-1958.

29 Catherine MacLeod, 1866-1907, Isabel MacLeod, 1859-1927, wives of Samuel Campbell. Sadie J., his daughter, 1898-1900. Samuel Campbell, 1864-1933.

31 Alexander D. MacLeod, died May 26, 1917, age 63. Dr. Donald MacLeod, died April 3, 1918, age 54. Mary MacLeod, 1857-1923. Christie MacLeod, 1849-1926.

32 Annie, daughter of Donald and Flora MacLeod, died Feb. 11, 1876, age 18 years.

33 Catherine, daughter of Donald and Flora MacLeod, died Jan. 27, 1875, age 22.

34 Donald McLeod, elder, Jan. 20, 1891, age 74. Flora, his wife, died Feb. 25, 1899, age 78. Angus McLeod, died Dec. 14, 1891, age 87.

35 Euphemia MacLeod, 1856-1939.

36 Donald I. MacLeod, died Aug. 16, 1889, age 40. Donald A., his son, died March 6, 1891, age 3 years.

38 Angus MacLeod, died June 9, 1876, age 45.

39 Margaret, wife of John MacLeod, died Nov. 28, 1874, age 52.

49 Malcolm McLeod, died Sept. 12, 1872, age 28. Malcolm McLeod, 1820-1887, died in Nebraska, U.S.A. Jessie Munroe, his wife, 1824-1904.

50 Malcolm A. MacLeod, 1830-1877. Christy Martin, his wife, 1832-1904. Their sons: Donald W., 1872-1895, and an infant, 1874.

56 Ann Martin, wife of Angus McLeod, died May 16, 1867, aged 26. Erected by her father, Angus Martin.

68 Alexander McDonald, died May 21, 1890, age 75. John MacDonald, died Aug. 10, 1936, age 83. His wife, Margaret Jane MacLeod, died Sept. 18, 1958, age 84. Also his wife Mary McDonald, died Dec. 23, 1897, age 73.

73 Christy McLeod, wife of Donald Campbell, Head of Montague, died Feb. 22, 1882, age 50. Also their daughter, Margaret Ann, died Feb. 23, 1876, age 6 mos.

78 Angus D. MacDonald, 1840-1930. Mary MacLeod, his wife, 1840-1885. Catherine MacDonald, 1850-1925. Duncan A. MacDonald, 1877-1943.

92 Margaret Ann, daughter of Angus R. and Annie McLeod, died May 23, 1892, age 11 yrs. 9 mos.

93 Angus MacLeod, 1849-1884. Annie MacLeod, his wife, 1850-1922. Their daughter, Margaret A., 1880-1892.

94 Margaret Martin, wife of Roderick McLeod, died July 26, 1886, age 72.

95 Roderick McLeod, died April 4, 1904, age 90. Margaret, his wife, died July 22, 1886, age 72. Laura May, daughter of J. R. and Christy McLeod, died April 5, 1904, age 16. John D. McLeod, died March 1, 1912, age 20. Lance Cpl. Everett McLeod, killed in action in France, Sept. 15, 1916, age 23. John R. McLeod, 1851-1925. His wife, Christie Bruce, 1857-1944.

97 Willie, son of Donald and Sarah McLeod, died June 8, 1890, age 1 yr. 11 mos.

98 Rachel, wife of William McLeod, died May 11, 1891, age 70. William McLeod, died June 9, 1906, age 91. Donald W. McLeod, died March 19, 1933, age 80. His wife, Sarah Martin, died Jan. 21, 1901, age 45.

111 Roderick McLeod, elder, died Jan. 26, 1907, age 84. His wife, Marjory Martin, died Jan. 31, 1909, age 87.

117 Elizabeth P. McLeod, wife of John Gillis, died Dec. 14, 1907, age 34. John A. [or R.] Gillis, died April 4, 1945, age 75. Minnie Stewart, his sister, died Feb. 23, 1965, age 80.

119 Isabella McLeod, wife of Angus Gillis, died Jan. 8, 1910, age 40. Angus Gillis, died May 5, 1950, age 83. His wife, Nora MacPherson, died June 5, 1953, age 83. John A. Gillis, died June 23, 1918, age 19.

120 Katie M., daughter of M. A. And G. McLeod and wife of A. A. Bruce, born April 9, 1868, died Jan. 20, 1897.

121 William M. McLeod, died Dec. 17, 1894, age 73. Mary McPherson, his wife, died March 1, 1895, age 67.

122 John McLeod, died Dec. 23, 1899, age 40. His children: Angus Martin, died Nov. 24, 1897, age 4 mos. Mary, died Jan. 13, 1898, age 9 mos. Catherine MacPherson, his wife, died Dec. 6, 1932, age 70.

123 John D. MacLeod, 1891-1942.

126 James M. MacDonald, 1853-1925. Also his wife, Annie MacLeod, 1854-1936. Roderick, 1881-1911. Mary A., 1892-1912. Margaret, 1890-1917.

128 Margaret McLeod, wife of Alexander Martin, died July 3, 1899, age 85. Alexander Martin, died Jan. 1, 1905, age 85. Emigrated from Isle of Skye 1829.

134 Charles McLeod, died Dec. 20, 1903, age 80. Rachel McDonald, his wife, died June 11, 1926, age 87. Roderick C. MacLeod, died June 8, 1956, age 79. Hector,

died 1874, age 2 mos. Roderick, died 1876, age 4 years. Hector, died 1876, age 8 mos. Donald R., died 1886, age 7 yrs.

136   Marion F. Hugh, 1901-1970, wife of Malcolm F. MacLeod, 1885-1980.

137   John J. MacLeod, 1852-1934. Mary A. Finlayson, his wife, 1854-1927, born Edinburgh, Scotland.

139   John I. MacLeod, 1853-1929. Flora Ann Docherty, his wife, 1856-1943.

145   Margaret, wife of John MacLeod, 1844-1929.

146   Angus R. MacLeod, May 6, 1885 - Dec. 5, 1955.

147   Jane W. MacLeod, 1860-1929. Margaret A. MacLeod, 1890-1933. Mrs. Rachel Buchanan, 1852-1938. Angus W. MacLeod, 1895-1971.

153   Malcolm MacLeod, 1855-1936, his wife, Janette MacRae, 1850-1936, their daughter, H. Florence, 1879-1945.

157   Alexander N. MacPherson, 1840-1927. Mary Martin, his wife, 1844-1924. Alexander MacPherson, 1881-1958. Christy MacLeod, his wife, 1885-1976. Their children: Neil J., 1912-1919. Mary E., 1910-1927.

162   David MacLeod, 1918-1949. Angus Alexander MacLeod, 1882-1967. His wife, Mary Catherine Lamont, 1890-1975.

164   Donald Campbell, born Feb. 22, 1850, died Aug. 3, 1938. Flora MacLeod, his wife, born May 15, 1855, died Feb. 23, 1941. William M. Campbell, born Nov. 14, 1882, died May 13, 1957.

169   Samuel M. MacLeod, Sept. 14, 1870 - June 27, 1950. Catherine MacLeod, his wife, Oct. 23, 1872 - Dec. 16, 1944. David Gordon, April 1, - ____ 4, 1939, son of Donald and Dorothy MacLeod.

180   Samuel A. MacLeod, 1892-1959. Agnes Mae MacPherson, his wife, 1897-1964.

181   Ellen Elizabeth MacLeod, 1915-1957, wife of Edison Taylor.

PETERS ROAD PRESBYTERIAN

146   Murdoch A. MacLeod, 1881-1961. Husband of the late Georgia Foster at rest in Melfort, Sask.

31   Albert Griffin, April 24, 1910 - Jan. 8, 1977. Laura MacLeod, his wife, July 14, 1906 - Nov. 2, 1974. Ruth Cairns, his wife, June 15, 1919—.

145   Joyce, daughter of J. W. and Mae MacLeod, died March 29, 1926, age 4.

85   Albert L. MacLeod, 1882—. Daisy E. Higginbotham, his wife, 1890—.

19   John William MacLeod, 1890-1949.

PORTAGE (BRACKLEY AREA) PIONEER

95   Richard Alden MacInnis, 1881-1918. Florence MacLeod, his wife, 1876-1963.

33   John C. MacLeod, Oct. 22, 1866 - Sept. 30, 1958.

17   Richard MacLeod, April 12, 1878 - March 14, 1925.

77   Christina, died Oct. 19, 1885, age 11 yrs. 3 mos., daughter of John and Margaret McLeod.

76   John MacLeod, died Jan. 21, 1896, age 70.

71   Mary MacLeod, wife of Roderick Matheson, died Oct. 9, 1893, aged 29. Also an infant.

64   Malcolm McLeod, died July 10, 1882, aged 49. Isabella, his wife, died Aug., 1873, aged 29. Their daughter, Martha, died March 1875, aged 12.

63   Murdoch McLeod, died Nov. 19, 1905, aged 41. Isabell McLeod (adopted daughter of the late Donald McKay) died at Colorado Springs, May 23, 1896, aged 24.

36   Charles McLeod, died Jan. 11, 1922, aged 55. Margaret C. McLeod, died Dec. 15, 1918, aged 25.

Port Hill, St. James Anglican

125   Gorvill—R. Henry, 1863-1933. His wife, Murinde MacLeod, 1867-1946. Their daughter, Thelma, 1904-1908.

Pownal

92   Charles N. MacLeod, died April 9, 1922, age 66. His wife Susan A. Gay, died June 20, 1927, age 70. Mildred MacLeod, wife of Charles Peters, 1886-1923.

118   Mary MacLeod, wife of Jacob D. Judson, died May 29, 1901, age 65.

Princetown United (Presbyterian)

45   Mabel Florence MacLeod, wife of F. S. Watts, 1873-1935, son, Freeman, 1912-1912.

260   MacLeod, William M., Feb. 11, 1871 - June 9, 1936. His wife, Laura K. Burns, Nov. 8, 1880 - Dec. 29, 1972.

349   George A. MacLeod, May 10, 1876 - Sept. 20, 1955. His wife, Mary P. MacKay, March 18, 1864, died June 3, 1919. Nephew, Ertel MacLeod (2nd side), May 17, 1898 - Feb. 20, 1969.

574   Norman McLeod Ramsay of Beach Point, died May 2, 1860, aged 52 years.

Rustico Road, Fairview Baptist

15   David Alfred Andrews, March 17,1866 - Sept. 29, 1939. His wife Catherine Jane MacLeod, Oct. 26, 1863 - June 3, 1939, and infant daughter.

St. Catherine's, Shaw Cemetery

21   William MacEachern, died May 28, 1902, age 74. Ann McLeod, his wife, died Aug. 19, 1866, age 33.

74   Catherine McLeod, wife of Malcolm Shaw, died Dec. 9, 1880, age 63. Ann, their daughter, died Oct. 1844, age 2 years.

101   Archibald K. MacLeod, 1866-1952. Margaret MacPhee, his wife, 1868-1960. Benjamin E. MacLeod, 1888-1947.

102   Lois A., daughter of Archibald and Margaret MacLeod, died Jan. 24, 1896, age 5.

St. George's Roman Catholic Cemetery

111   Joseph J. Campbell, Jan. 17, 1885 - May 20, 1959. Emma C. MacLeod, his wife, July 16, 1884 - July 30, 1925. Emma Josephine, Oct. 23, 1924 - April 19, 1925.

152   Charles McLeod, died June 10, 1903, aged 51.

155   Alex McAskill, born Sept. 28, 1834, died March 3, 1913. Margaret J. MacLeod, his wife, 1857-1942. Alex Morrison McAskill, born June 27, 1885, died June 8, 1913.

178   Catherine, beloved wife of John McLeod, died Dec. 10, 1867, age 37.

272   Elizabeth, wife of the late Neil MacLeod, died July 22, 1870, age 52.

Seven Mile Bay, St. Peter's Roman Catholic

187   Mary Cecilia MacLeod, wife of Neil McInnis, May 4, 1892 - April 23, 1969.

Sherwood

432   Malcolm McLeod, Q.C. who died Jan. 8, 1900, aged 65 years.
779   Amelia Parker, deceased wife of Rev. John M. McLeod, who departed this life May 2, 1870, aged 39 yrs. In memory of Anne, Fred, Blanche, who died on Jan. 29, 1877, aged 4 yrs. 7 mos.
247   Ella Maud Gill, wife of Alfred McLeod, died Sept. 15, 1894, aged 26.
434   Florence Julia, wife of Malcolm MacLeod, died May 10, 1899, aged 42.
425   George H. Jones, 1866-1940. His wife, Christina MacLeod, 1866-1947.
312   Jean MacLeod, Feb. 9, 1906 - Nov. 13, 1973, wife of F. Rundell Seaman.
497   Mary Isabel (MacLeod) Bentley, Oct. 14, 1883 - June 18, 1955.
450   John M. MacLeod, March 26, 1888 - Aug. 20, 1941. His wife, Emily MacKay, May 8, 1893 - March 27, 1967.
310   Paul Norman MacLeod, June 26, 1952 - June 3, 1970.
449   John D. MacLeod, died Dec. 29, 1904, aged 51. His wife, Jessie McMillan, died Aug. 19, 1927, aged 71 yrs. Vernon H. MacLeod, 1892-1938.
248   Elizabeth Sarah Davison, wife of Henry C. MacLeod, Jan. 2nd 1855 - May 17, 1881. Joseph Henry MacLeod, July 12 - Oct. 7, 1876. Edith MacLeod, 1877-1936.
101   106 393 598 Pte. James Allison MacLeod, Can. Forces, 17 April, 1970, aged 22.
479   Margaret, daughter of Donald and Margaret MacLeod, died at Glace Bay, C. B., June 12, 1902, aged 5 years.
102   James Allison MacLeod, 1948-1970. Margaret Jane MacDonald, wife of John I. MacLeod. Donald Allison MacLeod, May 21, 1925 - May 9, 1957. Heather Jean, 1955-1978. Allison MacLeod, April 12, 1895 - Oct. 8, 1972.

Souris West Cemetery United

3   Joseph H. Pope, 1862-1939. His wife, Sarah A. MacLeod, 1870-1938.

South Granville Presbyterian

5   John Corbett, 1850-1920. His wife, Sarah MacLeod, 1845-1934. Their daughter, Mrs. Margaret Thompson, 1884-1939. Their sons, Hector A., 1882. Hector A., 1883-1956.
11   Morrison—Catherine MacLeod, wife of George Morrison, 1864-1927. George Morrison, 1860-1933.
12   Morrison—Hector F., son of George and Katie (MacLeod), died April 24, 1899, aged 1 yr. 6 mos.
17   Hugh McLeod, died June 3, 1888, aged 63, his wife, Barbara Campbell, died Jan. 12, 1909, aged 63.
18   Maria B. MacLeod, wife of Malcolm A. MacLeod, 1884-1932, also three infant children.
19   MacLeod, Murdoch, 1829-1885. His wife, Barbara Keir, 1840-1925. Their children: Roderick, 1864-1917. Annabelle, 1874-1904.
20   McLeod, Elizabeth Ann, wife of Robert McLeod, died May 11, 1912, aged 35. Also their four infants.
21   Wesley McLeod, 1901-1942, also two infants. Robert McLeod, 1867-1943.

22   MacLeod, Cathel W., June 4, 1871 - May 2, 1956. His wife Euphemia MacLellan, June 10, 1873 - April 7, 1958.

23   Ethel MacLeod, Aug. 2, 1886 - Aug. 2, 1959. Peter MacLeod, Apr. 7, 1880 - Dec. 29, 1969.

24   MacLeod, Robert, June 10, 1867 - Apr. 13, 1943. His wife Ruth Weeks Davis, Sept. 28, 1893 - Sept. 10, 1974.

31   MacLeod, Donald, 1810-1897, his wife, Mary MacLeod. Both born in Sutherlandshire, Scotland.

34   Ann MacLeod, wife of James Falconer, died Jan. 11, 1908, aged 64.

39   John McLeod, native of Sutherlandshire, Scotland, died Oct. 16, 1886, aged 74 yrs.

43   McLeod, John McLeod, died 1934, aged 85. His wife, Wilhemina McKenzie, died 1923, aged 79. Children: Barbara, 1892, 15 yrs. Twin boys, 1879, 3 weeks. Charlotte, 1881, 7 mos. George, 1884, 9 mos. McLeod, Ethel, wife of W. P. Hiltz, born April 26, 1862, died Nov. 4, 1949, also his daughter. Jean A. McLeod, born June 8, 1912, died Feb. 12, 1927.

44   Donald McLeod, died Aug. 22, 1876, aged 8 mos.

45   MacLeod, Robert, 1831-1922. His wife, Lavinia Woolner, 1891-1945.

46   Donald McLeod, died Apr. 21, 1881, aged 74. His wife, Janet McKay, died Mar. 10, 1892, aged 84. Residents of [?] River. Effie McLeod, widow of late Alexander McDonald, died Jan. 17, 1893, aged 56.

69   John MacMillan, died May 1, 1903, aged 85. Also his wife, Annie MacLeod, died Mar. 14, 1885, aged 68. Their son, John, died Aug. 18, 1886, age 41.

75   Donald Corbett, April 1, 1838 - Mar. 16, 1914. Native of Sutherlandshire, Scotland. Also his wife, Robina McLeod, July 19, 1841 - May 21, 1904. Their son, John D., 1880 - July 31, 1896. Also an infant.

76   Murdoch Corbett, died June 16, 1889, aged 84. His wife, Annie MacLeod, died Dec. 27, 1890, aged 86. Their son, William, July 1, 1904, aged 74. Emigrated from Sutherlandshire, Scotland in 1840. Their son, Roderick, died Nov. 1900, age 55.

93   MacKenzie, Hector, 1852-1941. His wife, Margaret MacLeod, 1856-1936.

96   John R. MacLeod, 1862-1934. His wife, Alice McVane, 1860-1945.

101   Moreside—Rhoda Mae MacLeod, July 21, 1901 - May 8, 1959, wife of Wallace Moreside.

102   MacLeod, David Archibald, 1898-1960.

Springfield, Summerfield United

87   Robert MacKenzie, died Oct. 5, 1923, age 69. Mary Margaret MacLeod, his wife, died Feb. 16, 1953, age 90. Laura S. Haslam, died Oct. 7, 1943, age 50. Ruth Winnifred MacLeod, their adopted daughter, died Oct. 23, 1933, age 22.

89-1 Christy MacLeod, wife of William Campbell, died Feb. 17, 1895, age 44. John Duncan Campbell, 1870-1958.

Springfield West United Baptist

125   Daniel MacLeod, 1851-1917, also his wife, Alice Gay, 1897-1919.

141   Side 2—In memory of Tena, beloved wife of Norman MacLeod, died at Brighton, Mass., U.S.A., Jan. 19, 1912, aged 23.

Springton

19   Henry E. Dixon, 1866-1928. Flora MacLeod, his wife, 1864-1945.

57   John B. MacGregor, grandson of James F. and Mary MacLeod, died Dec. 25, 1918, age 15 years.

56   Donald McLeod, died Jan. 30, 1893, age 74. Isabella, his wife, died April 9, 1901, age 74.

52   Malcolm Matheson, 1842-1930. Flora MacLeod, his wife, 1849-1928. John R., their son, 1883-1917. Angus, their son, 1894-1916.

22   Donald P. MacLeod, died March 14, 1927, age 84. Annie MacPherson, his wife, died July 24, 1936, age 82.

54   Archibald McLeod, died May 6, 1901, age 35.

23   Flora A. MacLeod, June 22, 1879 - Nov. 20, 1969.

59   Jane Stewart, wife of John McLeod, died Dec. 30, 1869, age 53. John, their son, died April 21, 1873, age 19.

46   Kenneth Graham, died May 22, 1892, age 77. Rachel McLeod, his wife, died July 5, 1910, age 85. Emigrated from Isle of Raasay, Scotland, 1858.

55   Henry J., son of A. D. and Edith McLeod, died Jan. 8, 1897, age 17 mos.

58   John George McLeod, died Sept. 30, 1895, age 88. Catherine Gillis, his wife, died Jan. 4, 1893, age 76. Erected by son George.

77   Malcolm McLeod, died Feb. 13, 1867, age 67. Margaret Gillis, his wife, died Nov. 19, 1863, age 60. Malcolm, died April 3, 1866, age 4. Also 4 infant children of John G. and Sarah MacLeod.

79   Anne MacLeod, wife of Hector MacDonald, died May 27, 1902, age 52. Lavenia C., their daughter, died May 11, 1888, age 4 years. Garfield, their son, died April 9, 1908, age 26.

151   Angus A. Nicholson, 1841-1919. Mary A. MacLeod, his wife, 1854-1932. Allan, 1885-1908; Sadie, 1891-1921; Annie, 1893-1930; Malcolm, 1901-1930; Florence, 1883-1932; Alexander, 1895-1946; John age 5; Flora, age 3. Their children.

107   Allan Nicholson, born Aug. 21, 1801, died Sept. 15, 1881. Margaret MacLeod, his wife, born Oct. 25, 1815, died May 27, 1891. Emigrated from Isle of Skye, 1841. Alexander, born April 8, 1849, died Nov. 30, 1850. Alexander, born March 31, 1851, died May 30, 1855. John A., born July 3, 1853, died Sept. 4, 1894. John, born Oct. 3, 1833, died Dec. 4, 1854. Murdoch, born Feb. 21, 1840, died Feb. 20, 1884. He won one of the first Brenniel Scholarships granted in P.E.I., Homo-multarum Literarum. John M., born April 20, 1860, died Jan. 12, 1901. Sons of Allan and Margaret Nicholson.

177   William MacLean, 1855-1944. Flora Jane MacLeod, his wife, 1860-1959. Christie Isabell, 1888-1905.

176   Donald J. Munroe, Aug. 22, 1874 - Jan. 5, 1929. Mary J. MacLeod, his wife, March 4, 1877 - Dec. 9, 1924. Also 3 infants. Christena M., Feb. 28, 1909. Frank W., Feb. 26, 1920.

Springvale, Princetown Road United

21   Walter MacLeod, 1882-1970. Bertha Sentner, 1885-1960.

Sturgeon United (Methodist)

16   Lorne F. MacLeod, 1943-1969.

SUMMERSIDE, PEOPLE'S PROTESTANT CEMETERY

41   John MacLeod, died 1903.
197   Howard K. MacLeod, 1893-1970.
261   Rev. Merrill MacLeod, 1920-1977.
276   Charlotte Florence MacLeod, 1938-1961.
277   John D. MacLeod, 1879-1953.
400   Cmdr. A. D. MacLeod, 1884-1957.
400   James MacLeod, 1840-1899.
400   Valerie MacLeod, 1893-1897.
400   Cedric MacLeod, 1895-1897.
474   Christy Ann MacLeod, 1841-1925. (Neil MacKinnon, 1837-1907.)
481   Alexander Stirling MacKay, 1871-1961. Ruth Ella MacLeod, 1877-1961.
542   Catherine MacLeod, 1857-1918.
594   Robert C. M., 1851-1965. Margaret L. MacLeod, 1853-1929. A. Gwendolin, 1846-1889.
643   J. Alfred Cahill, 1868-1934. Phoebe Joan MacLeod, 1874-1956.
661   Neil MacLeod, 1844-1915.
690   Barbara MacLeod (among others) died 1919.
786   Donald MacLeod, 1841-1913.
807   Mary MacLeod, died 1892.
865   Mary Louise Ella MacLeod, died 1881.
869   Murdoch MacLeod, 1846-1930.
881   Neil MacLeod, 1900-1935. Cpl. John Malcolm MacLeod, 1896-1916. G. R. Allan Roderick MacLeod, 1897-1917. Neil MacLeod, 1853-1934.
886   Norman MacLeod, 1887-1958.
891   Allan R. MacLeod, died 1917.
983   Malcolm D. MacLeod, 1851-1937.
984   Daniel John MacLeod, 1880-1957.

TIGNISH, UNITED CHURCH CEMETERY

18   MacLeod, William D., 187[?]-1954.
21   MacLeod, Donald, died Dec. 29, 1953, age 5 mos.

TRYON PEOPLE'S

234   Hazel Walsh MacLeod, wife of Willard Thomas, 1907-1941.
268   Janie McLeod, wife of A. E. Mabey, died Dec. 3, 1898, aged 28.
305   Robert Carr, 1862-1923. His wife Catherine McLeod, 1865-1929.

TYNE VALLEY PRESBYTERIAN

9   Alma MacLeod, wife of Wm. E. Sheen, 1866-1951. Wm. Sheen, 1864-1930.

UIGG BAPTIST CHURCH CEMETERY

3   Donald, son of Donald and Mary McLeod, died Oct. 24, 1859.
4   Norman McLeod, died March 6, 1877, age 78. His wife, Ann McDonald, died Dec. 3, 1885, age 82, natives of Isle of Skye, emigrated to P.E.I. 1828. Mary MacPherson died March 13, 1903, age 52.

13   James McDonald, died Sept. 12, 1883, age 90. His wife, Ann MacLeod, died Oct. 7, 1884, age 84. Natives of Isle of Skye, Scotland, emigrated 1829.

14   3204141 Pte. Samuel M. McLeod, N.S. Regt. C.E.F., 5 Dec. 1918.

15   In memory of Neil McLeod, died Aug. 27, 1912, age 78. Buried at Edmonton, Alta. His wife, Mary McDonald, died April 25, 1919, age 79. Their son, Samuel M., died Dec. 13, 1918, age 36.

18   Murdoch Ewen MacLeod, 1859-1933. His wife, Elizabeth MacKinnon, 1865-1907. Their son, William R., 1902-1920. Also his wife, Georgie MacEachern, 1874-1944.

19   Roderick MacLeod, died Nov. 19, 1876, age 66. His wife, Flora, daughter of John McDonald of Pinette, died July 2, 1882, age 64.

20   Murdoch McLeod, born in Skye, Scotland, he came to P.E.I. 1829, one of the original settlers of Uigg, died March 16, 1859, age 84. His wife, Margaret, died April 1847, age 59. Their son, Murdoch, born in Skye, came to P.E.I. with his parents 1829, he resided in Australia from 1852 to 1870. Died at Charlottetown, Feb. 25, 1883, age 57. Neil MacLeod, son of Murdoch MacLeod, died Sept. 1841, age 26. Ewen MacLeod, his brother, died Aug. 1, 1857, age 39.

30   John J. MacLeod, died April 1, 1888, age 82. Also his daughter Annie, died March 18, 1889, age 38. May, died May 15, 1858, age 10 days. His grandchild, Katie, died Dec. 9, 1886, age 13 mos. Also his sons: Alexander, died May 25, 1859, age 12. Roderick, died June 15, 1861, age 2.

32   John Ernest Shaw, 1882-1958. His wife, M. Murdena MacLeod, 1895-1976. Infant son, Lloyd, 1928-1928.

53   Jessie MacLeod, wife of John D. McQueen, 1879-1949.

61   Norman S. MacLeod, born Dec. 9, 1838, died July 10, 1928. His second wife, Margaret MacNeill, born June 15, 1837, died Feb. 23, 1931. In memory of Sarah A. MacLeod, wife of Norman S. MacLeod, born March 17,1847, died Nov. 22, 1876. Their daughter Sadie MacLeod, born October 31, 1876, died July 10, 1897. George Roderick MacLeod, B.Sc., born Sept. 23, 1872, died Aug. 27, 1945. His wife Margaret M. Furness, born Oct. 6, 1883, died Feb. 21, 1977. Samuel S. MacLeod, born April 10, 1871, died June 1, 1931.

62   Margaret MacLeod, 1883-1977.

63   J. Ella MacLeod, Dec. 27, 1881 - Sept. 4, 1960. Her sister Margaret MacLeod, Dec. 16, 1888 - Dec. 29, 1967.

67   Hannah, beloved child of Samuel and Margaret McLeod, born April 2, died Nov. 8, 1847.

68   In loving memory of Margaret, widow of the late Rev. Samuel McLeod, died Feb. 27, 1902, aged 95.

69   Samuel McLeod, minister of Baptist Church, Uigg and Belfast from 1840 to 1870, died Aug. 23, 1881, aged 84. His daughter Mary, died Jan. 24, 1920, age 79.

70   Malcolm S. McLeod, died April 29, 1903, in 64th year of his age. Ester Robertson, his wife, died Sept. 12, 1923, age 70.

71   Esther Ella, died Sept. 3, 1923, age 8 yrs. Evelyn Louise, died March 13, 1916, age 2 mos. Children of Samuel E. and Mabel MacLeod.

72   Edwin R. MacLeod, Aug. 20, 1913 - May 6, 1955. Veteran of W.W.2, son of Samuel E. and Mabel MacLeod.

74   Robert A.McLeod, 1858-1927.

73   Samuel E. MacLeod, March 8, 1880 - March 7, 1959.

75   Murdoch McLeod, died July 29, 1889, age 74. A native of Isle of Skye. His wife, Margaret Gunn, died Aug. 26, 1916, age 99. His children: Norman, died at

Maine, Nov. 21, 1880, age 42. Hugh H., died March 16, 1858, age 8 days. Lizzie, died April 19, 1854, age 6 weeks. Mary Gillis, wife of Norman McLeod, died June 22, 1913, age 82.

76 John M. MacLeod, 1848-1937. His wife, Christine MacLeod, 1852-1932.

77 John Otis MacLeod, Aug. 7, 1890 - Oct. 12, 1965. Evelyn, wife of J. Otis MacLeod, April 1, 1898 - July 14, 1946.

78 Norman Russell MacLeod, Aug. 21, 1927 - April 12, 1964.

79 John Henry Jenkins, born Feb. 22, 1834, died Oct. 25, 1921. Catherine McLeod, his wife, born June 3, 1847, died July 24, 1921.

80 Neil McLeod, died at Vernon River, Oct. 19, 1888, age 77. Native of Skye, emigrated 1829. His wife Margaret Vaniderstine, died at Vernon River, June 13, 1890, age 71. Annabella McLeod, May 8, 1855 - April 28, 1938.

81 Neil James, son of Neil and Margaret McLeod, Vernon River, died Aug. 25, 1880, age 20 yrs. Also daughter Margaret, age 4 years.

85 Catherine MacLeod, died April 18, 1928. Mary Hamish MacLeod, died Jan. 15, 1931. John MacLeod, died 1895, and Rachel Gordon, his wife, died 1897.

86 Here rest from their labours after enduring and overcoming the hardships of early settlement in this colony Roderick McLeod, born in Isle of Skye, Scotland, emigrated 1829, died June 29, 1888, age 85, and Catherine, his wife, died Dec. 2, 1882, age 75. Margaret, daughter of Roderick McLeod, died May 9, 1862, age 18. John R. MacLeod, died Sept. 1913. Mary MacLeod, died Jan. 1914.

87 Norman MacLeod, 1762-1837. Margaret MacPhee, his second wife, 1778-1855, both born in Skye, Scotland. Erected on the occasion of the Uigg Centenary 1929. Catherine Cameron, daughter of Norman MacLeod and his first wife Mary, 1795-1882. Alexander Cameron, her husband, 1785-1845. Their son, William, 1815-1840. All born in the Isle of Skye.

UIGG, CHURCH OF SCOTLAND

2 Catherine McLeod, beloved wife of John McKenzie, died Aug. 22, 1871, age 64. Christiana, their daughter, died Dec. 1859, age 25.

4 Donald, son of Roderick and Marjorie McLeod, died Sept. 20, 1859.

5 Anna McPhee, beloved wife of Calum MacLeod.

6 MacLeod, Donald, died Sept. 10, 1862, age 4 yrs. 4 mos. Also Flora, died Nov. 1, 1863, age 1 yr., 4 mos. Children of Donald and Flora McLeod.

8 Archibald McLeod, died March 20, 1858, age 66. A native of Isle of Skye. Emigrated to P.E.I. 1829.

9 Duncan McLeod, died Feb. 1865, age 26. Angus McLeod, M.D., died at Cambridge, Mass., Feb. 12, 1873, aged 30 years.

10 Alexander MacLeod, died Aug. 17, 1867, age 81. His wife, Isabella Gillis, died Feb. 28, 1868, age 64.

11 Donald MacLeod, native of Isle of Skye, Scotland, died Sept. 17, 1851, age 72. Also his wife, Mary Martin, died Oct. 20, 1869, age 83.

13 Catherine, daughter of Alex and Isabella McLeod, died May 12, 1866, age 19 yrs. 6 mos.

14 Sarah, daughter of John and Mary McLeod, died June 12, 1867, age 11 yrs.

25 Catherine, wife of John McLeod, died Aug. 8, 1843, age 24 yrs. Also his second wife, Christie.

28 Jessie McDonald, wife of Donald McLeod, died March 6, 1855, age 33.

Valleyfield United (Presbyterian)

42   Jessie MacLeod, wife of Alexander Bruce, died Jan. 13, 1905, aged 77.

63   J. W. Bruce MacLeod, Feb. 23, 1924 - Feb. 16, 1948. Annie J. Bruce, 1892-1976.

211   Catherine MacDonald, wife of Donald MacLeod, died June 27, 1883, age 62. Their sons: Roderick, died Oct. 14, 1886, age 26. Alexander, died July 29, 1881, age 23.

147   Margaret McLeod, wife of John Matheson, died Feb. 11, 1899, age 75. Native of Isle of Skye.

590   Alexander A. MacPherson, died July 3, 1937, age 87. Mary MacLeod, his wife, died Oct. 5, 1917, age 71. Angus A. MacPherson died in Montana, U.S.A., Feb. 20, 1900, age 20.

588   Malcolm S. MacLeod, June 8, 1870 - April 14, 1942. Rachel Ross, his wife, Jan. 8, 1884 - Feb. 5, 1968.

82   John MacLeod, 1873-1943. Mary E. MacKay, his wife, 1871-1960. Mary M. MacLeod, 1910-1974. Betty Anne, infant daughter of Preston and Mary Peardon, April 9, 1951.

78   Murdoch Roderick MacLeod, Dec. 30, 1883 - July 29, 1973. Katherine Jessie MacKinnon, his wife, June 6, 1886 - Jan. 9, 1973.

608   Murdoch Fred MacDonald, 1864-1936. Isabelle MacLeod, his wife, 1870-1950. Fred, 1899-1909, Milton, 1903-1943, their sons. Catherine MacDonald, 1866-1912.

27   Donald McLeod, 1815-1896. Annie MacDonald, his wife, 1824-1860. Archibald, 1851-1868, Annie, 1857-1871, son and daughter of Donald and Annie. Flora McDonald, wife of Malcolm MacLeod, 1857-1921. Malcolm D. MacLeod, 1855-1924.

29   Jane MacLeod, wife of John Johnston, died Dec. 8, 1880, age 27.

552   Norman McLeod, died Sept. 23, 1872, age 54. Murdoch, his brother, died May 9, 1869, age 48. Natives of Isle of Skye.

366   Donald MacKay, 1840-1917. Annie McLeod, his wife, 1842-1929. Major Atwood T. MacKay, D.S.O. and Brigade, died of wounds, France, Oct. 26, 1918, age 34. Sarah Ann MacKay, 1874-1945.

414   Malcolm J. MacLeod, died March 17, 1902, age 55. Annabella MacKenzie, his wife, died Dec. 8, 1930, age 78. Sons: Malcolm J., died April 8, 1887, age 6 yrs. Daniel W., died Aug. 24, 1896, age 18 mos.

353   Alexander McLeod, 1824-1899. Christie Finlayson, his wife, 1826-1910. Their son, Donald, 1863-1891. Margaret McLeod, 1813-1894. Angus A. MacLeod, 1875 - 19—. M. Catherine MacDonald, his wife, 1877-1950. Eagle Pol. C., Quincy, Mass.

432   Alexander McLeod, died June 1, 1913, age 93. Margaret Ross, his wife, died Aug. 3, 1884, age 59. William, their son, died Feb. 2, 1884, age 19 yrs.

397   Donald Finlayson, died July 19, 1885, age 46. Catherine McLeod, his wife, died Feb. 3, 1911, age 71. Margaret Flora, their daughter, died Dec. 23, 1895, age 14. Also two infants.

391   Jessie Bruce, wife of Donald MacLeod, died Jan. 12, 1906, age 54.

127   Rachel McLeod, wife of Malcolm D. Gillis, died Feb. 28, 1908, age 70. Malcolm D. Gillis, died July 7, 1926, age 89. Their daughters: Maggie, died Dec. 16, 1879, age 4 yrs. Catherine, died Nov. 12, 1892, age 20.

404   Archibald McLeod, died Dec. 15, 1884, age 82. Jessie Campbell, his wife, died Dec. 22, 1879, age 69.

409   Isabella McPherson, wife of Angus McLeod, died Dec. 24, 1881, age 38.

400 John D. Munroe, 1898-1923. Alexander Munroe, 1866-1956. Effie, 1866-1962.

439 Alexander McDonald, died Feb. 23, 1904, age 81. Jane McQueen, his wife, died Sept. 2, 1901, age 76. Neil McLeod, died Sept. 27, 1901, age 85. Catherine McDonald, his wife, died Sept. 19, 1899, age 78.

416 James McLeod, 1861-1887. Murdoch McLeod, 1855-1923. Margaret Beaton, his wife, 1863-1944.

194 Jessie McDonald, wife of Malcolm McLeod, Douses Rd., died Jan. 15, 1869, age 43.

189 Neil McLeod, died April 17, 1893, aged 80. Jessie Nicholson, his wife, died Sept. 10, 1888, age 53. Natives of Isle of Skye, Scotland.

579 Ronald Nicholson, died March 1, 1918, age 82. Mary MacLeod, his wife, died March 29, 1925, age 78.

62 John P. MacLeod, 1890—. Annie J. Bruce, 1892-1976, his wife.

200 Dorothy McLeod, relict of the late Laughlin McDonald, died Feb. 6, 1887, age 81.

574 John M. MacLeod, 1850-1940. Alexina MacDonald, his wife, 1863-1927. Ada G., 1893-1911. David, 1907. Malcolm M. MacLeod, 1898-1958.

581 Kenneth MacKenzie, 1890-1953. Katie A. MacLeod, his wife, 1893-1971.

407 Donald J. McLeod, died Feb. 1, 1885, age 46.

380 Donald McLeod, died Jan. 19, 1880, age 41.

384 Daniel MacLeod, died Jan. 10, 1959, age 64.

363 Malcolm McLeod, died Sept. 17, 1887, age 72, native of Isle of Skye. Margaret, his wife, died March 26, 1895, age 76.

370 Norman N. McLeod, died April 2, 1911, age 55. Christina, his wife, died May 28, 1900, age 46.

324 Donald McLeod, died June 23, 1886, age 62. A native of Isle of Skye.

298 Roderick MacLeod, died Sept. 20, 1887, age 39. Sarah, his wife, died March 6, 1932, age 83. Minnie MacLeod, died April 10, 1904, age 21.

304 In memory of Sadie, died March 5, 1890, age 16. Katie, died Jan. 3, 1874, age 9. Alexander, died Oct. 1, 1877, age 3 weeks. Children of Angus and Jessie McLeod.

288 Mary McLeod, died Dec. 19, 1880, age 26.

287 Alexander McLeod, died June 20, 1895, age 83. Catherine, his wife, died June 10, 1894, age 75. Emigrated from Isle of Skye.

589 Milton R. MacLeod, 1910-1973.

277 Malcolm, son of Angus and Jessie McLeod, died Jan. 14, 1876, age 2 yrs. 10 mos.

164 Norman McPhee, died March 27, 1908, age 35. Alexina MacLeod, his wife, died April 3, 1934, aged 85.

415 William McLeod, died May 28, 1876, age 58. Allan, his son, died Jan. 20, 1878. Mary McLeod, 1821-1904.

601 Murdoch R. MacLeod, 1863-1940. Flora MacPherson, his wife, 1864-1956.

604 Angus Nicholson, 1856-1934. Katie MacLeod, his wife, 1856-1944.

214 Christy MacLeod, wife of John McDonald, died March 15, 1851, age 43.

557 Donald McLeod, died Nov. 4, 1890, age 71. Mary McDonald, his wife, died Nov. 24, 1883, age 57.

91 Angus N. MacLeod, 1858-1947. Catherine Martin, his wife, 1857-1934. Herbert MacKenzie, April 30, 1897 - May 12, 1878. Flora MacLeod, his wife, June 12, 1899 - June 13, 1971. John Sterling, their son, April 3, 1939 - June 1, 1969.

87 Neil M. MacBeth, died July 22, 1954, age 77. Augusenia MacLeod, his wife, died Dec. 20, 1970, age 86. Isabell MacLeod, died Feb. 27, 1969, age 86.

85 John J. MacLeod, 1851-1934. Elizabeth MacPhee, his wife, 1853-1934. William A. MacLeod, 1889-1971. Margaret A. Morrison, his wife, 1893-1978.

96 Katie McLeod, wife of William Matheson, died Feb. 27, 1902, age 28. Martin J. Matheson, student at Dalhousie, born Sept. 12, 1901, died July 26, 1926. William

Matheson, died March 19, 1951, age 86. John R. Matheson, his son, June 24, 1894 - June 3, 1964.

112 Christy McLeod, wife of Ronald McDonald, died May 16, 1909, age 69.

226 Alex R. MacLeod, died Jan. 8, 1848, age 21.

225 Murdoch McLeod, died April 12, 1875, age 72. Jessie, his wife, died Dec. 23, 1870.

107 John Murdoch, third son of Alexander M. and Mary McLeod, accidently killed in Bellows Falls, V.T., Aug. 15, 1902, age 19 yrs.

104 Murdoch J., son of Jonathan and Catherine McLeod, died Feb. 1, 1892, age 1 year.

111 John Daniel, son of Peter and Maria McLeod, died June 14, 1867, age 2 years.

227 Catherine McLeod, died Feb. 19, 1908, age 63.

232 John McLeod, died Feb. 6, 1861, age 63. Catherine, his wife, died Feb. 20, 1870, age 70.

249 Daniel, son of Alexander and Margaret McLeod, died Nov. 4, 1901, age 24. Alex McLeod, died Nov. 7, 1902, age 75. Margaret, wife of Alexander McLeod, died Nov. 30, 1901, age 68. Lizzie Penelope, 1873-1907. Malcolm McLeod, died 1876, age 101. Effie, his wife, died 1878, age 98. Natives of Isle of Skye.

250 Katie Ann, daughter of Alexander and Margaret McLeod, died at Stanley Bridge, May 27, 1888, age 20.

251 John A. MacLeod, died at Rona, July 24, 1881, age 28.

228 John McLeod, died Dec. 7, 1866, age 61. Catherine McKay, his wife, died Feb. 4, 1903, age 88. Murdoch, his son, died May 27, 1874. age 22.

560 John M. MacLeod, April 15, 1857 - Aug. 30, 1919. Annie MacPherson, his wife, Feb. 9, 1867 - July 17, 1938. Angus MacLeod, their son, May 19, 1905 - Sept. 12, 1922. Malcolm MacLeod, their son, April 20, 1902 - March 30, 1968.

28 John D. Bruce, 1852-1935. Annie MacLeod, his wife, 1857-1943. Their sons: Alexander J., 1886-1907. A. Munro, 1888-1903. John Samuel, 1896-1903.

509 Malcolm D. MacLean, 1859-1928. Flora MacLeod, his wife, 1853-1936. Daniel M. MacLean, 1892-1937.

513 Kenneth MacBeth, 1873-1955. Bessie MacLeod, his wife, 1876-1927. Jessie B., a daughter, 1908-1927. Daniel A. MacBeth, 1875-1950.

512 M. Arthur MacLeod, July 7, 1913 - April 7, 1966.

511 Alexander MacLeod, died Aug. 31, 1953, age 72. Mary Emily Martin, his wife, died Jan. 16, 1957, age 69. John MacLeod, their son, died Jan. 18, 1933, age 14.

448 Sarah Ployer, wife of William M. MacLeod, died Aug. 1, 1909, age 44. William MacLeod, died July 27, 1933, age 75.

447 John P. MacLeod, Deputy Attorney of B.C., 1910-1916, born at Valleyfield, Jan. 27, 1861, died at Victoria, B.C., Jan. 31, 1917.

537 Angus J. MacLeod, 1855-1944. Mary MacDonald, his wife, 1862-1902. Their children: E. Maynard, 1894-1901. Donald Alex, 1889-1895. Lizzie Belle, 1898-1905. D. A., 1896-1917.

510 Murdoch A. MacLeod, 1856-1942. Sarah Ann Gillis, his wife, 1874-1943.

520 Murdoch D. MacLeod, Feb. 18, 1877 - May 25, 1947. Marjory C. MacLeod, his wife, Oct. 31, 1876 - Dec. 14, 1945. Infant son, 1916. Lewis D., a son, Aug. 16, 1913 - Jan. 14, 1971.

449 Norman MacLeod, died Jan. 1, 1894, age 78.

618 Angus T. MacPherson, 1862-1941. Flora Ann MacLeod, his wife, 1864-1953.

450 Catherine, wife of Murdoch MacLeod, died May 9, 1909, age 81.

466 Lauchlin McLeod, died Dec. 13, 1888, age 58.

278 Angus McLeod, died Feb. 4, 1908, age 62. Jessie McDonald, his wife, March 15, 1923, age 73.

303 Annie McLeod, wife of Alex R. Matheson, died Feb. 4, 1892, age 43. Also their sons: Johnie, died Nov. 15, 1879, age 22 mos. John, Nov. 18, 1879, age 5.

329 Donald Stewart, died Oct. 8, 1876, age 67. Mary MacLeod, his wife, died 1877, age 82. She emigrated to P.E.I. 1863.

364 John Duncan McLeod, Heatherdale, born 1824, died 1887. Mary McKay, his wife, born 1828, died 1900.

347 Malcolm A. MacLeod, 1842-1896. Christy Matheson, his wife, 1847-1922. Angus Alexander, their son, 1886, age 3 mos.

485 Murdoch MacPherson,. Feb. 24, 1882 - July 1, 1971. Jessie MacLeod, his wife, March 18, 1890 - Feb. 2, 1967.

484 Isabella MacBeth, 1847-1925, wife of Murdoch R. MacLeod, Bellevue. Murdoch R. MacLeod, 1839-1930.

483 Donald Ernest MacLeod, May 21, 1878 - Aug. 9, 1960. Mary MacPherson, Jan. 26, 1891—.

468 Donald D. MacPherson, 1850-1932. Rachel MacLeod, his wife, 1848-1936. Their sons: Donald W., 1891-1940. Norman A., 1901-1948. Florence, their daughter, 1885-1976.

221 Christy, daughter of John and Jessie MacLeod, died March 6, 1880, age 23.

266 Mary Jessie, died Dec. 5, 1901, age 19. Hugh, died Dec. 26, 1896, age 21. Alexander, died Oct. 15, 1880, age 6. Children of Ronald and Catherine McPherson. Ronald McPherson, died Feb. 5, 1921, age 90. Catherine McLeod, his wife, died June 12, 1930, age 89. Christy Ann, died June 23, 1907, age 20.

86 Jonathan MacLeod, 1853-1938. Catherine MacLeod, his wife, 1854-1945.

90 Alexander W. MacLeod, M.M. Private 105th Batt. C.E.F., Aug 2, 1972, age 75.

95 Angus McLeod, died Aug. 16, 1871, age 87. Mary, his wife, died Jan. 26, 1883, age 107. Native of Isle of Skye, Scotland.

136 Flora, wife of Hugh McLeod, died Feb. 16, 1880, age 59. John, died June 20, 1877, age 28. Murdoch, died Sept. 3, 1873, age 22. Christy, died Sept. 9, 1856, age 3. Her children.

210 Angus D. McLeod (stone underground), died March 19, 1881, age 90.

25 Ann, wife of Angus McLeod of Green Marsh, died April 6, 1858, age 26.

26 Samuel McLeod, died Nov. 20, 1864, age 30.

103 Rev. Murdoch J. MacLeod, B.A., Nov. 16, 1889, age 28, son of John and Mary MacLeod.

102 Neil McLeod, died Nov. 19, 1880, age 22.

101 John McLeod, died Oct. 18, 1883, age 73. Mary, his wife, died Feb. 16, 1883, age 63. Emigrated from Isle of Skye 1840.

Vernon, St. Andrew's United

16 Walter A. MacLeod, 1910—. His wife, Marion L. MacLeod, 1917—. Their son, Winston M. MacLeod, 1941-1971.

4 Neil MacLeod, 1954-1974.

Vernon River Memorial Cemetery, United Methodist/B. Christian

4 William F. MacMillan, died June 9, 1932, aged 77. His wife, Priscilla MacLeod, died February 22, 1945, age 80. Their son, E. MacMillan, B.A., L.L.B., age 50.

38 Spurgeon McLeod, died May 4, 190[?], age 37 yrs.

53 Bruce—Callum J., 1886-1933. His wife, Effie McLeod, 1885-1971.

99 James Douse Furness, died Sept. 26, 1896, age 17. Thomas Furness, 1826-1918.

Elizabeth A. MacLeod, his wife, 1851-1912.

100 Frederick Vickerson, 1856-1943. His wife, Sophia McLeod, 1857-1919. L. Neil Vickerson, died at Bolivia, S.A., Feb. 1, 1924, age 25.

122 Ian W. died March 6, 1948, age 2 weeks, son of John A. and Evelyn MacLeod.

124 Reuben Masters, died Feb. 25, 1910, age 72. His wife, Emily MacLeod, died Oct. 5, 1915, age 73.

132 Lemuel C. Hayden, died Nov. 6, 1921, age 79. His wife, Margaret MacLeod, died Dec. 26, 1933, age 76.

VICTORIA WEST UNITED CHURCH, PEOPLE'S CEMETERY

39 Christine A. MacLeod, 1881-1965, wife of Alfred L. Frost, 1883-1966.

68 MacLeod—Father—Daniel, 1883-1961. Mother—Belle Smith, 1883-1968. Son—D. Elton, 1912-1914. Daughter—Margaret L. 1907-1928.

89 James MacLeod, 1853-1925. His wife Harriet E. MacDougall, 1869-1944.

90 MacLeod—Archibald, 1897-1939. MacLeod—Douglas, 1901-1946.

92 MacLeod—Mary, wife of Roderick MacLeod, died Aug. 13, 1898, aged 54 yrs.

94 MacLeod—Jessie, daughter of Roderick and Mary McLeod, died May 11, 1904, aged 28.

115 Flora Bell—daughter of Malcolm D. MacLeod, died Aug. 27, 1886, aged 2 yrs. 6 mos.

116 Mary MacLeod, wife of Samuel Dyment, died June 8, 1921, aged 72.

117 Donald MacLeod, died Feb. 27, 1884, aged 75.

155 Alexander MacLeod, Jan. 9, 1893 - May 23, 1977. His wife Lulu Blanche Ramsay, March 19, 1901 - June 13, 1952.

194 David Blair MacLeod, Aug. 7, 1956 - Dec. 23, 1977. Paula Maureen Gillis, Nov. 11, 1958—, their son Colin David MacLeod, Nov. 15, 1977.

200 MacLeod—Mary MacKenzie, wife of Malcolm A. MacLeod, 1879-1913. Malcolm A. MacLeod, 1876-1960. Their children: Mary, 1908-1911, James, 1910-1910, William Roy, 1912-1922.

257 MacLeod—Murdoch, 1871-1952. Mary J. 1884—.

264 MacLeod—Donald, 1889-1974. His wife Lilla Belle Ramsay, 1896-1940.

WESTMORELAND BAPTIST

94 Benjamin McLeod, 1846-1931. His wife, Sarah C. McNeill, 1849-1931.

120 Rogerson, James, 1869-1931. Christine MacLeod, 1868-1955. Adrian Rogerson, 1895-1974. Veteran of World War I, 105th Batt.

WHEATLEY RIVER, UNITED CHURCH

14 Catherine MacLeod, wife of James Smith, died May 10, 1897, aged 81.

WINSLOE, HIGHFIELD PRESBYTERIAN, LOWER MALPEQUE ROAD

B-29 Dawn Sharleen McLeod, Feb. 22, 1968 - Aug. 26, 1970, daughter of Donald and Colleen McLeod.

WOOD ISLANDS PRESBYTERIAN

37 Malcolm M. MacLeod, 1891-1964. Mary E. McLennan, his wife, 1904—.

39 Donald M. MacLean, 1870-1953. Margaret MacLeod, his wife, 1875-1953.

59 John Nicholson, 1870-1928. Annie MacLeod, his wife, 1868-1944. Catherine, infant daughter, 1908. Allan M. Nicholson, 1902-1966.

72 Ewen McMillan, 1834-1920. Rachel MacLeod, his wife, 1849-1931.

96 Alexander T. MacLeod, 1856-1933. Isabelle C. MacKenzie, his wife, 1866-1948.

108 Alexander T. MacLeod, died June 14, 1933, age 77.

150 Christina McLeod, wife of D. M. MacLeod, died April 11, 1931, age 59. Donald M. MacLeod, died Feb. 9, 1947, age 73. John G. MacLeod, died April 20, 1919, age 82. Sarah McSwain, his wife, died March 27, 1932, age 94. Kattie J. MacLeod, wife of Donald M. MacLeod, 1887-1973.

141 John Martin, 1837-1919. Catherine McLeod, his wife, died Nov. 6, 1905, age 65. John L. MacLeod, 1834-1926. Norman Martin, died at Pittsburgh, P.A., April 1904, age 29. John J. Martin, 1872-1939.

CPSIA information can be obtained
at www.ICGtesting.com
Printed in the USA
BVHW051407141021
618837BV00005B/51